Irish Drama

1900 — 1980

Irish Drama

1900 — 1980

Edited by
Cóilín D. Owens
and
Joan N. Radner

The Catholic University of America Press
Washington, D.C.

Arrangement and editorial matter
Copyright © 1990
The Catholic University of America Press
All rights reserved
Printed in the United States of America

The paper used in this publication meets the minimum
requirements of American National Standards for Information Sciences—
Permanence of Paper for Printed Library Materials, ANSI Z39.48—1984.

∞

Cover illustration from the design for the cover of Lennox Robinson's
The Round Table and *Crabbed Youth and Age,* 1924, by Harry Clarke,
courtesy of the Hugh Lane Municipal Art Gallery, Dublin.

The map on page vi was designed and produced by Lisa A. Rexrode,
under the direction of Prof. Robert A. Rundstrom, Geography
Program, George Mason University.

Library of Congress Cataloging-in-Publication Data
Irish drama, 1900–1980 / edited by Cóilín D. Owens
and Joan N. Radner.
p. cm.
Bibliography: p.
1. English drama—Irish authors.
2. English drama—20th century.
3. Ireland—Drama.
I. Owens, Cóilín.
II. Radner, Joan Newlon.
PR8869.I7 1990
822'.91'08089172—dc19 89-727
ISBN 0-8132-0705-3 (alk. paper)

To our students

IRELAND

Contents

Acknowledgments

To our many friends and colleagues who advised us as we prepared this collection, our gratitude. A special thanks to Maurice Harmon of University College Dublin, Robert Hogan of the University of Delaware, and David McGonagle and Peggy Leonard of The Catholic University of America Press for their encouragement and expert assistance.

We also wish to thank the Office for Research, George Mason University, Fairfax, Virginia, and the Mellon Faculty Development Fund of the College of Arts and Sciences of The American University, Washington, D.C., for grants towards the production of this book.

On Baile's Strand by W. B. Yeats is reprinted by permission of A. P. Watt Ltd. on behalf of Michael B. Yeats and Macmillan London Ltd.

The Only Jealousy of Emer is reprinted with permission of Macmillan Publishing Company from *Collected Plays* by W. B. Yeats. Copyright 1934, 1952 by Macmillan Publishing Company. Copyrights renewed 1962 by Bertha Georgie Yeats and 1980 by Anne Yeats. Permission has also been granted by A. P. Watt Ltd. on behalf of Michael B. Yeats and Macmillan London Ltd.

The Land by Padraic Colum is reprinted by permission of the estate of Padraic Colum.

Maurice Harte by T. C. Murray is reprinted with permission of the Authors Guild of Ireland.

Juno and the Paycock by Sean O'Casey is reprinted with permission of Macmillan London Ltd.

The Big House by Lennox Robinson is reprinted with permission of the National Theatre Society Ltd.

The Old Lady Says "No!" by Denis Johnston is reprinted with permission of Colin Smythe Ltd., Publishers.

As the Crow Flies by Austin Clarke is reprinted with permission of R. Dardis Clarke, 21 Pleasants St., Dublin 8, Ireland.

The Paddy Pedlar by M. J. Molloy is reprinted with permission of the author.

The Vision of Mac Conglinne by Padraic Fallon is reprinted with permission of Brian Fallon.

The Quare Fellow by Brendan Behan is reprinted by permission of Grove Press, a division of Wheatland Corporation, copyright © 1956 by Brendan Behan and Theatre Workshop, and by permission of Methuen London.

Irish Drama

1900 – 1980

General Introduction

"Drama is conversation arranged," wrote Lady Augusta Gregory, one of the founders of the modern Irish dramatic movement, with characteristic understatement. But despite Ireland's reputation for brilliant conversation and humor, the country had no indigenous tradition of theater. Not until the establishment of the Abbey Theatre at the beginning of this century was it possible for Irish playwrights to draw on native precedents, distinct from those supplied by England. For centuries, Irish-born dramatists looked towards London not only for their audiences, but also for theatrical conventions. But the Abbey Theatre—central arena of the cultural-political movement known as the Irish Literary Revival—finally placed the island's resources of myth, social custom, folklore, and language at the service of dramatists whose work is distinctively Irish. The success of this national theater continues, with some qualifications, to the present time; but by the 1920s a reaction to the preoccupation with national history and identity, rural life, and religion led to the internationalization of theater in Ireland. As a result of these developments, dramatic writing in Ireland now produces works of various character: either provincially British, distinctly national, or Continental. Similarly, a historical account of Irish drama falls into three main phases: Anglo-Irish, Irish national, and contemporary European.

After a small theater was founded in Werburgh Street in 1635, followed later in the century by the Smock Alley Theatre, Dublin had an unbroken presence of successful commercial theaters at which touring companies offered the standard fare of the London stage—including, often, plays written by Irishmen. It is ironic that many of the most distinguished dramatists writing in English between 1700 and 1900 were of Irish birth—typically, members of the Anglo-Irish Protestant Ascendancy, who attended Irish grammar schools and Trinity College Dublin before moving to London to carry on their careers. Although Ireland produced its share of Grub Street hacks—writers who churned out sentimental commercial comedies, melodramas, or farces—the best Irish dramatists pioneered significant innovations in English drama. The famous Irish gift for humor may have contributed to the satirical skill of William Congreve (1672–1729), whose *Love for Love* (1695) is the masterpiece of the comedy of manners, and George Farquhar (1678–1707), whose genial comedies include *The Recruiting Officer* (1706) and *The Beaux' Stratagem* (1707). Two more Irishmen, Sir Richard Steele (1672–1729) and Hugh Kelly (1739–1777), were the principal authors of eighteenth-century sentimental comedy. Their countryman, Oliver Goldsmith (1728–1774), author of *She Stoops to Conquer* (1773), effectively criticized the mélange of tragedy and comedy typical of the sentimental drama of the day. Goldsmith's purification of laughter on the English stage was continued by another Irish writer, Richard Brinsley Sheridan (1751–1816), author of *The Rivals* (1775) and *The School for Scandal* (1777).

Down to the end of the nineteenth century, the most distinctively Irish element of English-language drama was the conventional figure of the Stage Irishman, a comic character marked by hot temper, exaggerated and outrageous dialect, and a tendency to speak "Irish bulls" (hyperbolic expressions, usually faulty in logic). In his many manifestations—servant, soldier, priest, gentleman, fortune hunter—this popular caricature appears in English theater from Tudor times onward: as Roebuck, for instance, in Farquhar's *Love and a Bottle* (1698), as Sir Lucius O'Trigger in Sheridan's *The Rivals,* and as Conn in *The Shaughraun* (1881) by Dion Boucicault (1820–1890), the nineteenth century's most successful and prolific Irish dramatist, noted for his melodramas and comedies of manners.

Two other Anglo-Dubliners, George Bernard Shaw (1854–1950) and Oscar Wilde (1854–1900), had by the 1890s begun to establish themselves in the Irish stage comedy tradition. Shaw quickly became the leading social satirist of the British theater, and Wilde's brilliantly witty comedies, particularly *The Importance of Being Earnest* (1895), made him the most celebrated—and infamous—of the Decadents. As Irishmen, detached somewhat from the class system, the customs, and the speech of England, Shaw and Wilde (like so many of their Anglo-Irish predecessors) could view English life with skepticism. Nevertheless, with the exception of Shaw's *John Bull's Other Island* (1904), neither dramatist's work made explicit use of Irish themes.

By the turn of the century, however, a distinctively Irish dramatic movement was well under way in Dublin, led by the poet William Butler Yeats (1865–1939) and strongly marked by Yeats's interests in Irish folklore and peasant life and in the heroic mythology of Iron-Age Ireland. After Yeats had met in the summer of 1897 with Lady Augusta Gregory (1852–1932), a colonial governor's widow who was to become one of the Irish theater's most popular playwrights, and Edward Martyn (1859–1924), a wealthy Catholic landowner who had written plays reflecting his admiration for Ibsen, the Irish Literary Theatre was founded. Despite their diverse backgrounds and personal interests, the founders' goal, as they wrote in their first manifesto, was "to build up a Celtic and Irish school of dramatic literature . . . to bring upon the stage the deeper thoughts and emotions of Ireland."

Indeed, building up the Irish theater was a key goal. From the first, the dramatic movement was a matter of inspired experiment by amateurs, who began the Irish Literary Theatre knowing of no available plays other than two by Yeats and two by Martyn. The movement gambled—successfully—on its power to inspire Irish writers to create suitable scripts, trusting, as the first manifesto said, that the Irish audience would allow dramatists "that freedom to experiment which is not found in theatres of England, and without which no new movement in art or literature can succeed." War was declared on the Stage Irishman caricature: "We will show that Ireland is not the home of buffoonery and of easy sentiment, as it has been represented, but the home of an ancient idealism."

Small and local as it was at its beginnings, the Irish Literary Theatre was cosmopolitan in its perspective. Its founders were aware of several other national and experimental European theaters: Ole Bull's in Norway (1850), Antoine's Théâtre Libre in Paris (1887), Germany's Freie Bühne Theatre (1889), J. T. Grein's Independent Theatre in London (1891), and the Moscow Arts Theatre (1898). Requesting financial support, Lady Gregory drew upon her wide acquaintance, ranging from Irish nationalists to the British Viceroy of India. The Theatre was to be national and popular, but nonetheless "outside all the political questions that divide us." Its founders were committed to experimentation with an imaginative and poetic drama that would combine Irish subject matter with contemporary developments in European theater. "Let us learn construction from the masters and language from ourselves," Yeats advised aspiring playwrights. Yeats developed his own dramas from indigenous folk and mythic materials, the methods of the French symbolists, Ibsen's poetic dramas, and, after 1913, Japanese Noh drama; Martyn's work was modeled on Ibsen's more realistic social problem plays; Lady Gregory drew on Irish local legends, folk history, and heroic sources, shaping these materials with the techniques of French comedy and in the language of the Irish peasantry.

The Irish Literary Theatre found supporters of all political persuasions (though, thanks to Edward Martyn's decision to fund the first performances, Lady Gregory did not need to draw on the guarantors' pledged subscriptions). The Antient Concert Rooms in Dublin were rented for the week of May 8, 1899, and with the practical help of the novelist George Moore, who hired and organized rehearsals of English actors for the productions, Yeats's poetic *The Countess Cathleen* was presented along with Martyn's realistic problem play, *The Heather Field*. Both plays center on Irish landowners and their relations to their tenants. Martyn's protagonist, Carden Tyrrell, is so obsessed with his project to reclaim for cultivation a barren heather field that he becomes a hated, tyrannical landlord and goes mad; Yeats's Countess Cathleen, on the other hand, lives not in a realistic world but in a symbolic medieval dream environment, in which she offers her own soul to demons in order to save her famine-stricken tenants from death and damnation. The initial double bill foreshadowed the mixed character of the theater's future repertoire, in which plays commenting on contemporary social problems were juxtaposed to poetic and symbolic drama focused on timeless issues.

Indeed, the public reception of the first productions was also prophetic, showing at once both the hunger of the Irish audience for a national drama and the limits that would be set to the dramatists' "freedom to experiment." *The Countess Cathleen* was denounced in advance as heretical by an Irish cardinal (who, as it turned out, had not read the play), and was hissed on its opening night by a few youths. But in general the plays were well attended and enthusiastically received; they provided a focus for the romantic nationalism of many Dubliners, who attended the Literary Theatre in "Celtic" costume and sang patriotic songs in the intervals. (Mary Colum recalled wearing "a white garment with blue and green embroidery, a blue brath [cloak], copper broaches, and other archaeological adornments.") In the succeeding two years the Literary Theatre staged its performances in the much larger Gaiety Theatre. And in its third and last year, 1901, its bill included the first play in the Irish language ever performed by a trained acting company: *Casadh an tSúgáin* ("The Twisting of the Rope"), written by Douglas Hyde, founder of Conradh na Gaeilge (The Gaelic League), and acted by an Irish cast directed by W. G. Fay.

The connection with William G. Fay and his elder brother, Frank, proved the crucial turning point in the development of the theater movement. The Irish Literary Theatre had imported professional English actors from London for its productions; this meant not only that Irish playwrights could not develop their plays through direct work with actors, but also that the extent to which the group could realize its aim of creating a distinctively *Irish* theater was in several ways limited. The Fays were Dubliners, passionate about the theater, who had developed their own amateur acting company and had been producing short dramatic pieces in whatever Dublin halls they could gain access to. Yeats was impressed with them, and after the end of the three-year trial period of the Irish Literary Theatre he offered them a play of his own. In cooperation with the patriotic women's organization Inginidhe na hÉireann (The Daughters of Erin) the Fays' company produced in April 1902 a landmark double bill: George Russell's dreamy, symbolic *Deirdre* and Yeats's nationalistic *Cathleen Ni Houlihan*, in which Maud Gonne played the title role: a mysterious old woman who embodies Ireland, coming into a peasant household in 1798 to inspire the son of the family to leave his parents and fiancée in order to join the heroic, doomed Irish rebels and French invaders at Killala. Despite the drafty chill of St. Theresa's Hall, where the production took place, and the distracting clamor from the billiard parlor next door, the play was electrifying; in Maud Gonne, one viewer later wrote, "the youth of the country saw all that was magnificent in Ireland." Crowds seeking tickets were turned away from the theater doors every night.

The extraordinary success of this production led the Fays in February 1903 to form the Irish National Theatre Society, with Yeats as president and William G. Fay as stage manager. A brief tour to London the same year, during which the English reviewers were unrestrained in their praise of the "simplicity" and "dream-feeling" of the low-key, naturalistic style of the Irish actors, cemented the company's reputation. And in the following year an Englishwoman, Annie Horniman, became the financial patroness of the society, establishing it in its permanent theater in Abbey Street, Dublin. In a contentious shift in 1906, the informal, democratic management style inherited from the Fays' company was abandoned; the Society became a limited liability company directed by Yeats, Lady Gregory, and J. M. Synge, and Miss Horniman endowed the Theatre with an annual grant.

The combination of the Fays' training of native Irish actors, Yeats's ideals about reform of the theater, and the physical limitations of the Abbey Theatre itself led to the development of a distinctive dramatic presence. In an interview, Lady Gregory gave one view of the Abbey's development:

> We realized that the Irish are not light and graceful of movement and quick of manner and action, so we did not try to cultivate these traits in them. We realized that they had beautiful voices naturally, so we let gesticulation count for very little and developed the subtle shades of the voice and depended on this vocal power for dramatic effect.
> Our theme, since we began consciously to have one, has been to find what was essentially natural in the Irish people and characteristic of them and to develop those things to their utmost power of growth.

Yeats connected the need to develop "a stronger feeling for beautiful and appropriate language" not only with his interest in "the musical lineaments of verse or prose," but also with a demand for plays that would "make the theatre a place of intellectual excitement." And the founders' insistence that acting, sets, and costumes be simplified so as to highlight the spoken voice accorded well both with the company's small budget and with the physical limitations of its theater: the Abbey's proscenium opening was only twenty-one feet wide; the stage, only fifteen feet deep, allowed no room even for a backdrop; and the limitations of off-stage space often made it expedient to produce plays requiring only a single set.

By 1904 the success of the Irish National Theatre had inspired the founding of the Ulster Literary Theatre in Belfast under Bulmer Hobson. The dramatic movement in Dublin, meanwhile, was attracting many talented members of the rising generation, including John Millington Synge

(1871–1909), Padraic Colum (1881–1972), and William Boyle (1853–1923); Lady Gregory had not only begun to write successful plays for the Abbey, but had also published two books of translations of the early Irish myths and heroic legends, *Cuchulain of Muirthemne* (1902) and *Gods and Fighting Men* (1904), which instantly became important sources of material and inspiration for other Irish writers.

Yeats himself experimented with various subject matter and with several dramatic styles, including peasant realism, farce, and modern naturalism, but his genius found its best expression in a highly sophisticated combination of poetry, dance, masks, and symbolic action representing a world of ideals and pure passion. His plays often drew on Irish heroic tales for their subjects, and (after 1913) on the Japanese Noh drama for their form, and expressed his belief in the primacy of imaginative or spiritual realities, of which historical change and the differentiation of human personality are emanations. Yeats's enmity with modern realism and middle-class values shows in all of his work, but most comprehensively in his plays for masked actors—intensely ritualized expressions, having affinities with both ancient religious drama and modern absurdism. Yeats's plays speak the virtues of heroic individualism, eloquence, aristocracy, and passionate intensity—values he wished to convey to modern Ireland, along with a heightened awareness of the possibilities of verse drama. Following his example, verse drama has had a small but persistent tradition in Ireland, notably in the works of Austin Clarke (1896–1974) and Donagh Mac-Donagh (1912–1968) and in the productions of the Lyric Theater, Belfast.

A distinctive duality evolved in the Abbey repertoire, which included both Yeatsian verse drama and more popular and naturalistic peasant and village plays. The actors were trained to perform these in two different modes: stylized, statuesque, and "decorative" for the poetic plays, with lines often spoken in a chanting fashion, and far more realistic in gesture and speech for the peasant plays. Symbolic and abstract costume and stage design characterized productions of Yeats's poetic drama. In presenting the peasant plays, however, the Abbey strove for authenticity in costume (sending to the Aran Islands, for instance, for pampooties—moccasin-like footwear—for the wardrobe of Synge's *Riders to the Sea*) and in setting—typically, the interior of a western Irish cottage, scaled to actual dimensions. The dialogue of peasant plays was often couched in an approximation of a country dialect of Hiberno-English. Lady Gregory developed a literary "peasant" speech modeled on that of the Kiltartan district in the vicinity of her home near Gort in Co. Galway, and even chose to publish her translations from the early literature in this "Kiltartan" dialect; Synge made a rich, near-poetic language for his country characters out of a sampling of rural speech from different parts of Ireland; George Fitzmaurice (1877–1963) imitated the idiosyncratic dialect of his native north Kerry.

Typical themes of the peasant play included matchmaking and marriage, emigration, land ownership, and family ties. These plays quickly became the bread and butter of the Abbey Theatre, appealing to the nostalgia of urban audiences, themselves only a generation or two from the land, and to nationalists, for whom the Land War of the 1880s was a recent and important milestone in the campaign for independence. To non-Irish audiences, the folklore of Irish country people carried the fascination of the exotic; and Yeats saw, as well, that such subject matter, though parochial, could reach out more broadly, that universality in literature is possible only through "what is near you—your nation, or, if you be no traveller, your village and the cobwebs on your walls." To the Irish at home and to Irish emigrants abroad, the Abbey's peasant plays were (or were expected to be) true representations of Irish life, broadcasting to the world a serious picture of the country to contradict the enduring stereotype of the Stage Irishman. Such expectations help to explain the acrimony, sometimes extreme, which greeted productions felt to defame the national character— most notably, the rows over Synge's *The Playboy of the Western World* in Dublin in 1907, and in 1911 on the Abbey company's first tour in the United States.

Synge's plays wrought to a high level the Abbey's distinctive blend of peasant naturalism, romanticism, and rich, eloquent dialogue. Synge was the first Irish dramatist to combine successfully the influences of Molière's design and humor, Racine's musicality, Irish myth and folklore, and extravagant rural Irish dialect; his work was also the Abbey's first major success, realizing its artistic objectives and making the theater a focus of consciousness for the emerging nation. Three central themes dominate his work: the enmity between romantic dreams and life's hard necessities, the relationship between humankind and the natural world, and the mutability of all things. Synge had considerable influence in shaping the style and theme of such later Irish dramatists as George Fitzmaurice, Michael J. Molloy (b. 1917), and John B. Keane (b. 1928), and he also had some influence outside Ireland, most notably on the work of García Lorca and Eugene O'Neill.

While Synge's work was certainly the most accomplished dramatic transmutation of Irish rural life, the National Theatre Society in its early years also called forth other excellent contributions: Lady Gregory's many comedies and tragedies based on folklife and popular historical legends; Padraic Colum's realistic tragedies of peasant life set in the midlands; and George Fitzmaurice's quirky fantasies and realistic tragedies set in his native Kerry.

By the time of Synge's death in 1909, however, the Abbey Theatre had begun to lose its initial momentum. The Fays had withdrawn from the Abbey in 1908, after a long series of disagreements about management, and several other actors had departed with them. Yeats, exhausted from the strain of theater business and constant contention with the political demands of the nationalists, was beginning to take less interest in the Abbey, and within a few years would turn from the popular stage to write closet dramas intended for an aristocratic, elite audience. From the first primarily an admirer of the work of Yeats, and never a friend to Irish nationalism, Miss Horniman finally withdrew her support from the Abbey in 1910, when the theater refused to close on the occasion of King Edward VII's death. The new budgetary constraint, leaving the Abbey Theatre at the mercy of the box office, dictated presentation chiefly of popular plays, and moved the Abbey farther from Yeats's theatrical ideal ("a place of intellectual excitement") and closer to being a commercial playhouse. The Abbey continued its commitment to Irish themes and authors, however, and the decline in its repertoire was arrested by the advent of Sean O'Casey's work in 1923.

In many ways Synge's city equivalent, O'Casey (1880–1964) brought the language, humor and sufferings of the Dublin poor to the stage, especially in his three "Dublin plays": *The Shadow of a Gunman* (1923), *Juno and the Paycock* (1924), and *The Plough and the Stars* (1926). In these works—set against the political struggles of the previous decade—he showed himself a master of tragicomedy and a trenchant critic of personal and national self-deception. However, when he submitted his next play (*The Silver Tassie*, 1928) to the Abbey co-directors, Yeats and Lady Gregory rejected it for what they considered an ill-conceived expressionist second act; an acrimonious public exchange followed, and O'Casey severed his relations with the Abbey. His later plays are marked by a more strident Marxism and less certainty in the handling of the Irish materials with which he persisted throughout his long remove to the south of England.

During the 1920s a talented "second generation" of Abbey playwrights emerged, including T. C. Murray (1873–1959), Lennox Robinson (1886–1958), who also served the Abbey as producer and director for much of his life after 1909, and Brinsley McNamara (1890–1963). These dramatists helped to establish domestic realism as the hallmark of the Abbey Theatre—a preference shared in Belfast by the Ulster Group Theatre in the 1940s. In contrast to Murray's stark tragedies of life in rural Cork, Robinson's work ranges from farce to historical treatments of the decline of the Anglo-Irish class, and McNamara wrote many popular comedies of small-town life.

The Abbey's finances, increasingly precarious during the political crises of the emerging Irish nation, were finally stabilized by the institution of an annual government subsidy in 1925—the first such grant to a theater in the English-speaking world. The subsidy made possible renovations which created in 1927 a small experimental theater, the Peacock, which was made available for rental for amateur and semi-professional productions. Lady Gregory, who had been active, reading plays for the Abbey until the very end, died in 1932, and Yeats remained on the theater's board of directors until his own death in 1939. Despite four major tours to America in the 1930s, the Abbey company's work was not distinguished during this decade. Perhaps the most interesting new dramas produced at the Theatre in the 1940s were those of Michael J. Molloy, mainly historical folk dramas rich in dialogue, complex in plot. The original Abbey Theatre building was destroyed by a disastrous fire in 1951, causing a temporary removal until the completion in 1966 of a new, expanded Abbey Theatre at the same site, at last realizing the plans of Yeats and Lady Gregory for a large, commercial auditorium along with a pocket theater (the Peacock) for poetic and experimental works.

It was not entirely a coincidence that in 1928, the same year as O'Casey's falling-out with the Abbey directorate, Dublin got its second serious theater: the Gate. Founded by Hilton Edwards, an English actor, and the Irish actor and artist Micheál MacLiammóir, the Gate Theatre set out to bring international theater to Ireland; although it would produce some experimental Irish drama, its founders—emphasizing the strong cosmopolitan awareness that had been present in the Irish theater movement from the outset—rendered signal service to Irish audiences by importing contemporary Continental and American plays. As if to symbolize its complementary relationship to the Abbey, in its first two years the Gate presented its productions in the Peacock Theatre, where in 1929 it staged Denis Johnston's sensational expressionist play about Irish nationalism, *The Old Lady Says "No!"*—a play which (as its title's ironic allusion emphasizes) had been rejected by Lady Gregory for production at the Abbey. Since 1930 the Gate Theatre has been housed in Dublin's Rotunda Buildings.

During the 1950s three dramatists emerged representing quite different traditions and social sectors. Brendan Behan (1923–1954), political dramatist from Dublin's working class, gained an international reputation when his spirited tragicomedies *The Quare Fellow* (1954) and *The Hostage* (1958) were produced by Joan Littlewood's Theatre Workshop in London. John B. Keane, north Kerry pub owner and author of many popular folk melodramas, satirizes the shibboleths of traditional Irish society with grotesque energy, especially in *Sive* (1959) and *The Field* (1965). With inimitable theatrical genius, Dubliner and expatriate Samuel Beckett (b. 1906) blends some Anglo-Irish coloration into his dramas of persistence in the face of dissolution and death. Beckett's *All That Fall* (1957), commissioned by the BBC, is one of many excellent Irish dramatic works written expressly for radio broadcast; others represented in this volume, written for Radio Éireann, are the lyrical *As the Crow Flies* (1942) by Austin Clarke, and—never before published—*The Vision of Mac Conglinne* (1953) by poet Padraic Fallon (1906–1975). These latter two works illustrate a changing relationship between Irish writers and Ireland's early history and literature; whereas earlier Revival authors dramatized chiefly the epic and mythological stories of Ireland's past, seeking a heritage both admirably heroic and patently separate from modern political and religious dissensions, Clarke, Fallon, and other more recent writers have drawn on a broader range of material, including medieval satires and legends of the Irish Church.

Contemporary Ireland probably has more playwrights and better actors than any society of comparable size. State subventions to various theaters, touring companies, and individual dramatists, along with the nationwide amateur dramatic societies, encourage potential writers for the stage and cultivate audiences. While the Abbey remains the national flagship, its financial fortune guaranteed by Arts Council grants, its artistic hegemony is by no means taken for granted. Since the mid-1960s, there has been a resurgence in original work of high quality on the Abbey mainstage, at the Peacock, and in various regional theaters, all of which offer incentives to new dramatists. The Abbey Theatre is committed to producing a quota of Irish plays each season; but despite its annual state subvention, it still is heavily beholden to the box office and the tourist trade to attain solvency. For a period, it appeared to be overly dependent on revivals and adaptations from other media. But that is no longer the case: despite commercial pressure and the counterattractions of television and film, contemporary Irish drama is in a healthier state than at any time since the 1920s. This is due to several factors.

The annual Dublin Theatre Festival has been held in the autumn of all but a couple of years since its inauguration in 1957. Despite controversy and continuous organizational changes, the festival has contributed to the enormous rise in production standards over the period, and to the internationalization of theatrical taste. Each year, it features one or more home-grown premieres and, especially since 1980, numerous international companies, predominantly eastern European. With some 30 to 40 productions over a three-week period, it is perhaps the best festival of its kind in the world.

There are many new companies and young actors, both in Dublin and the provinces. The Lyric Theatre of Belfast has grown from a closet theater specializing in Yeats's poetic plays to a thriving public enterprise. Provincial theatrical companies, most significantly the Field Day Company (Derry City), the Druid Theatre (Galway), and Charabanc (Belfast), stage the output of dramatists with particular regional flavor; thus, Brian Friel, Thomas Murphy, and Marie Jones, respectively, find companies ideally suited to their work, just as Cork's Southern Theatre Group served John B. Keane in the 1960s.

In addition, many middle-sized towns now have fully equipped theaters, catering to touring and amateur companies: Limerick's Belltable, Sligo's Hawk's Well, Cork's Everyman and Ivernia, Waterford's Theatre Royal, and Tralee's *Siamsa Tíre*. These theaters and scores of community halls cater for the thriving amateur drama tradition, especially in the winter months, when a series of drama festivals are held.

Since the 1960s, Irish writing for the stage has been dominated by five dramatists: Brian Friel (b. 1929), Hugh Leonard (b. 1926), John B. Keane (b. 1928), Thomas Murphy (b. 1936), and Thomas Kilroy (b. 1934). Friel and Leonard have attained international standing. In an *oeuvre* of impressive range from his early success, *Philadelphia, Here I Come!* (1964), through *Making History* (1988), Friel's central preoccupation has been the relationship between the nation's history and its present anomie. Throughout these works his dominant mood is bittersweet, while technically he applies various nonrealistic techniques to realistic situations. Friel has written what is perhaps the best play on the Northern Ireland conflict, *The Freedom of the City* (1973).

Hugh Leonard's eye, on the other hand, is on contemporary Ireland's uncertain prosperity. Primarily a witty social satirist of considerable technical virtuosity (refined through much commercial television work), his most accomplished work in this dominant vein is *The Patrick Pearse Motel* (1971). His greatest critical success, however, is the autobiographical *Da* (1973), invested with more feeling than his broader satire and farces. Whereas Friel's concerns are with the relationships between past and present, and between Ireland and Irish-America, Leonard looks at contemporary suburban life with an eye to Britain and Europe. Friel's characters, moreover, as Robert Hogan observes, "have a broader social base, [whereas] Leonard's exist only on a plane of personal relations."

Thomas Murphy writes with exacting vehemence of life among Irish laborers in England in *Whistle in the Dark* (1961), or of the frustrations of rural life in the west of Ireland in *A Crucial Week in the Life of a Grocer's Assistant* (1969). Thomas Kilroy is a disciplined and literate dramatist whose most acclaimed work is the surrealist *Talbot's Box* (1977), a study of the Dublin laborer and mystic, Matt Talbot.

Over the past decade, many talented younger playwrights have emerged, including Bernard Farrell, Liam Lynch, Heno Magee, J. Graham Reid, Anne Devlin, and Marie Jones. The most consistent and innovative is Frank McGuinness, author of *Observe the Sons of Ulster Marching towards the Somme* (1985). *Theatre Ireland,* an all-Ireland theater journal founded in 1982, edited and produced in Northern Ireland but drawing for funds on both Northern and Southern Arts Councils, has been reflecting on the fortunes of this continuing tradition. Irish dramatists are not bereft of either subject or language, and the dramatic movement set in motion by Yeats and Lady Gregory shows every sign of continuing in years to come.

LADY GREGORY

1852 — 1932

"If ever there was a person doomed from the cradle to write for the stage, to break through every social obstacle to get to the stage—nay, to invent and create a theatre if no theatre existed—that person," wrote George Bernard Shaw, was Lady Isabella Augusta Gregory. For more than the first half of her life, however, such a prediction would have seemed laughable—no less to Augusta Gregory herself than to those who knew her.

She was born on March 15, 1852, the twelfth of sixteen children (and last and least-regarded daughter) of Dudley Persse, on the family estate, Roxborough, County Galway. Her Unionist family descended from all the layers of Ireland's conquerors, from the Old English onwards. Her mother, Frances Barry Persse, devoted herself to passionate proselytizing among the tenants (Augusta took no part in this); her father, autocratic and self-indulgent, ruled his large estate from a wheelchair, his gout having crippled him by the time Augusta knew him. Like the servants and tenants, Augusta referred to her father and mother as "the Master" and "the Mistress." Perhaps sensing a similarity between the historical oppression of the native Irish and her own undervalued life, she gave what charity and service she could to the poorest of the tenants, and collected Fenian publications.

From her unprepossessing start in childhood, least daughter and deputy nursemaid to four younger brothers, Augusta Persse at the age of 27 made a marriage that immediately established her in the highest social circles in Ireland, England, Europe and the Colonies: she married a neighboring widower, Sir William Gregory, 63, of Coole Park. Recently retired as Governor of Ceylon, a trustee of the National Gallery of Art, Sir William was a man of cosmopolitan views; their married years were full of foreign travel, though chiefly they lived in London for the social season and at Coole in the summers. In May, 1881, their only child, William Robert Gregory, was born.

Sir William died in March, 1892, when Lady Gregory was 40; for the rest of her life—forty more years—she dressed in widow's black. In retrospect, she saw both marriage and widowhood as occasions for growth: "If I had not married I should not have learned the quick enrichment of sentences that one gets in conversation; had I not been widowed I should not have found the detachment of mind, the leisure for observation necessary to give insight into character, to express and interpret it. Loneliness made me rich—'full' as Bacon says." It was during her widowhood, certainly, that she came into her own as a creative artist, translator, editor and powerful manager; that her sympathies with the Irish country people ripened into such unequivocal nationalism that during the Troubles, when great estates all around her (including Roxborough) were being destroyed, Coole was unharmed; that she found her life's chosen company and her life's chosen work.

Her friendship with W. B. Yeats, which began with a casual meeting in London in 1894, developed into an association of extraordinary benefit to both of them—one which can truly be said to have catalyzed the Irish literary movement of this century. "I doubt I should have done much with my life," Yeats wrote, "but for her firmness and care." She had a gift for spotting and encouraging genius, and her guests at Coole Park (their invited signatures carved in the bark of her demesne's "Autograph Tree") formed a roster of the creative minds of the age.

In 1897, when Yeats spent the first of twenty summers at Coole, their conversations founded the Irish Literary Theatre. Much of the work of organizing, promoting, and managing the theater was hers; she saw the theater through all its changes and growth, and until the very last year of her life she read and evaluated plays submitted to the Abbey. It was she who accompanied the players on their (sometimes tempestuous) tours abroad. The *New York Dramatic Mirror,* calling Lady Gregory the "Guiding Genius" of the 1911 tour, described her as "a figure in a trailing black gown, with a black lace mantilla over her grey hair, [who] hovered about the house like a sort of patron saint."

"During [the theater's] first years," Yeats wrote, "Lady Gregory was friend and hostess, a centre of peace, an adviser who never overestimated or underestimated trouble, but neither she nor we thought her a possible creator. And now all in a moment, as it seemed, she became the founder of modern Irish dialect literature." Her development *was* sudden, despite some creditable earlier writing—mainly journalistic and editorial. Beginning in 1896, when Yeats briefly visited at Coole, she collected folklore from the country people, and in the following few years she also studied the Irish language. (She was the only one of the Abbey playwrights who learned Irish well.) The time spent carefully listening to the language(s) of her peasant neighbors helped her develop the stylized literary peasant dialect she called (after the name of the district around Coole) "Kiltartan." When she turned her hand to translating the early Irish epics and myths in *Cuchulain of Muirthemne* (1902) and later volumes, she chose to render them in this dialect, thus at once making these vivid stories available to her contemporaries and connecting Ireland's ancient heritage with its modern oral tradition.

Lady Gregory began her playwriting career quietly, "helping" Yeats with the peasant dialogue for his plays (but in fact, generously coauthoring several, including *Cathleen Ni Houlihan*, *The Pot of Broth*, and *Where There Is Nothing*) and writing scenarios for Douglas Hyde to expand into plays in Irish. She claimed to have begun to write her own plays in order to supply what the Abbey needed: short comedies, adapted to the particular actors in the company and to its limited stage and funds, which could complement the more serious dramas in the repertoire. But once she started, she discovered that "the desire for experiment is like fire in the blood"—and she wrote incessantly, finishing nineteen original plays and seven translations between 1904 and 1912. Her plays were the Abbey's steadiest attraction, receiving 600 performances in the same eight years (more than twice as many as Yeats's, and three times as many as Synge's). By the time of her death in 1932 she had written some forty plays.

She was a versatile dramatist, writing comedies, tragicomedies, tragedies, folk history plays (including a series focused on tragic heroines in Ireland's history), wonder plays for children, and religious dramas; a successful translator, her adaptations of the sharp repartee of Molière into Kiltartan rhythms of speech created a pungent meeting of cultures. She drew her own subject matter from the folklore she collected around Gort, from Irish history and nationalist legends, from chance stories and encounters. She loved the imaginative power of the country people, and was often "moved by the strange contrast between the poverty of the tellers and the splendours of the tales." As Lady Gregory's career developed, it influenced the direction of the Abbey Theatre: introducing peasant dialect as a quasi-poetic medium, demonstrating the effectiveness of one-act dramas and of extremely simplified action among few characters, and, later, showing the vitality and the enduring interest of plays based on Irish history.

SELECT BIBLIOGRAPHY

Publications

The Coole Edition of the Collected Works of Lady Gregory. Gerrards Cross, Bucks.: Colin Smythe Ltd., 1970–.

Selected Plays of Lady Gregory. Washington, DC: The Catholic University of America Press/Gerrards Cross, Bucks.: Colin Smythe Ltd., 1983. (*The Travelling Man, Spreading the News, Kincora, Hyacinth Halvey, The Doctor In Spite of Himself, The Gaol Gate, The Rising of the Moon, Dervorgilla, The Workhouse Ward, Grania, The Golden Apple, The Story Brought by Brigit, Dave*)

Our Irish Theatre: A Chapter of Autobiography. London and New York: G. P. Putnam's, 1913; rpt. New York: Capricorn Books, 1965; ed. with a foreword by Roger McHugh, Gerrards Cross, Bucks. and New York: Oxford University Press, 1973.

Biography and Criticism

Adams, Hazard. *Lady Gregory.* Lewisburg, PA: Bucknell University Press, 1973.

Coxhead, Elizabeth. *Lady Gregory: A Literary Portrait.* Rev. ed. London: Secker and Warburg, 1966.

Knapp, James F. "History against Myth: Lady Gregory and Cultural Discourse." *Eire-Ireland* 22,3 (Fall 1987): 30–42.

Kohfeldt, Mary Lou. *Lady Gregory: The Woman Behind the Irish Renaissance.* New York: Atheneum, 1985.

Kopper, Edward A. *Lady Isabella Persse Gregory.* Boston: Twayne, 1976.

Mikhail, E. H. *Lady Gregory: An Annotated Bibliography of Criticism.* Troy, NY: Whitston, 1982.

———. *Lady Gregory: Interviews and Recollections.* Totowa, NJ: Rowman and Littlefield, 1977.

Saddlemyer, Ann. *In Defense of Lady Gregory, Playwright.* Chester Springs, PA: Dufour Editions, 1966.

Thuente, Mary Helen. "Lady Gregory and 'The Book of the People.'" *Éire-Ireland* 15,1 (Spring 1980): 86–99.

SPREADING THE NEWS

Spreading the News, a brilliantly constructed comedy of rumor and mis-interpretation, was written in 1904 and first produced, along with Yeats's *On Baile's Strand*, at the opening of the Abbey Theatre, December 27, 1904. Like several of Lady Gregory's best-known comedies, it is set in the fictitious town of Cloon, modeled on Coole's market-town of Gort, but in truth a representative Irish small town. ("It is the boundless country of comedy," Ann Saddlemyer writes.) Of the play's initial reception Lady Gregory wrote to Wilfrid Blunt that "the audience would laugh so much at 'Spreading the News' that they lost about half the dialogue. I mustn't be so amusing again!"

Her account of the origin of the play illustrates not only the dutiful posture which often accompanied her early playwriting, but also her famous observation about the relationship between comedy and character: "Character comes in, and why it is so I cannot explain, but as soon as one creates a character, he begins to put out little feet of his own and take his own way."

"The idea of this play first came to me as a tragedy. I kept seeing as in a picture people sitting by the roadside, and a girl passing to the market, gay and fearless. And then I saw her passing by the same place at evening, her head hanging, the heads of others turned from her, because of some sudden story that had risen out of a chance word, and had snatched away her good name.

"But comedy and not tragedy was wanted at our theatre to put beside the high poetic work . . . , and I let laughter have its way with the little play. I was delayed in beginning it for a while, because I could only think of Bartley Fallon as dull-witted or silly or ignorant, and the handcuffs seemed too harsh a punishment. But one day by the sea at Duras a melancholy man who was telling me of the crosses he had gone through at home said—'But I'm thinking if I went to America, it's long ago today I'd be dead. And it's a great expense for a poor man to be buried in America.' Bartley was born at that moment, and, far from harshness, I felt I was providing him with a happy old age in giving him the lasting glory of that great and crowning day of misfortune." (*Seven Short Plays*)

Spreading the News

PERSONS

BARTLEY FALLON
MRS. FALLON
JACK SMITH
SHAWN EARLY
TIM CASEY
JAMES RYAN
MRS. TARPEY
MRS. TULLY
A Policeman (JO MULDOON)
A REMOVABLE MAGISTRATE

SCENE. *The outskirts of a Fair. An Apple Stall. Mrs. Tarpey sitting at it. Magistrate and Policeman enter.*

MAGISTRATE. So that is the Fair Green. Cattle and sheep and mud. No system. What a repulsive sight!
POLICEMAN. That is so, indeed.
MAGISTRATE. I suppose there is a good deal of disorder in this place?
POLICEMAN. There is.
MAGISTRATE. Common assault?
POLICEMAN. It's common enough.
MAGISTRATE. Agrarian crime, no doubt?
POLICEMAN. That is so.
MAGISTRATE. Boycotting? Maiming of cattle? Firing into houses?
POLICEMAN. There was one time, and there might be again.
MAGISTRATE. That is bad. Does it go any farther than that?
POLICEMAN. Far enough, indeed.
MAGISTRATE. Homicide, then! This district has been shamefully neglected! I will change all that. When I was in the Andaman Islands,[1] my system never failed. Yes, yes, I will change all that. What has that woman on her stall?
POLICEMAN. Apples mostly—and sweets.

1. **Andaman Islands** some 200 islands in the Bay of Bengal; site of a British penal colony from 1858 to 1945

MAGISTRATE. Just see if there are any unlicensed goods underneath—spirits or the like. We had evasions of the salt tax in the Andaman Islands.

POLICEMAN (*sniffing cautiously and upsetting a heap of apples*). I see no spirits here—or salt.

MAGISTRATE (*to Mrs. Tarpey*). Do you know this town well, my good woman?

MRS. TARPEY (*holding out some apples*). A penny the half-dozen, your honour.

POLICEMAN (*shouting*). The gentleman is asking do you know the town! He's the new magistrate!

MRS. TARPEY (*rising and ducking*). Do I know the town? I do, to be sure.

MAGISTRATE (*shouting*). What is its chief business?

MRS. TARPEY. Business, is it? What business would the people here have but to be minding one another's business?

MAGISTRATE. I mean what trade have they?

MRS. TARPEY. Not a trade. No trade at all but to be talking.

MAGISTRATE. I shall learn nothing here.

(*James Ryan comes in, pipe in mouth. Seeing Magistrate he retreats quickly, taking pipe from mouth.*)

MAGISTRATE. The smoke from that man's pipe had a greenish look; he may be growing unlicensed tobacco at home. I wish I had brought my telescope to this district. Come to the post-office, I will telegraph for it. I found it very useful in the Andaman Islands.

(*Magistrate and Policeman go out left.*)

MRS. TARPEY. Bad luck to Jo Muldoon, knocking my apples this way and that way. (*Begins arranging them.*) Showing off he was to the new magistrate.

(*Enter Bartley Fallon and Mrs. Fallon.*)

BARTLEY. Indeed it's a poor country and a scarce country to be living in. But I'm thinking if I went to America it's long ago the day I'd be dead!

MRS. FALLON. So you might, indeed.

(*She puts her basket on a barrel and begins putting parcels in it, taking them from under her cloak.*)

BARTLEY. And it's a great expense for a poor man to be buried in America.

MRS. FALLON. Never fear, Bartley Fallon, but I'll give you a good burying the day you'll die.

BARTLEY. Maybe it's yourself will be buried in the graveyard of Cloonmara before me, Mary Fallon, and I myself that will be dying unbeknownst some night, and no one a-near me. And the cat itself may be gone straying through the country, and the mice squealing over the quilt.

MRS. FALLON. Leave off talking of dying. It might be twenty years you'll be living yet.

BARTLEY *(with a deep sigh)*. I'm thinking if I'll be living at the end of twenty years, it's a very old man I'll be then!

MRS. TARPEY *(turns and sees them)*. Good morrow, Bartley Fallon; good morrow, Mrs. Fallon. Well, Bartley, you'll find no cause for complaining to-day; they are all saying it was a good fair.

BARTLEY *(raising his voice)*. It was not a good fair, Mrs. Tarpey. It was a scattered sort of a fair. If we didn't expect more, we got less. That's the way with me always; whatever I have to sell goes down and whatever I have to buy goes up. If there's ever any misfortune coming to this world, it's on myself it pitches, like a flock of crows on seed potatoes.

MRS. FALLON. Leave off talking of misfortunes, and listen to Jack Smith that is coming the way, and he singing.

(Voice of Jack Smith heard singing:)

> I thought, my first love,
> There'd be but one house between you and me,
> And I thought I would find
> Yourself coaxing my child on your knee.
> Over the tide
> I would leap with the leap of a swan,
> Till I came to the side
> Of the wife of the Red-haired man!

(Jack Smith comes in; he is a red-haired man, and is carrying a hayfork.)

MRS. TARPEY. That should be a good song if I had my hearing.

MRS. FALLON *(shouting)*. It's "The Red-haired Man's Wife."

MRS. TARPEY. I know it well. That's the song that has a skin on it!

(She turns her back to them and goes on arranging her apples.)

MRS. FALLON. Where's herself, Jack Smith?

JACK SMITH. She was delayed with her washing; bleaching the clothes on the hedge she is, and she daren't leave them, with all the tinkers that do be passing to the fair. It isn't to the fair I came myself, but up to the Five Acre Meadow I'm going, where I have a contract for the hay. We'll get a share of it into tramps² to-day.

(He lays down hayfork and lights his pipe.)

BARTLEY. You will not get it into tramps to-day. The rain will be down on it by evening, and on myself too. It's seldom I ever started on a journey but the rain would come down on me before I'd find any place of shelter.

JACK SMITH. If it didn't itself, Bartley, it is my belief you would carry a leaky pail on your head in place of a hat, the way you'd not be without some cause of complaining.

(A voice heard, "Go on, now, go on out o' that. Go on I say.")

JACK SMITH. Look at that young mare of Pat Ryan's that is backing

---

2. **tramps** or tramp-cocks: haystacks

into Shaughnessy's bullocks with the dint of the crowd! Don't be daunted, Pat, I'll give you a hand with her.

(He goes out, leaving his hayfork.)

MRS. FALLON. It's time for ourselves to be going home. I have all I bought put in the basket. Look at there, Jack Smith's hayfork he left after him! He'll be wanting it. *(Calls.)* Jack Smith! Jack Smith!—He's gone through the crowd—hurry after him, Bartley, he'll be wanting it.

BARTLEY. I'll do that. This is no safe place to be leaving it. *(He takes up fork awkwardly and upsets the basket.)* Look at that now! If there is any basket in the fair upset, it must be our own basket!

(He goes out to right.)

MRS. FALLON. Get out of that! It is your own fault, it is. Talk of misfortunes and misfortunes will come. Glory be! Look at my new egg-cups rolling in every part—and my two pound of sugar with the paper broke——

MRS. TARPEY *(turning from stall).* God help us, Mrs. Fallon, what happened your basket?

MRS. FALLON. It's himself that knocked it down, bad manners to him. *(Putting things up.)* My grand sugar that's destroyed, and he'll not drink his tea without it. I had best go back to the shop for more, much good may it do him!

(Enter Tim Casey.)

TIM CASEY. Where is Bartley Fallon, Mrs. Fallon? I want a word with him before he'll leave the fair. I was afraid he might have gone home by this, for he's a temperate man.

MRS. FALLON. I wish he did go home! It'd be best for me if he went home straight from the fair green, or if he never came with me at all! Where is he, is it? He's gone up the road *(jerks elbow)* following Jack Smith with a hayfork.

(She goes out to left.)

TIM CASEY. Following Jack Smith with a hayfork! Did ever any one hear the like of that. *(Shouts.)* Did you hear that news, Mrs. Tarpey?

MRS. TARPEY. I heard no news at all.

TIM CASEY. Some dispute I suppose it was that rose between Jack Smith and Bartley Fallon, and it seems Jack made off, and Bartley is following him with a hayfork!

MRS.TARPEY. Is he now? Well, that was quick work! It's not ten minutes since the two of them were here, Bartley going home and Jack going to the Five Acre Meadow; and I had my apples to settle up, that Jo Muldoon of the police had scattered, and when I looked round again Jack Smith was gone, and Bartley Fallon was gone, and Mrs. Fallon's basket upset, and all in it strewed upon the ground—the tea here—the two pound of sugar there—the egg-cups there—Look, now, what a great hardship

the deafness puts upon me, that I didn't hear the commincement of the fight! Wait till I tell James Ryan that I see below; he is a neighbour of Bartley's, it would be a pity if he wouldn't hear the news!
(She goes out. Enter Shawn Early and Mrs. Tully.)
TIM CASEY. Listen, Shawn Early! Listen, Mrs. Tully, to the news! Jack Smith and Bartley Fallon had a falling out, and Jack knocked Mrs. Fallon's basket into the road, and Bartley made an attack on him with a hayfork, and away with Jack, and Bartley after him. Look at the sugar here yet on the road!
SHAWN EARLY. Do you tell me so? Well, that's a queer thing, and Bartley Fallon so quiet a man!
MRS. TULLY. I wouldn't wonder at all. I would never think well of a man that would have that sort of a mouldering look. It's likely he has overtaken Jack by this.
(Enter James Ryan and Mrs. Tarpey.)
JAMES RYAN. That is great news Mrs. Tarpey was telling me! I suppose that's what brought the police and the magistrate up this way. I was wondering to see them in it a while ago.
SHAWN EARLY. The police after them? Bartley Fallon must have injured Jack so. They wouldn't meddle in a fight that was only for show!
MRS. TULLY. Why wouldn't he injure him? There was many a man killed with no more of a weapon than a hayfork.
JAMES RYAN. Wait till I run north as far as Kelly's bar to spread the news!
(He goes out.)
TIM CASEY. I'll go tell Jack Smith's first cousin that is standing there south of the church after selling his lambs.
(Goes out.)
MRS. TULLY. I'll go telling a few of the neighbours I see beyond to the west.
(Goes out.)
SHAWN EARLY. I'll give word of it beyond at the east of the green.
(Is going out when Mrs. Tarpey seizes hold of him.)
MRS. TARPEY. Stop a minute, Shawn Early, and tell me did you see red Jack Smith's wife, Kitty Keary, in any place?
SHAWN EARLY. I did. At her own house she was, drying clothes on the hedge as I passed.
MRS. TARPEY. What did you say she was doing?
SHAWN EARLY *(breaking away)*. Laying out a sheet on the hedge.
(He goes.)
MRS. TARPEY. Laying out a sheet for the dead! The Lord have mercy on us! Jack Smith dead, and his wife laying out a sheet for his burying!
(Calls out.) Why didn't you tell me that before, Shawn Early? Isn't the

deafness the great hardship? Half the world might be dead without me knowing of it or getting word of it at all! *(She sits down and rocks herself.)* O my poor Jack Smith! To be going to his work so nice and so hearty, and to be left stretched on the ground in the full light of the day! *(Enter Tim Casey.)*

TIM CASEY. What is it, Mrs. Tarpey? What happened since?

MRS. TARPEY. O my poor Jack Smith!

TIM CASEY. Did Bartley overtake him?

MRS. TARPEY. O the poor man!

TIM CASEY. Is it killed he is?

MRS. TARPEY. Stretched in the Five Acre Meadow!

TIM CASEY. The Lord have mercy on us! Is that a fact?

MRS. TARPEY. Without the rites of the Church or a ha'porth![3]

TIM CASEY. Who was telling you?

MRS. TARPEY. And the wife laying out a sheet for his corpse. *(Sits up and wipes her eyes.)* I suppose they'll wake him[4] the same as another? *(Enter Mrs. Tully, Shawn Early, and James Ryan.)*

MRS. TULLY. There is great talk about this work in every quarter of the fair.

MRS. TARPEY. Ochone![5] cold and dead. And myself maybe the last he was speaking to!

JAMES RYAN. The Lord save us! Is it dead he is?

TIM CASEY. Dead surely, and the wife getting provision for the wake.

SHAWN EARLY. Well, now, hadn't Bartley Fallon great venom in him?

MRS. TULLY. You may be sure he had some cause. Why would he have made an end of him if he had not? *(To Mrs. Tarpey, raising her voice.)* What was it rose the dispute at all, Mrs. Tarpey?

MRS. TARPEY. Not a one of me knows. The last I saw of them, Jack Smith was standing there, and Bartley Fallon was standing there, quiet and easy, and he listening to "The Red-haired Man's Wife."

MRS. TULLY. Do you hear that, Tim Casey? Do you hear that, Shawn Early and James Ryan? Bartley Fallon was here this morning listening to red Jack Smith's wife, Kitty Keary that was! Listening to her and whispering with her! It was she started the fight so!

SHAWN EARLY. She must have followed him from her own house. It is likely some person roused him.

TIM CASEY. I never knew, before, Bartley Fallon was great with[6] Jack Smith's wife.

MRS. TULLY. How would you know it? Sure it's not in the streets they

---

3. **ha'porth** "or anything" (halfpennyworth: tiny amount of money) 4. **wake him** hold a traditional wake for him 5. **Ochone** Alas! 6. **great with** intimate with, close to

would be calling it. If Mrs. Fallon didn't know of it, and if I that have the next house to them didn't know of it, and if Jack Smith himself didn't know of it, it is not likely you would know of it, Tim Casey.

SHAWN EARLY. Let Bartley Fallon take charge of her from this out so, and let him provide for her. It is little pity she will get from any person in this parish.

TIM CASEY. How can he take charge of her? Sure he has a wife of his own. Sure you don't think he'd turn souper[7] and marry her in a Protestant church?

JAMES RYAN. It would be easy for him to marry her if he brought her to America.

SHAWN EARLY. With or without Kitty Keary, believe me it is for America he's making at this minute. I saw the new magistrate and Jo Muldoon of the police going into the post-office as I came up—there was hurry on them—you may be sure it was to telegraph they went, the way he'll be stopped in the docks at Queenstown![8]

MRS. TULLY. It's likely Kitty Keary is gone with him, and not minding a sheet or a wake at all. The poor man, to be deserted by his own wife, and the breath hardly gone out yet from his body that is lying bloody in the field!

(Enter Mrs. Fallon.)

MRS. FALLON. What is it the whole of the town is talking about? And what is it you yourselves are talking about? Is it about my man Bartley Fallon you are talking? Is it lies about him you are telling, saying that he went killing Jack Smith? My grief that ever he came into this place at all!

JAMES RYAN. Be easy now, Mrs. Fallon. Sure there is no one at all in the whole fair but is sorry for you!

MRS. FALLON. Sorry for me, is it? Why would anyone be sorry for me? Let you be sorry for yourselves, and that there may be shame on you for ever and at the day of judgment, for the words you are saying and the lies you are telling to take away the character of my poor man, and to take the good name off of him, and to drive him to destruction! That is what you are doing!

SHAWN EARLY. Take comfort now, Mrs. Fallon. The police are not so smart as they think. Sure he might give them the slip yet, the same as Lynchehaun.[9]

---

7. **souper** a Catholic convert to Protestantism (from the Famine missionary work, famous in folk tradition for offering food—"soup"—to converts) 8. **Queenstown** the deep-water port in Cork Harbour 9. **Lynchehaun** James Lynchehaun, peasant land agent on Achill Island, Co. Mayo, who brutally assaulted English landowner Agnes MacDonnell in 1894, was captured, and finally escaped to America. For the whole story, see James Carney, *The Playboy and the Yellow Lady* (Dublin: Poolbeg Press, 1987).

MRS. TULLY. If they do get him, and if they do put a rope around his neck, there is no one can say he does not deserve it!

MRS. FALLON. Is that what you are saying, Bridget Tully, and is that what you think? I tell you it's too much talk you have, making yourself out[10] to be such a great one, and to be running down[11] every respectable person! A rope, is it? It isn't much of a rope was needed to tie up your own furniture the day you came into Martin Tully's house, and you never bringing as much as a blanket, or a penny, or a suit of clothes with you and I myself bringing seventy pounds and two feather beds. And now you are stiffer than a woman would have a hundred pounds! It is too much talk the whole of you have. A rope is it? I tell you the whole of this town is full of liars and schemers that would hang you up for half a glass of whiskey. (Turning to go.) People they are you wouldn't believe as much as daylight from without you'd get up to have a look at it yourself. Killing Jack Smith indeed! Where are you at all, Bartley, till I bring you out of this? My nice quiet little man! My decent comrade! He that is as kind and as harmless as an innocent beast of the field! He'll be doing no harm at all if he'll shed the blood of some of you after this day's work! That much would be no harm at all. (Calls out.) Bartley! Bartley Fallon! Where are you? (Going out.) Did any one see Bartley Fallon?

(All turn to look after her.)

JAMES RYAN. It is hard for her to believe any such a thing, God help her!

(Enter Bartley Fallon from right, carrying hayfork.)

BARTLEY. It is what I often said to myself, if there is ever any misfortune coming to this world it is on myself it is sure to come!

(All turn round and face him.)

BARTLEY. To be going about with this fork and to find no one to take it, and no place to leave it down, and I wanting to be gone out of this— Is that you, Shawn Early? (Holds out fork.) It's well I met you. You have no call to be leaving the fair for a while the way I have, and how can I go till I'm rid of this fork? Will you take it and keep it until such time as Jack Smith——

SHAWN EARLY (backing). I will not take it, Bartley Fallon, I'm very thankful to you!

BARTLEY (turning to apple stall). Look at it now, Mrs. Tarpey, it was here I got it; let me thrust it in under the stall. It will lie there safe enough, and no one will take notice of it until such time as Jack Smith——

MRS. TARPEY. Take your fork out of that! Is it to put trouble on me and to destroy me you want? putting it there for the police to be rooting it out maybe.

10. **making yourself out** pretending   11. **running down** denigrating

(Thrusts him back.)

BARTLEY. That is a very unneighbourly thing for you to do, Mrs. Tarpey. Hadn't I enough care on me with that fork before this, running up and down with it like the swinging of a clock, and afeard to lay it down in any place! I wish I never touched it or meddled with it at all!

JAMES RYAN. It is a pity, indeed, you ever did.

BARTLEY. Will you yourself take it, James Ryan? You were always a neighbourly man.

JAMES RYAN *(backing)*. There is many a thing I would do for you, Bartley Fallon, but I won't do that!

SHAWN EARLY. I tell you there is no man will give you any help or any encouragement for this day's work. If it was something agrarian[12] now——

BARTLEY. If no one at all will take it, maybe it's best to give it up to the police.

TIM CASEY. There'd be a welcome for it with them surely! *(Laughter.)*

MRS. TULLY. And it is to the police Kitty Keary herself will be brought.

MRS. TARPEY *(rocking to and fro)*. I wonder now who will take the expense of the wake for poor Jack Smith?

BARTLEY. The wake for Jack Smith!

TIM CASEY. Why wouldn't he get a wake as well as another? Would you begrudge him that much?

BARTLEY. Red Jack Smith dead! Who was telling you?

SHAWN EARLY. The whole town knows of it by this.

BARTLEY. Do they say what way did he die?

JAMES RYAN. You don't know that yourself, I suppose, Bartley Fallon? You don't know he was followed and that he was laid dead with the stab of a hayfork?

BARTLEY. The stab of a hayfork!

SHAWN EARLY. You don't know, I suppose, that the body was found in the Five Acre Meadow?

BARTLEY. The Five Acre Meadow!

TIM CASEY. It is likely you don't know that the police are after the man that did it?

BARTLEY. The man that did it!

MRS. TULLY. You don't know, maybe, that he was made away with for the sake of Kitty Keary, his wife?

BARTLEY. Kitty Keary, his wife!

(Sits down bewildered.)

---

12. **something agrarian** an agrarian crime, such as would have been committed as a tactic in the Land War

MRS. TULLY. And what have you to say now, Bartley Fallon?

BARTLEY (*crossing himself*). I to bring that fork here, and to find that news before me! It is much if I can ever stir from this place at all, or reach as far as the road!

TIM CASEY. Look, boys, at the new magistrate, and Jo Muldoon along with him! It's best for us to quit this.

SHAWN EARLY. That is so. It is best not to be mixed in this business at all.

JAMES RYAN. Bad as he is, I wouldn't like to be an informer against any man.

(*All hurry away except Mrs. Tarpey, who remains behind her stall. Enter magistrate and policeman.*)

MAGISTRATE. I knew the district was in a bad state, but I did not expect to be confronted with a murder at the first fair I came to.

POLICEMAN. I am sure you did not, indeed.

MAGISTRATE. It was well I had not gone home. I caught a few words here and there that roused my suspicions.

POLICEMAN. So they would, too.

MAGISTRATE. You heard the same story from everyone you asked?

POLICEMAN. The same story—or if it was not altogether the same, anyway it was no less than the first story.

MAGISTRATE. What is that man doing? He is sitting alone with a hayfork. He has a guilty look. The murder was done with a hayfork!

POLICEMAN (*in a whisper*). That's the very man they say did the act; Bartley Fallon himself!

MAGISTRATE. He must have found escape difficult—he is trying to brazen it out. A convict in the Andaman Islands tried the same game, but he could not escape my system! Stand aside—Don't go far—have the handcuffs ready. (*He walks up to Bartley, folds his arms, and stands before him.*) Here, my man, do you know anything of John Smith?

BARTLEY. Of John Smith! Who is he, now?

POLICEMAN. Jack Smith, sir—Red Jack Smith!

MAGISTRATE (*coming a step nearer and tapping him on the shoulder*). Where is Jack Smith?

BARTLEY (*with a deep sigh, and shaking his head slowly*). Where is he, indeed?

MAGISTRATE. What have you to tell?

BARTLEY. It is where he was this morning, standing in this spot, singing his share of songs—no, but lighting his pipe—scraping a match on the sole of his shoes——

MAGISTRATE. I ask you, for the third time, where is he?

BARTLEY. I wouldn't like to say that. It is a great mystery, and it is hard to say of any man, did he earn hatred or love.

MAGISTRATE. Tell me all you know.

BARTLEY. All that I know—Well, there are the three estates; there is Limbo, and there is Purgatory, and there is——

MAGISTRATE. Nonsense! This is trifling! Get to the point.

BARTLEY. Maybe you don't hold with the clergy so? That is the teaching of the clergy. Maybe you hold with the old people. It is what they do be saying, that the shadow goes wandering, and the soul is tired, and the body is taking a rest—The shadow! *(Starts up.)* I was nearly sure I saw Jack Smith not ten minutes ago at the corner of the forge, and I lost him again—Was it his ghost I saw, do you think?

MAGISTRATE *(to policeman)*. Conscience-struck! He will confess all now!

BARTLEY. His ghost to come before me! It is likely it was on account of the fork! I to have it and he to have no way to defend himself the time he met with his death!

MAGISTRATE *(to policeman.)* I must note down his words. *(Takes out notebook.)* *(To Bartley.)* I warn you that your words are being noted.

BARTLEY. If I had ha' run faster in the beginning, this terror would not be on me at the latter end! Maybe he will cast it up against me at the day of judgment—I wouldn't wonder at all at that.

MAGISTRATE *(writing)*. At the day of judgment——

BARTLEY. It was soon for his ghost to appear to me—is it coming after me always by day it will be, and stripping the clothes off in the night time?—I wouldn't wonder at all at that, being as I am an unfortunate man!

MAGISTRATE *(sternly)*. Tell me this truly. What was the motive of this crime?

BARTLEY. The motive, is it?

MAGISTRATE. Yes; the motive; the cause.

BARTLEY. I'd sooner not say that.

MAGISTRATE. You had better tell me truly. Was it money?

BARTLEY. Not at all! What did poor Jack Smith ever have in his pockets unless it might be his hands that would be in them?

MAGISTRATE. Any dispute about land?

BARTLEY *(indignantly)*. Not at all! He never was a grabber[13] or grabbed from any one!

MAGISTRATE. You will find it better for you if you tell me at once.

BARTLEY. I tell you I wouldn't for the whole world wish to say what it was—it is a thing I would not like to be talking about.

MAGISTRATE. There is no use hiding it. It will be discovered in the end.

BARTLEY. Well, I suppose it will, seeing that mostly everybody knows

---

13. **grabber** one who rents a farm from which another family has been evicted

it before. Whisper here now. I will tell no lie; where would be the use? *(Puts his hand to his mouth, and Magistrate stoops.)* Don't be putting the blame on the parish, for such a thing was never done in the parish before— it was done for the sake of Kitty Keary, Jack Smith's wife.

MAGISTRATE *(to policeman)*. Put on the handcuffs. We have been saved some trouble. I knew he would confess if taken in the right way.

(Policeman puts on handcuffs.)

BARTLEY. Handcuffs now! Glory be! I always said, if there was ever any misfortune coming to this place it was on myself it would fall. I to be in handcuffs! There's no wonder at all in that.

(Enter Mrs. Fallon, followed by the rest. She is looking back at them as she speaks.)

MRS. FALLON. Telling lies the whole of the people of this town are; telling lies, telling lies as fast as a dog will trot! Speaking against my poor respectable man! Saying he made an end of Jack Smith! My decent comrade! There is no better man and no kinder man in the whole of the five parishes! It's little annoyance he ever gave to any one! *(Turns and sees him.)* What in the earthly world do I see before me? Bartley Fallon in charge of the police! Handcuffs on him! O Bartley, what did you do at all at all?

BARTLEY. O Mary, there has a great misfortune come upon me! It is what I always said, that if there is ever any misfortune——

MRS. FALLON. What did he do at all, or is it bewitched I am?

MAGISTRATE. This man has been arrested on a charge of murder.

MRS. FALLON. Whose charge is that? Don't believe them! They are all liars in this place! Give me back my man!

MAGISTRATE. It is natural you should take his part, but you have no cause of complaint against your neighbours. He has been arrested for the murder of John Smith, on his own confession.

MRS. FALLON. The saints of heaven protect us! And what did he want killing Jack Smith?

MAGISTRATE. It is best you should know all. He did it on account of a love affair with the murdered man's wife.

MRS. FALLON *(sitting down)*. With Jack Smith's wife! With Kitty Keary!—Ochone, the traitor!

THE CROWD. A great shame, indeed. He is a traitor indeed.

MRS. TULLY. To America he was bringing her, Mrs. Fallon.

BARTLEY. What are you saying, Mary? I tell you——

MRS. FALLON. Don't say a word! I won't listen to any word you'll say! *(Stops her ears.)* O, isn't he the treacherous villain? Ohone go deo!¹⁴

BARTLEY. Be quiet till I speak! Listen to what I say!

MRS. FALLON. Sitting beside me on the ass car coming to the town, so quiet and so respectable, and treachery like that in his heart!

14. **Ohone go deo!** "Alas forever!"

BARTLEY. Is it your wits you have lost or is it I myself that have lost my wits?

MRS. FALLON. And it's hard I earned you, slaving—and you grumbling, and sighing, and coughing, and discontented, and the priest wore out anointing[15] you, with all the times you threatened to die!

BARTLEY. Let you be quiet till I tell you!

MRS. FALLON. You to bring such a disgrace into the parish. A thing that was never heard of before!

BARTLEY. Will you shut your mouth and hear me speaking?

MRS. FALLON. And if it was for any sort of a fine handsome woman, but for a little fistful of a woman like Kitty Keary, that's not four feet high hardly, and not three teeth in her head unless she got new ones! May God reward you, Bartley Fallon, for the black treachery in your heart and the wickedness in your mind, and the red blood of poor Jack Smith that is wet upon your hand!

(Voice of Jack Smith heard singing.)

> The sea shall be dry,
> The earth under mourning and ban!
> Then loud shall he cry
> For the wife of the red-haired man!

BARTLEY. It's Jack Smith's voice—I never knew a ghost to sing before—. It is after myself and the fork he is coming! *(Goes back. Enter Jack Smith.)* Let one of you give him the fork and I will be clear of him now and for eternity!

MRS. TARPEY. The Lord have mercy on us! Red Jack Smith! The man that was going to be waked!

JAMES RYAN. Is it back from the grave you are come?

SHAWN EARLY. Is it alive you are, or is it dead you are?

TIM CASEY. Is it yourself at all that's in it?

MRS. TULLY. Is it letting on you were to be dead?

MRS. FALLON. Dead or alive, let you stop Kitty Keary, your wife, from bringing my man away with her to America!

JACK SMITH. It is what I think, the wits are gone astray on the whole of you. What would my wife want bringing Bartley Fallon to America?

MRS. FALLON. To leave yourself, and to get quit of you she wants, Jack Smith, and to bring them away from myself. That's what the two of them had settled together.

JACK SMITH. I'll break the head of any man that says that! Who is it says it? *(To Tim Casey.)* Was it you said it? *(To Shawn Early.)* Was it you?

ALL TOGETHER *(backing and shaking their heads)*. It wasn't I said it!

---

15. **anointing** administering the last rites to

JACK SMITH. Tell me the name of any man that said it!

ALL TOGETHER *(pointing to Bartley)*. It was *him* that said it!

JACK SMITH. Let me at him till I break his head!

(Bartley backs in terror. Neighbours hold Jack Smith back.)

JACK SMITH *(trying to free himself)*. Let me at him! Isn't he the pleasant sort of a scarecrow for any woman to be crossing the ocean with! It's back from the docks of New York he'd be turned *(trying to rush at him again)*, with a lie in his mouth and treachery in his heart, and another man's wife by his side, and he passing her off as his own! Let me at him can't you.

(Makes another rush, but is held back.)

MAGISTRATE *(pointing to Jack Smith)*. Policeman, put the handcuffs on this man. I see it all now. A case of false impersonation, a conspiracy to defeat the ends of justice. There was a case in the Andaman Islands, a murderer of the Mopsa tribe, a religious enthusiast——

POLICEMAN. So he might be, too.

MAGISTRATE. We must take both these men to the scene of the murder. We must confront them with the body of the real Jack Smith.

JACK SMITH. I'll break the head of any man that will find my dead body!

MAGISTRATE. I'll call more help from the barracks. *(Blows Policeman's whistle.)*

BARTLEY. It is what I am thinking, if myself and Jack Smith are put together in the one cell for the night, the handcuffs will be taken off him, and his hands will be free, and murder will be done that time surely!

MAGISTRATE. Come on! *(They turn to the right.)*

CURTAIN

THE GAOL GATE

First produced at the Abbey Theatre on October 20, 1906, *The Gaol Gate* was Lady Gregory's first tragedy and one of her favorite plays. It reflects the agrarian violence that she had seen in her own Galway neighborhood. That a woman of her lineage and background could so acutely portray the native Irish hatred of British law and of informers, and so vividly dramatize the glorification of a man who has protected the murderers of a landlord or his agent, testifies strongly to her sympathetic understanding. This is her own account of the incidents which led her to write the play:

"I was told a story some one had heard, of a man who had gone to welcome his brother coming out of gaol, and heard he had died there before the gates had been opened for him.

"I was going to Galway, and at the Gort station I met two cloaked and shawled countrywomen from the slopes of Slieve Echtge, who were obliged to go and see some lax official in Galway because of some money left them by a kinsman in Australia. They had never been in a train or to any place farther than a few miles from their own village, and they felt astray and terrified 'like blind beasts in a bog' they said, and I took care of them through the day.

"An agent was fired at on the road from Athenry, and some men were taken up on suspicion. One of them was a young carpenter from my old home, and in a little time a rumour was put about that he had informed against the others in Galway gaol. When the prisoners were taken across the bridge to the courthouse he was hooted by the crowd. But at the trial it was found that he had not informed, that no evidence had been given at all; and bonfires were lighted for him as he went home.

"These three incidents coming within a few months wove themselves into this little play, and within three days it had written itself, or been written. . . . I have never changed a word of it." (*Seven Short Plays*)

The Gaol Gate

PERSONS

MARY CAHEL, *an old woman*
MARY CUSHIN, *her daughter-in-law*
THE GATEKEEPER

SCENE. *Outside the gate of Galway Gaol. Two countrywomen, one in a long dark cloak, the other with a shawl over her head, have just come in. It is just before dawn.*

MARY CAHEL. I am thinking we are come to our journey's end, and that this should be the gate of the gaol.

MARY CUSHIN. It is certain it could be no other place. There was surely never in the world such a terrible great height of a wall.

MARY CAHEL. He that was used to the mountain to be closed up inside of that! What call had he to go moonlighting[1] or to bring himself into danger at all?

MARY CUSHIN. It is no wonder a man to grow faint-hearted and he shut away from the light. I never would wonder at all at anything he might be driven to say.

MARY CAHEL. There were good men were gaoled before him never gave in to anyone at all. It is what I am thinking, Mary, he might not have done what they say.

MARY CUSHIN. Sure you heard what the neighbours were calling the time their own boys were brought away. "It is Denis Cahel," they were saying, "that informed against them in the gaol."

MARY CAHEL. There is nothing that is bad or is wicked but a woman will put it out of her mouth, and she seeing them that belong to her brought away from her sight and her home.

MARY CUSHIN. Terry Fury's mother was saying it, and Pat Ruane's mother and his wife. They came out calling it after me, "It was Denis swore against them in the gaol!" The sergeant was boasting, they were telling me, the day he came searching Daire-caol, it was he himself got his confession with drink he had brought him in the gaol.

MARY CAHEL. They might have done that, the ruffians, and the boy

---

1. **go moonlighting** take part in outlawed agrarian violence

have no blame on him at all. Why should it be cast up against him, and his wits being out of him with drink?

MARY CUSHIN. If he did give their names up itself, there was maybe no wrong in it at all. Sure it's known to all the village it was Terry that fired the shot.

MARY CAHEL. Stop your mouth now and don't be talking. You haven't any sense worth while. Let the sergeant do his own business with no help from the neighbours at all.

MARY CUSHIN. It was Pat Ruane that tempted them on account of some vengeance of his own. Every creature knows my poor Denis never handled a gun in his life.

MARY CAHEL (*taking from under her cloak a long blue envelope*). I wish we could know what is in the letter they are after sending us through the post. Isn't it a great pity for the two of us to be without learning at all?

MARY CUSHIN. There are some of the neighbours have learning, and you bade me not bring it anear them. It would maybe have told us what way he is² or what time he will be quitting the gaol.

MARY CAHEL. There is wonder on me, Mary Cushin, that you would not be content with what I say. It might be they put down in the letter that Denis informed on the rest.

MARY CUSHIN. I suppose it is all we have to do so, to stop here for the opening of the door. It's a terrible long road from Slieve Echtge³ we were travelling the whole of the night.

MARY CAHEL. There was no other thing for us to do but to come and to give him a warning. What way would he be facing the neighbours, and he to come back to Daire-caol?

MARY CUSHIN. It is likely they will let him go free, Mary, before many days will be out. What call have they to be keeping him? It is certain they promised him his life.

MARY CAHEL. If they promised him his life, Mary Cushin, he must live it in some other place. Let him never see Daire-caol again, or Daroda or Druimdarod.⁴

MARY CUSHIN. O, Mary, what place will we bring him to, and we driven from the place that we know? What person that is sent among strangers can have one day's comfort on earth?

MARY CAHEL. It is only among strangers, I am thinking, he could be hiding his story at all. It is best for him to go to America, where the people are as thick as grass.

MARY CUSHIN. What way could he go to America and he having no

---

2. **what way he is** "how he is" (translation of Irish *cén chaoi a bhfuil sé*)   3. **Slieve Echtge** Slieve Aughty mountains, on the border of Cos. Galway and Clare   4. **Daire-caol, Daroda, Druimdarod** understood to be small townlands in the neighborhood of Slieve Echtge

means in his hand? There's himself and myself to make the voyage and the little one-een[5] at home.

MARY CAHEL. I would sooner to sell the holding than to ask for the price paid for blood. There'll be money enough for the two of you to settle your debts and to go.

MARY CUSHIN. And what would yourself be doing and we to go over the sea? It is not among the neighbours you would wish to be ending your days.

MARY CAHEL. I am thinking there is no one would know me in the workhouse at Oughterard. I wonder could I go in there, and I not to give them my name?

MARY CUSHIN. Ah, don't be talking foolishness. What way could I bring the child? Sure he's hardly out of the cradle; he'd be lost out there in the States.

MARY CAHEL. I could bring him into the workhouse, I to give him some other name. You could send for him when you'd be settled or have some place of your own.

MARY CUSHIN. It is very cold at the dawn. It is time for them open the door. I wish I had brought a potato or a bit of a cake or of bread.

MARY CAHEL. I'm in dread of it being opened and not knowing what will we hear. The night that Denis was taken he had a great cold and a cough.

MARY CUSHIN. I think I hear some person coming. There's a sound like the rattling of keys. God and His Mother protect us! I'm in dread of being found here at all!

(The gate is opened, and the Gatekeeper is seen with a lantern in his hand.)

GATEKEEPER. What are you doing here, women? It's no place to be spending the night time.

MARY CAHEL. It is to speak with my son I am asking, that is gaoled these eight weeks and a day.

GATEKEEPER. If you have no order to visit him it's as good for you to go away home.

MARY CAHEL. I got this letter ere yesterday. It might be it is giving me leave.

GATEKEEPER. If that's so he should be under the doctor, or in the hospital ward.

MARY CAHEL. It's no wonder if he's down with the hardship, for he had a great cough and a cold.

GATEKEEPER. Give me here the letter to read it. Sure it never was opened at all.

MARY CAHEL. Myself and this woman have no learning. We were loth to trust any other one.

5. little one-een baby

GATEKEEPER. It was posted in Galway the twentieth, and this is the last of the month.

MARY CAHEL. We never thought to call at the post office. It was chance brought it to us in the end.

GATEKEEPER *(having read letter)*. You poor unfortunate women, don't you know Denis Cahel is dead? You'd a right to[6] come this time yesterday if you wished any last word at all.

MARY CAHEL *(kneeling down)*. God and His Mother protect us and have mercy on Denis's soul!

MARY CUSHIN. What is the man after saying? Sure it cannot be Denis is dead?

GATEKEEPER. Dead since the dawn of yesterday, and another man now in his cell. I'll go see who has charge of his clothing if you're wanting to bring it away.

(He goes in. The dawn has begun to break.)

MARY CAHEL. There is lasting kindness in Heaven when no kindness is found upon earth. There will surely be mercy found for him, and not the hard judgment of men! But my boy that was best in the world, that never rose a hair of my head, to have died with his name under blemish, and left a great shame on his child! Better for him have killed the whole world than to give any witness at all! Have you no word to say, Mary Cushin? Am I left here to keen him alone?

MARY CUSHIN *(who has sunk on to the step before the door, rocking herself and keening[7])*. Oh, Denis, my heart is broken you to have died with the hard word upon you! My grief you to be alone now that spent so many nights in company!

What way will I be going back through Gort and through Kilbecanty? The people will not be coming out keening you, they will say no prayer for the rest of your soul!

What way will I be the Sunday and I going up the hill to the Mass? Every woman with her own comrade, and Mary Cushin to be walking her lone!

What way will I be the Monday and the neighbours turning their heads from the house? The turf[8] Denis cut lying on the bog, and no well-wisher to bring it to the hearth!

What way will I be in the night time, and none but the dog calling after you? Two women to be mixing a cake, and not a man in the house to break it!

What way will I sow the field, and no man to drive the furrow? The

6. **You'd a right to** you should have 7. *keening* delivering the traditional, spontaneously composed poetic chant of lamentation (Irish *caoineadh*) that was the particular responsibility of women 8. **turf** peat, cut from bogs and left to dry out till it can be hauled home to be burned as fuel

sheaf to be scattered before springtime that was brought together at the harvest!

I would not begrudge you, Denis, and you leaving praises after you. The neighbours keening along with me would be better to me than an estate.

But my grief your name to be blackened in the time of the blackening of the rushes! Your name never to rise up again in the growing time of the year! *(She ceases keening and turns towards the old woman.)* But tell me, Mary, do you think would they give us the body of Denis? I would lay him out with myself only; I would hire some man to dig the grave.

(The Gatekeeper opens the gate and hands out some clothes.)

GATEKEEPER. There now is all he brought in with him; the flannels and the shirt and the shoes. It is little they are worth altogether; those mountainy boys do be poor.

MARY CUSHIN. They had a right to give him time to ready himself the day they brought him to the magistrates. He to be wearing his Sunday coat, they would see he was a decent boy. Tell me where will they bury him, the way I can follow after him through the street? There is no other one to show respect to him but Mary Cahel, his mother, and myself.

GATEKEEPER. That is not to be done. He is buried since yesterday in the field that is belonging to the gaol.

MARY CUSHIN. It is a great hardship that to have been done, and not one of his own there to follow after him at all.

GATEKEEPER. Those that break the law must be made an example of. Why would they be laid out like a well behaved man? A long rope and a short burying, that is the order for a man that is hanged.

MARY CUSHIN. A man that was hanged! O Denis, was it they made an end of you and not the great God at all? His curse and my own curse upon them that did not let you die on the pillow! The curse of God be fulfilled that was on them before they were born! My curse upon them that brought harm on you, and on Terry Fury that fired the shot!

MARY CAHEL *(standing up)*. And the other boys, did they hang them along with him, Terry Fury and Pat Ruane that were brought from Dairecaol?

GATEKEEPER. They did not, but set them free twelve hours ago. It is likely you may have passed them in the night time.

MARY CUSHIN. Set free is it, and Denis made an end of ? What justice is there in the world at all?

GATEKEEPER. He was taken near the house. They knew his footmark. There was no witness given against the rest worth while.

MARY CAHEL. Then the sergeant was lying and the people were lying when they said Denis Cahel had informed in the gaol?

GATEKEEPER. I have no time to be stopping here talking. The judge got no evidence and the law set them free.

(He goes in and shuts gate after him.)

MARY CAHEL *(holding out her hands)*. Are there any people in the streets at all till I call on them to come hither? Did they ever hear in Galway such a thing to be done, a man to die for his neighbour?

Tell it out in the streets for the people to hear, Denis Cahel from Slieve Echtge is dead. It was Denis Cahel from Daire-caol that died in the place of his neighbour!

It is he was young and comely and strong, the best reaper and the best hurler.[9] It was not a little thing for him to die, and he protecting his neighbour!

Gather up, Mary Cushin, the clothes for your child; they'll be wanted by this one and that one. The boys crossing the sea in the springtime will be craving a thread for a memory.

One word to the judge and Denis was free, they offered him all sorts of riches. They brought him drink in the gaol, and gold, to swear away the life of his neighbour!

Pat Ruane was no good friend to him at all, but a foolish, wild companion; it was Terry Fury knocked a gap in the wall and sent in the calves to our meadow.

Denis would not speak, he shut his mouth, he would never be an informer. It is no lies he would have said at all giving witness against Terry Fury.

I will go through Gort and Kilbecanty and Druimdarod and Daroda; I will call to the people and the singers at the fairs to make a great praise for Denis!

The child he left in the house that is shook, it is great will be his boast in his father! All Ireland will have a welcome before him, and all the people in Boston.

I to stoop on a stick through half a hundred years, I will never be tired with praising! Come hither, Mary Cushin, till we'll shout it through the roads, Denis Cahel died for his neighbour!

(She goes off to the left, Mary Cushin following her.)

CURTAIN

9. **hurler** player of the Irish sport of hurling

W. B. YEATS
1865 – 1939

Although William Butler Yeats has been celebrated more as a poet than as a dramatist, from another angle of vision poetic drama was central to his artistic life. It is not simply that he wrote plays as well as poems throughout his lengthy career, from the early 1880s until the day before he died; he needed to express himself dramatically. "I believe myself to be a dramatist," he wrote in his fifties; "I desire to show events and not merely tell of them; . . . and I seem to myself most alive at the moment when a room full of people share the one lofty emotion." In his poetry as in his plays, he aimed for a language of passionate speech, conveying moments of crucial and ultimately irresolvable conflict. He tended to express his philosophy in dramatic metaphors: "We begin to live when we have conceived life as tragedy."

Born in Dublin on June 13, 1865, W.B. was the oldest of the four children of Susan Pollexfen and John Butler Yeats, both descended from old Anglo-Irish families. His father, who had trained for the bar but in his adulthood left law for painting, encouraged his children's artistic impulses. W.B. was educated at home until he was ten, as the family moved back and forth from Sligo to Dublin to London, then at the Godolphin School in Hammersmith, London, at the Erasmus Smith High School in Dublin, and thereafter at the Metropolitan School of Art and the School of the Royal Hibernian Academy. In the mid-eighties he decided on a writing career, and also developed strong Irish nationalist sympathies and a lifelong fascination with occult philosophy and experimentation—themes intertwined in his art thenceforward.

Yeats's determination to foster a genuinely Irish literature led him first to found the Irish Literary Society in London, in 1891, and then to collaborate with Lady Gregory, the Fays, and others to found the Irish theater movement in Dublin around the turn of the century, encouraging Irish writers to turn their talents to the creation of plays on Irish subjects (see the General Introduction). Although Yeats was a lifetime director of the Irish National Theatre Society, he was most intensely involved with the practical running of the Abbey Theatre prior to World War I. Thereafter, his dramatic experiments took other directions. He continued to reside alternately in London and in Dublin, although after his marriage he restored for summer use Thoor Ballylee, a Norman tower near Lady Gregory's home at Gort in County Galway, and in the final years of his life illness led him to spend much time in Italy and the south of France.

In 1917 Yeats married Georgie Hyde-Lees, and with her help completed *A Vision*, the culminating statement of the mystical system linking history, human personality, and natural symbols which lies behind much of his writing. In 1922 he was appointed a Senator of the new Irish Free State, and in the following year he received the Nobel Prize for Literature. In 1932 Yeats, Æ (George Russell), and George Bernard Shaw founded the Irish Academy of Letters. Yeats continued to write and revise his work until his death at Cap Martin in France on January 28, 1939; his body, first interred in France, was returned in 1948 for permanent burial at Drumcliff, County Sligo.

In his time Yeats was such an innovator in the theater that his work often baffled contemporary audiences. Though most of his plays are verse dramas—a form he set out to revive—they range enormously in form and style from early work with peasant plays and farce to later achievements stressing symbolism and ritual. Disliking the naturalistic British theater of the turn of the century (and working on tight budgets and tiny stages, with largely amateur actors), he first created plays in which the spoken word took primacy over stage action, sets, costume, and lighting. Psychological insights into character, social or philosophical messages, and realistic presentation of events were unimportant; whatever their individual differences of style and form, Yeats's plays tend toward symbolic ritual, presenting the intersection of the spiritual and temporal worlds. As the Abbey Theatre repertoire developed in the direction of realism, Yeats moved away from his early ambition to write popular plays—realized most fully in his nationalistic *Cathleen Ni Houlihan* (1902)—and turned to producing "closet drama" for a small, select audience. The highly stylized Japanese Noh drama, which Ezra Pound first brought to Yeats's attention in 1913, provided a symbolic form which could—with adaptations—accommodate many of the ritual elements Yeats wished to include in his drama: austere staging, masks, dance, incantatory styles of speech, choruses, simple music, the presence of supernatural and ghostly figures, a distanced and graceful formality. *Four Plays for Dancers* (1921) presents the first fruits of Yeats's work with Noh forms, and at least nine of the later plays reflect this influence.

Concerned on the one hand with the universal spiritual validity of his art, Yeats was concerned as well that the literature of Ireland reflect the particular history and culture of the country. In the face of the materialism and moral bankruptcy he saw in the modern world, he hoped to revive Ireland's ancient spiritual mission. He often looked to early Irish mythology and legend for the materials of his art, and he urged his contemporaries to do the same; in his introduction to Lady Gregory's *Cuchulain of Muirthemne*, his major source of early Irish narrative, he wrote,

> We Irish should keep these [legendary] personages much in our hearts, for they lived in the places where we ride and go marketing,

and sometimes they have met one another on the hills that cast their
shadows upon our doors at evening. If we will but tell these stories
to our children the Land will begin again to be a Holy Land, as it
was before men gave their hearts to Greece and Rome and Judea.

Between 1903 and 1939 Yeats wrote five plays based on the life of the
epic hero Cuchulain (Cú Chulainn in Old Irish): *On Baile's Strand* (published 1903, revised 1906); *The Golden Helmet* (produced 1908, revised in
verse as *The Green Helmet*, 1910); *At the Hawk's Well* (1917); *The Only
Jealousy of Emer* (1919); and—finished the day before he died—*The Death
of Cuchulain* (1939). His principal source of material for the cycle was Lady
Gregory's *Cuchulain of Muirthemne*, but he shaped his plots freely to fit
his own needs, and created the story for one of the plays, *At the Hawk's
Well*, completely from his own imagination. His Cuchulain is not the
young, impetuous war-hero of Irish epic; he is a man—and artist—of
modern complexity, who ages and changes through a lifetime. The two
plays chosen for this volume illustrate both a range of dramatic technique
and Yeats's concern with Irish myth as a vehicle for personal expression.

SELECT BIBLIOGRAPHY

Publications

The Collected Plays of W. B. Yeats. New York: Macmillan, 1953.
The Variorum Edition of the Plays of W. B. Yeats. Ed. Russell K. Alspach. New York:
    Macmillan, 1966.
The Poems of W. B. Yeats. Ed. Richard J. Finneran. New York: Macmillan, 1983.

Biography and Criticism

Bushrui, S. B. *Yeats's Verse Plays: The Revisions, 1900–1910.* Oxford: Clarendon Press,
    1965.
Ellmann, Richard. *Yeats: The Man and the Masks.* London: Macmillan, 1949.
Flannery, James W. *W. B. Yeats and the Idea of a Theatre.* New Haven: Yale University
    Press, 1976.
Hone, Joseph M. *W. B. Yeats, 1865–1939.* London: Macmillan, 1942.
Ishibashi, Hiro. *Yeats and the Noh.* Dublin: Dolmen Press, 1966.
Jeffares, A. Norman, and A. S. Knowland. *A Commentary on the Collected Plays of
    W. B. Yeats.* London: Macmillan, 1975.
Jochum, K. P. S. *W. B. Yeats: A Classified Bibliography of Criticism including Additions
    to Allan Wade's Bibliography of the Writings of W. B. Yeats and a Section on the
    Irish Literary and Dramatic Revival.* Urbana: University of Illinois Press, 1978.
Moore, John Rees. *Masks of Love and Death: Yeats as Dramatist.* Ithaca, N.Y.: Cornell
    University Press, 1971.
Skene, Reg. *The Cuchulain Plays of W. B. Yeats.* London: Macmillan, 1974.
Taylor, Richard. *A Reader's Guide to the Plays of W. B. Yeats.* New York: St. Martin's,
    1984.
Ure, Peter. *Yeats the Playwright.* London: Routledge and Kegan Paul, 1963.

ON BAILE'S STRAND

Finished in 1903, *On Baile's Strand* was first performed, to widespread acclaim, at the opening of the new Abbey Theatre on December 27, 1904, in a double bill with Lady Gregory's *Spreading the News*; it was considerably revised, however, in 1905, and it is this later version that is represented here. The story of Cuchulain's fight with his son came to Yeats from "The Only Son of Aoife" in *Cuchulain of Muirthemne*, but Yeats added many elements to the tale, including the Shakespearean comic subplot of the Fool and the Blind Man, which echoes, foreshadows, motivates, and symbolically comments upon the events of the plot. Yeats also greatly restructured the motivations in the story, deepening the father-son drama with the poignancy of the older man's growing fondness for the youth, and adding the bureaucratic materialism of Conchubar, Cuchulain's oathtaking, and the influence of witches.

The oscillating characterization of Cuchulain in this play reflects Yeats's own ambivalence at this period about the nature of the artist—dreamer, visionary, wild and free dancer in the woods, heroic man of action. Yeats himself thought of the play as "a little over-complicated when played by itself," "a kind of cross-road where too many interests meet and jostle for the hearer to take them in at first hearing unless he listen carefully, or know something of the story of the other plays of the cycle." But in fact *On Baile's Strand,* presenting all the complicated ironies of Cuchulain's self-destruction, has always been one of Yeats's most moving and successfully staged plays.

On Baile's Strand[1]

1904

To William Fay[2]
because of the beautiful fantasy of his
playing in the character of the Fool

PERSONS IN THE PLAY

A FOOL
A BLIND MAN
CUCHULAIN, *King of Muirthemne*[3]
CONCHUBAR, *High King of Uladh*[4]
A YOUNG MAN, *son of Cuchulain*
KINGS AND SINGING WOMEN

A great hall at Dundealgan,[5] not 'Cuchulain's great ancient house' but an assembly-house nearer to the sea. A big door at the back, and through the door the misty light as of sea-mist. There are many chairs and one long bench. One of these chairs, which is towards the front of the stage, is bigger than the others. Somewhere at the back there is a table with flagons of ale upon it and drinking-horns. There is a small door at one side of the hall. A Fool and Blind Man, both ragged, and their features made grotesque and extravagant by masks,[6] come in through the door at the back. The Blind Man leans upon a staff.

FOOL. What a clever man you are though you are blind! There's nobody with two eyes in his head that is as clever as you are. Who but you could have thought that the henwife sleeps every day a little at noon? I would never be able to steal anything if you didn't tell me where to look for it. And what a good cook you are! You take the fowl out of my hands after I have stolen it and plucked it, and you put it into the big pot at the

---

1. **Baile's Strand** on the northeastern coast of Ireland, near modern Dundalk, Co. Louth   2. **William Fay** W. G. Fay, the actor and producer who, with his brother Frank, founded the Irish National Theatre Society, and, in alliance with Yeats and Lady Gregory, founded the Abbey Theatre   3. **Muirthemne** Cuchulain's territory; the plain surrounding modern Dundalk   4. **Uladh** Ulster, the northeastern province of Ireland   5. **Dundealgan** the seat of Cuchulain's legendary kingship of Muirthemne; modern Dundalk   6. **masks** added in the 1905 revision of the play

fire there, and I can go out and run races with the witches at the edge of the waves and get an appetite, and when I've got it, there's the hen waiting inside for me, done to the turn.

BLIND MAN *(who is feeling about with his stick).* Done to the turn.

FOOL *(putting his arm round Blind Man's neck).* Come now, I'll have a leg and you'll have a leg, and we'll draw lots for the wish-bone. I'll be praising you, I'll be praising you while we're eating it, for your good plans and for your good cooking. There's nobody in the world like you, Blind Man. Come, come. Wait a minute. I shouldn't have closed the door. There are some that look for me, and I wouldn't like them not to find me. Don't tell it to anybody, Blind Man. There are some that follow me. Boann[7] herself out of the river and Fand[8] out of the deep sea. Witches they are, and they come by in the wind, and they cry, "Give a kiss, Fool, give a kiss," that's what they cry. That's wide enough. All the witches can come in now. I wouldn't have them beat at the door and say, "Where is the Fool? Why has he put a lock on the door?" Maybe they'll hear the bubbling of the pot and come in and sit on the ground. But we won't give them any of the fowl. Let them go back to the sea, let them go back to the sea.

BLIND MAN *(feeling legs of big chair with his hands).* Ah! *(Then, in a louder voice as he feels the back of it.)* Ah—ah—

FOOL. Why do you say "Ah-ah"?

BLIND MAN. I know the big chair. It is to-day the High King Conchubar is coming. They have brought out his chair. He is going to be Cuchulain's master in earnest from this day out. It is that he's coming for.

FOOL. He must be a great man to be Cuchulain's master.

BLIND MAN. So he is. He is a great man. He is over all the rest of the kings of Ireland.

FOOL. Cuchulain's master! I thought Cuchulain could do anything he liked.

BLIND MAN. So he did, so he did. But he ran too wild, and Conchubar is coming to-day to put an oath upon him that will stop his rambling and make him as biddable as a house-dog and keep him always at his hand. He will sit in this chair and put the oath upon him.

FOOL. How will he do that?

BLIND MAN. You have no wits to understand such things. *(The Blind Man has got into the chair.)* He will sit up in this chair and he'll say: "Take the oath, Cuchulain. I bid you take the oath. Do as I tell you. What are your wits compared with mine, and what are your riches compared with mine? And what sons have you to pay your debts and to put a stone over you when you die? Take the oath, I tell you. Take a strong oath."

---

7. **Boann** the eponymous Celtic goddess of the Boyne River, in northeastern Ireland   8. **Fand** the divine wife of the sea god, Manannan mac Lir

FOOL (*crumpling himself up and whining*). I will not. I'll take no oath. I want my dinner.

BLIND MAN. Hush, hush! It is not done yet.

FOOL. You said it was done to a turn.

BLIND MAN. Did I, now? Well, it might be done, and not done. The wings might be white, but the legs might be red. The flesh might stick hard to the bones and not come away in the teeth. But, believe me, Fool, it will be well done before you put your teeth in it.

FOOL. My teeth are growing long with the hunger.

BLIND MAN. I'll tell you a story—the kings have story-tellers while they are waiting for their dinner—I will tell you a story with a fight in it, a story with a champion in it, and a ship and a queen's son that has his mind set on killing somebody that you and I know.

FOOL. Who is that? Who is he coming to kill?

BLIND MAN. Wait, now, till you hear. When you were stealing the fowl, I was lying in a hole in the sand, and I heard three men coming with a shuffling sort of noise. They were wounded and groaning.

FOOL. Go on. Tell me about the fight.

BLIND MAN. There had been a fight, a great fight, a tremendous great fight. A young man had landed on the shore, the guardians of the shore had asked his name, and he had refused to tell it, and he had killed one, and others had run away.

FOOL. That's enough. Come on now to the fowl. I wish it was bigger. I wish it was as big as a goose.

BLIND MAN. Hush! I haven't told you all. I know who that young man is. I heard the men who were running away say he had red hair, that he had come from Aoife's[9] country, that he was coming to kill Cuchulain.

FOOL. Nobody can do that.

(To a tune)
Cuchulain has killed kings,
Kings and sons of kings,
Dragons out of the water,
And witches out of the air,

Banachas and Bonachas[10] and people of the woods.

BLIND MAN. Hush! hush!

FOOL (*still singing*).

---

9. **Aoife** (pronounced "Eefa") the woman warrior whom Cuchulain had conquered during his training in arms in Scotland, and with whom he had begotten a son   10. **Banachas and Bonachas** (Irish *bánánach, bonánach*) in folklore, supernatural beings often found haunting battlefields

> Witches that steal the milk,
> Fomor[11] that steal the children,
> Hags that have heads like hares,
> Hares that have claws like witches,
> All riding a-cock-horse
> *(Spoken)*

Out of the very bottom of the bitter black North.

BLIND MAN. Hush, I say!

FOOL. Does Cuchulain know that he is coming to kill him?

BLIND MAN. How would he know that with his head in the clouds?
He doesn't care for common fighting. Why would he put himself out, and
nobody in it but that young man? Now if it were a white fawn that might
turn into a queen before morning—

FOOL. Come to the fowl. I wish it was as big as a pig; a fowl with
goose grease and pig's crackling.

BLIND MAN. No hurry, no hurry. I know whose son it is. I wouldn't
tell anybody else, but I will tell you,—a secret is better to you than your
dinner. You like being told secrets.

FOOL. Tell me the secret.

BLIND MAN. That young man is Aoife's son. I am sure it is Aoife's
son, it flows in upon me that it is Aoife's son. You have often heard me
talking of Aoife, the great woman-fighter Cuchulain got the mastery over
in the North?

FOOL. I know, I know. She is one of those cross queens that live in
hungry Scotland.

BLIND MAN. I am sure it is her son. I was in Aoife's country for a
long time.

FOOL. That was before you were blinded for putting a curse upon the
wind.

BLIND MAN. There was a boy in her house that had her own red colour
on him, and everybody said he was to be brought up to kill Cuchulain,
that she hated Cuchulain. She used to put a helmet on a pillarstone and
call it Cuchulain and set him casting at it. There is a step outside—Cuchulain's step.

(Cuchulain passes by in the mist outside the big door.)

FOOL. Where is Cuchulain going?

BLIND MAN. He is going to meet Conchubar that has bidden him to
take the oath.

---

11. **Fomor** Fomorians (Ir. *Fomoire*), a race of demonic gods in early Irish mythology; Yeats described them as "Gods of night and death and cold, . . . [they]
were] misshapen and had now the heads of goats and bulls, and now but one leg,
and one arm that came out of the middle of their breasts."

FOOL. Ah, an oath, Blind Man. How can I remember so many things at once? Who is going to take an oath?

BLIND MAN. Cuchulain is going to take an oath to Conchubar who is High King.

FOOL. What a mix-up you make of everything, Blind Man! You were telling me one story, and now you are telling me another story. . . . How can I get the hang of it at the end if you mix everything at the beginning? Wait till I settle it out. There now, there's Cuchulain *(he points to one foot)*, and there is the young man *(he points to the other foot)* that is coming to kill him, and Cuchulain doesn't know. But where's Conchubar? *(Takes bag from side.)* That's Conchubar with all his riches—Cuchulain, young man, Conchubar.—And where's Aoife? *(Throws up cap.)* There is Aoife, high up on the mountains in high hungry Scotland. Maybe it is not true after all. Maybe it was your own making up. It's many a time you cheated me before with your lies. Come to the cooking-pot, my stomach is pinched and rusty. Would you have it to be creaking like a gate?

BLIND MAN. I tell you it's true. And more than that is true. If you listen to what I say, you'll forget your stomach.

FOOL. I won't.

BLIND MAN. Listen. I know who the young man's father is, but I won't say. I would be afraid to say. Ah, Fool, you would forget everything if you could know who the young man's father is.

FOOL. Who is it? Tell me now quick, or I'll shake you. Come, out with it, or I'll shake you.

(A murmur of voices in the distance.)

BLIND MAN. Wait, wait. There's something coming . . . It is Cuchulain is coming. He's coming back with the High King. Go and ask Cuchulain. He'll tell you. It's little you'll care about the cooking-pot when you have asked Cuchulain that . . .

(Blind Man goes out by side door.)

FOOL. I'll ask him. Cuchulain will know. He was in Aoife's country. *(Goes up stage.)* I'll ask him. *(Turns and goes down stage.)* But, no, I won't ask him, I would be afraid. *(Going up again.)* Yes, I will ask him. What harm in asking? The Blind Man said I was to ask him. *(Going down.)* No, no. I'll not ask him. He might kill me. I have but killed hens and geese and pigs. He has killed kings. *(Goes up again almost to big door.)* Who says I'm afraid? I'm not afraid. I'm no coward. I'll ask him. No, no, Cuchulain, I'm not going to ask you.

> He has killed kings,
> Kings and the sons of kings,
> Dragons out of the water,
> And witches out of the air,

Banachas and Bonachas and people of the woods.

(Fool goes out by side door, the last words being heard outside. Cuchulain and Conchubar enter through the big door at the back. While they are still outside, Cuchulain's voice is heard raised in anger. He is a dark man, something over forty years of age.[12] *Conchubar is much older and carries a long staff, elaborately carved or with an elaborate gold handle.)*

CUCHULAIN.
> Because I have killed men without your bidding
> And have rewarded others at my own pleasure,
> Because of half a score of trifling things,
> You'd lay this oath upon me, and now—and now
> You add another pebble to the heap,
> And I must be your man, well-nigh your bondsman,
> Because a youngster out of Aoife's country
> Has found the shore ill-guarded.

CONCHUBAR.
>   He came to land
> While you were somewhere out of sight and hearing,
> Hunting or dancing with your wild companions.

CUCHULAIN.
> He can be driven out. I'll not be bound.
> I'll dance or hunt, or quarrel or make love,
> Wherever and whenever I've a mind to.
> If time had not put water in your blood,
> You never would have thought it.

CONCHUBAR.
>   I would leave
> A strong and settled country to my children.

CUCHULAIN.
> And I must be obedient in all things;
> Give up my will to yours; go where you please;
> Come when you call; sit at the council-board
> Among the unshapely bodies of old men;
> I whose mere name has kept this country safe,
> I that in early days have driven out
> Maeve of Cruachan[13] and the northern pirates,[14]

12. **over forty years of age** roughly Yeats's own age at the time of the 1905 revision; the first version of the play described Cuchulain as "though still young, . . . a good deal older than" the young kings who kept him company; in the epic tradition Cuchulain was said to have died at age 27. 13. **Maeve of Cruachan** Queen Medb, queen of Connacht at its capital of Cruachan (now Rathcroghan, Co. Roscommon), leader of the Men of Ireland on the epic Cattle Raid of Cooley during which Cuchulain singlehandedly defended the entire province of Ulster 14. **the northern pirates** probably an allusion to the Vikings (an anachronism, since Cuchulain was said to have lived around the Birth of Christ and the Viking era began in Ireland *ca.* 800 A.D., but this anachronism was common in Irish folklore and romance)

The hundred kings of Sorcha,[15] and the kings
Out of the Garden in the East of the World.
Must I, that held you on the throne when all
Had pulled you from it, swear obedience
As if I were some cattle-raising king?
Are my shins speckled with the heat of the fire,
Or have my hands no skill but to make figures
Upon the ashes with a stick? Am I
So slack and idle that I need a whip
Before I serve you?

CONCHUBAR.
                              No, no whip, Cuchulain,
But every day my children come and say:
"This man is growing harder to endure.
How can we be at safety with this man
That nobody can buy or bid or bind?
We shall be at his mercy when you are gone;
He burns the earth as if he were a fire,
And time can never touch him."

CUCHULAIN.
                              And so the tale
Grows finer yet; and I am to obey
Whatever child you set upon the throne,
As if it were yourself!

CONCHUBAR.
                         Most certainly.
I am High King, my son shall be High King;
And you for all the wildness of your blood,
And though your father came out of the sun,[16]
Are but a little king and weigh but light
In anything that touches government,
If put into the balance with my children.

CUCHULAIN.
It's well that we should speak our minds out plainly,
For when we die we shall be spoken of
In many countries. We in our young days
Have seen the heavens like a burning cloud
Brooding upon the world, and being more
Than men can be now that cloud's lifted up,
We should be the more truthful. Conchubar,

15. **Sorcha** ("Brightness") a country in the pagan Irish Otherworld, often alluded
to in romances   16. **your father came out of the sun** Cuchulain's father was said
to have been the Celtic god Lug, often regarded by scholars contemporary with
Yeats as a manifestation of the sun god

I do not like your children—they have no pith,
No marrow in their bones, and will lie soft
Where you and I lie hard.

CONCHUBAR.

You rail at them
Because you have no children of your own.

CUCHULAIN.

I think myself most lucky that I leave
No pallid ghost or mockery of a man
To drift and mutter in the corridors
Where I have laughed and sung.

CONCHUBAR.

That is not true,
For all your boasting of the truth between us;
For there is no man having house and lands,
That have been in the one family, called
By that one family's name for centuries,
But is made miserable if he know
They are to pass into a stranger's keeping,
As yours will pass.

CUCHULAIN.

The most of men feel that,
But you and I leave names upon the harp.[17]

CONCHUBAR.

You play with arguments as lawyers do,
And put no heart in them. I know your thoughts,
For we have slept under the one cloak and drunk
From the one wine-cup. I know you to the bone,
I have heard you cry, aye, in your very sleep,
"I have no son," and with such bitterness
That I have gone upon my knees and prayed
That it might be amended.

CUCHULAIN.

For you thought
That I should be as biddable as others
Had I their reason for it; but that's not true;
For I would need a weightier argument
Than one that marred me in the copying,
As I have that clean hawk out of the air
That, as men say, begot this body of mine
Upon a mortal woman.

17. **leave names upon the harp** gain immortality in the epic songs of poets

CONCHUBAR.
Now as ever
You mock at every reasonable hope,
And would have nothing, or impossible things.
What eye has ever looked upon the child
Would satisfy a mind like that?

CUCHULAIN.
I would leave
My house and name to none that would not face
Even myself in battle.

CONCHUBAR.
Being swift of foot,
And making light of every common chance,
You should have overtaken on the hills
Some daughter of the air, or on the shore
A daughter of the Country-under-Wave.[18]

CUCHULAIN.
I am not blasphemous.

CONCHUBAR.
Yet you despise
Our queens, and would not call a child your own,
If one of them had borne him.

CUCHULAIN.
I have not said it.

CONCHUBAR.
Ah! I remember I have heard you boast,
When the ale was in your blood, that there was one
In Scotland, where you had learnt the trade of war,
That had a stone-pale cheek and red-brown hair;
And that although you have loved other women,
You'd sooner that fierce woman of the camp
Bore you a son than any queen among them.

CUCHULAIN.
You call her a "fierce woman of the camp,"
For, having lived among the spinning-wheels,
You'd have no woman near that would not say,
"Ah! how wise!" "What will you have for supper?"
"What shall I wear that I may please you, sir?"
And keep that humming through the day and night
For ever. A fierce woman of the camp!

---

18. **Country-under-Wave** *Tír fo Thuinn,* one of the names for the pagan Irish Otherworld, which was frequently conceived as located under the sea

But I am getting angry about nothing.
You have never seen her. Ah! Conchubar, had you seen her
With that high, laughing, turbulent head of hers
Thrown backward, and the bowstring at her ear,
Or sitting at the fire with those grave eyes
Full of good counsel as it were with wine,
Or when love ran through all the lineaments
Of her wild body—although she had no child,
None other had all beauty, queen or lover,
Or was so fitted to give birth to kings.

CONCHUBAR.

There's nothing I can say that drifts you farther
From the one weighty matter. That very woman—
For I know well that you are praising Aoife—
Now hates you and will leave no subtlety
Unknotted that might run into a noose
About your throat, no army in idleness
That might bring ruin on this land you serve.

CUCHULAIN.

No wonder in that, no wonder at all in that.
I never have known love but as a kiss
In the mid-battle, and a difficult truce
Of oil and water, candles and dark night,
Hillside and hollow, the hot-footed sun
And the cold, sliding, slippery-footed moon—
A brief forgiveness between opposites
That have been hatreds for three times the age
Of this long-'stablished ground.

CONCHUBAR.

                              Listen to me.
Aoife makes war on us, and every day
Our enemies grow greater and beat the walls
More bitterly, and you within the walls
Are every day more turbulent; and yet,
When I would speak about these things, your fancy
Runs as it were a swallow on the wind.

(Outside the door in the blue light of the sea-mist are many old and young Kings; amongst them are three Women, two of whom carry a bowl of fire. The third, in what follows, puts from time to time fragrant herbs into the fire so that it flickers up into brighter flame.)

Look at the door and what men gather there—
Old counsellors that steer the land with me,
And younger kings, the dancers and harp-players

That follow in your tumults, and all these
Are held there by the one anxiety.
Will you be bound into obedience
And so make this land safe for them and theirs?
You are but half a king and I but half;
I need your might of hand and burning heart,
And you my wisdom.

CUCHULAIN (*going near to door*). Nestlings of a high nest,
Hawks that have followed me into the air
And looked upon the sun, we'll out of this
And sail upon the wind once more. This king
Would have me take an oath to do his will,
And having listened to his tune from morning,
I will no more of it. Run to the stable
And set the horses to the chariot-pole,
And send a messenger to the harp-players.
We'll find a level place among the woods,
And dance awhile.

A YOUNG KING.
             Cuchulain, take the oath.
There is none here that would not have you take it.

CUCHULAIN.
      You'd have me take it? Are you of one mind?

THE KINGS.
      All, all, all, all!

A YOUNG KING.
           Do what the High King bids you.

CONCHUBAR.
      There is not one but dreads this turbulence
Now that they're settled men.

CUCHULAIN.
            Are you so changed,
Or have I grown more dangerous of late?
But that's not it. I understand it all.
It's you that have changed. You've wives and children now,
And for that reason cannot follow one
That lives like a bird's flight from tree to tree.—
It's time the years put water in my blood
And drowned the wildness of it, for all's changed,
But that unchanged.—I'll take what oath you will:
The moon, the sun, the water, light, or air,
I do not care how binding.

CONCHUBAR.
On this fire
That has been lighted from your hearth and mine;
The older men shall be my witnesses,
The younger, yours. The holders of the fire
Shall purify the thresholds of the house
With waving fire, and shut the outer door,
According to the custom; and sing rhyme
That has come down from the old law-makers
To blow the witches out. Considering
That the wild will of man could be oath-bound,
But that a woman's could not, they bid us sing
Against the will of woman at its wildest
In the Shape-Changers that run upon the wind.
(Conchubar has gone on to his throne.)
THE WOMEN. *(They sing in a very low voice after the first few words so that the others will all but drown their words.[19])*
May this fire have driven out
The Shape-Changers that can put
Ruin on a great king's house
Until all be ruinous.
Names whereby a man has known
The threshold and the hearthstone,
Gather on the wind and drive
The women none can kiss and thrive,
For they are but whirling wind,
Out of memory and mind.
They would make a prince decay
With light images of clay
Planted in the running wave;
Or, for many shapes they have,
They would change them into hounds
Until he had died of his wounds,
Though the change were but a whim;
Or they'd hurl a spell at him,
That he follow with desire
Bodies that can never tire
Or grow kind, for they anoint

19. ***They sing . . . words*** Yeats wrote that although "very little of the song of the three women can be heard, . . . it seemed right to take some trouble over them, just as it is right to finish off the statue where it is turned to the wall, and besides there is always the reader and one's own pleasure."

All their bodies, joint by joint,
With a miracle-working juice
That is made out of the grease
Of the ungoverned unicorn.
But the man is thrice forlorn,
Emptied, ruined, wracked, and lost,
That they follow, for at most
They will give him kiss for kiss
While they murmur, "After this
Hatred may be sweet to the taste."
Those wild hands that have embraced
All his body can but shove
At the burning wheel of love
Till the side of hate comes up.
Therefore in this ancient cup
May the sword-blades drink their fill
Of the home-brew there, until
They will have for masters none
But the threshold and hearthstone.

CUCHULAIN *(speaking, while they are singing)*.
I'll take and keep this oath, and from this day
I shall be what you please, my chicks, my nestlings.
Yet I had thought you were of those that praised
Whatever life could make the pulse run quickly,
Even though it were brief,[20] and that you held
That a free gift was better than a forced.—
But that's all over.—I will keep it, too;
I never gave a gift and took it again.
If the wild horse should break the chariot-pole,
It would be punished. Should that be in the oath?
(Two of the Women, still singing, crouch in front of him holding the bowl over their heads. He spreads his hands over the flame.)
I swear to be obedient in all things
To Conchubar, and to uphold his children.

CONCHUBAR.
We are one being, as these flames are one:
I give my wisdom, and I take your strength.
Now thrust the swords into the flame, and pray
That they may serve the threshold and the hearthstone
With faithful service.

20. **whatever life . . . brief** an allusion to Cuchulain's famous boyhood boast (akin to that of Achilles) that he cared not how brief his life might be, so long as it was glorious

(The Kings kneel in a semicircle before the two Women and Cuchulain, who thrusts his sword into the flame. They all put the points of their swords into the flame. The third Woman is at the back near the big door.)

CUCHULAIN.

O pure, glittering ones
That should be more than wife or friend or mistress,
Give us the enduring will, the unquenchable hope,
The friendliness of the sword!—

(The song grows louder, and the last words ring out clearly. There is a loud knocking at the door, and a cry of "Open! open!"*)*

CONCHUBAR.

Some king that has been loitering on the way.
Open the door, for I would have all know
That the oath's finished and Cuchulain bound,
And that the swords are drinking up the flame.

(The door is opened by the third Woman, and a Young Man with a drawn sword enters.)

YOUNG MAN.

I am of Aoife's country.

(The Kings rush towards him. Cuchulain throws himself between.)

CUCHULAIN.

Put up your swords.
He is but one. Aoife is far away.

YOUNG MAN.

I have come alone into the midst of you
To weigh this sword against Cuchulain's sword.

CONCHUBAR.

And are you noble? for if of common seed,
You cannot weigh your sword against his sword
But in mixed battle.

YOUNG MAN.

I am under bonds
To tell my name to no man; but it's noble.

CONCHUBAR.

But I would know your name and not your bonds.
You cannot speak in the Assembly House,
If you are not noble.

FIRST OLD KING.

Answer the High King!

YOUNG MAN.

I will give no other proof than the hawk gives
That it's no sparrow! *(He is silent for a moment, then speaks to all.)*

Yet look upon me, Kings.
I, too, am that ancient seed, and carry
The signs about this body and in these bones.

CUCHULAIN.

To have shown the hawk's grey feather is enough,
And you speak highly, too. Give me that helmet.
I'd thought they had grown weary sending champions.
That sword and belt will do. This fighting's welcome.
The High King there has promised me his wisdom;
But the hawk's sleepy till its well-beloved
Cries out amid the acorns, or it has seen
Its enemy like a speck upon the sun.
What's wisdom to the hawk, when that clear eye
Is burning nearer up in the high air?

(Looks hard at Young Man; then comes down steps and grasps Young Man by shoulder.)

Hither into the light.

(To Conchubar.)

The very tint
Of her that I was speaking of but now.
Not a pin's difference.

(To Young Man.)

You are from the North,
Where there are many that have that tint of hair—
Red-brown, the light red-brown. Come nearer, boy,
For I would have another look at you.
There's more likeness—a pale, a stone-pale cheek.
What brought you, boy? Have you no fear of death?

YOUNG MAN.

Whether I live or die is in the gods' hands.

CUCHULAIN.

That is all words, all words; a young man's talk.
I am their plough, their harrow, their very strength;
For he that's in the sun begot this body
Upon a mortal woman, and I have heard tell
It seemed as if he had outrun the moon
That he must follow always through waste heaven,
He loved so happily. He'll be but slow
To break a tree that was so sweetly planted.
Let's see that arm. I'll see it if I choose.
That arm had a good father and a good mother,
But it is not like this.

YOUNG MAN.

You are mocking me;

You think I am not worthy to be fought.
But I'll not wrangle but with this talkative knife.
CUCHULAIN.
       Put up your sword; I am not mocking you.
I'd have you for my friend, but if it's not
Because you have a hot heart and a cold eye,
I cannot tell the reason.
(To Conchubar.)
                  He has got her fierceness,
And nobody is as fierce as those pale women.
But I will keep him with me, Conchubar,
That he may set my memory upon her
When the day's fading.—You will stop with us,
And we will hunt the deer and the wild bulls;
And, when we have grown weary, light our fires
Between the wood and water, or on some mountain
Where the Shape-Changers of the morning come.
The High King there would make a mock of me
Because I did not take a wife among them.
Why do you hang your head? It's a good life:
The head grows prouder in the light of the dawn,
And friendship thickens in the murmuring dark
Where the spare hazels meet the wool-white foam.
But I can see there's no more need for words
And that you'll be my friend from this day out.
CONCHUBAR.
       He has come hither not in his own name
But in Queen Aoife's, and has challenged us
In challenging the foremost man of us all.
CUCHULAIN.
       Well, well, what matter?
CONCHUBAR.
                  You think it does not matter,
And that a fancy lighter than the air,
A whim of the moment, has more matter in it.
For, having none that shall reign after you,
You cannot think as I do, who would leave
A throne too high for insult.
CUCHULAIN.
               Let your children
Re-mortar their inheritance, as we have,
And put more muscle on.—I'll give you gifts,
But I'd have something too—that arm-ring, boy.
We'll have this quarrel out when you are older.

YOUNG MAN.

>There is no man I'd sooner have my friend
>Than you, whose name has gone about the world
>As if it had been the wind; but Aoife'd say
>I had turned coward.

CUCHULAIN.

>   I will give you gifts
>That Aoife'll know, and all her people know,
>To have come from me.

(Showing cloak.)

>   My father gave me this.
>He came to try me, rising up at dawn
>Out of the cold dark of the rich sea.
>He challenged me to battle, but before
>My sword had touched his sword, told me his name,
>Gave me this cloak, and vanished. It was woven
>By women of the Country-under-Wave
>Out of the fleeces of the sea. O! tell her
>I was afraid, or tell her what you will.
>No; tell her that I heard a raven croak
>On the north side of the house, and was afraid.

CONCHUBAR.

>Some witch of the air has troubled Cuchulain's mind.

CUCHULAIN.

>No witchcraft. His head is like a woman's head
>I had a fancy for.

CONCHUBAR.

>   A witch of the air
>Can make a leaf confound us with memories.
>They run upon the wind and hurl the spells
>That make us nothing, out of the invisible wind.
>They have gone to school to learn the trick of it.

CUCHULAIN.

>No, no—there's nothing out of common here;
>The winds are innocent.—That arm-ring, boy.

A KING.

>If I've your leave I'll take this challenge up.

ANOTHER KING.

>No, give it me, High King, for this wild Aoife
>Has carried off my slaves.

ANOTHER KING.

>   No, give it me,
>For she has harried me in house and herd.

ANOTHER KING.

    I claim this fight.

OTHER KINGS *(together)*.

                           And I! And I! And I!

CUCHULAIN.

    Back! back! Put up your swords! Put up your swords!
    There's none alive that shall accept a challenge
    I have refused. Laegaire, put up your sword!

YOUNG MAN.

    No, let them come. If they've a mind for it,
    I'll try it out with any two together.

CUCHULAIN.

    That's spoken as I'd have spoken it at your age.
    But you are in my house. Whatever man
    Would fight with you shall fight it out with me.
    They're dumb, they're dumb. How many of you would meet

(Draws sword.)

    This mutterer, this old whistler, this sand-piper,
    This edge that's greyer than the tide, this mouse
    That's gnawing at the timbers of the world,
    This, this—Boy, I would meet them all in arms
    If I'd a son like you. He would avenge me
    When I have withstood for the last time the men
    Whose fathers, brothers, sons, and friends I have killed
    Upholding Conchubar, when the four provinces[21]
    Have gathered with the ravens over them.
    But I'd need no avenger. You and I
    Would scatter them like water from a dish.

YOUNG MAN.

    We'll stand by one another from this out.
    Here is the ring.

CUCHULAIN.

                  No, turn and turn about.
    But my turn's first because I am the older.

(Spreading out cloak.)

    Nine queens out of the Country-under-Wave
    Have woven it with the fleeces of the sea
    And they were long embroidering at it.—Boy,
    If I had fought my father, he'd have killed me,
    As certainly as if I had a son

---

21. **four provinces** the rest of Ireland, that mustered against Ulster in the Cattle Raid of Cooley

And fought with him, I should be deadly to him;
For the old fiery fountains are far off
And every day there is less heat o' the blood.

CONCHUBAR *(in a loud voice)*.
No more of this. I will not have this friendship.
Cuchulain is my man, and I forbid it.
He shall not go unfought, for I myself—

CUCHULAIN.
I will not have it.

CONCHUBAR.
                    You lay commands on me?

CUCHULAIN *(seizing Conchubar)*.
You shall not stir, High King. I'll hold you there.

CONCHUBAR.
Witchcraft has maddened you.

THE KINGS *(shouting)*.
                              Yes, witchcraft! witchcraft!

FIRST OLD KING.
Some witch has worked upon your mind, Cuchulain.
The head of that young man seemed like a woman's
You'd had a fancy for. Then of a sudden
You laid your hands on the High King himself!

CUCHULAIN.
And laid my hands on the High King himself?

CONCHUBAR.
Some witch is floating in the air above us.

CUCHULAIN.
Yes, witchcraft! witchcraft! Witches of the air!
(To Young Man.)
Why did you? Who was it set you to this work?
Out, out! I say, for now it's sword on sword!

YOUNG MAN.
But . . . but I did not.

CUCHULAIN.
                    Out, I say, out, out!

*(Young Man goes out followed by Cuchulain. The Kings follow them out
with confused cries, and words one can hardly hear because of the noise. Some
cry, "Quicker, quicker!" "Why are you so long at the door?" "We'll be too
late!" "Have they begun to fight?" "Can you see if they are fighting?" and
so on. Their voices drown each other. The three Women are left alone.)*

FIRST WOMAN.
I have seen, I have seen!

SECOND WOMAN.

What do you cry aloud?

FIRST WOMAN.

The Ever-living have shown me what's to come.

THIRD WOMAN.

How? Where?

FIRST WOMAN.

In the ashes of the bowl.

SECOND WOMAN.

While you were holding it between your hands?

THIRD WOMAN.

Speak quickly!

FIRST WOMAN.

I have seen Cuchulain's roof-tree
Leap into fire, and the walls split and blacken.

SECOND WOMAN.

Cuchulain has gone out to die.

THIRD WOMAN.

O! O!

SECOND WOMAN.

Who could have thought that one so great as he
Should meet his end at this unnoted sword!

FIRST WOMAN.

Life drifts between a fool and a blind man
To the end, and nobody can know his end.

SECOND WOMAN.

Come, look upon the quenching of this greatness.

(The other two go to the door, but they stop for a moment upon the threshold and wail.)

FIRST WOMAN.

No crying out, for there'll be need of cries
And rending of the hair when it's all finished.

(The Women go out. There is the sound of clashing swords from time to time during what follows.)

(Enter the Fool, dragging the Blind Man.)

FOOL. You have eaten it, you have eaten it! You have left me nothing but the bones.

(He throws Blind Man down by big chair.)

BLIND MAN. Oh, that I should have to endure such a plague! O, I ache all over! O, I am pulled to pieces! This is the way you pay me all the good I have done you.

FOOL. You have eaten it! You have told me lies. I might have known you had eaten it when I saw your slow, sleepy walk. Lie there till the kings come. O, I will tell Conchubar and Cuchulain and all the kings about you! BLIND MAN. What would have happened to you but for me, and you without your wits? If I did not take care of you, what would you do for food and warmth? FOOL. You take care of me? You stay safe, and send me into every kind of danger. You sent me down the cliff for gulls' eggs while you warmed your blind eyes in the sun; and then you ate all that were good for food. You left me the eggs that were neither egg nor bird. *(Blind Man tries to rise; Fool makes him lie down again.)* Keep quiet now, till I shut the door. There is some noise outside—a high vexing noise, so that I can't be listening to myself. *(Shuts the big door.)* Why can't they be quiet? Why can't they be quiet? *(Blind Man tries to get away.)* Oh! you would get away, would you? *(Follows Blind Man and brings him back.)* Lie there! lie there! No, you won't get away! Lie there till the kings come. I'll tell them all about you. I will tell it all. How you sit warming yourself, when you have made me light a fire of sticks, while I sit blowing it with my mouth. Do you not always make me take the windy side of the bush when it blows, and the rainy side when it rains?

BLIND MAN. O, good Fool! listen to me. Think of the care I have taken of you. I have brought you to many a warm hearth, where there was a good welcome for you, but you would not stay there; you were always wandering about.

FOOL. The last time you brought me in, it was not I who wandered away, but you that got put out because you took the crubeen[22] out of the pot when nobody was looking. Keep quiet, now!

CUCHULAIN *(rushing in)*. Witchcraft! There is no witchcraft on the earth, or among the witches of the air, that these hands cannot break.

FOOL. Listen to me, Cuchulain. I left him turning the fowl at the fire. He ate it all, though I had stolen it. He left me nothing but the feathers.

CUCHULAIN. Fill me a horn of ale!

BLIND MAN. I gave him what he likes best. You do not know how vain this Fool is. He likes nothing so well as a feather.

FOOL. He left me nothing but the bones and feathers. Nothing but the feathers, though I had stolen it.

CUCHULAIN. Give me that horn. Quarrels here, too! *(Drinks.)* What is there between you two that is worth a quarrel? Out with it!

BLIND MAN. Where would he be but for me? I must be always thinking—thinking to get food for the two of us, and when we've got it, if the moon is at the full or the tide on the turn, he'll leave the rabbit in the snare till it is full of maggots, or let the trout slip back through his hands into the stream.

22. crubeen pig's foot

(The Fool has begun singing while the Blind Man is speaking.)
FOOL *(singing)*.

> When you were an acorn on the tree-top,
>   Then was I an eagle-cock;
> Now that you are a withered old block,
>   Still am I an eagle-cock.

BLIND MAN. Listen to him, now. That's the sort of talk I have to put up with day out, day in.

(The Fool is putting the feathers into his hair. Cuchulain takes a handful of feathers out of a heap the Fool has on the bench beside him, and out of the Fool's hair, and begins to wipe the blood from his sword with them.)

FOOL. He has taken my feathers to wipe his sword. It is blood that he is wiping from his sword.

CUCHULAIN *(goes up to door at back and throws away feathers)*. They are standing about his body. They will not awaken him, for all his witchcraft.

BLIND MAN. It is that young champion that he has killed. He that came out of Aoife's country.

CUCHULAIN. He thought to have saved himself with witchcraft.

FOOL. That Blind Man there said he would kill you. He came from Aoife's country to kill you. That Blind Man said they had taught him every kind of weapon that he might do it. But I always knew that you would kill him.

CUCHULAIN *(to the Blind Man)*. You knew him, then?

BLIND MAN. I saw him, when I had my eyes, in Aoife's country.

CUCHULAIN. You were in Aoife's country?

BLIND MAN. I knew him and his mother there.

CUCHULAIN. He was about to speak of her when he died.

BLIND MAN. He was a queen's son.

CUCHULAIN. What queen? what queen? *(Seizes Blind Man, who is now sitting upon the bench.)* Was it Scathach?[23] There were many queens. All the rulers there were queens.

BLIND MAN. No, not Scathach.

CUCHULAIN. It was Uathach,[24] then? Speak! speak!

BLIND MAN. I cannot speak; you are clutching me too tightly. *(Cuchulain lets him go.)* I cannot remember who it was. I am not certain. It was some queen.

FOOL. He said a while ago that the young man was Aoife's son.

CUCHULAIN. She? No, no! She had no son when I was there.

---

23. **Scathach** the warrior woman in Scotland to whom the young Cuchulain went for training in arms   24. **Uathach** Scathach's daughter, with whom Cuchulain slept while he was in training with Scathach

FOOL. That Blind Man there said she owned him for her son.

CUCHULAIN. I had rather he had been some other woman's son. What father had he? A soldier out of Alba?[25] She was an amorous woman—a proud, pale, amorous woman.

BLIND MAN. None knew whose son he was.

CUCHULAIN. None knew! Did you know, old listener at doors?

BLIND MAN. No, no; I knew nothing.

FOOL. He said a while ago that he heard Aoife boast that she'd never but the one lover, and he the only man that had overcome her in battle. *(Pause.)*

BLIND MAN. Somebody is trembling, Fool! The bench is shaking. Why are you trembling? Is Cuchulain going to hurt us? It was not I who told you, Cuchulain.

FOOL. It is Cuchulain who is trembling. It is Cuchulain who is shaking the bench.

BLIND MAN. It is his own son he has slain.

CUCHULAIN.

> 'Twas they that did it, the pale windy people.
> Where? where? where? My sword against the thunder!
> But no, for they have always been my friends;
> And though they love to blow a smoking coal
> Till it's all flame, the wars they blow aflame
> Are full of glory, and heart-uplifting pride,
> And not like this. The wars they love awaken
> Old fingers and the sleepy strings of harps.
> Who did it then? Are you afraid? Speak out!
> For I have put you under my protection,
> And will reward you well. Dubthach the Chafer?
> He'd an old grudge. No, for he is with Maeve.
> Laegaire did it! Why do you not speak?
> What is this house? *(Pause.)* Now I remember all.

(Comes before Conchubar's chair, and strikes out with his sword, as if Conchubar was sitting upon it.)

> 'Twas you who did it—you who sat up there
> With your old rod of kingship, like a magpie
> Nursing a stolen spoon. No, not a magpie,
> A maggot that is eating up the earth!
> Yes, but a magpie, for he's flown away.
> Where did he fly to?

BLIND MAN.

> He is outside the door.

CUCHULAIN..
Outside the door?
BLIND MAN.
Between the door and the sea.
CUCHULAIN.
Conchubar, Conchubar! the sword into your heart!
(He rushes out. Pause. Fool creeps up to the big door and looks after him.)
FOOL. He is going up to King Conchubar. They are all about the young man. No, no, he is standing still. There is a great wave going to break, and he is looking at it. Ah! now he is running down to the sea, but he is holding up his sword as if he were going into a fight. *(Pause.)* Well struck! well struck!
BLIND MAN. What is he doing now?
FOOL. Oh! he is fighting the waves!
BLIND MAN. He sees King Conchubar's crown on every one of them.
FOOL. There, he has struck at a big one! He has struck the crown off it; he has made the foam fly. There again, another big one!
BLIND MAN. Where are the kings? What are the kings doing?
FOOL. They are shouting and running down to the shore, and the people are running out of the houses. They are all running.
BLIND MAN. You say they are running out of the houses? There will be nobody left in the houses. Listen, Fool!
FOOL. There, he is down! He is up again. He is going out in the deep water. There is a big wave. It has gone over him. I cannot see him now. He has killed kings and giants, but the waves have mastered him, the waves have mastered him!
BLIND MAN. Come here, Fool!
FOOL. The waves have mastered him.
BLIND MAN. Come here!
FOOL. The waves have mastered him.
BLIND MAN. Come here, I say.
FOOL *(coming towards him, but looking backwards towards the door)*. What is it?
BLIND MAN. There will be nobody in the houses. Come this way; come quickly! The ovens will be full. We will put our hands into the ovens.
(They go out.)

THE END

THE ONLY JEALOUSY OF EMER

In Yeats's personal revision of the original tales of Cuchulain, the plot of *The Only Jealousy of Emer* picks up where *On Baile's Strand* leaves off; Cuchulain has fought the sea and lies between life and death, suspended between this world and the next. He is tempted to the quiet of oblivion, to an escape from the remorse of his memories into the aesthetic perfection promised by the goddess Fand; only his wife Emer, with her human love and hope, can resolve his dilemma and keep him in the world of heroic action, joy, and passion. Like *On Baile's Strand, Emer* is built upon ironies—the greatest being that Cuchulain's wife's renunciation of his love is in fact her greatest deed of love for him.

Although the plots of the two plays are continuous, their styles differ tremendously. Conceived in his new Noh style, *The Only Jealousy of Emer* demonstrates Yeats's use of music and dance to embody a climax that is beyond words. Yeats wrote *The Only Jealousy of Emer* in a period of recoil from the politics and nagging practical necessities of running the Abbey Theatre; he rejoiced in the creation of a private, aristocratic drama, far removed from the popular stage. *Emer* was finished in 1918 and first published the next year by the Cuala Press and in Chicago's *Poetry* magazine. Its first performance was not in Ireland, but in Amsterdam in 1922; it was finally produced at the Abbey in 1929. In his introduction to *Four Plays for Dancers,* Yeats explained that

> while writing these plays, intended for some fifty people in a drawing-room or a studio, I have so rejoiced in my freedom from the stupidity of an ordinary audience that I have filled "The Only Jealousy of Emer" with . . . little known convictions about the nature and history of a woman's beauty. . . . The soul through each cycle of its development is held to incarnate through twenty-eight typical incarnations, corresponding to the phases of the moon, the light part of the moon's disc symbolizing the subjective and the dark part the objective nature, the wholly dark moon (called Phase 1) and the wholly light (called Phase 15) symbolizing complete objectivity and complete subjectivity respectively. . . . The invisible fifteenth incarnation is that of the greatest possible bodily beauty, and the fourteenth and sixteenth those of the greatest beauty visible to human eyes. . . .

Esoteric lore, while it provides a symbolic level of meaning in the play, is less important, however, than the portraits of characters caught in their human dilemmas: Emer, looking towards a life without her husband's love, and Cuchulain, aging, facing inevitable decline from his heroic greatness.

The Only Jealousy
of Emer

THREE MUSICIANS *(their faces made up to resemble masks)*
THE GHOST OF CUCHULAIN *(wearing a mask)*
THE FIGURE OF CUCHULAIN *(wearing a mask)*
EMER
EITHNE INGUBA } *(masked, or their faces made up to resemble masks)*
WOMAN OF THE SIDHE[1] *(wearing a mask)*

*Enter Musicians, who are dressed and made up as in "At the Hawk's Well."
They have the same musical instruments, which can either be already upon the
stage or be brought in by the First Musician before he stands in the centre with
the cloth between his hands, or by a player when the cloth has been unfolded.
The stage as before can be against the wall of any room, and the same black
cloth can be used as in "At the Hawk's Well."*[2]

(Song for the folding and unfolding of the cloth)[3]
FIRST MUSICIAN.
      A woman's beauty is like a white
      Frail bird, like a white sea-bird alone

---

1. **Sidhe** the fairies, people of the Otherworld (pronounced "shee")   2. *"At the Hawk's Well"* Here are the full stage directions from *At the Hawk's Well*: "The stage is any bare space before a wall against which stands a patterned screen. A drum and a gong and a zither have been laid close to the screen before the play begins. If necessary, they can be carried in after the audience is seated, by the First Musician, who also can attend to the lights if there is any special lighting. We had two lanterns upon posts—designed by Mr. Dulac—at the outer corners of the stage, but they did not give enough light, and we found it better to play by the light of a large chandelier. Indeed, I think, so far as my present experience goes, that the most effective lighting is the lighting we are most accustomed to in our rooms. These masked players seem stranger when there is no mechanical means of separating them from us. The First Musician carries with him a folded black cloth and goes to the centre of the stage towards the front and stands motionless, the folded cloth hanging from between his hands. The two other Musicians enter and, after standing a moment at either side of the stage, go towards him and slowly unfold the cloth, singing as they do so."   3. *folding and unfolding of the cloth* Since the play was designed

At daybreak after stormy night
Between two furrows upon the ploughed land:
A sudden storm, and it was thrown
Between dark furrows upon the ploughed land.
How many centuries spent
The sedentary soul
In toils of measurement
Beyond eagle or mole,
Beyond hearing or seeing,
Or Archimedes'[4] guess,
To raise into being
That loveliness?

A strange, unserviceable thing,
A fragile, exquisite, pale shell,
That the vast troubled waters bring
To the loud sands before day has broken.
The storm arose and suddenly fell
Amid the dark before day had broken.
What death? what discipline?
What bonds no man could unbind,
Being imagined within
The labyrinth of the mind,
What pursuing or fleeing,
What wounds, what bloody press,
Dragged into being
This loveliness?

(When the cloth is folded again the Musicians take their place against the wall. The folding of the cloth shows on one side of the stage the curtained bed or litter on which lies a man in his grave-clothes. He wears an heroic mask. Another man with exactly similar clothes and mask crouches near the front. Emer is sitting beside the bed.)

FIRST MUSICIAN *(speaking)*.

I call before the eyes a roof
With cross-beams darkened by smoke;
A fisher's net hangs from a beam,
A long oar lies against the wall.
I call up a poor fisher's house;
A man lies dead or swooning,
That amorous man,

to be acted in a private space such as a drawing room rather than on a formal stage, a large cloth, unfolded between "stage" and audience, was substituted for the closing of a stage curtain to permit the changing of sets.   4. **Archimedes** third century B.C. Greek natural philosopher and mathematician

That amorous, violent man, renowned Cuchulain,
Queen Emer at his side.
At her own bidding all the rest have gone;
But now one comes on hesitating feet,
Young Eithne Inguba, Cuchulain's mistress.
She stands a moment in the open door.
Beyond the open door the bitter sea,
The shining, bitter sea, is crying out,
(singing) White shell, white wing!
I will not choose for my friend
A frail, unserviceable thing
That drifts and dreams, and but knows
That waters are without end
And that wind blows.

EMER *(speaking)*.
Come hither, come sit down beside the bed;
You need not be afraid, for I myself
Sent for you, Eithne Inguba.

EITHNE INGUBA.
                                      No, Madam,
I have too deeply wronged you to sit there.

EMER.
Of all the people in the world we two,
And we alone, may watch together here,
Because we have loved him best.

EITHNE INGUBA.
                                      And is he dead?

EMER.
Although they have dressed him out in his grave-clothes
And stretched his limbs, Cuchulain is not dead;
The very heavens when that day's at hand,
So that his death may not lack ceremony,
Will throw out fires, and the earth grow red with blood.
There shall not be a scullion but foreknows it
Like the world's end.

EITHNE INGUBA.
                                      How did he come to this?

EMER.
Towards noon in the assembly of the kings
He met with one who seemed a while most dear.
The kings stood round; some quarrel was blown up;
He drove him out and killed him on the shore
At Baile's tree, and he who was so killed

Was his own son begot on some wild woman
When he was young, or so I have heard it said;
And thereupon, knowing what man he had killed,
And being mad with sorrow, he ran out;
And after, to his middle in the foam,
With shield before him and with sword in hand,
He fought the deathless sea. The kings looked on
And not a king dared stretch an arm, or even
Dared call his name, but all stood wondering
In that dumb stupor like cattle in a gale,
Until at last, as though he had fixed his eyes
On a new enemy, he waded out
Until the water had swept over him;
But the waves washed his senseless image up
And laid it at this door.[5]

EITHNE INGUBA.
                                        How pale he looks!

EMER.
          He is not dead.

EITHNE INGUBA.
                              You have not kissed his lips
          Nor laid his head upon your breast.

EMER.
                                        It may be
An image has been put into his place.
A sea-borne log bewitched into his likeness,
Or some stark horseman grown too old to ride
Among the troops of Manannan,[6] Son of the Sea,
Now that his joints are stiff.

EITHNE INGUBA.
                                        Cry out his name.
All that are taken from our sight, they say,
Loiter amid the scenery of their lives
For certain hours or days, and should he hear
He might, being angry, drive the changeling out.

EMER.
          It is hard to make them hear amid their darkness,
          And it is long since I could call him home;
          I am but his wife, but if you cry aloud
          With the sweet voice that is so dear to him
          He cannot help but listen.

5. **Towards noon . . . this door** a summary of the plot of *On Baile's Strand*
6. **Manannan** pagan Irish god of the sea

EITHNE INGUBA.

> He loves me best,
> Being his newest love, but in the end
> Will love the woman best who loved him first
> And loved him through the years when love seemed lost.

EMER.

> I have that hope, the hope that some day somewhere
> We'll sit together at the hearth again.

EITHNE INGUBA.

> Women like me, the violent hour passed over,
> Are flung into some corner like old nut-shells.
> Cuchulain, listen.

EMER.

> No, not yet, for first
> I'll cover up his face to hide the sea;
> And throw new logs upon the hearth and stir
> The half-burnt logs until they break in flame.
> Old Manannan's unbridled horses[7] come
> Out of the sea, and on their backs his horsemen;
> But all the enchantments of the dreaming foam
> Dread the hearth-fire.

(She pulls the curtains of the bed so as to hide the sick man's face, that the actor may change his mask unseen. She goes to one side of the platform and moves her hand as though putting logs on a fire and stirring it into a blaze. While she makes these movements the Musicians play, marking the movements with drum and flute perhaps.

Having finished she stands beside the imaginary fire at a distance from Cuchulain and Eithne Inguba.)

> Call on Cuchulain now.

EITHNE INGUBA.

> Can you not hear my voice?

EMER.

> Bend over him;
> Call out dear secrets till you have touched his heart,
> If he lies there; and if he is not there,
> Till you have made him jealous.

EITHNE INGUBA.

> Cuchulain, listen.

EMER.

> Those words sound timidly; to be afraid
> Because his wife is but three paces off,
> When there is so great need, were but to prove

7. **Old Manannan's unbridled horses** the waves of the sea

> The man that chose you made but a poor choice:
> We're but two women struggling with the sea.

EITHNE INGUBA.

> O my beloved, pardon me, that I
> Have been ashamed. I thrust my shame away.
> I have never sent a message or called out,
> Scarce had a longing for your company
> But you have known and come; and if indeed
> You are lying there, stretch out your arms and speak;
> Open your mouth and speak, for to this hour
> My company has made you talkative.
> What ails your tongue, or what has closed your ears?
> Our passion had not chilled when we were parted
> On the pale shore under the breaking dawn.
> He cannot speak: or else his ears are closed
> And no sound reaches him.

EMER.

> Then kiss that image;
> The pressure of your mouth upon his mouth
> May reach him where he is.

EITHNE INGUBA (starting back).

> It is no man.
> I felt some evil thing that dried my heart
> When my lips touched it.

EMER.

> No, his body stirs;
> The pressure of your mouth has called him home;
> He has thrown the changeling out.

EITHNE INGUBA (going further off).

> Look at that arm;
> That arm is withered to the very socket.

EMER (going up to the bed).

> What do you come for; and from where?

FIGURE OF CUCHULAIN.

> I have come
> From Manannan's court upon a bridleless horse.

EMER.

> What one among the Sidhe has dared to lie
> Upon Cuchulain's bed and take his image?

FIGURE OF CUCHULAIN.

> I am named Bricriu[8]—not the man—that Bricriu,

---

8. **Bricriu** nicknamed "Poison-Tongue," legendary trickster figure of the Ulster stories, said to delight in creating strife

Maker of discord among gods and men,
Called Bricriu of the Sidhe.

EMER.

                                Come for what purpose?

FIGURE OF CUCHULAIN (*sitting up, parting curtain and showing its distorted face, as Inguba goes out*).

I show my face, and everything he loves
Must fly away.

EMER.

                        You people of the wind
Are full of lying speech and mockery:
I have not fled your face.

FIGURE OF CUCHULAIN.

                                You are not loved.

EMER.

And therefore have no dread to meet your eyes
And to demand him of you.

FIGURE OF CUCHULAIN.

                                For that I have come.
You have but to pay the price and he is free.

EMER.

Do the Sidhe bargain?

FIGURE OF CUCHULAIN.

                        When they would free a captive
They take in ransom a less valued thing.
The fisher, when some knowledgeable man
Restores to him his wife, or son, or daughter,
Knows he must lose a boat or net, or it may be
The cow that gives his children milk; and some
Have offered their own lives. I do not ask
Your life, or any valuable thing;
You spoke but now of the mere chance that some day
You'd be the apple of his eye again
When old and ailing, but renounce that chance
And he shall live again.

EMER.

                        I do not question
But you have brought ill-luck on all he loves;
And now, because I am thrown beyond your power
Unless your words are lies, you come to bargain.

FIGURE OF CUCHULAIN.

You loved your mastery, when but newly married,
And I love mine for all my withered arm;

You have but to put yourself into that power
And he shall live again.

EMER.

                         No, never, never.

FIGURE OF CUCHULAIN.

You dare not be accursed, yet he has dared.

EMER.

I have but two joyous thoughts, two things I prize.
A hope, a memory, and now you claim that hope.

FIGURE OF CUCHULAIN.

He'll never sit beside you at the hearth
Or make old bones, but die of wounds and toil
On some far shore or mountain, a strange woman
Beside his mattress.

EMER.

                  You ask for my one hope
That you may bring your curse on all about him.

FIGURE OF CUCHULAIN.

You've watched his loves and you have not been jealous,
Knowing that he would tire, but do those tire
That love the Sidhe? Come closer to the bed
That I may touch your eyes and give them sight.

(He touches her eyes with his left hand, the right being withered.)

EMER *(seeing the crouching Ghost of Cuchulain)*.

My husband is there.

FIGURE OF CUCHULAIN.

                I have dissolved the dark
That hid him from your eyes, but not that other
That's hidden you from his.

EMER.

                  O husband, husband!

FIGURE OF CUCHULAIN.

He cannot hear—being shut off, a phantom
That can neither touch, nor hear, nor see;
The longing and the cries have drawn him hither.
He heard no sound, heard no articulate sound;
They could but banish rest, and make him dream,
And in that dream, as do all dreaming shades
Before they are accustomed to their freedom,
He has taken his familiar form; and yet
He crouches there not knowing where he is
Or at whose side he is crouched.

(A Woman of the Sidhe has entered and stands a little inside the door.)
EMER.

Who is this woman?

FIGURE OF CUCHULAIN.

> She has hurried from the Country-under-Wave
> And dreamed herself into that shape that he
> May glitter in her basket; for the Sidhe
> Are dexterous fishers and they fish for men
> With dreams upon the hook.

EMER.

And so that woman

> Has hid herself in this disguise and made
> Herself into a lie.

FIGURE OF CUCHULAIN.

> A dream is body;
> The dead move ever towards a dreamless youth
> And when they dream no more return no more;
> And those more holy shades that never lived
> But visit you in dreams.

EMER.

I know her sort.

> They find our men asleep, weary with war,
> Lap them in cloudy hair or kiss their lips;
> Our men awake in ignorance of it all,
> But when we take them in our arms at night
> We cannot break their solitude.

(She draws a knife from her girdle.)
FIGURE OF CUCHULAIN.

No knife

> Can wound that body of air. Be silent; listen;
> I have not given you eyes and ears for nothing.

(The Woman of the Sidhe moves round the crouching Ghost of Cuchulain at front of stage in a dance that grows gradually quicker, as he slowly awakes. At moments she may drop her hair upon his head, but she does not kiss him. She is accompanied by string and flute and drum. Her mask and clothes must suggest gold or bronze or brass or silver, so that she seems more an idol than a human being. This suggestion may be repeated in her movements. Her hair, too, must keep the metallic suggestion.)
GHOST OF CUCHULAIN.

> Who is it stands before me there
> Shedding such light from limb and hair
> As when the moon, complete at last

With every labouring crescent past,
And lonely with extreme delight,
Flings out upon the fifteenth night?[9]

WOMAN OF THE SIDHE.

Because I long I am not complete.
What pulled your hands about your feet,
Pulled down your head upon your knees,
And hid your face?

GHOST OF CUCHULAIN.

Old memories:
A woman in her happy youth
Before her man had broken troth,
Dead men and women. Memories
Have pulled my head upon my knees.

WOMAN OF THE SIDHE.

Could you that have loved many a woman
That did not reach beyond the human,
Lacking a day to be complete,
Love one that, though her heart can beat,
Lacks it but by an hour or so?

GHOST OF CUCHULAIN.

I know you now, for long ago
I met you on a cloudy hill
Beside old thorn-trees and a well.
A woman danced and a hawk flew,
I held out arms and hands; but you,
That now seem friendly, fled away,
Half woman and half bird of prey.[10]

WOMAN OF THE SIDHE.

Hold out your arms and hands again;
You were not so dumbfounded when
I was that bird of prey, and yet
I am all woman now.

GHOST OF CUCHULAIN.

I am not
The young and passionate man I was,
And though that brilliant light surpass
All crescent forms, my memories
Weigh down my hands, abash my eyes.

9. **the fifteenth night** the full of the moon, symbol of Otherworld perfection in Yeats's system (see *A Vision*)   10. **I met you . . . prey** an allusion to the story of *At the Hawk's Well*

WOMAN OF THE SIDHE.

> Then kiss my mouth. Though memory
> Be beauty's bitterest enemy
> I have no dread, for at my kiss
> Memory on the moment vanishes;
> Nothing but beauty can remain.

GHOST OF CUCHULAIN.

> And shall I never know again
> Intricacies of blind remorse?

WOMAN OF THE SIDHE.

> Time shall seem to stay his course;
> When your mouth and my mouth meet
> All my round shall be complete[11]
> Imagining all its circles run;
> And there shall be oblivion
> Even to quench Cuchulain's drouth,
> Even to still that heart.

GHOST OF CUCHULAIN.

> Your mouth!

(They are about to kiss, he turns away.)

> O Emer, Emer!

WOMAN OF THE SIDHE.

> So then it is she
> Made you impure with memory.

GHOST OF CUCHULAIN.

> O Emer, Emer, there we stand;
> Side by side and hand in hand
> Tread the threshold of the house
> As when our parents married us.

WOMAN OF THE SIDHE.

> Being among the dead you love her
> That valued every slut above her
> While you still lived.

GHOST OF CUCHULAIN.

> O my lost Emer!

WOMAN OF THE SIDHE.

> And there is not a loose-tongued schemer
> But could draw you, if not dead,
> From her table and her bed.
> But what could make you fit to wive

11. **All . . . complete** She is about to reach the fifteenth phase, absolute mystical perfection, and escape the cycles of rebirth.

With flesh and blood, being born to live
Where no one speaks of broken troth,
For all have washed out of their eyes
Wind-blown dirt of their memories
To improve their sight?

GHOST OF CUCHULAIN.

Your mouth, your mouth!

(She goes out followed by Ghost of Cuchulain.)

FIGURE OF CUCHULAIN.

Cry out that you renounce his love; make haste
And cry that you renounce his love for ever.

EMER.

No, never will I give that cry.

FIGURE OF CUCHULAIN.

Fool, fool!

I am Fand's[12] enemy coming to thwart her will,
And you stand gaping there. There is still time.
Hear how the horses trample on the shore,
Hear how they trample! She has mounted up.
Cuchulain's not beside her in the chariot.
There is still a moment left; cry out, cry out!
Renounce him, and her power is at an end.
Cuchulain's foot is on the chariot-step.
Cry——

EMER.

I renounce Cuchulain's love for ever.

(The Figure of Cuchulain sinks back upon the bed, half-drawing the curtain. Eithne Inguba comes in and kneels by bed.)

EITHNE INGUBA.

Come to me, my beloved, it is I.
I, Eithne Inguba. Look! He is there.
He has come back and moved upon the bed.
And it is I that won him from the sea,
That brought him back to life.

EMER.

Cuchulain wakes.

(The figure turns round. It once more wears the heroic mask.)

CUCHULAIN.

Your arms, your arms! O Eithne Inguba,
I have been in some strange place and am afraid.

12. **Fand** the woman of the Sidhe; wife of Manannan mac Lir

(The First Musician comes to the front of stage, the others from each side, and unfold the cloth singing.)
(Song for the unfolding and folding of the cloth)
THE MUSICIANS.

> Why does your heart beat thus?
> Plain to be understood,
> I have met in a man's house
> A statue of solitude,
> Moving there and walking;
> Its strange heart beating fast
> For all our talking.
> O still that heart at last.
>
> O bitter reward
> Of many a tragic tomb!
> And we though astonished are dumb
> Or give but a sigh and a word,
> A passing word.
>
> Although the door be shut
> And all seem well enough,
> Although wide world hold not
> A man but will give you his love
> The moment he has looked at you,
> He that has loved the best
> May turn from a statue
> His too human breast.
>
> O bitter reward
> Of many a tragic tomb!
> And we though astonished are dumb
> Or give but a sigh and a word,
> A passing word.
>
> What makes your heart so beat?
> What man is at your side?
> When beauty is complete
> Your own thought will have died
> And danger not be diminished;
> Dimmed at three-quarter light,
> When moon's round is finished
> The stars are out of sight.
>
> O bitter reward
> Of many a tragic tomb!

And we though astonished are dumb
Or give but a sigh and a word,
A passing word.

(When the cloth is folded again the stage is bare.)

THE END

PADRAIC COLUM
1881 – 1972

Nothing in Padraic Colum's early life or family history could have given notice that he was to be one of the most prolific and versatile Irish writers of his generation. His parents, Patrick and Susan MacCormack Collumb, came from rural, peasant Roman Catholic families. Eldest of eight children, Padraic was born on December 8, 1881, in a workhouse in Longford where his father was teacher and then master. When Padraic was six, his father lost his job and went to America for a few years; the children were sent to their grandmother in County Cavan, and Padraic spent much of his time on the road and at markets with his uncle, Micky Burns, a fowl dealer who was an accomplished ballad-singer and storyteller. Much of the material and feeling of Colum's poetry and early plays derives from these childhood years with Irish country people.

His father returned from the United States in 1891, and moved his family to Sandycove, outside Dublin, where he found a job in the railway station. At the age of seventeen, Padraic left school and took a clerkship in the Irish Railway Clearing House in Dublin.

At this time he became involved in the political, cultural, and literary nationalist movements. He joined the Gaelic League, drilled with the Irish Republican Army, joined the literary society Cumann na nGaedheal, and published his first poems and plays in Arthur Griffith's *United Irishman* newspaper. His attraction to the theater was based on small experience of it; when he began writing, he had seen little more than some English comedies, a few sentimental Irish plays by Dion Boucicault, and the *tableaux vivants* of Inginidhe na hÉireann (The Daughters of Ireland), the sister organization of Cumann na nGaedheal. After he sent parts of a play, *Broken Soil,* to the secretary of Inginidhe, he was introduced to Willie and Frank Fay, who invited him to join their National Theatre Society. The members of this democratic group took part in all aspects of production, including acting; thus Colum got hands-on experience of the theater as he began to write in earnest. "He had but little time for literary work," W. G. Fay remembered,

> but whenever the spirit moved him he just jotted down at odd moments a poem or a scrap of dialogue on the first bit of paper that came handy—the back of an invoice or an envelope or the corner of some useless document. . . . He would come into the hall at Camden Street, either before or after rehearsal, and coming up to my

table, would empty his pockets of pieces of paper of all shapes and colours and sizes. . . . Then he would begin to shuffle the pack. "Here's the first bit . . . no, that's a bit of Act II, and that's another bit of it." . . . It took a deal of patience to get the jigsaw puzzle into shape, but he learned dramatic technique very quickly, and I think his playing with us helped him to understand very soon the limitations imposed by a stage and proscenium.

The National Theatre Society produced *Broken Soil* in 1903; Colum was immediately recognized for his ability to dramatize Irish country people realistically. "Yeats, Lady Gregory, Synge, and all were doing it," he wrote later, "but the truth of the matter is that I was the only one of the lot that knew what the real country speech sounded like. I wouldn't want to say a word against Synge's language, which is exquisite, very fine, but has no more to do with how people actually spoke than Oscar Wilde's dialogue in his comedies has to do with how people spoke in London drawing rooms in the eighteen-nineties."

Colum's popularity transcended all the factions developing in the theater movement. Despite his youth, he was put on the first reading committee of the National Theatre Society; he was welcomed at Æ's Sunday soirées; Yeats and Lady Gregory took an interest in him. An American, Thomas Hughes Kelly, gave him a five-year scholarship that enabled him to leave his railway job and devote full time to study and writing.

It was during these years that Colum wrote the three plays that founded the tradition of realistic drama in the Abbey Theatre. *The Land* was produced at the recently completed Abbey on June 9, 1905. In 1907 the Theatre of Ireland, a splinter group protesting Abbey policies, staged *The Fiddler's House*; a reworking of *Broken Soil*, its theme is the age-old conflict between settled family responsibility and the fluid life of the wandering artist. The play also reflects Colum's notable sympathy with women in its portrayal of the fiddler's daughter Maire; her "recoil from her lover," Colum wrote, "is due to her fear of masculine possessiveness—a recoil not extraordinary in a girl brought up in the Irish countryside." *Thomas Muskerry*, Colum's third major play, produced by the Abbey in 1910, introduced into the Abbey repertoire a new aspect of Ireland: small-town life. Muskerry, master of Garrisowen Workhouse, has (perhaps like Colum's own father) unintentionally mismanaged its funds, and his life hopes are destroyed by the malicious gossip of the townspeople and the self-interested ambitions of his own family; he dies a pauper in his own workhouse, lamented only by other paupers to whom he has been kind.

In 1912 Colum married Mary Catherine Gunning Maguire, who was later to have a distinguished career as a journalist and literary critic. When money ran short for the couple—Kelly's five-year scholarship having expired—they went to America in 1914 to visit Colum's aunt in Pittsburgh, found literary employment far easier to come by in the United States than in Ireland, and stayed (apart from frequent visits back to Ireland, and a few years' residence in France) for the rest of their lives. As they had done in Dublin, the Colums quickly made a wide circle of literary acquaintances in America. They lived primarily in New York, and taught for some time at Columbia University. Mary Colum died in 1957. Padraic continued to write throughout his life—a career of over seventy years. He wrote about seventy books, including novels, biographies, poetry volumes, books about Ireland, folklore surveys, plays, and the many titles for children which brought the couple their bread and butter; he also edited dozens of volumes, and published hundreds of articles, poems, stories, and other miscellaneous writings. During the 1960s he returned intensively to theater work, making major revisions of *Three Plays* in 1963, and beginning a new series of Noh-style dramas. In a late interview on Radio Éireann he said, "Anything I have written, whether verse or narrative, goes back to my first literary discipline, the discipline of the theatre." He died on January 11, 1972, and was buried in Ireland.

When *The Land* was produced in 1905, it was, in Colum's words, "The first popular success the Irish Theatre had." As *The Freeman's Journal* explained,

> What we have been waiting for was a play that should be at once good and popular. Mr. Yeats has proved a little too abstruse, and Mr. Synge a little too bizarre to get fully down to the hearts of the people. . . . Mr. Colum has caught up his play out of the mid-current of actual, Irish life.

The matter of the play was immediate for its first audience: Colum wrote it, he later said, to celebrate "the redemption of the soil of Ireland" by the Land Act (the Wyndham Act) of 1903, the legislation that finally put an end to the Land War by encouraging landlords to sell their entire estates to their tenants, who bargained as a group on the terms of the sale. (Tenants who, like Martin Douras, could not afford to purchase their land could continue to pay rent to the Land Commission, which executed the sales.)

The play's celebration is not simple, however. The characters represent (perhaps too schematically) the historical trends that render this final victory of the Irish countryman bitterly ironic. In Murtagh Cosgar's tough devotion to the land we see a typical post-Famine pattern: the refusal to subdivide the farm among children, insistence on maintaining dominion over the farm (thus denying his children the chance of marriage and inheritance until he retires)—in general, a set of principles that entail the sacrifice of children as individuals to the family's future good. Like Old Mahon in *The Playboy of the Western World*, Murtagh has driven away all his children but the youngest: Matt, who loves the land but can sacrifice it (amazing his father) for love, and Sally, who is little more than a drudge. The intellectual Martin Douras, whose efforts in the land agitation (for which he has been jailed) have brought him little respect from the self-made Murtaghs who are now reaping the rewards, likewise is given two children: Ellen, who having her father's intellectual independence can imagine a better world, and names it America, and the garrulous, vapid Cornelius, echoer of fine phrases.

There is no right answer to the dilemma of this struggle of generations; the issue is tragic, and the vital young are giving up their inheritance, abandoning the "redemption" of Ireland at the moment it arrives. *The Land*'s classic presentation of this theme marked its first appearance on the Irish stage.

SELECT BIBLIOGRAPHY

Publications

Three Plays. Dublin and London: Maunsel, 1916; revised ed., New York: Macmillan, 1925; revised ed., Dublin: Allen Figgis, 1963. (*The Land, Thomas Muskerry, The Fiddler's House*)
Balloon: A Comedy in Four Acts. New York: Macmillan, 1929.
Moytura: A Play for Dancers. Dublin: Dolmen, 1963.
The Flying Swans. New York: Crown, 1957. (Novel)
Poems. New York and London: Macmillan, 1932. [Includes *Wild Earth* (1907/1916), *Dramatic Legends* (1922), *Creatures* (1927), *Old Pastures* (1930)]
The Poet's Circuits: Collected Poems of Ireland. London: Oxford University Press, 1960.
Selected Short Stories of Padraic Colum. Ed. Sanford Sternlicht. Syracuse: Syracuse University Press, 1985.

Biography and Criticism

Bowen, Zack. *Padraic Colum: A Biographical-Critical Introduction*. Carbondale, IL: Southern Illinois University Press, 1970.
Colum, Mary. *Life and the Dream*. Garden City, NY: Doubleday, 1947.
Denson, Alan. "Padraic Colum: An Appreciation with a Check-List of His Publications." *The Dublin Magazine* 6 (Spring 1967): 50–67.
Journal of Irish Literature 2,1 (1973). (Special Padraic Colum issue)
Murphy, Ann. "Appréciation: Padraic Colum (1881–1972), National Poet." *Éire/Ireland* 17,4 (Winter 1982): 128–147.

The Land

An Agrarian Comedy
in Three Acts

CHARACTERS

MURTAGH COSGAR, *a farmer*
MATT, *his son*
SALLY, *his daughter*
MARTIN DOURAS, *a farmer*
CORNELIUS, *his son*
ELLEN, *his daughter*
A group of men
A group of boys and girls

The scene is laid in the Irish Midlands, present time.

ACT 1

The interior of Murtagh Cosgar's. It is a large flagged[1] kitchen with the entrance on the right. The dresser is below the entrance. There is a large fireplace in the back, and a room door to the left of the fireplace; the harness-rack is between room door and fireplace. The yard door is on the left. The table is down from the room door. There are benches around fireplace.

It is the afternoon of a May day. Sally Cosgar is kneeling near the entrance chopping up cabbage-leaves with a kitchen-knife. She is a girl of twenty-five, dark, heavily built, with the expression of a half-awakened creature. She is coarsely dressed, and has a sacking apron. She is quick at work, and rapid and impetuous in speech. She is talking to herself.

SALLY. Oh, you may go on grunting, yourself and your litter, it won't put me a bit past my own time. You oul' black baste[2] of a sow, sure I'm slaving to you all the spring. We'll be getting rid of yourself and your litter soon enough, and may the devil get you when we lose you.

(Cornelius comes to the door. He is a tall young man with a slight stoop. His manners are solemn, and his expression somewhat vacant.)

1. **flagged** floored with flagstones   2. **baste** beast

85

CORNELIUS. Good morrow, Sally. May you have the good of the day. *(He comes in.)*

SALLY *(impetuously)*. Ah, God reward you, Cornelius Douras, for coming in. I'm that busy keeping food to a sow and a litter of pigs that I couldn't get beyond the gate to see any one.

CORNELIUS *(solemnly)*. You're a good girl, Sally. You're not like some I know. There are girls in this parish who never put hands to a thing till evening, when the boys do be coming in. Then they begin to stir themselves the way they'll be thought busy and good about a house.

SALLY *(pleased and beginning to chop again with renewed energy)*. Oh, it's true indeed for you, Cornelius. There are girls that be decking themselves, and sporting are themselves all day.

CORNELIUS. I may say that I come over to your father's, Murtagh Cosgar's house, this morning, thinking to meet the men.

SALLY. What men, Cornelius Douras?

CORNELIUS. Them that are going to meet the landlord's people with an offer for the land. We're not buying ourselves, unfortunately, but this is a great day—the day of the redemption, my father calls it—and I'd like to have some hand in the work if it was only to say a few words to the men.

SALLY. It's a wonder Martin, your father isn't on the one[3] errand with you.

CORNELIUS. We came out together, but the priest stopped father and us on the road. Father Bartley wanted his advice, I suppose. Ah, it's a pity the men won't have some one like my father with them! He was in gaol for the Cause.[4] Besides, he's a well-discoursed man, and a reading man, and, moreover, a man with a classical knowledge of English, Latin, and the Hibernian vernacular.

(Martin Douras comes in. He is a man of about sixty, with a refined, scholarly look. His manner is subdued and nervous. He has a stoop, and is clean-shaven.)

CORNELIUS. I was just telling Sally here what a great day it is, father.

MARTIN DOURAS. Ay, it's a great day, no matter what our own troubles may be. I should be going home again. *(He takes a newspaper out of his pocket, and leaves it on the table.)*

CORNELIUS. Wait for the men, father.

MARTIN DOURAS. Maybe they'll be here soon. Is Murtagh in, Sally? *(Cornelius takes the paper up, and begins to read it.)*

SALLY. He's down at the bottoms,[5] Martin.

MARTIN DOURAS. He's going to Arvach Fair, maybe.

---

3. **the one** the same   4. **the Cause** the Land War, 1879 and after   5. **bottoms** low-lying field

SALLY. He is in troth.[6]

MARTIN DOURAS. I'll be asking him for a lift. He'll be going to the Fair when he come back from the lawyer's, I suppose?

SALLY. Ay, he'll be going to-night.

(She gathers the chopped cabbage into her apron, and goes to the door.)

SALLY *(at the door)*. Cornelius.

(Cornelius puts down the paper, and goes to the door. Sally goes out.)

MARTIN DOURAS. Cornelius!

(Cornelius goes to Martin.)

SALLY *(outside)*. Cornelius, give me a hand with this.

(Cornelius turns again.)

MARTIN DOURAS. Cornelius, I want to speak to you.

(Cornelius goes to him.)

MARTIN DOURAS. There is something on my mind, Cornelius.

CORNELIUS. What is it, father?

MARTIN DOURAS. It's about our Ellen. Father Bartley gave me news for her. "I've heard of a school that'll suit Ellen," says he. "It's in the County Leitrim."

CORNELIUS. If it was in Dublin itself, Ellen is qualified to take it on. And won't it be grand to have one of our family teaching in a school?

MARTIN DOURAS *(with a sigh)*. I wouldn't stand in her way, Cornelius; I wouldn't stand in her way. But won't it be a poor thing for an old man like me to have no one to discourse with in the long evenings? For when I'm talking with you, Cornelius, I feel like a boy who lends back all the marbles he's won, and plays again, just for the sake of the game.

CORNELIUS. We were in dread of Ellen going to America at one time, and then she went in for the school. Now Matt Cosgar may keep her from the school. Maybe we won't have to go further than this house to see Ellen.

MARTIN DOURAS. I'm hoping it'll be like that; but I'm in dread that Murtagh Cosgar will never agree to it. He's a hard man to deal with. Still Murtagh and myself will be on the long road to-night, and we might talk of it. I'm afeard of Ellen going.

CORNELIUS *(at the door)*. It's herself that's coming here, father.

MARTIN DOURAS. Maybe she has heard the news and is coming to tell us. *(Ellen comes in. She has a shawl over her head which she lays aside. She is about twenty-five, slightly built, nervous, emotional.)*

ELLEN. Is it only ourselves that's here?

MARTIN DOURAS. Only ourselves. Did you get any news to bring you over, Ellen?

ELLEN. No news. It was the shine of the day that brought me out; and

6. **in troth** truly, indeed

I was thinking, too, of the girls that are going to America in the morning, and that made me restless.

(Martin and Cornelius look significantly at each other.)

MARTIN DOURAS. And did you see Matt, Ellen?

ELLEN. He was in the field and I coming up; but I did not wait for him, as I don't want people to see us together. *(Restlessly)* I don't know how I can come into this house, for it's always like Murtagh Cosgar. There's nothing of Matt in it at all. If Matt would come away. There are little labourers' houses by the side of the road. Many's the farmer's son became a labourer for the sake of a woman he cared for!

CORNELIUS. And are you not thinking about the school at all, Ellen?

ELLEN. I'll hear about it some time, I suppose.

MARTIN DOURAS. You're right to take it that way, Ellen. School doesn't mean scholarship now. Many's the time I'm telling Cornelius that a man farming the land, with a few books on his shelf and a few books in his head, has more of the scholar's life about him than the young fellows who do be teaching in schools and teaching in colleges.

CORNELIUS. That's all very well, father. School and scholarship isn't the one. But think of the word "Constantinople!" I could leave off herding and digging every time I think on that word!

MARTIN DOURAS. Ah, it's a great word. A word like that would make you think for days. And there are many words like that.

ELLEN. It's not so much the long words that we've to learn and teach now. When will you be home, father? Will Cornelius be with you?

MARTIN DOURAS. Ellen, I have news for you. There is a school in Leitrim that Father Bartley can let you have.

ELLEN. In Leitrim! Did you tell Matt about it?

MARTIN DOURAS. I did not.

(Sally is heard calling "Cornelius." Cornelius goes to the door.)

CORNELIUS. Here's Matt now. The benefit of the day to you, Matt.

(He stands aside to let Matt enter. Matt Cosgar is a young peasant of about twenty-eight. He is handsome and well-built. He is dressed in a trousers, shirt, and coat, and has a felt hat on. Cornelius goes out.)

MATT *(going to Ellen)*. You're welcome, Ellen. Good morrow, Martin. It's a great day for the purchase, Martin.

MARTIN DOURAS. A great day, indeed, thank God.

MATT. Ah, it's a great thing to feel the ownership of the land, Martin.

MARTIN DOURAS. I don't doubt but it is.

MATT. Look at the young apple-trees, Ellen. Walking up this morning, I felt as glad of them as a young man would be glad of the sweetheart he saw coming towards him.

ELLEN. Ay, there's great gladness and shine in the day.

MATT. It seems to trouble you.

ELLEN. It does trouble me.

MATT. Why?

ELLEN. Everything seems to be saying, "There's something here, there's something going."

MATT. Ay, a day like this often makes you feel that way. It's a great day for the purchase though. How many years ought we to offer, Ellen?

(Martin goes out.)

ELLEN. Twenty years, I suppose—*(suddenly)* Matt!

MATT. What is it, Ellen?

MATT. I have got an offer of a school in the County Leitrim.

MATT. I wish they'd wait, Ellen. I wish they'd wait till I had something to offer you.

ELLEN. I'm a long time waiting here, Matt.

MATT. Sure we're both young.

ELLEN. This is summer now. There will be autumn in a month or two. The year will have gone by without bringing me anything.

MATT. He'll be letting me have my own way soon, my father will.

ELLEN. Murtagh Cosgar never let a child of his have their own way.

MATT. When the land's bought out, he'll be easier to deal with.

ELLEN. When he owns the land, he'll never let a son of his marry a girl without land or fortune.[7]

MATT. Ellen, Ellen, I'd lose house and land for you. Sure you know that, Ellen. My brothers and sisters took their freedom. They went from this house and away to the ends of the world. Maybe I don't differ from them so much. But I've put my work into the land, and I'm beginning to know the land. I won't lose it, Ellen. Neither will I lose you.

ELLEN. O Matt, what's the land after all? Do you ever think of America? The streets, the shops, the throngs?

MATT. The land is better than that when you come to know it, Ellen.

ELLEN. May be it is.

MATT. I've set my heart on a new house. Ay and he'll build one for us when he knows my mind.

ELLEN. Do you think he'd build a new house for us, Matt? I could settle down if we were by ourselves. Maybe it's true that there are things stirring and we could begin a new life, even here.

MATT. We can, Ellen, we can. Hush! father's without. *(Martin Douras and Murtagh Cosgar are heard exchanging greetings. Then Murtagh comes in, Martin behind him. Murtagh Cosgar is about sixty. He is a hard, strong man, seldom-spoken, but with a flow of words and some satirical power. He is still powerful, mentally and physically. He is clean shaven, and wears a sleeved waistcoat, heavy boots, felt hat. He goes towards Ellen.)*

7. **fortune** dowry

MURTAGH. Good morrow to you. *(Turning to Matt)* When I get speaking to that Sally again, she'll remember what I say. Giving cabbage to the pigs, and all the bad potatoes in the house. And I had to get up in the clouds of the night to turn the cows out of the young meadow. No thought, no care about me. Let you take the harness outside and put a thong where there's a strain in it.

(Murtagh goes to the fire. Matt goes to the harness-rack. Martin Douras and Ellen are at the door.)

MARTIN DOURAS. Ellen, I'll have news for you when I see you again. I've made up my mind to that.

ELLEN. Are you going to the fair, father?

MARTIN DOURAS. Ay, with Murtagh.

ELLEN. God be with you, father. *(She goes out.)*

MARTIN DOURAS. What purchase are you thinking of offering, Murtagh?

MURTAGH COSGAR. Twenty years.

MARTIN DOURAS. It's fair enough. Oh, it's a great day for the country, no matter what our own troubles may be.

(Matt has taken down the harness. He takes some of it up and goes out to yard.)

MURTAGH COSGAR *(with some contempt).* It's a pity you haven't a share in the day after all.

MARTIN DOURAS. Ay, it's a pity indeed.

(Murtagh goes to the door.)

MURTAGH COSGAR *(with suppressed enthusiasm).* From this day out we're planted in the soil.

MARTIN DOURAS. Ay, we're planted in the soil.

MURTAGH COSGAR. God, it's a great day.

(Cornelius comes back.)

CORNELIUS. This is a memorial occasion, Murtagh Cosgar, and I wish you the felicitations of it. I met the delegates and I coming in, and I put myself at the head of them. It's the day of the redemption, Murtagh Cosgar.

(Murtagh, without speaking, goes up to the room left.)

CORNELIUS. He's gone up to get the papers. Father, we must give the men understanding for this business. They must demand the mineral rights. Here they are. Men of Ballykillduff, I greet your entrance.

(Six men enter discussing.)

FIRST MAN. We'll leave it to Murtagh Cosgar. Murtagh Cosgar isn't a grazier or a shopkeeper.

SECOND MAN. It's the graziers and shopkeepers that are putting a business head on this.

THIRD MAN. If we're all on the one offer, we can settle it at the lawyer's.

FOURTH MAN. Sure it's settled for twenty years on the first-term rents.

FIFTH MAN. There are some here that would let it go as high as twenty-three.

SIXTH MAN. What does Murtagh Cosgar say?

SOME OF THE MEN. We'll take the word from him.

MARTIN DOURAS. He mentioned twenty years.

SECOND MAN. Not as a limit, surely?

OTHER MEN. We're not for any higher offer.

SECOND MAN. Well, men, this is all I have to say. If you can get it for twenty, take it, and my blessing with it. But I want to be dealing with the Government, and not with landlords and agents. To have a straight bargain between myself and the Government, I'd put it up to twenty-three, ay, up to twenty-five years' purchase.

THIRD MAN. More power to you, Councillor. There's some sense in that.

SIXTH MAN. I'm with the Councillor.

FIRST MAN. It's all very well for graziers and shopkeepers to talk, but what about the small farmer?

FOURTH MAN. The small farmer. That's the man that goes under.

FIFTH MAN *(knocking at the table)*. Murtagh Cosgar! Murtagh Cosgar!

CORNELIUS. I tell you, men, that Murtagh Cosgar is in agreement with myself. Twenty years, I say, first term, no more. Let my father speak.

MARTIN DOURAS. There's a great deal to be said on both sides, men.

FIRST MAN. Here's Murtagh now.

MURTAGH COSGAR. Twenty years first term, that's what I agreed to.

SECOND MAN. And if they don't rise to that, Murtagh?

MURTAGH COSGAR. Let them wait. We can wait. I won't be going with you, men. I had a few words with the agent about the turbary[8] this morning, and maybe you're better without me.

FIRST MAN. All right, Murtagh. We can wait.

FOURTH MAN. We know our own power now.

FIFTH MAN. Come on, men.

MURTAGH COSGAR. If they don't rise to it, bide a while. We can make a new offer.

SECOND MAN. We want to be settled by the Fall.

THIRD MAN. The Councillor is right. We must be settled by the Fall.

SIXTH MAN. A man who's a farmer only has little sense for a business like this.

SECOND MAN. We'll make the offer, Murtagh Cosgar, and bide a while. But we must be settled this side of the Fall. We'll offer twenty years first term.

MURTAGH COSGAR. Do, and God speed you.

8. **turbary** rights to cut turf for fuel

CORNELIUS *(to the men going out)*. I told you Murtagh Cosgar and myself are on the one offer. And Murtagh is right again when he says that you can bide your time. But make sure of the mineral rights, men; make sure of the mineral rights.

(The men go out; Cornelius follows them.)

MURTAGH COSGAR *(with irony)*. Musha, but that's a well-discoursed lad. It must be great to hear the two of you at it.

MARTIN DOURAS. God be good to Cornelius. There's little of the world's harm in the boy.

MURTAGH COSGAR. He and my Sally would make a great match of it. She's a bright one, too.

MARTIN DOURAS. Murtagh Cosgar, have you no feeling for your own flesh and blood?

MURTAGH COSGAR. Too much feeling, maybe. *(He stands at the door in silence. With sudden enthusiasm)* Ah, but that's the sight to fill one's heart. Lands ploughed and spread. And all our own; all our own.

MARTIN DOURAS. All our own, ay. But we made a hard fight for them.

MURTAGH COSGAR. Ay.

MARTIN DOURAS. Them that come after us will never see them as we're seeing them now.

MURTAGH COSGAR *(turning round)*. Them that come after us. Isn't that a great thought, Martin Douras? and isn't it a great thing that we're able to pass this land on to them, and it redeemed for ever? Ay, and their manhood spared the shame that our manhood knew. Standing in the rain with our hats off to let a landlord—ay, or a landlord's dog-boy—pass the way!

MARTIN DOURAS *(mournfully)*. May it be our own generation that will be in it. Ay, but the young are going fast; the young are going fast.

MURTAGH COSGAR *(sternly)*. Some of them are no loss.

MARTIN DOURAS. Ten of your own children went, Murtagh Cosgar.

MURTAGH COSGAR. I never think of them. When they went from my control, they went from me altogether. There's the more for Matt.

MARTIN DOURAS *(moistening his mouth, and beginning very nervously)*. Ay, Matt. Matt's a good lad.

MURTAGH COSGAR. There's little fear of him leaving now.

MARTIN DOURAS *(nervously)*. Maybe, maybe. But, mind you, Murtagh Cosgar, there are things—little things, mind you. Least, ways, what we call little things. And, after all, who are we to judge whether a thing—

MURTAGH COSGAR. Is there anything on your mind, Martin Douras?

MARTIN DOURAS *(hurriedly)*. No; oh, no. I was thinking—I was thinking, maybe you'd give me a lift towards Arvach, if you'd be going that way this night.

MURTAGH COSGAR. Ay, why not?

MARTIN DOURAS. And we could talk about the land, and about Matt, too. Wouldn't it be a heart-break if any of our children went—because of a thing we might——

MURTAGH COSGAR (*fiercely*). What have you to say about Matt?

MARTIN DOURAS (*stammering*). Nothing except in a—in what you might call a general way. There's many a young man left house and land for the sake of some woman, Murtagh Cosgar.

MURTAGH COSGAR. There's many a fool did it.

MARTIN DOURAS (*going to door*). Ay, maybe; maybe. I'll be going now, Murtagh.

MURTAGH COSGAR. Stop! (*clutching him*) You know about Matt. What woman is he thinking of ?

MARTIN DOURAS (*frightened*). We'll talk about it again, Murtagh. I said I'd be back.

MURTAGH COSGAR. We'll talk about it now. Who is she? What name has she?

MARTIN DOURAS (*breaking from him and speaking with sudden dignity*). It's a good name, Murtagh Cosgar; it's my own name.

MURTAGH COSGAR. Your daughter! Ellen! You're——

MARTIN DOURAS. Ay, a good name, and a good girl.

MURTAGH COSGAR. And do you think a son of mine would marry a daughter of yours?

MARTIN DOURAS. What great difference is between us, after all?

MURTAGH COSGAR (*fiercely*). The daughter of a man who'd be sitting over his fire reading his paper, and the clouds above his potatoes, and the cows trampling his oats. (*Martin is beaten down.*) Do you know me at all, Martin Douras? I came out of a little house by the roadway and built my house on a hill. I had many children. Coming home in the long evenings, or kneeling still when the prayers would be over, I'd have my dreams. A son in Aughnalee, a son in Ballybrian, a son in Dunmore, a son of mine with a shop, a son of mine saying Mass in Killnalee. And I have a living name—a name in flesh and blood.

MARTIN DOURAS. God help you, Murtagh Cosgar.

MURTAGH COSGAR. But I've a son still. It's not your daughter he'll be marrying. (*He strides to the door and calls Matt.*)

MARTIN DOURAS (*going to him*). Murtagh Cosgar—for God's sake—we're both old men, Murtagh Cosgar.

MURTAGH COSGAR. You've read many stories, Martin Douras, and you know many endings. You'll see an ending now, and it will be a strong ending, and a sudden ending.

(*Matt comes in.*)

MURTAGH COSGAR. You're wanted here.

MATT. I heard you call. (*He sits on table.*) So they're sticking to the twenty years.

MARTIN DOURAS (*eagerly*). Twenty years, Matt, and they'll get it for twenty. O, it's a great day for you both! Father and son, you come into a single inheritance. What the father wins the son wields.

MURTAGH COSGAR. What the father wins, the son wastes.

MATT. What's the talk of father and son?

MARTIN DOURAS. They're the one flesh and blood. There's no more strife between them than between the right hand and the left hand.

MURTAGH COSGAR (to Matt). We were talking about you. We were fixing a match for you.

MATT (startled, looking at Martin Douras). Fixing a match for me? (He rises.)

MURTAGH COSGAR. Ay, Matt. Don't you think it's time to be making a match for you?

MATT (sullenly, going to the door). Maybe it is. When you have the woman, call. I'll be without.

MURTAGH COSGAR (going to him). We haven't chosen yet. But it won't be Martin Douras' daughter, anyhow.

MATT. Stop. You drove all your living children away, except Sally and myself. You think Sally and myself are the one sort.

MURTAGH COSGAR (tauntingly). Martin's daughter, Corney's sister. That's the girl for you!

MATT. We're not the one sort, I tell you. Martin Douras, isn't he a foolish old man that would drive all his children from him? What would his twenty years' purchase be to him then?

MURTAGH COSGAR. It wasn't for my children I worked. No, no; thank God; it wasn't for my children I worked. Go, if you will. I can be alone.

MARTIN DOURAS. O Murtagh, Murtagh, sure you know you can't be alone. We're two old men, Murtagh.

MURTAGH COSGAR. He daren't go.

MATT. Because I'm the last of them he thinks he can dare me like that.

MURTAGH COSGAR. There was more of my blood in the others.

MATT. Do you say that?

MARTIN DOURAS. Don't say it again. For God's sake, don't say it again, Murtagh.

MURTAGH COSGAR. I do say it again. Them who dared to go had more of my blood in them!

MATT. Ah, you have put me to it now, and I'm glad, glad. A little house, a bit of land. Do you think they could keep me here?

MURTAGH COSGAR (to Martin Douras). It's his own way he wants. I never had my own way. (To Matt) You're my last son. You're too young to know the hardship there was in rearing you.

MATT (exultantly). Your last son; that won't keep me here. I'm the last of my name, but that won't keep me here. I leave you your lands, your twenty years' purchase. Murtagh Cosgar, Murtagh Cosgar! isn't that a great name, Martin Douras—a name that's well planted, a name for generations? Isn't he a lucky man that has a name for generations? *(He goes out.)*

MURTAGH COSGAR. He can't go. How could he go and he the last of the name. Close the door, I say.

MARTIN DOURAS. He'll go to Ellen, surely. We'll lose both of them. Murtagh Cosgar, God comfort you and me.

MURTAGH COSGAR. Ellen; who's Ellen? Ay, that daughter of yours. Close the door, I say.

(He sits down at fireplace. Martin Douras closes door and goes to him.)

CURTAIN

ACT 2

Interior of Martin Douras'. The entrance is at back left. There is a dresser against wall back; a table down from dresser; room doors right and left. The fireplace is below the room door right; there are stools and chairs about it. There is a little bookcase left of the dresser, and a mirror beside it. There are patriotic and religious pictures on the wall. There are cups and saucers on table, and a teapot beside fire. It is afternoon still. Ellen Douras is near the fire reading. Cornelius comes in slowly.

CORNELIUS. I left the men down the road a bit. We ought to take great pride out of this day, Ellen. Father did more than any of them to bring it about.

ELLEN. He suffered more than any of them. And it's little we'll get out of the day.

CORNELIUS. It's a great thing to have prophesied it, even. We'll be here to see a great change.

ELLEN. There will be no change to make things better!

CORNELIUS. Will you be taking that school, Ellen?

ELLEN. I'll wait a while.

(Sally coming in; she is hurried.)

SALLY *(breathlessly)*. Oh, God save you, Cornelius. Tell me, is my father gone? I dread going back and he there! It was all over that baste of a sow that has kept me slaving all through the spring till I don't know whether greens or potatoes is the fittest for her!

CORNELIUS. He didn't go, Sally. I went down a bit of the road myself with the men.

SALLY. Oh, God help me! And I'll have to be going back to boil meal for her now. How are you, Ellen. *(She goes to Ellen.)*

ELLEN. Sit down for a while, Sally; it's a long time since I was speaking to you.

(Sally sits down beside Ellen.)

CORNELIUS. I'll leave this paper where they won't be looking for pipe-lights. There are things in that paper I'd like to be saying. *(He takes a newspaper out of his pocket and goes to room right.)*

ELLEN *(to Sally, who has been watching Cornelius)*. Tell me, Sally, are they always that busy in your house? Is your father as harsh as they say?

SALLY. Father 'ud keep us all working. He's a powerful great man.

ELLEN. Matt will be bringing a wife into the house soon from all I hear. How would your father treat her?

SALLY. Oh, he'd have his way, and she'd have her way, I suppose.

ELLEN. And do you think your father will let him marry?

SALLY. Sure he must if the boy likes.

ELLEN. What would he say if Matt married a girl without a fortune?

SALLY. In my mother's country there are lots of girls with fortunes that Matt could have.

ELLEN. Supposing he wanted a girl that had no fortune?

SALLY. Oh, I suppose father would give in in the end. It wouldn't be clay against flint[9] when Matt and father would be to it.

ELLEN. You're a good girl, Sally. If I was Matt's wife, do you think you'd be fond of me?

SALLY. I'd like you as well as another, Ellen.

(Cornelius comes down from room.)

CORNELIUS. I suppose they'll be here soon.

ELLEN. I have tea ready for them.

SALLY. Who's coming at all?

CORNELIUS. Some of the boys and girls that are for America. They are going to Gilroy's to-night, and are leaving from that in the morning. They are coming in to see Ellen on their way down.

SALLY. There are a good many going this flight. The land never troubles them in America, and they can wear fine clothes, and be as free as the larks over the bogs. It's a wonder you never thought of going, Ellen.

ELLEN. Father wouldn't like me to be far from him, and so I went in for the school instead.

SALLY. And now you've got a fine boy like Matt. It was lucky for you to be staying here.

ELLEN. Hush, Sally.

SALLY. Oh, I knew all about it before you talked to me at all. Matt always goes to the place where he thinks you'd be.

ELLEN *(rising)*. I'll be in the room when the girls come, Cornelius. *(She goes into room left.)*

SALLY *(going to Cornelius)*. God help us, but she's the silent creature. Isn't it a wonder she's not filled with talk of him after seeing him to-day?

9. **clay against flint** a soft substance against a hard one

But Ellen's right. We shouldn't be talking about men, nor thinking about them either; and that's the way to keep them on our hands on the long run. I'll be going myself.

(She goes towards door.)

CORNELIUS *(going to her)*. Don't be minding Ellen at all, Sally.

SALLY. Well, as high as she is, and as mighty as she is, she came into his own house to see Matt. God between us and harm, Cornelius, maybe they'll be saying I came into your house to see you.

CORNELIUS. Who'll know you came at all? And what isn't seen won't be spoken of.

SALLY. Would you like me to stay, Cornelius?

CORNELIUS. Ay, I would.

SALLY. Divil mind the sow.[10]

(They sit down together.)

SALLY *(after a pause)*. Would you like me to knit you a pair of socks, Cornelius?

CORNELIUS. Oh, I would, Sally; I'd love to wear them.

SALLY. I'll knit them. We'll be getting rid of the sow tonight, maybe, and I'll have time after that.

CORNELIUS. And you come along the road when I'm herding. I don't want to be going near your father's house.

SALLY. O Cornelius, it won't be lucky for us when father hears about Ellen and Matt.

CORNELIUS. That's true. No man sees his house afire but looks to his rick.[11]

SALLY. Come down a bit of the road with me, Cornelius. The sow will be grunting and grunting, reminding father that I'm away. Och, a minute ago I was as contented as if there was no land or pigs, or harsh words to trouble one. *(She goes to the door.)* The boys and girls for America are coming here.

CORNELIUS. Give me your hands to hold, Sally. *(She gives him her hands.)* We are as young as any of them after all.

(They hold each other's hands, then stand apart.)

SALLY. It's a fine time for them to be going when the leaves are opening on the trees.

(Three boys and three girls enter. They are dressed for going away.)

SALLY. God save you, girls. Good-bye, Cornelius. I'll have to run like a redshank.[12]

(Sally goes out.)

---

10. **Divil mind the sow** mild expletive, between "Never mind the sow" and "To hell with the sow"   11. **rick** stack of hay   12. **redshank** wading bird of the snipe family, so called from the color of its legs

CORNELIUS. I'll call Ellen down to you. *(He goes to the room door and calls.)* I'm going herding myself. Herding is pleasant when you have thoughts with you.

(He takes up the rod and goes out. The girls begin whispering, then chattering.)

FIRST GIRL. Sure I know. Every night I'm dreaming of the sea and the great towns. Streets and streets of houses and every street as crowded as the road outside the chapel when the people do be coming from Mass.

FIRST BOY. I could watch the crowd in the street; I would think it better than any sight I ever knew.

SECOND GIRL. And the shops and the great houses.

SECOND BOY. There's no stir here. There's no fine clothes, nor fine manners, nor fine things to be seen.

THIRD BOY. There's no money. One could never get a shilling together here. In America there's money to have and to spend and to send home.

THIRD GIRL. Every girl gets married in America.

(Ellen comes down.)

ELLEN. I'm glad you came. I have tea ready for you. I can't go to Gilroy's to-night.

(Some come to the table and some remain near the door.)

A GIRL *(at table, to Ellen)*. They say that a peat fire like that will seem very strange to us after America. Bridget wondered at it when she came back. "Do civilized people really cook at the like of them?" said she.

A BOY. It's the little houses with only three rooms in them that will seem strange. I'm beginning to wonder myself at their thatch and their mud walls.

ANOTHER GIRL. Houses in bogs and fields. It was a heart-break trying to keep them as we'd like to keep them.

A GIRL *(at door)*. Ah, but I'll never forget Gortan and the little road to Aughnalee.

ANOTHER GIRL. I think I'll be lonesome for a long time. I'll be thinking on my brothers and sisters. I nursed and minded all the little ones.

FIRST BOY. A girl like you, Ellen, is foolish to be staying here.

SECOND BOY. She'll be coming in the fall. We'll be glad to see you, Ellen.

ELLEN. I have no friends[13] in America.

FIRST GIRL. I have no friends there, either. But I'll get on. You could get on better than any of us, Ellen.

SECOND GIRL. She's waiting for her school. It will be a little place by the side of a bog.

THIRD GIRL *(going to Ellen)*. There would be little change in that. And

13. **friends** relatives

isn't it a life altogether different from this life that we have been longing for? To be doing other work, and to be meeting strange people. And instead of bare roads and market-towns, to be seeing streets, and crowds, and theaters.

ELLEN *(passionately)*. O what do you know about streets and theaters? You have only heard of them. They are finer than anything you could say. They are finer than anything you could think of, after a story, when you'd be young.

A GIRL. You'll be going after all, Ellen.

ELLEN. I won't be going.

FIRST GIRL. Well, maybe you'll be down at Gilroy's. We must go now. *(The girls go to the door. Ellen goes with them.)*

ONE OF THE BOYS. Phil said that an egg was all he could touch while he was on the sea.

SECOND BOY. God help us, if that was all Phil could take.

THIRD BOY. Light your pipes now, and we'll go.

(Ellen has parted with the girls. The boys light their pipes at fire. They go to door, and shake hands with Ellen. The boys go out.)

ELLEN. Theaters! What do they know of theaters? And it's their like will be enjoying them.

(Sally comes back. She is more hurried than before.)

SALLY. Ellen! Ellen! I have wonders to tell. Where is Cornelius, at all? He's never here when you have wonders to tell.

ELLEN. What have you to tell?

SALLY. Oh, I don't know how I'll get it all out! Matt and father had an *odious* falling out, and it was about you. And Matt's going to America; and he's to bring you with him. And Cornelius was saying that if father found out about yourself and Matt——

ELLEN. Sally, Sally, take breath and tell it.

SALLY. Matt is going to America, like the others, and he's taking you with him.

ELLEN. Sally, Sally, is it the truth you're telling?

SALLY. It is the truth. Honest as day, it is the truth.

ELLEN. And I thought I'd be content with a new house. Now we can go away together. I can see what I longed to see. I have a chance of knowing what is in me. *(She takes Sally's hands.)* It's great news you've brought me. No one ever brought me such news before. Take this little cross. You won't have a chance of getting fond of me after all. *(She wears a cross at her throat; she breaks the string, and gives it to Sally.)*

SALLY. I don't know why I was so fervent to tell you. There's the stool before me that myself and Cornelius were sitting on, and he saying—*(She goes to the door.)* Here's Matt! Now we'll hear all about it.

ELLEN. So soon; so soon. *(She goes to the mirror. After a pause, turning to Sally)* Go down the road a bit, when he comes in. Sally, you have a simple mind; you might be saying a prayer that it will be for the best.

SALLY *(going to the door muttering).* Go down the road a bit! 'Deed and I will not till I know the whole ins and outs of it. Sure I'm as much concerned in it as herself! "No man sees his house afire but watches his rick," he was saying. Ah, there's few of them could think of as fine a thing as that.

(Matt comes in.)

MATT. Well, Sally, were you home lately?

SALLY. I was—leastways as far as the door. Father and oul' Martin were discoorsing.[14]

MATT. I've given them something to discoorse about. Maybe you'll be treated better from this day, Sally.

SALLY. O Matt, I'm sorry.

(She goes out.)

MATT *(going to Ellen).* It happened at last, Ellen; the height of the quarrel came.

ELLEN. It was bound to come. I knew it would come, Matt.

MATT. He was a foolish man to put shame on me after all I did for the land.

ELLEN. You had too much thought for the land.

MATT. I had in troth. The others went when there was less to be done. They could not stand him. Even the girls stole away.

ELLEN. There was the high spirit in the whole of you.

MATT. I showed it to him. "Stop," said I; "no more, or I fling lands and house and everything aside."

ELLEN. You said that.

MATT. Ay. "Your other children went for less," said I; "do you think there's no blood in me at all?"

ELLEN. What happened then?

MATT. "I'm your last son," I said; "keep your land and your twenty years' purchase. I'm with the others; and it's poor your land will leave you, and you without a son to bring down your name. A bit of land, a house," said I; "do you think these will keep me here?"

ELLEN. I knew they could not keep you here, Matt. You have broken from them at last; and now the world is before us. Think of all that is before us—the sea, and the ships, the strange life, and the great cities.

MATT. Ay—there before us—if we like.

ELLEN. Surely we like.

MATT. I was always shy of crowds. I'm simple, after all, Ellen, and have no thought beyond the land.

---

14. **discoorsing** conversing (sarcastic)

ELLEN. You said that house and land could not keep you. You told him you were going as your brothers went.

MATT. And I felt I was going. I frightened him. He'll be glad to see me back. It will be long before he treats me that way again.

ELLEN *(suddenly)*. Matt!

MATT. What is it, Ellen?

ELLEN. I don't know—I was upset—thinking of the quarrel *(putting her hands on his shoulders)*. My poor Matt. It was about me you quarrelled.

MATT. Ay, he spoke against you. I couldn't put up with that.

ELLEN. He does not know your high spirit. He does not know your strength.

MATT. Ellen, it's no shame for a man to have harsh words said to him when it's about a woman like you.

ELLEN. Let nothing come between us now. I saw you in the winter making drains and ditches, and it wet. It's a poor story, the life of a man on the land.

MATT. I had too much thought for the land.

ELLEN. You had. Have thought for me now. There is no one in fair or market but would notice me. I was never a favourite. I lived to myself. I did not give my love about. You have never offered me anything. In the song a man offers towns to his sweetheart. You can offer me the sights of great towns, and the fine manners, and the fine life.

MATT. Ellen! *(He draws a little away.)* It's not me that could offer the like of that. I never had anything to my hand but a spade.

ELLEN. Your brothers—think of them.

MATT. They all left some one behind them. I am the last of my name.

ELLEN. Why should that keep you back?

MATT. His name is something to a man. Could you hear of your own name melting away without unease? And you are a woman. A man feels it more.

ELLEN. I do not understand men. Will you go back to your father's house after he shaming you out of it?

MATT. He'll be glad to see me back. He'll never cast it up to me that I went.

ELLEN. Matt, your father said words against me. Will you go to him and take his hand after that?

MATT. It was little he said against you. It was against your father he spoke.

ELLEN *(sinking down on a chair, and putting hands before her face)*. My God! After all my waiting, you talk like that.

MATT *(going to her)*. Ellen, Ellen, tell me what I can do for you? There's land and houses to be had here. Father will let me have my own way after this.

ELLEN (*rising, with anger*). What does it matter to me whether he lets you have your own way or not? Do you think I could go into a farmer's house?

MATT. Ellen!

ELLEN. It's a bad hand I'd make of a farmer's house. I am not the sort to be in one. I'm not like Sally.

MATT (*getting angry*). Don't be talking that way, Ellen Douras.

ELLEN (*with great vehemence*). I must be talking like this. If you take me, you will have to go from your father's house. I always knew it. You ought to know it now, Matt Cosgar.

MATT. You didn't know it always. And you have let some one come between us when you talk like that.

ELLEN. I'm not one to be listening to what people say about you. Nor do I be talking in the markets about you.

MATT. I suppose not. You wouldn't have people think you gave any thought to me; I am not good enough for you. The people you know are better.

ELLEN. You are foolish to be talking like that. You are foolish, I say.

MATT. I know I am foolish. Fit only to be working in drains and ditches in the winter. That's what you think.

ELLEN. Maybe it is.

MATT. Ellen Douras! Ellen Douras! A farmer's roof will be high enough for you some day.

ELLEN. May I never see the day. Go back, go back. Make it up with your father. Your father will be glad of a labourer.

MATT. Maybe you won't be glad if I go back; thinking on what you've said.

ELLEN. I said too much. We don't know each other at all. Go back. You have made your choice.

(*She goes up to room left.*)

MATT. Very well then. God above, am I to be treated everywhere like a heifer strayed into a patch of oats? Neither man nor woman will make me put up with this any longer. (*Going to door*) When Ellen Douras wants me, she knows the place to send to. (*He stands at door. There is no sound from room. Going back he speaks loudly.*) I'll be waiting two days or three days to hear from Ellen Douras.

(*There is no sound. Matt goes out. The room door is thrown open, and Ellen comes down.*)

ELLEN (*furiously*). Two days or three days he'll wait for me. As if I'd go into Murtagh Cosgar's house. As if I'd go into any farmer's house. As if I'd get married at all, and the world before me. Two days or three days you'll wait. Maybe it's lonesome, weary years you'll be waiting, Matt Cosgar.

CURTAIN

ACT 3

Interior of Murtagh Cosgar's. It is towards sunset. Murtagh Cosgar is stand-
ing before the door looking out. Martin Douras is sitting at the fire in an
armchair.

MARTIN DOURAS. It's getting late, Murtagh Cosgar.

MURTAGH COSGAR. Ay, it's getting late.

MARTIN DOURAS. It's time for me to be going home. I should be
seeing Ellen. *(He rises.)*

MURTAGH COSGAR. Stay where you are. *(Turning round)* We're two
old men, as you say. We should keep each other's company for a bit.

MARTIN DOURAS. I should be going home to see Ellen.

MURTAGH COSGAR. If she's going, you can't stay her. Let you keep
here.

MARTIN DOURAS. She'll be wondering what happened to me.

MURTAGH COSGAR. Divil a bit[15] it will trouble her. You're going to
the fair anyway?

MARTIN DOURAS. I have no heart to be going into a fair.

MURTAGH COSGAR. It's myself used to have the great heart. Driving
in on my own side-car,[16] and looking down on the crowd of them. It's
twenty years since I took a sup of drink. Oh, we'll have drinking to-morrow
that will soften the oul' skin of you. You'll be singing songs about the
Trojans to charm every baste in the fair.

MARTIN DOURAS. We're both old men, Murtagh Cosgar.

MURTAGH COSGAR. And is there any reason in your scholarship why
oul' men should be dry[17] men? Answer me that!

MARTIN DOURAS. I won't answer you at all, Murtagh Cosgar. There's
no use in talking to you.

MURTAGH COSGAR. Put it down on a piece of paper that oul' men
should have light hearts when their care is gone from them. They should
be like——

MARTIN DOURAS. There's nothing in the world like men with their
rearing gone from them, and they old.

(Sally comes to the door. She enters stealthily.)

MURTAGH COSGAR. Ha, here's one of the clutch[18] home. Well, did
you see that brother of yours?

SALLY. I did. He'll be home soon, father.

MURTAGH COSGAR. What's that you say? Were you talking to him?
Did he say he'd be home?

SALLY. I heard him say it, father.

---

15. **Divil a bit** Not at all   16. **side-car** light horse-drawn vehicle, usually seating
two passengers who ride back-to-back, facing the sides of the road   17. **dry**
thirsty   18. **clutch** brood (of chickens)

MARTIN DOURAS. God bless you for the news, Sally.

MURTAGH COSGAR. How could he go and he the last of them? Sure it would be against nature. Where did you see him, Sally?

SALLY. At Martin Douras's, father.

MURTAGH COSGAR. It's Ellen Douras that's putting him up to all this. Don't you be said by[19] her, Sally.

SALLY. No, father.

MURTAGH COSGAR. You're a good girl, and if you haven't wit, you have sense. He'll be home soon, did you say?

SALLY. He was coming home. He went round the long way, I'm thinking. Ellen Douras was vexed with him, father. She isn't going either, Matt says, but I'm thinking that you might as well try to keep a corn-crake in the meadow for a whole winter, as to try to keep Ellen Douras in Aughnalee.

MURTAGH COSGAR. Make the place tidy for him to come into. He'll have no harsh words from me. *(He goes up to the room.)*

SALLY. Father's surely getting ould.

MARTIN DOURAS *(sitting down)*. He's gone up to rest himself, God help him. Sally, a stor,[20] I'm that fluttered, I dread going into my own house.

SALLY. I'll get ready now, and let you have a good supper before you go to the fair.

MARTIN DOURAS. Sit down near me, and let me hear everything, Sally. Was it Matt that told you, or were you talking to Ellen herself?

SALLY. O, indeed, I had a talk with Ellen, but she won't give much of her mind away. It was Matt that was telling me. "Indeed she's not going," said he, "and a smart young fellow like myself thinking of her. Ellen is too full of notions." Here's Matt himself. Father won't have a word to say to him. He's getting mild as he's getting ould, and maybe it's a fortune he'll be leaving to myself.

(Matt comes to the door. He enters.)

MATT. Where is he? He's not gone to the fair so early?

SALLY. He's in the room.

MATT. Were you talking to him at all? Were you telling him you saw myself?

SALLY. I was telling him that you were coming back.

MATT. How did he take it?

SALLY. Very quiet. God help us all; I think father's losing his spirit.

MATT *(going to Martin)*. Well, you see I've come back, Martin.

MARTIN DOURAS. Ay, you're a good lad. I always said you were a good lad.

MATT. How did father take it, Martin?

---

19. **be said by** take orders from   20. *a stor* Irish *stór* "treasure"; hence *a stór* "darling," a term of endearment

MARTIN DOURAS. Quietly, quietly. You saw Ellen?

MATT. Ay, I saw Ellen *(gloomily)*. She shouldn't talk the way she talks, Martin. What she said keeps coming into my mind, and I'm troubled. God knows I've trouble enough on my head.

MARTIN DOURAS *(eagerly)*. What did she say, Matt Cosgar?

MATT. It wasn't what she said. She has that school in her mind, I know.

MARTIN DOURAS. And is there anything to keep her here, Matt Cosgar?

MATT. I don't know that she thinks much of me now. We had a few words, but there's nothing in the world I put above Ellen Douras.

MARTIN DOURAS. I should be going to her.

MATT. Wait a bit, and I'll be going with you. Wait a bit. Let us talk it over. She wouldn't go from you, and you old.

MARTIN DOURAS. God forgive my age, if it would keep her here. Would I have my Ellen drawing turf, or minding a cow, or feeding pigs?

MATT. I'm fond of her, Martin. She couldn't go, and I so fond of her. What am I doing here? I should be making it up with her. What good will anything be if Ellen Douras goes? *(He turns to the door, then stops.)* I came to settle with him. I mustn't be running about like a frightened child.

(The room door opens, and Murtagh Cosgar is seen. Sally has hung a pot over the fire, and is cleaning the dishes at the dresser.)

MURTAGH COSGAR *(at the room door)*. Sally, it's time to be putting on the meal. If you have any cabbage left, put it through the meal. *(To Matt)* You put the thong in the harness?

MATT. I did. *(Pause.)* Well, I've come back to you.

MURTAGH COSGAR. You're welcome. We were making ready for the fair.

MATT. I'll be going out again before nightfall.

MURTAGH COSGAR. I'll not be wanting you here, or at the fair.

MATT *(sullenly)*. There's no good talking to me like that.

MURTAGH COSGAR. You said, "I've come back," and I said, "you're welcome." You said, "I'm going out again," and I said, "I'll not be wanting you."

MATT. Father, have you no feeling for me at all?

MURTAGH COSGAR. Sure the wild raven on the tree has thought for her young.

MATT. Ay, but do you feel for me, and I standing here, trying to talk to you?

MURTAGH COSGAR. You're my son, and so I feel sorry for you; and you beginning to know your own foolishness. *(He turns to Sally.)* I'm not taking the pigs. Put a fresh bedding under them to-night.

SALLY. I will, father.

MURTAGH COSGAR. Be up early, and let the cows along the road, or they'll be breaking into the young meadow.

SALLY. I'll do that, too.

MURTAGH COSGAR. Be sure to keep enough fresh milk for the young calf.

SALLY. I'll be sure to do it, father.

(She goes out. Martin takes out his paper, and begins to read it again.)

MATT *(turning on Murtagh)*. Before I go out again there's something I want settled.

MURTAGH COSGAR. What is it you want?

MATT. Would you have me go, or would you have me stay?

MURTAGH COSGAR. Don't be talking of going or staying, and you the last of them.

MATT. But I will be talking of it. You must treat me differently if you want me to stay. You must treat me differently to the way you treat Sally.

MURTAGH COSGAR. You were always treated differently, Matt. In no house that ever I remember was there a boy treated as well as you are treated here.

MATT. The houses that you remember are different from the houses that are now. Will you have me go, or will you have me stay?

MURTAGH COSGAR. You're very threatening. I'd have you stay. For the sake of the name, I'd have you stay.

MATT. Let us take hands on it, then.

MURTAGH COSGAR. Wait, we'll see what you want first.

MATT. You have no feeling. I'd go out of this house, only I want to give you a chance.

MURTAGH COSGAR. Stop. We can have kindness in this. We needn't be beating each other down, like men at a fair.

MATT. We're not men at a fair. May God keep the kindness in our hearts.

(Martin rises.)

MURTAGH COSGAR. Don't be going, Martin Douras.

MATT. Don't be going yet. I'll be with you, when you're going.

(Martin sits down.)

MURTAGH COSGAR *(to Matt)*. You'll be getting married, I suppose, if you stay?

MATT. Maybe I will.

MURTAGH COSGAR *(bitterly)*. In the houses that are now, the young marry where they have a mind to. It's their own business, they say.

MATT. Maybe it is their own business. I'm going to marry Ellen Douras, if she'll have me.

MURTAGH COSGAR. Ellen is a good girl, and clever, I'm told. But I would not have you deal before you go into the fair.[21]

---

21. **deal before you go into the fair** make a decision or bargain before you have seen all the possibilities

MATT. I'm going to marry Ellen Douras.

MURTAGH COSGAR. Her father is here, and we can settle it now. What fortune will you be giving Ellen, Martin? That £100 that was saved while you were in Maryborough gaol?

(Martin shakes his head.)

MATT *(stubbornly)*. I'm going to marry Ellen Douras, with or without a fortune.

MURTAGH COSGAR *(passionately)*. Boy, your father built this house. He got these lands together. He has a right to see that you and your generations are in the way of keeping them together.

MATT. I'll marry Ellen Douras, with or without a fortune.

MURTAGH COSGAR. Marry her, then. Marry Ellen Douras.

MATT. Now, Martin, we mustn't let an hour pass without going to her. *(He takes Martin's arm, and they go to the door.)*

MURTAGH COSGAR. Marry Ellen Douras, I bid you. Break what I have built, scatter what I have put together. That is what all the young will be doing.

(Ellen Douras comes to the door as Matt and Martin reach it.)

MATT. Ellen!

(She shrinks back.)

ELLEN. It's my father I came to speak to.

MURTAGH COSGAR *(going to the door, and drawing the bolt from the half-door)*. When you come to my house, Ellen Douras, you are welcome within.

(Ellen comes in.)

ELLEN. It's right that I should speak to you all. Matt Cosgar, I am going from here.

MATT. Ellen, Ellen, don't be saying that. Don't be thinking of the few words between us. It's all over now. Father agrees to us marrying. Speak, father, and let her hear yourself say it.

ELLEN. I can't go into a farmer's house.

MATT. You said that out of passion. Don't keep your mind on it any longer.

ELLEN. It's true, it's true. I can't go into a farmer's house. This place is strange to me.

MATT. How can you talk like that? I'm always thinking of you.

ELLEN. I've stayed here long enough. I want my own way; I want to know the world.

MATT. If you go, how will I be living, day after day? The heart will be gone out of me.

MURTAGH COSGAR. You'll be owning the land, Matt Cosgar.

MATT *(passionately)*. I've worked on the land all my days. Don't talk to me about it now.

(Ellen goes to Martin. Murtagh goes up to the door, and then turns and speaks.)

MURTAGH COSGAR. Listen to me, Matt Cosgar; and you listen too, Ellen Douras. It's a new house you want maybe. This house was built for me and my generations; but I'll build a new house for you both. It's hard for a man to part with his land before the hour of his death; and it's hard for a man to break his lands; but I'll break them, and give a share of land to you.

ELLEN. You were never friendly to me; but you have the high spirit, and you deserve a better daughter than I would make. The land and house you offer would be a drag on me. *(She goes to the door.)*

MATT. Ellen, what he offers is nothing, after all; but I care for you. Sure you won't go from me like that?

ELLEN. Oh, can't you let me go? I care for you as much as I care for any one. But it's my freedom I want.

MATT. Then you're going surely?

ELLEN. I am. Good-bye.

(She goes out, Martin follows her. Matt stands dazed. Murtagh closes the door, then goes and takes Matt's arm, and brings him down.)

MURTAGH COSGAR. Be a man. We offered her everything, and she went. There's no knowing what the like of her wants. The men will be in soon, and we'll drink to the new ownership.

MATT. Oh, what's the good in talking about that now? If Ellen was here, we might be talking about it.

MURTAGH COSGAR. To-morrow you and me might go together. Ay, the bog behind the meadow is well drained by this, and we might put the plough over it. There will be a fine, deep soil in it, I'm thinking. Don't look that way, Matt, my son.

MATT. When I meet Ellen Douras again, it's not a farmer's house I'll be offering her, nor life in a country place.

MURTAGH COSGAR. No one could care for you as I care for you. I know the blood between us, and I know the thoughts I had as I saw each of you grow up.

(Matt moves to the door.)

MURTAGH COSGAR. Where are you going?

MATT. To see the boys that are going away.

MURTAGH COSGAR. Wait till the fall and I'll give you money to go and come back. Farrell Kavanagh often goes to America. You could go with him.

MATT. I'll go by myself, unless Ellen Douras comes now. The creamery owes me money for the carting, and I'll get it.

MURTAGH COSGAR. Then go. Good-bye to you, Matt Cosgar.

MATT. Good-bye to you.

(He goes out. Murtagh stands, then moves about vaguely.)

MURTAGH COSGAR. The floor swept, the hearth tidied. It's a queer end to it all. Twenty years I bid them offer. Twenty years, twenty years!

(*Martin comes back.*)

MURTAGH COSGAR. The men will be coming back.

MARTIN DOURAS. I suppose they will.

MURTAGH COSGAR. You're a queer fellow, Martin Douras. You went to gaol for some meeting.

MARTIN DOURAS. Ay.

MURTAGH COSGAR. Them was the stirring times. I can't help but think of you in gaol, and by yourself. What brings you back now?

MARTIN DOURAS. Ellen told me to go back. I should say something to Matt, I think.

MURTAGH COSGAR. He went out as you came in.

MARTIN DOURAS. I'll go in when the house is quiet. I'll have a few prayers to be saying this night.

MURTAGH COSGAR. I'm going to the fair.

MARTIN DOURAS. I won't be going to the fair.

MURTAGH COSGAR. Why won't you be going to the fair? Didn't you ask me for a lift? You'll be going with me.

MARTIN DOURAS. I won't be going, and don't be overbearing me now, Murtagh Cosgar.

MURTAGH COSGAR. You will be going to the fair, if it was only to be showing that seemly face of yours. (*Going to the door, he calls* "Sally!" *He turns to Martin Douras.*) I've a daughter still, Martin Douras.

MARTIN DOURAS. You have, and I have a son.

MURTAGH COSGAR. What would you say to a match between them, Martin Douras?

MARTIN DOURAS. I have nothing to say again it.

MURTAGH COSGAR. Then a match it will be.

(*Sally comes in from yard.*)

SALLY. If you fed that baste on honey, she'd turn on you. Cabbage I gave her and got into trouble for it, and now she's gone and trampled the bad potatoes till they're hardly worth the boiling. I'll put the bush in the gap when I'm going out again, father.

MURTAGH COSGAR. Ay. Is that Cornelius Douras that's coming up the path?

SALLY. O faith it is. I'll get him to give me a hand with the trough.

(*Cornelius comes in.*)

CORNELIUS. Well, Murtagh Cosgar, a great and memorial day is ended. May you live long to enjoy the fruits of it. Twenty years on the first term, and the land is ours and our children's. I met the men.

MURTAGH COSGAR. Ours and our children's, ay. We've been making a match between yourself and Sally.

CORNELIUS. Between me and Sally?

SALLY. Between Cornelius and myself?

MURTAGH COSGAR. Ay, shake hands on it now.

CORNELIUS. And tell me one thing, Murtagh Cosgar. Is it true that Matt's going to America and that Ellen will wait for him for a year at the school? I met them together, and they told me that.

MURTAGH COSGAR. What they say is true, I'm sure. The land is yours and your children's.

SALLY *(wiping her hands in her apron)*. O Cornelius.

CORNELIUS. Aren't they foolish to be going away like that, father, and we at the mouth of the good times? The men will be coming in soon, and you might say a few words. *(Martin shakes his head.)* Indeed you might, father; they'll expect it of you. *(Martin shakes his head. Murtagh and Sally try to restrain him.)* "Men of Ballykillduff," you might say, "stay on the land, and you'll be saved body and soul; you'll be saved in the man and in the nation. The nation, men of Ballykillduff, do you ever think of it at all? Do you ever think of the Irish nation that is waiting all this time to be born?"

(He becomes more excited; he is seen to be struggling with words.)

END OF PLAY

J. M. SYNGE
1871 — 1909

Edmund John Millington Synge, the fifth child of a wealthy Anglo-Irish Protestant landowning family, was born on April 16, 1871, in Rathfarnham, County Dublin. He was educated privately and at Trinity College Dublin, where he won prizes in Irish and Hebrew even though music was his first love. During his adolescence he became disaffected from his mother's religious fervor, and developed the habit of taking long solitary walks through the Irish countryside, reflecting on its natural beauty and historic landmarks. In 1893 he went to Germany to study music, but the following year moved to Paris and attended lectures in European language and literature at the Sorbonne. Between 1894 and 1896 he traveled through Germany, Italy, and France; meanwhile he began to write his first verses and dramatic sketches, and studied French and Italian, returning to Dublin during the summers, where he pursued his interests in the Irish language and Irish antiquities.

In December 1896, W. B. Yeats encountered Synge in Paris, discerning immediately in him a literary talent in search of a subject. He advised Synge to go to the Aran Islands in the mouth of Galway Bay, where the inhabitants were still Irish speakers whose lives were yet unaffected by modern social conventions. Synge agreed, and for a portion of each summer from 1898 to 1902 he lived among these people, recording his observations with notebook and camera. He continued to sketch dramatic ideas and write literary reviews, while editing his notes under the title *The Aran Islands* (1907). After a couple of attempts at verse plays, Synge matured rapidly. During the summer of 1902 he wrote *Riders to the Sea* and *The Shadow of the Glen,* and began *The Tinker's Wedding.*

The Shadow of the Glen was a controversial treatment of sexual frustration in the lonely Irish countryside. Its premier production in October 1903 provoked an acrimonious public debate concerning its representation of Irish life. Synge's career was off to a rocky start. The following year, however, the first production of *Riders to the Sea* somewhat redeemed his reputation: it was hailed as a work of a genuine poet of the theater.

Of Synge's plays, *Riders to the Sea* is most closely based on his observations of life on the Aran Islands. His journals give a background to much of the local detail and the main incident in this brief tragedy. It was Synge's first successful use of Hiberno-English to serve his own dramatic and poetic purposes, and it is regarded by most commentators as one of the finest short plays in modern dramatic literature.

An indication of how far his reputation had come was his appointment in December 1904 as literary advisor (later director) of the new Abbey Theatre. During a number of visits to Counties Kerry, Galway, and Mayo, *The Playboy of the Western World,* his masterpiece, germinated in his imagination. And as he designed and revised this play throughout 1906, a romantic relationship was growing with Molly Allgood (known onstage as Máire O'Neill), the Abbey actress who was to play the role of Pegeen Mike in the first production on January 26, 1907. Amidst the controversy surrounding this play, Synge then undertook his last work, *Deirdre of the Sorrows,* based on the story of the Sons of Uisneach from the Ulster Cycle of Celtic tales. During the same year, the symptoms of Hodgkin's disease, which had first manifested themselves a decade before, reappeared. The resultant operations interfered with Synge's revisions of the play and caused his wedding to be postponed, but failed to arrest the disease. He died on March 24, 1909. In January 1910, the incomplete *Deirdre of the Sorrows* was first performed, with Molly Allgood in the role of its tragic heroine.

The Playboy of the Western World originated in an infamous incident which occurred on Achill Island, Co. Mayo, in 1894. A certain James Lynchehaun, in an attempt to murder his English landlady, left her maimed. He made a dramatic escape from the police, and was harbored by his relatives for a time before being rearrested, tried, and found guilty. However, he again escaped from jail and, with the help of various friends, fled to the United States. Around a plot germinating in this celebrated case, Synge wove many observations made during his western sojourns: the lonely landscapes of the western seaboard; the moodiness and rebellious temperament of the people; their religiosity, alcoholism and fanciful language. For the next two years, he worked steadily on the play under five successive titles, almost twenty scenarios, and a dozen complete drafts, before it was finally produced on January 26, 1907.

The play provoked immediate outrage at the Abbey. It was denounced as an assault on national pride, Catholicism, and common decency. Among a people hoping for a fair if not positive treatment, the play was a grievous insult. For his part, during rehearsals Synge had refused to tone down the play's oaths and indelicacies, even when privately appealed to by the actors and by his fellow directors, Yeats and Lady Gregory. The protests in the theater cumulated nightly, until the players were actually pelted on stage. The cue for this assault was Christy's reference to "a drift of chosen females standing in their shifts," which was considered a particularly outrageous obscenity. During the remainder of the run, the police protected the stage and players from nightly attack, Yeats defended the freedom of the stage in public debate, Synge himself granted an unfortunate interview to the press, and the newspapers were full of acrimonious argument. In retrospect, it is not difficult to understand why a Dublin audience, sensitive to signs of religious and ethnic derogation, should react so vehemently to the work of one of the Ascendancy at the new "national" theater. They were not disposed to acknowledge its original blend of Rabelaisian humor, lyricism, romance, and exaggeration.

In his preface to the play, Synge anticipated the hostile reaction he would arouse among the Irish bourgeoisie by praising the "popular imagination that is fiery and magnificent, and tender" that he found among their countrymen of the remote regions. He holds that the language and images are authentic, "that the wildest sayings and ideas in this play are tame indeed compared with the fancies one may hear in any little hillside cabin." While it is true that Synge's sources—in plot, language, and characterization—are personally documented, the combination here, more than in his other works, is uniquely his own creation. Just as the action and characterization of the *Playboy* lack the constraints imposed by urban socialization, so, too, is the language compressed and heightened.

Synge fashioned the Hiberno-English dialect into a malleable and piquant expression of his own passionate vision of the lonely outsider. Christy is the poet whose creative gifts are only superficially appreciated by a convention-bound society; he not only invests the language with zest and daring but also unknowingly transforms himself, by the same process of imaginative energy, from a cowering lout into a master of his own destiny. His transformation begins as the people of Mayo trust his story and continues as he realizes his own narrative skills; it is completed when, with full moral awareness, he strikes his father down a second time. His father is the first to recognize the new Christy; Pegeen Mike does so, too, but for her it is too late; for the rest, the episode is no more than a subject for gossip.

Christy's path to his apotheosis comes only after an erratic journey of surges and reversals; *The Playboy of the Western World* is exuberant comedy in its action as well as in its language and characterization. It contains moments of farce, satire, tragicomedy, and the mock heroic. The power of *The Playboy of the Western World* rests on more than its verbal pyrotechnics and comic structure; as many critics have argued, it exhibits features of the scapegoat archetype, the Oedipus myth, and the Messiah theme. It has relationships with Irish folk legend, with the early Irish Ulster Cycle of heroic tales, and with Ibsen's *Peer Gynt* (1867). Whatever the relevance of these sources or analogues to an appreciation of this great play, its distinction derives from the happy collaboration of Synge's instinctive sense of the dramatic and the quality of his material. He describes it thus to an admirer: "The wildness and, if you will, the vices of the Irish peasantry are due, like their extraordinary good points of all kinds, to the *richness* of their nature—a thing that is priceless beyond words."

SELECT BIBLIOGRAPHY

Publications

J. M. Synge: Collected Works. Ed. Robin Skelton, Alan Price and Ann Saddlemyer, 4 vols. London: Oxford University Press, 1962–68. (I, *Poems,* ed. Skelton, 1962; II, *Prose,* ed. Price, 1966; III, IV, *Plays,* ed. Saddlemyer, 1968). Rpt., Washington, DC: The Catholic University of America Press, 1983.

The Collected Letters of John Millington Synge, Volume 1: 1871–1907. Ed. Ann Saddlemyer. London: Oxford University Press, 1983.

Letters to Molly: John Millington Synge to Maire O'Neill, 1906–1909. Ed. Ann Saddlemyer. Cambridge, MA: Harvard University Press/London: Oxford University Press, 1971.

Biography and Criticism

Bushrui, J. B., ed. *A Centenary Tribute to John Millington Synge 1871–1909: Sunshine and the Moon's Delight.* Gerrards Cross, Bucks.: Colin Smythe Ltd./New York: Barnes and Noble, 1972.

Carney, James. *The Playboy and the Yellow Lady.* Dublin: Poolbeg Press, 1986.

Greene, David, and Edward M. Stephens. *John Millington Synge, 1871–1909.* New York: Macmillan, 1959.

Kilroy, James. *The "Playboy" Riots.* Dublin: Dolmen Press, 1971.

Kopper, Edward A., Jr., ed. *John Millington Synge: A Reference Guide.* Boston: G. K. Hall/London: George Prior, 1979.

———. *A J. M. Synge Literary Companion.* Westport, CT: Greenwood Press, 1988.

See discussions in Finneran (1976 and 1983), Krause, *The Profane Book of Irish Comedy,* and Deane, *Celtic Revivals.*

THE PLAYBOY OF THE WESTERN WORLD

Preface

In writing *The Playboy of the Western World*, as in my other plays, I have used one or two words only, that I have not heard among the country people of Ireland, or spoken in my own nursery before I could read the newspapers. A certain number of the phrases I employ I have heard also from herds and fishermen along the coast from Kerry to Mayo, or from beggar-women and ballad-singers nearer Dublin; and I am glad to acknowledge how much I owe to the folk-imagination of these fine people. Anyone who has lived in real intimacy with the Irish peasantry will know that the wildest sayings and ideas in this play are tame indeed compared with the fancies one may hear in any little hillside cabin in Geesala, or Carraroe, or Dingle Bay. All art is a collaboration; and there is little doubt that in the happy ages of literature striking and beautiful phrases were as ready to the story-teller's or the play-wright's hand as the rich cloaks and dresses of his time. It is probable that when the Elizabethan dramatist took his ink-horn and sat down to his work he used many phrases that he had just heard, as he sat at dinner, from his mother or his children. In Ireland, those of us who know the people have the same privilege. When I was writing *The Shadow of the Glen,* some years ago, I got more aid than any learning could have given me from a chink in the floor of the old Wicklow house where I was staying, that let me hear what was being said by the servant girls in the kitchen. This matter, I think, is of importance, for in countries where the imagination of the people, and the language they use, is rich and living, it is possible for a writer to be rich and copious in his words, and at the same time to give the reality, which is the root of all poetry, in a comprehensive and natural form. In the modern literature of towns, however, richness is found only in sonnets, or prose poems, or in one or two elaborate books that are far away from the profound and common interests of life. One has, on one side, Mallarmé and Huysmans producing this literature; and on the other, Ibsen and Zola dealing with the reality of life in joyless and pallid words. On the stage one must have reality, and one must have joy, and that is why the intellectual modern drama has failed, and people have grown sick of the false joy of the musical comedy, that has been given them in place of the rich joy found only in what is superb and wild in reality. In a good play every speech should be as fully flavoured as a nut or apple, and such speeches cannot be written by anyone who works among people who have shut their lips on poetry. In Ireland, for a few years more, we have a popular imagination that is fiery and magnificent, and tender; so that those of us who wish to write start with a chance that is not given to writers in places where the spring-time of the local life has been forgotten, and the harvest is a memory only, and the straw has been turned into bricks.

January 21st, 1907.   J.M.S.

The Playboy[1] of the Western World[2]

PERSONS*

CHRISTOPHER MAHON
OLD MAHON, *his father, a squatter*
MICHAEL JAMES FLAHERTY (called MICHAEL JAMES), *a publican*
MARGARET FLAHERTY (called PEGEEN MIKE), *his daughter*
SHAWN KEOGH, *her cousin, a young farmer*
PHILLY O'CULLEN,
JIMMY FARRELL, } *small farmers*
WIDOW QUIN, *a woman of about thirty*
SARA TANSEY,
SUSAN BRADY,
HONOR BLAKE, } *village girls*
NELLY MCLOUGHLIN,
A BELLMAN
SOME PEASANTS

The action takes place near a village, on a wild coast of Mayo. The first Act passes on an evening of autumn, the other two Acts on the following day.

ACT 1

SCENE: *Country public house or shebeen,[3] very rough and untidy. There is a sort of counter on the right with shelves, holding many bottles and jugs, just seen above it. Empty barrels stand near the counter. At back, a little to left of counter, there is a door into the open air, then, more to the left, there is a settle[4] with shelves above it, with more jugs, and a table beneath a window. At the left there is a large open fire-place, with turf[5] fire, and a small door into inner*

1. **Playboy** actor, athlete (from Ir. *buachaill báire*, "hurling boy") 2. **Western World** western Ireland, Connaught; America; Western Europe 3. **shebeen** a low-class or unlicensed wayside pub 4. **settle** a long wooden bench with a high back and a cupboard space under the seat 5. **turf** dried peat used for fuel

*In her standard edition of this play, Ann Saddlemyer restores the list of Persons to their full and proper order.

room. Pegeen, a wild-looking but fine girl, of about twenty, is writing at table. She is dressed in the usual peasant dress.

PEGEEN *(slowly as she writes)*. Six yards of stuff[6] for to make a yellow gown. A pair of lace boots with lengthy heels on them and brassy eyes. A hat is suited for a wedding-day. A fine tooth comb. To be sent with three barrels of porter[7] in Jimmy Farrell's creel cart[8] on the evening of the coming Fair[9] to Mister Michael James Flaherty. With the best compliments of this season. Margaret Flaherty.

SHAWN KEOGH *(a fat and fair young man comes in as she signs, looks round awkwardly, when he sees she is alone)*. Where's himself?[10]

PEGEEN *(without looking at him)*. He's coming. *(She directs letter.)* To Mister Sheamus Mulroy, Wine and Spirit Dealer, Castlebar.[11]

SHAWN *(uneasily)*. I didn't see him on the road.

PEGEEN. How would you see him *(licks stamp and puts it on letter)* and it dark night this half hour gone by?

SHAWN *(turning towards door again)*. I stood a while outside wondering would I have a right to pass on or to walk in and see you, Pegeen Mike *(comes to fire)*, and I could hear the cows breathing, and sighing in the stillness of the air, and not a step moving any place from this gate to the bridge.

PEGEEN *(putting letter in envelope)*. It's above[12] at the cross-roads he is meeting Philly Cullen; and a couple more are going along with him to Kate Cassidy's wake.[13]

SHAWN *(looking at her blankly)*. And he's going that length in the dark night?

PEGEEN *(impatiently)*. He is surely, and leaving me lonesome on the scruff[14] of the hill. *(She gets up and puts envelope on dresser, then winds clock.)* Isn't it long the nights are now, Shawn Keogh, to be leaving a poor girl with her own self counting the hours to the dawn of day?

SHAWN *(with awkward humour)*. If it is, when we're wedded in a short while you'll have no call[15] to complain, for I've little will to be walking off to wakes or weddings in the darkness of the night.

PEGEEN *(with rather scornful good humour)*. You're making mighty certain, Shaneen,[16] that I'll wed you now.

SHAWN. Aren't we after making a good bargain,[17] the way we're only

---

6. **stuff** material   7. **porter** dark beer   8. **creel cart** cart with temporary wicker sides and back   9. **Fair** monthly farmers' market   10. **himself** the man of the house   11. **Castlebar** principal town in Co. Mayo   12. **above** up there   13. **wake** communal watching of the dead the night before burial, combining prayer, drinking, and carousal   14. **scruff** back   15. **call** need   16. **Shaneen** little Shawn   17. **bargain** business arrangements connected with matchmaking

waiting these days on Father Reilly's dispensation[18] from the bishops, or the Court of Rome.

PEGEEN *(looking at him teasingly, washing up at dresser)*.[19] It's a wonder, Shaneen, the Holy Father'd[20] be taking notice of the likes of you; for if I was him I wouldn't bother with this place where you'll meet none but Red Linahan, has a squint in his eye, and Patcheen is lame in his heel, or the mad Mulrannies were driven from California and they lost in their wits. We're a queer lot these times to go troubling the Holy Father on his sacred seat.

SHAWN *(scandalized)*. If we are, we're as good this place as another, maybe, and as good these times as we were for ever.

PEGEEN *(with scorn)*. As good, is it? Where now will you meet the like of Daneen Sullivan knocked the eye from a peeler,[21] or Marcus Quin, God rest him, got six months for maiming ewes,[22] and he a great warrant[23] to tell stories of holy Ireland till he'd have the old women shedding down tears about their feet. Where will you find the like of them, I'm saying?

SHAWN *(timidly)*. If you don't, it's a good job, maybe; for *(with peculiar emphasis on the words)* Father Reilly has small conceit[24] to have that kind walking around and talking to the girls.

PEGEEN *(impatiently, throwing water from basin out of the door)*. Stop tormenting me with Father Reilly *(imitating his voice)* when I'm asking only what way[25] I'll pass these twelve hours of dark, and not take my death with the fear. *(Looking out of door.)*

SHAWN *(timidly)*. Would I fetch you the widow Quin, maybe.

PEGEEN. Is it the like of that murderer? You'll not, surely.

SHAWN *(going to her, soothingly)*. Then I'm thinking himself will stop along with you when he sees you taking on for it'll be a long night-time with great darkness, and I'm after feeling a kind of fellow above in the furzy ditch,[26] groaning wicked like a maddening[27] dog, the way[28] it's good cause you have, maybe, to be fearing now.

PEGEEN *(turning on him sharply)*. What's that? Is it a man you seen?

SHAWN *(retreating)*. I couldn't see him at all; but I heard him groaning out, and breaking his heart. It should have been a young man from his words speaking.

PEGEEN *(going after him)*. And you never went near to see was he hurted or what ailed him at all?

18. **dispensation** an ecclesiastical override of the ban on marriage between second cousins   19. **dresser** cupboard   20. **Holy Father** the Pope   21. **peeler** policeman (after Sir Robert Peel, who formed the Royal Irish Constabulary in 1812)   22. **maiming ewes** a tactic to intimidate landlords adopted during the "Land War" (1879–82)   23. **warrant** talent   24. **small conceit** little inclination   25. **what way** how   26. **furzy ditch** bank overgrown with gorse   27. **maddening** going mad   28. **the way** so that

SHAWN. I did not, Pegeen Mike. It was a dark lonesome place to be hearing the like of him.

PEGEEN. Well, you're a daring fellow, and if they find his corpse stretched above in the dews of dawn, what'll you say then to the peelers, or the Justice of the Peace?

SHAWN (*thunderstruck*). I wasn't thinking of that. For the love of God, Pegeen Mike, don't let on I was speaking of him. Don't tell your father and the men is coming above; for if they heard that story, they'd have great blabbing this night at the wake.

PEGEEN. I'll maybe tell them, and I'll maybe not.

SHAWN. They are coming at the door. Will you whisht,[29] I'm saying.

PEGEEN. Whisht yourself.

(*She goes behind counter. Michael James, fat jovial publican, comes in followed by Philly Cullen, who is thin and mistrusting, and Jimmy Farrell, who is fat and amorous, about forty-five.*)

MEN (*together*). God bless you. The blessing of God on this place.

PEGEEN. God bless you kindly.[30]

MICHAEL (*to men who go to the counter*). Sit down now, and take your rest. (*Cross to Shawn at the fire.*) And how is it you are, Shawn Keogh? Are you coming over the sands to Kate Cassidy's wake?

SHAWN. I am not, Michael James. I'm going home the short cut to my bed.

PEGEEN (*speaking across the counter*). He's right too, and have you no shame, Michael James, to be quitting off[31] for the whole night, and leaving myself lonesome in the shop?

MICHAEL (*good-humouredly*). Isn't it the same whether I go for the whole night or a part only; and I'm thinking it's a queer daughter you are if you'd have me crossing backward[32] through the Stooks of the Dead Women,[33] with a drop taken.

PEGEEN. If I am a queer daughter, it's a queer father'd be leaving me lonesome these twelve hours of dark, and I piling the turf with the dogs barking, and the calves mooing, and my own teeth rattling with the fear.

JIMMY (*flatteringly*). What is there to hurt you, and you a fine, hardy girl would knock the head of any two men in the place?

PEGEEN (*working herself up*). Isn't there the harvest boys[34] with their tongues red for drink, and the ten tinkers[35] is camped in the east glen, and the thousand militia[36]—bad cess[37] to them!—walking idle through the

---

29. **whisht** be silent   30. **kindly** a customary greeting   31. **quitting off** going away   32. **crossing backward** coming back   33. **Stooks of the Dead Women** foreshore rocks   34. **harvest boys** migrant workers returned from harvest work in Scotland or England   35. **tinkers** Irish gypsies   36. **militia** British garrison   37. **bad cess** bad luck

land. There's lots surely to hurt me, and I won't stop alone in it, let himself do what he will.

MICHAEL. If you're that afeard,[38] let Shawn Keogh stop[39] along with you. It's the will of God, I'm thinking, himself should be seeing to you now.

(They all turn on Shawn.)

SHAWN *(in horrified confusion)*. I would and welcome,[40] Michael James, but I'm afeard of Father Reilly; and what at all would the Holy Father and the Cardinals of Rome be saying if they heard I did the like of that?

MICHAEL *(with contempt)*. God help you! Can't you sit in by the hearth with the light lit and herself[41] beyond in the room? You'll do that surely, for I've heard tell there's a queer fellow above, going mad or getting his death, maybe, in the gripe[42] of the ditch, so she'd be safer this night with a person here.

SHAWN *(with plaintive despair)*. I'm afeard of Father Reilly, I'm saying. Let you not be tempting me, and we near married itself.[43]

PHILLY *(with cold contempt)*. Lock him in the west room.[44] He'll stay then and have no sin to be telling to the priest.

MICHAEL *(to Shawn, getting between him and the door)*. Go up now.[45]

SHAWN *(at the top of his voice)*. Don't stop me, Michael James. Let me out of the door, I'm saying, for the love of the Almighty God. Let me out *(trying to dodge past him)*. Let me out of it, and may God grant you His indulgence[46] in the hour of need.

MICHAEL *(loudly)*. Stop your noising, and sit down by the hearth.

(Gives him a push and goes to counter laughing.)

SHAWN *(turning back, wringing his hands)*. Oh, Father Reilly and the saints of God, where will I hide myself to-day? Oh, St. Joseph and St. Patrick and St. Brigid,[47] and St. James, have mercy on me now!

(Shawn turns round, sees door clear, and makes a rush for it.)

MICHAEL *(catching him by the coat-tail)*. You'd be going, is it?

SHAWN *(screaming)*. Leave me go, Michael James, leave me go, you old Pagan, leave me go, or I'll get the curse of the priests[48] on you, and of the scarlet-coated[49] bishops of the courts of Rome.

(With a sudden movement he pulls himself out of his coat, and disappears out of the door, leaving his coat in Michael's hands.)

38. **afeard** afraid   39. **stop** stay   40. **would and welcome** would gladly 41. **and herself** while she is   42. **gripe** hollow   43. **and we near married itself** even though we are about to be married   44. **west room** at western end of house, reserved for the aged and for family heirlooms   45. **Go up now** get back to the hearth   46. **indulgence** remission of punishment   47. **Brigid** abbess of Kildare (*ca.* 500): after St. Patrick, Ireland's most venerated saint   48. **curse of the priests** Catholic clergy were reputed to have special powers   49. **scarlet-coated** Roman Catholic cardinals wear red

MICHAEL (*turning round, and holding up coat*). Well, there's the coat of a Christian man. Oh, there's sainted glory this day in the lonesome west; and by the will of God I've got you a decent man, Pegeen, you'll have no call to be spying after if you've a score of young girls, maybe, weeding in your fields.

PEGEEN (*taking up the defence of her property*). What right have you to be making game[50] of a poor fellow for minding[51] the priest, when it's your own the fault is, not paying a penny pot-boy[52] to stand along with me and give me courage in the doing of my work?

(*She snaps the coat away from him, and goes behind counter with it.*)

MICHAEL (*taken aback*). Where would I get a pot-boy? Would you have me send the bell-man[53] screaming in the streets of Castlebar?

SHAWN (*opening the door a chink and putting in his head, in a small voice*). Michael James!

MICHAEL (*imitating him*). What ails you?

SHAWN. The queer dying fellow's beyond looking over the ditch. He's come up, I'm thinking, stealing your hens. (*Looks over his shoulder.*) God help me, he's following me now (*he runs into room*), and if he's heard what I said, he'll be having my life, and I going home lonesome in the darkness of the night.

(*For a perceptible moment they watch the door with curiosity. Some one coughs outside. Then Christy Mahon, a slight young man, comes in very tired and frightened and dirty.*)

CHRISTY (*in a small voice*). God save all here!

MEN. God save you kindly.

CHRISTY (*going to the counter*). I'd trouble you for a glass of porter, woman of the house.

(*He puts down coin.*)

PEGEEN (*serving him*). You're one of the tinkers, young fellow, is beyond camped in the glen?

CHRISTY. I am not; but I'm destroyed[54] walking.

MICHAEL (*patronizingly*). Let you come up then to the fire. You're looking famished[55] with the cold.

CHRISTY. God reward you. (*He takes up his glass and goes a little way across to the left, then stops and looks about him.*) Is it often the polis[56] do be coming into this place, master of the house?

MICHAEL. If you'd come in better hours, you'd have seen "Licensed for the sale of Beer and Spirits, to be consumed on the premises," written

50. **making game** making fun   51. **minding** paying attention to, obeying   52. **penny pot-boy** helper for pub cleanup   53. **bell-man** town crier   54. **destroyed** half-killed   55. **famished** dying   56. **polis** police

in white letters above the door, and what would the polis want spying on me, and not a decent house within four miles, the way every living Christian is a bona fide,[57] saving one widow alone.

CHRISTY *(with relief)*. It's a safe house, so.

(He goes over to the fire, sighing and moaning. Then he sits down putting his glass beside him and begins gnawing a turnip, too miserable to feel the others staring at him with curiosity.)

MICHAEL *(going after him)*. Is it yourself is fearing the polis? You're wanting,[58] maybe?

CHRISTY. There's many wanting.

MICHAEL. Many surely, with the broken[59] harvest and the ended wars.[60] *(He picks up some stockings, etc., that are near the fire, and carries them away furtively.)* It should be larceny, I'm thinking?

CHRISTY *(dolefully)*. I had it in my mind it was a different word and a bigger.

PEGEEN. There's a queer lad. Were you never slapped in school, young fellow, that you don't know the name of your deed?

CHRISTY *(bashfully)*. I'm slow at learning, a middling scholar[61] only.

MICHAEL. If you're a dunce itself, you'd have a right to know that larceny's robbing and stealing. Is it for the like of that you're wanting?

CHRISTY *(with a flash of family pride)*. And I the son of a strong[62] farmer *(with a sudden qualm)*, God rest his soul, could have bought up the whole of your old house a while since, from the butt of his tail-pocket,[63] and not have missed the weight of it gone.

MICHAEL *(impressed)*. If it's not stealing, it's maybe something big.

CHRISTY *(flattered)*. Aye; it's maybe something big.

JIMMY. He's a wicked-looking young fellow. Maybe he followed after a young woman on a lonesome night.

CHRISTY *(shocked)*. Oh, the saints forbid, mister; I was all times a decent lad.

PHILLY *(turning on Jimmy)*. You're a silly man, Jimmy Farrell. He said his father was a farmer a while since, and there's himself now in a poor state. Maybe the land was grabbed[64] from him, and he did what any decent man would do.

MICHAEL *(to Christy, mysteriously)*. Was it bailiffs?[65]

CHRISTY. The divil a one.[66]

57. **bona fide** according to the licensing laws, a genuine traveler of at least three miles had the right to be served at all times   58. **wanting** wanted by the law
59. **broken** bad   60. **ended wars** the Land War and Boer War (1899–1902)
61. **scholar** schoolboy   62. **strong** wealthy   63. **tail-pocket** in swallow-tail coat
64. **grabbed** to "grab" was to occupy the holding of an evicted tenant-farmer, a practice targeted by the Land League during the Land War   65. **bailiffs** tax collectors or landlords' agents   66. **divil a one** none

MICHAEL. Agents?[67]

CHRISTY. The divil a one.

MICHAEL. Landlords?

CHRISTY *(peevishly)*. Ah, not at all, I'm saying. You'd see the like of them stories on any little paper of a Munster[68] town. But I'm not calling to mind any person, gentle, simple,[69] judge or jury, did the like of me.

(They all draw nearer with delighted curiosity.)

PHILLY. Well, that lad's a puzzle-the-world.[70]

JIMMY. He'd beat Dan Davies' circus, or the holy missioners[71] making sermons on the villainy of man. Try him again, Philly.

PHILLY. Did you strike golden guineas out of solder,[72] young fellow, or shilling coins itself?

CHRISTY. I did not mister, not sixpence nor a farthing[73] coin.

JIMMY. Did you marry three wives maybe? I'm told there's a sprinkling have done that among the holy Luthers[74] of the preaching north.

CHRISTY *(shyly)*. I never married with one, let alone with a couple or three.

PHILLY. Maybe he went fighting for the Boers,[75] the like of the man beyond,[76] was judged to be hanged, quartered and drawn.[77] Were you off east, young fellow, fighting bloody wars for Kruger[78] and the freedom of the Boers?

CHRISTY. I never left my own parish till Tuesday was a week.[79]

PEGEEN *(coming from counter)*. He's done nothing, so. *(To Christy.)* If you didn't commit murder or a bad, nasty thing, or false coining, or robbery, or butchery, or the like of them, there isn't anything that would be worth your troubling for to run from now. You did nothing at all.

CHRISTY *(his feelings hurt)*. That's an unkindly thing to be saying to a poor orphaned traveller, has a prison behind him, and hanging before, and hell's gap gaping below.

PEGEEN *(with a sign to the men to be quiet)*. You're only saying it. You did nothing at all. A soft lad the like of you wouldn't slit the windpipe of a screeching sow.

CHRISTY *(offended)*. You're not speaking the truth.

67. **agents** landlords' process-servers   68. **Munster** Ireland's southwestern province (includes Kerry)   69. **gentle, simple** high or low class   70. **puzzle-the-world** total enigma   71. **missioners** Catholic preachers   72. **strike golden guineas out of solder** forge money   73. **farthing** a quarter penny, the smallest English coin   74. **holy Luthers** Presbyterians   75. **Boers** several Irish brigades opposed the British in this South African War   76. **the man beyond** apparently Major John MacBride, although the last person actually so sentenced was the Fenian Michael O'Brien in 1867   77. **quartered and drawn** under English law until 1870, evisceration and dismemberment were parts of the penalty for treason   78. **Kruger** Stephen Kruger (1825–1904), leader of the Boer Rebellion   79. **till Tuesday was a week** until a week ago last Tuesday

PEGEEN *(in mock rage)*. Not speaking the truth, is it? Would you have me knock the head of you with the butt of the broom?

CHRISTY *(twisting round on her with a sharp cry of horror)*. Don't strike me. I killed my poor father, Tuesday was a week, for doing the like of that.

PEGEEN *(with blank amazement)*. Is it killed your father?

CHRISTY *(subsiding)*. With the help of God I did surely, and that the Holy Immaculate Mother may intercede for his soul.

PHILLY *(retreating with Jimmy)*. There's a daring fellow.

JIMMY. Oh, glory be to God!

MICHAEL *(with great respect)*. That was a hanging crime, mister honey.[80] You should have had good reason for doing the like of that.

CHRISTY *(in a very reasonable tone)*. He was a dirty man, God forgive him, and he getting old and crusty,[81] the way I couldn't put up with him at all.

PEGEEN. And you shot him dead?

CHRISTY *(shaking his head)*. I never used weapons. I've no licence, and I'm a law-fearing man.

MICHAEL. It was with a hilted knife maybe? I'm told, in the big world, it's bloody knives they use.

CHRISTY *(loudly, scandalized)*. Do you take me for a slaughter-boy?

PEGEEN. You never hanged him, the way Jimmy Farrell hanged his dog from the licence,[82] and had it screeching and wriggling three hours at the butt of a string, and himself swearing it was a dead dog, and the peelers swearing it had life?

CHRISTY. I did not then. I just riz the loy[83] and let fall the edge of it on the ridge[84] of his skull, and he went down at my feet like an empty sack, and never let a grunt or groan from him at all.

MICHAEL *(making a sign to Pegeen to fill Christy's glass)*. And what way weren't you hanged, mister? Did you bury him then?

CHRISTY *(considering)*. Aye. I buried him then. Wasn't I digging spuds[85] in the field?

MICHAEL. And the peelers never followed after you the eleven days that you're out?

CHRISTY *(shaking his head)*. Never a one of them, and I walking forward facing hog, dog, or divil on the highway of the road.

PHILLY *(nodding wisely)*. It's only with a common week-day kind of a murderer them lads would be trusting their carcase, and that man should be a great terror when his temper's roused.

---

80. **mister honey** my dear man   81. **crusty** short-tempered   82. **from the licence** on account of the license fee   83. **riz the loy** raised the long, narrow turf-cutting spade   84. **ridge** top   85. **spuds** potatoes

MICHAEL. He should then. *(To Christy)* And where was it, mister honey, that you did the deed?

CHRISTY *(looking at him with suspicion)*. Oh, a distant place, master of the house, a windy corner of high distant hills.

PHILLY *(nodding with approval)*. He's a close[86] man, and he's right surely.

PEGEEN. That'd be a lad with the sense of Solomon[87] to have for a pot-boy, Michael James, if it's the truth you're seeking one at all.

PHILLY. The peelers is fearing him, and if you'd that lad in the house there isn't one of them would come smelling around if the dogs itself were lapping poteen[88] from the dung-pit of the yard.

JIMMY. Bravery's a treasure in a lonesome place, and a lad would kill his father, I'm thinking, would face a foxy divil with a pitchpike[89] on the flags of hell.

PEGEEN. It's the truth they're saying, and if I'd that lad in the house, I wouldn't be fearing the loosed kharki cut-throats,[90] or the walking dead.

CHRISTY *(swelling with surprise and triumph)*. Well, glory be to God!

MICHAEL *(with deference)*. Would you think well to stop here and be pot-boy, mister honey, if we gave you good wages, and didn't destroy you with the weight of work?

SHAWN *(coming forward uneasily)*. That'd be a queer kind to bring into a decent quiet household with the like of Pegeen Mike.

PEGEEN *(very sharply)*. Will you whisht? Who's speaking to you?

SHAWN *(retreating)*. A bloody-handed murderer the like of . . .

PEGEEN *(snapping at him)*. Whisht I am saying; we'll take no fooling from your like at all. *(To Christy with a honeyed voice.)* And you, young fellow, you'd have a right to stop, I'm thinking, for we'd do our all and utmost to content your needs.

CHRISTY *(overcome with wonder)*. And I'd be safe this place from the searching law?

MICHAEL. You would, surely. If they're not fearing you, itself, the peelers in this place is decent droughty[91] poor fellows, wouldn't touch a cur dog and not give warning in the dead of night.

PEGEEN *(very kindly and persuasively)*. Let you stop a short while anyhow. Aren't you destroyed walking with your feet in bleeding blisters, and your whole skin needing washing like a Wicklow[92] sheep.

CHRISTY *(looking round with satisfaction)*. It's a nice room, and if it's not humbugging me you are, I'm thinking that I'll surely stay.

JIMMY *(jumps up)*. Now, by the grace of God, herself will be safe this

86. **close** tight-lipped   87. **Solomon** King of Israel, renowned for his wisdom   88. **poteen** illicit whiskey   89. **pitchpike** pitchfork   90. **kharki cut-throats** disbanded British soldiers   91. **droughty** thirsty   92. **Wicklow** eastern county renowned for its sheep

night, with a man killed his father holding danger from the door, and let you come on, Michael James, or they'll have the best stuff drunk at the wake.

MICHAEL *(going to the door with men)*. And begging your pardon, mister, what name will we call you, for we'd like to know?

CHRISTY. Christopher Mahon.

MICHAEL. Well, God bless you, Christy, and a good rest till we meet again when the sun'll be rising to the noon of day.

CHRISTY. God bless you all.

MEN. God bless you.

(They go out except Shawn, who lingers at door.)

SHAWN *(to Pegeen)*. Are you wanting me to stop along with you and keep you from harm?

PEGEEN *(gruffly)*. Didn't you say you were fearing Father Reilly?

SHAWN. There'd be no harm staying now, I'm thinking, and himself in it too.

PEGEEN. You wouldn't stay when there was need for you, and let you step off nimble this time when there's none.

SHAWN. Didn't I say it was Father Reilly . . .

PEGEEN. Go on, then, to Father Reilly *(in a jeering tone),* and let him put you in the holy brotherhoods,[93] and leave that lad to me.

SHAWN. If I meet the Widow Quin . . .

PEGEEN. Go on, I'm saying, and don't be waking this place with your noise. *(She hustles him out and bolts door.)* That lad would wear the spirits from the saints of peace. *(Bustles about, then takes off her apron and pins it up in the window as a blind. Christy watching her timidly. Then she comes to him and speaks with bland good-humour.)* Let you stretch out now by the fire, young fellow. You should be destroyed travelling.

CHRISTY *(shyly again, drawing off his boots)*. I'm tired surely, walking wild eleven days, and waking fearful in the night.

(He holds up one of his feet, feeling his blisters and looking at them with compassion.)

PEGEEN *(standing beside him, watching him with delight)*. You should have had great people in your family, I'm thinking, with the little, small feet you have, and you with a kind of a quality name,[94] the like of what you'd find on the great powers and potentates of France and Spain.

CHRISTY *(with pride)*. We were great surely, with wide and windy acres of rich Munster land.

PEGEEN. Wasn't I telling you, and you a fine, handsome young fellow with a noble brow.

CHRISTY *(with a flash of delighted surprise)*. Is it me?

93. **holy brotherhoods** associations of men under religious vows of poverty, chastity and obedience   94. **quality name** aristocratic

PEGEEN. Aye. Did you never hear that from the young girls where you come from in the west or south?

CHRISTY (*with venom*). I did not then. Oh, they're bloody[95] liars in the naked parish where I grew a man.

PEGEEN. If they are itself, you've heard it these days, I'm thinking, and you walking the world telling out your story to young girls or old.

CHRISTY. I've told my story no place till this night, Pegeen Mike, and it's foolish I was here, maybe, to be talking free, but you're decent people, I'm thinking, and yourself a kindly woman, the way I wasn't fearing you at all.

PEGEEN (*filling a sack with straw*). You've said the like of that, maybe, in every cot[96] and cabin where you've met a young girl on your way.

CHRISTY (*going over to her, gradually raising his voice*). I've said it no-where till this night, I'm telling you, for I've seen none the like of you the eleven long days I am walking the world, looking over a low ditch or a high ditch on my north or south, into stony scattered fields, or scribes[97] of bog, where you'd see young, limber girls, and fine prancing women making laughter with the men.

PEGEEN. If you weren't destroyed travelling, you'd have as much talk and streeleen,[98] I'm thinking, as Owen Roe O'Sullivan[99] or the poets of the Dingle Bay,[100] and I've heard all times it's the poets are your like, fine fiery fellows with great rages when their temper's roused.

CHRISTY (*drawing a little nearer to her*). You've a power[101] of rings, God bless you, and would there be any offence if I was asking are you single now?

PEGEEN. What would I want wedding so young?

CHRISTY (*with relief*). We're alike, so.

PEGEEN (*she puts sack on settle and beats it up*). I never killed my father. I'd be afeard to do that, except I was the like of yourself with blind rages tearing me within, for I'm thinking you should have had great tussling when the end was come.

CHRISTY (*expanding with delight at the first confidential talk he has ever had with a woman*). We had not then.[102] It was a hard[103] woman was come over the hill, and if he was always a crusty kind when he'd a hard woman setting him on,[104] not the divil himself or his four fathers[105] could put up with him at all.

PEGEEN (*with curiosity*). And isn't it a great wonder that one wasn't fearing you?

95. **bloody** mild expletive   96. **cot** cottage   97. **scribes** strips   98. **streeleen** string of talk   99. **Owen Roe O'Sullivan** Kerry poet of the eighteenth century   100. **Dingle Bay** an area in west Kerry renowned for its Gaelic poets during the eighteenth century   101. **power** a lot   102. **then** indeed   103. **hard** aggressive   104. **setting him on** annoying him   105. **four fathers** whole family

CHRISTY *(very confidentially)*. Up to the day I killed my father, there wasn't a person in Ireland knew the kind I was, and I there drinking, waking, eating, sleeping, a quiet, simple poor fellow with no man giving me heed.[106]

PEGEEN *(getting a quilt out of cupboard and putting it on the sack)*. It was the girls were giving you heed maybe, and I'm thinking it's most conceit you'd have to be gaming[107] with their like.[108]

CHRISTY *(shaking his head, with simplicity)*. Not the girls itself, and I won't tell you a lie. There wasn't anyone heeding me in that place saving[109] only the dumb beasts of the field.

(He sits down at fire.)

PEGEEN *(with disappointment)*. And I thinking you should have been living the like of a king of Norway or the Eastern world.[110]

(She comes and sits beside him after placing bread and mug of milk on the table.)

CHRISTY *(laughing piteously)*. The like of a king, is it? And I after toiling, moiling,[111] digging, dodging[112] from the dawn till dusk with never a sight of joy or sport saving only when I'd be abroad[113] in the dark night poaching rabbits on hills, for I was a divil to poach, God forgive me, *(very naïvely)* and I near got six months for going with a dung fork[114] and stabbing a fish.[115]

PEGEEN. And it's that you'd call sport, is it, to be abroad in the darkness with yourself alone?

CHRISTY. I did, God help me, and there I'd be as happy as the sunshine of St. Martin's Day,[116] watching the light passing the north or the patches of fog, till I'd hear a rabbit starting to screech and I'd go running in the furze. Then when I'd my full share I'd come walking down where you'd see the ducks and geese stretched sleeping on the highway of the road, and before I'd pass the dunghill, I'd hear himself snoring out, a loud lonesome snore he'd be making all times, the while he was sleeping, and he a man'd be raging all times, the while he was waking, like a gaudy[117] officer you'd hear cursing and damning and swearing oaths.

PEGEEN. Providence and Mercy, spare us all!

CHRISTY. It's that you'd say surely if you seen him and he after drinking for weeks, rising up in the red dawn, or before it maybe, and going out into the yard as naked as an ash tree in the moon of May, and shying clods against the visage of the stars till he'd put the fear of death into the banbhs[118] and the screeching sows.

---

106. **giving me heed** noticing me   107. **gaming** fooling   108. **like** kind   109. **saving** except for   110. **Eastern world** in Irish folklore, an Oriental fantasy land   111. **moiling** working hard   112. **dodging** foot-dragging   113. **abroad** outside   114. **dung fork** three- or four-pronged fork   115. **fish** salmon   116. **St. Martin's Day** November 11   117. **gaudy** splendid   118. **banbhs** piglets

PEGEEN. I'd be well-nigh afeard of that lad myself, I'm thinking. And there was no one in it[119] but the two of you alone?

CHRISTY. The divil a one, though he'd sons and daughters walking[120] all great states and territories of the world, and not a one of them, to this day, but would say their seven curses on him, and they rousing[121] up to let a cough or sneeze, maybe, in the deadness of the night.

PEGEEN *(nodding her head)*. Well, you should have been a queer lot. I never cursed my father the like of that, though I'm twenty and more years of age.

CHRISTY. Then you'd have cursed mine, I'm telling you, and he a man never gave peace to any, saving when he'd get two months or three, or be locked in the asylums for battering peelers or assaulting men, *(with depression)* the way it was a bitter life he led me till I did up a Tuesday[122] and halve his skull.

PEGEEN *(putting her hand on his shoulder)*. Well, you'll have peace in this place, Christy Mahon, and none to trouble you, and it's near time a fine lad like you should have your good share of the earth.

CHRISTY. It's time surely, and I a seemly[123] fellow with great strength in me and bravery of . . .

(Some one knocks.)

CHRISTY *(clinging to Pegeen)*. Oh, glory! it's late for knocking, and this last while I'm in terror of the peelers, and the walking dead.

(Knocking again.)

PEGEEN. Who's there?

VOICE *(outside)*. Me.

PEGEEN. Who's me?

VOICE. The Widow Quin.

PEGEEN *(jumping up and giving him the bread and milk)*. Go on now with your supper, and let on[124] to be sleepy, for if she found you were such a warrant to talk, she'd be stringing gabble[125] till the dawn of day.

(He takes bread and sits shyly with his back to the door.)

PEGEEN *(opening door, with temper)*. What ails you, or what is it you're wanting at this hour of the night?

WIDOW QUIN *(coming in a step and peering at Christy)*. I'm after meeting Shawn Keogh and Father Reilly below, who told me of your curiosity man,[126] and they fearing by this time he was maybe roaring, romping on your hands with drink.

PEGEEN *(pointing to Christy)*. Look now is he roaring, and he stretched out drowsy with his supper and his mug of milk. Walk down and tell that to Father Reilly and to Shaneen Keogh.

---

119. **in it** there   120. **walking** wandering   121. **rousing** rising   122. **did up a Tuesday** rose up on a Tuesday   123. **seemly** good-looking   124. **let on** pretend 125. **stringing gabble** gossiping   126. **curiosity man** strange man

WIDOW QUIN *(coming forward)*. I'll not see them again, for I've their word[127] to lead that lad forward for to lodge with me.

PEGEEN *(in blank amazement)*. This night, is it?

WIDOW QUIN *(going over)*. This night. "It isn't fitting," says the priesteen,[128] "to have his likeness[129] lodging with an orphaned[130] girl." *(To Christy.)* God save you, mister!

CHRISTY *(shyly)*. God save you kindly.

WIDOW QUIN *(looking at him with half-amused curiosity)*. Well, aren't you a little smiling fellow? It should have been great and bitter torments did rouse your spirits to a deed of blood.

CHRISTY *(doubtfully)*. It should, maybe.

WIDOW QUIN. It's more than "maybe" I'm saying, and it'd soften my heart to see you sitting so simple with your cup and cake, and you fitter to be saying your catechism[131] than slaying your da.

PEGEEN *(at counter, washing glasses)*. There's talking when any'd see he's fit to be holding his head high with the wonders of the world. Walk on[132] from this, for I'll not have him tormented and he destroyed travelling since Tuesday was a week.

WIDOW QUIN *(peaceably)*. We'll be walking surely when his supper's done, and you'll find we're great company, young fellow, when it's of the like of you and me you'd hear the penny poets[133] singing in an August Fair.

CHRISTY *(innocently)*. Did you kill your father?

PEGEEN *(contemptuously)*. She did not. She hit himself[134] with a worn pick,[135] and the rusted poison did corrode his blood[136] the way he never overed[137] it, and died after. That was a sneaky kind of murder did win small glory[138] with the boys itself.

(She crosses to Christy's left.)

WIDOW QUIN *(with good-humour)*. If it didn't, maybe all knows a widow woman has buried her children and destroyed[139] her man is a wiser comrade[140] for a young lad than a girl, the like of you, who'd go helter-skeltering after any man would let you a wink upon the road.

PEGEEN *(breaking out into wild rage)*. And you'll say that, Widow Quin, and you gasping with the rage you had racing the hill beyond to look on his face.

WIDOW QUIN *(laughing derisively)*. Me, is it? Well, Father Reilly has

---

127. **word** orders   128. **priesteen** little priest (contemptuous)   129. **likeness** the like of him   130. **orphaned** left alone   131. **saying your catechism** repeating from memory the formulations of Catholic doctrine   132. **Walk on** go away   133. **penny poets** poets who sold their ballads at a penny a broadsheet   134. **himself** her husband   135. **pick** pickaxe   136. **did corrode his blood** gave him tetanus   137. **overed** recovered from   138. **win small glory** earn little admiration   139. **destroyed** killed   140. **comrade** wife

cuteness[141] to divide you now. *(She pulls Christy up.)* There's great temptation in a man did slay his da, and we'd best be going, young fellow; so
rise up and come with me.

PEGEEN *(seizing his arm)*. He'll not stir. He's pot-boy in this place, and
I'll not have him stolen off and kidnabbed[142] while himself 's[143] abroad.

WIDOW QUIN. It'd be a crazy pot-boy'd lodge him in the shebeen
where he works by day, so you'd have a right to come on, young fellow,
till you see my little houseen,[144] a perch[145] off on the rising hill.

PEGEEN. Wait till morning, Christy Mahon. Wait till you lay eyes on
her leaky thatch is growing more pasture[146] for her buck goat than her
square of fields, and she without a tramp itself to keep in order her place
at all.

WIDOW QUIN. When you see me contriving[147] in my little gardens,
Christy Mahon, you'll swear the Lord God formed me to be living lone,[148]
and that there isn't my match in Mayo for thatching, or mowing, or shear-
ing a sheep.

PEGEEN *(with noisy scorn)*. It's true the Lord God formed you to con-
trive indeed. Doesn't the world know you reared a black ram at your own
breast, so that the Lord Bishop of Connaught felt the elements of a Christian, and he eating it after in a kidney stew? Doesn't the world know
you've been seen shaving the foxy[149] skipper from France[150] for a threepenny bit[151] and a sop of grass tobacco[152] would wring the liver from a
mountain goat you'd meet leaping the hills?

WIDOW QUIN *(with amusement)*. Do you hear her now, young fellow?
Do you hear the way she'll be rating[153] at your own self when a week is
by?[154]

PEGEEN *(to Christy)*. Don't heed her. Tell her to go on into her pigsty
and not plague us here.

WIDOW QUIN. I'm going; but he'll come with me.

PEGEEN *(shaking him)*. Are you dumb, young fellow?

CHRISTY *(timidly, to Widow Quin)*. God increase you;[155] but I'm pot-
boy in this place, and it's here I'd liefer[156] stay.

PEGEEN *(triumphantly)*. Now you have heard him, and go on from this.

WIDOW QUIN *(looking round the room)*. It's lonesome this hour crossing
the hill, and if he won't come along with me, I'd have a right[157] maybe to

141. **cuteness** cleverness   142. **kidnabbed** kidnapped   143. **himself** Michael James
144. **houseen** little house   145. **perch** seven yards (Irish measure)   146. **pasture**
grass is growing in her rotting thatch roof   147. **contriving** working purposefully
148. **formed me to be living lone** made me to be independent   149. **foxy** red-
haired   150. **skipper from France** French trawlers frequented the coastal waters of
Ireland   151. **threepenny bit** a pittance   152. **sop of grass tobacco** a wisp of dried
but uncured tobacco   153. **rating** scolding   154. **when a week is by** after a
week   155. **God increase you** i.e., your wealth   156. **liefer** prefer to   157. **I'd have
a right** I ought

stop this night with yourselves. Let me stretch out on the settle, Pegeen Mike; and himself can lie by the hearth.

PEGEEN *(short and fiercely)*. Faith, I won't. Quit off or I will send you now.

WIDOW QUIN *(gathering her shawl up)*. Well, it's a terror to be aged a score. *(To Christy.)* God bless you now, young fellow, and let you be wary, or there's right torment will await you here if you go romancing with her like, and she waiting only, as they bade me say, on a sheepskin parchment[158] to be wed with Shawn Keogh of Killakeen.

CHRISTY *(going to Pegeen as she bolts door)*. What's that she's after saying?[159]

PEGEEN. Lies and blather,[160] you've no call to mind. Well, isn't Shawn Keogh an impudent fellow to send up spying on me? Wait till I lay hands on him. Let him wait, I'm saying.

CHRISTY. And you're not wedding him at all?

PEGEEN. I wouldn't wed him if a bishop came walking for to join us here.

CHRISTY. That God in glory may be thanked for that.

PEGEEN. There's your bed now. I've put a quilt upon you I'm after quilting a while since[161] with my own two hands, and you'd best stretch out now for your sleep, and may God give you a good rest till I call you in the morning when the cocks will crow.

CHRISTY *(as she goes to inner room)*. May God and Mary and St. Patrick bless you and reward you, for your kindly talk. *(She shuts the door behind her. He settles his bed slowly, feeling the quilt with immense satisfaction.)* Well, it's a clean bed and soft with it,[162] and it's great luck and company I've won me in the end of time—two fine women fighting for the likes of me— till I'm thinking this night wasn't I a foolish fellow not to kill my father in the years gone by.

CURTAIN

ACT 2

SCENE, *as before. Brilliant morning light. Christy, looking bright and cheerful, is cleaning a girl's boots.*

CHRISTY *(to himself, counting jugs on dresser)*. Half a hundred beyond. Ten there. A score that's above. Eighty jugs. Six cups and a broken one.

---

158. **sheepskin parchment** the dispensation   159. **after saying** has just said   160. **blather** noisy nonsense   161. **a while since** a while ago   162. **with it** too

Two plates. A power[163] of glasses. Bottles, a school-master'd be hard set[164] to count, and enough in them, I'm thinking, to drunken all the wealth and wisdom of the County Clare.[165] *(He puts down the boot carefully.)* There's her boots now, nice and decent for her evening use, and isn't it grand brushes she has? *(He puts them down and goes by degrees to the looking-glass.)* Well, this'd be a fine place to be my whole life talking out with swearing Christians,[166] in place of my old dogs and cat, and I stalking around, smoking my pipe and drinking my fill, and never a day's work but drawing a cork an odd time, or wiping a glass, or rinsing out a shiny tumbler for a decent man. *(He takes the looking-glass from the wall and puts it on the back of a chair; then sits down in front of it and begins washing his face.)* Didn't I know rightly I was handsome, though it was the divil's own mirror we had beyond, would twist a squint across an angel's brow, and I'll be growing fine from this day, the way I'll have a soft lovely skin on me and won't be the like of the clumsy young fellows do be[167] ploughing all times in the earth and dung. *(He starts.)* Is she coming again. *(He looks out.)* Stranger girls. God help me, where'll I hide myself away and my long neck naked to the world? *(He looks out.)* I'd best go to the room maybe till I'm dressed again.

(He gathers up his coat and the looking-glass, and runs into the inner room. The door is pushed open, and Susan Brady looks in, and knocks on door.)

SUSAN. There's nobody in it.

(Knocks again.)

NELLY *(pushing her in and following her, with Honor Blake and Sara Tansey)*. It'd be early for them both to be out walking the hill.

SUSAN. I'm thinking Shawn Keogh was making game of us and there's no such man in it at all.

HONOR *(pointing to straw and quilt)*. Look at that. He's been sleeping there in the night. Well, it'll be a hard case if he's gone off now, the way we'll never set our eyes on a man killed his father, and we after rising early and destroying ourselves running fast on the hill.

NELLY. Are you thinking them's his boots?

SARA *(taking them up)*. If they are, there should be his father's track on them. Did you never read in the papers the way murdered men do bleed and drip?

SUSAN. Is that blood there, Sara Tansey?

SARA *(smelling it)*. That's bog water,[168] I'm thinking, but it's his own they are surely, for I never seen the like of them for whity mud, and red

163. **a power** many   164. **hard set** challenged   165. **County Clare** on Munster's Atlantic coast   166. **swearing Christians** full-blooded people   167. **do be** are (habitual present)   168. **bog water** dark water lodging in trenches ("bog holes") after peat ("turf") has been removed

mud, and turf on them, and the fine sands of the sea. That man's been walking, I'm telling you.

(She goes down right, putting on one of his boots.)

SUSAN *(going to window)*. Maybe he's stolen off to Belmullet[169] with the boots of Michael James, and you'd have a right so to follow after him, Sara Tansey, and you the one yoked the ass cart and drove ten miles to set your eyes on the man bit the yellow[170] lady's nostril on the northern shore.[171]

(She looks out.)

SARA *(running to window, with one boot on)*. Don't be talking, and we fooled to-day. *(Putting on other boot.)* There's a pair do fit me well, and I'll be keeping them for walking to the priest, when you'd be ashamed this place, going up winter and summer with nothing worth while to confess at all.

HONOR *(who has been listening at door)*. Whisht! there's some one inside the room. *(She pushes door a chink open.)* It's a man.

(Sara kicks off boots and puts them where they were. They all stand in a line looking through chink.)

SARA. I'll call him. Mister! Mister! *(He puts in his head.)* Is Pegeen within?

CHRISTY *(coming in as meek as a mouse, with the looking-glass held behind his back)*. She's above on the cnuceen,[172] seeking the nanny goats, the way she'd have a sup[173] of goat's milk for to colour my tea.

SARA. And asking your pardon, is it you's the man killed his father?

CHRISTY *(sidling toward the nail where the glass was hanging)*. I am, God help me!

SARA *(taking eggs she has brought)*. Then my thousand welcomes to you, and I've run up with a brace[174] of duck's eggs for your food to-day. Pegeen's ducks is no use, but these are the real rich sort. Hold out your hand and you'll see it's no lie I'm telling you.

CHRISTY *(coming forward shyly, and holding out his left hand)*. They're a great and weighty size.

SUSAN. And I run up with a pat of butter, for it'd be a poor thing to have you eating your spuds dry, and you after running a great way since you did destroy your da.

CHRISTY. Thank you kindly.

HONOR. And I brought you a little cut[175] of a cake, for you should have a thin stomach on you,[176] and you that length walking the world.

NELLY. And I brought you a little laying pullet—boiled and all she

---

169. **Belmullet** small seaport in Mayo 170. **yellow** English 171. **northern shore** of Achill Island (see Introduction) 172. **cnuceen** little hill 173. **sup** small quantity (of liquid) 174. **brace** two 175. **cut** slice 176. **have a thin stomach on you** be hungry

is—was crushed at the fall of night by the curate's car.[177] Feel the fat of that breast, Mister.

CHRISTY. It's bursting, surely.

(He feels it with the back of his hand, in which he holds the presents.)

SARA. Will you pinch it? Is your right hand too sacred for to use at all? *(She slips round behind him.)* It's a glass he has. Well, I never seen to this day a man with a looking-glass held to his back. Them that kills their fathers is a vain lot surely.

(Girls giggle.)

CHRISTY *(smiling innocently and piling presents on glass)*. I'm very thankful to you all to-day . . .

WIDOW QUIN *(coming in quickly, at door)*. Sara Tansey, Susan Brady, Honor Blake! What in glory[178] has you here at this hour of day?

GIRLS *(giggling)*. That's the man killed his father.

WIDOW QUIN *(coming to them)*. I know well it's the man; and I'm after putting him down[179] in the sports[180] below for racing, leaping, pitching,[181] and the Lord knows what.

SARA *(exuberantly)*. That's right, Widow Quin. I'll bet my dowry that he'll lick the world.

WIDOW QUIN. If you will, you'd have a right to have him fresh and nourished in place of nursing a feast.[182] *(Taking presents.)* Are you fasting or fed, young fellow?

CHRISTY. Fasting, if you please.

WIDOW QUIN *(loudly)*. Well, you're the lot. Stir up now and give him his breakfast. *(To Christy.)* Come here to me *(she puts him on bench beside her while the girls make tea and get his breakfast)* and let you tell us your story before Pegeen will come, in place of grinning your ears off like the moon of May.

CHRISTY *(beginning to be pleased)*. It's a long story; you'd be destroyed listening.

WIDOW QUIN. Don't be letting on to be shy, a fine, gamey,[183] treacherous lad the like of you. Was it in your house beyond you cracked his skull?

CHRISTY *(shy but flattered)*. It was not. We were digging spuds in his cold, sloping, stony, divil's patch of a field.

WIDOW QUIN. And you went asking money of him, or making talk of getting a wife would drive him from his farm?

CHRISTY. I did not, then; but there I was, digging and digging, and

---

177. **curate's car** priest's horse-drawn sidecar   178. **glory** heaven   179. **putting him down** entering him   180. **sports** athletic competition   181. **pitching** tossing weights   182. **nursing a feast** because Christy's arms are full of his gifts   183. **gamey** plucky

"You squinting idiot," says he, "let you walk down now and tell the priest you'll wed the Widow Casey in a score of days."

WIDOW QUIN. And what kind was she?

CHRISTY *(with horror)*. A walking[184] terror from beyond the hills, and she two score and five years, and two hundredweights and five pounds[185] in the weighing scales, with a limping leg on her, and a blinded eye, and she a woman of noted misbehaviour with the old and young.

GIRLS *(clustering round him, serving him)*. Glory be.

WIDOW QUIN. And what did he want driving you to wed with her? *(She takes a bit of the chicken.)*

CHRISTY *(eating with growing satisfaction)*. He was letting on[186] I was wanting a protector from the harshness of the world, and he without a thought the whole while but how he'd have her hut to live in and her gold to drink.[187]

WIDOW QUIN. There's maybe worse than a dry hearth and a widow woman and your glass at night. So you hit him then?

CHRISTY *(getting almost excited)*. I did not. "I won't wed her," says I, "when all know she did suckle me for six weeks when I came into the world, and she a hag this day with a tongue on her has the crows and seabirds scattered, the way they wouldn't cast a shadow on her garden with the dread of her curse."

WIDOW QUIN *(teasingly)*. That one should be right company.

SARA *(eagerly)*. Don't mind her. Did you kill him then?

CHRISTY. "She's too good for the like of you," says he, "and go on now or I'll flatten you out like a crawling beast has passed under a dray."[188] "You will not if I can help it," says I. "Go on," says he, "or I'll have the divil making garters of your limbs to-night." "You will not if I can help it," says I.

(He sits up, brandishing his mug.)

SARA. You were right surely.

CHRISTY *(impressively)*. With that the sun came out between the cloud and the hill, and it shining green in my face. "God have mercy on your soul," says he, lifting a scythe; "or on your own," says I, raising the loy.

SUSAN. That's a grand story.

HONOR. He tells it lovely.

CHRISTY *(flattered and confident, waving bone)*. He gave a drive[189] with the scythe, and I gave a lep[190] to the east. Then I turned around with my back to the north, and I hit a blow on the ridge of his skull, laid him stretched out, and he split to the knob of his gullet.

---

184. **walking** living   185. **two hundredweights and five pounds** two hundred and twenty nine pounds   186. **letting on** pretending   187. **her gold to drink** her money to spend on alcohol   188. **dray** a little low cart   189. **gave a drive** made a sally   190. **lep** leap

(He raises the chicken bone to his Adam's apple.)

GIRLS *(together)*. Well, you're a marvel! Oh, God bless you! You're the lad surely!

SUSAN. I'm thinking the Lord God sent him this road to make a second husband to the Widow Quin, and she with a great yearning to be wedded, though all dread her here. Lift him on her knee, Sara Tansey.

WIDOW QUIN. Don't tease him.

SARA *(going over to dresser and counter very quickly, and getting two glasses and porter)*. You're heroes surely, and let you drink a supeen with your arms linked like the outlandish[191] lovers in the sailor's song. *(She links their arms and gives them the glasses.)* There now. Drink a health to the wonders of the western world, the pirates, preachers, poteen-makers, with the jobbing[192] jockies; parching peelers,[193] and the juries fill their stomachs selling judgments of the English law.[194]

(Brandishing the bottle.)

WIDOW QUIN. That's a right toast, Sara Tansey. Now Christy.

(They drink with their arms linked, he drinking with his left hand, she with her right. As they are drinking, Pegeen Mike comes in with a milk can and stands aghast. They all spring away from Christy. He goes down left. Widow Quin remains seated.)

PEGEEN *(angrily)*. What is it you're wanting *(to Sara)*?

SARA *(twisting her apron)*. An ounce of tobacco.

PEGEEN. Have you tuppence?[195]

SARA. I've forgotten my purse.

PEGEEN. Then you'd best be getting it and not be fooling us here. *(To the Widow Quin, with more elaborate scorn.)* And what is it you're wanting, Widow Quin?

WIDOW QUIN *(insolently)*. A penn'orth[196] of starch.

PEGEEN *(breaking out)*. And you without a white shift[197] or a shirt in your whole family since the drying of the flood. I've no starch for the like of you, and let you walk on now to Killamuck.

WIDOW QUIN *(turning to Christy, as she goes out with the girls)*. Well, you're mighty huffy[198] this day, Pegeen Mike, and, you young fellow, let you not forget the sports and racing when the noon is by.

(They go out.)

PEGEEN *(imperiously)*. Fling out that rubbish and put them cups away. *(Christy tidies away in great haste.)* Shove in the bench by the wall. *(He does so.)* And hang that glass on the nail. What disturbed it at all?

---

191. **outlandish** foreign   192. **jobbing** for hire   193. **parching peelers** thirsty policemen   194. **selling judgments of the English law** i.e., bribed juries   195. **tuppence** two pence   196. **penn'orth** pennyworth   197. **shift** petticoat   198. **huffy** arrogant/touchy

CHRISTY *(very meekly)*. I was making myself decent only, and this a fine country for young lovely girls.

PEGEEN *(sharply)*. Whisht your talking of girls.

(Goes to counter—right.)

CHRISTY. Wouldn't any wish to be decent in a place . . .

PEGEEN. Whisht I'm saying.

CHRISTY *(looks at her face for a moment with great misgivings, then as a last effort, takes up a loy, and goes towards her, with feigned assurance)*. It was with a loy the like of that I killed my father.

PEGEEN *(still sharply)*. You've told me that story six times since the dawn of day.

CHRISTY *(reproachfully)*. It's a queer thing you wouldn't care to be hearing it and them girls after walking four miles to be listening to me now.

PEGEEN *(turning round astonished)*. Four miles?

CHRISTY *(apologetically)*. Didn't himself say there were only bona fides living in the place?

PEGEEN. It's bona fides by the road[199] they are, but that lot came over the river lepping the stones. It's not three perches when you go like that, and I was down this morning looking on the papers the post-boy does have in his bag. *(With meaning and emphasis.)* For there was great news this day, Christopher Mahon.

(She goes into room left.)

CHRISTY *(suspiciously)*. Is it news of my murder?

PEGEEN *(inside)*. Murder, indeed.

CHRISTY *(loudly)*. A murdered da?

PEGEEN *(coming in again and crossing right)*. There was not, but a story filled half a page of the hanging of a man. Ah, that should be a fearful end, young fellow, and it worst of all for a man destroyed his da, for the like of him would get small mercies, and when it's dead he is, they'd put him in a narrow grave, with cheap sacking wrapping him round, and pour down quicklime[200] on his head, the way you'd see a woman pouring any frish-frash[201] from a cup.

CHRISTY *(very miserably)*. Oh, God help me. Are you thinking I'm safe. You were saying at the fall of night, I was shut of jeopardy[202] and I here with yourselves.

PEGEEN *(severely)*. You'll be shut of jeopardy no place if you go talking with a pack of wild girls the like of them do be walking abroad with the peelers, talking whispers at the fall of night.

---

199. **by the road** measured by the road   200. **quicklime** to burn the flesh from the corpse of the executed criminal   201. **frish-frash** a mixture of various ingredients in cooking   202. **shut of jeopardy** free of danger

CHRISTY *(with terror)*. And you're thinking they'd tell?

PEGEEN *(with mock sympathy)*. Who knows, God help you.

CHRISTY *(loudly)*. What joy would they have to bring hanging to the likes of me?

PEGEEN. It's queer joys they have, and who knows the thing they'd do, if it'd make the green stones cry itself to think of you swaying and swiggling[203] at the butt of a rope, and you with a fine, stout neck, God bless you! the way you'd be a half an hour, in great anguish, getting your death.

CHRISTY *(getting his boots and putting them on)*. If there's that terror of them, it'd be best, maybe, I went on wandering like Esau[204] or Cain and Abel[205] on the sides of Neifin[206] or the Erris plain.[207]

PEGEEN *(beginning to play with him)*. It would, maybe, for I've heard the Circuit Judges[208] this place is a heartless crew.

CHRISTY *(bitterly)*. It's more than Judges this place is a heartless crew. *(Looking up at her.)* And isn't it a poor thing to be starting again and I a lonesome fellow will be looking out on women and girls the way the needy fallen spirits[209] do be looking on the Lord?

PEGEEN. What call[210] have you to be that lonesome when there's poor girls walking Mayo in their thousands now?

CHRISTY *(grimly)*. It's well you know what call I have. It's well you know it's a lonesome thing to be passing small towns with the lights shining sideways when the night is down, or going in strange places with a dog noising before you and a dog noising behind, or drawn to the cities where you'd hear a voice kissing and talking deep love in every shadow of the ditch, and you passing on with an empty, hungry stomach failing from your heart.

PEGEEN. I'm thinking you're an odd man, Christy Mahon. The oddest walking fellow I ever set my eyes on to this hour to-day.

CHRISTY. What would any be but odd men and they living lonesome in the world?

PEGEEN. I'm not odd, and I'm my whole life with my father only.

CHRISTY *(with infinite admiration)*. How would a lovely handsome woman the like of you be lonesome when all men should be thronging around to hear the sweetness of your voice, and the little infant children should be pestering your steps I'm thinking, and you walking the roads.

PEGEEN. I'm hard set to know what way a coaxing fellow the like of yourself should be lonesome either.

---

203. **swiggle** swing plus wriggle   204. **Esau** son of Isaac and Rebecca who lost his birthright   205. **Cain and Abel** Cain was a fugitive murderer   206. **Neifin** mountain in Mayo   207. **Erris plain** north west Mayo   208. **Circuit Judges** judges who travel from one courthouse to another   209. **needy fallen spirits** souls in Purgatory   210. **What call** what right

CHRISTY. Coaxing?

PEGEEN. Would you have me think a man never talked with the girls would have the words you've spoken to-day? It's only letting on you are to be lonesome, the way you'd get around me now.

CHRISTY. I wish to God I was letting on; but I was lonesome all times, and born lonesome, I'm thinking, as the moon of dawn.

(Going to door.)

PEGEEN *(puzzled by his talk)*. Well, it's a story I'm not understanding at all why you'd be worse than another, Christy Mahon, and you a fine lad with the great savagery to destroy your da.

CHRISTY. It's little I'm understanding myself, saving only that my heart's scalded[211] this day, and I going off stretching out the earth[212] between us, the way I'll not be waking near you another dawn of the year till the two of us do arise to hope or judgment with the saints of God, and now I'd best be going with my wattle[213] in my hand, for hanging is a poor thing *(turning to go)*, and it's little welcome only is left me in this house to-day.

PEGEEN *(sharply)*. Christy! *(He turns round.)* Come here to me. *(He goes towards her.)* Lay down that switch and throw some sods[214] on the fire. You're pot-boy in this place, and I'll not have you mitch off[215] from us now.

CHRISTY. You were saying I'd be hanged if I stay.

PEGEEN *(quite kindly at last)*. I'm after going down and reading the fearful crimes of Ireland for two weeks or three, and there wasn't a word of your murder. *(Getting up and going over to the counter.)* They've likely not found the body. You're safe so with ourselves.

CHRISTY *(astonished, slowly)*. It's making game of me you were *(following her with fearful joy)*, and I can stay so,[216] working at your side, and I not lonesome from this mortal[217] day.

PEGEEN. What's to hinder you staying, except the widow woman or the young girls would inveigle you off?

CHRISTY *(with rapture)*. And I'll have your words from this day filling my ears, and that look is come upon you meeting my two eyes, and I watching you loafing around in the warm sun, or rinsing your ankles when the night is come.

PEGEEN *(kindly, but a little embarrassed)*. I'm thinking you'll be a loyal young lad to have working around, and if you vexed me a while since with your leaguing[218] with the girls, I wouldn't give a thraneen[219] for a lad hadn't a mighty spirit in him and a gamey heart.

---

211. **scalded** tormented　212. **stretching out the earth** lengthening the distance　213. **wattle** stick　214. **sods** chunks of peat　215. **mitch off** steal away　216. **so** in that case　217. **mortal** very　218. **leaguing** scheming together　219. **thraneen** a stalk of grass

(Shawn Keogh runs in carrying a cleeve[220] on his back, followed by the Widow Quin.)

SHAWN *(to Pegeen).* I was passing below, and I seen your mountainy sheep eating cabbages in Jimmy's field. Run up or they'll be bursting surely.

PEGEEN. Oh, God mend[221] them!

(She puts a shawl over her head and runs out.)

CHRISTY *(looking from one to the other. Still in high spirits).* I'd best go to her aid maybe. I'm handy with ewes.

WIDOW QUIN *(closing the door).* She can do that much, and there is Shaneen has long speeches for to tell you now.

(She sits down with an amused smile.)

SHAWN *(taking something from his pocket and offering it to Christy).* Do you see that, mister?

CHRISTY *(looking at it).* The half of a ticket to the Western States![222]

SHAWN *(trembling with anxiety).* I'll give it to you and my new hat *(pulling it out of hamper);* and my breeches with the double seat[223] *(pulling it out);* and my new coat is woven from the blackest shearings for three miles around *(giving him the coat);* I'll give you the whole of them, and my blessing, and the blessing of Father Reilly itself, maybe, if you'll quit from this and leave us in the peace we had till last night at the fall of dark.

CHRISTY *(with a new arrogance).* And for what is it you're wanting to get shut of me?

SHAWN *(looking to the Widow for help).* I'm a poor scholar with middling faculties to coin a lie,[224] so I'll tell you the truth, Christy Mahon. I'm wedding with Pegeen beyond, and I don't think well of having a clever fearless man the like of you dwelling in her house.

CHRISTY *(almost pugnaciously).* And you'd be using bribery for to banish me?

SHAWN *(in an imploring voice).* Let you not take it badly, mister honey, isn't beyond[225] the best place for you where you'll have golden chains and shiny coats and you riding upon hunters[226] with the ladies of the land.

(He makes an eager sign to the Widow Quin to come to help him.)

WIDOW QUIN *(coming over).* It's true for him, and you'd best quit off and not have that poor girl setting her mind on you, for there's Shaneen thinks she wouldn't suit you though all is saying that she'll wed you now.

(Christy beams with delight.)

SHAWN *(in terrified earnest).* She wouldn't suit you, and she with the divil's own temper the way you'd be strangling one another in a score of

220. **cleeve** a large basket   221. **God mend** God chastise   222. **half of a ticket to the Western States** a one-way ticket to the United States   223. **double seat** with extra durability and quality   224. **middling faculties to coin a lie** moderate talent to invent a story   225. **beyond** across in America   226. **hunters** hunting horses

days. *(He makes the movement of strangling with his hands.)* It's the like of me only that she's fit for, a quiet simple fellow wouldn't raise a hand upon her if she scratched itself.[227]

WIDOW QUIN *(putting Shawn's hat on Christy)*. Fit them clothes on you anyhow, young fellow, and he'd maybe loan them to you for the sports. *(Pushing him towards inner door.)* Fit them on and you can give your answer when you have them tried.

CHRISTY *(beaming, delighted with the clothes)*. I will then. I'd like herself to see me in them tweeds and hat.

(He goes into room and shuts the door.)

SHAWN *(in great anxiety)*. He'd like herself to see them. He'll not leave us, Widow Quin. He's a score of divils in him the way it's well nigh[228] certain he will wed Pegeen.

WIDOW QUIN *(jeeringly)*. It's true all girls are fond of courage and do hate the like of you.

SHAWN *(walking about in desperation)*. Oh, Widow Quin, what'll I be doing now? I'd inform again him,[229] but he'd burst from Kilmainham[230] and he'd be sure and certain to destroy me. If I wasn't so God-fearing, I'd near have courage to come behind him and run a pike[231] into his side. Oh, it's a hard case to be an orphan and not to have your father that you're used to, and you'd easy kill and make yourself a hero in the sight of all. *(Coming up to her.)* Oh, Widow Quin, will you find me some contrivance[232] when I've promised you a ewe?

WIDOW QUIN. A ewe's a small thing, but what would you give me if I did wed him and did save you so?

SHAWN *(with astonishment)*. You?

WIDOW QUIN. Aye. Would you give me the red cow you have and the mountainy ram, and the right of way[233] across your rye path, and a load of dung at Michaelmas,[234] and turbary[235] upon the western hill?

SHAWN *(radiant with hope)*. I would surely, and I'd give you the wedding-ring I have, and the loan of a new suit, the way you'd have him decent on the wedding-day. I'd give you two kids for your dinner, and a gallon of poteen, and I'd call the piper on the long car[236] to your wedding from Crossmolina or from Ballina.[237] I'd give you . . .

WIDOW QUIN. That'll do, so, and let you whisht, for he's coming now again.

227. **scratched itself** even if she scratched his face   228. **well nigh** almost
229. **inform again him** bear witness against him   230. **Kilmainham** Dublin jail   231. **pike** pitchfork   232. **contrivance** stratagem   233. **right of way** legal passage   234. **Michaelmas** September 29. Local custom frequently designated this date for the repayment of rents and debts.   235. **turbary** right to cut peat on another's land   236. **long car** stage coach   237. **Crossmolina . . . Ballina** Mayo market towns

(Christy comes in very natty in the new clothes. Widow Quin goes to him admiringly.)

WIDOW QUIN. If you seen yourself now, I'm thinking you'd be too proud to speak to us at all, and it'd be a pity surely to have your like sailing from Mayo to the Western World.

CHRISTY *(as proud as a peacock)*. I'm not going. If this is a poor place itself, I'll make myself contented to be lodging here.

(Widow Quin makes a sign to Shawn to leave them.)

SHAWN. Well, I'm going measuring the racecourse while the tide is low, so I'll leave you the garments and my blessing for the sports to-day. God bless you!

(He wriggles out.)

WIDOW QUIN *(admiring Christy)*. Well, you're mighty spruce,[238] young fellow. Sit down now while you're quiet till you talk with me.

CHRISTY *(swaggering)*. I'm going abroad on the hillside for to seek Pegeen.

WIDOW QUIN. You'll have time and plenty for to seek Pegeen, and you heard me saying at the fall of night the two of us should be great company.

CHRISTY. From this out I'll have no want of company when all sorts is bringing me their food and clothing *(he swaggers to the door, tightening his belt)*, the way they'd set their eyes upon a gallant orphan cleft his father with one blow to the breeches belt. *(He opens door, then staggers back.)* Saints of glory! Holy angels from the throne of light!

WIDOW QUIN *(going over)*. What ails you?

CHRISTY. It's the walking spirit of my murdered da!

WIDOW QUIN *(looking out)*. Is it that tramper?[239]

CHRISTY *(wildly)*. Where'll I hide my poor body from that ghost of hell?

(The door is pushed open, and old Mahon appears on threshold. Christy darts in behind door.)

WIDOW QUIN *(in great amusement)*. God save you, my poor man.

MAHON *(gruffly)*. Did you see a young lad passing this way in the early morning or the fall of night?

WIDOW QUIN. You're a queer kind to walk in not saluting[240] at all.

MAHON. Did you see the young lad?

WIDOW QUIN *(stiffly)*. What kind was he?

MAHON. An ugly young streeler[241] with a murderous gob[242] on him, and a little switch in his hand. I met a tramper seen him coming this way at the fall of night.

238. **mighty spruce** very smartly dressed   239. **tramper** tramp, vagrant   240. **saluting** greeting   241. **streeler** lazybones   242. **gob** mouth

WIDOW QUIN. There's harvest hundreds do be passing these days for the Sligo boat.[243] For what is it you're wanting him, my poor man?

MAHON. I want to destroy him for breaking the head on me with the clout of a loy. (*He takes off a big hat, and shows his head in a mass of bandages and plaster, with some pride.*) It was he did that, and amn't I a great wonder to think I've traced him ten days with that rent in my crown?

WIDOW QUIN (*taking his head in both hands and examining it with extreme delight*). That was a great blow. And who hit you? A robber maybe?

MAHON. It was my own son hit me, and he the divil a robber, or anything else, but a dirty, stuttering lout.

WIDOW QUIN (*letting go his skull and wiping her hands in her apron*). You'd best be wary of a mortified[244] scalp, I think they call it, lepping around with that wound in the splendour of the sun. It was a bad blow surely, and you should have vexed him fearful to make him strike that gash in his da.

MAHON. Is it me?

WIDOW QUIN (*amusing herself*). Aye. And isn't it a great shame when the old and hardened do torment the young?

MAHON (*raging*). Torment him is it? And I after holding out with the patience of a martyred saint till there's nothing but destruction on,[245] and I'm driven out in my old age with none to aid me.

WIDOW QUIN (*greatly amused*). It's a sacred wonder the way that wickedness will spoil a man.

MAHON. My wickedness, is it? Amn't I after saying it is himself has me destroyed, and he a lier on walls,[246] a talker of folly, a man you'd see stretched the half of the day in the brown ferns with his belly to the sun.

WIDOW QUIN. Not working at all?

MAHON. The divil a work, or if he did itself, you'd see him raising up a haystack like the stalk of a rush,[247] or driving our last cow till he broke her leg at the hip, and when he wasn't at that he'd be fooling over little birds he had—finches and felts[248]—or making mugs[249] at his own self in the bit of a glass we had hung on the wall.

WIDOW QUIN (*looking at Christy*). What way was he so foolish? It was running wild after the girls may be?

MAHON (*with a shout of derision*). Running wild, is it? If he seen a red petticoat coming swinging over the hill, he'd be off to hide in the sticks, and you'd see him shooting out his sheep's eyes between the little twigs and the leaves, and his two ears rising like a hare looking out through a gap. Girls, indeed!

243. **Sligo boat** point of embarkation for seasonal migrant workers en route to Scotland   244. **mortified** gangrenous   245. **destruction on** my ruination   246. **lier on walls** lounger   247. **raising . . . rush** building a haystack too narrowly   248. **felts** small birds   249. **making mugs** making faces

WIDOW QUIN. It was drink maybe?

MAHON. And he a poor fellow would get drunk on the smell of a pint. He'd a queer rotten stomach,[250] I'm telling you, and when I gave him three pulls from my pipe a while since,[251] he was taken with contortions till I had to send him in the ass cart[252] to the females' nurse.

WIDOW QUIN (clasping her hands). Well, I never till this day heard tell of a man the like of that!

MAHON. I'd take a mighty oath you didn't surely, and wasn't he the laughing joke of every female woman where four baronies[253] meet, the way the girls would stop their weeding if they seen him coming the road to let a roar at him, and call him the looney of Mahon's.

WIDOW QUIN. I'd give the world and all to see the like of him. What kind was he?

MAHON. A small low fellow.

WIDOW QUIN. And dark?

MAHON. Dark and dirty.

WIDOW QUIN (considering). I'm thinking I seen him.

MAHON (eagerly). An ugly young blackguard.

WIDOW QUIN. A hideous, fearful villain, and the spit[254] of you.

MAHON. What way is he fled?

WIDOW QUIN. Gone over the hills to catch a coasting steamer to the north or south.

MAHON. Could I pull up on[255] him now?

WIDOW QUIN. If you'll cross the sands below where the tide is out, you'll be in it as soon as himself, for he had to go round ten miles by the top of the bay. (She points to the door.) Strike[256] down by the head beyond and then follow on the roadway to the north and east.

(Mahon goes abruptly.)

WIDOW QUIN (shouting after him). Let you give him a good vengeance when you come up with him, but don't put yourself in the power of the law, for it'd be a poor thing to see a judge in his black cap reading out his sentence on a civil warrior[257] the like of you.

(She swings the door to and looks at Christy, who is cowering in terror, for a moment, then she bursts into a laugh.)

WIDOW QUIN. Well, you're the walking playboy of the western world, and that's the poor man you had divided to his breeches belt.

CHRISTY (looking out; then, to her). What'll Pegeen say when she hears that story? What'll she be saying to me now?

WIDOW QUIN. She'll knock the head of you, I'm thinking, and drive

250. **queer rotten stomach** very delicate stomach   251. **since** ago   252. **ass cart** small cart drawn by a donkey   253. **baronies** subdivisions of an Irish county   254. **spit** image   255. **pull up on** catch up with   256. **Strike** walk   257. **civil warrior** brave citizen

you from the door. God help her to be taking you for a wonder, and you a little schemer making up a story you destroyed your da.

CHRISTY *(turning to the door, nearly speechless with rage, half to himself)*. To be letting on he was dead, and coming back to his life, and following after me like an old weazel tracing a rat, and coming in here laying desolation[258] between my own self and the fine women of Ireland, and he a kind of carcase that you'd fling upon the sea[259] . . .

WIDOW QUIN *(more soberly)*. There's talking for a man's one only son.

CHRISTY *(breaking out)*. His one son, is it? May I meet him with one tooth and it aching, and one eye to be seeing seven and seventy divils in the twists of the road, and one old timber leg on him to limp into the scalding[260] grave. *(Looking out.)* There he is now crossing the strands, and that the Lord God would send a high wave to wash him from the world.

WIDOW QUIN *(scandalised)*. Have you no shame? *(Putting her hand on his shoulder and turning him round.)* What ails you? Near crying, is it?

CHRISTY *(in despair and grief)*. Amn't I after seeing the love-light of the star of knowledge[261] shining from her brow, and hearing words would put you thinking on the holy Brigid speaking to the infant saints, and now she'll be turning again, and speaking hard words to me, like an old woman with a spavindy ass[262] she'd have, urging on a hill.

WIDOW QUIN. There's poetry talk for a girl you'd see itching and scratching, and she with a stale stink of poteen on her from selling in the shop.

CHRISTY *(impatiently)*. It's her like is fitted to be handling merchandise in the heavens above, and what'll I be doing now, I ask you, and I a kind of wonder was jilted by the heavens when a day was by.

(There is a distant noise of girls' voices. Widow Quin looks from window and comes to him, hurriedly.)

WIDOW QUIN. You'll be doing like myself, I'm thinking, when I did destroy my man, for I'm above many's the day, odd times in great spirits, abroad in the sunshine, darning a stocking or stitching a shift, and odd times again looking out on the schooners, hookers,[263] trawlers is sailing the sea, and I thinking on the gallant hairy fellows are drifting beyond, and myself long years living alone.

CHRISTY *(interested)*. You're like me, so.

WIDOW QUIN. I am your like, and it's for that I'm taking a fancy to you, and I with my little houseen above where there'd be myself to tend you, and none to ask were you a murderer or what at all.

258. **desolation** a wasteland   259. **carcase . . . sea** dead animals were pushed into the ocean   260. **scalding** cruel: elaborate curses were a much feared part of the Irish poet's armament   261. **star of knowledge** conventional Gaelic love image   262. **spavindy ass** lame with spavin, a disease causing a tumor in the hock   263. **hookers** single-masted fishing boats

CHRISTY. And what would I be doing if I left Pegeen?

WIDOW QUIN. I've nice jobs you could be doing, gathering shells to make a white-wash for our hut within, building up a little goose-house, or stretching a new skin on an old curragh[264] I have, and if my hut is far from all sides, it's there you'll meet the wisest old men, I tell you, at the corner of my wheel,[265] and it's there yourself and me will have great times whispering and hugging. . . .

VOICES (outside, calling far away). Christy! Christy Mahon! Christy!

CHRISTY. Is it Pegeen Mike?

WIDOW QUIN. It's the young girls, I'm thinking, coming to bring you to the sports below,[266] and what is it you'll have me to tell them now?

CHRISTY. Aid me for to win Pegeen. It's herself only that I'm seeking now. (Widow Quin gets up and goes to window.) Aid me for to win her, and I'll be asking God to stretch a hand to you in the hour of death, and lead you short cuts through the Meadows of Ease,[267] and up the floor of Heaven to the Footstool of the Virgin's Son.

WIDOW QUIN. There's praying!

VOICES (nearer). Christy! Christy Mahon!

CHRISTY (with agitation). They're coming. Will you swear to aid and save me for the love of Christ?

WIDOW QUIN (looks at him for a moment). If I aid you, will you swear to give me a right of way I want, and a mountainy ram, and a load of dung at Michaelmas, the time that you'll be master here?

CHRISTY. I will, by the elements and stars of night.

WIDOW QUIN. Then we'll not say a word of the old fellow, the way Pegeen won't know your story till the end of time.

CHRISTY. And if he chances to return again?

WIDOW QUIN. We'll swear he's a maniac and not your da. I could take an oath I seen him raving on the sands to-day.

(Girls run in.)

SUSAN. Come on to the sports below. Pegeen says you're to come.

SARA TANSEY. The lepping's beginning, and we've a jockey's suit to fit upon you for the mule race on the sands below.

HONOR. Come on, will you.

CHRISTY. I will then if Pegeen's beyond.

SARA. She's in the boreen[268] making game of Shaneen Keogh.

CHRISTY. Then I'll be going to her now.

(He runs out followed by the girls.)

WIDOW QUIN. Well, if the worst comes in the end of all, it'll be great

---

264. **curragh** coracle, light boat of tarred canvas   265. **wheel** spinning wheel   266. **below** down there   267. **Meadows of Ease** Elysian Fields   268. **boreen** country lane

game to see there's none to pity him but a widow woman, the like of me, has buried her children and destroyed her man.

(She goes out.)

CURTAIN

ACT 3

SCENE, *as before. Later in the day. Jimmy comes in, slightly drunk.*

JIMMY *(calls)*. Pegeen! *(Crosses to inner door.)* Pegeen Mike! *(Comes back again into the room.)* Pegeen! *(Philly comes in in the same state.)* *(To Philly.)* Did you see herself?[269]

PHILLY. I did not; but I sent Shawn Keogh with the ass cart for to bear him home. *(Trying cupboards which are locked.)* Well, isn't he a nasty man to get into such staggers[270] at a morning wake? and isn't herself the divil's daughter for locking, and she so fussy after that young gaffer,[271] you might take your death[272] with drought and none to heed you?

JIMMY. It's little wonder she'd be fussy, and he after bringing bankrupt ruin on the roulette man, and the trick-o'-the-loop[273] man, and breaking the nose of the cockshot-man,[274] and winning all in the sports below, racing, lepping, dancing, and the Lord knows what! He's right luck, I'm telling you.

PHILLY. If he has, he'll be rightly hobbled[275] yet, and he not able to say ten words without making a brag of the way he killed his father, and the great blow he hit with the loy.

JIMMY. A man can't hang by his own informing,[276] and his father should be rotten by now.

(Old Mahon passes window slowly.)

PHILLY. Supposing a man's digging spuds in that field with a long spade, and supposing he flings up the two halves of that skull, what'll be said then in the papers and the courts of law?

JIMMY. They'd say it was an old Dane,[277] maybe, was drowned in the flood. *(Old Mahon comes in and sits down near door listening.)* Did you never hear tell of the skulls they have in the city of Dublin, ranged out like blue jugs[278] in a cabin of Connaught?

269. **herself** the woman of the house   270. **get into such staggers** get so drunk   271. **gaffer** strapping fellow   272. **take your death** die   273. **trick-o'-the-loop** a gamble based on sleight-of-hand   274. **cockshot man** a living target game   275. **hobbled** tripped up   276. **informing** evidence   277. **Dane** Vikings raided the Irish coasts *ca.* 800–1000   278. **blue jugs** Irish country cottages display their crockery

PHILLY. And you believe that?

JIMMY (*pugnaciously*). Didn't a lad see them and he after coming from harvesting in the Liverpool boat?[279] "They have them there," says he, "making a show[280] of the great people there was one time walking the world. White skulls and black skulls and yellow skulls, and some with full teeth, and some haven't only but one."

PHILLY. It was no lie, maybe, for when I was a young lad, there was a graveyard beyond the house with the remnants of a man who had thighs as long as your arm. He was a horrid man, I'm telling you, and there was many a fine Sunday I'd put him together for fun, and he with shiny bones, you wouldn't meet the like of these days in the cities of the world.

MAHON (*getting up*). You wouldn't is it? Lay your eyes on that skull, and tell me where and when there was another the like of it, is splintered only from the blow of a loy.

PHILLY. Glory be to God! And who hit you at all?

MAHON (*triumphantly*). It was my own son hit me. Would you believe that?

JIMMY. Well, there's wonders hidden in the heart of man!

PHILLY (*suspiciously*). And what way was it done?

MAHON (*wandering about the room*). I'm after walking hundreds and long scores of miles, winning clean beds and the fill of my belly four times in the day, and I doing nothing but telling stories of that naked truth. (*He comes to them a little aggressively.*) Give me a supeen and I'll tell you now.

(*Widow Quin comes in and stands aghast behind him. He is facing Jimmy and Philly, who are on the left.*)

JIMMY. Ask herself beyond. She's the stuff[281] hidden in her shawl.

WIDOW QUIN (*coming to Mahon quickly*). You here, is it? You didn't go far at all?

MAHON. I seen the coasting steamer passing, and I got a drought upon me and a cramping leg, so I said, "The divil go along with him," and turned again. (*Looking under her shawl.*) And let you give me a supeen, for I'm destroyed travelling since Tuesday was a week.

WIDOW QUIN (*getting a glass, in a cajoling tone*). Sit down then by the fire and take your ease for a space.[282] You've a right to be destroyed indeed, with your walking, and fighting, and facing the sun (*giving him poteen from a stone jar she has brought in*). There now is a drink for you, and may it be to your happiness and length of life.

MAHON (*taking glass greedily, and sitting down by fire*). God increase you!

WIDOW QUIN (*taking men to the right stealthily*). Do you know what?

---

279. **harvesting . . . boat** from England   280. **making a show** giving evidence of   281. **stuff** whiskey   282. **take your ease for a space** relax for a while

That man's raving from his wound to-day, for I met him a while since telling a rambling tale of a tinker had him destroyed. Then he heard of Christy's deed, and he up and says it was his son had cracked his skull. O isn't madness a fright, for he'll go killing someone yet, and he thinking it's the man has struck him so?

JIMMY *(entirely convinced)*. It's a fright[283] surely. I knew a party was kicked in the head by a red mare, and he went killing horses a great while, till he eat the insides of a clock and died after.

PHILLY *(with suspicion)*. Did he see Christy?

WIDOW QUIN. He didn't. *(With a warning gesture.)* Let you not be putting him in mind of him, or you'll be likely summoned if there's murder done. *(Looking round at Mahon.)* Whisht! He's listening. Wait now till you hear me taking him easy[284] and unravelling all. *(She goes to Mahon.)* And what way are you feeling, mister? Are you in contentment now?

MAHON *(slightly emotional from his drink)*. I'm poorly only, for it's a hard story the way I'm left to-day, when it was I did tend him from his hour of birth, and he a dunce never reached his second book, the way he'd come from school, many's the day, with his legs lamed under him, and he blackened with his beatings like a tinker's ass. It's a hard story, I'm saying, the way some do have their next and nighest raising up a hand of murder on them, and some is lonesome getting their death with lamentation in the dead of night.

WIDOW QUIN *(not knowing what to say)*. To hear you talking so quiet, who'd know you were the same fellow we seen pass to-day?

MAHON. I'm the same surely. The wrack and ruin of three score years; and it's a terror to live that length, I tell you, and to have your sons going to the dogs against you, and you wore out scolding them, and skelping[285] them, and God knows what.

PHILLY *(to Jimmy)*. He's not raving. *(To Widow Quin.)* Will you ask him what kind was his son?

WINDOW QUIN *(to Mahon, with a peculiar look)*. Was your son that hit you a lad of one year and a score maybe, a great hand at racing and lepping and licking the world?

MAHON *(turning on her with a roar of rage)*. Didn't you hear me say he was the fool of men, the way from this out he'll know the orphan's lot with old and young making game of him and they swearing, raging, kicking at him like a mangy cur.

(A great burst of cheering outside, some way off.)

MAHON *(putting his hands to his ears)*. What in the name of God do they want roaring below?

283. **fright** terrible thing   284. **taking him easy** handling him deftly   285. **skelping** hitting, beating

WIDOW QUIN *(with the shade of a smile)*. They're cheering a young lad, the champion playboy of the Western World.

(More cheering.)

MAHON *(going to window)*. It'd split my heart to hear them, and I with pulses in my brain-pan[286] for a week gone by. Is it racing they are?

JIMMY *(looking from door)*. It is then. They are mounting him for the mule race will be run upon the sands. That's the playboy on the winkered[287] mule.

MAHON *(puzzled)*. That lad, is it? If you said it was a fool he was, I'd have laid a mighty oath he was the likeness of my wandering son *(uneasily, putting his hand to this head)*. Faith, I'm thinking I'll go walking for to view the race.

WIDOW QUIN *(stopping him, sharply)*. You will not. You'd best take the road to Belmullet, and not be dilly-dallying in this place where there isn't a spot you could sleep.

PHILLY *(coming forward)*. Don't mind her. Mount there on the bench and you'll have a view of the whole. They're hurrying before the tide will rise, and it'd be near over if you went down the pathway through the crags below.

MAHON *(mounts on bench, Widow Quin beside him)*. That's a right view again the edge of the sea. They're coming now from the point. He's leading. Who is he at all?

WIDOW QUIN. He's the champion of the world, I tell you, and there isn't a hap'orth isn't falling lucky[288] to his hands to-day.

PHILLY *(looking out, interested in the race)*. Look at that. They're pressing him now.

JIMMY. He'll win it yet.

PHILLY. Take you time, Jimmy Farrell. It's too soon to say.

WIDOW QUIN *(shouting)*. Watch him taking[289] the gate. There's riding.

JIMMY *(cheering)*. More power to the young lad!

MAHON. He's passing the third.

JIMMY. He'll lick them yet!

WIDOW QUIN. He'd lick them if he was running races with a score itself.

MAHON. Look at the mule he has, kicking the stars.

WIDOW QUIN. There was a lep! *(Catching hold of Mahon in her excitement.)* He's fallen! He's mounted again! Faith, he's passing them all!

JIMMY. Look at him skelping her!

PHILLY. And the mountain girls hooshing[290] him on!

286. **brain-pan** skull   287. **winkered** Christy's mule wears blinkers because it's the most spirited, fastest, and hardest to control   288. **there isn't a hap'orth isn't falling lucky** everything is lucky   289. **taking** clearing   290. **hooshing** cheering, encouraging

JIMMY. It's the last turn! The post's cleared[291] for them now!

MAHON. Look at the narrow place. He'll be into the bogs! *(With a yell.)* Good rider! He's through it again!

JIMMY. He's neck and neck!

MAHON. Good boy to him! Flames, but he's in!

(Great cheering, in which all join.)

MAHON *(with hesitation)*. What's that? They're raising him up. They're coming this way. *(With a roar of rage and astonishment.)* It's Christy! by the stars of God! I'd know his way of spitting and he astride[292] the moon.

(He jumps down and makes a run for the door, but Widow Quin catches him and pulls him back.)

WIDOW QUIN. Stay quiet, will you. That's not your son. *(To Jimmy.)* Stop him, or you'll get a month for the abetting of manslaughter and be fined as well.

JIMMY. I'll hold him.

MAHON *(struggling)*. Let me out! Let me out the lot of you! till I have my vengeance on his head to-day.

WIDOW QUIN *(shaking him, vehemently)*. That's not your son. That's a man is going to make a marriage with the daughter of this house, a place with fine trade, with a licence, and with poteen too.

MAHON *(amazed)*. That man marrying a decent and a moneyed[293] girl! Is it mad yous are? Is it in a crazy-house[294] for females that I'm landed now?

WIDOW QUIN. It's mad yourself is with the blow upon your head. That lad is the wonder of the Western World.

MAHON. I seen it's my son.

WIDOW QUIN. You seen that you're mad. *(Cheering outside.)* Do you hear them cheering him in the zig-zags of the road? Aren't you after saying that your son's a fool, and how would they be cheering a true idiot born?

MAHON *(getting distressed)*. It's maybe out of reason that that man's himself. *(Cheering again.)* There's none surely will go cheering him. Oh, I'm raving with a madness that would fright[295] the world! *(He sits down with his hand to his head.)* There was one time I seen ten scarlet divils letting on they'd cork my spirit in a gallon can; and one time I seen rats as big as badgers sucking the life blood from the butt of my lug;[296] but I never till this day confused that dribbling idiot with a likely[297] man. I'm destroyed surely.

WIDOW QUIN. And who'd wonder when it's your brain-pan that is gaping[298] now?

291. **post's cleared** winning post cleared of spectators   292. **and he astride** even if he were riding   293. **moneyed** publicans were considered wealthy   294. **crazy-house** lunatic asylum   295. **fright** frighten   296. **butt of my lug** earlobe   297. **likely** promising   298. **gaping** broken open

MAHON. Then the blight of the sacred drought upon myself and him, for I never went mad to this day, and I not three weeks with the Limerick[299] girls drinking myself silly, and parlatic[300] from the dusk to dawn. *(To Widow Quin, suddenly.)* Is my visage astray?[301]

WIDOW QUIN. It is then. You're a sniggering maniac, a child could see.

MAHON *(getting up more cheerfully).* Then I'd best be going to the union[302] beyond, and there'll be a welcome before me, I tell you *(with great pride),* and I a terrible and fearful case, the way that there I was one time, screeching in a straightened waistcoat,[303] with seven doctors writing out my sayings in a printed book. Would you believe that?

WIDOW QUIN. If you're a wonder itself, you'd best be hasty, for them lads caught a maniac one time and pelted the poor creature till he ran out, raving and foaming, and was drowned in the sea.

MAHON *(with philosophy).* It's true mankind is the divil when your head's astray.[304] Let me out now and I'll slip down the boreen, and not see them so.

WIDOW QUIN *(showing him out).* That's it. Run to the right, and not a one will see.

(He runs off.)

PHILLY *(wisely).* You're at some gaming,[305] Widow Quin; but I'll walk after him and give him his dinner and a time to rest, and I'll see then if he's raving or as sane as you.

WIDOW QUIN *(annoyed).* If you go near that lad, let you be wary of your head, I'm saying. Didn't you hear him telling he was crazed at times?

PHILLY. I heard him telling a power; and I'm thinking we'll have right sport, before night will fall.

(He goes out.)

JIMMY. Well, Philly's a conceited and foolish man. How could that madman have his senses and his brain-pan slit? I'll go after them and see him turn on Philly now.

(He goes; Widow Quin hides poteen behind counter. Then hubbub outside.)

VOICES. There you are! Good jumper! Grand lepper! Darlint boy! He's the racer! Bear him on, will you!

(Christy comes in, in Jockey's dress, with Pegeen Mike, Sara, and other girls, and men.)

PEGEEN *(to crowd).* Go on now and don't destroy him and he drenching with sweat. Go along, I'm saying, and have your tug-of-warring till he's dried his skin.

---

299. **Limerick** city at the Shannon estuary   300. **parlatic** paralytic with drink
301. **visage astray** face mad-looking   302. **union** poorhouse   303. **straightened
waistcoat** straitjacket   304. **when your head's astray** when you're mad   305. **gaming** trickery

CROWD. Here's his prizes! A bagpipes! A fiddle was played by a poet in the years gone by! A flat and three-thorned blackthorn[306] would lick the scholars out of Dublin town!

CHRISTY *(taking prizes from the men)*. Thank you kindly, the lot of you. But you'd say it was little only I did this day if you'd seen me a while since striking my one single blow.

TOWN CRIER *(outside, ringing a bell)*. Take notice, last event of this day! Tug-of-warring on the green below! Come on, the lot of you! Great achievements for all Mayo men!

PEGEEN. Go on, and leave him for to rest and dry. Go on, I tell you, for he'll do no more. *(She hustles crowd out; Widow Quin following them.)*

MEN *(going)*. Come on then. Good luck for the while!

PEGEEN *(radiantly, wiping his face with her shawl)*. Well, you're the lad, and you'll have great times from this out when you could win that wealth of prizes, and you sweating in the heat of noon!

CHRISTY *(looking at her with delight)*. I'll have great times if I win the crowning prize I'm seeking now, and that's your promise that you'll wed me in a fortnight, when our banns is called.[307]

PEGEEN *(backing away from him)*. You've right daring to go ask me that, when all knows you'll be starting to some girl in your own town-land,[308] when your father's rotten in four months, or five.

CHRISTY *(indignantly)*. Starting from you, is it? *(He follows her)*. I will not, then, and when the airs is warming in four months, or five, it's then yourself and me should be pacing Neifin[309] in the dews of night, the times sweet smells do be rising, and you'd see a little, shiny new moon, maybe, sinking on the hills.

PEGEEN *(looking at him playfully)*. And it's that kind of a poacher's love you'd make, Christy Mahon, on the sides of Neifin, when the night is down?

CHRISTY. It's little you'll think if my love's a poacher's, or an earl's itself, when you'll feel my two hands stretched around you, and I squeezing kisses on your puckered lips, till I'd feel a kind of pity for the Lord God is all ages sitting lonesome in his golden chair.

PEGEEN. That'll be right[310] fun, Christy Mahon, and any girl would walk her heart out before she'd meet a young man was your like for eloquence, or talk, at all.

CHRISTY *(encouraged)*. Let you wait, to hear me talking, till we're astray[311] in Erris, when Good Friday's by,[312] drinking a sup from a well,

306. **blackthorn** walking stick *cum* cudgel   307. **banns is called** public announcement of marriage   308. **townland** division of land based on a group of cottages   309. **Neifin** Cf. the Gaelic lovesong "The Brow of Nefin"   310. **right** great   311. **astray** wandering   312. **when Good Friday's by** in springtime, after Good Friday

and making mighty kisses with our wetted mouths, or gaming[313] in a gap
of sunshine, with yourself stretched back unto your necklace, in the flowers
of the earth.

PEGEEN *(in a lower voice, moved by his tone)*. I'd be nice so, is it?

CHRISTY *(with rapture)*. If the mitred[314] bishops seen you that time,
they'd be the like of the holy prophets,[315] I'm thinking, do be straining
the bars of Paradise to lay eyes on the Lady Helen of Troy,[316] and she
abroad, pacing back and forward, with a nosegay in her golden shawl.

PEGEEN *(with real tenderness)*. And what is it I have, Christy Mahon,
to make me fitting entertainment for the like of you, that has such poet's
talking, and such bravery of heart?

CHRISTY *(in a low voice)*. Isn't there the light of seven heavens in your
heart alone, the way you'll be an angel's lamp to me from this out, and I
abroad in the darkness, spearing salmons in the Owen, or the Carrowmore?[317]

PEGEEN. If I was your wife, I'd be along with you those nights, Christy
Mahon, the way you'd see I was a great hand at coaxing bailiffs, or coining
funny nick-names for the stars of night.

CHRISTY. You, is it? Taking your death in the hailstones, or in the fogs
of dawn.

PEGEEN. Yourself and me would shelter easy in a narrow bush, *(with
a qualm of dread)* but we're only talking, maybe, for this would be a poor,
thatched place to hold a fine lad is the like of you.

CHRISTY *(putting his arm round her)*. If I wasn't a good Christian, it's
on my naked knees I'd be saying my prayers and paters[318] to every
jackstraw[319] you have roofing your head, and every stony pebble is paving
the laneway to your door.

PEGEEN *(radiantly)*. If that's the truth, I'll be burning candles[320] from
this out to the miracles of God that have brought you from the south to-
day, and I, with my gowns bought ready, the way that I can wed you, and
not wait at all.

CHRISTY. It's miracles, and that's the truth. Me there toiling a long
while, and walking a long while, not knowing at all I was drawing all
times nearer to this holy day.

PEGEEN. And myself, a girl, was tempted often to go sailing the seas
till I'd marry a Jew-man, with ten kegs of gold, and I not knowing at all
there was the like of you drawing nearer, like the stars of God.

CHRISTY. And to think I'm long years hearing women talking that talk,

313. **gaming** having fun   314. **mitred** formally attired   315. **prophets** of the
Old Testament   316. **Helen of Troy** the beautiful wife of Menelaus   317. **Owen
. . . Carrowmore** river and lake in northwest Mayo   318. **paters** Our Fathers
319. **jackstraw** worthless straw   320. **burning candles** votive lights

to all bloody fools, and this the first time I've heard the like of your voice talking sweetly for my own delight.

PEGEEN. And to think it's me is talking sweetly, Christy Mahon, and I the fright of seven townlands for my biting tongue. Well, the heart's a wonder; and, I'm thinking, there won't be our like in Mayo, for gallant lovers, from this hour, to-day. *(Drunken singing is heard outside.)* There's my father coming from the wake, and when he's had his sleep we'll tell him, for he's peaceful then.

(They separate.)

MICHAEL *(singing outside)*——

> The jailor and the turnkey[321]
> They quickly ran us down,
> And brought us back as prisoners
> Once more to Cavan town.[322]

(He comes in supported by Shawn.)

> There we lay bewailing
> All in a prison bound. . . .

(He sees Christy. Goes and shakes him drunkenly by the hand, while Pegeen and Shawn talk on the left.)

MICHAEL *(to Christy)*. The blessing of God and the holy angels on your head, young fellow. I hear tell you're after winning all in the sports below; and wasn't it a shame I didn't bear you along with me to Kate Cassidy's wake, a fine, stout lad, the like of you, for you'd never see the match of it for flows of drink, the way when we sunk[323] her bones at noonday in her narrow grave, there were five men, aye, and six men, stretched out retching[324] speechless on the holy stones.

CHRISTY *(uneasily, watching Pegeen)*. Is that the truth?

MICHAEL. It is then, and aren't you a louty[325] schemer to go burying your poor father unbeknownst[326] when you'd a right to throw him on the crupper[327] of a Kerry[328] mule and drive him westwards, like holy Joseph[329] in the days gone by, the way we could have given him a decent burial, and not have him rotting beyond, and not a Christian drinking a smart[330] drop to the glory of his soul?

CHRISTY *(gruffly)*. It's well enough he's lying, for the likes of him.

MICHAEL *(slapping him on the back)*. Well, aren't you a hardened slayer?

321. **turnkey** jailer's subordinate   322. **Cavan town** Ulster market town   323. **sunk** lowered   324. **retching** vomiting   325. **louty** loutish   326. **unbeknownst** secretly   327. **crupper** rump   328. **Kerry** Christy's native county in the extreme southwest   329. **Joseph** Joseph's elaborate funeral for his father (Genesis 50: 1–14)   330. **smart** strong

It'll be a poor thing for the household man[331] where you go sniffing for a female wife; and *(pointing to Shawn)* look beyond at that shy and decent Christian I have chosen for my daughter's hand, and I after getting the gilded dispensation this day for to wed them now.

CHRISTY. And you'll be wedding them this day, is it?

MICHAEL *(drawing himself up)*. Aye. Are you thinking, if I'm drunk itself, I'd leave my daughter living single with a little frisky rascal is the like of you?

PEGEEN *(breaking away from Shawn)*. Is it the truth the dispensation's come?

MICHAEL *(triumphantly)*. Father Reilly's after reading it in gallous[332] Latin, and "It's come in the nick of time," says he; "so I'll wed them in a hurry, dreading that young gaffer who'd capsize the stars."

PEGEEN *(fiercely)*. He's missed his nick of time, for it's that lad, Christy Mahon, that I'm wedding now.

MICHAEL *(loudly with horror)*. You'd be making him a son to me, and he wet and crusted with his father's blood?

PEGEEN. Aye. Wouldn't it be a bitter thing for a girl to go marrying the like of Shaneen, and he a middling kind of a scarecrow, with no savagery or fine words in him at all?

MICHAEL *(gasping and sinking on a chair)*. Oh, aren't you a heathen daughter to go shaking the fat of my heart, and I swamped and drownded with the weight of drink? Would you have them turning on me the way that I'd be roaring to the dawn of day with the wind upon my heart? Have you not a word to aid me, Shaneen? Are you not jealous at all?

SHANEEN *(in great misery)*. I'd be afeard to be jealous of a man did slay his da.

PEGEEN. Well, it'd be a poor thing to go marrying your like. I'm seeing there's a world of peril for an orphan girl, and isn't it a great blessing I didn't wed you, before himself came walking from the west or south?

SHAWN. It's a queer story you'd go picking a dirty tramp up from the highways of the world.

PEGEEN *(playfully)*. And you think you're a likely beau[333] to go straying along with, the shiny Sundays of the opening year, when it's sooner on a bullock's[334] liver you'd put a poor girl thinking than on the lily or the rose?

SHAWN. And have you no mind of my weight of passion, and the holy dispensation, and the drift[335] of heifers I am giving, and the golden ring?

PEGEEN. I'm thinking you're too fine for the like of me, Shawn Keogh of Killakeen, and let you go off till you'd find a radiant lady with droves

331. **household man** the man of the house   332. **gallous** eloquent, splendid
333. **likely beau** attractive lover   334. **bullock's** steer's   335. **drift** herd

of bullocks on the plains of Meath,[336] and herself bedizened[337] in the diamond jewelleries of Pharaoh's ma. That'd be your match, Shaneen. So God save you now!

(She retreats behind Christy.)

SHAWN. Won't you hear me telling you . . . ?

CHRISTY *(with ferocity)*. Take yourself from this, young fellow, or I'll maybe add a murder to my deeds to-day.

MICHAEL *(springing up with a shriek)*. Murder is it? Is it mad yous are? Would you go making murder in this place, and it piled with poteen for our drink to-night? Go on to the foreshore if it's fighting you want, where the rising tide will wash all traces from the memory of man.

(Pushing Shawn towards Christy.)

SHAWN *(shaking himself free, and getting behind Michael)*. I'll not fight him, Michael James. I'd liefer live a bachelor, simmering in passions to the end of time, than face a lepping savage the like of him has descended from the Lord knows where. Strike him yourself, Michael James, or you'll lose my drift of heifers and my blue bull from Sneem.[338]

MICHAEL. Is it me fight him, when it's father-slaying he's bred to now? *(Pushing Shawn.)* Go on you fool and fight him now.

SHAWN *(coming forward a little)*. Will I strike him with my hand?

MICHAEL. Take the loy is on your western side.[339]

SHAWN. I'd be afeard of the gallows if I struck with that.

CHRISTY *(taking up the loy)*. Then I'll make you face the gallows or quit off from this.

(Shawn flies out of the door.)

CHRISTY. Well, fine weather be after him, *(going to Michael, coaxingly)* and I'm thinking you wouldn't wish to have that quaking[340] blackguard in your house at all. Let you give us your blessing and hear her swear her faith to me, for I'm mounted on the spring-tide of the stars of luck, the way it'll be good for any to have me in the house.

PEGEEN *(at the other side of Michael)*. Bless us now, for I swear to God I'll wed him, and I'll not renege.[341]

MICHAEL *(standing up in the centre, holding on to both of them)*. It's the will of God, I'm thinking, that all should win an easy or a cruel end, and it's the will of God that all should rear up lengthy[342] families for the nurture of the earth. What's a single man, I ask you, eating a bit in one house and drinking a sup in another, and he with no place of his own, like an old braying jackass strayed upon the rocks? *(To Christy.)* It's many would be

336. **plains of Meath** fertile county in east central Ireland   337. **bedizened** adorned   338. **Sneem** Kerry village: Shawn's bull is one of the sturdy black breed native to Kerry   339. **western side** left side   340. **quaking** trembling   341. **renege** break a promise   342. **lengthy** large

in dread to bring your like into their house for to end them, maybe, with a sudden end; but I'm a decent man of Ireland, and I liefer face the grave untimely[343] and I seeing a score of grandsons growing up little gallant swearers by the name of God, than go peopling my bedside with puny weeds the like of what you'd breed, I'm thinking, out of Shaneen Keogh. *(He joins their hands.)* A daring fellow is the jewel of the world, and a man did split his father's middle with a single clout, should have the bravery of ten, so may God and Mary and St. Patrick bless you, and increase you from this mortal day.

CHRISTY AND PEGEEN. Amen, O Lord!

(Hubbub outside.)

(Old Mahon rushes in, followed by all the crowd, and Widow Quin. He makes a rush at Christy, knocks him down, and begins to beat him.)

PEGEEN *(dragging back his arm)*. Stop that, will you. Who are you at all?

MAHON. His father, God forgive me!

PEGEEN *(drawing back)*. Is it rose from the dead?

MAHON. Do you think I look so easy quenched[344] with the tap of a loy?

(Beats Christy again.)

PEGEEN *(glaring at Christy)*. And it's lies you told, letting on you had him slitted, and you nothing at all.

CHRISTY *(catching Mahon's stick)*. He's not my father. He's a raving maniac would scare the world. *(Pointing to Widow Quin.)* Herself knows it is true.

CROWD. You're fooling Pegeen! The Widow Quin seen him this day, and you likely knew! You're a liar!

CHRISTY *(dumbfounded)*. It's himself was a liar, lying stretched out with an open head on him, letting on he was dead.

MAHON. Weren't you off racing the hills before I got my breath with the start I had seeing you turn on me at all?

PEGEEN. And to think of the coaxing[345] glory we had given him, and he after doing nothing but hitting a soft blow and chasing northward in a sweat of fear. Quit off from this.

CHRISTY *(piteously)*. You've seen my doings this day, and let you save me from the old man; for why would you be in such a scorch[346] of haste to spur me to destruction now?

PEGEEN. It's there your treachery is spurring me, till I'm hard set to think you're the one I'm after lacing in my heart-strings half-an-hour gone by. *(To Mahon.)* Take him on from this, for I think bad the world should see me raging for a Munster liar, and the fool of men.

343. **untimely** prematurely   344. **quenched** killed   345. **coaxing** flattering
346. **scorch** blaze

MAHON. Rise up now to retribution, and come on with me.

CROWD *(jeeringly)*. There's the playboy! There's the lad thought he'd rule the roost in Mayo. Slate[347] him now, mister.

CHRISTY *(getting up in shy terror)*. What is it drives you to torment me here, when I'd asked the thunders of the might of God to blast me if I ever did hurt to any saving only that one single blow.

MAHON *(loudly)*. If you didn't, you're a poor good-for-nothing, and isn't it by the like of you the sins of the whole world are committed?

CHRISTY *(raising his hands)*. In the name of the Almighty God. . . .

MAHON. Leave troubling the Lord God. Would you have him sending down droughts, and fevers, and the old hen[348] and the cholera morbus?[349]

CHRISTY *(to Widow Quin)*. Will you come between us and protect me now?

WIDOW QUIN. I've tried a lot, God help me, and my share is done.

CHRISTY *(looking round in desperation)*. And I must go back into my torment is it, or run off like a vagabond straying through the Unions with the dusts of August making mudstains in the gullet of my throat, or the winds of March blowing on me till I'd take an oath I felt them making whistles of my ribs within?

SARA. Ask Pegeen to aid you. Her like does often change.

CHRISTY. I will not then, for there's torment in the splendour of her like, and she a girl any moon of midnight would take pride to meet, facing southwards on the heaths of Keel.[350] But what did I want crawling forward to scorch my understanding at her flaming brow?

PEGEEN *(to Mahon, vehemently, fearing she will break into tears)*. Take him on from this or I'll set the young lads to destroy[351] him here.

MAHON *(going to him, shaking his stick)*. Come on now if you wouldn't have the company to see you skelped.

PEGEEN *(half laughing, through her tears)*. That's it, now the world will see him pandied,[352] and he an ugly liar was playing off the hero, and the fright of men.

CHRISTY *(to Mahon, very sharply)*. Leave me go!

CROWD. That's it. Now Christy. If them two set fighting, it will lick the world.

MAHON *(making a grab at Christy)*. Come here to me.

CHRISTY *(more theateningly)*. Leave me go, I'm saying.

MAHON. I will maybe, when your legs is limping, and your back is blue.

---

347. **Slate** beat   348. **old hen** influenza   349. **cholera morbus** infectious cholera
350. **Keel** village on Achill island off the Mayo coast   351. **destroy** kill   352. **pandied** beaten like a schoolboy

CROWD. Keep it up the two of you. I'll back the old one. Now the playboy.

CHRISTY *(in low and intense voice)*. Shut your yelling, for if you're after making a mighty man of me this day by the power of a lie, you're setting me now to think if it's a poor thing to be lonesome, it's worse maybe go mixing with the fools of earth.

(Mahon makes a movement towards him.)

CHRISTY *(almost shouting)*. Keep off . . . lest I do show a blow unto the lot of you would set the guardian angels winking in the clouds above.

(He swings round with a sudden rapid movement and picks up a loy.)

CROWD *(half frightened, half amused)*. He's going mad! Mind yourselves! Run from the idiot!

CHRISTY. If I am an idiot, I'm after hearing my voice this day saying words would raise the topknot[353] on a poet in a merchant's town.[354] I've won your racing, and your lepping, and . . .

MAHON. Shut your gullet and come on with me.

CHRISTY. I'm going, but I'll stretch you first.

(He runs at old Mahon with the loy, chases him out of the door, followed by crowd and Widow Quin. There is a great noise outside, then a yell, and dead silence for a moment. Christy comes in, half dazed, and goes to fire.)

WIDOW QUIN *(coming in, hurriedly, and going to him)*. They're turning again you. Come on, or you'll be hanged, indeed.

CHRISTY. I'm thinking, from this out, Pegeen'll be giving me praises, the same as in the hours gone by.

WIDOW QUIN *(impatiently)*. Come by the back-door. I'd think bad to have you stifled[355] on the gallows tree.

CHRISTY *(indignantly)*. I will not, then. What good'd be my life-time, if I left Pegeen?

WIDOW QUIN. Come on, and you'll be no worse than you were last night; and you with a double murder this time to be telling to the girls.

CHRISTY. I'll not leave Pegeen Mike.

WIDOW QUIN *(impatiently)*. Isn't there the match of her in every parish public,[356] from Binghamstown[357] unto the plain of Meath? Come on, I tell you, and I'll find you finer sweethearts at each waning moon.

CHRISTY. It's Pegeen I'm seeking only, and what'd I care if you brought me a drift of chosen females, standing in their shifts itself, maybe, from this place to the Eastern World?

SARA *(runs in, pulling off one of her petticoats)*. They're going to hang him. *(Holding out petticoat and shawl.)* Fit these upon him, and let him run off to the east.

353. **raise the topknot** cause the hair to stand on end   354. **merchant's town** where poets found patrons at fairs   355. **stifled** throttled   356. **parish public** in every local pub   357. **Binghamstown** a west Mayo village

WIDOW QUIN. He's raving now; but we'll fit them on him, and I'll take him, in the ferry, to the Achill boat.

CHRISTY *(struggling feebly)*. Leave me go, will you? when I'm thinking of my luck to-day, for she will wed me surely, and I a proven hero in the end of all.

(They try to fasten petticoat round him.)

WIDOW QUIN. Take his left hand, and we'll pull him now. Come on, young fellow.

CHRISTY *(suddenly starting up)*. You'll be taking me from her? You're jealous, is it, of her wedding me? Go on from this.

(He snatches up a stool, and threatens them with it.)

WIDOW QUIN *(going)*. It's in the mad-house they should put him, not in jail, at all. We'll go by the back-door, to call the doctor, and we'll save him so.

(She goes out, with Sara, through inner room. Men crowd in the doorway. Christy sits down again by the fire.)

MICHAEL (in a terrified whisper). Is the old lad killed surely?

PHILLY. I'm after feeling the last gasps quitting his heart.

(They peer in at Christy.)

MICHAEL *(with a rope)*. Look at the way he is. Twist a hangman's knot on it, and slip it over his head, while he's not minding at all.

PHILLY. Let you take it, Shaneen. You're the soberest of all that's here.

SHAWN. Is it me to go near him, and he the wickedest and worst with me? Let you take it, Pegeen Mike.

PEGEEN. Come on, so.

(She goes forward with the others, and they drop the double hitch over his head.)

CHRISTY. What ails you?

SHAWN *(triumphantly, as they pull the rope tight on his arms)*. Come on to the peelers, till they stretch[358] you now.

CHRISTY. Me!

MICHAEL. If we took pity on you, the Lord God would, maybe, bring us ruin from the law to-day, so you'd best come easy, for hanging is an easy and a speedy end.

CHRISTY. I'll not stir. *(To Pegeen.)* And what is it you'll say to me, and I after doing it this time in the face of all?

PEGEEN. I'll say, a strange man is a marvel, with his mighty talk; but what's a squabble in your back-yard, and the blow of a loy, have taught me that there's a great gap between a gallous[359] story and a dirty deed. *(To Men.)* Take him on from this, or the lot of us will be likely put on trial for his deed to-day.

358. **stretch** hang   359. **gallous** powerful (with play on "gallows")

CHRISTY *(with horror in his voice)*. And it's yourself will send me off, to have a horny-fingered hangman hitching his bloody slip-knots at the butt of my ear.

MEN *(pulling rope)*. Come on, will you?

(He is pulled down on the floor.)

CHRISTY *(twisting his legs round the table)*. Cut the rope, Pegeen, and I'll quit the lot of you, and live from this out, like the madmen of Keel, eating muck and green weeds, on the faces of the cliffs.

PEGEEN. And leave us to hang, is it, for a saucy liar, the like of you? *(To men.)* Take him on, out from this.

SHAWN. Pull a twist on his neck, and squeeze him so.

PHILLY. Twist yourself. Sure he cannot hurt you, if you keep your distance from his teeth alone.

SHAWN. I'm afeard of him. *(To Pegeen.)* Lift a lighted sod, will you, and scorch his leg.

PEGEEN *(blowing the fire, with a bellows)*. Leave go now, young fellow, or I'll scorch your shins.

CHRISTY. You're blowing for to torture me? *(His voice rising and growing stronger.)* That's your kind, is it? Then let the lot of you be wary, for, if I've to face the gallows, I'll have a gay march down,[360] I tell you, and shed the blood of some of you before I die.

SHAWN *(in terror)*. Keep a good hold, Philly. Be wary, for the love of God. For I'm thinking he would liefest wreak his pains[361] on me.

CHRISTY *(almost gaily)*. If I do lay my hands on you, it's the way you'll be at the fall of night, hanging as a scarecrow for the fowls of hell. Ah, you'll have a gallous jaunt I'm saying, coaching out through Limbo[362] with my father's ghost.

SHAWN *(to Pegeen)*. Make haste, will you? Oh, isn't he a holy terror, and isn't it true for Father Reilly, that all drink's a curse that has the lot of you so shaky and uncertain now?

CHRISTY. If I can wring a neck among you, I'll have a royal judgment looking on the trembling jury in the courts of law. And won't there be crying out in Mayo the day I'm stretched upon the rope with ladies in their silks and satins snivelling in their lacy kerchiefs, and they rhyming songs and ballads on the terror of my fate?

(He squirms round on the floor and bites Shawn's leg.)

SHAWN *(shrieking)*. My leg's bit on me. He's the like of a mad dog, I'm thinking, the way that I will surely die.

---

360. **gay march down** lively exit   361. **liefest wreak his pains** most willingly lash out at me   362. **Limbo** abode of the unredeemed dead

CHRISTY (*delighted with himself*). You will then, the way you can shake out hell's flags of welcome for my coming in two weeks or three, for I'm thinking Satan hasn't many have killed their da in Kerry, and in Mayo too.

(*Old Mahon comes in behind on all fours and looks on unnoticed.*)

MEN (*to Pegeen*). Bring the sod, will you?

PEGEEN (*coming over*). God help him so.

(*Burns his leg.*)

CHRISTY (*kicking and screaming*). O, glory be to God!

(*He kicks loose from the table, and they all drag him towards the door.*)

JIMMY (*seeing old Mahon*). Will you look what's come in?

(*They all drop Christy and run left.*)

CHRISTY (*scrambling on his knees face to face with old Mahon*). Are you coming to be killed a third time, or what ails you now?

MAHON. For what is it they have you tied?

CHRISTY. They're taking me to the peelers to have me hanged for slaying you.

MICHAEL (*apologetically*). It is the will of God that all should guard their little cabins from the treachery of law, and what would my daughter be doing if I was ruined or was hanged itself?

MAHON (*grimly, loosening Christy*). It's little I care if you put a bag on her back, and went picking cockles[363] till the hour of death; but my son and myself will be going our own way, and we'll have great times from this out telling stories of the villainy of Mayo, and the fools is here. (*To Christy, who is freed.*) Come on now.

CHRISTY. Go with you, is it? I will then, like a gallant captain with his heathen slave. Go on now and I'll see you from this day stewing my oatmeal and washing my spuds, for I'm master of all fights from now. (*Pushing Mahon.*) Go on, I'm saying.

MAHON. Is it me?

CHRISTY. Not a word out of you. Go on from this.

MAHON (*walking out and looking back at Christy over his shoulder*). Glory be to God! (*With a broad smile.*) I am crazy again!

(*Goes.*)

CHRISTY. Ten thousand blessings upon all that's here, for you've turned me a likely gaffer in the end of all, the way I'll go romancing through a romping lifetime from this hour to the dawning of the judgment day.

(*He goes out.*)

MICHAEL. By the will of God, we'll have peace now for our drinks. Will you draw the porter,[364] Pegeen?

363. **picking cockles** foraging for shellfish on the foreshore   364. **draw the porter** pour the drinks

SHAWN *(going up to her)*. It's a miracle Father Reilly can wed us in the end of all, and we'll have none to trouble us when his vicious bite is healed.

PEGEEN *(hitting him a box on the ear)*. Quit my sight. *(Putting her shawl over her head and breaking out into wild lamentations.)* Oh my grief, I've lost him surely. I've lost the only playboy of the Western World.

CURTAIN

T. C. MURRAY
1873 – 1959

Addressing the Abbey Theatre Festival in 1938, Thomas Cornelius Murray, one of the leading exponents of the realistic drama with which the theater had by then become generally identified, had this to say of his own beginnings some 30 years before: "I knew the Irish Catholic peasant from my childhood, and while the work of Yeats and Synge and Lady Gregory charmed my imagination, I could never recognise the characters that moved on their stage as counterparts of the country-folk of South Munster, to which I belonged. They created, these three, a peasant world of their own, and one surrendered to it as to the mood of an old folktale. It offered some kind of escape from the humdrum commerce of everyday life, and we accepted their drama as an adventure in makebelieve." He credited Lennox Robinson with "sound[ing] a new note in the Irish theatre—a note in which the clamour of everyday concerns drowned the poetic idealism of his forerunners [and] revealed to us that in that very traffic of everyday life from which we turned our eyes there was potential comedy and tragedy as merry as *Twelfth Night,* as profoundly moving as *Hamlet* or *Lear.* In their way of thought, their speech, the accent, the people that he created were the people I knew. From the field, the farmhouse, the shop, the wayside tavern, they seemed to have wandered on to his stage." Murray could well have been describing his own work.

T. C. Murray was born in Macroom, a market town in the western part of County Cork. As *Spring Horizon,* his autobiographical novel records, he was in a good position to observe the character and regionalisms of the country folk who patronized his father's shop. He received an education at local schools and his teacher training at St. Patrick's College, Drumcondra, Dublin. His career as a primary teacher took him from schools in Cork to Inchicore Model Schools, Dublin, where he was headmaster from 1915 until 1932.

Among his first publications are translations of Irish poetry and essays on education in *The New Ireland Review.* In the drama, his earliest influences were Racine (he read *Athalie* in secondary school) and Shakespeare, which he saw performed by Sir Frank Benson at the Cork Opera House. Then in 1909, following the example of the Abbey in Dublin, he helped found the Cork Little Theatre (An Dún) with Terence MacSwiney, Daniel Corkery and others. The object of that theater was to produce work by Munster writers, and there his first play, *Wheel of Fortune*—a comedy about matchmaking—was produced in December of that year.

In 1910 the Abbey accepted his second play, *Birthright,* a bleak portrayal of rural poverty, fraternal jealousy and violence. When the Abbey company made its first American tour in 1911, *Birthright* and Synge's *Playboy* were on the playbill. Among those in attendance were theater critic Cornelius Weygandt and Eugene O'Neill. Weygandt reported that *Birthright* was generally regarded as "the best play new to America presented during the winter 1911–12," and O'Neill observed that the Abbey players "demonstrate the possibilities of naturalistic acting better than any other company."

The Abbey company gave his next play, *Maurice Harte,* its premiere at the Court Theatre, London, in 1912. It was immediately hailed as a new masterpiece of realism. Yeats wrote: "If Mr. Murray can give us more plays equal in intensity to *Maurice Harte* then we shall deserve, perhaps, as much attention as any contemporary theatre." Of Murray's later work, *Autumn Fire* (1924) and possibly *Michaelmas Eve* (1932) fulfilled Yeats's hopes. In these and other plays, Murray reveals a firm and disciplined, but relatively narrow, range. Within the confines of a poor rural life, his characters struggle for the basic necessities: shelter, land, inheritance, marriage partners. Murray meets these themes with certain powers: clear, simple characterization, solid construction, and faithful reproduction of the manners and speech of West Cork.

Through the 1930s he continued to contribute to Irish literary journals, *The Dublin Magazine* and *The Bell.* He was president of the Irish Playwrights' Association, and vice president of the Irish Academy of Letters. He was director of the Authors' Guild of Ireland and in 1949 he received an honorary D.Litt. from the National University of Ireland. He died on March 7, 1959, in Ballsbridge, Dublin.

Except for one play (*The Pipe in the Fields,* 1927), T. C. Murray's work is entirely in the mainstream of dramatic realism. His demonstrated strengths—technical and emotional control, searchingly accurate character portrayal, social conscience—ensure that his major themes—murder, insanity, generational and marital conflict, clerical influence, and incest—are treated without sensationalism, yet with palpable dramatic power. His vision is brooding, dark; his plays press on relentlessly to their tragic conclusions. They portray the deep frustrations resulting from the savage poverty of Irish country life with but a modicum of social decorum and a glimmer of conventional religion to relieve the gloom. But the convincing detail and the firm, simple design combine to produce a powerful sense of classical inevitability. This process, as J. J. Hogan observed, takes Murray's art beyond the usual limitations of dramatic realism: "[W]hat his characters do and say under the stress of great emotion and in desperate situations is a true revelation of the deeper instinct, the souls, of our people."

Maurice Harte exemplifies all of these qualities. As Joseph Holloway reports, it began when Murray "was told by a man of the sad fate of his son who tried in vain to become a priest. The tragic look in the spoiled priest's parent's face haunted [Murray] and set him thinking with the result—*Maurice Harte*." In writing this play, Murray felt that he "was doing something to relieve the Abbey's reputation for anti-Catholicism," and "that it introduce[d] for the first time perhaps the true note of Irish Catholic life on the Abbey stage."

In a deeply Catholic society such as Ireland—particularly rural Ireland—the priesthood is held in high esteem. With the lifting of restrictions on religious practice, the founding of St. Patrick's College, Maynooth (1795), and the "devotional revolution" of the mid-nineteenth century, the fervor of Irish Catholicism has been remarkable. Through the period of which Murray writes, religious vocations reached record proportions. Having a priest, nun, or brother in the family was not merely socially acceptable; it conferred a unique respectability, as well as presumed advantages in the order of grace. The social attitude towards the priesthood carried the further assumption that any young man who commenced a clerical career was, *ipso facto,* "called" to the priesthood: he had a "vocation." Therefore a clerical student who failed, for whatever reason, to proceed all the way to ordination was called a "spoiled priest." This particular Irish Catholic usage carried a certain social stigma.

Maurice Harte, then, sets social and psychological definitions of vocation against one another. But as a social realist, Murray is less interested in the forces at odds in Maurice's spirit than in the relationships between religion and social status. From one perspective, providing the material necessities of life is an undertaking beside which the conflicts of conscience seem effete or incomprehensible. And from another, hypocrisy exacts unbearable social and psychological prices. Murray's treatment of the contention between the claims of loyalty and conscience has an imaginative resonance which causes the play to transcend its limited social origins.

SELECT BIBLIOGRAPHY

Publications

Birthright. Dublin: Maunsel, 1911. Rpt. London: Allen and Unwin, 1928.

Maurice Harte. Dublin: Maunsel, 1912.

Spring and Other Plays (*Sovereign Love* and *The Briery Gap*). Dublin: Talbot Press, 1917.

Aftermath. Dublin: Talbot Press, 1922.

Autumn Fire. London: Allen and Unwin, 1928.

The Pipe in the Fields. The Dublin Magazine 2 (April–June 1927): 7–30. Rpt. London: Allen and Unwin, 1928.

Michaelmas Eve. London: Allen and Unwin, 1932.

Spring Horizon. London: Nelson, 1937. (Autobiographical novel)

Biography and Criticism

Connolly, Terence L. "T. C. Murray, the Quiet Man." *The Catholic World* 190 (March 1960): 364–69.

Fitzgibbon, T. Gerald. "The Elements of Conflict in the Plays of T. C. Murray." *Studies* 64 (Spring 1975): 59–65.

Hogan, Thomas. "T. C. Murray." *Envoy* 3 (November 1950): 138–48.

Macardle, Dorothy. "The Dramatic Art of T. C. Murray." *The Dublin Magazine* 2 (January 1925): 393–98.

Ó hAodha, Micheál. "T. C. Murray and Some Critics." *Studies* 47 (Summer 1958): 185–91.

See also discussion in Ellis-Fermor, *The Irish Dramatic Movement,* and Ó hAodha, *Theatre in Ireland.*

Maurice Harte

To my wife
and my little boy and girl,
my play's first audience

PERSONS IN THE PLAY

MICHAEL HARTE, *a farmer*
ELLEN, *his wife*
OWEN ⎱
MAURICE ⎰ *their sons*
MRS. O'CONNOR, *Ellen's sister*
FATHER MANGAN, *a parish priest*
PETER MANGAN, *a clerical student*
Another Student

The action takes place in the farmhouse of Michael Harte in the County Cork.[1] There is an interval of about nine months between Acts I and II.

ACT 1

The afternoon of a late August. A bright, comfortable farmhouse kitchen. The sunshine is streaming in through the open door, through which one catches a glimpse of green fields and yellowing corn.[2] Mrs. Harte is seen making preparations for ironing. She looks a cheery, robust woman, and the strongly-marked features, as well as the energy of her movements, seem to indicate some decision of character. As she puts a heater in the fire her sister comes in. Mrs. O'Connor is a thin, pale, overworked woman, but younger than Mrs. Harte.

MRS. O'CONNOR *(entering)*. Glory be to God, Ellen, but isn't it the wonderful weather for the country? I never saw anything like the gardens this year.

MRS. HARTE. 'Twill make a great year surely. The corn in the well-field below is already on the turn, and it always green till September.

---

1. **County Cork** in the south of Ireland   2. **corn** a collective term for the cereals wheat, oats, barley and rye

MRS. O'CONNOR. 'Tis so. . . . I just ran over to see if you'd have a bit of darning thread to spare. I want it very badly *(producing a piece of grey woollen thread)*. Anything like that would do me.

MRS. HARTE. Show me *(examining thread)*. I have then,[3] I think. *(She goes to a drawer and takes out some thread, which she compares with the pattern.)* 'Tis nearly the very same. Take the skein of it. But sit down for a bit and be telling us the news.

MRS. O'CONNOR. I can't, I'm afraid. I'm in a terrible hurry.

MRS. HARTE *(with slight asperity)*. O, 'tis ever and always the same story with you, Mary. You're hardly inside the door when you're off again. Sure anyone might think 'tis black strangers[4] we were, and not two sisters at all. *(With affected indifference.)* But have your own way—have your own way.

MRS. O'CONNOR *(extenuatingly)*. I don't know how it is, Ellen, but between one thing and another, I do be kept going from morning till night. The children are terrible trouble—for every kind o' wildness and crossness[5] there's not their beating anywhere.

MRS. HARTE *(dryly)*. All children are the same.

MRS. O'CONNOR. I don't know, then. There's Christie, now. 'Twas only yesterday I put a new pair o' stockings on him—fine, thick stockings they were, too—the same thread as that—an' glory be to God! if you only saw the state o' them when he came home from school in the evening. For all the world like a little tramp he was, with his skin out through them in half a dozen places. Running through the briery field, he said he was, playing "Hunt the Fox." *(Discontentedly.)* Sure my life is no good to me at all with them. . . . But is it any news you have yourself, Ellen?

MRS. HARTE *(more suavely)*. Wisha, no, then, except that Maurice got notice this morning to be going back to Maynooth[6] in a couple o' days.

MRS. O'CONNOR. Did he so? Well, sure, he had a good share o' rest. 'Tis half tired of it he was, I'm thinking?

MRS. HARTE. It isn't indeed, then. A week longer he was expecting, and glad he'd be to get it.

MRS. O'CONNOR. Well, now.

MRS. HARTE *(half confidentially)*. When he opened the letter 'tis half pale he turned, and he was that disappointed he got up from the table without ever finishing his breakfast.

MRS. O'CONNOR. Well, well! . . . But they have a terrible hard life up there by all accounts? Sure when William Kearney's son came home after being priested,[7] they said his mother went off in a weakness[8] when she saw him first.

3. **then** indeed   4. **black strangers** total strangers   5. **crossness** ill-humor
6. **Maynooth** St. Patrick's College, Co. Kildare, Ireland's national theological seminary   7. **priested** ordained   8. **went off in a weakness** fainted

MRS. HARTE. I heard them to say so. Everyone had it at the time.

MRS. O'CONNOR *(more cheerfully)*. But isn't it the fine thing for ye that 'twill soon be all over for Maurice?

MRS. HARTE. 'Tis, surely.

MRS. O'CONNOR *(half laughingly)*. Do you know 'twas of him I was thinking, God forgive me! all the time during the Mass last Sunday?

MRS. HARTE *(laughing)*. 'Tis small blame for me to be thinking of him, so.

MRS. O'CONNOR *(more gravely)*. Wondering I was how we'd all feel, and we seeing him coming on the altar for the first time. And look! . . . Almost as plain as you're standing there, I saw him in my mind, and he coming out the sacristy door, with the fine vestments on him, and all the little altar boys and they on before him. . . . That will be a proud day for you, Ellen, and for all of us.

MRS. HARTE. 'Twill so. But isn't it strange that I have a kind o' feel on me sometimes that 'tis how something queer'll happen, or the heart, maybe, stop altogether on me, when I'll see him turn round to read the Acts⁹ and everyone's eyes fixed on himself.

MRS. O'CONNOR *(with solemn emphasis)*. It must be the wonderful feel entirely for any mother to be looking and listening to her own son and he before her on the altar o' God for the first time. . . . May God preserve you, Ellen, to see that day!

MRS. HARTE. Wisha, Amen. 'Twould be hard on me to be called away before it.

MRS. O'CONNOR. 'Twould, surely.

MRS. HARTE. And I often say to myself, whenever the death'll come after, 'twont be so hard at all. 'Twould be great joy thinking of him saying the Mass for your soul, and all the priests and they chanting the great Latin, the same as if 'twas over one o' themselves. . . . God help us, they're the foolish thoughts, I suppose, but they'll be coming into my mind when I do be awake at night, sure as the stars.

MRS. O'CONNOR. An' where's the harm in them? Faith, if I had a son myself and he to be as good as priested 'tis the same thoughts I'd be thinking. . . . *(With a slight laugh)*. But do you know I do be building my own castles, too, young and wild as the children are yet?

MRS. HARTE *(encouragingly)*. An' sure why not? 'Tis surprising how the time'll slip by till you'll find yourself bothering your mind, and asking yourself what you'll do with this one, and that one, and the other one o' them.

MRS. O'CONNOR *(confidentially)*. What Diarmuid and myself was thinking was that our Patrick had such a great head for the learning we'd

9. **read the Acts** read the scriptural texts

try to put a little bit o' money by for his schooling, . . . *(half timidly)* and we were hoping that Maurice, maybe—after a couple o' years—knowing the road like—might—might help him along a bit?

MRS. HARTE *(in astonishment)*. 'Tisn't a priest you'd be thinking of making him, Mary?

MRS. O'CONNOR. 'Tis so.

MRS. HARTE *(decidedly)*. I wouldn't at all.

MRS. O'CONNOR *(taken aback)*. And why so, now?

MRS. HARTE *(enigmatically)*. Because I'd be advising you for your good.

MRS. O'CONNOR. Oh, there should be a reason for everything.

MRS. HARTE. And there *is* a reason—and a great reason for what I am saying to you. . . . Listen, Mary. If Michael and myself have our son nearly a priest this day, 'tis no small price at all we have paid for it. Many a time I thought to be telling you, but whatever you'll tell another woman—even your own sister—she's sure to tell it to her husband, and when the knowledge of anyone's affairs passes outside the four walls of their own house, it goes here and there like the wind, with nothing to stop it at all.

MRS. O'CONNOR *(protestingly)*. Oh, Diarmuid isn't like that at all, Ellen!—I could give you my hand and word on that.

MRS. HARTE. I'm not saying it about him in particular. . . . Isn't it the terrible thing, Mary, every time you look through that window to have the fear in your heart that 'tis the process-server[10] you'll see and he coming up the boreen?[11]

MRS. O'CONNOR. Yeh, glory be to God! and why so?

MRS. HARTE. Why so? . . . I'll tell you, then, soon enough.

(She goes into an inner room. She returns in a moment, and from a thick wrapper of brown paper securely fastened, draws two small account books. She opens one and hands it to her sister, indicating the entry denoting the total liability. There is a look of vague wonder and curiosity on the face of the second woman.)

MRS. HARTE. Look at that.

MRS. O'CONNOR *(scrutinizing it)*. The Lord save us, Ellen!

MRS. HARTE. And look at that, now.

(Mrs. O'Connor makes no comment, save closing her eyes and making the sign of the cross.)

MRS. HARTE *(after a pause)*. Well, now?

MRS. O'CONNOR. You've put a fright in my heart that I'll never forget. . . . *(Suddenly.)* In the name o' God, Ellen, what happened ye at all, at all, and to have such a terrible load o' debt on ye?

10. **process-server** sheriff's officer who serves summonses   11. **boreen** county laneway

MRS. HARTE *(dryly)*. What happened us? Faith, nothing at all. We couldn't help it.

MRS. O'CONNOR. And in the name of all that's good and gracious, how did that mountain o' money rise on ye so? *(referring to accounts)*. A hundred and forty pounds on ye by James McCarthy and Redmond Kelly, with fifty-three pounds on ye, besides!

MRS. HARTE. 'Tis little you know, Mary, or any other like you, the great money that goes to make a priest. From the first day your boy will be leaving your house for the College till he'll come back to you finished in nine years or ten years maybe, 'tis money, money, money, all the time. Shovelling it out you must be every other day.

MRS. O'CONNOR. 'Tis a fright, surely.

MRS. HARTE *(impressively)*. But don't be thinking at all, Mary, that because I'd be against my own sister following my example, that 'tis sorry I am, or Michael either, for our bargain.

MRS. O'CONNOR. But didn't Maurice win a share o' money in prizes and the like from time to time? Didn't I see his name on the newspapers again and again, and sure you showed me the cheques yourself?

MRS. HARTE. I did so, but they're only trifles in the end. What is a matter of five pounds or even ten pounds now and again?

MRS. O'CONNOR. That's true. . . . Oh, 'tis a fright entirely, and whatever fine notions Diarmuid and myself had for Patrick 'tis cured of them for ever we are from this day out. Well, may the Lord spare Maurice to pay it back to ye on the double![12]

MRS. HARTE. Whisht! Whisht! Here he's up the boreen. Don't pretend anything for the world. He don't know a sign about them books. And we're keeping it from Owen as well. *(Hastily wraps up books and put them into drawer of dresser.)*

MRS. O'CONNOR. There's no fear 'twill ever pass my lips.

MRS. HARTE. Ssh! Ssh!

(Maurice comes in. He is about twenty-two. His dress is the clerical broadcloth and collar of a Maynooth student in minor orders.[13] He has remarkably large dark eyes set in the pale intellectual features of an overwrought student. His expression gives one a sense of mental unrest. He has a large volume in his hand. Mrs. O'Connor gets up ready to leave.)

MAURICE. Good day, aunt. 'Tisn't running off you are, surely?

MRS. O'CONNOR. I left a cake in the pot-oven nearly half an hour ago, and 'tis destroyed 'twill be if I wait another minute, so you'll excuse me.

MAURICE *(half indifferently)*. Oh, very well, very well.

12. **on the double** doubly   13. **collar . . . minor orders** a variation on the Roman collar worn by clerical students in the preliminary stages of preparing for the priesthood

(Mrs. O'Connor goes out. Maurice throws himself into a chair near the open window. Mrs. Harte goes to the table and takes the box-iron[14] from the stand. She then goes to the fire-place, removes a heater from the fire, and inserts it in the box. She returns to the table.)

MAURICE. You're not going to iron, surely, on such a hot day, mother?

MRS. HARTE. Oh, 'tis only your father's shirt, and a collar or two for yourself. They'll only take me a short while.

MAURICE. Even so, wouldn't it be much better to wait till the cool of the evening?

MRS. HARTE. Oh, there's no time like the daylight for making up the linen. I often tried it by candlelight, an' 'tis quite proud of myself I'd be, seeing the collars and they so white and stiff, an' the grand gloss on them, an' maybe next morning 'tis a fright I'd get when I'd see the way they'd be. My sight isn't as good, I'm thinking, as it used to be. . . . But 'tisn't at the study you're going to be again, Maurice?

MAURICE. Why not?

MRS. HARTE. They're cutting the oats above at your uncle's, and they'll be expecting you; you ought to take a walk east before the dinner, if only for the fresh air.

MAURICE. Not now—not now. Later on, maybe.

MRS. HARTE. I tell you 'twould be a lot better for you than to be bending over them books. 'Tis no wonder the neighbours are making remarks about the way you're looking lately.

MAURICE *(startled)*. Remarks! How?

MRS. HARTE. Sure, glory be to God, you need only look at the glass to find out. Look at the colour that's on you this minute—you that used to have the fine, red, blushy cheeks. . . . Them books are killing you. Morning, noon and night you're over them.

MAURICE. Oh, nonsense.

MRS. HARTE. Faith, 'tis no nonsense at all, Maurice; you'll be sorry yet. 'Tisn't much comfort your great honours will be to yourself or to us if you lose your health over them.

MAURICE. I gave you credit for more sense, mother, than to mind what people say.

MRS. HARTE. And neither do I, except when they say the very thing that's on my own mind. . . . Throw them aside for this week, anyway? Sure, 'tis only a matter of a few days now till you'll be back in the College again; *(with warm conviction)* and the Lord knows 'tis plenty o' the books you'll get up there—and maybe too much!

(Maurice gives a slight laugh.)

MRS. HARTE *(laying down her iron)*. Sure, if you don't care to take a

---

14. **box-iron** smoothing iron with a cavity to contain a heater

turn[15] east to the mowing, you might take out the little mare, as she's idle, and go for a bit of a ride up to the mountain, or you might be riding to the town to see if any letters came for you by the evening post—or be doing anything at all rather than be destroying yourself with them blessed books.

MAURICE. This book, mother, I—I should like to tell you about it.

MRS. HARTE *(somewhat ungraciously)*. Yeh, don't mind. To tell you the truth I'd rather a lot to see you above with the men in the corn-field, and you making diversions for[16] them, the same as you used to be every other year. Sure, what they're saying now is that you're getting a bit proud and distant in yourself for the last year or so.

MAURICE *(with a slight laugh)*. Proud! Proud, is it?

MRS. HARTE. Sure, glory be to goodness, you used to be the life and soul o' the place when you came home every other year?

MAURICE *(gravely)*. If I am changed I cannot help it. Circumstances are not always the same.

MRS. HARTE. No, surely. 'Twould hardly do, I suppose, for one that's nearly a priest now, to be too—too airy like in himself? But sure, not minding that at all, 'tis enough to give anyone a pain in the heart to see the poor appetite you have lately. Your father and Owen would go through as much in one meal as you would in a month. *(Going to him.)* Here, now, throw away that book, and be off with yourself!

MAURICE *(with a mirthless laugh)*. Very well, very well. But you'll give me just a few minutes to tell you what I've been reading? You'll not grudge me that time, will you?

MRS. HARTE. Yeh, I haven't learning enough to understand the things that would be in such a great book as that.

MAURICE. Oh, nonsense! Why, a child could understand it. It is only a novel—a mere story—and a very simple one at that. I got it from Father Mangan.

MRS. HARTE *(surprised)*. A novel, is it? An' would the priest be reading the like o' that?

MAURICE. Of course. Why not?

MRS. HARTE *(innocently)*. But, Maurice, sure them story-books do be all lies, and love, and the like o' that?

MAURICE. This is a true story.

MRS. HARTE *(dimly curious)*. Is it, now? Well!

MAURICE *(uncertainly)*. 'Tis about a country boy, the—the son of a farmer in middling circumstances. His name was—let me see? *(turns hastily a few pages.)* It doesn't matter about his name—but from his earliest years he was a rare[17] lad at his books.

15. **take a turn** set out   16. **making diversions for** entertaining   17. **rare** gifted

MRS. HARTE. Sure, and to do his best he couldn't be more gifted than you were, Maurice?

MAURICE *(unheeding)*. It happened one day—he was just twelve at the time—the parish priest visited the school. The teacher pressed him to examine the boy. He did so.

MRS. HARTE. Well, then.

MAURICE *(after a slight pause)*. Those old Jewish rabbis who listened long ago in the Temple to the wisdom of another Boy of twelve,[18] could not have been one bit more astonished than was this parish priest. He turned to the schoolmaster in wonder. "Surely," said he, "God never put such brains into a child's head without some very good purpose!"

MRS. HARTE. Well, well. . . . But sure the bishop, when he came here for the confirmation, singled yourself out from all the rest that was there. And didn't he call over Canon O'Grady and three other priests to hear you answering the catechism. Sure, the like was never known before or since, and everyone in the parish was talking of it. Don't you remember it?

MAURICE *(mechanically nodding assent.)* That evening the schoolmaster went to the boy's parents. He told them what the priest had said, and urged them to give the lad a chance—to send him to college.

MRS. HARTE. And they did, I suppose?

MAURICE. They were only struggling farmers.

MRS. HARTE. Wisha, what a pity now!

MAURICE. The schoolmaster was disappointed. He reasoned with them, he used every argument he could think of—he almost begged them in the end to do as he suggested.

MRS. HARTE. And they wouldn't?

MAURICE. They could ill spare the money.

MRS. HARTE *(genuinely interested)*. Well! well! And what became of him?

MAURICE. The priest himself came to the boy's father.

MRS. HARTE. He did, now?

MAURICE. Yes, and he—he succeeded where the schoolmaster failed.

MRS. HARTE *(in surprise)*. Well, now, look at that! The priests have great power surely. Sure, only for Father Mangan 'tis long till we'd think of sending yourself to the college either.

MAURICE. You see, he assured the parents that their boy would practically pay his own way if they sent him for the Church.

MRS. HARTE. Father Mangan prophesied the *very same thing* about yourself. . . . And what way did he get on, now?

MAURICE. Oh, very well, indeed—almost brilliantly—till—till *(he be-*

18. **another Boy of twelve** Jesus (Luke, 2: 41–52)

comes slightly confused)—let me see? Yes—till some eight or nine years had passed.

MRS. HARTE. Sure, by right he should be ordained by that time—or else he'd be very near it, judging by yourself?

MAURICE. There's the sorrow of it, mother. . . . He—he was never ordained.

MRS. HARTE. Glory! he wasn't?

MAURICE. No.

MRS. HARTE. Yeh, an' why so at all? 'Twasn't how he died?

MAURICE. No, though it would have been better for him—a thousand times better!—if he had. He found too late he—he had no vocation.[19]

MRS. HARTE. Well! Well! Well!

MAURICE *(with hidden emotion).* He—he couldn't face home. He couldn't endure to see the disappointment of—of those who—who had built all the hopes of their life on him.

MRS. HARTE. 'Twas terrible entirely, and he to go so far. And all that was lost on him!—and his poor people only in a middling fair kind of way, you tell me, like ourselves? But what became of him?

MAURICE. What became of him? He—he—I don't quite know *(he becomes nervous and confused)*—you see the—the end of the story isn't known to me yet—I'll soon be at the last chapter, . . . but I should think it will end by—by his going off to America.

MRS. HARTE. Oh, Maurice, wouldn't it be wrong of him entirely to do that? Sure the neighbours would be thinking everything queer of him— or that he did some disgraceful thing, maybe—and he not to show himself at home. And his poor people, hadn't they plenty trouble in their hearts, God help them, without that suspicion to be on their boy? 'Tis the sad story, surely. And you tell me 'tis all true.

MAURICE. Too true, mother.

MRS. HARTE. Well, well, 'tis little any man or woman knows, and they rising up in the dawn, what's between them an' the next dawn.

(There is a short pause.)

MAURICE *(with a laugh).* Mother, if—if that happened to me—if I walked in that door to you one day with that poor fellow's story—what would you say?

MRS. HARTE *(laughingly).* Well, indeed, 'twould be very hard for me to tell that. *(More seriously.)* I suppose I'd try to say, "Welcome be the will o' God," but they'd be the hardest words, surely, that ever came out of a woman's mouth. *(Fervently.)* But thank God and His Blessed Mother this day, 'tisn't that way with us, Maurice! . . . The poor old people, wasn't it the cruel blow entirely for them. God help us! God help us!

19. **vocation** personal call from God

MAURICE *(after a slight pause).* And the wretched student himself, mother?

MRS. HARTE *(lightly).* Wisha, the young get over these things in a short time. . . . But sure, it may be that he suffered his share, too?

MAURICE. Suffered? Suffered, is it, mother? What agony he endured no one knows but himself and his Maker!

MRS. HARTE *(in surprise).* God help us! isn't it thankful to God people ought to be when the trouble keeps away from their doors?

MAURICE *(with intensity of feeling).* Mother, he often wished he had never been born.

MRS. HARTE. Yeh, an' why didn't he go on, so?

MAURICE *(in profound astonishment).* Why, surely, you wouldn't have him take Orders without a vocation?

MRS. HARTE *(dryly).* Oh, sure, it might come to him in time. There's no fear but it would. God is good. 'Tis only talk about a vocation?

MAURICE *(shocked).* What! *Talk—only talk* about a vocation?

MRS. HARTE. Yeh, don't take me up like that! Sure, what I only meant to say was this——

MAURICE. I'm amazed at you! Why, mother, a priest without a vocation is a—a traitor to God and to man. Every priestly function he performs is, in a sense, sacrilege. He had escaped that horror, and it was that one thought alone saved him from madness. . . . Surely, mother, he did the right thing in the end? *(Appealingly.)* You think so—don't you?

MRS. HARTE. But, sure, 'twas the queer thing entirely for him, Maurice, to be going on and on like that year after year, deceiving his own an' deceiving everyone else? If he was that great scholar you tell me, wouldn't he know his own mind long before that?

MAURICE. He *did* know it—he knew it well, but you see, he—he was wretchedly sensitive—constitutionally so—and he—he hadn't the courage to confess it.

MRS. HARTE *(censoriously).* Oh, sure, there was no sense at all in that! . . . *(Wonderingly.)* And would yourself be taking pity on the like of him, Maurice?

MAURICE. Oh, surely, surely.

MRS. HARTE. Well, maybe you're right. 'Tis hard to be finding fault with anyone, and people shouldn't be saying anything but be thankful to God 'tisn't their own story. . . . Listen to them calves outside. A sup o' sweet milk they're wanting. They've almost the sense of a Christian, God bless them. *(She takes a can of milk and goes toward the open door.)* The poor people, 'twas a terrible blow for them. *(As she steps outside her voice can be heard calling to the calves.)*

MAURICE *(he flinging the book from him in self-disgust).* I'll . . . *(rises suddenly, strides towards the door, and hesitates).* Yet, my God, how can I do

it? *(He returns to his place, and sits down, speaking in distracted whispers.)*
What shall I do! What shall I do at all? Merciful God, direct me!

(He sits in troubled thought, his hands to his brow. He is in this attitude when Father Mangan appears in the doorway and walks in. Father Mangan is a bright, genial-tempered warm-complexioned little man of about sixty-five. He has a newspaper in one hand, in the other he carries a walking-stick.)

FATHER MANGAN *(breezily)*. Good-day, Maurice.

MAURICE *(with a slight start)*. Oh, good-day, Father Mangan.

FATHER MANGAN *(with a twinkle)*. Day-dreaming, I see?—or is it formulating a thesis for the D.D.?[20] *(Maurice forces a smile.)* Ah, Maurice, my boy, 'tis matter for confession[21] to be indoors on such a day as this. I shook a dozen years off my old shoulders the moment I stepped outside the hall door this morning.

MAURICE *(with sudden resolve)*. Strange, Father, you are the one person of all the world I wanted to see this minute.

FATHER MANGAN. There, now, and I just wanted to see you, too. I'll expect you up about four tomorrow evening. Father John Burke is driving over, and Hackett and a few young scoundrels like yourself, to make war to the knife[22] on those fat chickens your good mother sent up on Saturday last. . . . But you wanted to see me?

MAURICE *(with earnest conviction)*. 'Twas God Himself directed you here. . . . Father Mangan, I'm about to beg a great favour of you?

FATHER MANGAN. Granted already, boy.

MAURICE *(after a pause)*. I'm—I'm in trouble, Father—in terrible trouble.

FATHER MANGAN. Trouble, is it, Maurice? *You?*

MAURICE. Trouble that is killing me, body and soul.

FATHER MANGAN. God bless us, boy, don't say that! If you've been plucked for[23] your degree, or anything like that——

MAURICE. No, no! Oh, no, no! Would to God it were only something like that! . . . Oh, Father, isn't it a terrible thing to be fated to bring life-long sorrow on those whom one—one cares most for in the world?

FATHER MANGAN *(mystified)*. 'Tis, surely, boy, but I—I really don't understand what it has to do with you. What is wrong?

MAURICE. Oh, everything—everything is wrong! . . . Father Mangan, God help me, I—I have no vocation.

FATHER MANGAN *(aghast)*. My God, Maurice!

MAURICE *(sadly)*. 'Tis true.

FATHER MANGAN. Don't say it, boy—don't say it! 'Tis some insane delusion.

20. **D.D.** Doctor of Divinity, a theological degree   21. **matter for confession** a sin   22. **make war to the knife** usually "with the knife": to eat heartily   23. **been plucked for** failed

MAURICE *(dejectedly)*. 'Tis no delusion, Father. 'Tis only too true.

FATHER MANGAN. Oh, nonsense, man, I won't believe it! 'Tis folly—'tis downright folly. Some absurd scruples you have that are easily got over. Why, man, 'tis out of the question at this hour.

MAURICE. Father——

FATHER MANGAN *(emphatically)*. I won't listen to it! 'Tis madness!

MAURICE *(quietly)*. There is no use, Father. There isn't a doubt in my mind.

FATHER MANGAN. Oh, nonsense.

MAURICE. My conscience——

FATHER MANGAN. Rubbish, Maurice, rubbish! Why every great saint in the Church had these misgivings. It is one of the best proofs of a true vocation. Those who never have these scruples make but indifferent priests.

MAURICE. That may be so, Father, but——

FATHER MANGAN. I won't listen to any "buts." My God, man, I never knew in all my experience a young fellow cut out so distinctly for the ministry as yourself! . . . Look here, Maurice, *(placing his hand paternally on his shoulder)*, take my advice and go down there to the chapel, and go on your knees, and talk to Him who is waiting there to comfort you. In His divine mercy He will dispel every doubt that is darkening your mind, and you'll come back to me like him who was blind and recovered his sight. Do, Maurice. . . . Do, my poor fellow.

MAURICE. There is no use, Father. You don't understand the whole truth.

FATHER MANGAN. How? How?

MAURICE. 'Tisn't to-day nor yesterday I—I realized my own nature. . . . But I buried my wretched secret in my soul. . . . Those two, my poor father and mother, I thought to tell them again and again. But my heart failed in the attempt. I can defer it no longer. It must be told them this day—this very hour.

FATHER MANGAN. I am shocked—I am simply overwhelmed. Think, boy, of the misery, the—the heartbreaking disappointment.

MAURICE. Think? *Think,* Father? . . . *(Bitterly.)* Many a night have I lain down in my bed in Maynooth, and my eye and my mind never closed till I heard intoned the *Benedicamus Domino.*[24]

FATHER MANGAN *(moved)*. Poor fellow! Poor fellow!

MAURICE *(wistfully)*. Father, you'll—you'll help me to—to break it to them?

FATHER MANGAN. Look here, Maurice, my poor boy. I'm an old man, with an old man's life experience. Don't act precipitately. Don't, I beg of you. Let us talk it over to-night. I'm too disturbed to reason calmly now.

24. *Benedicamus Domino* "Let us bless the Lord": morning call

The mercy of God is beyond our thoughts. Wait just a little longer, boy. Make up your mind to that. You must wait.

MAURICE *(half passionately)*. No, Father, no! Waiting has been the curse of my life. I have waited too long. I will not wait any longer. *(Mrs. Harte is seen slowly passing the window outside.)* There! she's coming now, and I know 'tis God himself that sends her.

FATHER MANGAN. You shall not!—You must not! To-morrow—to-night—any time but now.

MAURICE. No! No!

FATHER MANGAN *(earnestly)*. Only half an hour's time? I tell you, you must.

MAURICE *(doggedly)*. I cannot. I will not, Father.

FATHER MANGAN *(in low, earnest tones)*. You *must*, Maurice. Look, I beg of you! If you don't, I—I shall never be your friend again.

MAURICE. I don't care. I must, Father.

(Mrs. Harte appears at the door. Seeing the priest, she comes in with bustling eagerness.)

MRS. HARTE. Wisha, Father Mangan, and is it there you are? And, Maurice, aren't you queer not to take the priest down in the parlour? Tch! tch! tch!

FATHER MANGAN. My dear woman, your kitchen is good enough for the Queen herself, not to mind a plain old man like Father Mangan. 'Tis a lot better than my own.

MAURICE *(quiveringly)*. Mother?

MRS. HARTE. Well, Maurice?

MAURICE. Do you think you—you could bear to hear bad news from me—very bad news?

MRS. HARTE. The Lord save us! What bad news would I be hearing at all?

FATHER MANGAN *(striving to divert her attention)*. Bad news enough for you, then, this day, and for many another man and woman in this parish. Pork that has fallen—eh—six shillings a hundredweight, and flour that's up three shillings a sack.

MRS. HARTE *(to Father Mangan)*. That's bad, surely, Father, and Michael with six pigs at the fair[25] to-day—and the yellow meal[26] nearly a pound a bag all along. . . . But sure, thank God, after all 'tis nothing worse!

MAURICE. Mother, it *is* worse——

FATHER MANGAN *(breaking in)*. Now, couldn't you keep it from her? Mrs. Harte, it is worse. . . . Look at this paper. *(Unfolds newspaper.)* See here—butter and eggs going down, I may say, to nothing. 'Tis on account of the Australian trade——

---

25. **fair** farmer's market   26. **yellow meal** American corn meal, ground maize

MRS. HARTE. Oh, glory! Sure 'tis destroyed in earnest we'll all be so, Father?

MAURICE *(arrestingly)*. Mother——

FATHER MANGAN *(abruptly seizing her arm)*. Look! Mrs. Harte. Look over there—there beyond the well-field! Aren't those your cows in Kenny's clover?

MRS. HARTE. Oh, blessed hour!

FATHER MANGAN. Up at the sessions[27] you'll be again for trespass as sure as I'm alive!

MRS. HARTE *(in a state of trepidation)*. Oh, we'll be destroyed entirely this time. A torment to them for heifers! Like wild deer they are for going over the bounds *(going)*.

MAURICE. Mother? Mother? Just one moment.

MRS. HARTE *(on the doorstep)*. I'll be back in half a minute. My heart is up in my mouth with the fright.

(She goes away hurriedly. Maurice sits down dejectedly. He remains silent, with drooped head. There is a pause.)

FATHER MANGAN *(going to him)*. Come, come, boy, I did it for the best. Don't be offended, Maurice. Hardened as I am I was not quite prepared to see that poor woman's desolation. . . . Come up to the house. We'll be alone there. We can thrash the whole matter out, and see what is best to be done. . . . *(Tenderly.)* Come, Maurice. Come, boy. *(Maurice stands up dejectedly.)* That's right . . . That's right, Maurice.

(They both go out. Mrs. Harte returns out of breath. She sits down to recover herself. Her sister comes in a few moments after. She has a grocer's parcel in her hand.)

MRS. O'CONNOR *(entering)*. O'Brien's van that called above while I was out, and he left this for you. I thought I'd run down with it for fear you might be wanting anything that's in it *(lays down parcel)*. Yeh, what's the matter with you at all?

MRS. HARTE *(half gaspingly)*. Don't talk to me till—till I get my breath.

MRS. O'CONNOR. The Lord save us!

MRS. HARTE *(after a pause)*. Such a start! I'm not worth anything after it!

MRS. O'CONNOR. The breath is gone from you altogether.

MRS. HARTE. Such a queer thing. Father Mangan he was standing there. "Look," says he (we were talking about the rise in flour, or something), "look at your cows east there in Kenny's clover!"

MRS. O'CONNOR. That was terrible—so soon again.

MRS. HARTE. I ran till I was nearly dead, there was that fright in my heart. And what do you think, Ellen?—there wasn't the sign of a cow or even one heifer out o' bounds.

27. **Up at the sessions** summoned to appear in court

MRS. O'CONNOR. That was very strange entirely. . . . But he's getting a bit old, and the sight mightn't be too good with him.

MRS. HARTE. That's likely enough. He's getting slow at the Mass, too. The years are beginning to tell on him, God bless him. But he took the heart out o' me with the fright.

MRS. O'CONNOR. Faith, and no wonder. You'll be wanting to keep a good eye on them cows all the same. Once they get the taste of the young clover mad out[28] they do be for it. . . . There's a car[29] after stopping outside.

MRS. HARTE. Michael and Owen, I suppose, that's after coming from the fair.

MRS. O'CONNOR *(looking out)*. Sure enough, 'tis themselves.

(Michael Harte comes in. He is a fresh-faced, mild-looking man, with light-blue eyes, and fair hair and beard.)

MRS. O'CONNOR. 'Tis early in the day you're home, Michael. How were prices? I see you sold.

MICHAEL. Bad then. Very bad. Everyone was complaining. A lot more people brought home their pigs than sold them.

MRS. O'CONNOR. Well, well, that's a bad story.

MICHAEL. I saw your neighbour above, the Widow Carroll, about a mile outside the town, an' she bringing home her little pig again.

MRS. O'CONNOR *(with feeling)*. Wisha, God help us! Sure one o' the loneliest things in the world is to see a poor widow woman like that with her little donkey an' crib,[30] an' her slip of a pig not sold, an' she coming home the long road by herself after the fair.

MICHAEL. 'Tis so.

MRS. O'CONNOR. Well, the Lord send that prices will be up against the next fair. We're expecting to have a couple o' stores[31] fattened by then. But you're killed with the hunger, I'm sure.

(She goes out. Mrs. Harte, who has been busy preparing the meal, suddenly suspends her work and comes to Michael. She speaks with the eagerness of one whose curiosity had to be repressed in the presence of a third party.)

MRS. HARTE. Well, and how did you get on at all?

MICHAEL. Middling then, Ellen. Middling.

MRS. HARTE *(disappointed)*. But didn't you pay him the fifteen pounds out o' what you got for the pigs?

MICHAEL. I did, of course. But he wasn't satisfied with that at all.

MRS. HARTE. He wasn't, is it? Wisha, bad manners to him! . . . Don't tell me you had to sign that note of his, Michael.

MICHAEL. I had so. I held out tough as long as I could, but 'twas no use.

---

28. **mad out** very mad   29. **car** horsedrawn sidecar   30. **crib** small donkey cart with high sides   31. **stores** young cattle ready for fattening

MRS. HARTE *(hotly)*. 'Tis the bad right then, James McCarthy had to make you do that! Many the pound of our money he got for the last twenty years! . . . I'm sorry in my heart I didn't go with you, Michael. 'Tis long till he'd get you to do it and I to be there. You're always too soft and easy going. Wasn't it a good thing for him to be getting his fifteen pounds all in a lump?

MICHAEL. 'Twas so. But, you see, he looked at it a very different way from us, Ellen.

MRS. HARTE. An' what different way could he look at it?

MICHAEL. He made out 'twas as good as insulting him making such a small payment, and the money that's on us to be so heavy. "If you don't wish to sign that note," says he, "you needn't. It don't matter at all to me one way or the other, for before the next Quarter Sessions 'tis Andy Driscoll, the process server, will be marching up to your door." So what could I do but sign?

MRS. HARTE *(solemnly)*. As long as I live I'll never again in my life take as much as one ha'porth[32] from him!—that's as true as if I swore it. . . . *(Reproachfully.)* But 'tis your fault, Michael, taking him so easy.[33] That's plain to be seen.

MICHAEL. When your hand is in the dog's mouth, Ellen, 'tis better to draw it out easy. James McCarthy knows well he can be very stiff in himself with all that money on us.

MRS. HARTE. Maybe he can, an' maybe he can't! . . . Ah, sure, you made a great mistake entirely letting him slip that rope round our necks.

MICHAEL. Sure, what could I do?

MRS. HARTE. Yeh, couldn't you let on your hand was sprained or something like that. You're no way knowing at all, Michael. But sure 'tis idle talking when the harm is done.

MICHAEL. Yeh, Ellen, you don't understand at all the way he went on over it. Wild out he was. And when I told how Owen would be settling down next year and a tidy fortune coming in to us, what he did was to shake his head an' say, "Live horse, Michael Harte, and you'll eat grass."

MRS. HARTE. Glory be to God! One would think 'tis robbers we were! And we that never in our lives wronged anyone as much as the black o' your nail.

MICHAEL. So, then, I thought I'd explain to him the terrible expenses Maurice was to us all along, and how that would be all over next June, and, with the help o' God, a share o' money likely to be coming in to us instead of going out.

MRS. HARTE. Well, an' didn't that quieten him?

32. **ha'porth** halfpenny worth: very little   33. **taking him so easy** being so civil with him

MICHAEL. *Quieten him,* is it? Why, 'twas how he turned on me in a red passion. "And isn't it a scandal, Michael Harte," says he, "for the likes o' you, with your name on them books there for a hundred and fifty pounds, and you with only the grass of nine or ten cows, to be making your son a priest? The like of it," says he, "was never heard of before."

MRS. HARTE *(overwhelmed).* Glory be to God! *(Hotly.)* The bostoon![34] What business was it of his, I'd like to know? Jealous of us, he is! There's no fear any of *his* sons will ever be anything much! Laughing at them the others used to be and they in the college. Maurice himself that often told me. *(Reproachfully.)* But 'tis your fault entirely, Michael. You're too quiet in yourself dealing with the like of him.

MICHAEL. Maybe so, maybe so. But I was afraid, like, it might be the means o' creating talk; and I was thinking it might do Maurice some harm with the Bishop if it came out on the papers that we were up before the judge for a civil bill.

MRS. HARTE *(reflectively).* Well, now, looking at it that way, maybe you weren't very far astray.

MICHAEL *(encouraged).* And do you know, Ellen, I was thinking of a great way entirely out o' the trouble an' I coming home?

MRS. HARTE *(hopefully).* Wisha, maybe you were?

MICHAEL. What I was saying to myself was that as we're in such great want o' the money, if we tried to get Owen settled down after the harvest instead of waiting till next year. The fortune would come in just in time to meet the bill?

MRS. HARTE *(decidedly).* Oh, there's no sense in that at all.

MICHAEL. An' why so, now?

MRS. HARTE *(with a touch of anger).* God knows, Michael, 'twill be soon enough for the two of us, after all our years, to see another woman mistress of this house!

MICHAEL. 'Twill, sure enough.

MRS. HARTE. But 'tisn't that altogether, maybe, so much as another thing. . . . 'Tisn't once or twice I told you that I had my heart set on hearing Maurice say the marriage words over his own brother. Whatever the bill will do there'll be no marriage in this house till the ordination. 'Twas the great misfortune you to sign that note. *(With a twinge of conscience.)* But sure, you did what you could, poor man, and 'tis weak you must be with the hunger. What's keeping Owen so long?

MICHAEL. I left him to untackle the horse, and he said he'd ride her down to the well to give her a drink. Here he is now.

(Owen comes in. He looks about thirty. He is a good-looking young fellow, has a bright, ruddy complexion, and a head of crisp dark curls. There is a suggestion of soft, shy pleasantry in the expression of the eyes.)

34. **bostoon** ignoramus, boor

OWEN *(on the doorstep)*. There's old Tom Kenny walking round already to see if anything happened while he was at the fair. I hope you kept a good eye on them vagabonds of cows of ours, mother?

MRS. HARTE. Don't talk to me about them!

OWEN. For the Lord's sake don't say 'tis how they went out o' bounds again?

MRS. HARTE *(in the manner of a story-teller)*. I was giving a sup[35] o' milk to the calves outside in the haggart.[36] When I came back here who was before me but the priest himself and he conversing with Maurice. He turned to talk to me for a little bit—telling me he was about the bad prices at the markets—when something made him look out that window. "Look! Look, woman!" says he, all of a sudden, "aren't them your cows gone over the bounds' ditch?"[37]

MICHAEL. Almighty! that was a fright.

MRS. HARTE. The eyes spread on me, and I nearly lost my life running. But when I came to the place, sure, thanks be to God! there wasn't a cow nor a heifer but was safe inside in the rath field.

OWEN. A mistake he made.

MRS. HARTE. Mary was saying 'twas how the sight was beginning to fail a bit with him. I got such a start I wasn't worth anything after it. . . . Here, sit down and be eating now. 'Tis dead with the hunger ye must be, and the two of ye on the road since daybreak. *(They sit down at the table.)*

OWEN. We're in fine humour for it, I tell you, mother.

MICHAEL. 'Tis seldom now I felt so hungry before.

(They begin the meal and have eaten only a mouthful when Father Mangan appears in the open doorway.)

MRS. HARTE *(apologetically)*. There's bother for you now, Father Mangan, coming back for your stick. I was going to send it up by Owen the minute he was done.

FATHER MANGAN. Oh, thanks, thanks. I quite I forgot I had left it here.

(Michael and Owen rise from the table.)

FATHER MANGAN. Sit down—sit down, Michael. Sit down, Owen. Don't let me disturb you.

OWEN. We were just finished, Father.

MICHAEL. I could hardly eat another bite if I was paid for it.

FATHER MANGAN. Oh, very well, then, very well. . . . I just ran down to see yourself and Michael on—a little private matter. *(Owen goes out.)*

MICHAEL *(handing him a chair)*. Sit down, Father.

FATHER MANGAN. Thanks, Michael, thanks.

---

35. **sup** small drink　36. **haggart** farmyard　37. **ditch** raised earthen fence covered with bushes

(He sits down. There is a slight pause.)

FATHER MANGAN. As I was coming along the lane up to the house do you know what I was puzzling at? Trying to reckon the years that have passed since I stepped inside this door.

MICHAEL. 'Twould be no small share o' time, I'm thinking, Father.

MRS. HARTE. 'Tis I can tell that, for 'twas the very night Maurice was born. Twenty-two years this Michaelmas[38] it is. You remember we had to send for you to baptize him in the house—the women thought he'd die he was such a weak little bit of a child—and you were only in the parish since that morning.

FATHER MANGAN. That's so. I remember now. *(There is another pause.)*

MICHAEL *(smiling)*. You put the good hand on him that night, Father?

MRS. HARTE. Michael never said truer words. 'Tis often on my two knees I thank God that sent you to us, for only for you, Father, 'tis a common boy working on the farm Maurice would likely be this day.

FATHER MANGAN *(enigmatically)*. Maybe, Mrs. Harte, it would have been better for him—and better for you—and better for us all?

MICHAEL *(protestingly)*. God bless us, Father, don't say that at all! We don't deny the money came a bit heavy on us all along—but sure that's as good as over now.

MRS. HARTE *(suspiciously)*. Father Mangan, someone with a long tongue is after telling you about Michael signing that note in the town to-day. . . . Don't be thinking, Father, that either one or the other of us is ever regretting the bit o' money that's lost on Maurice, or is anything but thankful to God this minute that we followed your advice.

MICHAEL. 'Tis the truth she's telling you, Father.

FATHER MANGAN *(passing his hand uneasily over his brow)*. I believe you, but—but——

MRS. HARTE. Sure—not interrupting you, Father, 'tis many a strong farmer in your parish puts his name to a note as well as Michael. And Owen's wife will be bringing in a decent fortune next year, so there's no fear the thought of it will ever come between us and our night's rest.

MICHAEL *(earnestly)*. To tell you the honest truth, if it was twice as much expense he was we'd still be more than thankful to ourselves.

FATHER MANGAN. I know that, Michael, I know, but——

MRS. HARTE *(impressively)*. Father Mangan, I'm a strong, healthy woman, with a healthy woman's appetite, and yet I could live for the rest o' my days on a bit o' bread and a sup o' sour milk for the wonderful joy that comes rushing down on me night and day, and I thinking of him a priest of God like yourself.

FATHER MANGAN *(hesitatingly)*. One—one can never be sure—quite sure, Mrs. Harte.

38. **Michaelmas** September 29

MICHAEL. That's true, then. 'Tis many a man and woman that's called away[39] in nine months or ten.

MRS. HARTE *(optimistically)*. Oh, God is good. The Hartes were always a long-lived family. Michael's father here—the Lord have mercy on him!—was over ninety when he died, and his mother, God rest her soul, was long past eighty, and 'twas just the same with my own people. Maurice has the tough, wholesome breed in him, Father, and that's everything.

FATHER MANGAN *(awkwardly)*. Yes—yes, but—but, you see, there are possible accidents—accidents of another nature that sometimes befall those—those going for the Church. Many a young man has discovered almost on the—the very threshold of his ordination, that he has no real vocation.

MICHAEL *(with conviction)*. They must be *bad*, Father, and to be like that!

FATHER MANGAN. Oh, no! no! no! Don't think that at all, Michael. It is quite otherwise.

MRS. HARTE. 'Tisn't for a mother to be saying it, Father, but sure Maurice is a born saint if ever there was one.

FATHER MANGAN. He is, but he has one fault, poor fellow.

MRS. HARTE *(taken aback)*. Has he, now?

FATHER MANGAN. A very grave fault.

MICHAEL. Yeh, Father.

MRS. HARTE. Is it Maurice, Father?

FATHER MANGAN *(after a pause)*. 'Tis a good thing for any son to love his parents, and to feel for them. 'Tis a bad thing for a son to love and feel for them so intensely that he fears to—to tell them of a disease that is eating his heart in secret.

MRS. HARTE *(vaguely uneasy)*. Is there anything wrong with Maurice, Father?

FATHER MANGAN. Wrong?

MRS. HARTE. For the love o' God, if there is tell us!

FATHER MANGAN. The two of you must promise me first——

MICHAEL. What bad news have you, Father?

MRS. HARTE *(trembling)*. Father, Father, don't keep me in this state! What's wrong with Maurice?

FATHER MANGAN *(after a slight pause)*. I'm sorry to tell you he's not returning to Maynooth. He has asked me to break it to you. He has no vocation.

(They look at him in stupefied amazement. There is a painful pause.)

MRS. HARTE *(hoarsely)*. 'Tis not true, Father.

FATHER MANGAN. It is, indeed, poor woman—only too true.

39. **called away** dies

MRS. HARTE *(crushed)*. A Mhuire![40] Mhuire! Mhuire!

FATHER MANGAN *(deeply moved)*. God help ye, poor people, I'm sorry in my soul for this!

MRS. HARTE *(in a high note of despair)*. A Mhuire! Mhuire! Mhuire!

FATHER MANGAN. Don't, Mrs. Harte, don't. You must try to be more patient. . . . Think of Mary and her Seven Sorrows.[41]

MRS. HARTE *(wildly)*. Don't give me any of that talk, Father, and my heart breaking! What did we ever do to God that He should give us this blow?

MICHAEL *(gently)*. Whisht, Ellen, whisht.

MRS. HARTE. The curse o' the Lord is on this house this day! . . . *(In sudden desperation.)* You must make him go back, Father! For the love of Christ you'll do it. Won't you? Won't you?

FATHER MANGAN. I have already done all that any man could do.

MICHAEL *(piteously)*. Talk to him again, Father?

FATHER MANGAN. There is no use, Michael. His mind is finally made up. There is no moving him. You might as well try to move that mountain beyond.

MRS. HARTE *(in a strained, unfamiliar voice)*. Do you know what it is you're saying at all, Father? Would you kill us dead this day?

FATHER MANGAN *(raising his hand as if to reason with her)*. Mrs. Harte——

MRS. HARTE *(hysterically)*. No! No! I won't believe it! I won't, till I hear it from his own two lips.

FATHER MANGAN *(persuasively)*. Mrs. Harte——

MRS. HARTE. I won't! I won't! I won't! He couldn't do it—he couldn't! You don't know him as we do. He couldn't—No! No! No!

FATHER MANGAN. Don't blind yourself with false hopes. 'Tis very hard, I know, but God has His own wise ends in everything. . . . Take the poor fellow gently. 'Tis wrong, remember, to interfere in such a matter. God comfort you both this day.

(He goes out slowly. They sit in dreary silence. There is a long pause.)

MRS. HARTE *(with a sob)*. Oh, Michael, Michael, isn't it terrible, terrible, altogether! . . . The Lord in Heaven pity us, 'tis the cruellest blow He ever sent on any man or woman since the beginning o' the world!

(There is another pause. Owen returns.)

OWEN *(entering)*. Upon my word I thought he'd never go. *(Seating himself at table.)* I'm dead out with the hunger.

(They return no answer.)

OWEN. What's the matter at all?

---

40. **A Mhuire!** O Mary!   41. **Mary and her Seven Sorrows** the sufferings of Mary

(Mrs. Harte gives a broken sob.)

OWEN *(wonderingly)*. In the name o' God what's wrong with ye? What is it, father?

MICHAEL. Your brother that says he won't go back to Maynooth any more.

OWEN. Good God!

MICHAEL. He sent the priest to tell us.

OWEN. And, in God's name, why? Why, father? What happened him at all?

MICHAEL. Nothing. He says something about not having a vocation.

OWEN. Upon my soul, that's the strangest thing I ever heard in all my life! 'Tis mad he must be. Sure no man in his right senses would think o' doing the like o' that. Here he is himself.

(Maurice comes in deadly pale. Michael remains with his back turned to him. Mrs. Harte sits with drooped head, her apron to her eyes. She gives a stifled sob.)

MAURICE *(quiveringly)*. Mother? . . . Father?

(They give no answer.)

MAURICE *(distressfully)*. For God's sake don't let me see you like that. I can't bear it. 'Twill set me mad.

MICHAEL *(after a short pause)*. 'Tisn't true, Maurice?

MAURICE. It is, father. I would to God it weren't so.

MRS. HARTE *(rising with the air of one who has formed a desperate resolution and going to him)*. And with the help o' God it won't be so either, Maurice. *(Persuasively.)* You'll go back again? You will, Maurice? You will, boy?

MAURICE *(bracing himself)*. There is no use. I cannot.

MRS. HARTE. But why? Why, Maurice?

MAURICE. There is no use explaining. You would not understand. It is a matter of conscience.

MRS. HARTE *(striving to subdue her feelings)*. Look here, Maurice. I don't understand that kind o' talk at all.

MICHAEL *(with affected incredulity)*. Yeh, Ellen, 'tis only a passing notion he's got, you'll find. 'Twill be gone out of his mind like a bad dream to-morrow morning.

MAURICE. God help me this hour! I thought he made everything plain for you. He promised he would. . . . *(With impressive deliberation.)* Listen to me. I can never go back. *Never*. It's impossible. . . . *(They look at him imploringly.)* Don't ask me. Don't, don't, I beg of you.

MICHAEL *(gravely)*. Maurice, would you break our hearts?

MAURICE. Father, would you have your son live a life of sacrilege? Would you, father? Would you?

MRS. HARTE. That's only foolish talk. Aren't you every bit as good as the next?

MAURICE. I may be, but I haven't a vocation. . . . God has spoken to me in my soul.

MRS. HARTE. In the name o' the Lord, boy, what kind o' talk at all is that? Aren't you that was ever and always so good and graceful as likely to make as good a priest as Father Kelly over any day? And wouldn't one like you, with all the wonders you did at the learning, make a better priest than many another of them?

MAURICE. That's only a mother's opinion. . . . My mind is finally made up.

MRS. HARTE. Maurice, listen to me—listen to me!

OWEN *(restrainingly)*. Ah, let him alone, mother; let him alone. What's the use?

MRS. HARTE *(passionately)*. What's the use, Owen? What's the use? Is it out o' your mind you are to ask? If it went out about him this day isn't it destroyed for ever we'd be? Look! the story wouldn't be east in Macroom[42] when we'd have the bailiffs walking in that door. The whole world knows he's to be priested next June, and only for the great respect they have for us through the means o' that, 'tisn't James M'Carthy alone, but every other one o' them would come down on us straight for their money. In one week there wouldn't be a cow left by us, nor a horse, nor a lamb, nor anything at all!

OWEN *(incredulously)*. Yeh, not at all, not at all. . . . Leave him alone.

MRS. HARTE. Leave him alone, is it? If I will 'tis you'll have the good cause to regret it! . . . Look at them books *(producing the two account books from drawer)*. 'Tis about time you should know how we stand here.

OWEN *(staggered)*. Is—is this the way 'tis with us?

MRS. HARTE. 'Tis so, and if your brother is going to bring the bailiffs to this house, tell me who's the girl would be willing to walk in here ever after with a fortune? Not Bride Burke, anyway—much as she thinks of you. *(To Maurice.)* God knows, I wouldn't be hard on you at all, but look at the great load o' money that's on us this day, and mostly all on your account.

MAURICE. Mother, don't make my cross harder to bear.

MRS. HARTE. An' would you be seeing a heavier cross put on them that did all that mortal man and woman could do for you?

MAURICE. Look! I'll wear the flesh off my bones, but in pity spare me!

MRS. HARTE *(bitterly)*. And will you have no pity at all on us and on Owen here, that have slaved for you all our lives? And will you have no pity either on your three brothers who sent home, for your sake, the money that they earned in sweat and hard labour in the city of Boston? And, Maurice——

MAURICE. Don't, mother, don't, I beseech you.

42. **Macroom** market town in west Cork

MRS. HARTE. Will you be talking wild, frightening, foolish talk about your conscience, and not think at all of them, nor of us, and all we done for you?

MAURICE (*distressfully*). Mother! Mother!

MRS. HARTE. You'll go back? 'Tis only a mistake?

MAURICE. Great God of Heaven! . . . you'll kill me.

MICHAEL. You'll go back, Maurice? The vocation will come to you in time with the help o' God. It will, surely.

MAURICE. Don't ask me! Don't ask me!

OWEN. 'Twould be better for you, Maurice. 'Twould surely.

MRS. HARTE (*passionately*). If you don't how can I ever face outside this door or lift up my head again?

MAURICE (*piteously*). Mother!

MRS. HARTE. How could I listen to the neighbours making pity for me, and many a one o' them only glad in their hearts? How could I ever face again into the town o' Macroom?

MAURICE. Oh, don't!

MRS. HARTE. I tell you, Maurice, I'd rather be lying dead a thousand times in the graveyard over at Killnamartyra——

MAURICE (*with a sudden cry*). Stop, mother, stop! . . . (*There is a tense pause.*) I'll—I'll go back—as—as you all wish it.

(*He sinks into a seat with an air of hopeless dejection.*)

MICHAEL (*drawing a long, deep breath*). God bless you, boy, for that! I knew you would.

OWEN. 'Tis the best thing, surely.

MRS. HARTE (*kneeling*). Oh, thanks be to the Almighty God and His Blessed Mother this day!

CURTAIN

ACT 2

Nine months later. The same scene. The new window-screens and the general air of things suggest preparations for some event of unusual importance. The rich light of a late afternoon fills the room, but very gradually fades as the action progresses. Mrs. Harte is engaged darning a man's sock when her sister comes in.

MRS. O'CONNOR (*eagerly*). I ran over to know if ye've settled with them. I couldn't do a stir o' work with thinking of it.

MRS. HARTE. 'Tis all settled now, thank God, only the writing of the marriage papers, and if everything goes all right 'tis more than likely they are done by this.

Mrs. O'Connor. That's great.

Mrs. Harte. Michael and Owen, they're to meet the other parties in the town to-day. Eleven o'clock they were to be in Mr. Shannon's office. . . . I'm getting a small bit uneasy. They were expecting to be home a good while before this. You didn't see any sign o' them and you coming down?

Mrs. O'Connor. No, then. But 'tis early yet, and they'd be in no great hurry having the long day.

Mrs. Harte. What I'd be afraid of is that her people might be changing their minds since last night. *(With a sigh.)* A person can't make sure of anything at all in this world.

Mrs. O'Connor. That's true. But didn't they seem agreeable like about the settlement?

Mrs. Harte. Oh, there was no bother at all about that—they agreed to everything at once. 'Tis very thankful to themselves they seemed to be and they leaving.

Mrs. O'Connor. Oh, sure, that's enough! Well, hadn't ye the wonderful luck to meet them? She's a grand girl, and by all accounts she's every bit as good as she's graceful. 'Tis blessed you'll be with her, Ellen.

Mrs. Harte. Wisha, I don't know. 'Tis a lonely thing for a woman after all her years to be giving up everything to the stranger.

Mrs. O'Connor. It is, sure enough.

Mrs. Harte. 'Tis a hard thing, Mary, to be depending on your own son's wife for the handful o' flour, and the bit o' butter, and the drop o' milk, and all the things that used to be ever an' always your own.

Mrs. O'Connor. Yeh, I wouldn't be looking at it that way at all.

Mrs. Harte. 'Tis very easy to talk.

Mrs. O'Connor. Well, of course——

Mrs. Harte. Whatever you say or think, Mary, 'twill be the big change here.

Mrs. O'Connor. But sure, whatever'll happen won't Michael an' yourself have a warm room to yourselves always, an' your own share of butter an' milk, and a small bit o' money every year according to the settlement? And in a couple o' years' time, when ye'll be getting the pension, sure 'tis as stiff as themselves the two of ye can be.

Mrs. Harte. 'Tis the queer feel for all to have only the right to one room in the house that was yours for over forty years.

Mrs. O'Connor. 'Tis, of course, but when a girl has the decent drop o' blood in her like her that's coming here, 'tisn't much a person would notice the change at all.

Mrs. Harte. Maybe so. I don't know.

Mrs. O'Connor *(argumentatively)*. When yourself walked in here, Ellen, and Michael's own mother before you—God rest her soul!—what difference did it make for her?

MRS. HARTE. That's true.

MRS. O'CONNOR. This girl of Owen's, you'll find, she's just like one of ourselves.

MRS. HARTE *(more optimistically)*. Oh, I must say I liked her greatly. She was as nice and as friendly as anyone could be, and she didn't go asking questions about one thing or another, or finding fault with this or that, as many another would do. I took to her very much, somehow, though there was a kind o' pain in my heart all the time.

MRS. O'CONNOR *(dismissing the argument as settled)*. You needn't say another word about her now! What you tell me is enough. 'Tis a little thing shows what kind people are.

(A pause. Mrs. Harte goes to the door, looks toward the high road, shading her eyes, and returns. She seems slightly anxious.)

MRS. O'CONNOR *(taking up the thread of the conversation again)*. And Owen seems to be gone about her altogether?

MRS. HARTE *(with a gesture of scorn)*. Yeh, don't bother me with him! Wild out he's about her. I never saw anyone so foolish out and out. 'Twould upset a person.

MRS. O'CONNOR. I always said 'twould be that way with him, he has that nice, soft, grauvar[43] way with him. When he takes a turn east the children do be wild about him, and you'd see one o' them, maybe, an' they riding his knee, and another, maybe, climbing up his back, and the little fist of him stuck in his curls, and 'tis a hundred miles away they'd keep from their own father. *(Sighing.)* 'Tis often I thought how different they were.

MRS. HARTE. 'Twouldn't do for the father to be too easy with them.

MRS. O'CONNOR. Maybe so. But 'tis bad to be too severe. 'Tis only wild it makes them. . . . But about Owen, is it true about his people-in-law having the big connections?

MRS. HARTE *(with unconscious pride)*. 'Tis so. Dr. Burke over at Carrigdonal is a first cousin of her own.

MRS. O'CONNOR *(surprised)*. Her first cousin, is it?

MRS. HARTE. Owen has her own word for it.

MRS. O'CONNOR *(much impressed)*. Well, well!

MRS. HARTE. But for all that, Mary, don't you think, between ourselves, that the Burkes haven't the worst o' the bargain at all?

MRS. O'CONNOR *(dubiously)*. They haven't, of course. . . . But 'tis a fine fortune, all the same, coming into a place like this, that's not over big altogether.

MRS. HARTE. I don't know, then. I don't think so at all.

MRS. O'CONNOR. Well, then.

43. **grauvar** affectionate

MRS. HARTE. 'Tisn't a penny more than we were expecting. An' 'tis all wanted, as you know yourself. 'Tis only right that Owen should get a fair start after his time.

MRS. O'CONNOR. Oh, sure, of course.

MRS. HARTE. If the farm isn't too big sure 'tis nearly a freehold since we went into the Land Court?[44]

MRS. O'CONNOR. That's true, but for all now, Ellen——

MRS. HARTE *(nettled)*. Isn't a tidy bit of a place like this, with only a trifle of rent on it and every spade of it in good heart,[45] a sight more profitable than a hundred acres o' mountainy land, the like o' that yourself have above?

MRS. O'CONNOR. Maybe you're right and maybe—— *(pulling herself up)*. Well, we won't fall out over it. . . .

(The heavy rumble of a farm cart is heard.)

MRS. O'CONNOR. See, they weren't too long after all.

(Mrs. Harte hurries to the door and looks out eagerly.)

MRS. HARTE *(disappointed)*. Oh, wisha![46] wisha! . . .

MRS. O'CONNOR. What's the matter?

MRS. HARTE. 'Tis only Donal Murphy. . . . *(Hailing someone at a distance)*. Hey, Donal.

(The car jogs on a moment, then stops.)

A VOICE *(answering)*. Hey?

MRS. HARTE. Would you see Michael on the road home? And Owen?

A VOICE. I passed them a short while ago. A bit west o' the cross.

MRS. HARTE. Thanks, Donal.

(The car is heard moving on.)

MRS. O'CONNOR. Your mind is at rest now. . . . And the wedding, is it settled that 'tis Maurice himself—— Oh, sure, I knew there was something on my mind to tell you.

MRS. HARTE. Was there so?

MRS. O'CONNOR *(effusively)*. Diarmuid that was telling me last night after he coming from the funeral. An O'Brien man from near Millstreet[47] that came over to him and he in the graveyard. "I'm told," says he to Diarmuid, "that your wife's a near friend of young Mr. Harte that's up with my son in Maynooth."

MRS. HARTE *(deeply interested)*. Yes, faith.

MRS. O'CONNOR. "Well," said he, "I had a letter from my son three or four days ago, and he mentioned in it that the young man had bested[48] every blessed one o' them at the examinations. 'He's such a wonder at the

44. **'tis nearly . . . Land Court** the holding has almost been repurchased from the former landlords, with the assistance of the Land Acts   45. **in good heart** fertile   46. **wisha!** a euphemism for "O Mary!"   47. **Millstreet** market town in northwest Cork   48. **bested** beaten

learning,' says he, 'that they're all thinking 'tis most likely he'll be something very high—a bishop or something, maybe, one day, if God will only
spare him the health.'"

MRS. HARTE *(breathlessly)*. The Lord be praised! . . . *(Suddenly.)* And
for God's sake, Mary, why didn't you run down straight an' tell us?

MRS. O'CONNOR. Sure I would, but that ye were all in bed. Diarmuid
had a small share o' drink taken, and he fell asleep in the settle[49] shortly
after coming in. 'Twas only when he woke up near ten o'clock, and the
two of us were having a sup o' tea by ourselves that he told me. There
wasn't the sign of a light down here then. . . . Isn't it great?

MRS. HARTE *(after a pause)*. And, I suppose, there's no doubt of it,
Mary?

MRS. O'CONNOR. Yeh, glory be to God, what reason could a stranger
like that have for telling lies? A fine respectable looking man he was too,
Diarmuid said.

MRS. HARTE *(fervently)*. Thanks be to the good God for everything!

MRS. O'CONNOR. 'Tis wonderful, surely. And is it settled and all that
'tis himself is to marry them?

MRS. HARTE. 'Tis so. . . . I can't get that news out o' my head. We
had a letter from him only a week ago, and he'll be down. I'll show it to
you. *(Stands on stool to take letter from shelf.)* 'Tis wonderful—wonderful
entirely. Wasn't it great luck, now—Diarmuid to be at the funeral! *(Searching for the letter.)* I thought I put it there in the clevy.[50] That's queer, surely.
(Giving up search.) Telling us he was about all the goings on an' the great
ceremonies that'll be at the ordination next Sunday. He sent two cards—
tickets like—for his father and the priest. *(Resumes search again.)* I'd nearly
swear I put it there under the tea-drawer. *(Gets off stool again.)*

MRS. O'CONNOR. 'Tis somewhere about, you'll find. Never fear but
'twill turn up. Michael might be after taking it, or Owen?

MRS. HARTE. Maybe so, then. I wouldn't mind the letter only for the
two cards. I'd be afraid 'tis how they wouldn't let Michael in at all to the
ceremonies, and he not to have his own. His name was on it and all.

MRS. O'CONNOR *(astonished)*. But you don't tell me that Michael is
going up after all?

MRS. HARTE. He is so—himself and Father Mangan.

MRS. O'CONNOR. Glory! An' what made him change his mind at all,
an' he so stubborn like against going all along?

MRS. HARTE. Myself, then, an' no one else.

MRS. O'CONNOR *(admiringly)*. Well, well, you're great, Ellen! 'Tis long
till I could get Diarmuid to do a thing like that for me, and he to have

49. **settle** a long wooden bench with a high back and a cupboard space under
the seat   50. **clevy** cubbyhole beside the fireplace

his mind made up like Michael. *(Half confidentially.)* Terrible black an' stubborn he is in himself. How different the men do be.

MRS. HARTE. They do, then, but I tell you 'twasn't too easy at all to persuade Michael into it, quiet as he is in himself.

MRS. O'CONNOR. Well, then.

MRS. HARTE *(confidentially)*. Terribly shy and backward like he felt he'd be up there with the crowds o' strangers—an' the priests an' bishops—and all their eyes on himself, maybe.

MRS. O'CONNOR *(sympathetically)*. Wisha, no wonder at all. I'd be half frightened like, myself. Sure, the morning we have the Stations[51] in the house I can't eat a sign[52] and the priest at the table. And up there 'twill be a show for grandeur.

MRS. HARTE. Well, whatever way he'll pull along, sure 'twould be nothing short of a disgrace for Maurice not to have one of his own there besides the parish priest.

MRS. O'CONNOR. Oh, 'twouldn't do at all.

MRS. HARTE. He's bringing the new suit with him to-day, and a top coat—he'd be wanting them, anyway, for the wedding; and I tell you when they'll be on him, Mary, 'tis more respectable he'll look, maybe, than many another one o' them next Sunday. But he's terrible shy.

MRS. O'CONNOR. Yeh, not at all. I never noticed it.

MRS. HARTE. He is, then. Look! I'm as sure as you're sitting there, 'tis glad in his heart he'd be if the clothes wouldn't be finished to-day. 'Twould be the finest excuse in the world for not going, and no blame to be on himself at all. They're coming now, I think. That's like the car. *(Hurries to the door and sees Owen. Calls eagerly.)* Owen, come here a minute. Hurry! *(He comes to the door beaming.)*

MRS. HARTE *(anxiously)*. Well, and did ye meet them?

OWEN. We did, of course.

MRS. HARTE. And is everything settled?

OWEN. 'Tis so, mother, and well settled. *(Smiling.)* Everything now but the words o' the Church. I hope Maurice'll take good care to have them off an' no mistake.

(They move from the doorway into the kitchen.)

MRS. HARTE *(to Mrs. O'Connor, eagerly)*. Everything is settled now, Mary, he tells me—the writing[53] an' all.

MRS. O'CONNOR. That's grand news, entirely! *(To Owen.)* 'Tis wonderful luck you have, Owen, by all accounts, and *(shaking hands)* I hope 'twill thrive with you.[54]

---

51. **Stations** the celebration of Mass in private homes   52. **a sign** anything, only a token   53. **the writing** the details of the match   54. **'twill thrive with you** that you will do well

OWEN. Thank you for the good wish, aunt.

MRS. O'CONNOR *(banteringly)*. And tell me, how did herself look to-day, Owen?

OWEN *(smiling)*. Oh, lovely—lovely, altogether.

MRS. O'CONNOR. I always said you had the bit o' taste. But some o' the neighbours will be having your life for going outside the parish for the mistress.[55]

OWEN *(radiant)*. When they'll put their eyes on her once they'll forgive me. If Bride was only like one o' themselves 'twould be different.

MRS. HARTE *(impatiently)*. Yeh, hush up that kind o' talk and have a bit o' sense! *(Anxiously.)* Tell me, did your father get his clothes?

OWEN. They're outside in the car by him.

MRS. HARTE. That's the greatest relief to my mind. And the top-coat, did he bring it with him?

OWEN. He did, faith, an' the hat, an' the collar an' tie, and all the rest o' the tackling as well.

MRS. O'CONNOR. 'Tis the proud man he must be this day with one of his boys going to be priested, and the other making a great match— and all nearly within the one week!

OWEN *(laughing)*. I don't know then about that. Faith, anyone would think and we coming home that 'twas to the gallows he was going. *(Half-confidentially)*. Now and then you'd see him and he giving a kind o' side-look at the parcels, and when we were passing over Carrigaphooka Bridge I think 'twas half on his mind to fling them over into the river.

MRS. O'CONNOR *(sympathetically)*. Wisha, the poor man. *(Michael appears at the door.)*

OWEN. Ssh!

(Michael comes in moodily. He is laden with parcels. Mrs. Harte hastens to relieve him of some of them. She lays them on the table.)

MRS. HARTE. So everything is all right?

MICHAEL. 'Tis so.

MRS. HARTE. An' short as you were away 'tis the great news we have before you.

MICHAEL *(curious)*. Great news, is it?

MRS. HARTE. Mary, that's just after telling me. Diarmuid that had it last night for her after coming from the funeral. Some man from the West, it seems, that came up to him in the graveyard——

MRS. O'CONNOR. An O'Brien man from near Millstreet, he was, Michael.

MRS. HARTE *(continuing)*. There's a son of his up in Maynooth with Maurice, and he told them the other day in a letter that Maurice bested

55. **mistress** wife

the world at the examinations, and that 'tis how they're all prophesying he'll be something great yet—a bishop, maybe, or something very high.

MICHAEL. That's wonderful news, surely *(taking off his hat reverently)*. Thanks be to the Almighty God!

OWEN. Bride will be every bit as proud of it as ourselves.

MRS. O'CONNOR. What I was saying a minute ago, Michael, was, that 'tis you have the good right in all earnest to be the proud man this day.

MICHAEL *(after a pause)*. God is very good to us. . . . There's no doubt but the priest was a great prophet after all. He said, and Maurice only that height *(illustrating with his hand)*, that 'twould be that way with him some day.

MRS. O'CONNOR *(a little envious)*. Our Patrick is a fright,[56] too, at the books. 'Tis like a miracle the way everything comes to him. But Jimmy has no stomach at all for the learning. He's like the father's people that way.

MRS. HARTE. Yeh, sure what is he but a child yet? *(Undoing one of the parcels.)* This is the suit, I suppose? What kind is it? *(Owen goes into parlour.)*

MICHAEL. 'Tis all right.

MRS. HARTE. You must try the coat on you before you sit down, Michael.

MICHAEL *(graciously)*. Yeh, give us a bit to eat first! There's plenty time for that.

MRS. HARTE *(persuasively)*. 'Twon't take half a minute. I'd like greatly to have Mary see it on you.

MICHAEL. Yeh, what nonsense, woman? They'll do finely.

MRS. HARTE. Wisha, glory be to goodness, what work you're making about it! You're the queer man to be so black in yourself and we having such tidings before you.

MRS. O'CONNOR. Wisha, Ellen, don't mind. Maybe the poor man is tired.

MRS. HARTE. Yeh, not at all. What 'ud be making him tired? Come, Michael. Do. *(Unfolds the coat and holds it up to him.)*

MICHAEL *(yielding)*. Very well, then. I suppose 'tis as good to be done with it.

(He takes off his coat and tries on the new one, Mrs. Harte assisting the while. She smooths it down very carefully.)

MICHAEL. Well?

MRS. HARTE *(critically)*. 'Tis a fine fit entirely. Come here, Mary, and look at the stuff.

MRS. O'CONNOR *(examining it closely)*. 'Tis elegant.

56. **fright** genius

MRS. HARTE. I got it a great bargain. A remnant it was.

MRS. O'CONNOR. 'Tis for all the world like what Mr. Armstrong, the land commissioner,[57] had on him and he here Lady Day.[58]

MRS. HARTE. 'Twill look very respectable when he'll have everything to match. Turn round, Michael, this way.

MICHAEL *(turning round)*. Well?

MRS. HARTE. 'Tis grand out—if it wouldn't be a small bit tight there round the collar?

MICHAEL. Yeh, that's nothing. 'Twill stretch.

MRS. O'CONNOR. Sure, you could remove that upper button yourself, Ellen? 'Twould ease it a bit.

MICHAEL *(with a hint of eagerness)*. Wouldn't it be a lot safer for the tailor to do the like o' that? Maybe 'tis only destroying the coat she'd be meddling with it. 'Tis likely we'll see some one going east that would take it to him?

MRS. HARTE. Yes, an' sure as day never get it back in time for your journey! Isn't it long enough he kept them from you. *(Holding up overcoat.)* I'd like to see this on you now.

MRS. O'CONNOR *(with conviction)*. Well, isn't it grand entirely it looks on him? And so comfortable? *Years younger* you're looking this minute, Michael.

MICHAEL *(sceptically)*. Wisha, I don't know.

MRS. O'CONNOR. God knows you are, Michael!

MRS. HARTE. 'Tis elegant it looks on you—elegant. When Maurice'll set his eyes on you Sunday 'tis a great start he'll get. . . . Well, there's no doubt in the world but there's a lot in clothes. Walk over towards the door.

(He is about to do so when he suddenly catches sight of the priest coming towards the house.)

MICHAEL *(excitedly)*. Ellen, Ellen, the priest! *(Hurriedly unbuttoning overcoat.)* Laughing his sides he'd be at me and he to see me like this. What a time he should come!

MRS. HARTE. Take care, or 'tis how you'll tear it!

(He gets out of his overcoat, which he flings on the table, and hurries into the parlour.)

MRS. HARTE *(following him with his old coat)*. Here, take this with you.

MRS. O'CONNOR *(in dismay)*. An' glory be to God, look at the way I am before him! I wouldn't have him see me with this apron on me for all the world.

MRS. HARTE. You'll find one o' mine in the room above.

57. **the land commissioner** the bureaucrat charged with distributing divided estates and overseeing the collection of annuities   58. **Lady Day** May 1

MRS. O'CONNOR. I'd rather not be meeting him and I in this state. I'll slip out, by the way not seeing him at all.

(Mrs. O'Connor goes out. Mrs. Harte tidies up the room, flicking imaginary dust off tables and chairs. She leaves the parcels on the table with the overcoat carefully folded on top. Owen returns to the kitchen.)

MRS. HARTE *(to Owen)*. 'Tis for that card for the ordination he's coming surely, and I don't know under heaven where I put that letter. I'm half blind from looking for it. You didn't see e'er a sign of it, I suppose?

OWEN. Oh, sure I took it with me. I was anxious like for Bride to see it. I didn't know you were looking for it. *(Takes out letter from inner breast pocket of his coat, and gives her the two cards, retaining the letter.)* Here they're for you.

MRS. HARTE *(relieved)*. Oh, thanks be to God! 'Twas troubling me in a fright, as I couldn't find them.

(Father Mangan comes in. He looks unusually grave. He has an open letter in his hand.)

MRS. HARTE *(effusively)*. Welcome, Father.

FATHER MANGAN. Is Michael at home, Mrs. Harte?

MRS. HARTE. He is, Father. He went down the room there this minute. *(Calls.)* Michael, Michael.

MICHAEL *(from room)*. Just half a minute, Ellen.

MRS. HARTE *(going to the door and opening it)*. Hurry, can't you, and don't be keeping the priest. He's here to settle everything about your going.

(Michael returns dressed as usual.)

MICHAEL *(heartily)*. Good evening, Father. 'Tis early you got home from the Conference.[59] There must be a good bit o' breeding in that new little cob[60] of yours.

FATHER MANGAN. I'm very sorry, Michael, to be the bearer of rather disappointing news this evening.

MICHAEL. What news, Father?

FATHER MANGAN. I've got a note here from the President of Maynooth. He says that Maurice, poor fellow, is not—eh—quite well for the last day or two.

MRS. HARTE *(troubled)*. Is it sick he is, Father?

FATHER MANGAN. Ye—s, a—a kind of—of breakdown from overstudy.

OWEN. And no wonder at all! Sure no one could stand it.

MRS. HARTE *(half bitterly)*. 'Tisn't once or twice I warned him how 'twould be with him.

FATHER MANGAN. The unfortunate part of it is that the authorities

59. **Conference** regional clerical meeting   60. **cob** horse

have been obliged to—to postpone his ordination—but merely for a little time, of course.

MRS. HARTE *(with a gasp)*. What's that you say, Father?

MICHAEL. That's terrible, Father.

FATHER MANGAN. 'Tis a great disappointment, Michael, to us all. . . . I can't tell you how I feel myself this moment over it.

MRS. HARTE *(struggling with her fears)*. He must be very bad, and they to do the like o' that to him.

OWEN. And it must be awful sudden, Father, and to say we had that letter *(producing Maurice's letter)* less than a week ago.

FATHER MANGAN. It *was* very sudden, Owen—alarmingly so. *(To Mrs. Harte.)* There is no use in keeping the truth from you. Dr. Hynes, the President, says the poor fellow is seriously ill.

MRS. HARTE. Blessed Mother o' God!

MICHAEL. You're keeping something from us, Father?

FATHER MANGAN. 'Tis always better, Michael, to—to be prepared for the worst.

MRS. HARTE *(crying out wildly)*. My God, 'tis dead he is surely! Christ in Heaven pity us this day!

FATHER MANGAN. Mrs. Harte——

MRS. HARTE *(distracted)*. God of Heaven, only to think of him dying with no one but the strangers about him!

OWEN *(appealingly)*. Mother . . . don't!

MRS. HARTE. Son o' God, isn't it terrible, terrible altogether! My boy to be lying dead, and not one of his own to know it at all. *A Mhuire! Mhuire! Mhuire!*

FATHER MANGAN *(half angrily)*. Woman, are you mad? . . . Your son is *not* dead. Who told you he was?

MICHAEL. Is—is that the truth, Father?

FATHER MANGAN. It *is* the truth, of course. He's no more dead than yourself. He's ill—he's not quite himself—that's all.

MICHAEL *(fervently)*. God bless you for that word, Father.

FATHER MANGAN. The doctors ordered him home at once. Complete rest is what they prescribed. He has left the College this morning. He'll be here any minute now.

MICHAEL *(thunderstruck)*. What's that you say, Father? *Here? Here,* is it?

FATHER MANGAN. There are two students—special friends of his—with him. One of them is my nephew. They'll do everything possible for the poor fellow on the way. Rest assured of that, Michael.

MRS. HARTE. And what time is this to be telling us this terrible news, Father, and you knowing, as well as ourselves, how all the friends are looking to have him say Mass in the chapel below, Sunday week, and it settled with yourself to have him say the marriage words for his brother here the week after?

FATHER MANGAN (*with a hint of annoyance*). I assure you, poor woman, 'tis no fault of mine. I had left for the Conference before the post arrived, and I hurried down the moment I got this letter.

MRS. HARTE. 'Tis the heart-breaking story you always bring with you!

MICHAEL (*reproachfully*). Hush, Ellen, hush! (*To Father Mangan.*) Don't mind her, Father. She don't mean it at all.

FATHER MANGAN. I understand her feelings, poor woman. I have no blame whatever to her. None, indeed.

(*Mrs. Harte is seen to throw a big shawl about her as if to go out.*)

OWEN. Where are you going, mother?

MRS. HARTE. I'm going where I'd be gone many an hour this morning if them that ought to know better hadn't treated me worse than a beggar on the road! . . . 'Tis the cold home-coming for him and he dying, surely.

FATHER MANGAN (*persuasively*). Wait a minute.

MRS. HARTE. No, Father, I can't.

FATHER MANGAN. One moment only.

(*She makes no answer, but goes resolutely towards the open door.*)

FATHER MANGAN (*laying his hand restrainingly on her arm*). Stop! Stop, I say!

MRS. HARTE. Take your hand off me, Father. Let me go to my boy. . . . Oh, Maurice, Maurice!

MICHAEL (*in a low voice*). For God's sake, Ellen, can't you do as the priest bids you? Sure, it isn't his fault at all.

OWEN. Wait, mother. Wait, can't you?

FATHER MANGAN (*earnestly*). Listen, Mrs. Harte—I speak for your good. Your boy's illness is such that if you go to him in this agitated condition you may do him a hurt from which he may never recover. As you love your son keep calm and collected.

MRS. HARTE. I don't care! I don't care! I'll go.

OWEN (*barring her way*). You won't go, mother.

MRS. HARTE (*sobbing wildly*). I must! I must! I must!

(*Michael goes to her. He appeals to her in a low tone of mingled pain and reproach.*)

MICHAEL. 'Tis a shame for you, Ellen, after the priest's words. 'Tis mad you are! . . . (*Persuasively.*) Sit down there (*pointing to a stool*), and be said by the priest. Do, Ellen. Do.

(*She hesitates.*)

OWEN (*appealingly*). Do, mother.

FATHER MANGAN. Do, Mrs. Harte, like a good woman. Do, I beg of you. (*Consulting his watch.*) He'll be with you now any moment.

(She sits down without speaking. The shawl slips from her shoulder and falls to the ground. She makes no effort to replace it.)

FATHER MANGAN. That's right, my poor woman, that's right. . . . And now that we're all more—more resigned to this—this very painful disappointment, 'tis but right——

(He is interrupted by the noise of a hurried footstep approaching the door. They all look in the direction of the doorway with questioning anxiety.)

FATHER MANGAN. Peter!—and alone?

(He hastens to meet a young clerical student who appears in the doorway. They shake hands very quietly.)

FATHER MANGAN *(wonderingly)*. Where is he, Peter?

PETER *(slightly out of breath)*. In the covered car with a friend. They're coming round by the lane. I just ran up the short cut through the fields to have a word with you all first.

MICHAEL. How is he, Mr. Mangan?

PETER. Oh, better, Mr. Harte—much better—but very tired, of course.

FATHER MANGAN. The long train journey is exhausting.

PETER. Oh, fearfully. *(To Michael.)* Our President, Dr. Hynes, gave me particular instructions to tell you in person how deeply sorry he is. The awful suddenness of the whole thing prevented him acquainting you earlier. And he thought the kindest way to let you know was through my uncle.

MICHAEL. We're very thankful, indeed, to the good gentleman, Mr. Magnan, an' tell him so.

PETER. I can assure you it was almost as great a disappointment to Dr. Hynes as to yourselves. You could hardly understand how grieved he was. Maurice, poor chap, had done such brilliant things, he was to be attached to the Dunboyne[61] after his ordination. 'Twas desperately hard luck. Everyone got a most painful shock.

FATHER MANGAN. Poor lad! Poor lad! *(Mrs. Harte tries to stifle a sob.)*

PETER *(touched)*. Oh, don't take it like that, Mrs. Harte. There are very good grounds for believing it to be only a temporary thing. . . . Pray, don't. 'Twould upset him awfully to see you taking it so much to heart. A month or two at home——

MICHAEL *(puzzled)*. What kind o' complaint did the doctors say he was suffering from, Mr. Mangan?

OWEN. He was very thin and white at Easter. . . . And coughing. 'Tisn't in a decline he is?

MICHAEL. He was saying that was only after the long fast o' Lent.[62]

(Father Mangan vainly endeavours to catch his nephew's eye.)

61. **the Dunboyne** Maynooth's postgraduate and post-ordination residence
62. **Lent** 40-day period of penitence preceding Easter

PETER *(to Father Mangan, turning round in full)*. I—I thought you told them.

FATHER MANGAN *(awkwardly)*. Yes, yes, so I did—of course in—in a general way. I was about to enter into details just as you came in.

MRS. HARTE *(distractedly)*. In the name o' God, what mystery is it that ye have between ye? . . . Is it some disgrace that's after coming upon us or what?

PETER. *Disgrace?* No, indeed, Mrs. Harte.

(As he speaks a car arrives at the door. Maurice, assisted by his companion, another young student, is seen to alight.)

FATHER MANGAN *(to Mrs. Harte)*. Stay there a moment. And for God's sake try to control yourself.

(He advances to meet Maurice.)

FATHER MANGAN *(with excessive heartiness)*. Welcome home, Maurice! Welcome, a thousand times, my dear fellow!

MAURICE *(half audibly)*. Oh, yes—yes. . . . Yes—yes. . . . Thanks. . . . Thanks.

(He passes into the centre of the apartment. Peter and his fellow student are seen to converse for a moment in whispers with Father Mangan, and then go away very quietly.)

MRS. HARTE *(tenderly)*. Maurice. . . . How are you, my poor boy? . . . What happened you at all? *(He smiles wearily and mutters something in an undertone.)* Don't be troubled one bit. We're well content to wait. We are, indeed, Maurice. *(With forced cheerfulness.)* Sure what signifies a month or two—or, for the matter of that, a whole year?

(He gives a profound sigh, and looks at her somewhat strangely.)

MICHAEL *(bringing him a chair)*. You're dead tired, boy, after the long journey. Sit here, Maurice. Your mother'll have a bit to eat for you this minute.

(Maurice sits down wearily. Father Mangan draws a chair beside him. As the priest speaks he gives you the impression of one striving desperately to be natural.)

FATHER MANGAN. By the by, Maurice *(placing his hand on his shoulder)*, and how is my old friend, Tom Morgan—Dr. Morgan, you know? We read together in the sixties. Boon companions, Tom and I, in those days.

MAURICE. Dr. Morgan? Dr.? . . . Yes—yes. . . .

FATHER MANGAN. Ah, a rare genius, Tom! A profound thinker, and a brilliant theologian, Maurice. . . . But a child at heart for all his wisdom. A Kempis[63] we nicknamed him. Of course you read his work on the Immaculate Conception?[64] A great thing that. . . . And he's wearing well, you

63. **A Kempis** Thomas A Kempis *(ca.* 1380–1471), Augustinian canon, famous for his unworldliness and simplicity of life, and author of *The Imitation of Christ* 64. **the Immaculate Conception** the article of Catholic dogma asserting that Mary was conceived without original sin

tell me? Ah, a fine fellow, Tom Morgan. A fine fellow, Maurice.

(Maurice sits gazing intently into the heart of the fire. In his profound absorption he seems dead to externals. Mrs. Harte approaches as if to speak. The priest stands up very quietly, and motions her to leave him undisturbed. They all speak in half-whispers and look at one another piteously.)

FATHER MANGAN *(to Mrs. Harte)*. A cup of hot tea. . . . Quickly as you can.

(Mrs. Harte takes Michael's overcoat from the table and hangs it up, sighing deeply. There is something inexpressibly touching in the action. She removes each of the other parcels slowly one by one. There is a tragic significance in every movement. As she spreads the tablecloth Maurice is heard suddenly speaking to himself in a voice and manner startling in their indefinable strangeness.)

MAURICE. I can't! I can't, mother! . . . I'll wear the flesh off my bones. . . . A life of sacrilege. . . . Would you, would you, Father?

(There is a great silence. Maurice drops suddenly into the same attitude of absorption and aloofness as before. The priest goes to Mrs. Harte and tries to break the spell that seems to hold her. As he speaks to her, Maurice is seen to open his breviary, and to read a portion of the day's Office. His voice, as he reads, is an audible whisper.)

MICHAEL *(in a low voice that hides a sob)*. His mind that's gone, Father.

FATHER MANGAN *(in the same low tone)*. No. Michael. It is only a temporary breakdown. Overstrung nerves. It happens every day.

MICHAEL. 'Twas wrong to force him the way we did.

FATHER MANGAN. Hush, Michael. How could anyone have foreseen this?

MICHAEL *(piteously)*. 'Tis the punishment of the Almighty on us. I know it.

FATHER MANGAN. No, no, Michael. Don't think that. . . . How could you have known?

OWEN *(to himself, desolately)*. She'll never come into this house now.

FATHER MANGAN. Have sense, man, have sense.

OWEN. She won't, Father. . . . Never.

(Maurice is seen to rise from the chair abstractedly. With his eyes deep in the book, and still reciting fragments of his office in fitful whispers, he goes out the open door very slowly.)

FATHER MANGAN *(in a low voice)*. Follow him, Michael. *(Michael goes out.)*

MRS. HARTE *(tottering towards a seat)*. My God! My God! My God!

(The priest looks at her with a pained sense of his own helplessness. The curtain falls very slowly.)

CURTAIN

GEORGE FITZMAURICE
1877 – 1963

On January 28, 1877, George Fitzmaurice was born in Bedford House, near Listowel, Co. Kerry. He was the tenth of twelve children of the Reverend George Fitzmaurice, Church of Ireland minister and younger son of an old Hiberno-Norman family, who in his fortieth year had made an astonishing—and, by most lights, imprudent—marriage to a local country girl half his age, Roman Catholic, daughter of one of his tenants. Their children, home-educated, were cut off from the professions typical of the gentry, and when Parson Fitzmaurice died in 1891, his wife and children were left so badly off that they had to move into a small farmhouse at Kilcara-beg, near Duagh. From this time onwards George had much more contact with the O'Connors, his mother's Catholic peasant relatives, than with the Fitzmaurices. Thus he grew up between cultures—Protestant and Catholic, gentry and peasantry—and also to some degree between languages, for during his youth the area around Duagh was moving from Irish- to English-speaking.

Though he returned for family visits in later years, Fitzmaurice left Kerry and in 1901 moved to Dublin, where he spent the rest of his life (apart from World War I service in the British Army) as a low-ranking clerk in the civil service. He saw and was inspired by the Abbey Theatre's early productions, though later he ceased to attend the theater, avoiding even his own plays; however, he was a lifelong devotee of the music halls. An extremely shy man, he lived an unsociable life, never married (nor did any of his siblings), and had no close friends. He generally avoided his fellow writers, and in later years hardly ever discussed his plays and several times refused or ignored requests to let them be produced. Maurice Kennedy, the only man known to have been granted an interview with him, commented after their conversation in 1951 that Fitzmaurice was "as easy to interview as an oyster."

On his sixty-fifth birthday, in 1942, Fitzmaurice retired from his job in the Department of Agriculture. Increasingly reclusive, for the last two decades of his life he lived on his small pension in rented rooms in central Dublin. When he died at 3 Harcourt Street on May 12, 1963, his meager effects amounted to personal clothing, copies of his published plays and a few books, and various papers including manuscripts of his unpublished plays, drafts of letters (never sent) concerning productions of plays, and a penciled note: "Author is prepared to sell outright all rights in 14 plays dealing intimately with life in the Irish countryside. Most have already been either printed or published. Suitable to which to build musical, television, etc. Pass to anyone interested."

Fitzmaurice actually left behind a corpus of seventeen plays, written (in what order is uncertain) over a period of fifty years. His career as a dramatist began with the striking success of the Abbey's 1907 production of *The Country Dressmaker*, a three-act drama about country matchmaking. In the wake of the riots over *The Playboy of the Western World*, the instant popularity of *The Country Dressmaker*, which presents a harsh picture of Irish peasant materialism and credulity, surprised the Abbey directors; although the *Evening Telegraph* complained that the author "might . . . have introduced a few more lofty and more Irish types" into the play, it remained a staple of the Abbey repertoire for many years.

The next Fitzmaurice plays produced at the Abbey—*The Pie-Dish* in 1908 and *The Magic Glasses* in 1913, both of them fantastic, cynical and farcical—met with generally negative receptions; Joseph Holloway, the theater's architect, who attended all Abbey performances and wrote about them in an extensive journal, called *The Magic Glasses* "the silliest production ever attempted on the Abbey stage." The theater directors refused to put on two further plays—*The Dandy Dolls*, a masterly, extravagant folk fantasy which seems to have been Fitzmaurice's favorite play, and *The Moonlighter*, a four-act play set in the 1880s during the Land War. All five were published by Maunsel in Dublin in 1914 in a volume that was reviewed favorably, and after the war, in 1923, the Abbey staged one more Fitzmaurice play, *'Twixt the Giltinans and the Carmodys*, a fairly weak matchmaking comedy—the last of his plays to be produced there during his lifetime. (Ironically, the Abbey put on *The Dandy Dolls*, to rave reviews, six years after his death.) Seumas O'Sullivan, editor of *The Dublin Magazine*, took an interest in Fitzmaurice's work and published eight of his plays between 1924 and 1957. Austin Clarke's Lyric Theatre Company produced *The Dandy Dolls* in 1945, and thereafter there were a few other productions, some by amateur groups. But Fitzmaurice, always outside the gregarious Dublin literary world, sank into determined obscurity, though he continued to write. His funeral drew only ten mourners.

Fitzmaurice's plays came to public attention once more when Dolmen Press published all seventeen in three volumes between 1967 and 1970; since that time, the playwright's reputation has grown significantly. Although Austin Clarke supposed that Yeats had kept Fitzmaurice's plays off the Abbey stage from jealousy of their popularity, it seems much more likely that Fitzmaurice's lifetime obscurity stemmed partly from his own personality and partly from the difficult language and unconventional nature of his plays. He was writing beyond the comprehension of most of his Irish contemporaries. (It is noteworthy that English reviews of his fantasy plays performed on tour by the Abbey Company were far more enthusiastic than the reviews in his own country.)

With the exception of two late compositions, *One Evening Gleam* and *The Coming of Ewn Andzale,* both set in Dublin, all of Fitzmaurice's plays take place in the north Kerry region around Listowel and Duagh where he grew up. Perhaps taking his cue from Synge and Lady Gregory, Fitzmaurice fashioned the language of his plays from local dialect; "Sure," he told Maurice Kennedy, "anybody who could write down the sayings of Kerry people could fool anyone he was a poet." So extravagantly idiomatic is his dialogue, however, and so full of Gaelic expressions, that it occasionally defeated the Dublin audiences, and reviews typically complained of "a plethora of colloquialisms" despite (as two Kerrymen in the audience attested to Joseph Holloway one evening) the accuracy with which Fitzmaurice had reproduced Kerry speech.

On the surface Fitzmaurice's plays conform to the norms of the "peasant play" which quickly evolved as a popular staple of the Abbey: they are set in peasant cottages, feature folklore in their plots, use a version of rural dialect, and deal with such common themes as marriage, duty to family, land hunger, emigration. Nevertheless, most of these plays—even those generally described as "realistic"—are very different in mood and effect from other Irish peasant plays. Like Fitzmaurice himself, their protagonists (whom he once referred to as "wicked old children") are men and women cut off from their communities by their obsessions. Old Leum Donoghue in *The Pie-Dish* has spent twenty years single-mindedly making a pie-dish (a sort of casserole); for longer than that, Jaymony Shanahan in *The Magic Glasses* has retreated to the top loft of his family cottage, contemplating the visions he sees in his marvelous glasses; Roger Carmody in *The Dandy Dolls* ignores his family and passes his time making dolls that arouse the envy of the supernatural world; Jamesie Kennelly, respectable farmer in *The Linnaun Shee,* suddenly abandons his responsibilities to follow a fairy woman who appears in the guise of a horrid hag. Even in the earliest of the so-called "realistic" plays, there are hints of this same pattern of obsession. Julia Shea, the country dressmaker, has waited a decade for Pats Connor to return from America and marry her, in the interim so shaping her expectations from the romantic images of lovers in sensational periodicals (*"English"* ones, sniffed the nationalist *Evening Telegraph*) that when Pats actually comes back she can no longer love him, for "he is what he is."

By and large, the community sees no value, much madness and sometimes even demonic possession in these dreamers' blinkered pursuit of the impossible—and to their kindred they are embarrassments at best, and at worst, threats to the family's social and economic future. It is hard to see where value resides in the plays: certainly not in the established members of the community—priests, farmers, matchmakers, wives, and others—whose small-minded materialism abundantly merits Jaymony's condemnation of them as "ignorant, grumpy, and savage." But not in the self-centered, often childish visionaries, either, or in the deliberately incomprehensible objects of their obsessions. Many of the plays end in apocalyptic destruction of both visionary and object, leaving behind, in Jaymony's words, "the same old thing every day." John Cooke has suggested that Fitzmaurice's plays are often concerned "with the quality and function of imagination in a world which cannot accept its artists: society and artist each hide behind impenetrable masks—one of reactionary belief, the other of impotence and solipsistic fantasy." Considering Fitzmaurice's own biography, the suggestion is doubly plausible.

SELECT BIBLIOGRAPHY

Publications

Five Plays. London and Dublin: Maunsel, 1914; Boston: Little, Brown, 1917.

The Plays of George Fitzmaurice. Vol. 1, *Dramatic Fantasies* (Introduction by Austin Clarke). Dublin: Dolmen, 1967. (*The Magic Glasses, The Dandy Dolls, The Linnaun Shee, The Green Stone, The Enchanted Land, The Waves of the Sea*)

The Plays of George Fitzmaurice. Vol. 2, *Folk Plays* (Introduction by Howard K. Slaughter). Dublin: Dolmen, 1969. (*The Ointment Blue or The King of the Barna Men, The Pie-Dish, The Terrible Baisht, There Are Tragedies and Tragedies, The Moonlighter*)

The Plays of George Fitzmaurice. Vol. 3, *Realistic Plays* (Introduction by Howard K. Slaughter). Dublin: Dolmen, 1970. (*The Toothache, The Country Dressmaker, One Evening Gleam, 'Twixt the Giltinans and the Carmodys, The Simple Hanrahans, The Coming of Ewn Andzale*)

The Wonderful Wedding. Written with John Guinan. Newark, DE: Proscenium, 1978.

The Crows of Mephistopheles and Other Stories. Ed. Robert Hogan. Dublin: Dolmen, 1970.

Biography and Criticism

Achilles, Jochen. "George Fitzmaurice's Dramatic Fantasies: Wicked Old Children in a Disenchanting Land." *Irish University Review* 15,2 (1985): 148–63.

———. "'The Glame from That Old Lamp': The Unity of George Fitzmaurice's Plays." *Éire-Ireland* 20,4 (Winter 1985): 106–29.

Cooke, John. "'Tis Mysterious Surely and Fantastic Strange': Art and Artists in Three Plays of George Fitzmaurice." *Irish Renaissance Annual* 1 (1980): 32–55.

Gelderman, Carol W. *George Fitzmaurice*. Boston: Twayne, 1979.

Hogan, Robert. "The Genius of George Fitzmaurice." In *After the Irish Renaissance*, pp. 164–75. London: Macmillan, 1968.

Kennedy, Maurice. "Sketch for a Portrait." *Irish Writing* (June 1951): 38–46.

McGuinness, Arthur E. *George Fitzmaurice*. Lewisburg, PA: Bucknell University Press, 1975.

Slaughter, Howard K. *George Fitzmaurice and his Enchanted Land*. Dublin: Dolmen, 1972.

The Magic Glasses

CHARACTERS

Jaymony Shanahan
Padden, *his father*
Maineen, *his mother*
Mr. Quille
Aunt Jug
Aunt Mary

scene. *Padden Shanahan's kitchen. Maineen comes down from room. Padden comes in. Maineen places glasses and a bottle on table.*

Maineen. See now, Padden, all is in readiness for Mr. Quille, let him come what hour 'twill match him. And, oh hierna![1] the heart is rising in me at the thought of his putting Jaymony off that habit of his of going up in the top loft,[2] our fine sons, Roger and Frynk, lighting with shame on account of it, and saying they'll come home to us no more on their holydays if their brother don't get shut of his canter.[3]

Padden. Still, 'tis meself is thinking 'tis a reckless thing to be hysing[4] this Mr. Quille here on a false pretence that Jaymony has his breast bone down.[5] 'Tis unknown what the stranger will do when he'll know the truth, he an almighty passionate man, they do be saying, that don't like to be deceived.

Maineen. What croaking have you now, and as rejoiced as you were to coax the great man here? 'Tisn't a face we'd have surely[6] to send for a stranger twenty miles away with a high-diddle story of a lad going up in a top loft—'twould take pains to make Mr. Quille believe the like of that.

Padden. Faith, from what I'm after hearing[7] 'twill take pains to please him, whatever way you take him. And 'tisn't alone having the punch steaming on the table to him almost he's over the threshold will do; for Mary

1. **oh hierna!** (Ir. *a Thiarna*) Oh Lord! 2. **top loft** partial attic of planking over one end of the kitchen, accessible by a ladder 3. **get shut of his canter** get rid of his crazy habit 4. **hysing** luring, coaxing 5. **his breast bone down** fallen breastbone, *an cléithín do thuitim,* a folk affliction whose treatment by charms and cupping (applying heated glasses to the skin) is attested of folk healers in many areas of Gaelic Ireland 6. **'Tisn't a face we'd have surely** we wouldn't have the temerity 7. **I'm after hearing** I've just heard

Sofine says the half-sovereign must be slipped to him half unbeknownst,[8] the pride is that big in him. To put all words into one, Maineen, the notions and capers of the devil is in this Mr. Quille.

MAINEEN. 'Tis the same with all them geniuses, Padden, every mother's son of them nothing but notions and capers since the world began itself.[9]

PADDEN. But, maybe, he isn't the big genius we thought him after all. Sure, some say 'twas the great fame he got the first day from curing the breast bone down made people go running to him with this and that in the line of diseases, and, the pride and gumption rising in him, he couldn't renayge[10] himself attempting all before him—things he was as dull of[11] as the biggest fool walking the road.

MAINEEN. Glory! Listen to that, and yourself his biggest praiser—drawing down[12] but a few nights ago itself how he cured Mary Canty of the dropsies and the swellings with his dilution of the white heather that does be growing in the bogs; likewise how he set a charm for Looney Carroll put him from going around every tree he'd meet, the fool thinking there was money under it; and making tapes you were itself[13] of the marvel he did entirely with a blue lozenge that made Josie Patt keep his big tongue back in his mouth, and it ever and always going out that length in spite of him with every third syllable he'd speak.

PADDEN. Maybe I got another account puts a different colour on[14] some of his miracles. Morisheen Quirke wouldn't give in that dilution would cure a boil, and, he told me in private, 'twas no dropsies or swellings Mary Canty had at all, but a bully ball of wind in her stomach, that came up in a hurry, believe you me, at the fright Mr. Quille gave her, he to coagle[15] her into a corner, gave her a thump in the middle, and stuck out his tongue at her in the dark.

MAINEEN. Morisheen is a prime boy.[16]

PADDEN. If he is itself, 'tisn't Morisheen but another man was eyewitness to the way he managed Looney Carroll, chasing him through a wood in the dead hour of the night till the fool ran up again a tree unbeknownst, was flung back on his back, the blood of a pig spouting out of his nostrils, and, signs by, the fool won't go around a tree since, and it stuck in him[17] that every tree has got a divil. A queerer thing itself

---

8. **half unbeknownst** so that he is hardly aware of it (alluding to the idea that the power to cure is a supernatural gift, which must not be spoiled by the healer's accepting explicit payment for services)   9. **since the world began itself** ever since the world began   10. **renayge** refuse, deny   11. **as dull of** as ignorant of   12. **drawing down** making speeches about   13. **making tapes you were itself** you were even making a fuss about   14. **puts a different colour on** gives a different interpretation to   15. **coagle** coax   16. **a prime boy** a trickster, not to be trusted   17. **it stuck in him** he being convinced

he did on Josie Patt. Hit him on the head with a mallet, I hear, when the big tongue was out and the teeth coming together—the Lord save us, half the big tongue fell down on the ground!

MAINEEN. A likely story! And Josie's people blowing about Mr. Quille all over the world, nothing in their mouths but that blue lozenge, talking of it from dusk till dawn at every hour of the day.

PADDEN. Because they believed Mr. Quille, and Josie can't tell whether or which,[18] and nothing but gibberish coming from him since. Sure, they went to Mr. Quille about the way he was pronouncing, and what did my boy say but that it was French he was talking—that they all speak French for a while after being cured—and he'd come into the English again in the course of forty weeks. And, when this Mr. Quille comes along, I'm thinking it's wise people we'd be if we put the bed and dresser to the door and keep the divil out.

MAINEEN. Indeed, Padden, we'll do no such thing, and I'm thinking it's something must be rising in your brain to believe the fables going lately about Mr. Quille. Isn't it myself heard fables and didn't give ear to them, and isn't it yourself heard fables and didn't give ear to them, and what's come over you all in a hop?

PADDEN. He's a rogue, Maineen, and a divil of a variegated rogue itself! And with respect to his great speciality entirely of curing the breast bone down—God help you!—a man from his own quarter told me, "You have a better hand at it," said he, "up to your own door—a man there's no talk of at all, Michaeleen James O'Toole."

MAINEEN. Oh, my shame, Padden, to dare compare Mr. Quille with Michaeleen James. Padden, you'll make me say it, but it's a bad sign on you entirely to be losing your respect for the great. 'Twould be better you'd lose the brain itself than lose your respect. But it's shivering you are, shaky and shivery all over you are, Padden Shanahan.

PADDEN. Why wouldn't I be shivering, the ground a cake of frost, and the bitter breeze blowing from the North would perish the Danes or skin a flea itself.

MAINEEN. Shivering and shaking, and there's a skyon[19] in your eye, Padden Shanahan, glory be to God! 'Tisn't anything, anything airy or fearsome you seen and you are at the fort?[20]

PADDEN *(hesitatingly)*. I seen a man, then, a strange man, and he rising like a cloud over the gap in Peg Caxty's bounds ditch.[21]

18. **can't tell whether or which** can't give a true account   19. **skyon** (Ir. sceon) sign of terror   20. **the fort** Probably the remains of an early Christian *ráth*, or "ringfort," on Padden's farmland; such ruins are common in the Irish countryside, and were often believed to be the dwellings of the fairies, and thus to be places where supernatural ("airy") events and insights could occur.   21. **bounds ditch** earthen wall marking a property boundary

MAINEEN. Sure, maybe 'tis Mr. Quille himself you seen?

PADDEN. Well, there's no good in denying it, 'twas the very customer. I couldn't mistake him by the descriptions I got of him—a long black coat on him, and a hat like a parson. Believe you me, 'tisn't long I was putting the legs under me and skelping[22] home by the hedges, for it's a huge man he is, glory be to God! Taking up a big streak of the land itself he was, and he coming and walking through Aeneas Canty's square field. Holy Father, Maineen, he's the biggest and the blackest man I ever seen!

MAINEEN (soothingly). What harm, Padden. Like a good man, now, don't let his size be frightening you. Sure, for all we know, though being big he might be as soft in himself as a fool. And, Padden, think of our gintlemen. Be brave in yourself for the sake of having Jaymony cured before our fine respectable sons. Be thinking of Robin, the acting-sergeant, and 'twill put great heart in you to face Mr. Quille.

PADDEN. I'll be thinking of Robin, then, the rosy shine on his face, the clean shoe to his foot, and he sitting down to his bread, butter, tea, and two eggs. A great man for law and order is Robin. Let me be thinking of Robin, Maineen.

MAINTEEN. And Frynk in the London peelers,[23] a bigger man still. Be thinking of Frynk and the night at Mrs. Quinlan's wake, and the way he made an ape of Poet O'Rourke in the argument about Dublin and London.

PADDEN. I will, and how the poet turned as black as the hob,[24] and hadn't a word out of him for the rest of the night when Frynk turned on him in the heel and said, "You ain't got no 'Yde Park;[25] you ain't got no Rotten Row."[26]

MAINEEN. And the chicken, Padden. You mind he didn't know what to make of the chicken and she walking across the floor?[27]

PADDEN. Frynk lying back in his chair, and he breaking his heart laughing, "There she goes agin," said Frynk, said he; "there she goes agin."

MAINEEN. 'Tisn't "agin," Padden, but "agyne."[28] "There she goes agyne," said Frynk, and the lovely way he has of talking.

PADDEN (rising, pointing out door). Oh, Maineen, look at Mr. Quille, look at him now, and he marching down our triangle. Holy Father, you'd

22. **skelping** hurrying   23. **peelers** police (so nicknamed in Ireland after Sir Robert Peel, who was responsible for the establishment of police forces in both Ireland and England)   24. **hob** (smoke-blackened) projection at the back or side of a kitchen fireplace, on which a pot or kettle might be set to keep warm   25. **'Yde Park** Hyde Park (the dropped "h" is Cockney pronunciation), a large and fashionable park in central London   26. **Rotten Row** a fashionable bridle path in Hyde Park   27. **walking across the floor** It was common in Irish cottages (such as Maineen and Padden's, in which "Frynk" had grown up) for chickens to have access to the kitchen.   28. **agyne** "again" with a Cockney accent (lower-class London, but exotic and fine to Maineen and Padden, who have also come to say "Frynk," the Cockney pronunciation of "Frank")

think the wide world wasn't in it but himself,[29] he brooding and his head under him!

MAINEEN. 'Tis the proper way for him to come marching, Padden, and all he ever seen retained in his great brain. 'Tis no faith I'd have in him at all if he was going in a little boat peeping about him like a codger. Oh, glory! It must be a wonderful great man he is, surely, and almighty marvels running in his mind.

PADDEN *(handing her money)*. Here! Shove the half-sovereign to him yourself whatever, as you can do it nicely, having the slippery fingers of a female. I'll go up in the room[30] for a while, as 'tis an awkward man I am, and shy in myself before strangers. You to be introducing yourself to him, Maineen, and I'll come down after a bit.

MAINEEN *(running after him and catching him)*. For the love of God, Padden, stay and welcome Mr. Quille! The fine respectable man, what would he think of the boss of the house chambering[31] on a fine day? Sit down in the chair now, for yourself; rise up in your dignity when he comes in, and bow your respects to him with a fine smile on your face.

PADDEN *(looking out window)*. He has lepped[32] off the stile. He is coming up the bawn.[33] A swarthy devil! Holy Father, the cut of him and he blowing out of his two yellow cheeks! Let me go, will you!

(They struggle.)

MAINEEN. Padden!

PADDEN. Maineen!

(Quille comes in; he stands with his back to dresser facing Padden and Maineen. He utters a long loud sound through his nose.)

QUILLE *(in a deep mournful voice)*. Twenty miles of a tramp to cure a boy with the breast bone down! Twenty miles, and starting with the streak of dawn! *(Harshly.)* Yet there's devils would say the fame of Morgan Quille would never pass the bounds of Beenahorna[34]—doctors, priests, and jealous devils would say Morgan Quille was a quack—a quack, Padden Shanahan, if it's to you I'm speaking!

PADDEN. It is, sir; welcome here, sir. *(Aside.)* Speak, Maineen!

QUILLE. But look at me flourishing like a heap of dock leaves you'd vainly strive to smother by covering up with stones, for no man can wither the root or blast the fame of Morgan Quille of Beenahorna.

(Blows nose.)

---

29. **the wide world wasn't in it but himself** nothing existed but himself   30. **up in the room** into "the room"—a bedroom, or a parlor used only on the most ceremonial occasions—next to the kitchen ("up" indicates the end of the kitchen where the cooking hearth is; "down," the end away from the hearth)   31. **chambering** staying indoors in "the room"   32. **lepped** leaped   33. **bawn** (Ir. *bán*) the field in front of the house   34. **Beenahorna** a townland three miles east of Duagh, Co. Kerry (Fitzmaurice's childhood home was in Duagh)

PADDEN *(aside)*. Maineen, the punch!

QUILLE. Twenty miles to cure a boy with the breast bone down! I would, then, and a hundred miles itself flaking over a side of a country to come at the stiffest case of that disease! Where's the patient?

PADDEN. The thing is up in the top loft, sir. Speak, Maineen! In the name of God explain to his honour about the top loft!

QUILLE. Is it giggling and sniggering ye are? Giggling and sniggering at Morgan Quille?

PADDEN. Oh, God forbid, sir! Maineen!—alluding to the top loft, sir . . .

QUILLE *(taking a step forward)*. To the devil with yourself and your top loft! Ha! Maybe it's a doubt ye have on the powers of Morgan Quille? Some one has belied me about the case of Michaeleen O'Rourke.

PADDEN. That I may be dead and damned if I ever heard a syllable!

QUILLE. You lie, you sheefra![35] But did Michaeleen obey my instruction and come to me the nine mornings fasting to be cupped? Didn't the villain do for a twopenny loaf on the ninth morning unbeknownst, that made the breast bone fail to rise and I having the tumbler full of the flesh of his bosom, you brat? The blackguards and liars didn't tell you that maybe, the blackguards and liars that Christ Almighty will wither off the face of the earth as Christ Almighty has withered more that slandered my name!

(Faces Padden, who hides behind Maineen.)

MAINEEN. Mr. Quille—God forgive me!—'tis no breast bone down that's wrong with Jaymony; but 'tis well known to us there is no complaint you can't cure through means of that inspiration you get when you let yourself into the falling sickness. *(Gives him punch.)* We know 'tis only for special people you does it. *(Giving him money.)* But having the big heart, you might have mercy on us and the way we are, Mr. Quille.

QUILLE. Your faith opens my heart, and what can be done will be done, Mrs. Shanahan.

PADDEN *(coming forward confidentially)*. And maybe 'tis more merciful you'd be to us still when we tell you it's as humble in ourselves we are now in our riches and four cows as when we hadn't a cow or a calf; and we does good turns for neighbours without looking to be paid back—'tisn't like the born farmers that would have to get a return if it went to the fourth generation itself.

QUILLE *(sharply)*. What are you saying? Isn't all the world born farmers in the way you allude, and, God help you, if you haven't a few tricks of your own!

PADDEN *(meaning to please)*. 'Tis you must have some fine tricks surely, Mr. Quille.

35. **sheefra** (Ir. *síofra*) changeling, weakling

QUILLE. You snake! *(Catching him and flinging him across floor.)* Is it me have tricks? Is it me? Me to stoop to the dirty ways of the things that do be daubing each other in the puddles and the gutters and the sewers of the world! Me that can sweep them clean in the battlefield of the intellect, making them run like rats fleeping into their dirty holes, or cockroaches racing for their dirty lives before the glint of dawn! *(Music in top loft; he starts.)* Heavenly Father! What queer music is that upstairs?

MAINEEN. It's Jaymony, Mr. Quille; and that's what we want him cured of, and his fancy for going up in that top loft and making that noise in it.

QUILLE *(taken aback)*. Why, that's a fancy complaint entirely. *(Going and sitting at fire.)* Hum! But we'll see. *(Speaking in a professional way.)* Come here now, and give me the exact rudiments of his case. How long has he recourse to that top loft?

MAINEEN. God knows, sir, our little boy is going up in that top loft most every day since he was in the fifth book.[36]

PADDEN. He kept out of it for a while, Maineen, the time he was in his bloom.

MAINEEN. What signify was that? God knows, sir, counting every absence, he didn't keep clear of it for a twelvemonth.

QUILLE. His age?

MAINEEN. What age is on the boy, Padden? He was born whatever the year the bog ran at Cloranmadkeen; the same year that Rourke's son of Meenscubawn[37] knocked the eye out of Timothy Mascal at the election between Hassett and Dayse in the town of Listowel.[38]

PADDEN. The year the tinkers had the battle with the Moynsha people on the bridge of Lyre.[39]

QUILLE *(pondering and counting on his fingers)*. That makes him thirty-eight—a long and a chronic case, faith. Well, what does he be playing in that top loft?

MAINEEN. I'm dull of it, Mr. Quille, for I'm too wide in the girth to get into it, and Padden is too shy in himself to seek out the hidden mystery.

QUILLE *(meaningly)*. Maybe 'tis shy for him, Mrs. Shanahan. For it's the strange music that is entirely like what they do be playing in Teernanogue,[40] or what they hear them that do be drowning to their death. *(Rises.)*

PADDEN. Holy Father! Maineen, is it a fairy, then, that's in the top loft and our Jaymony swept away?

QUILLE *(walking up and down floor with hands behind his back)*. We must

---

36. **in the fifth book** in the fifth year of school, about eleven years old   37. **Meenscubawn** townland between Duagh and Abbeyfeale, Co. Kerry   38. **Listowel** town in north Kerry, a few miles north of Duagh   39. **Lyre** Lyracrumpane, on Smearlagh River nine miles southwest of Duagh   40. **Teernanogue** Irish *Tír na nÓg*, "the Land of the Young," the Otherworld, fairyland

make out if it is a Christian he is or if it isn't a Christian he is. *(Looking up at top loft.)* Is there ere a chance of getting a peep at him now?

MAINEEN. The dickens a chance, but it's up to the tips for[41] his tea, and, believe you me, he won't forget that whatever else will escape him. There's some stir out of him as it is and you'd hear the boards creaking.

QUILLE *(walking up and down as before)*. I'm saying we must first make out if it is a Christian he is or if it isn't a Christian he is. Let me think now—I have it. Put the tongs in the fire and redden it.[42]

PADDEN *(as Maineen puts tongs in fire)*. Holy Father, Maineen!

QUILLE. Put the tongs in the fire and redden it.

JAYMONY *(loudly in top loft)*. Is the tea drawn[43] yet?

MAINEEN *(putting tea in teapot)*. 'Tis drawn and shallow drawn.

JAYMONY. 'Tis not drawn, and 'tisn't wet itself, for it's after washing up the chaney[44] you are with the boiling water, and putting cold water in the kettle. Don't be trying to blink[45] me, for I heard the cover rattling, and 'tis the same with you every day, using the water and leaving me waiting for my tea. The selfishness of this world is a terror, but I'm warning you if the tea isn't drawn the minute I hop down out of this, there isn't a mug in the dresser I won't smash, and I'll break the window, and so every divil around the house will make it the sorry day to you you got into the habit of renayging me in the tea.

MAINEEN *(to Quille)*. As peevish as a cat always when coming out of that top loft. *(Loudly.)* Here now, you vagabone. *(Going to table with teapot.)* Isn't it on the table it is itself, and listen to me putting the sugar into it and stirring the sugar in the cup.

JAYMONY *(coming down)*. And the white bread and the jam?

MAINEEN. And the white bread and the jam. *(He comes down.)* There now, isn't it quick enough for you, my walking gentleman upstairs?

JAYMONY. 'Twill do, and 'tis to be hoped you'll be as regular for the future. 'Twould be a great boon to me. *(Takes off cap and eats and drinks rapidly, Quille from corner watching him intently. When done he blesses himself and puts on cap. Meditatively.)* That jam was damn nice, mother dear.

(Lights pipe; rises; walks across towards dresser. Sees Quille. Takes pipe out of mouth and turns his face away from Quille as if ashamed. Quille goes stealthily towards Jaymony. Puts hand behind back motioning with finger. Padden hands him tongs.)

QUILLE. Down on your knees now, you haunted thing. *(Jaymony drops*

---

41. **up to the tips for** almost time for   42. **Put the tongs in the fire and redden it** Threatening them with red-hot iron was believed to frighten away fairy changelings masquerading as human beings.   43. **drawn** steeped   44. **chaney** china   45. **blink** hoodwink, trick

on his knees.) Keep looking at me or I'll send this red-hot tongs fizzling down into your baistly[46] guts. Sacramento, Dominus vobiscum, mea culpa, mea maxime culpa, kyrie eleison, excelsior![47] I abjure thee by these words, tell me what you are and what you aren't. Are you Catholic?

JAYMONY *(meekly)*. I am, sir.

QUILLE *(softly)*. Are you, faith? Very good. And now, my bucko, if you are, maybe you'll say what I say after me: In the name of the Father.

JAYMONY. In the name of the Father.

QUILLE. In the name of the Son.

JAYMONY. In the name of the Son.

QUILLE. In the name of the Holy Ghost. *(Short pause.)* Ha!

JAYMONY. In the name of the Holy Ghost.

QUILLE *(pulling Jaymony towards hearth)*. Come along here, you're some sort of a Christian. Here, take this medicine and talk to me.

JAYMONY *(drinking)*. 'Tis you I'd like to be talking to, then, and you a knowledgeable man.

PADDEN. Holy Father, Maineen! 'Tis working him—the medicine.

QUILLE. Hush! hush! *(To Jaymony.)* Come, tell me, what's your meaning in going up in that top loft?

JAYMONY *(shrugging his shoulders)*. Wisha,[48] 'tis better than being in the slush—same old thing every day—this an ugly spot, and the people ignorant, grumpy, and savage.

QUILLE. By the way, they aren't double as bad above in Beenahorna; and I'm telling you it's a happy man you'd be out in the green fields for yourself with the sunny sky over you, if you knew the inside of Tralee[49] Jail where I was landed for six months—*(rising in great anger and excitement)*—on a false charge brought against me by devils during the time of the Agitation.[50] By devils, I'm saying, by devils!

(Subsides.)

JAYMONY *(sadly)*. Times I know it's a fool I am, surely, but the fancy's got stuck in me for them Magic Glasses, and the sport I had with them up in that top loft.

QUILLE. From whence, may I inquire, did you procure them Magic Glasses?

JAYMONY. From a brown woman, sir.

QUILLE *(meaningly)*. From a brown woman, ha!

JAYMONY. 'Twas on a summer's day and we going to the pattern[51] of

46. **baistly** beastly   47. **Sacramento . . . excelsior** "Bog Latin": scraps of the Latin and Greek of the Mass, intended to awe the ignorant country people   48. **Wisha** (Ir. *mhuise*) well; indeed   49. **Tralee** the nearest major town, seventeen miles southwest of Listowel, at the eastern end of the Dingle Peninsula   50. **Agitation** the Land War, 1879 and after   51. **pattern** festival associated with a patron saint

Lyre—myself and them two brothers of mine that are now ignorant peelers.

MAINEEN. Oh hierna! Is it reflecting you are on my two fine gentlemen
of sons? What learning had you beyond them yourself and you barely out
of the sixth book?

PADDEN. Too much learning he has, Maineen. Too much for sense, sir,
and too little for common sense.

QUILLE (waving his hand). Be easy now, my good people, and let me
examine the patient. (To Jaymony.) Proceed!

JAYMONY. It's through a wood the brown woman came to me, and it
wasn't a crackle or a noise at all she made and she walking on the grass
so green. She stood for a while where the bluebells grow.[52]

QUILLE. Hum! She stood for a while.

JAYMONY. Going she was and selling her wares at the pattern of Lyre.
And didn't I give her all I had for a set of the Magic Glasses! It put her
in great blood,[53] and, said she, "'Tis the like of you I always want to meet
that has the spunk in you, and I'm thinking you won't get tired of your
purchase and fling it away from you in a week like many that haggles over
the price of a glass or two, for 'tisn't one in a thousand buys of me the
whole set."

QUILLE (wisely). I see!

JAYMONY. "For it's the pleasure and diversion of the world," said she,
"you'll hear and see in them Magic Glasses."

QUILLE. Ha! It's more than music is in the glasses maybe?

JAYMONY (laughing). Hold your tongue!—the seven wonders of the
world, seas and mountains and cities, grand horses and carriages, and all
the wild animals of the earth. Gold and white money you'd see in heaps.
Palaces, with the finest furniture inside in them, the best of eating and
drinking laid out on tables with the loveliest chaney—all that and more is
to be seen in the three brown glasses. Then there's the three red glasses,
and the three blue glasses that makes up the set.

QUILLE. What's in the three red glasses?

JAYMONY. Women. Full of the purtiest women was ever seen on the
globe. It's myself got very fond of one of them, and maybe of two. And
in the glass I could see myself and the one I was doting on, and we together
for the six days of the week. Times we'd be talking and times there wouldn't
be a word out of us at all, our two mouths in one kiss and we in a sort
of a daze. It's after saying I am we'd be together for the six days of the
week. But that wouldn't satisfy us, and we'd be together for the three
hundred and sixty-five days of the year; and it wouldn't satisfy us, and for
ages and ages we'd be in Tirnanogue, and it isn't satisfied we'd be still.

52. **It's through a wood . . . the bluebells grow** language evocative of the Irish
poetic *aisling* convention, in which a mortal man is approached by a fairy
woman   53. **in great blood** in high spirits

MAINEEN *(rushing forward)*. You shameless thing! Don't mind him,[54] Mr. Quille, it's ravelling[55] he is in his immoral talk.

PADDEN. Two months now since he was at church or chapel, and 'tis years since he seen a priest.

QUILLE *(rising and bending towards Maineen and Padden, who shrink back)*. Them three blue glasses: in God's name what might be in them?

JAYMONY *(excitedly)*. Ha! it's the rousing wonders is in them entirely. You'd see a dandy army in the grey of the night rising out of the dark glens, and the places where the herons do be screeching.

QUILLE *(rising suddenly)*. The inspiration is coming on me, for I knew a sort of a poet—"Out of the mists they come," said he, "one by one— out of the mists and the fantastic quagmires of the South, their sabres gleaming in the light of the moon." *(Turning to Jaymony.)* Isn't it them you see?

JAYMONY. The same. *(In great excitement.)* Ah, but I seen more, for 'tis myself I see on a noble horse, spangled and grey; I seen my own bright sabre flashing and I leading the army on, and we driving the Saxon invader before us—through the plains of Desmond,[56] and on and on, even to the Eastern sea.

QUILLE *(flourishing arms)*. The cloth! The cloth! It's getting convulsed I am! It's getting convulsed I am!

(Padden and Maineen lay a sheet on floor. Quille falls on his back on sheet, and works as if in convulsions.)

PADDEN. Holy Father! Look at the two terrible eyes rolling in his head, he having no sight in them at all and he convulsed.

MAINEEN. 'Tis like a man of God he is, looking through the rafters, and seeing, maybe, the dome of Paradise itself.

QUILLE. Jaymony, Jaymony Shanahan! Let Jaymony Shanahan drink one wineglassful of the bottle left on the table by one Morgan Quille of Beenahorna—three times a day let him drink one wineglass, in the morning and in the noon-time and coming on the fall of night. And the price of that bottle is four-and-six—*(Padden fumbles in pocket, hands money to Maineen, who slips it into Quille's hand)*—and at the dawn of day let Jaymony Shanahan hop on one leg and make a bow East and West and North and South, and let him pick fourteen red roses and make a garland with ferny leaves and eglantine, and leave it on the thatch.[57] *(Works again in convulsions.)* Jaymony, Jaymony Shanahan! Let Jaymony Shanahan go turn the red earth every day will rise over him seven hours between dawn and the time the sun goes down, and in the dusk he'll ramble to the neighbours' houses and discourse on cattle and on crops and all things in the agricul-

54. **mind him** pay attention to him 55. **ravelling** rambling, nonsensical 56. **Desmond** south Munster 57. **on the thatch** on the house roof

tural way. He'll go to market and to fair—take drink—a little—and ketch a woman if he wants to when he is coming home. On the twenty-first day a farmer's daughter is to be made out for[58] Jaymony Shanahan.

(Works in convulsions.)

PADDEN. We never thought of a wife for him, Maineen.

MAINEEN. Hush, Padden! The great man's jaws are working towards speech.

QUILLE. Who is the woman to be made out for Jaymony Shanahan? A lovely woman for a man with four cows, no blemish on her beauty, but a slight impediment in her speech. The birthmarks on her are a pimple under her left ear, three black hairs on her buzzom and one brown. In Beenahorna this damsel does dwell, and on the twenty-first day—if Jaymony obey all the instructions given—one Morgan Quille will bring her to Jaymony Shanahan, and on the twenty-second day he'll be cured for ever and live in the grace of God.

JAYMONY *(clapping his hands)*. Is it cured I am to be in the heel?[59] Is it cured I am to be in the heel? *(Runs and takes up spade.)* I will go and turn the red earth! I will go and turn the red earth!

(Runs out.)

PADDEN *(running out)*. And I will rush and tell the neighbours the marvel of the world done for us this day.

(Maineen goes and makes more punch; she gives it to Quille, who rises; he drinks and hands her back the tumbler.)

QUILLE. Off with me now and flaking up the long, long country to Beenahorna; no time have I to waste, and a witch to prophesy my time was limited. Devils and curs would say 'tis myself invented the prophecy—devils and curs! But I am telling you, my good woman, my time is limited, my time is limited.

(Makes a spring out of the door.)

MAINEEN *(rushing to door)*. Oh, Mr. Quille, God keep you a thousand years to work miracles—God keep you a thousand years! *(She goes to fireplace. Re-enter Jaymony; she turns and sees him. Wringing her hands.)* For the love of God! 'Tisn't renaying you are to turn the red earth?

JAYMONY *(shrugging his shoulders)*. Sick I got of turning it, a dismal feeling to come over me, after Thade Martin telling me my two brothers had arrived in the village, are giving out porter and the people making much of them.

MAINEEN. Did you hop on the leg itself?

JAYMONY. I did not.

MAINEEN. Here, take the medicine in the name of God! It might prevent the charm from being cancelled, and maybe after a while you'd go out and hop on that leg. Is it better you feel?

58. **made out for** betrothed to   59. **in the heel** in the end, finally

JAYMONY. 'Tis better I feel.

MAINEEN. Thank God the charm isn't cancelled! Go out now and hop on that leg in the name of God!

JAYMONY *(with sudden elation)*. To-morrow I'll do it—to-morrow I'll follow out all the instructions, and it's a great effort I'll make entirely— *(sighs)*—if it isn't too far gone I am to be cured by quackery or the power of man.

(Padden re-enters with Jug and Mary. He goes to table and drinks whisky.)

PADDEN *(giving the women whisky)*. Drink, Aunt Jug—drink, Aunt Mary—'tisn't you should be to take a sup the glorious day that's in it. 'Tis in great blood I am, Maineen, I couldn't keep from waving my hat and shouting of the cure to the crowd of labourers on Peg Caxty's turnip garden.

AUNT JUG *(drinking)*. Isn't it me screeched the good news to Jane Quinlan, the boolumshee[60] that will spread the good news over the known world.

AUNT MARY *(drinking)*. I found time to screech it to Marse Doolen over her half-door, grigging[61] her I was and a hump on her own son, for 'tis often she was reflecting on Jaymony.

(Jaymony slips up to top loft.)

MAINEEN. And maybe she'll reflect again and the cure not rightly working in him yet. Isn't it up in the top loft he is and playing the music itself?

PADDEN. The villain of the world, it's now he has us scandalised. *(Going towards ladder.)* But maybe he don't know the courage the drop puts in a man. *(Catching ladder.)* Come down, will you, from your tingling and your jig-acting, or I'll leather[62] you within an inch of your life!

AUNT JUG AND AUNT MARY. That's the style, Padden, up to him and drill the devil out of him itself.

PADDEN. But I can't go up. I can't even raise a leg. Holy Father, it's paralysed I am, and it must be the devil himself is in the top loft!

AUNT JUG AND AUNT MARY *(at ladder)*. Mother of God, save and shield us! The devil himself above in the top loft!

MAINEEN *(going to ladder)*. What devil above in the top loft? It's drunk you're all and dazzled drunk itself. The house is creaking—leave go the ladder, I'm saying, or you'll pull the top loft down.

PADDEN. Holy Father! Isn't it the way I can't let go and I glued to it, Maineen?

AUNT JUG AND AUNT MARY. And likewise glued are we.

---

60. **boolumshee** braggart, windbag (Ir. *buailim,* "I strike," and *sciath,* "shield" —perhaps alluding to Irish legendary heroes' practice of striking their shields in issuing battle challenges) 61. **grigging** (Ir. *griogadh*) teasing, annoying 62. **leather** (Ir. *leadair*) thrash, beat

PADDEN. 'Tis the devil has us fast. Look through the top loft door. Holy Father! He's up on the table and having every wheel about!

AUNT JUG AND AUNT MARY. Mother of God! On the table and having every wheel about!

(Music in loft.)

MAINEEN. I'm telling you it's Jaymony is on the table, and better let him be. For it's playing wild he is, and his eyes gone curious mad.

PADDEN. It's a devil that's there, and a terrible devil too.

AUNT JUG AND AUNT MARY. The devil surely.

PADDEN. Don't I see the horns and the horrid hoofs?

AUNT JUG AND AUNT MARY. We see the horns and the horrid hoofs.

PADDEN. Brimstone I smell!

AUNT JUG AND AUNT MARY. Brimstone we smell!

PADDEN. The flags[63] of hell I see and the flames for ever!

AUNT JUG AND AUNT MARY. The flags of hell we see and the flames for ever!

(They sway about, clinging to ladder, Maineen still exhorting them to leave go and endeavouring to pull them away from it. Suddenly ladder gives way, and top loft tumbles down, Padden, Maineen, Jug and Mary falling on their backs, in different directions.)

PADDEN, AUNT JUG, AUNT MARY. In the name of God, we're kilt![64]

(They all get up.)

MAINEEN *(observing Jaymony's legs, which are seen sticking up above debris of top loft)*. More likely it's Jaymony is kilt. *(Goes to ruins of top loft. With considerable surprise, throwing her arms wide.)* And he is kilt! *(Bringing her hands together with a slap.)* Glory be, if it isn't kilt entirely he is, and his jugular cut by the Magic Glasses!

PADDEN *(in terror and excitement)*. In the name of God don't lay a hand to him, or it's taken up we'll be for murder, or manslaughter in the first degree. Leave him in the position he's in, Maineen, and start rising your lamentations, and likewise you, Aunt Jug. And let myself and Aunt Mary go running through the county, tearing our hair, and calling to the people, wide, the house fell down on Jaymony.

(Padden and Aunt Mary rush out.)

PADDEN AND AUNT MARY *(outside)*. Our Jaymony is kilt! the house fell down on Jaymony! Our Jaymony is kilt! the house fell down on Jaymony!

(Maineen and Aunt Jug commence to ullagone.[65] They keen[66] louder and louder as tumultuous voices are heard approaching.)

CURTAIN

63. **flags** flagstones   64. **kilt** killed   65. **ullagone** (Ir. *olagón*) wail, lament   66. **keen** (Ir. *caoin*) lament

SEAN O'CASEY
1880 – 1964

From its Abbey premiere in 1925, Sean O'Casey's *Juno and the Paycock* was a popular and critical success wherever it was staged: Dublin, London, New York. Lady Gregory praised O'Casey's gift for characterization, *The London Times* proclaimed the play's "rediscovery of words," and James Agate called it "the greatest play written in English since the days of Queen Elizabeth." Down through the years its virtues have been variously acclaimed: its accurate representation of Dublin speech, its allusive richness, its brilliant blend of tragedy and comedy, and its social conscience. Sean O'Casey's own introduction directs our attention to these latter qualities:

> This play is Ireland of the tenement houses of Dublin, where the poorer workers lived, and where many of them are living still. It is 1922, the time of the Troubles, the Civil War. Within the tenement there were those who drank too much, there were those who loved too much. There was much singing and a lot of laughter. But beyond the singing and within the echoes of the laughter and the singing, and beyond and within the light that love gave, there were darkness and sorrow, and death.
>
> This, then, is Ireland: Ireland of the Dublin tenements, in the time of the hateful Civil War, when those who had fought so long together as comrades became bitter enemies, and Irishmen again tore the cords of Ireland's heart asunder.

Sean O'Casey was born John Casey to a poor Protestant family in Dublin on March 30, 1880, the youngest of thirteen children. His early life was affected by poverty and the deaths of his father and of the majority of his siblings. Poorly educated, he became a laborer and threw himself into a series of organizations with strong appeal among the working class. These included the Gaelic League, the Irish Republican Brotherhood, the newly formed Irish Transport and General Workers' Union, and its political arm, the Irish Citizen Army. However, despite his initial enthusiasm, he soon grew disenchanted and withdrew successively from each of these associations.

Meanwhile, he was reading literature eclectically—Shakespeare, Goldsmith, Sheridan, the Romantic poets, Balzac, Dickens, Ruskin, Shaw—and attending the Abbey and the Dublin commercial theatres, where he was impressed by the work of Synge and Boucicault. His writing career began with labor journalism, included casual verses and a brief history of the Irish Citizen Army, and moved on to dramatic sketches for the Gaelic League. These efforts led to several unsuccessful submissions to the Abbey, until *The Shadow of a Gunman* was produced in 1923. Its humorous treatment of inner-city life under the stress of the War of Independence made it an immediate success. He was quick to learn from that experience, so that his next play, *Juno and the Paycock,* made striking advances in construction and complexity on the rather loose design of *The Shadow.*

His next work, *The Plough and the Stars* (1926), again set in Dublin's slums, but this time against the background of the 1916 Easter Rising, is a further advance into density of dramatic texture. But its satirical treatment of the self-deception of Irish patriots struck a raw nerve in the audience, so that the production was disrupted for a week, much as Synge's *Playboy* had been nineteen years before. Shortly thereafter, visiting London to accept the Hawthornden Prize for *Juno,* O'Casey found himself invited into the best circles. Taken by the adulation, he remained on in London, married the actress Eileen Carey, and thereafter visited Ireland only on occasion.

His decision not to return to Ireland was confirmed in 1928, when, much to his surprise, his next play, *The Silver Tassie,* was rejected by the Abbey directorate (Yeats, Lady Gregory and Lennox Robinson). In its theme (the sufferings of World War I) and technique (the expressionism of its second act), it was a departure from the "Dublin plays" which had made him famous. He took his case to the newspapers, who published his acidic exchanges with Yeats. A London production of *The Silver Tassie* was mounted, and although it was critically well received, it was not a commercial success.

To supplement his declining income, he turned to journalism, and moved to Devon for the sake of his children's education. None of his subsequent plays of the thirties and forties added to his income: *Within the Gates* (1934), *The Star Turns Red* (1940), *Red Roses for Me* (1943), *Purple Dust* (1945), *Oak Leaves and Lavender* (1947), and *Cock-a-Doodle Dandy* (1949). But meanwhile he was publishing his six-volume autobiography (1939–54).

The 1950s brought fresh controversy in Ireland, first with *The Bishop's Bonfire* (1955), and again in 1958 when his next play, *The Drums of Father Ned,* was accepted for production in the Dublin Theatre Festival. But Archbisop McQuaid objected to a dramatized version of Joyce's *Ulysses* as well as to references in *Drums* sympathetic to communism. This led to a confused debate, the upshot of which was that Samuel Beckett withdrew his *All That Fall* and O'Casey his play, and the entire festival was cancelled. In 1964, Sean O'Casey died in Devon.

O'Casey's literary reputation, by general consensus, rests on his first three "Dublin" plays. His later work, for various reasons (mainly his removal from his subject and his doctrinaire communism), is flawed by over-writing, rancor and caricature. But *The Shadow, Juno* and *The Plough* are sufficient to claim a major place in the history of Irish drama. In these plays, O'Casey writes of the lives of the inner-city poor caught up in celebrated historical conflicts. And from his plays emerge heroes other than those remembered in ballad and official history: the stouthearted defenders of domestic virtue. The paragon of these figures, most of whom are women, is Juno Boyle, whose no-nonsense grasp of proximate realities contrasts with the feckless talk of the men in her life. O'Casey's distinctive talent lies in his capacity to join these diverse elements, the tragic and the pathetic, so as to achieve several degrees of ironic and tragicomic counterpoint.

The comedy in *Juno* derives mainly from language and character. As regards language, O'Casey is often called a "Synge of the city": the distinctive O'Casey idiom is derived from authentic rhythms of Dublin speech, with its penchant for alliteration, malaprop and exaggeration. Loaded with emotion, it is a language that readily turns to song, as we see in the "hooley" of Act II. O'Casey's characters, well observed and particular though they are, derive from thoroughly traditional sources in Western comedy, in a line extending back through Dickens, Jonson and Shakespeare to the techniques of Plautus and Terence. As Jack Lindsay has observed, the stage Irishman of Boucicault has his roots in folk-humor and in the immemorial line that runs back through the Commedia dell'Arte to the ancient world. By purging the sentimentalities and falsities that had gathered round such types in the nineteenth century, O'Casey reached back to the origins and achieved what may be called the only true recreation of Aristophanic comedy ever made; for he found the links not in literature but in life itself and in a folk-tradition from which he himself had emerged.

Directors of *Juno and the Paycock* have not always resisted the temptation to yield to the playability of the broad comedy. Nevertheless, there is a growing sense of doom as the play progresses, a development that the interpolations of broad comedy and verbal understatement do not relieve, but heighten, so that the effect is one of a moving tragedy. The apotheosis of these effects is the incomparable final scene. Similarly, what appears at first to be a mock-heroic treatment of the mythic story of jealous Juno turns out to be quite the reverse: in O'Casey's words, *Juno and the Paycock* is the story of "a heroine who will never have her name in the papers, never have a memorial; nonetheless, [she is] one of Whitman's heroines among greatest heroines known."

SELECT BIBLIOGRAPHY

Publications

Collected Plays, Vol. 1. London: Macmillan, 1949. (*Juno and the Paycock, The Shadow of a Gunman, The Plough and the Stars, The End of the Beginning, A Pound on Demand*)

Collected Plays, Vol. 2. London: Macmillan, 1949. (*The Silver Tassie, Within the Gates, The Star Turns Red*)

Collected Plays, Vol. 3. London: Macmillan, 1951. (*Purple Dust, Red Roses for Me, Hall of Healing*)

Collected Plays, Vol. 4. London: Macmillan, 1951. (*Oak Leaves and Lavender, Cock-a-Doodle Dandy, Bedtime Story, Time to Go*)

The Bishop's Bonfire. New York: Macmillan, 1955.

The Drums of Father Ned. New York: St. Martin's Press, 1960.

Mirror in My House: The Autobiographies of Sean O'Casey. 2 vols. New York: Macmillan, 1956. Reprinted as *Autobiographies.* 2 vols. London: Macmillan, 1956.

Blasts and Benedictions: Articles and Stories. Ed. Ronald Ayling. London: Macmillan/New York: St. Martin's Press, 1967.

The Sean O'Casey Reader: Plays, Autobiographies, Opinions. Ed. Brooks Atkinson. New York: St. Martin's Press/London: Macmillan, 1968.

Biography and Criticism.

Ayling, Ronald. *Sean O'Casey: Modern Judgments.* London: Macmillan, 1969; Nashville, TN: Aurora, 1970.

———, and Michael J. Durkan. *Sean O'Casey: A Bibliography.* London: Macmillan, 1978.

Hogan, Robert. *The Experiments of Sean O'Casey.* New York: St. Martin's Press, 1960.

Kilroy, Thomas, Ed. *Sean O'Casey: A Collection of Critical Essays.* Englewood Cliffs, NJ: Prentice-Hall, 1975.

Krause, David. *Sean O'Casey: The Man and His Work.* New York: Macmillan/London: Collier Macmillan, 1975.

O'Connor, Garry. *Sean O'Casey: A Life.* London: Hodder and Stoughton/New York: Atheneum, 1988.

Juno and the Paycock

A Tragedy in Three Acts

CHARACTERS IN THE PLAY

"Captain" Jack Boyle
Juno Boyle, *his wife*
Johnny Boyle ⎫
Mary Boyle ⎬ *their children* ⎱ *Residents in*
"Joxer" Daly ⎰ *the Tenement*
Mrs. Maisie Madigan
"Needle" Nugent, *a tailor*
Mrs. Tancred ⎭
Jerry Devine
Charles Bentham, *a school teacher*
An Irregular Mobilizer
Two Irregulars
A Coal-Block Vendor
A Sewing Machine Man
Two Furniture Removal Men
Two Neighbours

SCENE

Act 1.—The living apartment of a two-roomed tenancy of the Boyle family, in a tenement house in Dublin.

Act 2.—The same.

Act 3.—The same.

A few days elapse between Acts 1 and 2 and two months between Acts 2 and 3.

During Act 3 the curtain is lowered for a few minutes to denote the lapse of one hour.

Period of the play, 1922.[1]

---

1. **1922** the new Irish Free State—made up of twenty-six of Ireland's thirty-two counties—has just been set up. But a civil war is in progress between those who accept this compromise (the Free Staters) and the Republicans (known as Diehards, or Irregulars), who insist on the independence of the whole of Ireland.

ACT 1

The living-room of a two-room tenancy occupied by the Boyle family in a tene-
ment house in Dublin. Left, a door leading to another part of the house; left of
door a window looking into the street; at back a dresser[2]; farther to right at
back, a window looking into the back of the house. Between the window and the
dresser is a picture of the Virgin; below the picture, on a bracket, is a crimson
bowl in which a floating votive light is burning. Farther to the right is a small
bed partly concealed by cretonne hangings strung on a twine. To the right is
the fireplace; near the fireplace is a door leading to the other room. Beside the
fireplace is a box containing coal. On the mantelshelf is an alarm clock lying
on its face. In a corner near the window looking into the back is a galvanized[3]
bath. A table and some chairs. On the table are breakfast things for one. A
teapot is on the hob[4] and a frying-pan stands inside the fender.[5] There are a
few books on the dresser and one on the table. Leaning against the dresser is a
long-handled shovel—the kind invariably used by labourers when turning con-
crete or mixing mortar. Johnny Boyle is sitting crouched beside the fire. Mary
with her jumper[6] off—it is lying on the back of a chair—is arranging her hair
before a tiny mirror perched on the table. Beside the mirror is stretched out the
morning paper, which she looks at when she isn't gazing into the mirror. She is
a well-made and good-looking girl of twenty-two. Two forces are working in her
mind—one, through the circumstances of her life, pulling her back; the other,
through the influence of books she has read, pushing her forward. The opposing
forces are apparent in her speech and her manners, both of which are degraded
by her environment, and improved by her acquaintance—slight though it be—
with literature. The time is early forenoon.

MARY *(looking at the paper)*. On a little bye-road,[7] out beyant[8] Finglas,[9]
he was found.

(Mrs. Boyle enters by door on right; she has been shopping and carries a
small parcel in her hand. She is forty-five years of age, and twenty years ago she
must have been a pretty woman; but her face has now assumed that look which
ultimately settles down upon the faces of the women of the working-class; a look
of listless monotony and harassed anxiety, blending with an expression of me-
chanical resistance. Were circumstances favourable, she would probably be a
handsome, active and clever woman.)

MRS. BOYLE. Isn't he come in yet?

MARY. No, mother.

MRS. BOYLE. Oh, he'll come in when he likes; struttin' about the town

2. **dresser** cupboard   3. **galvanized** iron coated with zinc   4. **hob** metal stand
beside the grate in a fireplace   5. **fender** metal guard on the floor around the
fireplace   6. **jumper** sweater   7. **bye-road** minor road   8. **beyant** beyond   9. **Fin-**
glas village on the northwest outskirts of Dublin

like a paycock[10] with Joxer, I suppose. I hear all about Mrs. Tancred's son is in this mornin's paper.

MARY. The full details are in it this mornin'; seven wounds he had— one entherin' the neck, with an exit wound beneath the left shoulder- blade; another in the left breast penethratin' the heart, an' . . .

JOHNNY *(springing up from the fire)*. Oh, quit that readin', for God's sake! Are yous losin' all your feelin's? It'll soon be that none of you'll read anythin' that's not about butcherin'!

(He goes quickly into the room on left.)

MARY. He's gettin' very sensitive, all of a sudden!

MRS. BOYLE. I'll read it myself, Mary, by an' by, when I come home. Everybody's sayin' that he was a Diehard—thanks be to God that Johnny had nothin' to do with him this long time. . . . *(Opening the parcel and taking out some sausages, which she places on a plate)* Ah, then, if that father o' yours doesn't come in soon for his breakfast, he may go without any; I'll not wait much longer for him.

MARY. Can't you let him get it himself when he comes in?

MRS. BOYLE. Yes, an' let him bring in Joxer Daly along with him? Ay, that's what he'd like, an' that's what he's waitin' for—till he thinks I'm gone to work, an' then sail in with the boul'[11] Joxer, to burn all the coal an' dhrink all the tea in the place, to show them what a good Samaritan[12] he is! But I'll stop here till he comes in, if I have to wait till to-morrow mornin'.

VOICE OF JOHNNY INSIDE. Mother!

MRS. BOYLE. Yis?

VOICE OF JOHNNY. Bring us in a dhrink o' wather.

MRS. BOYLE. Bring in that fella a dhrink o' wather, for God's sake, Mary.

MARY. Isn't he big an' able enough to come out an' get it himself?

MRS. BOYLE. If you weren't well yourself you'd like somebody to bring you in a dhrink o' wather.

(She brings in drink and returns.)

MRS. BOYLE. Isn't it terrible to have to be waitin' this way! You'd think he was bringin' twenty poun's a week into the house the way he's going on. He wore out the Health Insurance long ago, he's afther wearin' out the unemployment dole, an', now, he's thryin' to wear out me! An' con- stantly singin', no less, when he ought always to be on his knees offerin' up a Novena[13] for a job!

MARY *(tying a ribbon fillet-wise around her head)*. I don't like this ribbon, ma; I think I'll wear the green—it looks betther than the blue.

10. **paycock** peacock 11. **boul'** bold, shameless 12. **good Samaritan** as in Je- sus' parable (Luke 10: 33–37) 13. **Novena** a nine days' program of prayer

MRS. BOYLE. Ah, wear whatever ribbon you like, girl, only don't be botherin' me. I don't know what a girl on strike wants to be wearin' a ribbon round her head for, or silk stockins on her legs either; it's wearin' them things that make the employers think they're givin' yous too much money.

MARY. The hour is past now when we'll ask the employers' permission to wear what we like.

MRS. BOYLE. I don't know why you wanted to walk out for Jennie Claffey; up to this you never had a good word for her.

MARY. What's the use of belongin' to a Trades Union if you won't stand up for your principles? Why did they sack her? It was a clear case of victimization. We couldn't let her walk the streets, could we?

MRS. BOYLE. No, of course yous couldn't—yous wanted to keep her company. Wan victim wasn't enough. When the employers sacrifice wan victim, the Trades Union go wan betther be sacrificin' a hundred.

MARY. It doesn't matther what you say, ma—a principle's a principle.

MRS. BOYLE. Yis; an' when I go into oul' Murphy's to-morrow, an' he gets to know that, instead o' payin' all, I'm goin' to borry more, what'll he say when I tell him a principle's a principle? What'll we do if he refuses to give us any more on tick?[14]

MARY. He daren't refuse—if he does, can't you tell him he's paid?

MRS. BOYLE. It's lookin' as if he was paid, whether he refuses or no.

(Johnny appears at the door on left. He can be plainly seen now; he is a thin, delicate[15] fellow, something younger than Mary. He has evidently gone through a rough time. His face is pale and drawn; there is a tremulous look of indefinite fear in his eyes. The left sleeve of his coat is empty, and he walks with a slight halt.)

JOHNNY. I was lyin' down; I thought yous were gone. Oul' Simon Mackay is thrampin' about like a horse over me head,[16] an' I can't sleep with him—they're like thunder-claps in me brain! The curse o'—God forgive me for goin' to curse!

MRS. BOYLE. There, now; go back an' lie down again, an' I'll bring you in a nice cup o' tay.[17]

JOHNNY. Tay, tay, tay! You're always thinkin' o' tay. If a man was dyin', you'd thry to make him swally a cup o' tay!

(He goes back.)

MRS. BOYLE. I don't know what's goin' to be done with him. The bullet he got in the hip in Easter Week[18] was bad enough, but the bomb that shatthered his arm in the f_ɛ_nt in O'Connell Street put the finishin'

14. **tick** credit   15. **delicate** sickly   16. **over me head** on the floor above
17. **tay** tea   18. **Easter Week** the 1916 Easter Rising centered in Dublin's O'Connell Street

touch on him. I knew he was makin' a fool of himself. God knows I went
down on me bended knees to him not to go agen the Free State.

MARY. He stuck to his principles, an', no matther how you may argue,
ma, a principle's a principle.

VOICE OF JOHNNY. Is Mary goin' to stay here?

MARY. No, I'm not goin' to stay here; you can't expect me to be always
at your beck an' call, can you?

VOICE OF JOHNNY. I won't stop[19] here be meself!

MRS. BOYLE. Amn't I nicely handicapped with the whole o' yous! I
don't know what any o' yous ud do without your ma. *(To Johnny.)* Your
father'll be here in a minute, an' if you want anythin', he'll get it for you.

JOHNNY. I hate assin' him for anythin'. . . . He hates to be assed to
stir. . . . Is the light lightin' before the picture o' the Virgin?

MRS. BOYLE. Yis, yis! The wan inside to St. Anthony[20] isn't enough,
but he must have another wan to the Virgin here!

*(Jerry Devine enters hastily. He is about twenty-five, well set, active and
earnest. He is a type, becoming very common now in the Labour Movement,[21]
of a mind knowing enough to make the mass of his associates, who know less, a
power, and too little to broaden that power for the benefit of all. Mary seizes
her jumper and runs hastily into room left.)*

JERRY *(breathless)*. Where's the Captain, Mrs. Boyle, where's the Captain?

MRS. BOYLE. You may well ass a body that: he's wherever Joxer Daly
is—dhrinkin' in some snug[22] or another.

JERRY. Father Farrell is just afther stoppin' to tell me to run up an' get
him to go to the new job that's goin' on in Rathimines[23]; his cousin is
foreman o' the job, an' Father Farrell was speakin' to him about poor
Johnny an' his father bein' idle so long, an' the foreman told Father Farrell
to send the Captain up an' he'd give him a start—I wondher where I'd
find him?

MRS. BOYLE. You'll find he's ayther in Ryan's or Foley's.[24]

JERRY. I'll run round to Ryan's—I know it's a great house o' Joxer's.
(He rushes out.)

MRS. BOYLE *(piteously)*. There now, he'll miss that job, or I know for
what! If he gets win' o' the word, he'll not come back till evenin', so that
it'll be too late. There'll never be any good got out o' him so long as he
goes with that shouldher-shruggin' Joxer. I killin' meself workin', an' he
sthruttin' about from mornin' till night like a paycock!

(The steps of two persons are heard coming up a flight of stairs. They

19. **stop** stay   20. **St. Anthony** of Padua, Portuguese (1195–1231)   21. **Labour
Movement** founded in 1912, the Irish Labour Party developed rapidly in the cities
until 1922   22. **snug** private drinking booth in a bar   23. **Rathmines** Dublin City
district   24. **Ryan's or Foley's** neighborhood bars

are the footsteps of Captain Boyle and Joxer. Captain Boyle is singing in a deep, sonorous, self-honouring voice.)

THE CAPTAIN. Sweet Spirit, hear me prayer![25] Hear . . . oh . . . hear . . . me prayer . . . hear, oh, hear . . . Oh, he . . . ar . . . oh, he . . . ar . . . me . . . pray . . . er!

JOXER (outside). Ah, that's a darlin' song, a daaarlin' song!

MRS. BOYLE (viciously). Sweet spirit hear his prayer! Ah, then, I'll take me solemn affeydavey,[26] it's not for a job he's prayin'!

(She sits down on the bed so that the cretonne hangings hide her from the view of those entering.)

(The Captain comes slowly in. He is a man of about sixty; stout, grey-haired and stocky. His neck is short, and his head looks like a stone ball that one sometimes sees on top of a gate-post. His cheeks, reddish-purple, are puffed out, as if he were always repressing an almost irrepressible ejaculation. On his upper lip is a crisp, tightly cropped moustache; he carries himself with the upper part of his body slightly thrown back, and his stomach slightly thrust forward. His walk is a slow, consequential strut. His clothes are dingy, and he wears a faded seaman's-cap with a glazed peak.)

BOYLE (to Joxer, who is still outside). Come on, come on in, Joxer; she's gone out long ago, man. If there's nothing else to be got, we'll furrage[27] out a cup o' tay, anyway. It's the only bit I get in comfort when she's away. 'Tisn't Juno should be her pet name at all, but Deirdre of the Sorras,[28] for she's always grousin'.

(Joxer steps cautiously into the room. He may be younger than the Captain but he looks a lot older. His face is like a bundle of crinkled paper; his eyes have a cunning twinkle; he is spare and loosely built; he has a habit of constantly shrugging his shoulders with a peculiar twitching movement, meant to be ingratiating. His face is invariably ornamented with a grin.)

JOXER. It's a terrible thing to be tied to a woman that's always grousin'. I don't know how you stick it—it ud put years on me. It's a good job she has to be so often away, for (with a shrug) when the cat's away, the mice can play!

BOYLE (with a commanding and complacent gesture). Pull over to the fire, Joxer, an' we'll have a cup o' tay in a minute.

JOXER. Ah, a cup o' tay's a darlin' thing, a daaarlin' thing—the cup that cheers but doesn't . . .[29]

25. **Sweet Spirit, Hear My Prayer** from the opera *Lurline* (1860) by Edward Fitzball and William Vincent Wallace   26. **affeydavey** oath, affidavit   27. **furrage out** forage for, make   28. **Deirdre of the Sorras** Dierdre of the Sorrows, the tragic heroine of the classic Irish myth, who brought death to her lover and his two brothers and then committed suicide   29. **the cup that cheers but doesn't . . .** commercial slogan for tea, after William Cowper's "the cups / That cheer but not inebriate," *The Task*, iv, 39–40

*(Joxer's rhapsody is cut short by the sight of Juno coming forward and con-
fronting the two cronies. Both are stupefied.)*

MRS. BOYLE *(with sweet irony—poking the fire, and turning her head to
glare at Joxer).* Pull over to the fire, Joxer Daly, an' we'll have a cup o' tay
in a minute! Are you sure, now, you wouldn't like an egg?

JOXER. I can't stop, Mrs. Boyle; I'm in a desperate hurry, a desperate
hurry.

MRS. BOYLE. Pull over to the fire, Joxer Daly; people is always far
more comfortabler here than they are in their own place.

*(Joxer makes hastily for the door. Boyle stirs to follow him; thinks of something
to relieve the situation—stops, and says suddenly):* Joxer!

JOXER *(at door ready to bolt).* Yis?

BOYLE. You know the foreman o' that job that's goin' on down in
Killesther,[30] don't you, Joxer?

JOXER *(puzzled).* Foreman—Killesther?

BOYLE *(with a meaning look).* He's a butty o' yours, isn't he?

JOXER *(the truth dawning on him).* The foreman at Killesther—oh yis,
yis. He's an oul' butty[31] o' mine—oh, he's a darlin' man, a daarlin' man.

BOYLE. Oh, then, it's a sure thing. It's a pity we didn't go down at
breakfast first thing this mornin'—we might ha' been working now; but
you didn't know it then.

JOXER *(with a shrug).* It's betther late than never.

BOYLE. It's nearly time we got a start, anyhow; I'm fed up knockin'
round, doin' nothin'. He promised you—gave you the straight tip?

JOXER. Yis. "Come down on the blow o' dinner,"[32] says he, "an' I'll
start you, an' any friend you like to brin' with you." "Ah," says I, "you're
a darlin' man, a daaarlin' man."

BOYLE. Well, it couldn't come at a betther time—we're a long time
waitin' for it.

JOXER. Indeed we were; but it's a long lane that has no turnin'.

BOYLE. The blow up for dinner is at one—wait till I see what time it
'tis.

(He goes over to the mantelpiece, and gingerly lifts the clock.)

MRS. BOYLE. Min' now, how you go on fiddlin' with that clock—you
know the least little thing sets it asthray.

BOYLE. The job couldn't come at a betther time; I'm feelin' in great
fettle, Joxer. I'd hardly believe I ever had a pain in me legs, an' last week
I was nearly crippled with them.

JOXER. That's betther an' betther; ah, God never shut wan door but
He opened another!

---

30. **Killesther** Dublin City district   31. **butty** friend   32. **blow o' dinner** at
lunchtime

BOYLE. It's only eleven o'clock; we've lashins o' time. I'll slip on me oul' moleskins[33] afther breakfast, an' we can saunther down at our ayse.[34] *(Putting his hand on the shovel.)* I think, Joxer, we'd betther bring our shovels?

JOXER. Yis, Captain, yis; it's betther to go fully prepared an' ready for all eventualities. You bring your long-tailed shovel, an' I'll bring me navvy.[35] We mighten' want them, an', then agen, we might: for want of a nail the shoe was lost, for want of a shoe the house was lost, an' for want of a horse the man was lost—aw, that's a darlin' proverb, a daarlin' . . .

(As Joxer is finishing his sentence, Mrs. Boyle approaches the door and Joxer retreats hurriedly. She shuts the door with a bang.)

BOYLE *(suggestively)*. We won't be long pullin' ourselves together agen when I'm working for a few weeks.

(Mrs. Boyle takes no notice.)

BOYLE. The foreman on the job is an oul' butty o' Joxer's; I have an idea that I know him meself. (Silence.) . . . There's a button off the back o' me moleskin trousers. . . . If you leave out a needle an' thread I'll sew it on meself. . . . Thanks be to God, the pains in me legs is gone, anyhow!

MRS. BOYLE *(with a burst)*. Look here, Mr. Jacky Boyle, them yarns won't go down with Juno. I know you an' Joxer Daly of an oul' date,[36] an' if you think you're able to come it over me[37] with them fairy tales, you're in the wrong shop.[38]

BOYLE *(coughing subduedly to relieve the tenseness of the situation)*. U-u-u-ugh!

MRS. BOYLE. Butty o' Joxer's! Oh, you'll do a lot o' good as long as you continue to be a butty o' Joxer's!

BOYLE. U-u-u-ugh!

MRS. BOYLE. Shovel! Ah, then, me boyo, you'd do far more work with a knife an' fork than ever you'll do with a shovel! If there was e'er a genuine job goin' you'd be dh'other way about—not able to lift your arms with the pains in your legs! Your poor wife slavin' to keep the bit[39] in your mouth, an' you gallivantin' about all the day like a paycock!

BOYLE. It ud be betther for a man to be dead, betther for a man to be dead.

MRS. BOYLE *(ignoring the interruption)*. Everybody callin' you "Captain," an' you only wanst on the wather, in an oul' collier from here to Liverpool,[40] when anybody, to listen or look at you, ud take you for a second Christo For Columbus!

33. **moleskins** working trousers with a heavy weave   34. **ayse** ease   35. **navvy** spade or shovel for digging   36. **of an oul' date** for a long time   37. **come it over me** fool me   38. **in the wrong shop** mistaken   39. **the bit** a bit to eat   40. **an oul' collier from here to Liverpool** most of Ireland's coal from England via Liverpool (120 miles)

BOYLE. Are you never goin' to give us a rest?

MRS. BOYLE. Oh, you're never tired o' lookin' for a rest.

BOYLE. D'ye want to dhrive me out o' the house?

MRS. BOYLE. It ud be easier to dhrive you out o' the house than to dhrive you into a job. Here, sit down an' take your breakfast—it may be last you'll get, for I don't know where the next is goin' to come from.

BOYLE. If I get this job we'll be all right.

MRS. BOYLE. Did ye see Jerry Devine?

BOYLE *(testily)*. No, I didn't see him.

MRS. BOYLE. No, but you seen Joxer. Well, he was here lookin' for you.

BOYLE. Well, let him look!

MRS. BOYLE. Oh, indeed, he may well look, for it ud be hard for him to see you, an' you stuck in Ryan's snug.

BOYLE. I wasn't in Ryan's snug—I don't go into Ryan's.

MRS. BOYLE. Oh, is there a mad dog there? Well, if you weren't in Ryan's you were in Foley's.

BOYLE. I'm telling you for the last three weeks I haven't tasted a dhrop of intoxicatin' liquor. I wasn't in ayther wan snug or dh'other—I could swear that on a prayer-book—I'm as innocent as the child unborn!

MRS. BOYLE. Well, if you'd been in for your breakfast you'd ha' seen him.

BOYLE *(suspiciously)*. What does he want me for?

MRS. BOYLE. He'll be back any minute an' then you'll soon know.

BOYLE. I'll dhrop out an' see if I can meet him.

MRS. BOYLE. You'll sit down an' take your breakfast, an' let me go to me work, for I'm an hour late already waitin' for you.

BOYLE. You needn't ha' waited, for I'll take no breakfast—I've a little spirit left in me still!

MRS. BOYLE. Are you goin' to have your breakfast—yes or no?

BOYLE *(too proud to yield)*. I'll have no breakfast—yous can keep your breakfast. *(Plaintively.)* I'll knock out a bit⁴¹ somewhere, never fear.

MRS. BOYLE. Nobody's goin' to coax you—don't think that.

(She vigorously replaces the pan and the sausages in the press.⁴²)

BOYLE. I've a little spirit left in me still.

(Jerry Devine enters hastily.)

JERRY. Oh, here you are at last! I've been searchin' for you everywhere. The foreman in Foley's told me you hadn't left the snug with Joxer ten minutes before I went in.

MRS. BOYLE. An' he swearin' on the holy prayer-book that he wasn't in no snug!

---

41. **knock out a bit** find something to eat   42. **press** cupboard

BOYLE *(to Jerry)*. What business is it o' yours whether I was in a snug or no? What do you want to be gallopin' about afther me for? Is a man not to be allowed to leave his house for a minute without havin' a pack o' spies, pimps an' informers[43] cantherin' at his heels?

JERRY. Oh, you're takin' a wrong view of it, Mr. Boyle; I simply was anxious to do you a good turn. I have a message for you from Father Farrell: he says that if you go to the job that's on in Rathmines, an' ask for Foreman Managan, you'll get a start.

BOYLE. That's all right, but I don't want the motions of me body to be watched the way an asthronomer ud watch a star. If you're folleyin' Mary aself, you've no pereeogative to be folleyin' me. *(Suddenly catching his right thigh.)* U-ugh, I'm afther gettin' a terrible twinge in me right leg!

MRS. BOYLE. Oh, it won't be very long now till it travels into your left wan. It's miraculous that whenever he scents a job in front of him, his legs begin to fail him! Then, me bucko, if you lose this chance, you may go an' furrage for yourself!

JERRY. This job'll last for some time too, Captain, an' as soon as the foundations are in, it'll be cushy enough.

BOYLE. Won't it be a climbin' job? How d'ye expect me to be able to go up a ladder with these legs? An', if I get up aself, how am I goin' to get down agen?

MRS. BOYLE *(viciously)*. Get wan o' the labourers to carry you down in a hod![44] You can't climb a laddher, but you can skip like a goat into a snug!

JERRY. I wouldn't let myself be let down that easy, Mr. Boyle; a little exercise, now, might do you all the good in the world.

BOYLE. It's a docthor you should have been Devine—maybe you know more about the pains in me legs than meself that has them?

JERRY *(irritated)*. Oh, I know nothin' about the pains in your legs; I've brought the message that Father Farrell gave me, an' that's all I can do.

MRS. BOYLE. Here, sit down an' take your breakfast, an' go an' get ready; an' don't be actin' as if you couldn't pull a wing out of a dead bee.

BOYLE. I want no breakfast, I tell you; it ud choke me afther all that's been said. I've a little spirit left in me still.

MRS. BOYLE. Well, let's see your spirit, then, an' go in at wanst an' put on your moleskin trousers!

BOYLE *(moving towards the door on left)*. It ud be betther for a man to be dead! U-ugh! There's another twinge in me other leg! Nobody but meself knows the sufferin' I'm goin' through with the pains in these legs o' mine!

---

43. **informers** sellers of political information   44. **hod** implement for carrying bricks or mortar

(He goes into the room on left as Mary comes out with her hat in her hand.)

MRS. BOYLE. I'll have to push off now, for I'm terrible late already, but I was determined to stay an' hunt[45] that Joxer this time.

(She goes off.)

JERRY. Are you going out, Mary?

MARY. It looks like it when I'm putting on my hat, doesn't it?

JERRY. The bitther word agen, Mary.

MARY. You won't allow me to be friendly with you; if I thry, you deliberately misundherstand it.

JERRY. I didn't always misundherstand it; you were often delighted to have the arms of Jerry around you.

MARY. If you go on talkin' like this, Jerry Devine, you'll make me hate you!

JERRY. Well, let it be either a weddin' or a wake! Listen, Mary, I'm standin' for the Secretaryship of our Union. There's only one opposin' me; I'm popular with all the men, an' a good speaker—all are sayin' that I'll get elected.

MARY. Well?

JERRY. The job's worth three hundred an' fifty pounds a year, Mary. You an' I could live nice an' cosily on that; it would lift you out o' this place an' . . .

MARY. I haven't time to listen to you now—I have to go.

(She is going out, when Jerry bars the way.)

JERRY *(appealingly)*. Mary, what's come over you with me for the last few weeks? You hardly speak to me, an' then only a word with a face o' bitthernes on it. Have you forgotten, Mary, all the happy evenins that were as sweet as the scented hawthorn that sheltered the sides o' the road as we sauntered through the country?

MARY. That's all over now. When you get your new job, Jerry, you won't be long findin' a girl far betther than I am for your sweetheart.

JERRY. Never, never, Mary! No matther what happens, you'll always be the same to me.

MARY. I must be off; please let me go, Jerry.

JERRY. I'll go a bit o' the way with you.

MARY. You needn't, thanks; I want to be by meself.

JERRY *(catching her arm)*. You're goin' to meet another fella; you've clicked with someone else, me lady!

MARY. That's no concern o' yours, Jerry Devine; let me go!

JERRY. I saw yous comin' out o' the Cornflower Dance Class, an' you hangin' on his arm—a thin, lanky strip of a Mickey Dazzler,[46] with a walkin'-stick an' gloves!

---

45. **hunt** rout 46. **Micky Dazzler** dude, dandy

VOICE OF JOHNNY (*loudly*). What are you doin' there—pullin' about everything!

VOICE OF BOYLE (*loudly and viciously*). I'm puttin' on me moleskin trousers!

MARY. You're hurtin' me arm! Let me go, or I'll scream, an' then you'll have the oul' fella out on top of us!

JERRY. Don't be so hard on a fella, Mary, don't be so hard.

BOYLE (*appearing at the door*). What's the meanin' of all this hillabaloo?

MARY. Let me go, let me go!

BOYLE. D'ye hear me—what's all this hillabaloo about?

JERRY (*plaintively*). Will you not give us one kind word, one kind word, Mary?

BOYLE. D'ye hear me talkin' to yous? What's all this hillabaloo for?

JERRY. Let me kiss your hand, your little, tiny, white hand!

BOYLE. Your little, tiny, white hand—are you takin' leave o' your senses, man?

(*Mary breaks away and rushes out.*)

BOYLE. This is nice goins on in front of her father!

JERRY. Ah, dhry up, for God's sake!

(*He follows Mary.*)

BOYLE. Chiselurs[47] don't care a damn now about their parents, they're bringin' their fathers' grey hairs down with sorra to the grave, an' laughin' at it, laughin' at it. Ah, I suppose it's just the same everywhere—the whole worl's in a state o' chassis![48] (*He sits by the fire.*) Breakfast! Well, they can keep their breakfast for me. Not if they were down on their bended knees would I take it—I'll show them I've a little spirit left in me still! (*He goes over to the press, takes out a plate and looks at it.*) Sassige! Well, let her keep her sassige. (*He returns to the fire, takes up the teapot and gives it a gentle shake.*) The tea's wet right enough.

(*A pause; he rises, goes to the press, takes out the sausage, puts it on the pan, and puts both on the fire. He attends the sausage with a fork.*)

BOYLE (*singing*):

When the robins nest agen,[49]
And the flowers are in bloom,
When the Springtime's sunny smile seems to banish all sorrow an' gloom;
Then me bonny blue-ey'd lad, if me heart be true till then——
He's promised he'll come back to me,
When the robins nest agen!

(*He lifts his head at the high note, and then drops his eyes to the pan.*)

47. **Chiselurs** children   48. **chassis** chaos   49. **When the robins nest agen!** popular song (1883) by Frank Howard

BOYLE *(singing)*:

When the . . .

(Steps are heard approaching; he whips the pan off the fire and puts it under the bed, then sits down at the fire. The door opens and a bearded man looking in says:)

You don't happen to want a sewin' machine?

BOYLE *(furiously)*. No, I don't want e're a sewin' machine!

(He returns the pan to the fire, and commences to sing again.)

BOYLE *(singing)*:

> When the robins nest agen,
> And the flowers they are in bloom,
> He's . . .

(A thundering knock is heard at the street door.)

BOYLE. There's a terrible tatheraraa—that's a stranger—that's nobody belongin' to the house.

(Another loud knock.)

JOXER *(sticking his head in at the door)*. Did ye hear them tatherarahs?

BOYLE. Well, Joxer, I'm not deaf.

JOHNNY *(appearing in his shirt and trousers at the door on left; his face is anxious and his voice is tremulous)*. Who's that at the door; who's that at the door? Who gave that knock—d'ye yous hear me—are yous deaf or dhrunk or what?

BOYLE *(to Johnny)*. How the hell do I know who 'tis? Joxer, stick your head out o' the window an' see.

JOXER. An' mebbe get a bullet in the kisser? Ah, none o' them thricks for Joxer! It's better to be a coward than a corpse!

BOYLE *(looking cautiously out of the window)*. It's a fella in a thrench coat.

JOHNNY. Holy Mary, Mother o' God, I . . .

BOYLE. He's goin' away—he must ha' got tired knockin'.

(Johnny returns to the room on left.)

BOYLE. Sit down an' have a cup o' tay, Joxer.

JOXER. I'm afraid the missus ud pop in on us agen before we'd know where we are. Somethin's tellin' me to go at wanst.

BOYLE. Don't be superstitious, man; we're Dublin men, an' not boyos that's only afther comin' up from the bog o' Allen[50]—though if she did come in, right enough, we'd be caught like rats in a thrap.

JOXER. An' you know the sort she is—she wouldn't listen to reason—an' wanse bitten twice shy.

---

50. **bog o' Allen** Ireland's central turf (peat) bog: Dubliners consider natives of this region ignorant and uncouth

BOYLE *(going over to the window at back).* If the worst came to the worst, you could dart out here, Joxer; it's only a dhrop of a few feet to the roof of the return room,[51] an' the first minute she goes into dh'other room I'll give you the bend,[52] an' you can slip in an' away.

JOXER *(yielding to the temptation).* Ah, I won't stop very long anyhow. *(Picking up a book from the table.)* Whose is the buk?

BOYLE. Aw, one o' Mary's; she's always readin' lately—nothin' but thrash, too. There's one I was lookin' at dh'other day: three stories, The Doll's House, Ghosts, an' The Wild Duck[53]—buks only fit for chiselurs!

JOXER. Didja ever rade *Elizabeth, or Th' Exile o' Sibayria?*[54] . . . Ah, it's a darlin' story, a daarlin' story!

BOYLE. You eat your sassige, an' never min' *Th' Exile o' Sibayria.*

(Both sit down; Boyle fills[55] *out tea, pours gravy on Joxer's plate, and keeps the sausage for himself.)*

JOXER. What are you wearin' your moleskin trousers for?

BOYLE. I have to go to a job, Joxer. Just afther you'd gone, Devine kem runnin' in to tell us that Father Farrell said if I went down to the job that's goin' on in Rathmines I'd get a start.

JOXER. Be the holy, that's good news!

BOYLE. How is it good news? I wondher if you were in my condition, would you call it good news?

JOXER. I thought . . .

BOYLE. You thought! You think too sudden sometimes, Joxer. D'ye know, I'm hardly able to crawl with the pains in me legs!

JOXER. Yis, yis; I forgot the pains in your legs. I know you can do nothin' while they're at you.

BOYLE. You forgot; I don't think any of yous realize the state I'm in with the pains in me legs. What ud happen if I had to carry a bag o' cement?

JOXER. Ah, any man havin' the like of them pains id be down an' out, down an' out.

BOYLE. I wouldn't mind if he had said it to meself; but, no, oh no, he rushes in an' shouts it out in front o' Juno, an' you know what Juno is, Joxer. We all know Devine knows a little more than the rest of us, but he doesn't act as if he did; he's a good boy, sober, able to talk an' all that, but still . . .

JOXER. Oh ay; able to argufy, but still . . .

BOYLE. If he's runnin' afther Mary, aself, he's not goin' to be runnin'

51. **return room** an extension at the back of the house   52. **bend** sign   53. **The Doll's House, Ghosts, an' The Wild Duck** Henrik Ibsen's social dramas of the 1880s   54. **Elizabeth, or Th' Exile o' Sibayria** *Elizabeth; or, the Exiles of Siberia: A Tale Founded upon Facts,* from the French by Madame (Marie) Cottin (1770–1807), went through dozens of editions during the nineteenth century   55. **fills** pours

afther me. Captain Boyle's able to take care of himself. Afther all, I'm not gettin' brought up on Virol.[56] I never heard him usin' a curse; I don't believe he was ever dhrunk in his life—sure he's not like a Christian at all!

JOXER. You're afther takin' the word out o' me mouth—afther all, a Christian's natural, but he's unnatural.

BOYLE. His oul' fella was just the same—a Wicklow[57] man.

JOXER. A Wicklow man! That explains the whole thing. I've met many a Wicklow man in me time, but I never met wan that was any good.

BOYLE. "Father Farrell," says he, "sent me down to tell you." Father Farrell! . . . D'ye know, Joxer, I never like to be beholden to any o' the clergy.

JOXER. It's dangerous, right enough.

BOYLE If they do anything for you, they'd want you to be livin' in the Chapel.[58] . . . I'm goin' to tell you somethin', Joxer, that I wouldn't tell to anybody else—the clergy always had too much power over the people in this unfortunate country.

JOXER. You could sing that if you had an air to it!

BOYLE *(becoming enthusiastic)*. Didn't they prevent the people in "'47" from seizin' the corn, an' they starvin';[59] didn't they down Parnell;[60] didn't they say that hell wasn't hot enough nor eternity long enough to punish the Fenians?[61] We don't forget, we don't forget them things, Joxer. If they've taken everything else from us, Joxer, they've left us our memory.

JOXER *(emotionally)*. For mem'ry's the only friend that grief can call its own, that grief . . . can . . . call . . . its own![62]

BOYLE. Father Farrell's beginnin' to take a great intherest in Captain Boyle; because of what Johnny did for his country, says he to me wan day. It's a curious way to reward Johnny to be makin' his poor oul' father work. But that's what the clergy want, Joxer—work, work, work for me an' you; havin' us mulin' from mornin' till night, so that they may be in bether fettle when they come hoppin' round for their dues! Job! Well, let him give his job to wan of his hymn-singin', prayer-spoutin', craw-thumpin' Confraternity men![63]

56. **Virol** a brand-name tonic   57. **Wicklow** a mountainous county just south of Dublin   58. **Chapel** Catholic church   59. **Didn't they prevent the people . . . starvin'** corn (cereals) were used to pay rents; 1847 was the height of the Irish potato famine   60. **Parnell** Charles Stewart Parnell (1846–1891), leader of the Irish Party in Westminster. His political career ended when a divorce scandal eroded his support, which included a majority of the Irish bishops.   61. **didn't they say . . . Fenians?** the Fenian Brotherhood, a secret revolutionary organization responsible for the abortive rising of 1867 and other violence. It was opposed by most of the Catholic hierarchy, especially Bishop Moriarty of Kerry, who was credited with these literal terms of condemnation.   62. **For mem'ry . . . its own!** "The Heart Bowed Down," a popular ballad from William Balfe's opera *The Bohemian Girl* (1843)   63. **Confraternity men** members of a voluntary association of Catholics, engaged in pious or charitable works

(The voice of a coal-block vendor[64] is heard chanting in the street.)

VOICE OF COAL VENDOR. Blocks . . . coal-blocks! Blocks . . . coal-blocks!

JOXER. God be with the young days when you were steppin' the deck of a manly ship, with the win' blowin' a hurricane through the masts, an' the only sound you'd hear was, "Port your helm!"[65] an' the only answer, "Port it is, sir!"

BOYLE. Them was days, Joxer, them was days. Nothin' was too hot or too heavy for me then. Sailin' from the Gulf o' Mexico to the Antanartic Ocean.[66] I seen things, I seen things, Joxer, that no mortal man should speak about that knows his Catechism.[67] Ofen, an' ofen, when I was fixed to the wheel with a marlin-spike,[68] an' the wins blowin' fierce an' the waves lashin' an' lashin', till you'd think every minute was goin' to be your last, an' it blowed, an' blowed—blew is the right word, Joxer, but blowed is what the sailors use. . . .

JOXER. Aw, it's a darlin' word, a daarlin' word.

BOYLE. An', as it blowed an' blowed, I ofen looked up at the sky an' assed meself the question—what is the stars, what is the stars?

VOICE OF COAL VENDOR. Any blocks, coal-blocks; blocks, coal-blocks!

JOXER. Ah, that's the question, that's the question—what is the stars?

BOYLE. An' then, I'd have another look, an' I'd ass meself—what is the moon?

JOXER. Ah, that's the question—what is the moon, what is the moon?

(Rapid steps are heard coming towards the door. Boyle makes desperate efforts to hide everything; Joxer rushes to the window in a frantic effort to get out; Boyle begins to innocently lilt "Oh, me darlin' Jennie, I will be thrue to thee," when the door is opened, and the black face of the Coal Vendor appears.)

THE COAL VENDOR. D'yes want any blocks?

BOYLE *(with a roar)*. No, we don't want any blocks!

JOXER *(coming back with a sigh of relief)*. That's afther puttin' the heart across me—I could ha' sworn it was Juno. I'd betther be goin', Captain; you couldn't tell the minute Juno'd hop in on us.

BOYLE. Let her hop in; we may as well have it out first as at last. I've made up me mind—I'm not goin' to do only what she damn well likes.

JOXER. Them sentiments does you credit, Captain; I don't like to say anything as between man an' wife, but I say as a butty, as a butty, Captain,

---

64. **coal-block vendor** street vendor of synthetic blocks of coal or pitch, used as fuel   65. **Port your helm!** steer to the right (nautical)   66. **Antanartic Ocean** portmanteau malapropism: Antarctica plus Arctic Ocean   67. **Catechism** a question-and-answer primer of Catholic doctrine   68. **marlin-spike** pointed iron tool for splicing ropes

that you've stuck it too long, an' that it's about time you showed a little spunk.

> How can a man die bctther than facin' fearful odds,
> For th' ashes of his fathers an' the temples of his gods?[69]

BOYLE. She has her rights—there's no one denyin' it, but haven't I me rights too?

JOXER. Of course you have—the sacred rights o' man![70]

BOYLE. Today, Joxer, there's goin' to be issued a proclamation be me, establishin' an independent Republic,[71] an' Juno'll have to take an oath of allegiance.[72]

JOXER. Be firm, be firm, Captain; the first few minutes'll be the worst:—if you gently touch a nettle it'll sting you for your pains; grasp it like a lad of mettle, an' as soft as silk remains!

VOICE OF JUNO OUTSIDE. Can't stop, Mrs. Madigan—I haven't a minute!

JOXER *(flying out of the window).* Holy God, here she is!

BOYLE *(packing the things away with a rush in the press).* I knew that fella ud stop till she was in on top of us!

(He sits down by the fire.)

(Juno enters hastily; she is flurried and excited.)

JUNO. Oh, you're in—you must have been only afther comin' in?

BOYLE. No, I never went out.

JUNO. It's curious, then, you never heard the knockin'.

(She puts her coat and hat on bed.)

BOYLE. Knockin'? Of course I heard the knockin'.

JUNO. An' why didn't you open the door, then? I suppose you were so busy with Joxer that you hadn't time.

BOYLE. I haven't seen Joxer since I seen him before. Joxer! What ud bring Joxer here?

JUNO. D'ye mean to tell me that the pair of yous wasn't collogin'[73] together here when me back was turned?

BOYLE. What ud we be collogin' together about? I have somethin' else to think of besides collogin' with Joxer. I can swear on all the holy prayer-books . . .

MRS. BOYLE. That you weren't in no snug! Go on in at wanst now,

69. **How can a man . . . temples of his gods?** Lord Macaulay, "Horatius," *Lays of Ancient Rome* (1842), Stanza 27　70. **sacred rights o' man!** Thomas Paine's *The Rights of Man* (1791)　71. **issued a proclamation . . . an independent Republic** Cf. Proclamation issued on Easter Monday 1916, asserting Ireland's claim to independence　72. **oath of allegiance** a major cause of the Irish civil war was the oath of allegiance to the British crown included in the Anglo-Irish Treaty of 1922　73. **collogin'** talking

an' take off that moleskin trousers o' yours, an' put on a collar an' tie to smarten yourself up a bit. There's a visitor comin' with Mary in a minute, an' he has great news for you.

BOYLE. A job, I suppose; let us get wan first before we start lookin' for another.

MRS. BOYLE. That's the thing that's able to put the win' up you. Well, it's no job, but news that'll give you the chance o' your life.

BOYLE. What's all the mysthery about?

MRS. BOYLE. G'win an' take off the moleskin trousers when you're told!

(Boyle goes into room on left.)

(Mrs. Boyle tidies up the room, puts the shovel under the bed, and goes to the press.)

MRS. BOYLE. Oh, God bless us, looka the way everything's thrun about! Oh, Joxer was here, Joxer was here!

(Mary enters with Charlie Bentham; he is a young man of twenty-five, tall, good-looking, with a very high opinion of himself generally. He is dressed in a brown coat, brown knee-breeches, grey stockings, a brown sweater, with a deep blue tie; he carries gloves and a walking-stick.)

MRS. BOYLE *(fussing round)*. Come in, Mr. Bentham; sit down, Mr. Bentham, in this chair; it's more comfortabler than that, Mr. Bentham. Himself 'll be here in a minute; he's just takin' off his trousers.

MARY. Mother!

BENTHAM. Please don't put yourself to any trouble, Mrs. Boyle—I'm quite all right here, thank you.

MRS. BOYLE. An' to think of you knowin' Mary, an' she knowin' the news you had for us, an' wouldn't let on; but it's all the more welcomer now, for we were on our last lap!

VOICE OF JOHNNY INSIDE. What are you kickin' up all the racket for?

BOYLE *(roughly)*. I'm takin' off me moleskin trousers!

JOHNNY. Can't you do it, then, without lettin' th' whole house know you're takin' off your trousers? What d'ye want puttin' them on an' takin' them off again?

BOYLE. Will you let me alone, will you let me alone? Am I never goin' to be done thryin' to please th' whole o' yous?

MRS. BOYLE *(to Bentham)*. You must excuse th' state o' th' place, Mr. Bentham; th' minute I turn me back that man o' mine always makes a litther o' th' place, a litther o' th' place.

BENTHAM. Don't worry, Mrs. Boyle; it's all right, I assure . . .

BOYLE *(inside)*. Where's me braces[74]; where in th' name o' God did I leave me braces? . . . Ay, did you see where I put me braces?

74. **braces** suspenders

JOHNNY *(inside, calling out)*. Ma, will you come in here an' take da away ou' o' this or he'll dhrive me mad.

MRS. BOYLE *(going towards the door)*. Dear, dear, dear, that man'll be lookin' for somethin' on th' day o' Judgement. *(Looking into room and calling to Boyle.)* Look at your braces, man, hangin' round your neck!

BOYLE *(inside)*. Aw, Holy God!

MRS. BOYLE *(calling)*. Johnny, Johnny, come out here for a minute.

JOHNNY. Ah, leave Johnny alone, an' don't be annoyin' him!

MRS. BOYLE. Come on, Johnny, till I inthroduce you to Mr. Bentham. *(To Bentham.)* My son, Mr. Bentham; he's afther goin' through the mill. He was only a chiselur of a Boy Scout in Easter Week, when he got hit in the hip; and his arm was blew off in the fight in O'Connell Street. *(Johnny comes in.)* Here he is, Mr. Bentham; Mr. Bentham, Johnny. None can deny he done his bit for Irelan', if that's goin' to do him any good.

JOHNNY *(boastfully)*. I'd do it agen, ma, I'd do it agen; for a principle's a principle.

MRS. BOYLE. Ah, you lost your best principle, me boy, when you lost your arm; them's the only sort o' principles that's any good to a workin' man.

JOHNNY. Ireland only half free'll never be at peace while she has a son left to pull a trigger.

MRS. BOYLE. To be sure, to be sure—no bread's a lot betther than half a loaf. *(Calling loudly in to Boyle.)* Will you hurry up there?

(Boyle enters in his best trousers, which aren't too good, and looks very uncomfortable in his collar and tie.)

MRS. BOYLE. This is me husband; Mr. Boyle, Mr. Bentham.

BENTHAM. Ah, very glad to know you, Mr. Boyle. How are you?

BOYLE. Ah, I'm not too well at all; I suffer terrible with pains in me legs. Juno can tell you there what . . .

MRS. BOYLE. You won't have many pains in your legs when you hear what Mr. Bentham has to tell you.

BENTHAM. Juno! What an interesting name! It reminds one of Homer's glorious story of ancient gods and heroes.[75]

BOYLE. Yis, doesn't it? You see, Juno was born an' christened in June; I met her in June; we were married in June, an' Johnny was born in June, so wan day I says to her, "You should ha' been called Juno," an' the name stuck to her ever since.

MRS. BOYLE. Here, we can talk o' them things agen; let Mr. Bentham say what he has to say now.

75. **Homer's glorious story of ancient gods and heroes** Juno (Roman) or Hera (Greek) goddess of motherhood, nurturance, and childbearing

BENTHAM. Well, Mr. Boyle, I suppose you'll remember a Mr. Ellison of Santry[76]—he's a relative of yours, I think.

BOYLE *(viciously)*. Is it that prognosticator an' procrastinator! Of course I remember him.

BENTHAM. Well, he's dead, Mr. Boyle. . . .

BOYLE. Sorra many'll[77] go into mournin' for him.

MRS. BOYLE. Wait till you hear what Mr. Bentham has to say, an' then, maybe, you'll change your opinion.

BENTHAM. A week before he died he sent for me to write his will for him. He told me that there were two only that he wished to leave his property to: his second cousin, Michael Finnegan of Santry, and John Boyle, his first cousin, of Dublin.

BOYLE *(excitedly)*. Me, is it me, me?

BENTHAM. You, Mr. Boyle; I'll read a copy of the will that I have here with me, which has been duly filed in the Court of Probate.

(He takes a paper from his pocket and reads:)

6th February 1922

This is the last Will and Testament of William Ellison, of Santry, in the County of Dublin. I hereby order and wish my property to be sold and divided as follows——

£20 to the St. Vincent de Paul Society.[78]

£60 for Masses for the repose of my soul (5s. for each Mass).

The rest of my property to be divided between my first and second cousins.

I hereby appoint Timothy Buckly, of Santry, and Hugh Brierly, of Coolock,[79] to be my Executors.

> *(Signed)* WILLIAM ELLISON.
> HUGH BRIERLY.
> TIMOTHY BUCKLY.
> CHARLES BENTHAM, N.T.[80]

BOYLE *(eagerly)*. An' how much'll be comin' out of it, Mr. Bentham?

BENTHAM. The Executors told me that half of the property would be anything between £1500 and £2000.

MARY. A fortune, father, a fortune!

JOHNNY. We'll be able to get out o' this place now, an' go somewhere we're not known.

MRS. BOYLE. You won't have to trouble about a job for a while, Jack.

BOYLE *(fervently)*. I'll never doubt the goodness o' God agen.

76. **Santry** district north of Dublin City   77. **Sorra many** not many   78. **St. Vincent de Paul Society** Catholic charitable society   79. **Coolock** district north of Dublin   80. **N.T.** National Teacher (grade/primary school)

BENTHAM. I congratulate you, Mr. Boyle.

(They shake hands.)

BOYLE. An' now, Mr. Bentham, you'll have to have a wet.

BENTHAM. A wet?

BOYLE. A wet—a jar—a boul![81]

MRS. BOYLE. Jack, you're speakin' to Mr. Bentham, an' not to Joxer.

BOYLE *(solemnly)*. Juno . . . Mary . . . Johnny . . . we'll have to go into mournin' at wanst. . . . I never expected that poor Bill ud die so sudden. . . . Well, we all have to die some day . . . you, Juno, to-day . . . an' me, maybe, to-morrow. . . . It's sad, but it can't be helped. . . . Requiescat in pace[82] . . . or, usin' our oul' tongue like St. Patrick or St. Bridget, Guh sayeree jeea ayera![83]

MARY. Oh, father, that's not Rest in Peace; that's God save Ireland.

BOYLE. U-u-ugh, it's all the same—isn't it a prayer? . . . Juno, I'm done with Joxer; he's nothin' but a prognosticator an' a . . .

JOXER *(climbing angrily through the window and bounding into the room)*. You're done with Joxer, are you? Maybe you thought I'd stop on the roof all the night for you! Joxer out on the roof with the win' blowin' through him was nothin' to you an' your friend with the collar an' tie!

MRS. BOYLE. What in the name o' God brought you out on the roof; what were you doin' there?

JOXER *(ironically)*. I was dhreamin' I was standin' on the bridge of a ship, an' she sailin' the Antartic Ocean, an' it blowed, an' blowed, an' I lookin' up at the sky an' sayin', what is the stars, what is the stars?

MRS. BOYLE *(opening the door and standing at it)*. Here, get ou' o' this, Joxer Daly; I was always thinkin' you had a slate off.[84]

JOXER *(moving to the door)*. I have to laugh every time I look at the deep-sea sailor; an' a row on a river ud make him sea-sick!

BOYLE. Get ou' o' this before I take the law into me own hands!

JOXER *(going out)*. Say aw rewaeawr,[85] but not good-bye. Lookin' for work, an' prayin' to God he won't get it!

(He goes.)

MRS. BOYLE. I'm tired tellin' you what Joxer was; maybe now you see yourself the kind he is.

BOYLE. He'll never blow the froth off a pint o' mine agen, that's a sure thing. Johnny . . . Mary . . . you're sure to keep yourselves to yourselves for the future. Juno, I'm done with Joxer. . . . I'm a new man from this out. . . .

(Clasping Juno's hand, and singing emotionally:)

81. **a wet—a jar—a boul!** a drink 82. **Requiescat in pace** may he rest in peace 83. **Guh sayeree jeea ayera**— *Go saoradh Dia Éire!* 84. **had a slate off** were a little crazy 85. **aw rewaeawr** *au revoir* until we meet again

O, me darlin' Juno, I will be thrue to thee;
Me own, me darlin' Juno, you're all the world to me.

CURTAIN

ACT 2

The same, but the furniture is more plentiful, and of a vulgar nature. A glaringly upholstered armchair and lounge;[86] *cheap pictures and photos everywhere. Every available spot is ornamented with huge vases filled with artificial flowers. Crossed festoons of coloured paper chains stretch from end to end of ceiling. On the table is an old attaché case. It is about six in the evening, and two days after the First Act. Boyle, in his shirt-sleeves, is voluptuously stretched on the sofa; he is smoking a clay pipe. He is half asleep. A lamp is lighting on the table. After a few moments' pause the voice of Joxer is heard singing softly outside at the door—"Me pipe I'll smoke, as I dhrive me moke*[87]—*are you there, Mor . . . ee . . . ar . . . i . . . teee!"*[88]

BOYLE *(leaping up, takes a pen in his hand and busies himself with papers).*
Come along, Joxer, me son, come along.

JOXER *(putting his head in).* Are you be yourself ?

BOYLE. Come on, come on; that doesn't matther; I'm masther now, an' I'm goin' to remain masther.

(Joxer comes in.)

JOXER. How d'ye feel now, as a man o' money?

BOYLE *(solemnly).* It's a responsibility, Joxer, a great responsibility.

JOXER. I suppose 'tis now, though you wouldn't think it.

BOYLE. Joxer, han' me over that attackey case on the table there. *(Joxer hands the case.)* Ever since the Will was passed I've run hundhreds o' dockyments through me hans—I tell you, you have to keep your wits about you.

(He busies himself with papers.)

JOXER. Well, I won't disturb you; I'll dhrop in when . . .

BOYLE *(hastily).* It's all right, Joxer, this is the last one to be signed today. *(He signs a paper, puts it into the case, which he shuts with a snap, and sits back pompously in the chair.)* Now, Joxer, you want to see me; I'm at your service—what can I do for you, me man?

JOXER. I've just dhropped in with the £3:5s.[89] that Mrs. Madigan riz[90]

---

86. **lounge** chaise longue   87. **moke** donkey   88. **Me pipe I'll smoke . . . i . . . teee!** "Are You There Moriar-i-tee?" a popular comic song   89. **£3:5s.** three pounds and five shillings sterling   90. **riz** raised

on the blankets an' table for you, an' she says you're to be in no hurry payin' it back.

BOYLE. She won't be long without it; I expect the first cheque for a couple o' hundhred any day. There's the five bob for yourself—go on, take it man; it'll not be the last you'll get from the Captain. Now an' agen we have our differ, but we're there together all the time.

JOXER. Me for you, an' you for me, like the two Musketeers.

BOYLE. Father Farrell stopped me to-day an' tole me how glad he was I fell in for[91] the money.

JOXER. He'll be stoppin' you often enough now; I suppose it was "Mr." Boyle with him?

BOYLE. He shuk me be the han' . . .

JOXER *(ironically)*. I met with Napper Tandy, an' he shuk me be the han'![92]

BOYLE. You're seldom asthray, Joxer, but you're wrong shipped this time. What you're sayin' of Father Farrell is very near to blasfeemey. I don't like any one to talk disrespectful of Father Farrell.

JOXER. You're takin' me up wrong, Captain; I wouldn't let a word be said agen Father Farrell—the heart o' the rowl,[93] that's what he is; I always said he was a darlin' man, a daarlin' man.

BOYLE. Comin' up the stairs who did I meet but that bummer,[94] Nugent. "I seen you talkin' to Father Farrell," says he, with a grin on him. "He'll be folleyin' you," says he, "like a Guardian Angel from this out"— all the time the oul' grin on him, Joxer.

JOXER. I never seen him yet but he had that oul' grin on him!

BOYLE. "Mr. Nugent," says I, "Father Farrell is a man o' the people, an', as far as I know the History o' me country, the priests was always in the van[95] of the fight for Irelan's freedom."

JOXER *(fervently)*:

Who was it led the van, Soggart Aroon?[96]
Since the fight first began, Soggart Aroon?

BOYLE. "Who are you tellin'?" says he. "Didn't they let down the Fenians, an' didn't they do in Parnell? An' now . . ." "You ought to be ashamed o' yourself," says I, interruptin' him, "not to know the History o' your country." An' I left him gawkin' where he was.

JOXER. Where ignorance 's bliss 'tis folly to be wise; I wondher did he ever read the Story o' Irelan'.

91. **fell in for** happened on   92. **I met with Napper Tandy, an' he shuk me be the han'!** first line of the patriotic song about the 1798 rebellion, "The Wearing of the Green"   93. **the heart o' the rowl** the most flavorful center of a wad of chewing tobacco   94. **bummer** sponger   95. **van** forefront   96. **Soggart Aroon?** "Soggart Aroon" ("Priest Dear"), title of a patriotic ballad by John Banim (1798–1842) commemorating Fr. John Murphy, leader of the 1798 rebellion in Wexford

BOYLE. Be J. L. Sullivan?[97] Don't you know he didn't.

JOXER. Ah, it's a darlin' buk, a daarlin' buk!

BOYLE. You'd better be goin', now, Joxer; his Majesty, Bentham, 'll be here any minute, now.

JOXER. Be the way things is lookin', it'll be a match between him an' Mary. She's thrun over[98] Jerry altogether. Well, I hope it will, for he's a darlin' man.

BOYLE. I'm glad you think so—I don't. *(Irritably.)* What's so darlin' about him?

JOXER *(nonplussed)*. I only seen him twiced; if you want to know me, come an' live with me.

BOYLE. He's too dignified for me—to hear him talk you'd think he knew as much as a Boney's Oraculum.[99] He's given up his job as teacher, an' is goin' to become a solicitor[100] in Dublin—he's been studyin' law. I suppose he thinks I'll set him up, but he's wrong shipped.[101] An' th' other fella—Jerry's as bad. The two o' them ud give you a pain in your face, listenin' to them; Jerry believin' in nothin', an' Bentham believin' in everythin'. One that says all is God an' no man; an' th' other that says all is man an' no God!

JOXER. Well, I'll be off now.

BOYLE. Don't forget to dhrop down afther awhile; we'll have a quiet jar, an' a song or two.

JOXER. Never fear.

BOYLE. An' tell Mrs. Madigan that I hope we'll have the pleasure of her organization at our little enthertainment.

JOXER. Righto; we'll come down together.

(He goes out.)

(Johnny comes from room on left, and sits down moodily at the fire. Boyle looks at him for a few moments, and shakes his head. He fills his pipe.)

VOICE OF JUNO AT THE DOOR. Open the door, Jack; this thing has me nearly kilt with the weight.

(Boyle opens the door. Juno enters carrying the box of a gramophone, followed by Mary carrying the horn and some parcels. Juno leaves the box on the table and flops into a chair.)

JUNO. Carryin' that from Henry Street[102] was no joke.

BOYLE. U-u-ugh, that's a grand-lookin' insthrument—how much was it?

---

97. **J. L. Sullivan** Boyle is referring to A. M. Sullivan's *The Story of Ireland*. He has confused its author with J. L. Sullivan, the Irish-American boxer. 98. **thrun over** jilted, rejected 99. **Boney's Oraculum** *Boneparte's Oraculum* was a popular penny-pamphlet containing interpretations of dreams, fortune-telling cards and various signs and wonders 100. **solicitor** lawyer 101. **wrong shipped** mistaken 102. **Henry Street** shopping street in central Dublin

JUNO. Pound down, an' five to be paid at two shillins a week.

BOYLE. That's reasonable enough.

JUNO. I'm afraid we're runnin' into too much debt; first the furniture, an' now this.

BOYLE. The whole lot won't be much out of £2000.

MARY. I don't know what you wanted a gramophone for—I know Charlie hates them; he says they're destructive of real music.

BOYLE. Desthructive of music—that fella ud give you a pain in your face. All a gramophone wants is to be properly played; its thrue wondher is only felt when everythin's quiet—what a gramophone wants is dead silence!

MARY. But, father, Jerry says the same; afther all, you can only appreciate music when your ear is properly trained.

BOYLE. That's another fella ud give you a pain in your face. Properly thrained! I suppose you couldn't appreciate football unless your fut was properly thrained.

MRS. BOYLE *(to Mary)*. Go on in ower that an' dress, or Charlie'll be in on you, an' tea nor nothing'll be ready.

(Mary goes into room left.)

MRS. BOYLE *(arranging table for tea)*. You didn't look at our new gramophone, Johnny?

JOHNNY. 'Tisn't gramophones I'm thinking of.

MRS. BOYLE. An' what is it you're thinkin' of, allanna?[103]

JOHNNY. Nothin', nothin', nothin'.

MRS. BOYLE. Sure, you must be thinkin' of somethin'; it's yourself that has yourself the way y'are; sleepin' wan night in me sisther's, an' the nex' in your father's brother's—you'll get no rest goin' on that way.

JOHNNY. I can rest nowhere, nowhere, nowhere.

MRS. BOYLE. Sure, you're not thryin' to rest anywhere.

JOHNNY. Let me alone, let me alone, let me alone, for God's sake.

(A knock at street door.)

MRS. BOYLE *(in a flutter)*. Here he is; here's Mr. Bentham!

BOYLE. Well, there's room for him; it's a pity there's not a brass band to play him in.

MRS. BOYLE. We'll han' the tea round, an' not be clusthered round the table, as if we never seen nothin'.

(Steps are heard approaching, and Juno, opening the door, allows Bentham to enter.)

JUNO. Give your hat an' stick to Jack, there . . . sit down, Mr. Bentham . . . no, not there . . . in th' easy chair be the fire . . . there, that's betther. Mary'll be out to you in a minute.

103. **allanna** dear child [Ir.]

BOYLE *(solemnly)*. I seen be the paper this mornin' that Consols[104] was down half per cent. That's serious, min' you, an' shows the whole counthry's in a state o' chassis.

MRS. BOYLE. What's Consols, Jack?

BOYLE. Consols? Oh, Consols is—oh, there's no use tellin' women what Consols is—th' wouldn't undherstand.

BENTHAM. It's just as you were saying, Mr. Boyle . . .

(Mary enters, charmingly dressed.)

BENTHAM. Oh, good evening, Mary; how pretty you're looking—

MARY *(archly)*. Am I?

BOYLE. We were just talkin' when you kem in, Mary; I was tellin' Mr. Bentham that the whole counthry's in a state o' chassis.

MARY *(to Bentham)*. Would you prefer the green or the blue ribbon round me hair, Charlie?

MRS. BOYLE.Mary, your father's speakin'.

BOYLE *(rapidly)*. I was jus' tellin' Mr. Bentham that the whole counthry's in a state o' chassis.

MARY. I'm sure you're frettin', da, whether it is or no.

MRS. BOYLE. With all our churches an' religions, the worl's not a bit the betther.

BOYLE *(with a commanding gesture)*. Tay!

(Mary and Mrs. Boyle dispense the tea.)

MRS. BOYLE. An' Irelan's takin' a leaf out o' the worl's buk; when we got the makin' of our own laws I thought we'd never stop to look behind us, but instead of that we never stopped to look before us! If the people ud folley up[105] their religion betther there'd be a betther chance for us— what do you think, Mr. Bentham?

BENTHAM. I'm afraid I can't venture to express an opinion on that point, Mrs. Boyle; dogma has no attraction for me.

MRS. BOYLE. I forgot you didn't hold with us: what's this you said you were?

BENTHAM. A Theosophist,[106] Mrs. Boyle.

MRS. BOYLE. An' what in the name o' God's a Theosophist?

BOYLE. A Theosophist, Juno, 's a—tell her, Mr. Bentham, tell her.

BENTHAM. It's hard to explain in a few words: Theosophy's founded on The Vedas,[107] the religious books of the East. Its central theme is the existence of an all-pervading Spirit—the Life-Breath. Nothing really exists but this one Universal Life-Breath. And whatever even seems to exist separately from this Life-Breath, doesn't really exist at all. It is all vital force

---

104. **Consols** Consolidated Annuities (British Government securities)   105. **folly up** practice   106. **Theosophist** a religious sect emphasizing mystical experience incorporating elements of Buddhism and Brahminism   107. **The Vedas** the sacred writings of Hinduism

in man, in all animals, and in all vegetation. This Life-Breath is called the Prawna.[108]

MRS. BOYLE. The Prawna! What a comical name!

BOYLE. Prawna; yis, the Prawna. *(Blowing gently through his lips.)* That's the Prawna!

MRS. BOYLE. Whist, whist, Jack.

BENTHAM. The happiness of man depends upon his sympathy with this Spirit. Men who have reached a high state of excellence are called Yogi.[109] Some men become Yogi in a short time, it may take others millions of years.

BOYLE. Yogi! I seen hundhreds of them in the streets o' San Francisco.

BENTHAM. It is said by these Yogi that if we practise certain mental exercises that we would have powers denied to others—for instance, the faculty of seeing things that happen miles and miles away.

MRS. BOYLE. I wouldn't care to meddle with that sort o' belief; it's a very curious religion, altogether.

BOYLE. What's curious about it? Isn't all religions curious?—if they weren't, you wouldn't get any one to believe them. But religions is passin' away—they've had their day like everything else. Take the real Dublin people, f 'rinstance: they know more about Charlie Chaplin an' Tommy Mix[110] than they do about SS.[111] Peter an' Paul!

MRS. BOYLE. You don't believe in ghosts, Mr. Bentham?

MARY. Don't you know he doesn't, mother?

BENTHAM. I don't know that, Mary. Scientists are beginning to think that what we call ghosts are sometimes seen by persons of a certain nature. They say that sensational actions, such as the killing of a person, demand great energy, and that that energy lingers in the place where the action occurred. People may live in the place and see nothing, when someone may come along whose personality has some peculiar connection with the energy of the place, and, in a flash, the person sees the whole affair.

JOHNNY *(rising swiftly, pale and affected)*. What sort o' talk is this to be goin' on with? Is there nothin' betther to be talkin' about but the killin' o' people? My God, isn't it bad enough for these things to happen without talkin' about them!

(He hurriedly goes into the room on left.)

BENTHAM. Oh, I'm very sorry, Mrs. Boyle; I never thought . . .

MRS. BOYLE *(apologetically)*. Never mind, Mr. Bentham, he's very touchy.

(A frightened scream is heard from Johnny inside.)

108. **Prawna** Buddhist term for insight into the forces of nature   109. **Yogi** Buddhist ascetics given to meditation   110. **Tommy Mix** American cowboy film star (1880–1940) at the height of his popularity 1917–28   111. **SS.** Saints

MRS. BOYLE. Mother of God, what's that?

(He rushes out again, his face pale, his lips twitching, his limbs trembling.)

JOHNNY. Shut the door, shut the door, quick, for God's sake! Great God, have mercy on me! Blessed Mother o' God, shelter me, shelther your son!

MRS. BOYLE *(catching him in her arms)*. What's wrong with you? What ails you? Sit down, sit down, here, on the bed . . . there now . . . there now.

MARY. Johnny, Johnny, what ails you?

JOHNNY. I seen him, I seen him . . . kneelin' in front o' the statue . . . merciful Jesus, have pity on me!

MRS. BOYLE *(to Boyle)*. Get him a glass o' whisky . . . quick, man, an' don't stand gawkin'.[112]

(Boyle gets the whisky.)

JOHNNY. Sit here, sit here, mother . . . between me an' the door.

MRS. BOYLE. I'll sit beside you as long as you like, only tell me what was it came across you at all?

JOHNNY *(after taking some drink)*. I seen him. . . . I seen Robbie Tancred kneelin' down before the statue . . . an' the red light shinin' on him . . . an' when I went in . . . he turned an' looked at me . . . an' I seen the wouns bleedin' in his breast. . . . Oh, why did he look at me like that? . . . it wasn't my fault that he was done in.[113] . . . Mother o' God, keep him away from me!

MRS. BOYLE. There, there, child, you've imagined it all. There was nothin' there at all—it was the red light you seen, an' the talk we had put all the rest into your head. Here, dhrink more o' this—it'll do you good. . . . An', now, stretch yourself down on the bed for a little. *(To Boyle.)* Go in, Jack, an' show him it was only in his own head it was.

BOYLE *(making no move)*. E-e-e-eh; it's all nonsense; it was only a shadda he saw.

MARY. Mother o' God, he made me heart lep!

BENTHAM. It was simply due to an over-wrought imagination—we all get that way at times.

MRS. BOYLE. There, dear, lie down in the bed, an' I'll put the quilt across you . . . e-e-e-eh, that's it . . . you'll be as right as the mail in a few minutes.

JOHNNY. Mother, go into the room an' see if the light's lightin' before the statue.

MRS. BOYLE *(to Boyle)*. Jack, run in an' see if the light's lightin' before the statue.

BOYLE *(to Mary)*. Mary, slip in an' see if the light's lightin' before the statue.

112. **gawkin'** staring   113. **done in** murdered

(Mary hesitates to go in.)

BENTHAM. It's all right; Mary, I'll go.

(He goes into the room; remains for a few moments, and returns.)

BENTHAM. Everything's just as it was—the light burning bravely before the statue.

BOYLE. Of course; I knew it was all nonsense.

(A knock at the door.)

BOYLE *(going to open the door)*. E-e-e-e-eh.

(He opens it, and Joxer, followed by Mrs. Madigan, enters. Mrs. Madigan is a strong, dapper little woman of about forty-five; her face is almost always a widespread smile of complacency. She is a woman who, in manner at least, can mourn with them that mourn, and rejoice with them that do rejoice. When she is feeling comfortable, she is inclined to be reminiscent; when others say anything, or following a statement made by herself, she has a habit of putting her head a little to one side, and nodding it rapidly several times in succession, like a bird pecking at a hard berry. Indeed, she has a good deal of the bird in her, but the bird instinct is by no means a melodious one. She is ignorant, vulgar and forward, but her heart is generous withal.[114] For instance, she would help a neighbour's sick child; she would probably kill the child, but her intention would be to cure it; she would be more at home helping a drayman[115] to lift a fallen horse. She is dressed in a rather soiled grey dress and a vivid purple blouse; in her hair is a huge comb, ornamented with huge coloured beads. She enters with a gliding step, beaming smile and nodding head. Boyle receives them effusively.)

BOYLE. Come on in, Mrs. Madigan; come on in; I was afraid you weren't comin' . . . *(Slyly.)* There's some people able to dhress, ay, Joxer?

JOXER. Fair as the blossoms that bloom in the May, an' sweet as the scent of the new-mown hay. . . . Ah, well she may wear them.

MRS. MADIGAN *(looking at Mary)*. I know some as are as sweet as the blossoms that bloom in the May—oh, no names, no pack dhrill![116]

BOYLE. An' now I'll inthroduce the pair o' yous to Mary's intended: Mr. Bentham, this is Mrs. Madigan, an oul' back-parlour neighbour,[117] that, if she could help it at all, ud never see a body shuk![118]

BENTHAM *(rising, and tentatively shaking the hand of Mrs. Madigan)*. I'm sure, it's a great pleasure to know you, Mrs. Madigan.

MRS. MADIGAN. An' I'm goin' to tell you, Mr. Bentham, you're goin' to get as nice a bit o' skirt[119] in Mary, there, as ever you seen in your puff.[120] Not like some of the dhressed-up dolls that's knockin' about lookin' for men when it's a skelpin'[121] they want. I remember, as well as I remember

114. **withal** nonetheless   115. **drayman** cart driver   116. **pack dhrill** military punishment involving marching in full gear   117. **back-parlour neighbour** from the adjoining apartment in the converted townhouse   118. **a body shuk** a person taken advantage of   119. **a bit o' skirt** girl, woman   120. **puff** life   121. **skelpin'** spanking

yestherday, the day she was born—of a Tuesday, the 25th o' June, in the year 1901, at thirty-three minutes past wan in the day be Foley's clock, the pub at the corner o' the street. A cowld day it was too, for the season o' the year, an' I remember sayin' to Joxer, there, who I met comin' up th' stairs, that the new arrival in Boyle's ud grow up a hardy[122] chiselur if it lived, an' that she'd be somethin' one o' these days that nobody suspected, an' so signs on it, here she is to-day, goin' to be married to a young man lookin' as if he'd be fit to commensurate[123] in any position in life it ud please God to call him!

BOYLE *(effusively)*. Sit down, Mrs. Madigan, sit down, me oul' sport. *(To Bentham.)* This is Joxer Daly, Past Chief Ranger of the Dear Little Shamrock Branch of the Irish National Foresters,[124] an oul' front-top neighbour, that never despaired, even in the darkest days of Ireland's sorra.

JOXER. Nil desperandum,[125] Captain, nil desperandum.

BOYLE. Sit down, Joxer, sit down. The two of us was often in a tight corner.

MRS. BOYLE. Ay, in Foley's snug!

JOXER. An' we kem out of it flyin',[126] we kem out of it flyin', Captain.

BOYLE. An' now for a dhrink—I know yous won't refuse an oul' friend.

MRS. MADIGAN *(to Juno)*. Is Johnny not well, Mrs. . . .

MRS. BOYLE *(warningly)*. S-s-s-sh.

MRS. MADIGAN. Oh, the poor darlin'.

BOYLE. Well, Mrs. Madigan, is it tea or what?

MRS. MADIGAN. Well, speakin' for meself, I jus' had me tea a minute ago, an' I'm afraid to dhrink any more—I'm never the same when I dhrink too much tay. Thanks, all the same, Mr. Boyle.

BOYLE. Well, what about a bottle o' stout[127] or a dhrop o' whisky?

MRS. MADIGAN. A bottle o' stout ud be a little too heavy for me stummock afther me tay. . . . A-a-ah, I'll thry the ball o' malt.[128]

(Boyle prepares the whisky.)

MRS. MADIGAN. There's nothin' like a ball o' malt occasional like— too much of it isn't good. *(To Boyle, who is adding water.)* Ah, God, Johnny, don't put too much wather on it! *(She drinks.)* I suppose yous'll be lavin' this place.

BOYLE. I'm looking for a place near the sea; I'd like the place that you might say was me cradle, to be me grave as well. The sea is always callin' me.

JOXER. She is callin', callin', callin', in the win' an' on the sea.

BOYLE. Another dhrop o' whisky, Mrs. Madigan?

122. **hardy** healthy   123. **to commensurate** malaprop: commence plus commensurate with   124. **Irish National Foresters** fraternal social service club   125. **Nil desperandum** Despair of nothing   126. **flyin'** with flying colors, in style   127. **stout** dark beer brewed in Ireland   128. **ball o' malt** shot of whiskey

MRS. MADIGAN. Well, now, it ut be hard to refuse seein' the suspicious times that's in it.

BOYLE *(with a commanding gesture)*. Song! ... Juno ... Mary ... "Home to Our Mountains"![129]

MRS. MADIGAN *(enthusiastically)*. Hear, hear!

JOXER. Oh, tha's a darlin' song, a daarlin' song!

MARY *(bashfully)*. Ah no, da; I'm not in a singin' humour.

MRS. MADIGAN. Gawn with you, child, an' you only goin' to be married; I remember as well as I remember yesterday,—it was on a lovely August evenin', exactly, according to date, fifteen years ago, come the Tuesday folleyin' the nex' that's comin' on, when me own man—*the Lord be good to him*[130]—an' me was sittin' shy together in a doty[131] little nook on a counthry road, adjacent to The Stiles. "That'll scratch your lovely, little white neck," says he, ketchin' hould of a danglin' bramble branch, holdin' clusters of the loveliest flowers you ever seen, an' breakin' it off, so that his arm fell, accidental like, roun' me waist, an' as I felt it tightenin', an' tightenin', an' tightenin', I thought me buzzom was every minute goin' to burst out into a roystherin' song about

> The little green leaves that were shakin' on the threes,
> The gallivantin' buttherflies, an' buzzin' o' the bees!"

BOYLE. Ordher for the song!

JUNO. Come on, Mary—we'll do our best.

(Juno and Mary stand up, and choosing a suitable position, sing simply "Home to Our Mountains.")

(They bow to company, and return to their places.)

BOYLE *(emotionally, at the end of song)*. Lull ... me ... to ... rest!

JOXER *(clapping his hands)*. Bravo, bravo! Darlin' girulls, darlin' girulls!

MRS. MADIGAN. Juno, I never seen you in betther form.

BENTHAM. Very nicely rendered indeed.

MRS. MADIGAN. A noble call, a noble call!

MRS. BOYLE. What about yourself, Mrs. Madigan?

(After some coaxing, Mrs. Madigan rises, and in a quavering voice sings the following verse:)

> If I were a blackbird I'd whistle and sing;[132]
> I'd follow the ship that my thrue love was in;
> An' on the top riggin', I'd there build me nest,
> An' at night I would sleep on me Willie's white breast!

---

129. **Home to Our Mountains** by Charles Jeffreys   130. *the Lord be good to him* customary prayer for the deceased   131. **doty** cute   132. **If I were a blackbird ... sing** traditional English song

(Becoming husky, amid applause, she sits down.)

MRS. MADIGAN. Ah, me voice is too husky now, Juno; though I remember the time when Maisie Madigan could sing like a nightingale at matin' time. I remember as well as I remember yesterday, at a party given to celebrate the comin' of the first chiselur to Annie an' Benny Jimeson—who was the barber, yous may remember, in Henrietta Street, that, afther Easter Week, hung out a green, white an' orange[133] pole, an', then, when the Tans[134] started their Jazz dancin', whipped it in agen, an' stuck out a red, white an' blue[135] wan instead, givin' as an excuse that a barber's pole was strictly nonpolitical—singin' "An' You'll Remember Me," with the top notes quiverin' in a dead hush of pethrified attention, folleyed be a clappin' o' hans that shuk the tumblers on the table, an' capped by Jimeson, the barber, sayin' that it was the best rendherin' of "You'll Remember Me" he ever heard in his natural!

BOYLE *(peremptorily)*. Ordher for Joxer's song!

JOXER. Ah no, I couldn't; don't ass me, Captain.

BOYLE. Joxer's song, Joxer's song—give us wan of your shut-eyed[136] wans.

(Joxer settles himself in his chair; takes a drink; clears his throat; solemnly closes his eyes, and begins to sing in a very querulous voice:)

> She is far from the lan' where her young hero sleeps,[137]
> An' lovers around her are sighing

(He hesitates.)

> An' lovers around her are sighin' . . . sighin' . . . sighin . . .

(A pause.)

BOYLE *(imitating Joxer)*:

> And lovers around her are sighing!

What's the use of you thryin' to sing the song if you don't know it?

MARY. Thry another one, Mr. Daly—maybe you'd be more fortunate.

MRS. MADIGAN. Gawn, Joxer; thry another wan.

JOXER *(starting again)*:

> I have heard the mavis singin' his love song to the morn;[138]
> I have seen the dew-dhrop clingin' to the rose jus' newly born; but . . .
> but . . . *(frantically)* To the rose jus' newly born . . . newly born . . . born.

JOHNNY. Mother, put on the gramophone, for God's sake, an' stop Joxer's bawlin'.

---

133. **green, white an' orange** Irish national colors   134. **Tans** British auxiliary forces used to suppress the Irish rebellion (1919–21)   135. **red, white an' blue** British colors   136. **shut-eyed** sentimental   137. **She is far from the land . . . sleeps** song about Irish patriot Robert Emmet, by Thomas Moore   138. **I have heard the mavis . . . morn** song thrush, from "Mary of Argyle," by Charles Jeffreys

BOYLE *(commandingly)*. Gramophone! . . . I hate to see fellas thryin' to do what they're not able to do.

(Boyle arranges the gramophone, and is about to start it, when voices are heard of persons descending the stairs.)

MRS. BOYLE *(warningly)*. Whisht, Jack, don't put it on, don't put it on yet; this must be poor Mrs. Tancred comin' down to go to the hospital— I forgot all about them bringin' the body to the church to-night. Open the door, Mary, an' give them a bit o' light.

(Mary opens the door, and Mrs. Tancred—a very old woman, obviously shaken by the death of her son—appears, accompanied by several neighbours. The first few phrases are spoken before they appear.)

FIRST NEIGHBOUR. It's a sad journey we're goin' on, but God's good, an' the Republicans won't be always down.

MRS. TANCRED. Ah, what good is that to me now? Whether they're up or down—it won't bring me darlin' boy from the grave.

MRS. BOYLE. Come in an' have a hot cup o' tay, Mrs. Tancred, before you go.

MRS. TANCRED. Ah, I can take nothin' now, Mrs. Boyle—I won't be long afther him.

FIRST NEIGHBOUR. Still an' all, he died a noble death, an' we'll bury him like a king.

MRS. TANCRED. An' I'll go on livin' like a pauper. Ah, what's the pains I suffered bringin' him into the world to carry him to his cradle, to the pains I'm sufferin' now, carryin' him out o' the world to bring him to his grave!

MARY. It would be better for you not to go at all, Mrs. Tancred, but to stay at home beside the fire with some o' the neighbours.

MRS. TANCRED. I seen the first of him, an' I'll see the last of him.

MRS. BOYLE. You'd want a shawl, Mrs. Tancred; it's a cowld night, an' the win's blowin' sharp.

MRS. MADIGAN *(rushing out)*. I've a shawl above.

MRS. TANCRED. Me home is gone now; he was me only child, an' to think that he was lyin' for a whole night stretched out on the side of a lonely counthry lane, with his head, his darlin' head, that I often kissed an' fondled, half hidden in the wather of a runnin' brook. An' I'm told he was the leadher of the ambush where me nex' door neighbour, Mrs. Mannin', lost her Free State soldier son. An' now here's the two of us oul' women, standin' one on each side of a scales o' sorra, balanced be the bodies of our two dead darlin' sons. *(Mrs. Madigan returns, and wraps a shawl around her.)* God bless you, Mrs. Madigan. . . . *(She moves slowly towards the door.)* Mother o' God, Mother o' God, have pity on the pair of us! . . . O Blessed Virgin, where were you when me darlin' son was riddled with bullets, when me darlin' son was riddled with bullets! . . . Sacred

Heart of the Crucified Jesus, take away our hearts o' stone . . . an' give us hearts o' flesh! . . . Take away this murdherin' hate . . . an' give us Thine own eternal love![139] *(They pass out of the room.)*

MRS. BOYLE *(explanatorily to Bentham)*. That was Mrs. Tancred of the two-pair back[140]; her son was found, e'er yestherday, lyin' out beyant Fing-las riddled with bullets. A Die-hard he was, be all accounts. He was a nice quiet boy, but lattherly[141] he went to hell, with his Republic first, an' Republic last an' Republic over all. He ofen took tea with us here, in the oul' days, an' Johnny, there, an' him used to be always together.

JOHNNY. Am I always to be havin' to tell you that he was no friend o' mine? I never cared for him, an' he could never stick me. It's not because he was Commandant of the Battalion that I was Quarther-Masther of,[142] that we were friends.

MRS. BOYLE. He's gone now—the Lord be good to him! God help his poor oul' creature of a mother, for no matther whose friend or enemy he was, he was her poor son.

BENTHAM. The whole thing is terrible, Mrs. Boyle; but the only way to deal with a mad dog is to destroy him.

MRS. BOYLE. An' to think of me forgettin' about him bein' brought to the church to-night, an' we singin' an' all, but it was well we hadn't the gramophone goin', anyhow.

BOYLE. Even if we had aself. We've nothin' to do with these things, one way or t'other. That's the Government's business, an' let them do what we're payin' them for doin'.

MRS. BOYLE. I'd like to know how a body's not to mind these things; look at the way they're afther leavin' the people in this very house. Hasn't the whole house, nearly, been massacreed? There's young Dougherty's husband with his leg off; Mrs. Travers that had her son blew up be a mine in Inchegeela, in Co. Cork; Mrs. Mannin' that lost wan of her sons in ambush a few weeks ago, an' now, poor Mrs. Tancred's only child gone west with his body made a collandher[143] of. Sure, if it's not our business, I don't know whose business it is.

BOYLE. Here, there, that's enough about them things; they don't affect us, an' we needn't give a damn. If they want a wake,[144] well, let them have

---

139. **Sacred Heart . . . eternal love!** devotion to the Sacred Heart was popular in Catholic Ireland, as expressed in this hymn: "Sacred Heart of Jesus, fount of love and mercy / Today we come thy blessing to implore; / Oh, touch our hearts, so cold and so ungrateful, / And make them, Lord, thine forever more." 140. **two-pair back** two-room apartment 141. **lattherly** recently 142. **Commandant . . . Quarther-Masther of** Robbie Tancred and Johnny Boyle were former comrades in the Irish Republican Army 143. **collandher** strainer 144. **wake** communal watching of the dead the night before burial, combining prayer, drinking, and carousal

a wake. When I was a sailor, I was always resigned to meet with a wathery grave; an' if they want to be soldiers, well, there's no use o' them squealin'[145] when they meet a soldier's fate.

JOXER. Let me like a soldier fall—me breast expandin' to th' ball![146]

MRS. BOYLE. In wan way, she deserves all she got; for lately, she let th' Die-hards make an open house of th' place; an' for th' last couple of months, either when th' sun was risin' or when th' sun was settin', you had C.I.D.[147] men burstin' into your room, assin' you where were you born, where were you christened, where were you married, an' where would you be buried!

JOHNNY. For God's sake, let us have no more o' this talk.

MRS. MADIGAN. What about Mr. Boyle's song before we start th' gramophone?

MARY (*getting her hat, and putting it on*). Mother, Charlie and I are goin' out for a little sthroll.

MRS. BOYLE. All right, darlin'.

BENTHAM (*going out with Mary*). We won't be long away, Mrs. Boyle.

MRS. MADIGAN. Gwan, Captain, gwan.

BOYLE. E-e-e-e-eh, I'd want to have a few more jars in me, before I'd be in fettle for singin'.

JOXER. Give us that poem you writ t'other day. (*To the rest.*) Aw, it's a darlin' poem, a daarlin' poem.

MRS. BOYLE. God bless us, is he startin' to write poetry!

BOYLE (*rising to his feet*). E-e-e-e-eh.

(*He recites in an emotional, consequential manner the following verses:*)

Shawn an' I were friends, sir, to me he was all in all.
His work was very heavy and his wages were very small.
None betther on th' beach as Docker, I'll go bail,
'Tis now I'm feelin' lonely, for to-day he lies in jail.
He was not what some call pious—seldom at church or prayer;
For the greatest scoundrels I know, sir, goes every Sunday there.
Fond of his pint—well, rather, but hated the Boss by creed
But never refused a copper to comfort a pal in need.

E-e-e-e-eh.

(*He sits down.*)

MRS. MADIGAN. Grand, grand; you should folly that up,[148] you should folly that up.

145. **squealing** complaining   146. **Let me like a soldier . . . ball!** "Yes, Let Me Like a Soldier Fall," from *Maritana* (1846) by William Vincent Wallace and Edward Fitzball   147. **C.I.D.** term derived from Scotland Yard's Criminal Investigation Department; actually, the Free State police investigators   148. **folly that up** write more like that

JOXER. It's a daarlin' poem!

BOYLE *(delightedly).* E-e-e-e-eh.

JOHNNY. Are yous goin' to put on th' gramophone to night, or are yous not?

MRS. BOYLE. Gwan, Jack, put on a record.

MRS. MADIGAN. Gwan, Captain, gwan.

BOYLE. Well, yous'll want to keep a dead silence.

(He sets a record, starts the machine, and it begins to play "If you're Irish, come into the Parlour."[149] *As the tune is in full blare, the door is suddenly opened by a brisk, little bald-headed man, dressed circumspectly in a black suit; he glares fiercely at all in the room; he is "Needle Nugent," a tailor. He carries his hat in his hand.)*

NUGENT *(loudly, above the noise of the gramophone).* Are yous goin' to have that thing bawlin' an' the funeral of Mrs. Tancred's son passin' the house? Have none of yous any respect for the Irish people's National regard for the dead?

(Boyle stops the gramophone.)

MRS. BOYLE. Maybe, Needle Nugent, it's nearly time we had a little less respect for the dead, an' a little more regard for the livin'.

MRS. MADIGAN. We don't want you, Mr. Nugent, to teach us what we learned at our mother's knee. You don't look yourself as if you were dyin' of grief; if y'ass Maisie Madigan anything, I'd call you a real thrue Diehard an' live-soft Republican, attendin' Republican funerals in the day, an' stoppin' up half the night makin' suits for the Civic Guards![150]

(Persons are heard running down to the street, some saying, "Here it is, here it is." Nugent withdraws, and the rest, except Johnny, go to the window looking into the street, and look out. Sounds of a crowd coming nearer are heard; portion are singing:)

> To Jesus' Heart all burning[151]
> With fervent love for men,
> My heart with fondest yearning
> Shall raise its joyful strain.
> While ages course along,
> Blest be with loudest song
> The Sacred Heart of Jesus
> By every heart and tongue.

MRS. BOYLE. Here's the hearse, here's the hearse!

149. **"If you're Irish, come into the Parlour"** popular party song (1920), by Shaun Glenville and Frank Miller 150. **Civic Guards** Free State police force formed in late 1922 151. **To Jesus Heart all burning** hymn to Sacred Heart by Aloys Schlor

BOYLE. There's t'oul' mother walkin' behin' the coffin.

MRS. MADIGAN. You can hardly see the coffin with the wreaths.

JOXER. Oh, it's a darlin' funeral, a daarlin' funeral!

MRS. MADIGAN. W'd have a betther view from the street.

BOYLE. Yes—this place ud give you a crick in your neck.

(They leave the room, and go down. Johnny sits moodily by the fire.)

(A young man enters; he looks at Johnny for a moment.)

THE YOUNG MAN. Quarther-Masther Boyle.

JOHNNY *(with a start)*. The Mobilizer![152]

THE YOUNG MAN. You're not at the funeral?

JOHNNY. I'm not well.

THE YOUNG MAN. I'm glad I've found you; you were stoppin' at your aunt's; I called there but you'd gone. I've to give you an ordher to attend a Battalion Staff meetin' the night afther to-morrow.

JOHNNY. Where?

THE YOUNG MAN. I don't know; you're to meet me at the Pillar at eight o'clock; then we're to go to a place I'll be told of to-night; there we'll meet a mothor that'll bring us to the meeting. They think you might be able to know somethin' about them that gave the bend where Commandant Tancred was shelterin'.

JOHNNY. I'm not goin', then. I know nothing about Tancred.

THE YOUNG MAN *(at the door)*. You'd betther come for your own sake—remember your oath.[153]

JOHNNY *(passionately)*. I won't go! Haven't I done enough for Ireland! I've lost me arm, an' me hip's desthroyed so that I'll never be able to walk right agen! Good God, haven't I done enough for Ireland?

THE YOUNG MAN. Boyle, no man can do enough for Ireland!

(He goes.)

(Faintly in the distance the crowd is heard saying:)

> Hail, Mary, full of grace, the Lord is with Thee;
> Blessed art Thou amongst women, and blessed, etc.

CURTAIN

ACT 3

The same as Act 2. It is about half-past six on a November evening; a bright fire burns in the grate; Mary, dressed to go out, is sitting on a chair by the fire, leaning forward, her hands under her chin, her elbows on her knees. A look of dejection, mingled with uncertain anxiety, is on her face. A lamp, turned low,

152. **The Mobilizer** officer charged with calling soldiers to action   153. **remember your oath** to obey Volunteer orders

is lighting on the table. The votive light under the picture of the Virgin gleams more redly than ever. Mrs. Boyle is putting on her hat and coat. It is two months later.

MRS. BOYLE. An' has Bentham never even written to you since—not one line for the past month?

MARY *(tonelessly)*. Not even a line, mother.

MRS. BOYLE. That's very curious. . . . What came between the two of yous at all? To leave you so sudden, an' yous so great[154] together. . . . To go away t' England, an' not to even leave you his address. . . . The way he was always bringin' you to dances, I thought he was mad afther[155] you. Are you sure you said nothin' to him?

MARY. No, mother—at least nothing that could possibly explain his givin' me up.

MRS. BOYLE. You know you're a bit hasty at times, Mary, an' say things you shouldn't say.

MARY. I never said to him what I shouldn't say, I'm sure of that.

MRS. BOYLE. How are you sure of it?

MARY. Because I love him with all my heart and soul, mother. Why, I don't know; I often thought to myself that he wasn't the man poor Jerry was, but I couldn't help loving him, all the same.

MRS. BOYLE. But you shouldn't be frettin' the way you are; when a woman loses a man, she never knows what she's afther losin', to be sure, but, then, she never knows what she's afther gainin', either. You're not the one girl of a month ago—you look like one pinin' away. It's long ago I had a right[156] to bring you to the doctor, instead of waitin' till to-night.

MARY. There's no necessity, really, mother, to go to the doctor; nothing serious is wrong with me—I'm run down and disappointed, that's all.

MRS. BOYLE. I'll not wait another minute; I don't like the look of you at all. . . . I'm afraid we made a mistake in throwin' over poor Jerry. . . . He'd have been betther for you than that Bentham.

MARY. Mother, the best man for a woman is the one for whom she has the most love, and Charlie had it all.

MRS. BOYLE. Well, there's one thing to be said for him—he couldn't have been thinkin' of the money, or he wouldn't ha' left you . . . it must ha' been somethin' else.

MARY *(wearily)*. I don't know . . . I don't know, mother . . . only I think . . .

MRS. BOYLE. What d'ye think?

MARY. I imagine . . . he thought . . . we weren't . . . good enough for him.

154. **great** intimate, in love   155. **mad afther** infatuated with   156. **had a right** should have

MRS. BOYLE. An' what was he himself, only a school teacher? Though I don't blame him for fightin' shy[157] of people like that Joxer fella an' that oul' Madigan wan—nice sort o' people for your father to inthroduce to a man like Mr. Bentham. You might have told me all about this before now, Mary; I don't know why you like to hide everything from your mother; you knew Bentham, an' I'd ha' known nothin' about it if it hadn't bin for the Will; an' it was only to-day, afther long coaxin', that you let out that he's left you.

MARY. It would have been useless to tell you—you wouldn't understand.

MRS. BOYLE *(hurt)*. Maybe not. . . . Maybe I wouldn't understand. . . . Well, we'll be off now.

(She goes over to door left, and speaks to Boyle inside.)

MRS. BOYLE. We're goin' now to the doctor's. Are you goin' to get up this evenin'?

BOYLE *(from inside)*. The pains in me legs is terrible! It's me should be poppin' off to the doctor instead o' Mary, the way I feel.

MRS. BOYLE. Sorra mend you![158] A nice way you were in last night—carried in in a frog's march,[159] dead to the world.[160] If that's the way you'll go on when you get the money it'll be the grave for you, an asylum for me and the Poorhouse for Johnny.

BOYLE. I thought you were goin'?

MRS. BOYLE. That's what has you as you are—you can't bear to be spoken to. Knowin' the way we are, up to our ears in debt, it's a wondher you wouldn't ha' got up to go to th' solicitor's an' see if we could ha' gotten a little o' the money even.

BOYLE *(shouting)*. I can't be goin' up there night, noon an' mornin', can I? He can't give the money till he gets it, can he? I can't get blood out of a turnip, can I?

MRS. BOYLE. It's nearly two months since we heard of the Will, an' the money seems as far off as ever. . . . I suppose you know we owe twenty pouns to oul' Murphy?

BOYLE. I've a faint recollection of you tellin' me that before.

MRS. BOYLE. Well, you'll go over to the shop yourself for the things in future—I'll face him no more.

BOYLE. I thought you said you were goin'?

MRS. BOYLE. I'm goin' now; come on, Mary.

BOYLE. Ey, Juno, ey!

MRS. BOYLE. Well, what d'ye want now?

BOYLE. Is there e'er a bottle o' stout left?

157. **fightin' shy** avoiding   158. **Sorra mend you!** God help you!   159. **frog's march** face down, feet dragging   160. **dead to the world** insensible

MRS. BOYLE. There's two o' them here still.

BOYLE. Show us in one o' them an' leave t'other there till I get up.
An' throw us in the paper that's on the table, an' the bottle o' Sloan's
Liniment that's in th' drawer.

MRS. BOYLE *(getting the liniment and the stout)*. What paper is it you
want—the *Messenger*?[161]

BOYLE. *Messenger*! The *News o' the World*![162]

(Mrs. Boyle brings in the things asked for, and comes out again.)

MRS. BOYLE *(at door)*. Mind[163] the candle, now, an' don't burn the
house over our heads. I left t'other bottle o' stout on the table.

*(She puts bottle of stout on table. She goes out with Mary. A cork is heard
popping inside.)*

*(A pause; then outside the door is heard the voice of Joxer lilting softly: "Me
pipe I'll smoke, as I dhrive me moke . . . are you . . . there . . . Mor . . . ee . . .
ar . . . i . . . teee!" A gentle knock is heard, and after a pause the door opens,
and Joxer, followed by Nugent, enters.)*

JOXER. Be God, they must be all out; I was thinkin' there was somethin' up when he didn't answer the signal. We seen Juno an' Mary goin',
but I didn't see him, an' it's very seldom he escapes me.

NUGENT. He's not goin' to escape me—he's not goin' to be let go to
the fair altogether.

JOXER. Sure, the house couldn't hould them lately; an' he goin' about
like a masthperiece[164] of the Free State counthry; forgettin' their friends;
forgettin' God—wouldn't even lift his hat passin' a chapel! Sure they were
bound to get a dhrop! An' you really think there's no money comin' to
him afther all?

NUGENT. Not as much as a red rex,[165] man; I've been a bit anxious
this long time over me money, an' I went up to the solicitor's to find out
all I could—ah, man, they were goin' to throw me down the stairs. They
toul' me that the oul' cock himself had the stairs worn away comin' up
afther it, an' they black in the face tellin' him he'd get nothin'. Some way
or another that the Will is writ he won't be entitled to get as much as a
make![166]

JOXER. Ah, I thought there was somethin' curious about the whole
thing; I've bin havin' sthrange dhreams for the last couple o' weeks. An' I
notice that that Bentham fella doesn't be comin' here now—there must be
somethin' on the mat[167] there too. Anyhow, who, in the name o' God, ud
leave anythin' to that oul' bummer? Sure it ud be unnatural. An' the way

---

161. *Messenger* **Messenger of the Sacred Heart** a pious periodical   162. *News
o' the World* an English sensational tabloid   163. **Mind** Be careful with   164. **mas-
therpiece** chief excellence   165. **red rex** penny   166. **make** halfpenny   167. **on the
mat** the matter

Juno an' him's been throwin' their weight about for the last few months! Ah, him that goes a borrowin' goes a sorrowin'!

NUGENT. Well, he's not goin' to throw his weight about in the suit I made for him much longer. I'm tellin' you seven pouns aren't to be found growin' on the bushes these days.

JOXER. An' there isn't hardly a neighbour in the whole street that hasn't lent him money on the strength of what he was goin' to get, but they're after backing the wrong horse. Wasn't it a mercy o' God that I'd nothin' to give him! The softy I am, you know, I'd ha' lent him me last juice! I must have had somebody's good prayers. Ah, afther all, an honest man's the noblest work o' God!

(Boyle coughs inside.)

JOXER. Whisht, damn it, he must be inside in bed.

NUGENT. Inside o' bed or outside of it, he's goin' to pay me for that suit, or give it back—he'll not climb up my back as easily as he thinks.

JOXER. Gwan in at wanst, man, an' get it off him, an' don't be a fool.

NUGENT *(going to door left, opening it and looking in)*. Ah, don't disturb yourself, Mr. Boyle; I hope you're not sick?

BOYLE. Th' oul' legs, Mr. Nugent, the oul' legs.

NUGENT. I just called over to see if you could let me have anything off the suit?

BOYLE. E-e-e-eh, how much is this it is?

NUGENT. It's the same as it was at the start—seven pouns.

BOYLE. I'm glad you kem, Mr. Nugent; I want a good heavy topcoat—Irish frieze,[168] if you have it. How much would a topcoat like that be, now?

NUGENT. About six pouns.

BOYLE. Six pouns—six an' seven, six an' seven is thirteen—that'll be thirteen pouns I'll owe you.

(Joxer slips the bottle of stout that is on the table into his pocket. Nugent rushes into the room, and returns with suit on his arm; he pauses at the door.)

NUGENT. You'll owe me no thirteen pouns. Maybe you think you're betther able to owe it than pay it!

BOYLE *(frantically)*. Here, come back to hell ower that—where're you goin' with them clothes o' mine?

NUGENT. Where am I goin' with them clothes o' yours? Well, I like your damn cheek!

BOYLE. Here, what am I goin' to dhress meself in when I'm goin' out?

NUGENT. What do I care what you dhress yourself in! You can put yourself in a bolshter cover, if you like.

(He goes towards the other door, followed by Joxer.)

JOXER. What'll he dhress himself in! Gentleman Jack an' his frieze coat!

---

168. **frieze** coarse woolen cloth with uncut nap

(They go out.)

BOYLE *(inside)*. Ey, Nugent; ey, Mr. Nugent, Mr. Nugent!

(After a pause Boyle enters hastily, buttoning the braces of his moleskin trousers; his coat and vest are on his arm; he throws these on a chair and hurries to the door on right.)

BOYLE. Ey, Mr. Nugent, Mr. Nugent!

JOXER *(meeting him at the door)*. What's up, what's wrong, Captain?

BOYLE. Nugent's been here an' took away me suit—the only things I had to go out in!

JOXER Tuk your suit—for God's sake! An' what were you doin' while he was takin' them?

BOYLE. I was in bed when he stole in like a thief in the night, an' before I knew even what he was thinkin' of, he whipped them from the chair an' was off like a redshank![169]

JOXER. An' what, in the name o' God, did he do that for?

BOYLE. What did he do it for? How the hell do I know what he done it for?—jealousy an' spite, I suppose.

JOXER. Did he not say what he done it for?

BOYLE. Amn't I afther tellin' you that he had them whipped up an' was gone before I could open me mouth?

JOXER. That was a very sudden thing to do; there mus' be somethin' behin' it. Did he hear anythin', I wondher?

BOYLE. Did he hear anythin'?—you talk very queer, Joxer—what could he hear?

JOXER. About you not gettin' the money, in some way or t'other?

BOYLE. An' what ud prevent me from gettin' th' money?

JOXER. That's jus' what I was thinkin'—what ud prevent you from gettin' the money—nothin', as far as I can see.

BOYLE *(looking round for bottle of stout, with an exclamation)*. Aw, holy God!

JOXER. What's up, Jack?

BOYLE. He must have afther lifted[170] the bottle o' stout that Juno left on the table!

JOXER *(horrified)*. Ah no, ah no; he wouldn't be afther doin' that now.

BOYLE. An' who done it then? Juno left a bottle o' stout here, an' it's gone—it didn't walk, did it?

JOXER. Oh, that's shockin'; ah, man's inhumanity to man makes countless thousands mourn![171]

MRS. MADIGAN *(appearing at the door)*. I hope I'm not disturbin' you

169. **redshank** red-legged seagull of no fixed abode   170. **lifted** stolen   171. **man's inhumanity to man makes countless thousands mourn!** Robert Burns's "Man Was Made to Mourn"

in any discussion on your forthcomin' legacy—if I may use the word—
an' that you'll let me have a barny[172] for a minute or two with you, Mr.
Boyle.

BOYLE *(uneasily)*. To be sure, Mrs. Madigan—an oul' friend's always
welcome.

JOXER. Come in the evenin', come in th' mornin'; come when you're
assed, or come without warnin', Mrs. Madigan.

BOYLE. Sit down, Mrs. Madigan.

MRS. MADIGAN *(ominously)*. Th' few words I have to say can be said
standin'. Puttin' aside all formularies,[173] I suppose you remember me len-
din' you some time ago three pouns that I raised[174] on blankets an' furniture in me uncle's?

BOYLE. I remember it well. I have it recorded in me book—three pouns
five shillins from Maisie Madigan, raised on articles pawned; an', item:
fourpence, given to make up the price of a pint, on th' principle that no
bird ever flew on wan wing[175]; all to be repaid at par, when the ship comes
home.

MRS. MADIGAN. Well, ever since I shoved in[176] the blankets I've been
perishing with th' cowld, an' I've decided, if I'll be too hot in th' nex'
world aself, I'm not goin' to be too cowld in this wan; an' consequently,
I want me three pouns, if you please.

BOYLE. This is a very sudden demand, Mrs. Madigan, an' can't be met;
but I'm willin' to give you a receipt in full, in full.

MRS. MADIGAN. Come on, out with th' money, an' don't be jack-
actin'.[177]

BOYLE. You can't get blood out of a turnip, can you?

MRS. MADIGAN *(rushing over and shaking him)*. Gimme me money,
y'oul' reprobate, or I'll shake the worth of it out of you!

BOYLE. Ey, houl' on, there; houl' on, there! You'll wait for your money
now, me lassie!

MRS. MADIGAN *(looking around the room and seeing the gramophone)*.
I'll wait for it, will I? Well, I'll not wait long; if I can't get th' cash, I'll get
th' worth of it.

(She catches up the gramophone.)

BOYLE. Ey, ey, there, wher'r you goin' with that?

MRS. MADIGAN. I'm goin' to th' pawn to get me three quid[178] five
shillins; I'll brin' you th' ticket, an' then you can do what you like, me
bucko.

---

172. **barny** chat, talk   173. **formularies** malaprop: preliminaries plus formalities
174. **raised** by pawning   175. **no bird ever flew on wan wing** to buy a second
drink   176. **shoved in** pawned   177. **jack-actin'** playing the fool   178. **three quid**
three pounds

BOYLE. You can't touch that, you can't touch that! It's not my property, an' it's not ped for yet!

MRS. MADIGAN. So much th' betther. It'll be an ayse to me conscience, for I'm takin' what doesn't belong to you. You're not goin' to be swankin'[179] it like a paycock with Maisie Madigan's money—I'll pull some o' th' gorgeous feathers out o' your tail!

(She goes off with the gramophone.)

BOYLE. What's th' world comin' to at all? I ass you, Joxer Daly, is there any morality left anywhere?

JOXER. I wouldn't ha' believed it, only I seen it with me own two eyes. I didn't think Maisie Madigan was that sort of woman; she has either a sup taken, or she's heard somethin'.

BOYLE. Heard somethin'—about what, if it's not any harm to ass you?

JOXER. She must ha' heard some rumour or other that you weren't goin' to get th' money.

BOYLE. Who says I'm not goin' to get th' money?

JOXER. Sure, I don't know—I was only sayin'.

BOYLE. Only sayin' what?

JOXER. Nothin'.

BOYLE. You were goin' to say somethin'—don't be a twisther.[180]

JOXER *(angrily)*. Who's a twisther?

BOYLE. Why don't you speak your mind, then?

JOXER. You never twisted yourself—no, you wouldn't know how!

BOYLE. Did you ever know me to twist; did you ever know me to twist?

JOXER *(fiercely)*. Did you ever do anythin' else! Sure, you can't believe a word that comes out o' your mouth.

BOYLE. Here, get out, ower o' this; I always knew you were a prognosticator an' a procrastinator!

JOXER *(going out as Johnny comes in)*. The anchor's weighed, farewell, ree ... mem ... ber ... me. Jacky Boyle, Esquire,[181] infernal rogue an' damned liar.

JOHNNY. Joxer an' you at it agen?—when are you goin' to have a little respect for yourself, an' not be always makin' a show of us all?

BOYLE. Are you goin' to lecture me now?

JOHNNY. Is mother back from the doctor yet, with Mary?

(Mrs. Boyle enters; it is apparent from the serious look on her face that something has happened. She takes off her hat and coat without a word and puts them by. She then sits down near the fire, and there is a few moments' pause.)

---

179. **swankin'** acting in style 180. **twisther** liar or swindler 181. **Esquire** gentleman

BOYLE. Well, what did the doctor say about Mary?

MRS. BOYLE *(in an earnest manner and with suppressed agitation)*. Sit down here, Jack; I've something to say to you . . . about Mary.

BOYLE *(awed by her manner)*. About . . . Mary?

MRS. BOYLE. Close that door there and sit down here.

BOYLE *(closing the door)*. More throuble in our native land, is it? *(He sits down.)* Well, what is it?

MRS. BOYLE. It's about Mary.

BOYLE. Well, what about Mary—there's nothin' wrong with her, is there?

MRS. BOYLE. I'm sorry to say there's a gradle[182] wrong with her.

BOYLE. A gradle wrong with her! *(Peevishly.)* First Johnny an' now Mary; is the whole house goin' to become an hospital! It's not consumption,[183] is it?

MRS. BOYLE. No . . . it's not consumption . . . it's worse.

JOHNNY. Worse! Well, we'll have to get her into some place ower this, there's no one here to mind her.

MRS. BOYLE. We'll all have to mind her now. You might as well know now, Johnny, as another time. *(To Boyle.)* D'ye know what the doctor said to me about her, Jack?

BOYLE. How ud I know—I wasn't there, was I?

MRS. BOYLE. He told me to get her married at wanst.

BOYLE. Married at wanst! An' why did he say the like o' that?

MRS. BOYLE. Because Mary's goin' to have a baby in a short time.

BOYLE. Goin' to have a baby!—my God, what'll Bentham say when he hears that?

MRS. BOYLE. Are you blind, man, that you can't see that it was Bentham that has done this wrong to her?

BOYLE *(passionately)*. Then he'll marry her, he'll have to marry her!

MRS. BOYLE. You know he's gone to England, an' God knows where he is now.

BOYLE. I'll folly him, I'll folly him, an' bring him back, an' make him do her justice. The scoundrel, I might ha' known what he was, with his yogees an' his prawna!

MRS. BOYLE. We'll have to keep it quiet till we see what we can do.

BOYLE. Oh, isn't this a nice thing to come on top o' me, an' the state I'm in! A pretty show I'll be to Joxer an' to that oul' wan, Madigan! Amn't I afther goin' through enough without havin' to go through this!

MRS. BOYLE. What you an' I'll have to go through'll be nothin' to what poor Mary'll have to go through; for you an' me is middlin' old, an' most of our years is spent; but Mary'll have maybe forty years to face an' handle, an' every wan of them'll be tainted with a bitther memory.

182. **gradle** great deal   183. **consumption** tuberculosis

BOYLE. Where is she? Where is she till I tell her off? I'm tellin' you when I'm done with her she'll be a sorry girl!

MRS. BOYLE. I left her in me sister's till I came to speak to you. You'll say nothin' to her, Jack; ever since she left school she's earned her livin', an' your fatherly care never throubled the poor girl.

BOYLE. Gwan, take her part agen her father! But I'll let you see whether I'll say nothin' to her or no! Her an' her readin'! That's more o' th' blasted nonsense that has the house fallin' down on top of us! What did th' likes of her, born in a tenement house, want with readin'? Her readin's afther bringin' her to a nice pass—oh, it's madnin', madnin', madnin'!

MRS. BOYLE. When she comes back say nothin' to her, Jack, or she'll leave this place.

BOYLE. Leave this place! Ay, she'll leave this place, an' quick too!

MRS. BOYLE. If Mary goes, I'll go with her.

BOYLE. Well, go with her! Well, go, th' pair o' yous! I lived before I seen yous, an' I can live when yous are gone. Isn't this a nice thing to come rollin' in on top o' me afther all your prayin' to St. Anthony an' The Little Flower![184] An' she's a Child o' Mary,[185] too—I wonder what'll the nuns think of her now? An' it'll be bellows'd[186] all over th' disthrict before you could say Jack Robinson[187]; an' whenever I'm seen they'll whisper, "That's th' father of Mary Boyle that had th' kid be th' swank she used to go with; d'ye know, d'ye know?" To be sure they'll know—more about it than I will meself!

JOHNNY. She should be dhriven out o' th' house she's brought disgrace on!

MRS. BOYLE. Hush, you, Johnny. We needn't let it be bellows'd all over the place; all we've got to do is to leave this place quietly an' go somewhere where we're not known, an' nobody'll be th' wiser.

BOYLE. You're talkin' like a two-year-oul', woman. Where'll we get a place ou' o' this?—places aren't that easily got.

MRS. BOYLE. But, Jack, when we get the money . . .

BOYLE. Money—what money?

MRS. BOYLE. Why, oul' Ellison's money, of course.

BOYLE. There's no money comin' from oul' Ellison, or any one else. Since you've heard of wan throuble, you might as well hear of another. There's no money comin' to us at all—the Will's a wash-out![188]

MRS. BOYLE. What are you sayin', man—no money?

JOHNNY. How could it be a wash-out?

---

184. **The Little Flower** St. Therese of Lisieux (1873–97), venerated for her simplicity and sanctity, canonized in 1925   185. **Child o' Mary** a member of the Sodality of Our Lady, an association which cultivated spiritual devotion and charitable work   186. **bellows'd** talked about   187. **Jack Robinson** instantly   188. **wash-out** failure

BOYLE. The boyo that's afther doin' it to Mary done it to me as well. The thick[189] made out the Will wrong; he said in th' Will, only first cousin an' second cousin, instead of mentionin' our names, an' now any one that thinks he's a first cousin or second cousin t'oul' Ellison can claim the money as well as me, an' they're springin' up in hundreds, an' comin' from America an' Australia, thinkin' to get their whack[190] out of it, while all the time the lawyers is gobblin' it up, till there's not as much as ud buy a stockin' for your lovely daughter's baby!

MRS. BOYLE. I don't believe it, I don't believe it, I don't believe it!

JOHNNY. Why did you say nothin' about this before?

MRS. BOYLE. You're not serious, Jack; you're not serious!

BOYLE. I'm tellin' you the scholar, Bentham, made a banjax[191] o' th' Will; instead o' sayin', "th' rest o' me property to be divided between me first cousin, Jack Boyle, an' me second cousin, Mick Finnegan, o' Santhry," he writ down only, "me first an' second cousins," an' the world an' his wife are afther th' property now.

MRS. BOYLE. Now I know why Bentham left poor Mary in th' lurch; I can see it all now—oh, is there not even a middlin' honest man left in th' world?

JOHNNY *(to Boyle)*. An' you let us run into debt, an' you borreyed money from everybody to fill yourself with beer! An' now you tell us the whole thing's a wash-out! Oh, if it's thrue, I'm done with you, for you're worse than me sisther Mary!

BOYLE. You hole your tongue, d'ye hear? I'll not take any lip from you. Go an' get Bentham if you want satisfaction for all that's afther happenin' us.

JOHNNY. I won't hole me tongue, I won't hole me tongue! I'll tell you what I think of you, father an' all as you are . . . you . . .

MRS. BOYLE. Johnny, Johnny, Johnny, for God's sake, be quiet!

JOHNNY. I'll not be quiet, I'll not be quiet; he's a nice father, isn't he? Is it any wondher Mary went asthray, when . . .

MRS. BOYLE. Johnny, Johnny, for my sake be quiet—for your mother's sake!

BOYLE. I'm goin' out now to have a few dhrinks with th' last few makes I have, an' tell that lassie o' yours not to be here when I come back; for if I lay me eyes on her, I'll lay me hans on her, an' if I lay me hans on her, I won't be accountable for me actions!

JOHNNY. Take care somebody doesn't lay his hands on you—y'oul' . . .

MRS. BOYLE. Johnny, Johnny!

BOYLE *(at door, about to go out)*. Oh, a nice son, an' a nicer daughter, I have. *(Calling loudly upstairs.)* Joxer, Joxer, are you there?

189. **thick** stupid person   190. **whack** portion   191. **banjax** botch, mess

JOXER (*from a distance*). I'm here, More . . . ee . . . aar . . . i . . . tee!

BOYLE. I'm goin' down to Foley's—are you comin'?

JOXER. Come with you? With that sweet call me heart is stirred; I'm only waiting for the word, an' I'll be with you, like a bird!

(*Boyle and Joxer pass the door going out.*)

JOHNNY (*throwing himself on the bed*). I've a nice sisther, an' a nice father, there's no bettin' on it. I wish to God a bullet or a bomb had whipped me ou' o' this long ago! Not one o' yous, not one o' yous, have any thought for me!

MRS. BOYLE (*with passionate remonstrance*). If you don't whisht, Johnny, you'll drive me mad. Who has kep' th' home together for the past few years—only me? An' who'll have to bear th' biggest part o' this throuble but me?—but whinin' an' whingin'[192] isn't goin' to do any good.

JOHNNY. You're to blame yourself for a gradle of it—givin' him his own way in everything, an' never assin' to check him, no matther what he done. Why didn't you look afther th' money? why . . .

(*There is a knock at the door; Mrs. Boyle opens it; Johnny rises on his elbow to look and listen; two men enter.*)

FIRST MAN. We've been sent up be th' Manager of the Hibernian Furnishing Co., Mrs. Boyle, to take back the furniture that was got a while ago.

MRS. BOYLE. Yous'll touch nothin' here—how do I know who yous are?

FIRST MAN (*showing a paper*). There's the ordher, ma'am. (*Reading.*) A chest o' drawers, a table, wan easy an' two ordinary chairs; wan mirror; wan chestherfield divan, an' a wardrobe an' two vases. (*To his comrade.*) Come on, Bill, it's afther knockin'-off[193] time already.

JOHNNY. For God's sake, mother, run down to Foley's an' bring father back, or we'll be left without a stick.

(*The men carry out the table.*)

MRS. BOYLE. What good would it be?—you heard what he said before he went out.

JOHNNY. Can't you thry? He ought to be here, an' the like of this goin' on.

(*Mrs. Boyle puts a shawl around her, as Mary enters.*)

MARY. What's up, mother? I met men carryin' away the table, an' everybody's talking about us not gettin' the money after all.

MRS. BOYLE. Everythin's gone wrong, Mary, everythin'. We're not gettin' a penny out o' the Will, not a penny—I'll tell you all when I come back; I'm goin' for your father.

(*She runs out.*)

192. **whingin'** whining, snivelling   193. **knockin'-off** quitting

JOHNNY (*to Mary, who has sat down by the fire*). It's a wondher you're not ashamed to show your face here, afther what has happened.

(*Jerry enters slowly; there is a look of earnest hope on his face. He looks at Mary for a few moments.*)

JERRY (*softly*). Mary!

(*Mary does not answer.*)

JERRY. Mary, I want to speak to you for a few moments, may I?

(*Mary remains silent; Johnny goes slowly into room on left.*)

JERRY. Your mother has told me everything, Mary, and I have come to you. . . . I have come to tell you, Mary, that my love for you is greater and deeper than ever. . . .

MARY (*with a sob*). Oh, Jerry, Jerry, say no more; all that is over now; anything like that is impossible now!

JERRY. Impossible? Why do you talk like that, Mary?

MARY. After all that has happened.

JERRY. What does it matter what has happened? We are young enough to be able to forget all those things. (*He catches her hand.*) Mary, Mary, I am pleading for your love. With Labour, Mary, humanity is above everything; we are the Leaders in the fight for a new life. I want to forget Bentham, I want to forget that you left me—even for a while.

MARY. Oh, Jerry, Jerry, you haven't the bitter word of scorn for me after all.

JERRY (*passionately*). Scorn! I love you, love you, Mary!

MARY (*rising, and looking him in the eyes*). Even though . . .

JERRY. Even though you threw me over for another man; even though you gave me many a bitter word!

MARY. Yes, yes, I know; but you love me, even though . . . even though . . . I'm . . . goin' . . . goin' . . . (*He looks at her questioningly, and fear gathers in his eyes.*) Ah, I was thinkin' so. . . . You don't know everything!

JERRY (*poignantly*). Surely to God, Mary, you don't mean that . . . that . . . that . . .

MARY. Now you know all, Jerry; now you know all!

JERRY. My God, Mary, have you fallen as low as that?

MARY. Yes, Jerry, as you say, I have fallen as low as that.

JERRY. I didn't mean it that way, Mary . . . it came on me so sudden, that I didn't mind what I was sayin'. . . . I never expected this—your mother never told me. . . . I'm sorry . . . God knows, I'm sorry for you, Mary.

MARY. Let us say no more, Jerry; I don't blame you for thinkin' it's terrible. . . . I suppose it is. . . . Everybody'll think the same . . . it's only as I expected—your humanity is just as narrow as the humanity of the others.

JERRY. I'm sorry, all the same. . . . I shouldn't have troubled you. . . .

I wouldn't if I'd known. . . . If I can do anything for you . . . Mary . . . I will.

(He turns to go, and halts at the door.)

MARY. Do you remember, Jerry, the verses you read when you gave the lecture in the Socialist Rooms some time ago, on Humanity's Strife with Nature?

JERRY. The verses—no; I don't remember them.

MARY. I do. They're runnin' in me head now—

> An' we felt the power that fashion'd[194]
> All the lovely things we saw,
> That created all the murmur
> Of an everlasting law,
> Was a hand of force an' beauty,
> With an eagle's tearin' claw.
>
> Then we saw our globe of beauty
> Was an ugly thing as well,
> A hymn divine whose chorus
> Was an agonizin' yell;
> Like the story of a demon,
> That an angel had to tell;
>
> Like a glowin' picture by a
> Hand unsteady, brought to ruin;
> Like her craters, if their deadness
> Could give life unto the moon;
> Like the agonizing horror
> Of a violin out of tune.

(There is a pause, and Devine goes slowly out.)

JOHNNY *(returning)*. Is he gone?

MARY. Yes.

(The two men re-enter.)

FIRST MAN. We can't wait any longer for t'oul' fella—sorry, Miss, but we have to live as well as th' nex' man.

(They carry out some things.)

JOHNNY. Oh, isn't this terrible! . . . I suppose you told him everything . . . couldn't you have waited for a few days? . . . he'd have stopped th' takin' of the things, if you'd kep' your mouth shut. Are you burnin' to tell every one of the shame you've brought on us?

MARY *(snatching up her hat and coat)*. Oh, this is unbearable!

(She rushes out.)

194. **An' we felt the power that fashion'd** from O'Casey's own juvenilia

FIRST MAN *(re-entering)*. We'll take the chest o' drawers next—it's the heaviest.

(The votive light flickers for a moment, and goes out.)

JOHNNY *(in a cry of fear)*. Mother o' God, the lights afther goin' out!

FIRST MAN. You put the win' up[195] me the way you bawled that time. The oil's all gone, that's all.

JOHNNY *(with an agonizing cry)*. Mother o' God, there's a shot I'm afther gettin'!

FIRST MAN. What's wrong with you, man? Is it a fit you're takin'?

JOHNNY. I'm afther feelin' a pain in me breast, like the tearin' by of a bullet!

FIRST MAN. He's goin' mad—it's a wondher they'd leave a chap like that here by himself.

(Two Irregulars enter swiftly; they carry revolvers; one goes over to Johnny; the other covers the two furniture men.)

FIRST IRREGULAR *(to the men, quietly and incisively)*. Who are you?—what are yous doin' here?—quick!

FIRST MAN. Removin' furniture that's not paid for.

IRREGULAR. Get over to the other end of the room an' turn your faces to the wall—quick!

(The two men turn their faces to the wall, with their hands up.)

SECOND IRREGULAR *(to Johnny)*. Come on, Sean[196] Boyle, you're wanted; some of us have a word to say to you.

JOHNNY. I'm sick, I can't—what do you want with me?

SECOND IRREGULAR. Come on, come on; we've a distance to go, an' haven't much time—come on.

JOHNNY. I'm an oul' comrade—yous wouldn't shoot an oul' comrade.

SECOND IRREGULAR. Poor Tancred was an oul' comrade o' yours, but you didn't think o' that when you gave him away to the gang that sent him to his grave. But we've no time to waste; come on—here, Dermot, ketch his arm. *(To Johnny.)* Have you your beads?[197]

JOHNNY. Me beads! Why do you ass me that, why do you ass me that?

SECOND IRREGULAR. Go on, go on, march!

JOHNNY. Are yous goin' to do in a comrade?—look at me arm, I lost it for Ireland.

SECOND IRREGULAR. Commandant Tancred lost his life for Ireland.

JOHNNY. Sacred Heart of Jesus, have mercy on me! Mother o' God, pray for me—be with me now in the agonies o' death! . . . Hail, Mary, full o' grace . . . the Lord is . . . with Thee.

(They drag out Johnny Boyle, and the curtain falls. When it rises again the most of the furniture is gone. Mary and Mrs. Boyle, one on each side, are sitting in a darkened room, by the fire; it is an hour later.)

195. **put the win' up** frightened   196. **Sean** John (Irish)   197. **beads** Rosary

MRS. BOYLE. I'll not wait much longer . . . what did they bring him away in the mothor for? Nugent says he thinks they had guns . . . is me throubles never goin' to be over? . . . If anything ud happen to poor Johnny, I think I'd lose me mind. . . . I'll go to the Police Station, surely they ought to be able to do somethin'.

(Below is heard the sound of voices.)

MRS. BOYLE. Whisht, is that something? Maybe, it's your father, though when I left him in Foley's he was hardly able to lift his head. Whisht!

(A knock at the door, and the voice of Mrs. Madigan, speaking very softly:) Mrs. Boyle, Mrs. Boyle.

(Mrs. Boyle opens the door.)

MRS. MADIGAN. Oh, Mrs. Boyle, God an' His Blessed Mother be with you this night!

MRS. BOYLE *(calmly)*. What is it, Mrs. Madigan? It's Johnny—something about Johnny.

MRS. MADIGAN. God send[198] it's not, God send it's not Johnny!

MRS. BOYLE. Don't keep me waitin', Mrs. Madigan; I've gone through so much lately that I feel able for anything.

MRS. MADIGAN. Two polismen[199] below wantin' you.

MRS. BOYLE. Wantin' me; an' why do they want me?

MRS. MADIGAN. Some poor fella's been found, an' they think it's, it's . . .

MRS. BOYLE. Johnny, Johnny!

MARY *(with her arms round her mother)*. Oh, mother, mother, me poor, darlin' mother.

MRS. BOYLE. Hush, hush, darlin'; you'll shortly have your own throuble to bear. *(To Mrs. Madigan.)* An' why do the polis think it's Johnny, Mrs. Madigan?

MRS. MADIGAN. Because one o' the doctors knew him when he was attendin' with his poor arm.

MRS. BOYLE. Oh, it's thrue, then; it's Johnny, it's me son, me own son!

MARY. Oh, it's thrue, it's thrue what Jerry Devine says—there isn't a God, there isn't a God; if there was He wouldn't let these things happen!

MRS. BOYLE. Mary, Mary, you musn't say them things. We'll want all the help we can get from God an' His Blessed Mother now! These things have nothin' to do with the Will o' God. Ah, what can God do agen the stupidity o' men!

MRS. MADIGAN. The polis want you to go with them to the hospital to see the poor body—they're waitin' below.

MRS. BOYLE. We'll go. Come, Mary, an' we'll never come back here

---

198. **send** ensure   199. **polismen** policemen, Civic Guards

agen. Let your father furrage for himself now; I've done all I could an' it was all no use—he'll be hopeless till the end of his days. I've got a little room in me sisther's where we'll stop till your throuble is over, an' then we'll work together for the sake of the baby.

MARY. My poor little child that'll have no father!

MRS. BOYLE. It'll have what's far betther—it'll have two mothers.

A ROUGH VOICE SHOUTING FROM BELOW. Are yous goin' to keep us waitin' for yous all night?

MRS. MADIGAN. *(going to the door, and shouting down).* Take your hour,[200] there, take your hour! If yous are in such a hurry, skip off, then, for nobody wants you here—if they did yous wouldn't be found. For you're the same as yous were undher the British Government—never where yous are wanted! As far as I can see, the Polis as Polis, in this city, is Null an' Void![201]

MRS. BOYLE. We'll go, Mary, we'll go; you to see your poor dead brother, an' me to see me poor dead son!

MARY. I dhread it, mother, I dhread it!

MRS. BOYLE. I forgot, Mary, I forgot; your poor oul' selfish mother was only thinkin' of herself. No, no, you mustn't come—it wouldn't be good for you. You go on to me sisther's an' I'll face th' ordeal meself. Maybe I didn't feel sorry enough for Mrs. Tancred when her poor son was found as Johnny's been found now—because he was a Die-hard! Ah, why didn't I remember that then he wasn't a Diehard or a Stater, but only a poor dead son! It's well I remember all that she said—an' it's my turn to say it now: What was the pain I suffered, Johnny, bringin' you into the world to carry you to your cradle, to the pains I'll suffer carryin' you out o' the world to bring you to your grave! Mother o' God, Mother o' God, have pity on us all! Blessed Virgin, where were you when me darlin' son was riddled with bullets? Sacred Heart o' Jesus, take away our hearts o' stone, and give us hearts o' flesh! Take away this murdherin' hate, an' give us Thine own eternal love!

(They all go slowly out.)

(There is a pause. Then a sound of shuffling steps on the stairs outside. The door opens and Boyle and Joxer, both of them very drunk, enter.)

BOYLE. I'm able to go no farther. . . . Two polis, ey . . . what were they doin' here, I wondher? . . . Up to no good, anyhow . . . an' Juno an' that lovely daughter o' mine with them. *(Taking a sixpence from his pocket and looking at it.)* Wan single, solitary tanner left out of all I borreyed. . . . *(He lets it fall.)* The last o' the Mohicans.[202] . . . The blinds is down, Joxer, the blinds is down![203]

---

200. **hour** time 201. **Null an' Void** invalid 202. **The last o' the Mohicans** Cf. James Fenimore Cooper's novel (1826) 203. **The blinds is down** because of Johnny's death

JOXER *(walking unsteadily across the room, and anchoring at the bed.)* Put all . . . your throubles . . . in your oul' kit-bag . . . an' smile . . . smile . . . smile![204]

BOYLE. The counthry'll have to steady itself . . . it's goin' . . . to hell. . . . Where'r all . . . the chairs . . . gone to . . . steady itself, Joxer. . . . Chairs'll . . . have to . . . steady themselves. . . . No matther . . . what any one may . . . say. . . . Irelan' sober . . . is Irelan' . . . free.[205]

JOXER *(stretching himself on the bed)*. Chains . . . an' slaveree[206] . . . that's a darlin' motto . . . a daaarlin' . . . motto!

BOYLE. If th' worst comes . . . to th' worse . . . I can join a . . . flyin' . . . column.[207] . . . I done . . . me bit . . . in Easther Week . . . had no business . . . to . . . be . . . there . . . but Captain Boyle's Captain Boyle!

JOXER. Breathes there a man with soul . . . so . . . de . . . ad . . . this . . . me . . . o . . .wn, me nat . . . ive l . . . an'![208]

BOYLE *(subsiding into a sitting posture on the floor)*. Commandant Kelly died . . . in them . . . arms . . . Joxer. . . . Tell me Volunteer Butties . . . says he . . . that . . . I died for . . . Irelan'!

JOXER. D'jever rade Willie . . . Reilly . . . an' his own . . . Colleen . . . Bawn?[209] It's a darlin' story, a daarlin' story!

BOYLE. I'm telling you . . . Joxer . . . th' whole worl's . . . in a terr . . .ible state o' . . . chassis!

CURTAIN

---

204. **Put all . . . smile!** "Pack All Your Troubles" song popular among Allied soldiers during World War I   205. **Irelan' sober . . . is Irelan' free** slogan of Fr. Theobald Mathew's temperance movement of the 1840s   206. **Chains . . . an' . . . slaveree** Robert Burns's song "Scots, Wha Hae"   207. **flyin' column** mobile unit of the Irish Volunteers or I.R.A. during the Irish War of Independence   208. **Breathes there a man . . . native l . . . an'** "Breathes there a man, with soul so dead, / Who never to himself hath said, / This is my own, my native land!" Sir Walter Scott, "The Lay of the Last Minstrel" (1805)   209. **Willie . . . Bawn** characters in the Irish folk ballad "Willy Reilly"

LENNOX ROBINSON
1886 – 1958

Esmé Stuart Lennox Robinson was born the son of a Protestant clergyman in Douglas, Co. Cork in 1886. The Robinsons were conservative in
religion and unionist in politics. Poor health prevented young Lennox
from getting much schooling beyond a limited time at Bandon Grammar
School. But his imagination was sparked when in 1907 he attended a production by the touring Abbey players in Cork. Their production of W. B.
Yeats's *Cathleen Ni Houlihan* and Lady Gregory's *The Rising of the Moon*
decided Robinson on a theatrical career. Thereafter, although his literary
career was primarily as a playwright and director, he also wrote fiction,
biography, autobiography, essays, and a history of the Abbey.

His own first effort for the stage, *The Clancy Name* (1908) was a well
designed social play which showed a penchant for melodrama. The following year, Robinson was apprenticed by Lady Gregory and Yeats as a manager and director at the Abbey; arrangements were made for his theatrical
education in London under the auspices of Bernard Shaw and Granville
Barker. Back in Dublin the next year, his decision not to close the Abbey
in mourning for the death of Edward VII led to a dispute between the
directors and their English benefactress Miss A. E. F. Horniman. An unsuccessful Abbey tour of the United States in 1914 led to Robinson's resignation. The plays of Robinson's early career—*The Clancy Name* (1908),
The Cross Roads (1909), *Harvest* (1910), and *Patriots* (1912)—register a
strongly realistic critique of Irish life, but they all overreach themselves for
theatrical effect.

He returned to West Cork, where his work for the Carnegie Union
Trust took him through small-town Ireland and deepened his appreciation
of the ordinary people of the countryside. This contact was the basis of
his most famous work, the satirical comedy *The Whiteheaded Boy* (1916).
Following his return to the Abbey in 1919, he was appointed to the Board
of Directors (1923), a post he held for thirty-five years; and he also served
as director-producer until 1935. Although his energy and vision moved him
to found the Dublin Drama League in 1919 to present works by American
and European authors, he found that his own work was governed by what
he termed "this strange Irish thing, the commanding force in my life."

In his later years, he expended more energy on interests allied to his
playwriting: editing, writing autobiography, reminiscences of his life in
the theater, and going on lecture tours. During his long association with

the Abbey—longer than that of either Yeats or Lady Gregory—Robinson frequently traveled abroad with the company or on lecture tours. In 1948 he was granted an honorary doctorate from Trinity College Dublin. He died in 1958 and was buried in St. Patrick's Cathedral.

Robinson's long and productive career made him a central figure in the Irish theatrical scene. As director, producer and playwright he was responsible for bringing a sophistication and diversification to the stage: with twenty-two plays staged at the Abbey and three more at the Gate, he was one of the most productive Irish dramatists. His best works were expressly written to be directed by himself at the Abbey—a company and a stage he knew from long experience. But these familiarities did not curtail his versatility, from his early realistic plays of rural and small-town life through the political drama of his middle period, to his later fantasies, comedies of manners, and psychological plays. As a major theme connecting all of this work, his own persona, the idealist, grapples with the indignities of ordinary life.

The Big House is a major theme in modern Irish literature. It is concerned with the political and social position of the landlord class in the new democratic republic. Unlike their European equivalents, Irish landlords were colonials, so that any aspect of life in the drawing room or library was likely to run into political considerations. The Anglo-Irish ascendancy and their English cousins were divided from the Catholic natives by differences in religion, class, culture, and even language, attitudes towards colonial conquest, and views of the political future. Forty years before the establishment of the Irish Free State, the Land Wars served notice to the landed gentry that their position was no longer secure; and with the passage of the Land Acts and the Anglo-Irish Treaty, the economic and political base on which they had depended for three hundred years was broken. For some, the eviction notice came as abruptly as the incendiary's torch; and for others, life continued circumspectly in the light reflected from a bygone age. Meanwhile, outside the demesne walls, in the midst of the rejoicing for the triumph of democracy, a few cautionary voices were raised in lament for what was being destroyed. Yeats, for example, in his poetry and public statements protested the loss of houses such as Lady Gregory's family home ("Coole Park, 1929"); later, in his play *Purgatory* (1938), the Big House is praised as a symbol of the traditions of cultured leadership, and its destroyers denounced: "to kill a house / Where great men grew up, married, died, / I here declare a capital offense."

While Yeats is primarily responsible for the elevation of this theme to mythic status, Lennox Robinson's play is the most graphic and balanced dramatization of the dilemmas facing the ascendancy during the turbulent years of the national struggle.

In the course of his work for the Carnegie Trust, Lennox Robinson lived for a time at the estate of the O'Briens of Cahirmoyle, Co. Limerick, where he absorbed the atmosphere of a country estate from the inside. In his autobiography, *Curtain Up*, he recalls driving home to Dublin after a visit to Wicklow and seeing in the distance a derelict Big House across the fields. He was immediately impressed by its air of mystery, by what he took to be the hoard of memories held by this Georgian or sham Gothic castle. He was taken by the idea of developing a play of a disintegrating social order, set against the background of Ireland's struggle for independence. A nationalist like Yeats, Robinson admired the Anglo-Irish class, and lamented its eclipse in Irish life. Thus *The Big House* reflects these sympathies as a reservation to his sympathy with the new directions the nation was taking in the 1920s.

The Big House (1926) is set during the period between the end of World War I and the Irish Civil War. It gives a sympathetic view of the Alcocks' attempts to preserve their position in a rapidly changing political scene. Robinson has invested the figures of Kate and her brother Ulick with his claim for the ascendancy's place in the new order. Like O'Casey's Boyle family, the Alcocks are caught up in forces turbulent beyond their control; yet Robinson's approach is more detached, intellectual, and sociological, the characters less individuated, the conclusion less pessimistic than that of his great Dublin counterpart. In a Chekhovian sequel, *Killycreggs at Twilight* (1937), however, there is none of Kate Alcock's buoyancy.

The Big House is the work of a fine craftsman. It bears out Christopher Murray's general observation regarding Robinson's work: "lacking the passion of Synge or O'Casey, nevertheless [it] takes its inspiration from the source that gives these writers places among the greatest of Irish writers: national feeling. It takes its significance, however, from its value as theatrical art, unremittingly pursued."

SELECT BIBLIOGRAPHY

Publications

Selected Plays of Lennox Robinson. Ed. and intro., Christopher Murray. Gerrards Cross, Bucks.: Colin Smythe/Washington, 'DC: The Catholic University of America Press, 1982. (*Patriots, The Whiteheaded Boy, Crabbed in Youth and Age, The Big House, Drama at Inish, Church Street*)
Curtain Up: An Autobiography. London: Michael Joseph, 1942.
Ireland's Abbey Theatre: A History, 1899–1951. London: Sidgwick and Jackson/New York: Samuel French, 1951.

Biography and Criticism

Hoover, Ronald G. "Lennox Robinson." *Dictionary of Literary Biography* 10: 116–21.
O'Neill, Michael. *Lennox Robinson*. New York: Twayne Publishers, 1964.
The Journal of Irish Literature. 9,1 (January 1980): A Lennox Robinson Number.

See also discussions in Hunt, *The Abbey*; Hogan, *After the Irish Renaissance*; Krause, *The Profane Book of Irish Comedy*; and Maxwell, *Modern Irish Drama*.

The Big House

*Four scenes
in its life*

*To Rutherford Mayne
of the Ulster Players
this play of County Cork[1]*

THE SCENES

SCENE 1. The drawing-room at Ballydonal House. A November morning, 1918.

SCENE 2. The dining-room at Ballydonal House. A June evening, 1921.

SCENE 3. The same. A February night, 1923.

SCENE 4. A corner of the garden early the next morning.

CHARACTERS

In the order of their appearance

ATKINS
REV. HENRY BROWN
CAPTAIN MONTGOMERY DESPARD
KATE ALCOCK
ST. LEGER ALCOCK
VANDALEUR O'NEILL
MRS. ALCOCK
ANNIE DALY
THREE YOUNG MEN

SCENE 1

The large drawing-room at Ballydonal House. The room must give the impression of size, on a small stage one of its sides must not be seen but should be

1. **County Cork** in Munster, southern Ireland

"masked" by a large Chinese screen. At the back are two large windows, they can be either Georgian[2] type or mock-Gothic,[3] there are heavy curtains on them. On the side of the room which is seen is a door up stage and, lower down, a fireplace. A profusion of furniture, some good, some bad, profusion of small unimportant pictures, photographs, china on the walls; the effect of all being a comfortable room containing the vestigia[4] of generations, the mid-Victorian vestigia prevailing. There is a bright fire and bright sunshine outside the windows. It is about ten-thirty on a November morning, 1918.[5] The room is empty. A door on the unseen side of the room opens and the voice of Atkins, the butler, is heard.

ATKINS. Mr. Brown to see you, sir.
(Mr. Brown appears round the screen, a middle-aged, bearded clergyman.)
BROWN *(looking round the room).* Atkins! Atkins!
ATKINS *(coming back but still unseen).* Did you call, sir?
BROWN. Mr. Alcock isn't here.
ATKINS *(coming into sight round the screen and looking round the room. He is a small stout man of sixty-five, his gait is a little rolling, his voice a little thick, he is obviously a little drunk).* I beg your pardon, your reverence, he was here a minute ago. *(He crosses to the door above the fireplace, opens it and looks into the next room. He shuts it again.)* There's no one in the small drawing-room but Captain Despard. I'll send looking for him.
BROWN. Thank you.
ATKINS. He'll likely have walked out to the yard to see do they understand about the bell.
BROWN. What bell?
ATKINS. The big bell, Father—your reverence, I mean—the yard bell. It's to be rung at eleven o'clock and it's not been rung these twenty years.
BROWN. I see. Part of the celebrations?[6]
ATKINS. But indeed he needn't be bothering. I have Paddy O'Reilly tutored in the bell. He's to be there since ten o'clock, the rope in his hand, the cook's alarm clock hanging on the wall in front of his face and on the stroke of eleven he's to start bell-ringing, ring for a quarter of an hour and then walk into the kitchen for the bottle of stout[7] the master's after ordering for him.
BROWN. I see. Well, it's a great day.
ATKINS. It is, Father.

---

2. **Georgian** eighteenth-century, from the time of the four Georges (1714–1830) 3. **mock-Gothic** nineteenth-century Gothic revival 4. **vestigia** furnishings, effects 5. **It is about ten-thirty on a November morning, 1918** World War I came to an end at 11 a.m. on November 11, 1918, Armistice Day. 6. **celebrations** of the conclusion of the war 7. **stout** dark beer

BROWN. You'll be expecting your grandson home now. Is he still in Salonika?[8]

ATKINS. He is. When he couldn't get through them Dardanelles[9] he gev up and he's sitting in Salonika ever since.

BROWN. He's been luckier than some. . . . Will you try and find Mr. Alcock? I can't wait long, I have a lot to do this morning.

ATKINS. I will, your reverence. There's the papers—this morning's "Constitution"[10] and Saturday's "Irish Times."[11] We don't get it till the morning now since the second post[12] was cut off, bad luck to it. But I suppose it's the same way at the rectory.

BROWN. It is indeed.

ATKINS. Ah well, please God now the Germans are bet[13] we'll have posts and sugar and everything back the way it used to be long ago. Will I bring you a glass of sherry while you're waiting?

BROWN. No, thank you.

ATKINS. You'll excuse me for asking, Father—your reverence, I mean— I forgot you were so mad for the temperance. I'll have the master for you now as fast as I can get him.

(He ambles out. Mr. Brown opens the "Irish Times" and glances at it. From the door above the fire enters Captain Despard, twenty-five years old, in uniform, he limps a little. He stops on seeing Brown.)

BROWN *(going to him, holding out his hand)*. How d'ye do? You are Captain Despard, I'm sure.

DESPARD. Oh—ah—yes.

BROWN. My name is Brown, I'm the parson[14] here. St. Leger—Mr. Alcock—told me you were coming here.

DESPARD. Oh—yes.

BROWN. You've been having a nasty time with your foot, haven't you? Is it better?

DESPARD. Nearly all right. I hope I'll be able to go back in another week or ten days.

BROWN. But fortunately there'll be nothing to go back to.

DESPARD. Nothing?

BROWN. No war. Only half an hour more of it, thank goodness.

DESPARD. I doubt if it's as over as people think it is.

BROWN. But President Wilson's terms—

DESPARD. Those damned Yankees—beg your pardon—but this Ar-

---

8. **Salonika** Thessaloniki, a port in northern Greece, a British base during World War I   9. **Dardanelles** the straits joining the eastern Mediterranean and the Black Sea, scene of a disastrous British defeat in 1915   10. **"Constitution"** Unionist Cork newspaper (1823–1924)   11. **"Irish Times"** Unionist Dublin newspaper, founded in 1859   12. **second post** the second of two daily mail deliveries   13. **bet** beaten   14. **parson** Church of Ireland clergyman in charge of a parish

mistice business[15] is a bad mistake, we should have marched through to Berlin.

BROWN. Hm! But if we get all we want without losing another man or killing another man—

DESPARD. Oh, losing! Killing! It's not a picnic.

BROWN. No, indeed, it isn't. . . . You were very good to poor Reginald. It made a great difference to Mrs. Alcock to know there was a friend with him when he died.

DESPARD. There wasn't much I could do.

BROWN. Still, it made a difference. Have you ever come across her other boy, Ulick?

DESPARD. Only once. A rather quiet dull sort of chap, isn't he? Not like poor old Reg.

BROWN. No, he's very different from Reginald. . . . I suppose you have no idea where Mr. Alcock is?

DESPARD. I haven't seen him since breakfast.

BROWN. Atkins is supposed to be looking for him, but Atkins is a little—well, he started to celebrate early.

DESPARD. Atkins? Oh, that's the butler. Why, he started to celebrate last night. You should have seen him handing round the soup. It was a marvel, but not a drop spilled.

BROWN. Poor Atkins. It's his one failing.

DESPARD. Typically Irish old fellow, isn't he?

BROWN. I hope not.

DESPARD. Oh, but he's a delightful old chap. And the rest of it doesn't seem to be so awfully Irish.

BROWN. The rest of it?

DESPARD. Well, the house itself, the way it's run, and—and everything.

BROWN. Do they read "Castle Rackrent"[16] in the trenches?

DESPARD (*staring*). I don't think so, never heard of it. What do you mean?

BROWN. Nothing. I withdraw my insinuation. I started by thinking how blunderingly English your conclusions were. I beg your pardon. Second thoughts make me give you credit for exceedingly sharp penetration.

DESPARD. Oh, thank you.

BROWN. I'm sure you're thinking that we haven't known each other long enough for me to say that sort of thing to you. But here in the country fresh acquaintances are so rare that I've got into the impolite habit of taking short cuts. You must forgive me.

---

15. **Armistice business** Woodrow Wilson, the architect of the terms of the Armistice, limited the Allies' claims on the Central Powers   16. **"Castle Rackrent"** Maria Edgeworth's novel (1800) of the decline of an Irish ascendancy house through excess, mismanagement and neglect

DESPARD. Oh, rot. There's nothing to forgive. I suppose I was a bit taken aback by your talking of my penetration. What the dickens have I penetrated?

BROWN. Mr. Alcock told me you have never been in Ireland before. You've been in this house for a day and two nights and in that short time you've put your finger on the great fact that it is not typical. It isn't. It's a protest against the type.

DESPARD. The type being?

BROWN. Not quite what you think it is. Not always slovenly and ramshackle. The difference doesn't lie in the obvious things you've seen, it's not that this room is clean and decent and comfortable. Irish country houses frequently are that, it's not that your dinner was eatable and your bath hot—

DESPARD. Oh well, Irish hospitality—it's traditional, you know.

BROWN. But is St. Leger traditional, is Kate—Miss Alcock?

DESPARD. She's a jolly fine girl.

BROWN. You won't realize how fine until you see the others!

DESPARD. What others? She's the only daughter.

BROWN. I mean the types. Without an idea. With no culture. Ignorant. Don't know whether the portraits that hang in their dining rooms are eighteenth-century masterpieces[17] or photo-gravures,[18] don't know if the silver they use every day is old Irish[19] or modern Brummagem.[20] Don't know the history of their own family, don't know Irish history. Have nothing but a few religious prejudices and very good health. Can't even grow decent flowers.

DESPARD. Well, they're great sportswomen, Irish sportswomen are traditional, you know.

BROWN. That's the least Irish thing about them, your real Irish-woman despises sport, she thinks its only use is keeping the men out of mischief. And the Irish gentleman! Ignorant. Asleep. Look at their libraries. A splendid collection of eighteenth-century classics, twenty volumes of sermons of the early nineteenth century—after that nothing. They're divorced from all reality.

DESPARD. Oh, I say!

BROWN. Absurd of me to blaze out like this, isn't it? But I know what I'm talking about. My name's as common as dirt, but I'm from County Wexford,[21] and County Wexford Browns fancy themselves. They came over

---

17. **eighteenth-century masterpieces** Anglo-Irish culture was at its height during the Georgian period   18. **photogravures** printing made from an etching made according to a photographic original   19. **old Irish** sterling silver   20. **Brummagem** silver plated (from Birmingham)   21. **County Wexford** county in southeast Ireland, scene of the Anglo-Norman landing (1169)

with your people[22] once upon a time. I'm attacking my own class. And I'm extraordinarily interested in watching this house and the fight it's making.

DESPARD. Fight? What the dickens is it fighting for?

BROWN. Its life.

(Kate Alcock comes in, her arms are full of Michaelmas daisies.)[23]

Ah, Kate! Good morning.

KATE. Mr. Brown! I haven't a finger. Aren't they lovely? They're lasting so long this year. What a morning. Such sunshine. You've made each other's acquaintance?

BROWN. Yes.

KATE. You've heard the great news of course. Aunt Kat wired to father from London first thing this morning, we knew at breakfast time.

BROWN. Miss Doyle at the Post Office made no bones of sharing the news, the whole village knew it before you did and she sent a messenger to the rectory on a bicycle.

KATE. Well, I don't blame her. Can you believe that the horrible thing will be killed dead at eleven o'clock, in less than half an hour?

BROWN. Captain Despard doesn't believe it will be killed.

KATE. Oh, soldiers are such optimists. Where's the boss?

BROWN. He's being looked for.

KATE. You're coming to dinner tonight, I hope. With this news it's going to be a celebration.

BROWN. That's what I called in to say. Alice's cold is almost gone, and she'll be delighted to come, for, as you say, it will be an occasion.

KATE. It's only ourselves, you know, not a dinner-party.

BROWN. Gracious, we didn't expect a dinner-party. When were you at a dinner-party last, Kate? Here, in County Cork, I mean?

KATE. Mother and I were counting up the other day. Not since the first winter of the war when those people took Knock for the shooting.[24] They were awful bounders,[25] but they did manage to gather fifteen people for a dinner. . . . My goodness, Monty, you're going to have a dull time of it here. . . . I told the boss it was cruel to invite you.

DESPARD. You forget. I invited myself.

KATE. Well, on your own head be it. We tried having Colonials[26] here for their leave, men, you know, who had no relations or friends to go to. The South Africans didn't mind much, but the Australians always, after one day, sent themselves telegrams recalling themselves to the front. . . . I must get some more vases. Here's the boss.

---

22. **your people** the Normans   23. **Michaelmas daisies** species of aster   24. **took Knock for the shooting** rented a neighboring big house for the hunting season   25. **bounders** unmannerly cads   26. **Colonials** soldiers from British Commonwealth nations

(Mr. Alcock comes in, Kate goes out.)

ALCOCK. Henry!

BROWN. Good morning, St. Leger. I couldn't let you know yesterday whether Alice would be well enough to come over tonight. I've come now to tell you that she can.

ALCOCK. Good. You've heard the news?

BROWN. Yes.

ALCOCK. In our quiet way we're going to let things rip tonight, I depend on Captain Despard to make things lively.

DESPARD. Don't expect too much from me.

ALCOCK. Oh, I've another string to my bow. *(To Brown.)* I've just been down to that place you don't approve of—the wine-cellar.

BROWN. Atkins has been looking for you.

ALCOCK. I didn't see him, and I should have thought his feet would have turned instinctively in that direction. If anyone knows the way to the cellar he does. I haven't been there for six months or more but, thanks to Atkins, it's like Mother Hubbard's cupboard. You know all we take—a little claret[27] at dinner, my small whiskey before I go to bed—but Atkins! My dear Despard, that old chap has an unerring palate. I bought a couple of dozen of cheap Burgundy, not bad at all, but cheap, I thought I'd buy him off with them. He tried one bottle but then concentrated on my best Pommard,[28] and there's only one bottle of brandy left. He seems to have a conscience about champagne, it is sacred in his sight and you shall have plenty of it tonight.

BROWN. You can leave my name out of it.

ALCOCK. Hang it all, the night of the Armistice you must make an exception. Mrs. Brown is T.T.,[29] but I'm sure she'll drink her glass tonight like a good 'un.[30]

BROWN. I wouldn't put it past her.[31] Women seem to be able to square their consciences in a way we can't.

ALCOCK. By the way, I'm glad I've seen you beforehand. Tonight *is* an occasion and we'll drink a toast—the King and Victory. But not a word. No speeches or anything like that. Mary's feeling it a bit, of course, I know Reg is very much in her mind and if we once started to say things anything might happen.

BROWN. You needn't be afraid, I won't want to say anything, I couldn't trust myself. I'll be thinking of Dick.

ALCOCK. Of course. *(To Despard.)* He lost his only boy at Gallipoli.[32] Such a splendid chap.

27. **claret** dry red wine from Bordeaux   28. **Pommard** red French burgundy from the Côte d'Or district   29. **T.T.** teetotaler   30. **like a good 'un** with zest   31. **put it past her** disbelieve it of her   32. **Gallipoli** the attempted British landing in the Dardanelles

DESPARD. Rotten luck.

BROWN. When did you hear from Ulick?

ALCOCK. Yesterday. Fit as a fiddle. Only a few lines, things had been pretty strenuous of course.

BROWN. I wonder how soon you can expect him back.

ALCOCK. His mother has set her heart on having him for Christmas.

ATKINS *(Unseen)*. Mr. O'Neill.

(A gawky common-looking young man comes in.)

ALCOCK. Hallo, Vandaleur.

VANDALEUR *(in a very marked brogue)*.[33] Good morning, Alcock. Good morning, Mr. Brown.

ALCOCK. Mr. O'Neill, Captain Despard.

(They shake hands.)

DESPARD. How d'ye do?

VANDALEUR. I hope ye're well. *(To Alcock.)* I was riding in this direction and me mother asked me to leave in a note, she and the gerr'ls want Mrs. Alcock and Kate to go over to tea next week. Here it is. 'Tis a bit crushed I'm afraid.

ALCOCK *(ringing the bell)*. I'll get it sent to Mary. Will you wait for the answer? Sit down.

VANDALEUR *(sitting)*. Thank ye'. . . . Me fawther's sick.

BROWN. I am sorry to hear that. Is he seriously ill?

VANDALEUR. I don't know' . . . I sold the black mare.

ALCOCK. Oh, did you get a good price?

VANDALEUR. Rotten.

BROWN. I'll go over and see your father this afternoon.

VANDALEUR. Ye needn't then.

BROWN. I can quite easily go, and if he's ill—

VANDALEUR. Sure he went to Cork by the morning train.

BROWN. Oh! Will he be back tonight?

VANDALEUR. Well, he was going to the doctor, and it would depind on what he said whether he'd end up the day in the hospital or in the County Club,[34] but I think meself he'll be for the club.

BROWN. Oh! *(Enter Atkins.)*

ALCOCK. Take this to the mistress please, and tell her that Mr. O'Neill is waiting for the answer.

ATKINS. Yes, sir. *(He takes the note and goes.)*

ALCOCK. Well, this is a great day, Vandaleur.

VANDALEUR. Indeed, 'tis wonderful weather for this time of year.

ALCOCK. I wasn't thinking of the weather.

33. **brogue** Irish country accent   34. **County Club** club for the ascendancy of the county

VANDALEUR. There was a great turn-out for Dicky Smith's funeral a-Choosday, why weren't you there?

ALCOCK. I meant the war—the Armistice.

VANDALEUR. Oh, to be sure. Is it to be today or tomorrow?

ALCOCK. Within an hour.

VANDALEUR. Fancy that now. I suppose they'll fire off a big gun like or ring a bell.

DESPARD. Were you fighting?

VANDALEUR. I was not. *(To Alcock.)* I met Michael Dempsey on the avenue and he was telling me that you have some sheep sick and that one's after dying on you.

ALCOCK. Yes, Kate's in a great stew about it. But I've written to the vet and I heard from him this morning. He's going to wire this morning and let me know if he can come today or tomorrow.

VANDALEUR. Is it the fella from Knock you mean?

ALCOCK. Yes.

VANDALEUR. He is a bloody bad vet. He lost me a mare and a foal last year. I'd rather have the district nurse than that fella. When they told me at home 'tother day that a cow was sick "Send for Mrs. Maguire," says I. "Send for Mrs. Maguire." That's all I'd say. Wasn't I right, Captain?

(Despard merely looks contemptuous.)

BROWN. Well, I hope the cow survived.

VANDALEUR. Of course she did, she's lepping[35] round giving gallons of milk. 'Tis all a cod,[36] inspectors and departments and tillage. What the divil do the lads that make the regulations know about tillage? They wouldn't know the difference between wheat and oats.

ALCOCK. Well, we don't want to starve.

VANDALEUR. There's planty to ate[37] in this part of the country.

ALCOCK. But in the towns, in England—

VANDALEUR. Ah, let them go to the divil.

(Mrs. Alcock and Kate come in.)

MRS. ALCOCK. Good morning, Van. Will you wait a minute while I write a note to your mother? I won't be long.

VANDALEUR. Sure there's no hurry. Good morning, Kate.

KATE. Good morning, Van. Sit down, don't mind me, I'm only doing these flowers.

VANDALEUR *(sitting)*. Flossie and Maggie and Helana and Gertie sent you their love.

KATE. Please give them my love.

VANDALEUR *(after a pause)*. Sissy sent you her love too.

KATE. Give my love to Sissy.

---

35. **lepping** leaping   36. **a cod** nonsense   37. **ate** eat

ALCOCK *(to Despard)*. Do you feel up to a stroll?

DESPARD. I'm afraid not. I've got to rest my foot as much as possible.

VANDALEUR. Are you after hurting your foot?

DESPARD. Yes.

ALCOCK. He got a nasty knock in France.

VANDALEUR. France?

DESPARD. There happens to be a war on there.

VANDALEUR. Sure I know. . . . Jerry Mangan's not the better of the fall he got, yet.

KATE. Oh, did he get a fall? I hadn't heard.

VANDALEUR. Lepping a small bit of a fence on that old red mare of his. Sure he's the rottenest rider in the country.

ALCOCK. I wish I had a horse to offer you, Despard, the only beast in the stables is the old carriage mare.

KATE. I'm sure the Goods or the O'Sullivans would lend him a horse.

VANDALEUR. Sure me fawther would lend him one. What about Prince Chawming?[38]

DESPARD *(shortly)*. No, thank you.

VANDALEUR. He's quiet but a good goer and a very handy lepper. . . . You know him, Kate?

KATE. Yes. . . . Have you any flowers left, Van?

VANDALEUR. I don't know. 'Tis the gerr'ls looks after the flowers.

MRS. ALCOCK *(getting up)*. There, Van. Now don't forget it in your pocket.

VANDALEUR. I won't, Mrs. Alcock. Me mother sent you her love.

MRS. ALCOCK. Thank you.

VANDALEUR. And so did the gerr'ls. At least I didn't see Helana when I was leaving, but I'm sure she would have if I had seen her.

MRS. ALCOCK. Give them all my love and say I'm looking forward to seeing them next week. How's your father?

VANDALEUR. Sick.

BROWN. Are you in a great hurry, Van, or will you walk down the avenue with me?

VANDALEUR. Sure I'm in no hurry.

BROWN. Well, unfortunately, I am, so if you don't mind we'll be off now. I want to talk to you about the graveyard at Kilbeg. Good bye, Mrs. Alcock, till this evening.

MRS. ALCOCK. Seven-thirty. I'm so glad Alice is better, make her wrap up well.

ALCOCK. I'm sending the brougham[39] for you at seven o'clock. Now don't start to protest, it's all been arranged.

38. **Prince Chawming** mimicking Despard's English accent   39. **brougham** automobile with open driver's seat

BROWN. It's very kind of you. The little walk really wouldn't have done her any harm. . . . *Au revoir.*

(Brown goes to the door, while Vandaleur awkwardly and formally shakes hands with everyone. He finishes with Despard.)

VANDALEUR. You're sure you won't have Prince Chawming?

DESPARD. Certain. . . . Thanks.

BROWN. Come on, Vandaleur.

(They go out.)

KATE. Go on, Monty, say it. Don't spare our feelings. "What a lout!" Or was it something worse, something unprintable?

DESPARD. In present company "lout" will have to do. Who is he? A farmer's son?

KATE *(laughing)*. Farmer's son! Vandaleur O'Neill!

ALCOCK. If family counts for anything he gets full marks. A quarter of him is Irish—the best old Irish, the other three-quarters are successive English invasions. Compared to him we're second-rate interlopers. His father is first cousin and heir to Lord Rathconnell, but the father is drinking himself to death, he won't last a twelvemonth longer. Van doesn't drink, Van will be the next lord.

DESPARD. That clodhopper?[40]

MRS. ALCOCK. Poor boy, it's not his fault, and he's really a good boy.

ALCOCK. No, it's not his fault, it's his wicked old father and his foolish mother. He was sent to a preparatory school[41] in England; at the end of the first term he refused to go back, and his father and mother gave in. That's all the education he ever had. He can just sign his name, I suppose he can read. He's lived at home ever since with his father and mother and his five sisters.

KATE. Flossie and Sissy and Maggie and Gertie and "Helana"! And we've got to have tea with them all next week. Why did you say we'd go, mother?

MRS. ALCOCK. My dear, what could I do? Mrs. O'Neill asked me for *any* day next week. I couldn't say I was engaged for the whole week, that's simply unbelievable in Ballydonal.

KATE. I don't mind Van, I like poor Van. It's the "gerr'ls," as he calls them. What day did you say you'd go?

MRS. ALCOCK. Wednesday.

KATE. Thank God.

MRS. ALCOCK. Why?

KATE. I've two committees 'ı at afternoon.

MRS. ALCOCK. I don't believe it.

---

40. **clodhopper** bumpkin   41. **preparatory school** junior school to prepare sons of gentlemen for secondary school or university

KATE. It's quite true. Poultry Society and Library.

MRS. ALCOCK. You and your committees!

KATE. They're better than tea with the O'Neills.

(Atkins appears.)

ATKINS. There's a lad of the O'Flynns wishful to speak to your ladyship.

MRS. ALCOCK. Who?

ATKINS. One of the O'Flynns from the cross.

MRS. ALCOCK. Are you sure he doesn't want the master?

ATKINS. He asked specially for your ladyship.

MRS. ALCOCK. All right, I'll come. *(Atkins goes.)* Atkins is drunk, St. Leger. He always ladyships me when he's drunk.

ALCOCK. Yes, my dear.

MRS. ALCOCK. Can't you do something? Can't you speak to him?

ALCOCK. Not much use while he's drunk. And I suppose there is some excuse this morning.

MRS. ALCOCK. If there wasn't you'd invent one. You're too easy-going.

ALCOCK. He's been here for more than forty years.

MRS. ALCOCK. Will you do what I've been asking you to do for the last twenty years? Will you get him to give you his key of the cellar?

ALCOCK. My dear, that would hurt his feelings.

MRS. ALCOCK. What about *my* feelings? Captain Despard will go back to England talking about us being so Irish. And I'm not Irish, Captain Despard, thank God. I'm a Hampshire[42] woman, a respectable Hampshire woman, in exile, with a drunken Irish butler, and now I've got to go and talk to a "lad of the O'Flynns." Even after living here for twenty years I won't understand half of what he says. I suppose he wants a bottle of medicine for his old grandmother, or he wants to sell me a rabbit he's poached a hundred yards from our own front-door.

(Half vexed, half amused, she goes out.)

DESPARD. Mrs. Alcock's quite wrong, I'm enjoying myself immensely.

ALCOCK. Ah, but that's just what you mustn't do. You mustn't "enjoy" us as if we were a comic story or a play. My wife would like you to take us as seriously as you'd take any country-house in England. She tries— she's tried for twenty-five years—to keep us serious, but always at our most proper moments Atkins or a lad of the O'Flynns keeps breaking in. You remember Dr. Johnson's friend?[43]

DESPARD *(not remembering)*. Yes, oh yes.

ALCOCK. There's a great deal to be said for marrying out of your race.

42. **Hampshire** on England's south coast, one of the country's oldest shires, and considered socially superior 43. **Dr. Johnson's friend** Oliver Edwards: see Boswell's *Life of Samuel Johnson*, 17 April 1778

I like every now and then seeing Ballydonal through her foreign, hostile eyes. A touch of Hampshire does us no harm, keeps us from becoming like the O'Neills.

KATE. They married the foreigner, as you said yourself, but it didn't save them.

ALCOCK. True, it doesn't always work.

DESPARD. It's all part of what the padre was saying—that you're not the type.

ALCOCK. Oh, Brown talks a lot of nonsense. I keep telling him that we *are* the type, people like the O'Neills are the dreadful variants.

DESPARD. Is the padre himself up to type?

ALCOCK. He's a gentleman by birth and education—no, I'm afraid he's no longer the typical Irish parson. I believe you can be ordained now without having been to college—to what you and I would call a college. And the priests are as bad. Old Canon[44] Maguire, who was here for forty years, was a travelled, cultivated gentleman, it was a pleasure and an honour to have him to dinner, but he's dead and gone and the new parish priest—impossible—a barbarian.

KATE. I'm sure priests are like soldiers. Didn't Bernard Shaw say that there are only two kinds of soldiers—young soldiers and old soldiers?[45] There are only three kinds of priests, young, old and middle-aged. The old are, as father says, charmers, the middle-aged are rather dreadful generally, but I adore the curates,[46] especially the Republican[47] ones, they're such splendid workers.

DESPARD. Kate!

ALCOCK. Yes, she's hand-in-glove with them. The other day I came round a corner of the road, between here and the village, and I found a curate sitting on a pile of stones giving my daughter a lesson in Irish[48] while she mended a puncture in his bicycle.

KATE. Well, he had cut his hand; I didn't want him to get the cut full of dirt. And he was a very old friend, a great pet, he got into trouble with the bishop in 1916.

DESPARD. About what?

ALCOCK *(dryly)*. Not theology!

KATE *(airily)*. Drilling and guns and a plan to blow up a military barracks.

44. **Canon** Catholic priest attached to the diocesan cathedral, an honorific title   45. **two kinds of soldiers—young soldiers and old soldiers** G. B. Shaw's *Arms and the Man*   46. **curates** priests assistant to the pastor   47. **Republican** supporting the aggressive Irish independence movement popular since the 1916 Easter Rising. Sinn Féin ("Ourselves") the committed republican party, won a sweeping victory in the general election of December 1918.   48. **a lesson in Irish** since the foundation of the Gaelic League (1893), the learning of Irish Gaelic became a mark of cultural nationalism

DESPARD. Oh, no! Good God!

KATE. A fact.

DESPARD. Are the Protestant curates as bad as that?

KATE. Worse. They play tennis.

(Mrs. Alcock comes.)

MRS. ALCOCK. You must come, St. Leger, the boy is trying to get at you through me. Something about a brother of his who's been arrested. One of those Sinn Feiners, I think. He wants you to write "a bit of a note" to somewhere or someone, he's not sure to whom.

ALCOCK. Oh, these notes! Do you want a character, Despard, for some brother or cousin of yours whom I have never seen? I shall be delighted to give you one, I am a past master in the art of describing and praising the unknown. I'll come, Mary.

KATE *(to him as he goes out)*. Any wire from the vet?

ALCOCK. No, nothing so far.

(Mr. and Mrs. Alcock go out.)

KATE. Poor father!

DESPARD. Why poor?

KATE. Oh, I don't know. . . . Yes, I do. It's not his *métier*,[49] all this.

DESPARD. This?

KATE. Notes to magistrates, sick sheep and general rural uplift. His place is in the music room, at his piano.

DESPARD. Does he play the piano?

KATE. Does he play—? Why, it's what he does do, much too well to be quite respectable in an Irish country gentleman. He was never intended for Ballydonal, he was in the Foreign Office, but his elder brother broke his neck hunting, and so he had to come back here.

DESPARD. Yes, it's no sort of a life for him or for you.

KATE. Oh, I'm not like father, I love it. . . . There's something I want you to tell me—how soon do you think we may expect Ulick home, not on leave, for good and all I mean? Supposing this armistice means peace, how soon is he likely to be able to get clear of the army?

DESPARD. Awfully hard to say. Three or four months perhaps, if he pushes hard.

KATE. Oh, he'll push like the dickens. . . . December, January, February . . . he might be home in March.

DESPARD. Of course he might get some leave before then. Your mother told me he's due leave.

KATE. Yes, he hates fighting so much that he has a sort of conscience about pressing for leave and allows himself to be passed over. But if the war is over he'll have no conscience, he'll move heaven and earth to get out of the army.

49. *métier* specialty

DESPARD. To come and live here?

KATE. Yes . . . And you go back to the law, I suppose?

DESPARD. Not if I can help it. I'll move heaven and earth to stay in the army.

KATE. You like it so much, Monty?

DESPARD. It's taught me what living is.

KATE. It seems to me like four years stolen out of life.

DESPARD. Yes, I know, it's been hard on girls, not much fun and all the men away. . . . Do you remember, Kate, what I said to you that night in London, the night before I went back to France?

KATE. I'm sure we all said a lot of silly things.

DESPARD. I said a lot of things to you, but I didn't say one thing. . . . I don't believe it's right for a chap to get engaged—married perhaps—when there's a war on. It's not fair to the girl. That's why I didn't ask you to marry me.

KATE. Oh, there were lots of other reasons. Feminine ones. That pretty Scotch girl, for instance.

DESPARD. Lulu Mackenzie? Nonsense. I liked you better than all the others rolled together.

KATE. That's only because I was Reggie's sister, your best friend's sister.

DESPARD. No, really. Do you remember Billie Dale? Vulgar little chap, but he had a knack of hitting the nail on the head. Well *he* said to me that night, "Monty, the little Irish girl has all the others beaten to a frazzle."

KATE. That dreadful Mr. Dale!

DESPARD. As dreadful as you like, but it's God's truth.

KATE. To begin with, I'm not particularly little, I haven't gray eyes and long dark lashes, I don't speak with a fascinating brogue—

DESPARD. Your voice—

KATE. Stop! I remember you telling me that your favourite play was *Peg o' my Heart.*[50] Well, I'm none of your Pegs. I don't go about with an Irish terrier under my arm, I don't much like dogs, I've no April[51] moods, I don't go from tears to laughter in a moment, I don't believe I've cried once in ten years.

DESPARD. You're charming!

KATE. Much you know what I'm like! You've only known me in London spending a giddy fortnight there, on a holiday and consequently exactly the opposite of what I really am. I'm quite different here. Before you were out of your bath this morning I had fed my hens, when I've finished these flowers I'm going to garden till lunch—not a lady-like snipping off of dead flowers, really hard digging with a spade, forking dung probably.

---

50. *Peg o' My Heart* American musical (1913) by Alfred Bryan and Fred Fisher 51. **April** capricious

After lunch I go to the creamery[52] for a committee meeting. I ride to the committee. I don't ride there on an unbroken pony, bare-backed, with my hair flying, I ride on a bicycle, a rather old and dirty bicycle, and I wear a rather old and dirty tweed coat and skirt. After the meeting I go to a poultry lecture, after the lecture to an Irish class. I'll have to leave the class early because you're here, and dinner tonight is an affair. If you weren't here I wouldn't be home in time for dinner, and I'd have tea and bread and jam when I came back. That's the real me, the me I like to be.

DESPARD. Yes, because you've never had the chance to be anything else.

KATE. I think I could have been other things.

DESPARD. You can be other things now.

KATE. Monty, are you asking me to marry you?

DESPARD. Of course.

KATE. I wish you wouldn't.

DESPARD. I can't help myself.

KATE. Oh, yes, you can. It's all sentimentalism, pegofmyheartiness.

DESPARD. You liked me in London. Don't you like me here?

KATE. It's different here, you're not part of my life here, you're part of the London holiday—a very nice part, Monty.

DESPARD. Make London your life, have Ballydonal for holiday.

KATE. Ah, there's Ulick.

DESPARD. What the devil—beg your pardon—what has your brother got to do with it?

KATE. Everything.

DESPARD. Everything?

KATE. He's like me; we think Ballydonal *is* life, our life. Of course, as long as Reggie was alive he was the eldest and he'd inherit, but he hated the country, he went straight from school into the army; he'd never want to live here. We planned that Ulick should rent the place from him or live here as sort of manager-agent. Ulick's all father isn't, a born farmer, a born public man, but he didn't depend merely on his instincts; he spent five years learning the newest and best ways of farming, and I've learnt lots of things you'd think silly and dull about poultry and milk and vegetables and bees, we were just ready to start here together—Ballydonal Limited— and then this horrible war came and upset everything, and I've been carrying on as best I could and Ulick's been drilling and marching and breaking his heart to be back, but now the war's over and Reggie's dead and—

DESPARD. Well?

52. **creamery** a dairy-farmers' cooperative plant for the manufacture of butter and cheese

KATE. I don't see why I shouldn't say it, even to his best friend. I'm glad Reggie's dead, glad he died like that, honourably, with letters after his name and mentioned in despatches and all that sort of thing. You knew him well, better than I did probably, and you knew he was handsome and popular, and that he gambled too much and drank too much and got himself mixed up in at least one very shady affair—

DESPARD. Reg was a bit reckless, but there was no harm in him. Just Irish high spirits.

KATE. Just Irish dissipation. Just what has tumbled the big houses into ruins or into the hands of the big graziers[53] or into the hands of the Roman Catholic Church. Vandaleur O'Neills! Not poor Van himself, but the generations of your Irish high spirits that have gone to the making of Van. Reggie wouldn't have cared if he had dragged Ballydonal down. But Ulick and I do care—tremendously. We're going to hold our heads above water, hold Ballydonal above water, proudly and decently.

DESPARD. Milk and hens and turnips! It seems a poor ambition.

KATE. Oh, it's not milk for milk's sake exactly. Everything's mixed up in it, the country, the people, the whole thing.

DESPARD. Good Lord, you're not a Nationalist,[54] are you?

KATE. I thought fervent Nationalism was part of the make-up of your little gray-eyed Irish girl. . . . But no, I don't think I'm a Nationalist, I don't bother about politics, they crop up sometimes at committee meetings and are a great nuisance, and that's all I know about them.

DESPARD. But you learn Irish.

KATE. Yes. You learnt Latin.

DESPARD. I had to. It was part of the make-up of my career.

KATE. Irish is part of my make-up. I don't like it much; I don't suppose you liked Latin much. Ulick's better at it than I am; he really likes it, he even has managed to keep it up in spite of the war; he'll fit perfectly into the Ballydonal picture.

DESPARD. Hasn't it occurred to you that Ulick may marry? Where would you come in then?

KATE. I wouldn't come in, I'd go out.

DESPARD. So you'd much better marry me. I believe we'd make a good thing of marriage. I'd understand you. After all, my grandmother was Irish—from Ulster.[55]

KATE. Ulster!

DESPARD. That's where I get my sense of humour from.

KATE. I see. . . . These Irish grandmothers!

53. **big graziers** large-scale cattle farmers   54. **Nationalist** one who supports either Irish Home Rule or the more extreme Republicanism   55. **Ulster** heavily settled by Scots and English "planters" in the seventeenth-century: predominantly Unionist in politics

DESPARD. Think it over, give me a chance. I'm here for a week anyway.

KATE. If I answered you now, Monty, I'd say "no." If you want me to think it over you must wait until I've seen Ulick.

DESPARD. I don't see the necessity of talking it over with him.

KATE. Oh, maybe I won't talk it over with him, but I just want to see him, see him here, and—and—oh, I do like you very much, Monty, but to live and work here with Ulick—!

DESPARD. Ten to one after France and the army this place will seem so desperately slow that he'll chuck it after a year.

KATE. If you only knew him! . . . Why, he comes here sometimes—I don't mean on leave—that's the only really Irish bit of me, I see him sometimes when he's not here at all.

DESPARD. What? Do you mean a ghost? Is this place haunted?

KATE. Sometimes. By Ulick. The night he enlisted he came, he stood on the gravel outside the hall-door, he looked so sad, so very sad. And twice I've seen him in the library standing at the bookcase where all the farming books are. And then only three nights ago.

DESPARD. Where?

KATE. I was coming back from the village, it was dusk, I had pushed my bicycle through the gate between the park and the grass-garden. I was closing the gate when I saw him coming up the drive towards me. He was walking very fast and he was looking very happy. He passed me, and I said "Ulick," I couldn't help it, he seemed so real. By that time he was on the hall-door steps, he turned round, gave me a smile and was gone.

DESPARD. By Jove!

KATE. That was just when the Armistice had begun to seem inevitable. He was dreaming it all over, you see, he was dreaming he was home. And you think he'd chuck it! How he's managed all this time to keep himself from deserting—!

DESPARD. He must be a rum[56] chap. Well, everyone to their taste. But if you're right and he does stick here he'll be certain to marry. It will be part of his programme; he'll marry one of O'Neill's sisters.

KATE. Monty, your Irish grandmother has given you a revolting imagination.

(*Mr. Alcock comes back, the others separate a little self-consciously.*)

DESPARD. It's such a ripping morning, I think, foot or no foot, I must go out for a bit. I'll go and put on a pair of stronger shoes. May I come and watch you gardening, Kate?

KATE. Certainly.

(*He goes.*)

Well, what did young O'Flynn want?

56. **rum** odd

ALCOCK. Oh, just a note to the R.M.[57] at Carrig. His brother has got himself into a bad mess, I'm afraid. He was suspected of being mixed up in that raid for arms[58] at Carrigmore, and now three shotguns were found in the mattress of his bed.

KATE. What an uncomfortable place to put them. Did you give his brother the note?

ALCOCK. Of course. . . . I like Despard.

KATE. Do you?

ALCOCK. Don't you?

KATE. Oh, yes, quite.

ALCOCK. You saw a good deal of him in London last spring, didn't you?

KATE. Yes, he was staying with Aunt Kat for his leave, and then he got measles, and that kept him there longer so we saw a lot of each other.

ALCOCK. I know he was a great friend of Reggie's but Reggie never told us much about him. Who are his people?

KATE. Oh, the usual respectable English people with public-school temperaments.[59] They think they're very poor, we'd call them quite rich.

ALCOCK. He's been a barrister, hasn't he? He'll go back to it after the war, I suppose?

KATE. Darling, don't try and be diplomatic. Have him into the library and ask him his income and his intentions. They are both entirely honourable. As you most obviously suspect—he wants to marry me.

ALCOCK. And you?

KATE. Am not at all sure that I want to marry him, and am not going to be rushed.

ALCOCK. I'd like you to marry, Kitty.

KATE. Thanks.

ALCOCK. That's the worst of living here. You meet no one you could, decently, marry.

KATE. I don't think I want to get married at all. I'm quite happy here, especially now Ulick's coming home.

ALCOCK. Ulick must marry, of course. You wouldn't be so happy then.

KATE. That's what Captain Despard threatened me with.

ALCOCK. I think if you really like Despard you'd be wise to take the chance of getting out of all this. Ballydonal's no life for an unmarried woman.

57. **R.M.** Resident Magistrate: under colonial administration, a judge presiding over a district in which he resided   58. **raid for arms** at this time, the Irish Volunteers were being formed to back up the Sinn Féin political party, and requisitioned arms where they could be found, including "Big Houses" such as Carrigmore   59. **public-school temperaments** snobbish and supercilious: traits cultivated in prestigious private English boarding schools

KATE. It's my life. I don't like marrying out of my life, out of my class—
I don't mean that in a snobbish way, I'm sure the Despards are as good
as we are—but they're different, they're English.

ALCOCK. You're half English yourself.

KATE. The English half of me seems swamped.

ALCOCK. How can you, if you stay here, marry into your class? Who
is there to choose? Vandaleur?

KATE. No, not poor Van.

ALCOCK. There's not another house left within visiting distance except
Carrigmore, and there are only two old women there. Get out of it, get
away. You've done your duty by Ballydonal splendidly in Ulick's absence;
now that he's coming back, quit.

KATE. Are you going to quit?

ALCOCK. Your mother would like to, but I think I'm too old to change.
But, gracious, I'm going to quit in all kinds of other ways. My mind is
full of letters of resignation.

KATE. From what?

ALCOCK. Everything. Every blessed committee and board I'm on. The
Old Age Pensions, the Creamery, the Library, the District Council,[60] the
Hospital, the Select Vestry,[61] the Diocesan Synod,[62] the Agricultural Show,
and all the other fifty committees. Ulick must take my place on them all.
The moment he comes back I retire. I'm going then to play scales, nothing
but scales, for a month.

KATE. Disgusting self-indulgence.

(Atkins comes in.)

ATKINS *(presenting a telegram)*. The boy is waiting in case there's answer.

ALCOCK *(taking it)*. Thank you. This will be from the vet. *(A loud bell
is heard.)* By Jove, we were forgetting! *(He looks at his watch.)* Eleven
o'clock! Thank God.

KATE *(raising her arms with a gesture of relief)*. Oh, at last, at last.

ATKINS. He's ringing it too slow, the young divil. Wait till I talk to
him. *(He hurries out.)*

KATE. We can begin to live again.

ALCOCK. Poor Reginald!

KATE. Yes, poor old Reg. *(They are silent for a little.)*

ALCOCK. Imagine London and Paris, how the flags must be flying and
the bells ringing.

KATE. And imagine poor Berlin.

ALCOCK. I don't want to think about that. I spent such happy years

60. **District Council** local government council   61. **Select Vestry** Church of
Ireland lay body   62. **Diocesan Synod** advisory to the bishop

there long ago—and Vienna too. Oh, well, they must be glad it's over. But they won't be junketing.

KATE. I'm glad we're here and that it's quiet. I'm so slow, I'll only take it in by degrees. I couldn't throw down my work and start ragging.[63] It wouldn't mean anything to me. I'll take a week to realise.

ALCOCK. The sunshine and your gay flowers will help us to take it in.

KATE. Yes. Michael Dempsey says—oh, the vet, when is he coming, I promised to let Michael know the moment we heard.

ALCOCK. I forgot. *(He opens and reads the telegram, Kate has turned away.)*

KATE. I searched all through the sheep-book[64] again last night, and I know a lot of things it's *not,* but I'm blessed if I know what it *is.* Michael persists in calling it a "blasht."[65] Well, is he coming today? *(She turns and looks at her father, he looks at her strangely.)* What is it? . . . My darling, has anything happened?

ALCOCK *(with difficulty).* Ulick.

KATE. Ulick? *(She snatches the telegram.)* "His Majesty deeply regrets . . . of wounds." Ulick? But the war is over.

ALCOCK. The eighth . . . three days ago.

KATE. Dead? . . . Ulick? . . . *(She begins to laugh hysterically.)* Listen to the bell, listen to the bell!

ALCOCK. My dear!

KATE. Victory! Victory!

ALCOCK. It *is.* For King, for Empire. That's what matters.

KATE. Damn King and Empire. They don't matter, not to us.

ALCOCK *(his arm round her).* Hush, my dear, hush.

KATE *(breaking from him).* I won't hush. Why should I? Ulick's life was here, here. All he loved, all he worked for.

ALCOCK. We must try and be proud—

KATE *(passionately).* Never. Never in this world. I'll never be proud of it, I'll never pretend that it was anything but stupid and hateful. You and your King and your Empire! Much good they ever did Ulick, or me, or you.

ALCOCK. Stop, Kate, stop—

KATE. Stop your damned bell then.

(Mrs. Alcock hurries in, she goes straight to her husband and throws her arms round his neck.)

MRS. ALCOCK. Do you hear it? Peace! Victory!

ALCOCK. Yes, yes, dear. *(Over her shoulder to Kate.)* Kate, please.

(Kate goes out.)

63. **ragging** making a mess (celebrating)   64. **sheep-book** to diagnose ailments   65. **"blasht"** erysipelas

MRS. ALCOCK. Isn't it wonderful? But—so silly of me—I feel I want to cry. . . . It's Reggie, my poor dead Reggie.

ALCOCK. Of course, dear, of course.

MRS. ALCOCK. But I won't cry, I won't cry. I'll be proud of my dead, I'll think of my living. I'll think of Ulick.

ALCOCK. Yes . . . Ulick. . . .

MRS. ALCOCK. Won't Ulick laugh at us when he hears that we rang the poor old bell?

ALCOCK *(leading her to the sofa)*. My dear . . . I have something to tell you.

MRS. ALCOCK. Yes, but listen to the bell, it's ringing faster now, Paddy is ringing it *con amore*;[66] he must be thinking of his beloved "Masther Ulick."

ALCOCK. I want to tell you . . .

(He stops.)

MRS. ALCOCK. Yes?

ALCOCK. I have had a telegram from the War Office.

MRS. ALCOCK. About Ulick?

ALCOCK. Yes, about Ulick.

MRS. ALCOCK. He's coming back? When?

ALCOCK. No. He's never coming back.

ALCOCK. Never? What do you mean? . . . What do you mean, St. Leger?

ALCOCK. My poor darling.

(She stares at him, tries to say something, can't. His arm is round her and as he draws her to him the curtain falls. The bell is ringing quite merrily by this time.)

CURTAIN

SCENE 2

The dining-room at Ballydonal. An evening in the latter part of June, 1921.[67] *Dinner is over, everything has disappeared from the table except dessert—a dish of strawberries. Mr. and Mrs. Alcock are sitting at the table, he wears a dinner jacket.*

MRS. ALCOCK. A few more strawberries, St. Leger?

ALCOCK. No, thank you.

MRS. ALCOCK. Just two or three—this big one. There are plenty left for Kate.

66. **con amore** with love   67. **June, 1921** during the Irish War of Independence

(She helps him to a few.)

ALCOCK. Thanks. Take some yourself.

MRS. ALCOCK. I never remember having them so early as this, and so sweet.

ALCOCK. Of course the weather is exceptional.

MRS. ALCOCK. Yes. Brady says if we haven't rain soon these will be the last as well as the first. I wonder why weather is so difficult. It seems as if no weather was just the right weather. The roses are hardly worth the picking, they fade in a few hours.

ALCOCK. I love it. I love the heat. Do you remember that June in Rome—ninety-four or ninety-five, was it?—the heat and the roses?

MRS. ALCOCK. I remember. But even then the weather was wrong for the children, and I had to take them up to that horrible place in the hills.

ALCOCK. . . . How long ago it seems. . . . Like a different existence. . . .

MRS. ALCOCK. Yes. . . . It's nine years since we were abroad. Couldn't we manage to go this summer, even for a few weeks? There are such cheap trips again. I don't care how I go. I'll be a Polytechnic[68]—whatever that means—or a Free Churcher,[69] I'll stay at the scrubbiest *pensions*,[70] I'll submit to being shown the Eiffel Tower from a charabanc[71]—anything to get away.

ALCOCK. Isn't your sister going next month? Go with her.

MRS. ALCOCK. Not without you.

ALCOCK. I can't.

MRS. ALCOCK. What good does your staying here do?

ALCOCK. I'd be miserable away.

MRS. ALCOCK. You're miserable enough here in the middle of it, we're both miserable. Imagine the relief of being in a country whose politics mattered nothing to us.

ALCOCK. I don't believe I'd find it any relief. I'd always think I might have been able to do something if I'd stayed.

MRS. ALCOCK. You know you can't do anything. You can only wring your hands. It's much better to wash your hands of the whole thing.

ALCOCK. You're almost making an epigram.

MRS. ALCOCK. Am I? I know I'm talking common sense. I know that we're living in a community of criminal lunatics and that the sooner we get out of it the better.

ALCOCK. I'll wait till I'm put out.

MRS. ALCOCK. Burned out?

ALCOCK. Yes . . . or starved out—that seems more likely.

---

68. **Polytechnic** devoted to many arts: a free thinker   69. **Free Churcher** Nonconformist, an English Protestant outside the Church of England   70. *pensions* small hotels   71. **charabanc** large sightseeing bus

MRS. ALCOCK *(with a sigh)*. Sometimes I envy the O'Neills. Kate had a letter today from Sissy O'Neill. They are with some relations in London and having a wonderfully gay time. Everyone makes no end of them because they've been burned out of the ancestral home. If London only knew what the ancestral home was like!

ALCOCK. Such an ugly house.

MRS. ALCOCK. Such a filthy house. Mrs. O'Neill once told me that the drawing-room carpet had never been up[72] in *her* time—and I believe her.

ALCOCK. I suppose the Irish refugees will soon become as *distingués*[73] as the Russians.[74] I understand that all the Russians are counts and princesses, all the Irish will be the descendants of kings. I can see the O'Neills having quite a success. I can see chivalrous young Englishmen laying their hearts at the large feet of Flossie and Helana.

MRS. ALCOCK. I can't quite see that. Englishmen at least know a pretty girl when they see one; no one could call those red-faced O'Neills pretty.

ALCOCK. Being burned out will have paled their cheeks. Kate, unburned, wouldn't have a look-in beside them, so, not to spoil her chances of matrimony, I'll stay.

MRS. ALCOCK. Don't talk rubbish. What good can you do? Your being here didn't save poor Maggie Leahy this afternoon.

ALCOCK *(sighing)*. No.

MRS. ALCOCK. All this murder has got to be put down ruthlessly. *You* can't be ruthless, so you'd better not be here while it's being put down.

ALCOCK. Ah, you admit it was murder.

MRS. ALCOCK. I admit nothing of the kind. Maggie's death was an accident—a most distressing one—but the ambush last night was murder pure and simple.

ALCOCK. I envy you, you have a wonderful power of discrimination.

MRS. ALCOCK. Right is right and wrong is wrong.

ALCOCK. Agreed.

MRS. ALCOCK. There are the eternal verities.

ALCOCK. No doubt there are, but what are they

MRS. ALCOCK. You refuse to recognise them when you meet them, when they're as plain as the nose on your face.

ALCOCK. Oh, of course, England is right and Ireland is wrong, the Republicans commit murder, the Black and Tans[75] commit—accidents.

MRS. ALCOCK. That's stupid—and unkind. I'm not as crude as that.

ALCOCK. Forgive me, my dear. I'm all on edge. Maggie Leahy's death

---

72. **never been up** lifted for beating   73. *distingués* distinguished   74. **Russians** aristocratic refugees from the Bolshevik Revolution (1917)   75. **Black and Tans** a force notorious for its brutality, recruited from among British ex-soldiers to support the Royal Irish Constabulary during the Irish War of Independence

seems the last straw. Let's talk of something else, something quite off the point—avalanches or irregular French verbs.

MRS. ALCOCK. I suppose I'm on edge too, that's why I say we both want a holiday. . . . Shall we have coffee here on the chance of Kate coming in?

ALCOCK. Yes.

(Mrs. Alcock rings.)

Even If I'd go away, Kate wouldn't.

MRS. ALCOCK. Kate, more than either of us, should go away. I'll try again to persuade her to go. The horrible affair this afternoon may have shaken her nerve.

ALCOCK. After all—though one would never have wanted them to come, all these horrors I mean, though one would have done everything in one's power to stop them—now that they're here it's all, in a sense, enriching. I mean Kate's life has been a richer, graver life than if she'd just played games and danced herself into matrimony. I don't believe she'd change places with her London cousins.

MRS. ALCOCK. More fool she then. They're all married, at least they will be next month when May marries, and Kate won't even go over to be bridesmaid! I've no patience with her.

(Enter a parlourmaid—Annie.)

We'll have coffee here, please, Annie.

ANNIE. Yes, ma'am.

MRS. ALCOCK. I suppose Miss Kate hasn't come in yet?

ANNIE. I haven't seen her, ma'am.

MRS. ALCOCK. I wish she was safely home.

ALCOCK. There's been nothing fresh about poor Mrs. Leahy?

ANNIE. I'm told the husband is nearly demented.

ALCOCK. Poor fellow, no wonder! But it's not true, is it, that the baby was shot too?

ANNIE. I don't think so, sir. But of course I'd put nothing past them Tans.

MRS. ALCOCK. Bring us the coffee, please. Is cook keeping something hot for Miss Kate?

ANNIE. Yes, ma'am. . . . Father Doyle says they're a disgrace to civilisation.

(She goes out.)

MRS. ALCOCK. I don't trust that girl. Sly, like all Irish servants.

ALCOCK. Oh, I don't think so. But I must say I miss poor old Atkins. I often wish I hadn't pensioned him off. I met him in the village yesterday, he looked so extraordinarily well, I was strongly tempted to bring him back here with me.

MRS. ALCOCK. He's well because he hasn't the run of the cellar. A week here and he'd be as bad as ever.

ALCOCK. For all he'd find in the cellar now! I wonder if my grandfather is turning in his grave.

MRS. ALCOCK. Why should he?

ALCOCK. Oh, we must seem shockingly degenerate. No hunters[76] in the stables, no swilling of claret, no card-playing. In this part of the country the eighteenth century lasted right down to the seventies, society even in my father's time was like one of Balzac's provincial novels.[77] . . . Well, if grandfather upbraids me in the next world I'll retaliate by upbraiding him for stripping this room of its pictures. There was a Romney[78] there, just opposite to me, my father remembered it as a child, and my great-grand-uncle hung over the fire—a dashing portrait of him in his admiral's dress with a sea-fight in the background, and they and all the others were sold to a little Jew in Limerick for a few beggarly pounds—they didn't even pay grandfather's racing debts.

MRS. ALCOCK. It was shameful of him to strip the house the way he did.

ALCOCK. I'm afraid I can't take a very high line about it. I grumble because he left me so little that *I* can sell. I really must get money somewhere.

MRS. ALCOCK. It made me simply furious this morning when I was walking back from the village and the Goods flashed past me in their motor choking me with dust. To think of all the rent they owe us! And their car isn't a Ford either, oh dear me no, some very expensive make Mrs. Brown told me. Is there no way of making them and all the others pay?

ALCOCK. None.

MRS. ALCOCK. I call them common thieves.

ALCOCK. Well, we can console ourselves with the thought that either the Republicans or the Black and Tans will commandeer[79] their car one of these days.

(Annie comes in with the coffee, which she puts before Mrs. Alcock and goes out.)

ALCOCK *(taking his coffee from Mrs. Alcock.)* Thank you. . . . Aren't you having any?

MRS. ALCOCK. I don't think so.

ALCOCK. Why not?

MRS. ALCOCK. It would keep me awake.

ALCOCK. It never used to. Aren't you sleeping well?

MRS. ALCOCK. Not very—lately.

ALCOCK. Ah! lying awake imagining you hear the tread of strange feet on the gravel, a hammering on the door, a rattle of petrol tins, there's a click of a revolver, a scratch of a match, a—

76. **hunters** horses   77. **Balzac's provincial novels** The *Comédie humaine* of Honoré de Balzac (1799–1850)   78. **Romney** George Romney (1734–1802), English historical and portrait painter   79. **commandeer** to force into military service

MRS. ALCOCK. Don't, don't, St. Leger, *please!*

ALCOCK. My dear, are you really frightened?

MRS. ALCOCK. Terrified.

ALCOCK. I had no idea. . . . You really lie awake—?

MRS. ALCOCK. Listening. Till the light comes. Thank God the nights are short.

ALCOCK. How long has this been going on?

MRS. ALCOCK. Since the spring. No, always.

ALCOCK. Always?

MRS. ALCOCK. Never as bad as now, of course, but I've always felt strange, felt afraid.

ALCOCK. Good God! You've never got used to Ballydonal?

MRS. ALCOCK. Never quite used.

ALCOCK. It's always seemed a little foreign, a little queer? My dear Mary, why didn't you tell me?

MRS. ALCOCK. Oh, it's nothing to fuss about. I can stand it. I've stood it for more than twenty years. But I feel—just for the sake of sleeping again—I'd like to spend a month or two in some very dull London suburb; Ealing, I think, for choice.

(Kate comes in very pale and tired.)

My dear, how late you are, I was getting anxious. Do they know you're in? Mrs. Moloney is keeping something hot for you.

KATE. I came in the back way. Mrs. Moloney knows. She's sending me up some tea.

MRS. ALCOCK. Oh nonsense, you must have some dinner.

KATE. I couldn't, mother, really. I couldn't eat anything.

(She sits at the table.)

MRS. ALCOCK. Just a little soup?

KATE. No really, thanks.

(Alcock goes to the sideboard and pours something into a glass.)

ALCOCK. Here, drink this.

KATE. What is it?

ALCOCK. Whiskey.

KATE. Oh, no, I couldn't, I don't want it—

ALCOCK. Now, no nonsense. Drink it down.

(She does so. Suddenly she's afraid she's going to cry and gets up and goes to the window and stands looking out with her back to the room. Her mother is about to go to her.)

ALCOCK *(in a low voice)*. Let her alone, she'll pull herself together.

MRS. ALCOCK *(low)*. She shouldn't have gone, we shouldn't have let her.

KATE *(turning round)*. I'm sorry. I'm all right now.

(She comes and sits down at the table.)

ALCOCK. Do you want to talk, my dear, or would you rather be all alone?

KATE. I don't mind. . . . It was very dreadful but I don't think she can have suffered, Dr. Hennessy is sure it was instantaneous. She was sitting on the bank by the road with the baby in her arms, Pat was working in the field behind her. He never heard the lorry till it came round the corner from the cross. They only fired two shots he says. One of them hit her in the breast, I don't know how the poor baby escaped.

ALCOCK. But—but—the whole thing seems incredible. . . . Were they blind drunk?

KATE. Nobody knows. I suppose they're in an awful state of nerves and fury after the ambush last night. Father Doyle is afraid they'll burn the village tonight.

ALCOCK. He was there—at the Leahy's cottage, I mean?

KATE. Yes, and Mrs. Brown came. Mr. Brown is away until tomorrow. Mrs. Brown was splendid with all the children—six of them, imagine, and all so young. Pat was useless, simply blubbered like a child. Mrs. Murphy's taken the baby, its arm got bruised when poor Maggie fell off the bank.

MRS. ALCOCK. Can we send down anything? Food?

KATE. I think they've everything. I'll bring down a lot of flowers tomorrow, Maggie likes flowers. *(Enter Annie with the tea.)* Thank you, Annie.

(Annie goes.)

MRS. ALCOCK. Take a few strawberries, Kate. The first this year.

KATE. Thanks.

(But she doesn't take any.)

MRS. ALCOCK *(pouring her out some tea)*. That will do you good.

KATE. Don't bother about me, I'll be all right. Go to the drawing-room, mother, please, I'd rather you would.

MRS. ALCOCK. I'd like to stay and see you eat a good tea.

KATE. I'll do that all right. Please don't wait, do go.

MRS. ALCOCK. Will you promise me to eat something?

KATE. Yes, I promise.

MRS. ALCOCK. And if you feel you'd like something more substantial, you've only got to ring the bell and Mrs. Moloney will send you up something nice.

KATE. Yes, I know.

MRS. ALCOCK. And you'll come to the drawing-room when you've finished?

KATE. Yes, I'll come. I won't be long.

MRS. ALCOCK. Come, St. Leger.

(She goes. Alcock follows her as far as the door and turns back.)

ALCOCK. I don't like leaving you, Kitty.

KATE. I'm all right now. I was silly for a minute.

ALCOCK. Well, no wonder.

KATE. "And no one but the baby cried for poor Lorraine, Loree." That's been running in my head all the evening. So silly, for we all cried. . . . I suppose I'll see some meaning in it some time. Of course we read of much worse horrors in the war, but to see it—and she was my nurse—a friend really—I gave her her wedding dress, do you remember? and the first baby was called after me.

ALCOCK. Yes, and Pat's father was gardener here for thirty years. They're really part of the family, one of ourselves.

KATE *(sombrely)*. No, that's just what they're not.

ALCOCK. Not?

KATE. Not us, we're not them. That was the awful thing I realised this evening. There I was in that cottage with the neighbours and Father Doyle and Dr. Hennessy and I knew Maggie better than any of them, and I—I was an outsider.

ALCOCK. What do you mean?

KATE. Just what I say. An outsider. Something outside, different, away from them.

ALCOCK. When death is in question one feels, of course, that religion makes such a difference.

KATE. Yes, there was religion to make me feel outside but lots of other things too; education, I suppose, and tradition and—and everything that makes me me and them them. Between us and them, like the people in the Bible, there was a "great gulf fixed."[80]

ALCOCK. I know no one who has made less of the gulf than you, Kitty. Your democracy shocks your mother.

KATE *(impatiently)*. Oh, yes, I threw a bridge across the gulf and ran across it and called Pat, Mick, and Larry by their Christian names, and hobnobbed with priests and creamery managers and Gaelic teachers—but it was only a bridge, the gulf remained and when the moment came they instinctively forced me to stand on the farther side. Oh, it wasn't only tonight I've felt it. I've been conscious of it ever since I've been conscious of anything, but I thought it could be broken down.

ALCOCK. Your politics aren't extreme enough.

KATE. It's not that. They could forgive me for not being an out-and-out Republican. There's something deeper, something that none of us can put into words, something instinctive, this "them" and "us" feeling.

ALCOCK. History.

KATE. I think I'd like it better if they hated us. That at least would make me feel that we had power, that we counted for something; it's very hard to forgive toleration.

80. **"great gulf fixed"** between rich and poor (Luke 16: 26)

ALCOCK. And it's hard for us not to seem to patronise.

KATE. I don't patronise, I never have. I sit on committees like every ordinary member. I sit with schoolchildren at the Gaelic classes because I'm such a dunce at Gaelic. We're as poor as mice, we don't keep up any style. We're as Irish as most of them, we're honest and hard working.

ALCOCK. I suppose they feel—

KATE. "They, they, they!" Why should there be any "they?" I was made to feel in that cottage this evening that *I* had shot Mary, and yet they know perfectly well that I've no sympathy with the Auxiliaries.[81]

ALCOCK. You're overwrought, my dear. You're exaggerating very much.

KATE. No, I'm not. What I'm saying is true, and you know it is. Van O'Neill is an ignorant clod, Father Doyle compared with him is a paragon of culture, but you're uncomfortable when Father Doyle comes here, you're not speaking your full mind to him, he's not speaking his full mind to you, but you're quite happy and easy with poor ignorant Van.

ALCOCK. I've known Van all his life.

KATE. I've known the people in the village all my life. I've worked with them, quarrelled with them, loved them, but at the end of it all I find myself—just different.

ALCOCK. Maybe it's right we should be different.

KATE. How can it be right? I want to be the same.

ALCOCK. You'll never be that.

KATE. Why not?

ALCOCK. It will be always "them" and "us."

KATE. I feel sick and discouraged.

ALCOCK. And your mother feels frightened.

KATE. Frightened? Of what?

ALCOCK. Everything. She says she's never felt quite at home here.

KATE. Yes, it must be worse for her—no, it's worse for me with the Irish side of me tormenting me. Let's give up, chuck up the sponge.

ALCOCK. Kate!

KATE. We're "going, going, going—" like a battered old piece of furniture at an auction. Let's smash the hammer down ourselves and cry "gone."

ALCOCK. Yes, go, Kate, go. You and your mother.

KATE. And you?

ALCOCK. No, no, I can't go yet.

KATE. Yet? What worse are you waiting for?

ALCOCK. I don't know.

81. **Auxiliaries** recruited to help the depleted R.I.C. from among demobilized British army officers British army, they were notorious for indiscriminate reprisals against the civilian population

KATE. I know. It's your devilish pride.

ALCOCK. I don't think so.

KATE. It's your devilish pride.

ALCOCK. No, no. It's—somehow I'd feel it physically impossible to go just now.

KATE. Yes. You're devilishly proud.

ALCOCK. Nonsense. . . . Your mother will be wondering where I am. I'd better join her. Come to the drawing room as soon as you can.

KATE. All right.

(Alcock goes out. Left to herself Kate drinks a little tea disheartedly. A minute later Annie comes in.)

ANNIE *(planting an egg on the table)*. Mrs. Moloney sent this up, miss.

KATE. Oh, thanks, thank Mrs. Moloney.

ANNIE. Aren't you cold with the window open, miss?

KATE. I don't think so.

ANNIE. There's a terrible breeze blowing in.

(She half closes the casement window.)

KATE. It's getting very dark, isn't it, or is it very late?

ANNIE. 'Tis like as if there was going to be a storm, or thunder maybe. *(She is going out.)*

KATE *(suddenly and decisively)*. Annie!

ANNIE. Yes, miss.

KATE. Shut the door. Come here. I want you to tell me something.

ANNIE *(wonderingly)*. Yes, miss?

KATE. If the Black and Tans burn the village tonight will we be burned out the next night?

ANNIE. Oh, miss!

KATE. Will we?

ANNIE. Such a thing to say!

KATE. Will we, will we?

ANNIE. Sure how could I say?

KATE. I know you can't say definitely "yes" or "no." But you can tell me whether you think it's likely. Your brother—well, I know what he is as well as you do—is he likely to look on us as a suitable reprisal?

ANNIE *(vaguely)*. Miss!

KATE. He burned the O'Neills.

ANNIE *(with contempt)*. Ah, sure, the O'Neills!

KATE. That's what I want to know. Will there be any difference made between them and us? Will all the master has done for the district count for anything?

ANNIE. Everyone has a great respect for the master and for yourself too, miss.

KATE. I know. But how much respect? Enough to save us? I'm only asking as a matter of curiosity; if you tell me they will burn us I shan't do anything about it—as a matter of fact there's nothing to be done—but I just want to know.

ANNIE. I don't know why you ask me, miss.

KATE. I don't know why I shouldn't ask you. We've known each other ever since we were children; you know as much about what's going on in the village as any girl in it. I suspect that you know more than any girl. I want a straight answer to a straight question.

ANNIE. Ah, don't bother your head about such things, miss.

KATE. I see. . . . You won't answer me. . . . You're probably right not to. Thank you, you needn't wait. Thank Mrs. Moloney for sending me the egg.

ANNIE. Yes, miss.

(She goes out.)

KATE *(to herself)*. A great gulf fixed.

(She remains brooding, she makes no attempt to eat anything but drinks a little tea. The door opens, Despard appears in the uniform of the Auxiliary Police. Kate doesn't stir, they look at each other silently for half a minute.)

Why have you come? I told you not to.

DESPARD *(thickly, rather drunkenly)*. Professionally.

KATE. What?

DESPARD. Professionally. In the discharge of my duties.

KATE. Do you mean you're stationed here—in Ballydonal? I thought you were in Gormanstown?[82]

DESPARD. Left. Why don't you read my letters?

KATE. I told you why.

DESPARD. Forgot. Shockin' memory.

KATE. I don't correspond with Auxiliaries.

DESPARD. No?

KATE. And I don't want them in this house.

DESPARD. No?

KATE. So will you please go?

DESPARD. This wonderful Irish hospitality! And I've come such a long way today, all the way from County Limerick.[83]

KATE. Limerick?

DESPARD. Yes. The hell of a distance, but, as you were about to remark, lovely day for a drive.

KATE. Why? Why do you come?

DESPARD. Pleasure—and a duty. Pleasure to see you, duty to drop across and tell Ballydonal what we think of it.

---

82. **Gormanstown** Gormanston, Co. Meath, a military camp   83. **County Limerick** west Munster county

KATE. To tell—? You—? I understand. How many of you are there?

DESPARD. Cars an' cars an' cars.

KATE. You're going to burn the village, I suppose?

DESPARD. Don't know. Depends.

KATE. Depends on whether you're drunk enough. You're drunk now but not very drunk.

DESPARD. You are going it, Kate.

KATE. What do you want here, in this house?

DESPARD. Stayed here once. Finding myself passing your gate felt it was only commonly polite to call on you.

KATE. Passing the gate . . . were you on the road between this and the village about four o'clock this afternoon?

DESPARD. No. Only just arrived.

KATE. Ah!

DESPARD. Why d'you ask?

KATE. Nothing.

DESPARD. My chaps searching your yard.

KATE. Searching the yard? In the name of goodness, for what?

DESPARD. Anything in trousers that might be hiding in loft or coach-house. Said I'd wait for them here. Damned rude, Kate, you might ask me to sit down or have a drink—*and* have a drink I mean.

KATE *(getting up)*. Take your men away, Captain Despard, take them away. You'll scare mother out of her wits. I give you my word of honour we're hiding no one in the house or in the yard.

DESPARD. Your word! My dear Kate! I said to the driver as we passed your gate "Taylor" (that's his name), "Taylor, that's Ballydonal House and there's a girl there who's as damned a little Sinn Féiner as any I know. Stop the car, turn round—"

KATE. Captain Despard—

DESPARD. Monty, Kate, Monty. This standoffishness, so uncalled for, unexpected—

KATE. Will you please, for the sake of the good friends we were once, go quietly away?

DESPARD. Remarked before—wonderful Irish hospitality, traditional. Well, I've learned not to wait to be asked.

(He sits down and pours himself out some whiskey.)

KATE *(reaching for the decanter)*. Please, please, Monty—

DESPARD. Hands off! The dust of these roads. You wouldn't grudge an old friend a drink. *(He drinks.)* As you remarked, we were good friends. *(Kate moves towards the door, Despard gets between her and it.)* Where are you going?

KATE. To mother.

DESPARD. No. No warnings. Not allowed. You stay here, see? My business keep you here. House must be searched.

KATE. How ridiculous.

DESPARD *(suddenly blazing out)*. Yes, damned funny, like the ambush last night. Frightfully funny joke for the fellows who went west.[84]

KATE. You know perfectly well we had nothing to do with the ambush.

DESPARD. Not guts enough. 'Scuse my language. But true. Whiners, that's what you are. "Why doesn't the Government. . . . Must establish law and order. . . . But Black and Tans are rather naughty." Compromise, conference, save your bacon. Wow, wow.

(Kate turns away from the door and walks to the other side of the room. Despard goes back to the table and drinks again.)

Your father used to brag of his cellar, I remember. How's the old boy?

KATE *(turning round)*. You realise that if you burn the village as a reprisal we'll probably be burned as another reprisal?

DESPARD. Unfortunate. Got to think of the murder of those chaps. Must punish. Must make Ballydonal squeal.

KATE. It was strangers did it, no one from this village.

DESPARD. Yes, always the naughty boys in the next parish. Heard that tale too often. Cuts no ice.

KATE. Monty, if I could bring those poor men back from the dead I'd do so, believe me I would. But they've been avenged. This afternoon a poor woman sitting by the road nursing a baby was shot dead by some Auxiliaries who were passing in a lorry. Won't you take that as your vengeance, and let the village alone?

DESPARD. Spying. I know these women.

KATE. She wasn't spying, she was only a poor labourer's wife sitting in the sunshine with her baby. I've known her all my life, she was my nurse when *I* was a baby.

DESPARD. Your nurse?

KATE. Yes. How would you feel if it had been your nurse.

DESPARD. Damnable.

KATE. Yes, damnable. It's all damnable, Monty, you and us and everything, but it won't be so damnable if because poor Maggie is dead you turn round your cars and go quietly home.

DESPARD. Home? What the hell d'you mean?

KATE. Home to Limerick.

DESPARD. Limerick? Home? Up Garryowen![85] More Irish than the Irish,[86] you see.

KATE. Go home altogether, back to England, and we can be friends again.

DESPARD. Friends? Only friends?

---

84. **went west** were killed 85. **Up Garryowen!** Limerick rugby team cheer 86. **More Irish than the Irish** *Hibernis ipsis Hiberniores*, first observed of fourteenth-century Anglo-Norman assimilation into Irish life and custom

KATE. Good friends.

DESPARD. I'd do a lot for you, Kitty.

KATE. I know you would. Do this.

DESPARD. Damn me, we will be friends again, Kitty, damn me, we will. Give me a kiss and say you forgive and forget.

KATE. Oh, Monty, nonsense.

DESPARD. It's not nonsense. It's God truth. Say you forget and forgive, kiss me and say you'll marry me and I'll spare the damned village.

KATE. Rubbish.

DESPARD. How rubbish?

KATE. This is County Cork, not third-rate melodrama.

DESPARD. What d'you mean?

KATE. You're behaving like the hero—or the villain—in a cheap novel.

DESPARD. You're damned superior.

KATE. You're not.

DESPARD. Won't quarrel with you, improves you to lose your temper. I'll kiss and be friends.

KATE. I won't.

DESPARD. Oh, yes, you will. . . . Come here.

KATE. Don't be silly.

DESPARD (*going to her*). I mean it. Kiss me.

KATE. No.

DESPARD. Kiss me, you—(*He struggles with her, overpowers her, kisses her violently, repeatedly, suddenly he softens, grows tearfully tender.*) Kitty, Kitty, Kitty.

KATE. Monty, poor Monty.

DESPARD (*crying*). Kitty, Kitty.

KATE (*soothing him*). Hush, hush.

DESPARD. It's hell, Kitty, it's hell.

KATE. I know, I know.

DESPARD. You can't know how hellish.

KATE. My poor Monty.

DESPARD. The hot nights—that awful little barracks, the rotten chaps that are there, and never knowing when—who—

KATE. Yes, yes, I know.

DESPARD. It wasn't like this in France. I wish I were back there, I'd give my soul to be back there.

KATE. Get out of it. Give it up. Go back to England.

DESPARD (*shaking himself free of her*). I'll see it through. The lice! We'll give 'em as hard as they give us and just a little bit harder.

(*Mr. Alcock comes in.*)

ALCOCK. Your mother is wondering—Good gracious!

KATE. It's Captain Despard, father.

DESPARD. Evening, Mr. Alcock, how are you? Unexpected pleasure.

KATE. Captain Despard's men are just having a look round the yard. I explained, of course, that there was nobody—nothing—there for them to find and they will be gone in a few minutes. Perhaps you had better go to mother in case she hears anything and is frightened.

DESPARD. Not an unfriendly visit, Alcock, don't take it unfriendly.

ALCOCK. I'll take it as I please.

KATE. Will you go, father? I'll look after Captain Despard.

DESPARD. Yes, Kitty's turning duty into pleasure.

ALCOCK. Come on, Kitty.

DESPARD *(holding her arm)*. No, no, cruel—

ALCOCK *(suddenly exploding)*. Let my daughter alone.

KATE *(getting to Alcock)*. Father!

ALCOCK. Do your duty, damn you, as quickly as you can, and clear out of my house.

DESPARD. Mind what you're saying, Alcock.

ALCOCK. Mind your own business.

DESPARD. You're all my business. You and your lovely village and Kitty—

ALCOCK. Leave my daughter. . . . *(Kate is trying to quiet him.)* Let me alone, Kitty.

KATE. Come to mother, father.

DESPARD. Yes, clear out of this, do you hear? Clear out, the two of you.

(He whips out his revolver.)

ALCOCK. By God, if you threaten me—

KATE. Father, hush. . . .

DESPARD. Upstairs with you. Hide. Under the bed.

ALCOCK. I see. You are drunk. Very pretty. Kate!

(He opens the door for her.)

KATE. Not without you.

ALCOCK. I'm coming. *(To Despard.)* If you want us you will find us in the drawing-room, my wife, my daughter and myself. You know the way, you have been a welcome guest here—when your uniform was a different one.

(Alcock and Kate go out.)

DESPARD. Old fool! *(The light has been fading, the room is full of shadows. He gropes for his glass and knocks it over, it breaks.)* Damn! *(He drinks straight from the decanter, spilling the whiskey down his face. There is a sudden gust of wind, the casement behind him blows open, the curtain blows out into the room. He starts violently and swings round to the window, his revolver in his hand.)* Hands up! Who are you? Who are you, I say?

A WHISPER OUT OF THE DARKNESS. Ulick!

DESPARD. Ulick? Who are you? I warn you, don't come in through that window, don't, I say. Hands up or I fire. *(He fires rapidly in the direction of the windows two or three shots. The glass splinters and falls. He blows a whistle.)* Taylor! Taylor! *(He fires again.)*

CURTAIN

SCENE 3

An evening in February, 1923.[87] *The same scene as the previous one, but the room is somewhat changed, it is less emphatically a dining-room and more of a sitting room. A comfortable armchair is above the fire, and in it Mrs. Alcock is sitting knitting and reading, the room is lit by an oil lamp on the dining-room table, and there is a pair of candles on a little table beside Mrs. Alcock. Half a minute after the curtain rises Annie comes into the room, she has a large bundle of letters, newspapers, and postal packages in her hand.*

ANNIE *(bringing them to Mrs. Alcock).* The post, ma'am.

MRS. ALCOCK. Letters! Oh, what a surprise!

ANNIE. And the postman said Miss Doyle told him to tell you that there'd be likely be a post going out tomorrow about twelve o'clock.

MRS. ALCOCK. Tomorrow? I see. I'll have a lot of letters to go. Will you tell the master that letters have come? He's in the library.

ANNIE. Yes, ma'am. *(She goes out.)*

(Mrs. Alcock sorts the mail and starts to open her own letters. Alcock comes in, he is dressed in a dark lounge suit, he has a sheet of paper—an unfinished letter in his hand.)

MRS. ALCOCK. Letters, St. Leger. But only two from Kate.

ALCOCK. How is she?

MRS. ALCOCK. I haven't had time to read them yet. Those are yours, they don't look very exciting, and there are all these "Times"[88] and the "Lit. Sup."[89] and "Punch"[90] and "The Saturday Review"[91]—plenty of reading anyhow.

ALCOCK *(a little petulantly throwing the newspapers on the table).* I'll give up the "Times." Newspapers are bad enough taken in small daily doses, but when they arrive *en masse*[92] they are completely indigestible, they're only waste of money.

87. **February, 1923** during the Irish Civil War between the defenders of the Anglo-Irish Treaty (the "Free Staters") and its opponents (the Republicans) 88. **"Times"** *London Times* 89. **"Lit. Sup"** *The Times Literary Supplement* 90. **"Punch"** British weekly satirical magazine 91. **"The Saturday Review"** London weekly periodical (1855–1938) 92. *en masse* all together

MRS. ALCOCK. Only a few lines from Kate . . . had a bit of a cold and very busy at the office . . . oh, she's changing her rooms, going to a boarding house just off Bloomsbury Square.[93] . . . Oh, imagine, St. Leger! Van O'Neill is going to be married! Isn't that amazing?

ALCOCK. Well, why shouldn't he? Who's he marrying?

MRS. ALCOCK. Kate doesn't know, Sissy just sent her a card asking her to go round to dinner and she'd tell her about Van who was engaged to be married . . . That is exciting. . . . The next letter will tell me.

(She searches for it and opens it.)

ALCOCK *(opening and tearing up letters)*. No, I do *not* want to lay down a hard tennis-court . . . *nor* install central heating . . . nor do I want to restock my cellar . . . stupid advertisers are, have they no imagination, do they never read the papers? . . . ah, a moneylender, he's more in the picture . . . *(But he tears it up.)* . . . your subscription . . . due. . . . Yes, I expect it is, don't they wish they may get it. . . . Your subscription. . . . What a post, I can't face it tonight.

MRS. ALCOCK *(having glanced through Kate's other letter)*. This one is written earlier than the other, so we'll have to wait to hear about Van. It would be just like him to go and make a grand match. Look at Flossie marrying that Bradford millionaire.[94] *(She attacks other letters, Alcock bundles his torn papers into the fire.)* . . . Oh, Margaret's gone to Bournemouth,[95] she likes the rooms and it's very mild she says. She'll stay there till Easter, then she's due at the Coddingtons, I must write to her tonight. . . . Did Annie tell you that there's a post out tomorrow, at twelve?

ALCOCK. No.

MRS. ALCOCK. So if you have anything it must be ready by eleven. Have you finished your letter to Cosgrave?[96]

ALCOCK *(troubled, getting the sheet of paper he has carried in with him)*. No. It doesn't satisfy me, I feel it's so inadequate. I'm sure he won't pay any attention to it—a letter from someone he's never seen, probably never heard of—in his place and with as much to do as he has, *I'd* pay no attention.

MRS. ALCOCK. Well, by writing you've done all you can do.

ALCOCK. You talk as if I was writing just to satisfy myself, not really with the object of saving Nicholas. You know it's come back on us like a boomerang—all these letters I've written for years and years recommending idle wastrels as being sober, industrious and entirely trustworthy. Now when I write something that's true, and when it's a matter of life and

---

93. **Bloomsbury Square** near the British Museum, London   94. **Bradford millionaire** Bradford, Yorkshire, is the home of the British textile industry   95. **Bournemouth** coastal city in Hampshire   96. **Cosgrave** William T. Cosgrave, first President of the Executive Council of the Irish Free State (1922–23)

death, no attention will be paid to it. I really think I should go to Dublin and try to see the President myself.

MRS. ALCOCK. What nonsense. In this weather. It's a terrible journey.

ALCOCK. I hate to leave you alone—if only Kitty wasn't in London. You wouldn't come with me?

MRS. ALCOCK. It's unnecessary.

ALCOCK. It's a matter of life and death, and Nicholas is such a sterling fine fellow.

MRS. ALCOCK. Oh, they won't execute him. Condemning him to death is only to scare people. He'll be kept in prison for a couple of months and then he'll be made a cabinet minister. They're all in the same gang.

ALCOCK. My dear, it's not all bluff; they *have* executed people. There's no shutting our eyes to the fact that Nicholas is in very grave danger.

MRS. ALCOCK. Well, he's got no one but himself to thank for the scrape he's in. You're not pretending you approve of what he's done?

ALCOCK. Of course not. But if I could make the President realise that he's not just disorderly, not the common kind of gun-man, that he's a man of very high principles and fine motives—

MRS. ALCOCK. Oh, every murder no doubt committed from the highest motives!

ALCOCK (*sighs, gives it up*). I'll think it over tonight, if I could be even sure of the post getting quickly through to Dublin, but the mail might be raided, the letters might never get through at all.

MRS. ALCOCK. The letters are going all right now. Don't worry about it tonight anyway. Give me "Punch" and play me something.

ALCOCK (*handing her "Punch"*). Here you are. (*He goes to a cottage piano.*[97]) What shall I play?

MRS. ALCOCK. Anything you like.

(*He sits at the piano, worrying, he doesn't play.*)

MRS. ALCOCK (*discovering something in "Punch"*). Listen to this, St. Leger, this is rather good. "According to an evening paper Mr. G. F. Preston, London Telephone Controller, who is retiring at the end of this month, has held the post for eleven years. We congratulate him in spite of our suspicions that this is the wrong number." Really, "Punch" is very witty.

ALCOCK (*not listening*). Yes.

MRS. ALCOCK. And listen to this: "A garden party on a gigantic scale is to be held at Los Angeles. We understand that tickets will be issued to admit 'bearer and one wife.'" Isn't that amusing? (*She notices that he is paying no attention.*) Do play something, dear, take your mind off things.

ALCOCK. Yes. (*He plays for a moment or two.*) This beastly piano, it's

___

97. **cottage piano** small upright piano

out of tune too. *(He gets up.)* I can't play it. There must be a fire in the music-room tomorrow, the Steinway[98] is getting damp.

MRS. ALCOCK. Very well.

ALCOCK. This is cold too.

MRS. ALCOCK. You got perished sitting all the evening in that icy library. Sit near the fire and poke it up.

ALCOCK. Would you think it horrible of me to go to bed? I feel cold and cross. I'll only snap if I stay here.

MRS. ALCOCK. Yes, do go to bed, you look wretched. I'll bring you a hot drink in bed.

ALCOCK. Ah, you needn't bother.

MRS. ALCOCK. I'll bring it in a quarter of an hour. Take something to read, the "Saturday Review"—or take "Punch," I can read it tomorrow.

ALCOCK. No, thanks, too contemporary. I have "Tristram Shandy"[99] upstairs. Sterne is pleasantly remote. Are you coming to bed soon?

MRS. ALCOCK. Yes, I won't be very long after you.

(Kate has entered very quietly, she is in hat and coat.)

ALCOCK. Really I feel inclined never to get up, just lie in bed till the summer and read the classics, and never, never look at a newspaper or hear any horrible "news."

KATE. No, you're not going to bed as early as you think.

ALCOCK.   ⎱ Good gracious!
MRS. ALCOCK. ⎰ Kate!

(Kate flings herself round her father, and then on her another.)

ALCOCK. Kitty, is it possible?

KATE. Looks like it.

MRS. ALCOCK. My dear! How? Why?

KATE. Sorry to take you by surprise like this—

ALCOCK. Oh, don't apologise.

KATE. But everything's so uncertain, I didn't know if I'd ever arrive.

MRS. ALCOCK. How did you get here? You're starving, I'm sure. Ring for Annie.

KATE. They know, they're bringing tea. I came on Lordan's lorry from Cork; my, such a jolting, three bridges down, and we had to take to the fields and pay toll to every farmer. I walked up from the village lugging my suitcase. *(To her mother.)* You're looking blooming. *(Looking at her father.)* The boss is a little—a little wizened—I think that's the word.

ALCOCK. I'll get my bloom back now that you've come.

KATE *(taking off her hat and coat and flinging herself into a chair)*. My, it's good to be back. As the man said when he saw Rome—"You can 'ave

---

98. **Steinway** concert grand piano, manufactured by Steinway and Sons, New York   99. **"Tristram Shandy"** comic novel (1760) by Laurence Sterne

Rome." Well, you can 'ave London. Never again, my dears, never again, except for a fortnight's holiday once a year.

MRS. ALCOCK. Do you mean you've left for good—not just for a little holiday? But Mr. Scholes—?

KATE. I'm afraid you have me for good and all. Yesterday—or the day before—all this slow travelling has muddled my dates, I just felt I could bear it no longer. Columns in the paper about country houses going up in flames, Senators being kidnapped[100] and all kinds of thrilling goings-on, and there I was secretarying for Scholes, dear siring and dear madaming and referring to theirs of the ult. and the inst.[101] No, it was not to be borne. So I just up and told him I was going and swept out.

MRS. ALCOCK. But surely you had to give him a month's notice?

KATE. Of course. That was what made him so cross. He didn't much mind my going—I'm a rotten secretary I expect—but he did mind my not giving him a month's notice. It hurt his sense of decency. Your countrymen are very queer, mother, the things that shock them—and the things that don't.

MRS. ALCOCK. Well, a bargain is a bargain.

KATE. Of course it is, darling.

ALCOCK. Oh, damn Scholes. You're here, that's the great thing.

MRS. ALCOCK. It's so disorderly, so—so Irish to run away like that.

KATE. I know it is, but I just felt "Oh, damn Scholes," and said it.

MRS. ALCOCK. You didn't, Kate.

KATE. Practically; getting back here was all that mattered. I suppose he can have the law on me if he likes but he won't, he's too decent, he's got a nice tame English secretary by this time and is blessing his stars to be rid of me. But you're quite right, mother, in saying it was so Irish of me to cut and run, that's why I ran, because I felt myself going to pieces.

MRS. ALCOCK. How, Kate?

KATE. Morally, mamma dear. You've no idea what it's like in London now, how an Irish girl feels, the things people say, the things the papers say, the "we-told-you-so-ness" of them all. Well you can take it in either of two ways, either you're a martyred émigré like Margaret de Burgh and are shown off and have people asked to meet you, and carry pictures of your castle *before* the fire and *after* the fire (so like an advertisement for a hair restorer or a baby food—why doesn't Shell or Pratts[102] take it up "Before using our No. 1 spirit the castle was like this—after—!"), and you dress very plainly and get asked out to very good luncheons and talk of being betrayed by England, thrown to the wolves, call yourself an outpost

---

100. **Senators being kidnapped** a Republican tactic in the Civil War was the kidnapping of members of the Free State Senate, which was largely composed of members of the ascendancy   101. **ult. and the inst.** "last month" and "this month"   102. **Shell or Pratts** petroleum companies

of the Empire and how you made a gallant last stand and, altogether, are more "I-told-you-so" than anyone else.

(*She pauses for breath.*)

ALCOCK. Jealous! *You* had no photographs, we're still intact.

KATE. Exactly. I had no photographs. So I had to take it the other way, which means that I simply went livid green. I just damned people, I insulted the émigrés, I loathed their long, gloomy, Protestant faces, their whines and their appetite for luncheons; I insulted the English, I told them it was none of their business what we did with our own country, and anyway as we'd beaten them it would be more becoming if they kept their mouths shut. I made myself thoroughly objectionable to everyone and then I suddenly realised that I was behaving like any Irish girl in a tenth-rate novelette written by some horrible Colonial, that I was being "so Irish" as mother calls me. That shocked me profoundly, and I knew that for my soul's salvation the sooner I left the better, and I realised I'd better leave quick or maybe there'd be nothing to come back to. And here I am.

ALCOCK. We're not likely to be burned, I'm not a Senator.

MRS. ALCOCK. Thank God.

KATE. Well, anyway I'm here, and now I'll be able to be myself again. I'll criticise and dislike Irish people—some of them—and be either a Free Stater or a Republican, I suppose I've got to be one or the other. In London, you know, I was just blatantly Irish, I wouldn't stand a word against De Valera *or* Cosgrave.[103] . . . Oh, mother darling, I know I'm a disappointment to you coming back like this after all the trouble you took and the strings you pulled to get Scholes to take me and I know you wanted me to marry some nice quiet Englishman—but I've stood it for nearly a year and I couldn't bear it any longer and no nice Englishman wanted to marry me—not even a nasty one—I've had no followers, not one. I'm a failure, I'm back on your hands—for keeps.

MRS. ALCOCK. It's lovely to have you.

ALCOCK. By Jove, it is. It's not been fun—this winter.

KATE. I suppose it hasn't. I suppose we've all been telling lies to each other for the last six months, you telling me everything was splendid and not to mind what the papers said, and I telling you that there was no place like London. . . . Well, we needn't pretend any more to each other. God, it's grand to be back to real things even if they're hideous things. In London—apart from the struggle to make a living—everything seems just sentimental play-acting. It's—it's fuzzy.

MRS. ALCOCK (*bitterly*). Sentimental? If you want sentiment in its essence you have it here.

103. **De Valera** *or* **Cosgrave** Eamon de Valera and William T. Cosgrave, the political leaders of the Republican and Free State sides in the Civil War

KATE. Yes, I know. But you'll die for it. It's not fuzzy to die.

ALCOCK. Oh, Kate—no, I won't bother you with it tonight.

KATE. What is it? No, do tell me. I'm back for everything bad and good.

ALCOCK. It's Nicholas O'Connor—you remember Nicholas, Jer O'Connor's son?

KATE. Of course. Ulick thought so much of him, he got you to send him to the Model Farm. I thought you had put him in charge of the farms at Ballymacduff.

MRS. ALCOCK. He left early in the summer. He went very Republican you know. I lost sight of him, apparently he was in the West fighting all the autumn. He's been captured and condemned to death.

KATE. Nicholas! Oh, father!

ALCOCK. Yes. I only heard today. A three days' old paper I saw.

KATE. But can't something be done? Nicholas was one in a thousand.

ALCOCK. I know. I've written a letter to Cosgrave—half written it, but it seems inadequate, I don't believe he'll pay much attention to it, he doesn't know me. I thought I ought to go to Dublin and see him but I didn't like leaving your mother.

KATE. Oh, go, I'm here now. Mother—imagine Nicholas—oh, it's too horrible.

ALCOCK. You've not come home to a picnic.

KATE. No. Forgive me for saying all those silly things, that was the end of the novelette, I'll try and be decent now. Yet I do like real things, if there has to be a battle. I don't want it to be a sham fight. . . . How fond Ulick was of Nicholas. They used to fish together as boys, do you remember?

ALCOCK. Yes.

KATE. And they worked at Gaelic together in Ulick's holidays—but Ulick was better at Gaelic than Nick.

ALCOCK. I must save him, he was a decent fine fellow. Of course I don't approve of what he's done but— (To Mrs. Alcock.) My dear, you won't mind my going now?

MRS. ALCOCK. No. It was wicked of me to try to stop your going before. God knows I don't wish his death . . . there's been enough killing. . . . His mother. . . . (She pulls herself together, she won't be "sentimental.") Why don't they bring your tea, Kate?

KATE. No hurry. I'm not hungry, too excited. Oh, Sissy O'Neill saw me off. You'll not be surprised to hear that she "sent her love." The amount of love the O'Neills are always sending, I wonder they have any left.

MRS. ALCOCK. And what's this about Van? I only got your letter tonight—five minutes before you came.

KATE. Oh, my dear, Van is making a splendid match.

MRS. ALCOCK. There, St. Leger! Who is she?

KATE. American, the usual millions but not the usual American, lives in England altogether and likes to be thought English, has an English accent which Sissy speaks of as "magnificent." She's crazy about horses, Van was at Rathconnell's hunting—he *can* ride, poor Van—they met in the hunting field, he courted her from the back of a horse, he proposed to her from the back of a horse—the only place he'd have any courage—and they're to be married next month.

MRS. ALCOCK. Well, if she admires the English accent what does she think of Van's?

KATE. She's obviously very much in love. But Van's has improved. You really wouldn't know any of the O'Neills, burning them out has done wonders for them. There's Flossie with her Bradford woollen man—countless thousands; Sissy in an office, her boss told me the other day she was "invaluable"; Gertie in Bond Street[104] doing people's faces—Gertie who never washed her own! Maggie in a very comfortable little flat looking after her mother, and Helana in musical comedy. Can you beat it?

MRS. ALCOCK. It's wonderful, it's unbelievable.

KATE. Compared to them I feel I'm a thorough failure, a returned empty. *(She looks round the room.)* But—I knew there was something odd and queer—why are you sitting here? What's that armchair doing and the table out of the small drawing-room, why the school-room piano?

MRS. ALCOCK. Well, we haven't been using the drawing-room this winter.

KATE. Why not?

MRS. ALCOCK. Oh, it doesn't seem worth while. Your father is out or in the library all day, we go to bed very early, no one ever calls—there's no one *to* call except the Browns, and they don't mind sitting in here—

ALCOCK. Don't mind her, Kitty; she's making decent, needless excuses. The truth is we're pretty nearly broke, and she's trying to run the house with only two servants, Annie and the cook. Every room less means a fire less.

KATE. I see. . . . You're eating next to nothing, of course; you always had the appetite of wrens, no wonder the boss looks pinched; it's about time I came home.

ALCOCK. Nonsense, we've plenty to eat.

MRS. ALCOCK. But he would give up wine—even his glass of thin grog[105] before going to bed.

KATE. I've saved ten pounds; I wish it was more, but it's awfully hard to save in London. We'll go on a burst, *pâté de foie gras*[106] for you and champagne for the boss.

104. **Bond Street** London fashion center.   105. **grog** rum or spirits   106. *pâté de foie gras* paste made from goose liver and truffles

MRS. ALCOCK. Darling!

KATE. I suppose no rents are coming in?

ALCOCK. Not a penny for three years.

KATE. Hm. . . . We are shrinking, aren't we? Do you remember the first winter of the war we shut up the north wing and did without two servants, the next winter we cut off the central heating, that meant never sitting in the hall, now the drawing-room's gone and the music-room, too, I suppose. Soon we'll be reduced to a single bed-sitting room. . . . Do you think it all minds it—feels it—the house itself, I mean—Ballydonal?

ALCOCK. In all the generations it's seen, it must have learnt patience.

KATE. Yes, I suppose an immense toleration for the animals who run about through its passages and rooms, and who pull down a bit here and build it up again fifty years later, and cover its walls with paper and then wash the paper all off, who tear out its vitals to put in hot water pipes and then let the pipes go cold. And feather beds are banished to lofts and wax candles give place to lamps, and they should have gone before this to make place for acetylene[107] or electric light, and none of us live any longer or are any the happier, but we scratch and alter, scratch and alter, generation after generation.

ALCOCK. You're becoming quite lyric, Kitty.

KATE. Sorry. But you see when I was away from it I could see it in a way I never could before. When I lived here I couldn't see the house for the rooms.

MRS. ALCOCK. They're awful, all those empty rooms on every side of us—above us all those garrets, below us cellars and empty cellars.

ALCOCK. Never mind, one of these days I'll sell it to the priests or the nuns.

MRS. ALCOCK. I wish you would.

KATE. Is it true that Castle Bewley is to be a training college for South African missionaries?

ALCOCK. Quite true. And Carrigmore, of course, has dedicated itself to the task of converting China. . . . One of these days Ireland will wake up and realise that all its best houses and much of its best land have passed into the hands of landlords who are entirely self-contained, who give no employment, who hold themselves aloof from the life of the community. A curious situation.

KATE. Well, the big houses have had their fling, drank claret deeply in their youth, gambled and horse-raced in their middle-age, so it's right they should be converted and turn pious in their old age. But I should think Castle Bewley would need not conversion but exorcism.

MRS. ALCOCK. I hear Annie coming. Here's your supper at last.

(*The door opens, three young men in trench coats and soft hats appear. The leader of them has a revolver.*)

107. acetylene gas

LEADER. Mr. Alcock, you have five minutes to leave the house.

(The Alcocks have risen, speechless.)

ALCOCK. What do you want?

LEADER. You have five minutes to get out.

ALCOCK. You—you're going to—

LEADER. Blow it up and burn it. You have five minutes. Will you please leave as quickly as you can, you can take with you anything you like.

ALCOCK *(bewildered)*. Mary—

MRS. ALCOCK *(blazing with indignation, to the Leader)*. You dare? You dare? I don't expect you to have sense, that would be asking too much, but have you no decency? Do you know what house you're in, do you know who you're speaking to? Have you ever heard of Ballydonal House? Have you ever heard of Mr. St. Leger Alcock?

LEADER. You have five minutes to leave.

MRS. ALCOCK. Don't stand there prating of your five minutes. I'm English, thank God, if I'd my way I'd have been out of this house five years ago, five and twenty years ago.

ALCOCK *(restraining her)*. Mary, my dear—

MRS. ALCOCK *(shaking him off)*. No, St. Leger. . . . *(To the Leader.)* I don't know your face, are you a stranger here? If you are, before you destroy Ballydonal House go down to the village and ask the first person you meet what this house means, ask if anyone was ever turned away hungry from its door, ask them about Mr. Alcock, what he's done for them, the years of his life he's spent on them, the money, the—the—oh, it's monstrous. What was he doing this very evening? Writing a letter to Cosgrave to try and save one of you—one of you who come now to—

ALCOCK. Stop, Mary. We're not begging off.

LEADER. I have my orders. Ye're to go and the sooner the better; I've other work to do tonight.

MRS. ALCOCK. Nicholas O'Connor. He was writing to save his life, and now you—

LEADER. He's after the fair. Nick was executed yesterday.

MRS. ALCOCK. Oh.

ALCOCK. Yesterday? Poor Nicholas!

MRS. ALCOCK. Is that why we're to be burnt! It won't bring him back to life!

LEADER. I'm not here to argue. . . . *(To Alcock.)* Will you get the women out? They'd better get some coats or something, the night is dry but it's cold.

(Annie appears at the door in coat and hat.)

ANNIE *(to Leader)*. Me box and the cook's is in me room corded[108] and all. Will you send the lads to fetch them down.

---

108. **corded** roped

LEADER (*shortly*). All right.

ANNIE (*insolently taking out a cigarette*). Give me a light.

LEADER. A light?

ANNIE (*with a grin*). You needn't tell me you've no matches. (*He gives her a box, she lights her cigarette.*) I suppose you'll give us a lift to the village.

LEADER. I will not. We're going the other way; I'll leave the boxes at the lodge.

ANNIE. You're not very civil. . . . (*To Mrs. Alcock.*) You owe me a fortnight's wages. You can send it to me, care of Miss Doyle.

(*She goes.*)

MRS. ALCOCK. She was packed and ready, she knew!

ALCOCK. Come, my dear. Come, Kate.

KATE (*blazing*). No! they can blow me up here.

ALCOCK. Hush. No use talking like that. On with your coat. (*He helps her into her coat.*)

MRS. ALCOCK. St. Leger! The birds!

ALCOCK. Oh. . . . (*To Leader.*) It sounds quite ridiculous, but my wife has some canaries—two large cages—they're upstairs in the old nursery, if we could—?

LEADER (*to the men*). Let ye bring them down and hurry. Where are they?

KATE. No.

ALCOCK. I'll show the way myself. . . . See that your mother wraps up well. Now come. . . . (*He gets the women out, their heads are high; he turns at the door to the Leader.*) It's up two flights, I'm afraid, and the cages are awkward things to carry—I'll just see that my wife has her warm coat.

(*He disappears.*)

LEADER (*to men*). When you have the birds and the servants' boxes out come back here. We'll put one mine here and another at the library door where Annie Daly showed us. I'll want two tins of petrol[109] here and as many again in the hall, and. . . .

(*He is continuing his orders when the curtain falls.*)

CURTAIN

SCENE 4

A corner of the garden. Two high stone walls form a right angle across which has been built a summerhouse—a roof supported by a couple of pillars. Below

109. **tins of petrol** cans of gasoline

the stone walls are flower borders, empty now except for some withered stems of plants, on the walls some withered creepers and perhaps some evergreen ones, rose-trees gone a little wild. In the summerhouse and outside it on the path is a medley of furniture. It is just before sunrise, the morning after the previous scene, a cold light which grows brighter as the scene progresses. Atkins, collarless, dressed very hastily, and Mr. Brown, also hastily dressed and very dirty, enter carrying between them a sofa.

BROWN *(dropping his end)*. Just here, Atkins, we won't take it any further.

ATKINS. I'd like to get it into the summerhouse.

BROWN. There's not room. We'll get a cart later on and get all these things over to the rectory.

ATKINS *(rather futilely dusting the sofa)*. The murdering rascals. Will we bring the rest of the things, your reverence?

BROWN. I think they're as well on the gravel as they are here—now the summerhouse is full. For a wonder it doesn't look like rain. Michael will have an eye to them.

ATKINS. Oh, then, I know the sort of an eye Michael Dempsey will have to them, a covetous, thieving eye.

BROWN. Atkins!

ATKINS. Faith, Mary Dempsey will be living like a lady from this out, lolling back on her ladyship's cushions and drinking her tea out of her ladyship's cups.

BROWN. Nonsense. Michael is as honest as the day.

ATKINS. God help you, your reverence, 'tis little you know the class of people that's in this place. I was as innocent as yourself until I went to live beyond in the village. There's neither religion nor decency in the village, a low, thieving, murdering lot. Oh, my eyes were opened, I assure you. I learned things that surprised me, indeed and I did. Thanks be to God I come from the County Tipperary[110] and never set foot in County Cork till I took service with the poor master's father.

BROWN *(sitting on the sofa and lighting a pipe)*. I thought I remembered hearing that Tipperary had a reputation for wildness.

ATKINS. To be sure it has, but it's a decent kind of wildness; you wouldn't find a thing happening there like what happened here last night— burning Ballydonal House! God forgive me, I could curse like a tinker when I think of it. They're a low, mean, murdering crew, the people in this place, not a one of them would come up with me to lend a hand when the blaze of light on the window woke me this morning, but you'll see

110. **County Tipperary** mid-Munster county

they'll be up in an hour's time, nosing around, picking up this thing and that, "saving them" moryah,[111] "keeping them safe for Mr. Alcock against[112] the time he'll be wanting them." Do you know what I'd like to see this minute better than anything else in the world?

BROWN. What?

ATKINS. A regiment of English soldiers and my grandson in the middle of them marching into the village, horse, foot and artillery, and making smithereens[113] of the dirty little houses is there and the dirty little people is living in them, and maybe then they'd know what it is to feel the way the poor mistress feels this minute with her lovely house destroyed on her and she without a roof to shelter her.

BROWN. No, no, you wouldn't wish them that. They're not responsible for what's happened.

ATKINS. Bedad, then, I'd make them responsible, and mark you me, it will come to that yet, and maybe quicker than any of us expect.

BROWN. Come to what?

ATKINS. People high up and low down screeching to the English to come back and protect them from themselves.

BROWN. I don't think that day will ever come.

ATKINS. Indeed and it will. God knows we need protection. How can we live in peace in a little country where everyone knows everyone else and every third man you meet is your second cousin? Sure, 'tis well known that relations never agree and every man in Ireland is his own relation.

(Enter Kate.)

KATE. Here you are. I've been looking everywhere for you. Wouldn't you like a cup of tea? Michael kindled a fire in the coach-house and we've all been having tea.

BROWN. No, thanks, I'm having a pipe instead.

KATE. We've all been washing under the pump. I'm rather proud of the result.

BROWN. I've sent a message to the Goods asking them to send over a car to bring you all across to the rectory.

KATE. Oh, we could walk.

BROWN. The Goods may as well do that much for you.

ATKINS. Them Goods!

BROWN. You might have a look and see whether the car is there, Atkins. They won't know where to find us.

ATKINS. Very well, your reverence. *(He goes out.)*

BROWN. Poor old Atkins is in a state of tearing indignation. He takes it all as a personal insult to the family.

KATE. Yes. . . . What an amount of stuff you've got here!

---

111. **moryah** pretending   112. **against** until   113. **smithereens** small pieces

BROWN. I gave up when the summerhouse was full, we'll get it all up to the rectory before night, there are plenty of empty houses in the yard.

KATE *(looking into the summerhouse)*. What a mixture!

BROWN. It is, rather.

KATE. My God, look! *(She pulls out a picture—Leighton's "Wedded.")*[114] *I* saved that, Mr. Brown, *I* saved it, a picture I've always hated and at any rate it's only a cheap reprint. I struggled through smoke and flame to save it and I never remembered till too late those fine Hones[115] in the hall.

BROWN. How could you remember in all the excitement? I do wish I had known an hour earlier than I did.

KATE. Yes, if we'd had someone with a clear head—father was no use, once he found that there was no chance of saving the beloved Steinway, he just went numb. Mother, though you'd never have thought it, was the best of us, she kept her head and her sense, she made for the right things, made me get the miniatures[116] and made father get at the safe and the papers.

BROWN. And Atkins?

KATE. Instinctively went for big pieces of furniture, things he'd known all his life, it meant that the nice Chippendale[117] stuff was saved but also this hideous sofa. *(She sits on it.)* I suppose I'm a little hysterical but I can only feel everything—since the horror of the mine—as supremely ridiculous. If you could have seen us—but you can easily imagine it—literally risking our lives for the sake of certain bits of wood and china and glass. And we're supposed to be educated and intelligent and (as you'd remind me) we have immortal souls, but savages from darkest Africa couldn't have fought more desperately for some uncouth image of their god than we did for some piece of wood absurdly carved, for miniatures of our forebears, for Leighton's "Wedded." Pure fetish worship. Now that the excitement is over I realise what savages we were and what a nuisance this jetsam is going to be, so much better if everything had been burned. It's awful to think that we'll have to start again to live up to the Chippendale suite. Couldn't we—oh, don't you think we could—have a little private bonfire here of the contents of the summerhouse?

BROWN. The complications with the insurance people would be awful.

KATE. I suppose so. And anyway mother has the Chippendale in the coach-house. Joking apart, I'd like to have saved some of the books, a few of Ulick's for old sake's sake.[118]

BROWN. Could you get nothing from the library?

KATE. Nothing. The explosion blocked the door and it went on fire at

114. *Leighton's "Wedded"* by Baron Frederick Leighton, English (1830–1896) 115. **Hones** paintings by William Hone, Anglo-Irish painter (1718–84) 116. **miniatures** small, detailed paintings 117. **Chippendale** furniture by Thomas Chippendale, English cabinetmaker (1718–79) 118. **for old sake's sake** as keepsakes

once. Oh, well, a lot of them were very dusty, and most of them I had
never read, and God with amazing foresight has created Mr. Andrew Carnegie.[119]

BROWN. I'm glad that Ulick didn't live to see this, it would have broken
his heart.

KATE. I wonder would it. We thought very much alike, Ulick and I,
and do I look as if my heart was broken?

BROWN. I can't say you do. . . . I expect in your inmost soul you're
glad to be quit of it all.

KATE. Glad? I feel—exalted! If only you knew what I feel and I'll tell
you—but not now, here's father. Poor darling, he doesn't look exalted, we
must get him to the rectory as soon as possible.

(Enter Alcock.)

ALCOCK. Your mother is wondering where you are.

KATE. I'll go to her. Is she still in the coach-house?

ALCOCK. Yes. I left her feeding the birds.

KATE. Right. I'll be back again.

(She goes.)

BROWN. Sit down, St. Leger.

ALCOCK *(sitting on the sofa)*. I feel tired.

BROWN. Of course. Have a pipe.

ALCOCK. No, thanks. *(Feeling in his pocket.)* I don't believe I have a
pipe.

BROWN. I have a second one—if you don't mind.

ALCOCK. I feel a pipe would make me sick—like a schoolboy. Silly,
isn't it. But I'll try a cigarette.

BROWN. The Goods are sending a conveyance to bring you to the
rectory and after breakfast I shall pack you all off to bed.

ALCOCK. Yes.

BROWN. Kate is fine.

ALCOCK. Yes. I'm not and I'm not going to try to be fine. I feel as if
nothing matters any more, as if everything was over.

BROWN. Ay.

ALCOCK. And that I'm just damned glad it's all over and that there's
no reason to make an effort any more, no need to pretend ever again.

BROWN. To pretend what?

ALCOCK. That all this—all life here mattered—to me personally I
mean, that I really cared what happened.

BROWN. You cared a lot, my dear man, you've been breaking your
heart for four years.

119. **Mr. Andrew Carnegie** Scottish-American industrialist (1835–1919) who
created a public lending library system

ALCOCK. Because I hate cruelty and stupidity and waste, but not for any other reason. I'd have felt just the same if this had been Abyssinia.[120]

BROWN. I doubt it. . . . And what happens now?

ALCOCK. I haven't an idea. I don't intend to have an idea.

BROWN. Kate—?

ALCOCK. Exactly. Kate. I feel it's Kate's show. I leave it all to her and to my wife. My God, it's a relief to have it all over. I've felt for so many years like a bad actor cast for a part far too heroic for his talents, I haven't had technique enough for it, I haven't in any way been big enough for it, the audience has realised at last what I realised years go, it's hissed me off the stage and sitting here in the wings wiping off my make-up I'm feeling devilishly relieved, almost happy, but at the same time I feel distinctly sick in the stomach.

BROWN. You want a nip of spirits—whiskey or brandy.

ALCOCK. Henry, I'm surprised at you!

BROWN. Oh, for your stomach's sake. There's some at the rectory. For years I've been preaching total abstinence and boasting that I'd never let a drop of the accursed stuff under my roof and I discovered the other day that all the time my wife was squirrelling a bottle of brandy—on the top of the wardrobe in my dressing-room of all places—keeping it for emergencies, she said. It's been there for twenty years. Aren't women the dickens?

ALCOCK. Excellent Alice! It was probably twenty years old to start with. It will be worth drinking. Do you think she'll consider me an emergency?

BROWN. Surely.

(Enter Mrs. Alcock and Kate.)

MRS. ALCOCK *(fussily)*. Now, St. Leger, there's a message from the Goods to say they're sending a car, it will be here in five minutes. Are you ready to come?

ALCOCK. Quite.

MRS. ALCOCK. We'll take the birds with us, they're all right, I fed them just now. Kate has arranged with Michael to have all the things brought over to the rectory and stored there for the present, of course we couldn't trust them here for an hour, and we'll order a motor to take us to Cork this afternoon.

BROWN. Oh, won't you stay at the rectory? We've plenty of room, you're all welcome as long as ever you like to stay.

MRS. ALCOCK. I know it sounds rude but I'd rather go. They've burned us out, we've our pride still, I hope—at least I have—I know when

---

120. **Abyssinia** Ethiopia, East Africa. In 1919 Italy proposed a scheme for the conquest of Ethiopia to Britain, which the British evaded.

I'm not wanted, I take the hint and go and I hope to goodness I never come back.

(Brown sighs.)

Yes, I know it sounds horrible to you, dear Mr. Brown, our best friend here, our oldest friend, but it's because you're such an old friend I can't pretend. But we'll only be parted from you for a little while. You must follow us, we'll get you some lovely quiet English parish with an ancient beautiful church and you'll be able to put flowers and a crucifix on the altar without your congregation thinking that you are heading straight for Rome.

BROWN. Dear Mrs. Alcock!

MRS. ALCOCK. I mean it. You can't pretend that you'd prefer the horrible bare barrack of a church you have here. St. Leger sits here as if he was dead, but I don't feel a bit dead, I'm an old woman, I suppose, but I feel as if life was just beginning for me. Even if we never get a penny of compensation for all this—and I suppose we'll get something—we can't be worse off than we've been here trying to support this white elephant of a house. We'll go to Bournemouth, my sister's there, we'll go to furnished lodgings. Oh, the peace of English furnished lodgings, the beautiful dull respectability of Bournemouth.

ALCOCK. Bournemouth after Ballydonal!

MRS. ALCOCK. Don't get sentimental, St. Leger. Or do, if you like. Have a broken heart, it's quite a comfortable thing to have in a place like Bournemouth.

ALCOCK. What does Kate say?

KATE. It sounds a good plan.

MRS. ALCOCK. Of course it's a good plan.

BROWN. You can leave my English parish out of it. I've been fighting with my Select Vestry for twenty years, they'd think they'd won if I left.

KATE. Oh, I meant for mother and the boss.

MRS. ALCOCK. It's easy to run up to London from Bournemouth, Kate. You can go up for the weekends.

KATE. Don't bother about me. I'm not in that picture.

MRS. ALCOCK. Where are you then?

KATE. Here. Right here.

MRS. ALCOCK. Rubbish.

KATE. We'll get to Cork this evening, we sleep there and go on to England tomorrow or the next day. We go to Bournemouth, I find you really nice, stuffy, respectable lodgings, I hire a good piano, I stay with you till the Vicar calls on you—that launches you into society—and then I'm coming back.

MRS. ALCOCK. My dear! Nonsense.

KATE *(low, almost singing it)*. I'm coming back, I'm coming back, I'm coming back.

MRS. ALCOCK. Where to?

KATE. Atkins' pantry, I think. Did you notice how wonderfully Providence almost completely spared it? I want three pieces of corrugated iron to make a roof and a few little odds and ends—Mr. Brown must get them for me.

(Brown laughs.)

MRS. ALCOCK. Oh, I see it's a joke.

KATE. No, it isn't. The corrugated iron part is but the rest isn't. As we are planning our futures I may as well say what I have to say now as later. I am coming back to live here at Ballydonal.

ALCOCK. Is this bravado or mere obstinacy?

MRS. ALCOCK. As I said before, I have my pride, I know when I'm not wanted.

KATE. I have my pride too. Until last night I thought we were not wanted, that's what sickened me, that's what drove me to work in London, I saw everything sweeping past us and leaving us behind, high and dry like some old wreck, useless and forgotten, I couldn't bear that—my beastly conceit, I suppose.

MRS. ALCOCK. And after last night do you feel you're wanted?

KATE. I can't flatter myself that we're wanted, but we're not forgotten—ignored.

MRS. ALCOCK. I could have put up with being forgotten, there are some ways of being remembered—

KATE. I know. "Say it with petrol!" But still, even to have it said that way, to have it said any way—

BROWN. By Jove, I see. Last night showed you that you still mattered.

KATE. More than ever we mattered before. When those men came in I was furiously angry, I'd have shot them if I had a gun, but deep down in me there was something exulting, something saying, "This is real."

ALCOCK. Your passion for reality, Kitty!

KATE. I mean it was sincere. I've seen time after time father having interviews with people like those young men about one thing or another, but they were never quite real interviews, father wasn't real or they weren't real, but last night!—Did you notice they kept their hats on?

MRS. ALCOCK. I've no doubt they did.

KATE. I don't think they meant to be rude, it was just typical of their attitude towards us, they sort of kept on their hats in their minds. We were equals—except that they had revolvers and we hadn't. It was—it was grand.

MRS. ALCOCK. Well, if it pleases you to know that you're hated, to know that there's no gratitude in the country for all your father has done, you have ample reason for rejoicing. I suppose Annie's falseness and insolence was a great pleasure to you too.

KATE. No, Annie was hateful. But they didn't like her falseness, you could feel they didn't. . . . It's not quite that they hate us, it's fear. They're afraid of us.

ALCOCK. "They," "us"! Do you remember, Kate, the evening after Maggie Leahy was shot?

KATE. Yes. But now I don't want to give up the "they" and "us," I glory in it. I was wrong, we were all wrong, in trying to find a common platform, in pretending we weren't different from every Pat and Mick in the village. Do you remember that gray filly we had long ago that I christened "Pearl" and Michael always called it "Perr'l" and so we all called it "Perr'l" not to seem to criticise Michael's pronunciation? That's a trifling example, but it's the sort of democratic snobbishness we went in for. We were ashamed of everything, ashamed of our birth, ashamed of our good education, ashamed of our religion, ashamed that we dined in the evenings and that we dressed for dinner, and, after all, our shame didn't save us or we wouldn't be sitting here on the remnants of our furniture.

ALCOCK. And what can save you now, it's too late?

KATE. If it was too late they wouldn't have bothered to burn us; *they* don't think it's too late so why should we? They're afraid of us still.

MRS. ALCOCK *(with a bitter laugh)*. We do look formidable, don't we?

KATE. We are formidable if we care to make ourselves so, if we give up our poor attempt to pretend we're not different. We must glory in our difference, be as proud of it as they are of theirs.

BROWN. But why?

KATE. Why? What do you mean?

BROWN. Why "must" you glory?

KATE. Why, because we're what we are. Ireland is not more theirs than ours.

BROWN. Or ours than theirs.

KATE. Exactly. But do let's leave them to see their own point of view. We've spent so much time sympathetically seeing theirs that we've lost sight of our own. Ah, Mr. Brown, you've been as bad as any.

BROWN. As bad?

KATE. How many converts have you made during the twenty years you've been rector of Ballydonal?

BROWN. Converts? I'm not ministering among the heathen.

KATE. Shouldn't you feel, as a Protestant parson, that Roman Catholics are next thing to heathens? If you don't feel like that why are you a parson?

BROWN *(smiling)*. Do you want me to turn to souperism?[121]

KATE. Why not? You used to rail at the Irish country gentleman and say that he was putting up no fight. What sort of a fight have you put up?

121. **souperism** winning converts to Protestantism with handouts of food, a term dating from the Famine (1845–48)

If you really believed in your Protestantism you wouldn't hesitate at a trifle like souperism.

BROWN. You'll never get me to stoop to that.

KATE. Oh, well, religion's not my business and I'm too fond of you to quarrel with you but you'll have to go, all you amiable Protestant parsons, and make room for parsons who believe in their religion enough to fight for souls with every weapon that God has put into their hands. If they don't come, Protestantism itself goes.

ALCOCK. It's going now.

KATE. Because the Mr. Browns are letting it slip through their fingers just as you'd let Ballydonal slip through yours.

ALCOCK. It seems to me it's been snatched.

KATE. Pooh! What's a house? Bricks and stones. Aren't there plenty of both in the world. We'll build it up again.

MRS. ALCOCK. Nonsense. Never. Not for me.

KATE. I'll build it for myself. I'll build it with my own hands if I'm put to it. I believe in Ballydonal, it's my life, it's my faith, it's my country.

ALCOCK. My dear, don't. Don't waste your life here. If you were a man, if you were Ulick, I wouldn't say a word to stop you, but a single woman!—

KATE. I must marry if I can. That's another thing Mr. Brown must look out for me; three pieces of corrugated iron and a husband, please, Mr. Brown.

BROWN. I wish I could get you the husband as easily as the other. What sort of husband do you want?

KATE. Well, I ought to marry someone like Van O'Neill but I'd like to marry wildly, out of all reason, I'd . . . like to marry a—

(She stops.)

MRS. ALCOCK. Well Kate, who?

KATE. No, it's a dream, it's quite impossible. But I should like to marry a Republican Catholic curate.

MRS. ALCOCK. Kate!

KATE. I've always adored them.

(Atkins comes in.)

ATKINS. The Goods' car is here now, sir.

MRS. ALCOCK. Thank goodness, it puts an end to this ridiculous conversation. St. Leger, wake up, come along.

ALCOCK *(getting up slowly)*. Yes, I suppose so.

MRS. ALCOCK. Take my arm.

ALCOCK. My dear, you should take mine.

MRS. ALCOCK. I don't need it. Come.

ALCOCK *(as he goes out)*. Bournemouth after Ballydonal!

MRS. ALCOCK. Ssh!

(They go out.)

BROWN. I believe you mean it, Kate; I see it in your eye.

KATE. Every word of it. Go after them, I have a word to say to Atkins.

(Mr. Brown goes out.)

We're going to Cork this afternoon, Atkins, and then to England. The master will send you your money as usual. Here's something to go on with.

(She hands him a pound note.)

ATKINS. You're going away, miss? Ah, sure, it had to be.

KATE. But in a few weeks, in a month or two, I'm coming back.

ATKINS. You're what, miss?

KATE. Coming back to live here for good.

ATKINS. Thank God for that.

KATE. You can tell it in the village.

(She goes out.)

ATKINS *(looking after her)*. God bless Miss Kate. *(He looks at the furniture.)* The murdering ruffians! *(He is lifting a chair into the summerhouse, he drops it and starts back in terror.)* Miss Kate, Miss Kate, Miss Kate!

KATE *(coming back quickly)*. What is it, Atkins? What's the matter?

ATKINS *(babbling)*. I seen him there—in the summerhouse—as clear as the day—Master Ulick—

KATE. Ulick? Go away, Atkins, go away. *(She pushes him out. She turns to the summerhouse and speaks softly.)* Ulick! Are you there? . . . *(Her face lights up.)* Oh, my dear, you've come to me again, after all these years. . . . And you're smiling, so I'm right, it's what you'd have done. . . . *(A pause, she seems to listen to someone talking.)* Yes. . . . Yes. . . . So—kiss me, my dear. . . . *(She raises her face as if she were being kissed, she closes her eyes.)*

CURTAIN

DENIS JOHNSTON
1901 – 1984

Dubliner William Denis Johnston was educated at Cambridge and Harvard. A lawyer, journalist, college teacher, and theater director, he began his career as playwright with *The Old Lady Says "No!"* (1929). A BBC writer and director during the 1930s, he was a war correspondent, and on the faculty of Amherst, Mount Holyoke and Smith Colleges during the 1950s. He has written extensively for stage, radio and television, as well as literary scholarship and philosophical speculation. One of his four children is the distinguished novelist Jennifer Johnston. "Opus One" is his own introduction to this expressionist masterpiece.

SELECT BIBLIOGRAPHY

Publications

The Dramatic Works of Denis Johnston, 2 vols. Toronto: Macmillan, 1977.
Selected Plays of Denis Johnston, introduced by Joseph Ronsley. Gerrard's Cross, Bucks.: Colin Smythe; Washington, DC: The Catholic University of America Press, 1983. (*The Old Lady Says "No!," "The Moon in the Yellow River, The Golden Cuckoo, The Dreaming Dust, The Scythe and the Sunset*)
In Search of Swift. Dublin: Hodges, 1959.
Nine Rivers from Jordan: The Chronicle of a Journey and a Search. London: Verschoyle, 1953; Boston, Toronto: Little, Brown, 1955.
The Brazen Horn. Dublin: Dolmen, 1976.

Biography and Criticism

Barnett, Gene A. *Denis Johnston.* Boston: Twayne, 1980.
Canfield, Curtis. *Plays of Changing Ireland.* New York: Macmillan, 1936.
Ferrar, Harold. *Denis Johnston's Irish Theatre.* Dublin: Dolmen, 1973.
Henderson, Gordon. Interview with Denis Johnston, *Journal of Irish Literature,* II (1973): 30–44.
Hogan, Robert. *After the Irish Renaissance.* Minneapolis: University of Minnesota Press, 1967; London: Macmillan, 1986: 133–46.
Maxwell, D. E. S. *Modern Irish Drama.* Cambridge University Press, 1984: 114–30.
Ronsley, Joseph, ed. *Denis Johnston: A Retrospective.* Gerrard's Cross, Bucks.: Colin Smythe; Totowa, NJ: Barnes and Noble, 1981.

Opus One

One of the best loved figures of Irish romantic literature is Robert Emmet. The story of his rebellion of 1803 has all of the elements that make for magic. It was very high-minded, and completely unsuccessful. It was picturesquely costumed and insufficiently organized. Its leader—a young protestant university man of excellent social background—having failed to achieve anything more than an armed street riot, remained behind to bid goodbye to his forbidden sweetheart, instead of taking flight as any sensible rebel should do. In consequence of this, he was captured by an ogre of melodrama called Major Sirr, and was hanged after making one of the finest speeches from the dock in the annals of the criminal courts—and we have had some pretty good ones in Ireland.

So we all love Robert Emmet. Yeats and De Valera[1] loved him, each in his own fashion. I do too; and so did Sarah Curran. Even the hoardings along the Canal have been known to display a chalked inscription, "UP EMMET." We all agree that it was a pity that some of his supporters had to murder one of the most liberal judges on the bench, Lord Kilwarden, and that the only practical outcome of his affray was to confirm the Union with England for about a hundred and twenty years. Our affection is not affected by these details.

The tragedy of his love has been immortalized by Tom Moore[2] in one of his finest ballads:

> She is far from the land
> Where her young hero sleeps,
> And lovers around her are sighing.
> But coldly she turns from their gaze, and weeps,
> For her heart in his grave is lying.

Who cares that this reason for her absence from the land is the fact that she subsequently married an English officer,[3] and ended her days happily with him elsewhere? For us, her heart will always be lying in Robert's grave. And lying is the operative word.

The whole episode has got that delightful quality of story-book unreality that creates a glow of satisfaction without any particular reference to the facts of life. To put it into conflict with those facts ought to be an

---

1. **De Valera** Eamon De Valera (1882–1975) Republican, Prime Minister and President of Ireland 2. **Tom Moore** Thomas Moore (1779–1852), poet and composer, friend of Robert Emmet, author of *Irish Melodies* (1808–21) 3. **English officer** following Emmet's execution, Sarah Curran (1782–1808) married Captain R. H. Sturgeon of the Royal Staff Corps

easy proposition in the theatre, and particularly so back in 1926, when several years of intermittent and unromantic civil war[4] had soured us all a little towards the woes of Cathleen Ni Houlihan.[5] It was inevitable that such a play would be written in Ireland by someone or other at about that time.

Although it is by no means my favourite play, and is my only work that might fairly be described as anti-Irish, it is by far the best spoken-of in its native habitat. In Dublin it is now generally regarded as a strongly nationalistic piece, full of sound popular sentiments and provided with a title calculated to annoy Lady Gregory and the Abbey Theatre. It is true that on the occasion of its first production at the Gate, some tentative efforts were made to have me prosecuted—for what, I cannot at present remember. But those days are long past, and the only acrimony that the play evokes today is among the cast, the older members of which argue strongly during rehearsals over business and movements that were used on previous occasions, and must not now be altered.

As for the title, I cannot be held responsible for this. It was written by somebody on a sheet of paper attached to the front of the first version, when it came back to me from the Abbey. Whether it was intended to inform me that the play had been rejected, or whether it was being offered as an alternative to my own coy little name for the play—*Shadowdance*—is a question that I never liked to ask. So it remained, thereafter, as the title of the work—a definite improvement for which I have always been grateful. Lennox Robinson used to complain bitterly about any suggestion that Lady G. was against the play, but all I know of the matter is the distaste she expressed to me in the back sitting-room of her hotel in Harcourt Street. I was never invited to Gort.[6]

It is, of course, a director's play, written very much in the spirit of "Let's see what would happen" if we did this or that. We were tired of the conventional three-act shape, of conversational dialogue, and of listening to the tendentious social sentiments of the stage of the 'twenties, and we wanted to know whether the emotional appeal of music could be made use of in terms of theatrical prose, and an opera constructed that did not have to be sung. Could dialogue be used in lieu of some of the scenery, or as a shorthand form of character-delineation? Could the associations and thought-patterns already connected with the songs and slogans of our city be used deliberately to evoke a planned reaction from a known audience?

The opening playlet—which was felt by Lady G. to be an all-too-brief

---

4. **civil war** 1922–23, between forces of the new Irish Free State and irreconcilable Republicans   5. **Cathleen Ni Houlihan** traditional personification of Ireland as in Yeats's patriotic play of that title (1902)   6. **Gort** Lady Gregory's home in Co. Galway

preliminary to a vein of "coarseness" that was to follow—is made up almost entirely from lines by Mangan, Moore, Ferguson, Kickham, Todhunter, and the romantic school of nineteenth-century Irish poets, still well known to everybody although no longer imitated. So too, the final speech of the play contains some easily recognizable sections of Pearse's funeral oration for O'Donovan Rossa,[7] together with a large portion of Emmet's actual speech from the dock, which concludes:

"When my country takes her place amongst the nations of the earth, then, and not till then, let my epitaph be written."

There are both handicaps and benefits to be derived from writing for so specialized an audience. A phrase such as "When in the course of human events" will spontaneously call up an association-pattern when uttered in the United States, where it belongs.[8] An Englishman, prodded with the expression "Kiss me, Hardy,"[9] may react in a variety of ways, but some response is usually noticeable. On the other hand, outside Ireland, a reference to "my four beautiful green fields"[10] will not wring any withers, but becomes instead a mere literary reference that may or may not be recognized as an echo from Yeats.[11]

Thus, although written in a language common to all three countries, *The Old Lady* is not quite the same play in London or New York as it is in Dublin. Across the sea its intentional clichés are no longer clichés, and the various daggers concealed within its lacy sentiments find no flesh into which to probe. For this reason, apart from one production in New York, a couple in London, and a few presentations in colleges with *avant garde*[12] theatre departments, it has never been performed outside Ireland. There the pattern devised by Hilton Edwards and Micheál MacLiammóir for its first production in 1929 has become as much an integral part of the play as is the text.

Although many of its expressionist tricks[13] are now commonplace, especially in radio production, it was, at the time of writing, a fairly original type of play, and technically it owes less to other dramatists than anything that I have written since. The play's actual foster parents are neither Evreinov, O'Neill nor Georg Kaiser. Nor has Joyce got much to do with it, although I gratefully acknowledge the presence of his finger in the stirring

7. **Pearse's funeral oration for O'Donovan Rossa** Poet and 1916 leader Padraic Pearse (1879–1916) delivered a famous incendiary oration in 1915 at the burial of Republican Jeremiah O'Donovan Rossa (1831–1915) 8. Declaration of Independence, Preamble 9. **Kiss me, Hardy** reputedly Nelson's last words 10. **my four beautiful green fields** Ireland's four provinces 11. **echo from Yeats** Cathleen Ni Houlihan's words 12. *avant garde* progressive 13. **expressionist tricks** techniques which reject external appearances in order to render inner realities

of some of my later pies. I have once or twice been written to by students of the drama who feel that they can trace the influence of *Finnegans Wake*[14] upon *The Old Lady*. This is a book that I first attempted to read through about ten years ago, and the only part of it that has got into my play did so by a most circuitous route. This is the *Thuartpeatrick*[15] phrase, misspelled *St Peetrick* by me in the party scene. Its presence there is a surprising reminder that Tuohy,[16] the artist who painted both Joyce and his old father, had sentences from Joyce's own lips that he was bandying around Dublin as early as the Nine Arts Ball of 1925. In this very second-hand condition the expression has found its way into my text, as a quotation from a section of a book that had then hardly been begun. There are, of course, two short quotes from *Ulysses*[17] in *The Old Lady,* together with a phrase or two, such as "Jacobs Vobiscuits." But any resemblances to the *Wake* have nothing to do with me.

The two plays to which this experiment does owe something are, firstly, Kaufman and Connelly's *Beggar on Horseback*[18]—a superb piece of American expressionism that I have always admired—and secondly, a Continental satire called *The Land of Many Names*[19] that I once saw in the 'twenties. Who wrote it, and where it came from, I have often since wondered. I think it may have been one of the Capeks.

14. **Finnegans Wake** by James Joyce, 1939   15. **Thuartpeatrick** *Finnegans Wake* 3.22   16. **Touhy** Patrick Touhy, Irish portrait painter (1894–1930)   17. *Ulysses* novel by James Joyce, 1922   18. **Kaufman and Connelly's** *Beggar on Horseback* New York (1924), by George Kaufman and Marc Connelly   19. *The Land of Many Names* by Josef Capek (1887–1945), London (1926)

The Old Lady Says "No!"

SARAH CURRAN *and* FLOWER WOMAN*
THE SPEAKER (ROBERT EMMET)
FIRST REDCOAT *and* GENERAL*
SECOND REDCOAT
MAJOR SIRR[20] *and* GRATTAN*[21]
STAGE HAND *and* MINISTER FOR ARTS AND CRAFTS*
DOCTOR
BLIND MAN
CHORUS

Voices and Forms, Newsboys, Passer-By, Bus Man, Flapper, Medical, Well-Dressed Woman, Businessman, Carmel, Bernadette, An Older Man, Two Touts, Handshakers, Younger Man, A Man, Second Man, Joe, Maeve, Lady Trimmer, O'Cooney, O'Mooney, O'Rooney, Minister's Wife, He, She
First Shadow, Second Shadow,
Third Shadow, Fourth Shadow

*Both characters to be played by the same performer.

The action of the play opens in the garden of The Priory, the home of John Philpot Curran,[22] close to Rathfarnham (now a suburb of Dublin), on the night of August 25th, 1803.[23]

PART 1

To the left the dark gable of a building can be seen with a light burning behind the blind in the first-floor window. It is the house of John Philpot Curran, The

---

20. **Major Sirr** Dublin City police chief, responsible for the arrest of several United Irishmen, including Robert Emmet   21. **Grattan** Henry Grattan (1746–1820), patriotic politician and orator, whose statue stands outside Trinity College Dublin   22. **John Philpot Curran** (1750–1817) Lawyer and defender of prominent United Irishmen; father of Sarah, whose relationship with Robert Emmet he bitterly opposed   23. **August 25th, 1803** the date of Emmet's capture

Priory, close to Rathfarnham, a village outside Dublin. To the centre and to the right are the trees of the garden, and behind them the profile of Kilmashogue and the hills beyond. It is the night of August 25th in the year 1803, and the sound of men's voices is dying away into the distance as the Curtain rises.

VOICES.

> With their pikes in good repair,
>   Says the Shan Van Vocht,
> To the Curragh of Kildare
> The boys they will repair,
> And Lord Edward will be there,
>   Says the Shan Van Vocht.[24]

(The window opens and Sarah Curran gazes out towards the mountains.)
SARAH.

The air is rich and soft—the air is mild and bland.
Her woods are tall and straight, grove rising over grove.
Trees flourish in her glens below and on her heights above,
Oh, the fair hills of Eire, oh.[25]
Down from the high cliffs the rivulet is teeming
To wind around the willow banks that lure him from above.
Ah, where the woodbines with sleepy arms have
        wound him . . .[26]

(She starts.)

Who is there? I heard a rustling in the trees!
Who is there, I say?

(The Speaker emerges from among the trees. He is dressed as Robert Emmet in a green tunic, white-plumed hat, white breeches and Wellington boots[27] with gold tassels. At his side hangs a large cavalry sword.)

SPEAKER *(with an appropriate gesture)*. Hush beloved, it is I.

SARAH. Robert! I think, oh my love, 'tis thy voice from the kingdom of souls![28]

SPEAKER. Was ever light of beauty shed on loveliness like thine![29]

---

24. **Shan Van Vocht** famous patriotic ballad written in 1796. "Shan Van Vocht" (*Sean Bhean Bhocht*) means "the poor old woman" and is symbolic of Ireland. Hence the significance of the play's title. (Curtis Canfield, *Plays of Changing Ireland*, hereafter "CC") 25. **Oh, the fair hills of Eire, oh** "The Fair Hills of Eire, O!" by James Clarence Mangan (1803–1849). The original has "The soil is rich and soft . . . etc." (CC) 26. **with sleepy arms have wound him . . .** "Serenade of a Loyal Martyr" by George Darley (1795–1846) (CC) 27. **Wellington boots** boots extending to the knee in front and cut lower in the back 28. **kingdom of souls!** "At the Mid Hour of Night" by Thomas Moore (1779–1852) (CC) 29. **loveliness like thine!** "An Ancient Tale" by John O'Hagan (1822–1890) has ". . . was ever light of evening shed . . ." (CC)

SARAH. Oh, Robert, Robert, why have you ventured down? You are in danger.

SPEAKER. My bed was the ground, my roof the greenwood above: and the wealth that I sought, one far, kind glance from my love.[30]

SARAH. My love, for a vision of fanciful bliss to barter thy calm life of labour and peace![31]

SPEAKER. What matters life! Deirdre is mine: she is my queen, and no man now can rob me!

SARAH. The redcoats are everywhere. Last night they were around the house and they will come again.

SPEAKER. Let them come! A million a decade![32] Let me be persuaded that my springing soul may meet the eagle on the hills, and I am free.[33]

SARAH. Ah, go, forget me. Why should sorrow o'er that brow a shadow fling?[34]

SPEAKER. My strong ones have fallen from the bright eye of day.[35] Their graves are red, but their souls are with God in glory.[36]

SARAH. Ah, love, love! Where is thy throne? It is gone in the wind![37]

SPEAKER. A dark chain of silence is thrown o'er the deep.[38] No streak of dawning is in the sky. It is still unriven, that clanking chain.[39] Yet, am I the slave they say?[40]

SARAH. A lost dream to us now in our home! Ullagone! Gall to our heart![41]

SPEAKER. But there is lightning in my blood—red lightning tightening in my blood! Oh, if there was a sword in every Irish hand! If there was a flame in every Irish heart to put an end to slavery and shame! Oh, I would end these things![42]

SARAH. It is too late! Large, large affliction unto me and mine, that one of his majestic bearing, his fair and stately form, should thus be tor-

30. **kind glance from my love** "The Outlaw of Loch Lene," translated from the Irish by Jeremiah Joseph Callanan (1795–1829) (CC)   31. **life of labour and peace!** "Hy Breasail—the Isle of the Blest" by Gerald Griffin (1803–1840) has "Rash fool! For a vision . . ."   32. **A million a decade!** "The Exodus" by Lady Wilde (1826–1896) (CC)   33. **and I am free** "Sonnet Written during His Residence in College" by Charles Wolfe (1791–1823) (CC)   34. **a shadow fling?** "Go! Forget Me" by Charles Wolfe (CC)   35. **the bright eye of day** "Oh, Say, My Brown Drimin" by J. J. Callanan (CC)   36. **with God in glory.** "Plorans Ploravit" by Aubrey Thomas De Vere (1814–1902) (CC)   37. **It is gone in the wind!** "Gone in the Wind" by James Clarence Mangan (CC)   38. **thrown o'er the deep** "Eire" by William Drennan (1754–1820) (CC)   39. **that clanking chain** "To Erin" by Mary "Eva" Kelly (CC)   40. **the slave they say?** "Soggarth Aroon" (Priest Dear) by John Banim (1798–1842) (CC)   41. **Gall to our heart!** "The Swan's Lament for the Desolation of Lir" by John Todhunter (1839–1916) (CC)   42. **But there is lightning . . . end these things!** "Dark Rosaleen" by James Clarence Mangan (from the Irish). The Speaker's excitement evidently causes him to misquote here. The original has ". . . red lightning lightened through my blood. . . ." (CC)

tured and o'erborne—that this unsparing storm should wreak its wrath on head like this![43]

SPEAKER *(softly)*. My earthly comforter, whose love so indefeasible might be![44] Your holy, delicate, white hands shall girdle me with steel. You'll pray for me, my flower of flowers! You'll think of me through daylight hours, my virgin flower![45]

SARAH. At least I'll love thee till I die.

SPEAKER. How long, ah, Sarah, can I say how long my life will last?

SARAH. Cease boding doubt, my gentlest love; be hushed that struggling sigh.[46]

SPEAKER. When he who adores thee has left but a name, ah say, wilt thou weep?[47]

SARAH. I shall not weep. I shall not breathe his name.[48] For my heart in his grave will be lying.[49] I shall sing a lament for the Sons of Usnach.[50]

SPEAKER. But see, she smiles, she smiles! Her rosy mouth dimples with hope and joy; her dewy eyes are full of pity![51]

SARAH. Ah, Robert, Robert, come to me.

SPEAKER *(climbing up)*. I have written my name in letters of fire across the page of history. I have unfurled the green flag in the streets and cried aloud from the high places to all the people of the Five Kingdoms: "Men of Eire, awake to be blest! Rise, Arch of the Ocean[52] and Queen of the West!" I have dared all for Ireland and I will dare all again for Sarah Curran. Ah, it is a glorious thing to dare!

(He is about to touch her outstretched hand when—)

A VOICE. Halt! Who goes there?

SARAH. Ah God! The yeomen!

VOICES. The countersign.

　　　Stand.

　　　Front point.

　　　Advance.[53]

---

43. **on head like this!** "O'Hussey's Ode to the Maguire" by James Clarence Mangan (CC)　44. **so indefeasible might be!** "True Loveliness" by George Darley. This poem is known also by the title "It is Not Beauty I Demand." (CC)　45. **my virgin flower!** "Dark Rosaleen" by James Clarence Mangan (CC) 46. **I'll love thee till I die . . . be hushed that struggling sigh"** "Dry Be That Tear" by Richard Brinsley Sheridan (1751–1816) (CC)　47. **ah say, wilt thou weep?** "Wnen He Who Adores Thee" by Thomas Moore (CC)　48. **I shall not breathe his name** "Oh, Breathe not his Name" by Thomas Moore (CC)　49. **For my heart in his grave will be lying** "She Is Far from the Land" by Thomas Moore (CC)　50. **I shall sing a lament for the Sons of Usnach** John Todhunter is the author of a poem "Deirdre's Great Lamentation for the Sons of Usnach." (CC) 51. **her dewy eyes are full of pity!** "The Benumbed Butterfly" by Sir Aubrey De Vere (1788–1846) (CC)　52. **Rise, Arch of the Ocean . . .** "Eire" by William Drennan (CC)　53. **The Countersign . . . Advance** "Rory of the Hill" by Charles Joseph Kickham (1828–1882) (CC)

SPEAKER. The flint-hearted Saxon![54]

(He makes a gesture to her. She disappears and the light goes out.)

SARAH. . . . in their fearful red array![55]

FIRST REDCOAT *(rushing forward)*. Hold! Surrender or I fire!

SECOND REDCOAT. We hold this house for our lord the King.

FIRST REDCOAT. Amen, says I. May all traitors swing.[56]

SPEAKER *(springing down and folding his arms)*. Slaves and dastards, stand aside![57]

(Major Sirr enters.)

SIRR. Spawn of treason,[58] bow down thy humbled head to him, the King![59]

SPEAKER. A nation's voice, a nation's voice, 'tis stronger than the King.[60]

SIRR. Silence rebel! Do you not know who I am?

SPEAKER. A jackal of the Pale.

SIRR. Major Sirr.

SPEAKER. Who trapped Lord Edward?

SIRR. The same.

SPEAKER *(drawing his sword)*. I am honoured. Ireland will remember. Look well to your soul, Major Sirr, for the dawn of the Gael is still to break; when they that are up will be down[61] and they that are down will be up. I tell you, Major Sirr, we'll be a glorious nation yet—redeemed, erect, alone![62]

(He leaps upon them. One of the Redcoats clubs his musket and strikes him a resounding blow upon the head. The lights flicker momentarily and he lies still. Sarah Curran appears once more at the window.)

SARAH. A star is gone! There is a blank in heaven.[63] The last great tribune of the world is dead.[64]

SIRR *(seemingly a little surprised)*.

The sport of fools—the scoff of knaves,
Dead ere they blossomed, barren, blighted.

54. **The flint-hearted Saxon!** "Oh, Say, My Brown Drimin" by J. J. Callanan (CC) 55. **their fearful red array!** "Kathleen ban Adair" by Francis Davis (1810–1885) (CC) 56. **We hold this house for our lord the King . . . swing** "The Croppy Boy, a Ballad of '98" by William B. McBurney (CC) 57. **Slaves and dastards, stand aside!** "Fág an Bealach" (Clear the Road) by Sir Charles Gavan Duffy (1816–1903) (CC) 58. **Spawn of treason** "Oliver's Advice" by Colonel William Blacker (1777–1855) (CC) 59. **. . . bow down . . . King!** "The Land Betrayed" by Sir Stephen E. De Vere (1812–1904) (CC) 60. **stronger than the King** "Nationality" by Thomas Osborne Davis (1814–1845) (CC) 61. **when they that are up will be down . . .** These sentiments are expressed by the well-known play *The Rising of the Moon* (1907) by Lady Gregory. (CC) 62. **redeemed, erect, alone!** "Ourselves Alone" by John O'Hagan (1822–1890) (CC) 63. **A star is gone! There is a blank in heaven** "The Fallen Star" by George Darley (CC) 64. **The last great tribune of the world is dead** "The Great Tribune" by Denis Florence McCarthy (1817–1882) (CC)

They came, whose counsels wrapped the land in foul rebellion's flame,
Their hearts unchastened by remorse, their cheeks untinged by shame,[65]
To sue for a pity they shall not—shall not—[66]
Er—

(One of the Redcoats kneels beside the Speaker and shakes him by the shoulder. Sirr looks helplessly into the wings from which he receives a whispered prompt.)

PROMPT. Find.

FIRST REDCOAT. Ay!

SECOND REDCOAT. What's up?

SIRR *(to the wings)*. Curtain . . . curtain . . . I say.

STAGE HAND. Is he hurted?

VOICES. He's hurt. Hurt. He's hurt. Hurted.

FIRST REDCOAT. It wasn't my fault. I only . . .

SIRR. Curtain, please. Do stand back for a moment and give him a chance.

VOICES. Loosen his collar. What do you think you're doing? How did it happen? What's the matter? He'll be all right. Give him brandy. Take those boots off. Stand back, please. Did you see the skelp[67] he gave him? Can I help?

(The Curtain comes jerkily down and there is a heavy tramping behind upon the stage. Presently Sirr comes through the Curtain. House lights up.)

SIRR *(beckoning to someone in the audience)*. Is there a doctor in . . . I say . . . can you?

DOCTOR. Me?

SIRR. Just come through for a minute. I think he'll be all right.

DOCTOR. It looked a heavy enough . . .

SIRR. I don't think it is . . .

DOCTOR. . . . blow from the front.

SIRR. . . . very serious, really.

DOCTOR. I hope not. Anyhow you had better see whether you can't . . .

(They disappear through the Curtain, talking. Presently Sirr re-appears.)

SIRR. Ladies and gentlemen . . . he . . . er . . . the doctor would like the curtains up again . . . the draught blows through from the scene dock when it's across. We're really very sorry that the performance should be held up . . . but you see . . . it's nothing really . . . He . . . er . . . says he will be all right in a moment if he's kept quiet and not moved . . . if you would only be so good as to keep your seats and stay perfectly quiet for a few moments . . . just a few moments . . . while the doctor is . . . er . . . busy . . . I'm sure we'll be able to go on . . . if you don't mind . . . curtain

65. **They came . . . untinged by shame** "Oliver's Advice" by Colonel William Blacker (CC)   66. **To sue for a pity they shall not . . .** "The Ballad of the Bier that Conquered: or O'Donnell's Answer," by Sir Aubrey De Vere (CC)   67. **skelp** blow

please . . . quite quiet please . . . just for a few minutes . . . thank you so much.

(He hurries off. The Curtain is slowly drawn again, disclosing the Speaker where we left him, now attended by the Doctor, the Stage Hand and one of the Redcoats. A black gauze curtain has been drawn behind him through which we can see dim figures moving about and hear the thumping of heavy weights.)

DOCTOR. That's better now. Can you get them off?

STAGE HAND. Yes, sir. They're coming now.

(He draws off one of the Speaker's boots.)

REDCOAT. How could I know anyway? It wasn't my fault. I tell you I only . . .

DOCTOR. That's all right. Hold up his head a little. That's better. Oh, they've got it up.

(He refers to the Curtain.)

REDCOAT. Ah, God, isn't it awful!

DOCTOR. Ask those people to keep quiet there while he's coming round.

STAGE HAND. Ay, Barnie, tell them to shut up! Give us a hand with this boot. I can't get a grip on it at all.

REDCOAT. I don't know how it could have happened at all. You pull now.

STAGE HAND. Ah, will you hold on? How the hell . . .

DOCTOR. Ssssssh!

STAGE HAND. There she comes.

DOCTOR. See if you can get something to cover his legs with. He must be kept warm. And ask them to turn down that light a bit. He'll be all right soon if he's kept quiet and allowed to come round.

(The Stage Hand goes out obligingly.)

REDCOAT. I swear to God I hit him no harder than I was shown yesterday. I only . . . look . . .

DOCTOR. Ah, be quiet you, and be off. You're more of a hindrance than a help.

REDCOAT. It's all very well blaming me, but I only did what I was shown bef . . .

DOCTOR. Sssssssh!

(The Redcoat goes off muttering protestations. The lights are dimmed, making the forms behind the gauze clearer still. Presently the Stage Hand enters with a pair of gaudy carpet slippers.)

STAGE HAND. Would these be any use? They were all I could find. They belong to Mr . . . er . . .

DOCTOR. He's stirring a little.

(He examines the Speaker while the Stage Hand puts the slippers on his feet.)

STAGE HAND. Is the lights O.K. now?

DOCTOR. What's that? Oh, fine. You'd better . . .

STAGE HAND. I brought a sup[68] of brandy.

DOCTOR. Brandy! Good heavens, no! He has a slight concussion.

STAGE HAND. Is that a fact? A what?

DOCTOR. But I tell you what. Go and see if you can manage to get a little ice.

STAGE HAND *(dubiously)*. An ice?

DOCTOR. Yes. You know. In a basin of cold water. For a compress.

STAGE HAND. Oh, for a . . . Oh I see.

(He goes out slowly.)

DOCTOR. And . . . *(He notices the slippers.)* My God, what are those? I told you to bring something for his legs. Do you hear? A rug.[69] *(He rises and crosses).* Has anybody got a rug? *(He goes off and his voice is heard faintly.)* A rug for his legs. Ah, thanks so much. That will . . .

(Silence. The figures behind the Curtain have ceased to move and are clustered in a silent group peering through towards the spot where the Speaker is lying. Presently the latter stirs and his lips begin to move. There is a dim and distant boom-boom-boom as of someone tapping on a big drum. The lights pulse.)

SPEAKER. Redeemious . . . Oh . . . be a redeemious . . . re . . . warmest core I said . . . we'll *(He opens his eyes and stares weakly ahead.)* . . . I love thee . . . love thee bosom my head bosom my head's all . . . Oh, God! *(There is a pause while he stares out into the auditorium.)* They that are down will be down . . . down . . . up . . . erect . . . redeemiable . . . love thee, Sarah . . . redeemiablecurran . . . I see you. *(Pause—then with a great effort)* I am the Speaker . . . Deadbosom I see you.

THE FORMS *(answering on behalf of the audience with unctuous friendliness.)*

A.	Quirke	present
B.	Quinn	present
C.	Foley	present
D.	Byrne	present
E.	Ryan	present
F.	Carrol	present
G.	Lynch	present
H.	Dwyer	present
I.	Burke	present
J.	Farrell	present
K.	Gleeson	present
L.	Mooney	present
M.	Quigley	present

SPEAKER *(holding up his hand peremptorily)*. Stop! *(Pause. He bows solemnly.)* Thank you.

68. **sup** small drink   69. **rug** blanket

THE FORMS *(whispering in rhythm)*.

> Poor poor poor poor
> Hit him hit him
> With a gun
> Butt end butt end
> Dirty dirty
> Give him water
> For a compress
> Calf 's foot jelly[70]
> Fever fever
> Ninety-nine point ninety ninety
> Fahrenheit Centigrade
> Centigrade Fahrenheit
> Very unsettled unsettled unsettled
> Take his boots off
> Milk and soda
> Patrick Dun's and
> Cork Street Mater
> Adelaide and
> Vincent's Elpis
> Baggot Street and
> Mercer's Meath[71] and
> Is his better?
> How's the headache?
> Ambulance ambulance
> S.O.S.
> S.O.S. S.O.S.
> Tut tut tut tut
> Tut tut tut tut
> Poor poor poor poor . . .

SPEAKER *(with an impatient flap of his hand)*. Slaves and dastards stand aside, a nation's voice . . . nation's voice is stronger than a Speaker . . . I am an honored gloriable nationvoice your Sirrflinthearted Saxons . . . Oh! . . . if it would only stop going round . . . round . . . up . . . down . . . up will be down . . . O God, I am the Unspeakerable.

THE FORMS *(relentlessly)*.

> On with the performance
> Programmes Tenpence
> No Smoking

70. **Calf's foot jelly** gelatine food for convalescents   71. **Patrick Dun's . . . Meath** Dublin hospitals

> Spitting Coughing
> Nobody admitted
> Till after the Performance
> After nine
> Point ninety ninety
> For further particulars
> Apply to the Manager
> N. Moore
> O. Callan
> Q. O'Reilly
> R. Donovan
> S. Muldoon

SPEAKER *(with the rhythm).* Yes . . . yes . . . yes . . . yes . . .
THE FORMS.

> T. Cosgrave
> U. O'Toole
> V. Kelly
> W. Fogarty

SPEAKER.

> Red lightning tightening through my blood
> Red tightening lightning tightening through my blood
> My tightening blood . . .

(The voices are merged in a clanking, shrieking concatenation that swells up . . . the throb of petrol engines, the hoot of motor horns, the rattle and pounding of lorries, and, above all, the cry of the newsboys.)
NEWSBOYS.

> Hegler Press
> Late Buff Hegler Press
> Weekly Honesty
> Hegler Press

SPEAKER *(commencing to act again, at the top of his voice).* Their graves are red but their souls are with God in glory. A dark chain of silence is thrown o'er the deep. Silence . . . silence I say. O Ireland, Ireland, it is still unriven, that clanking chain . . . still unriven. O Ireland, Ireland, no streak of dawning is in the sky.

(As he has been declaiming the crowd breaks up and passes to and fro as in the street. The gauze parts. Headlights of motor cars. A policeman with a white baton is directing the traffic, while behind him upon a pedestal stands Grattan with arm outstretched. He has the face of Major Sirr.)

SPEAKER *(now in the midst of the traffic)*. Men of Eire, awake to be blest! Do you hear? *(He fiercely accosts a Passer-by.)* Do you hear? Awake!

PASSER-BY *(politely disengaging himself)*. Sorry. The banks close at half two.[72]

SPEAKER. At the loud call of freedom why don't they awake? Come back! . . . Rise Arch of the Ocean . . . Let me be persuaded that my springing soul may meet the eagle on the hills . . . the hills . . . the hills . . . I say . . . *(He shouts.)* I say! Look here!

(The Stage Hand enters with the script.)

STAGE HAND. What's the trouble?

SPEAKER. The hills!

STAGE HAND. What hills?

SPEAKER. Yes, what hills? Where?

STAGE HAND. Where's which?

SPEAKER. Don't be so stupid. You know I must have them. The eagle on the . . .

STAGE HAND. Did the Artistic Director say you were to have hills?

SPEAKER. I don't know what you mean. I can't go on like this. This is not right.

STAGE HAND. Well it's the first I heard of it. Wait now till I get the place.

SPEAKER. Down from the high cliff the rivulet is teeming. Go away! Be off!

STAGE HAND. Where had you got to?

SPEAKER. Not very far. I was with Sarah. She was up there. I was talking to her.

STAGE HAND *(producing a dirty programme)*. Scene One. Wait now till I see. Who did you say you were?

SPEAKER. Robert Emmet. See there.

STAGE HAND. Oh is that you? I thought I rekernized the unyform.

SPEAKER. "The action of the play opens in the garden of 'The Priory,' the home of John Philpot Curran close to Rathfarnham." You see. This is not Rathfarnham.

STAGE HAND. No. I suppose not.

SPEAKER. I can't go on here. Can't you stop this noise?

STAGE HAND. Well you know I'd be glad to do all I can, but . . . well, you see, it's all very well telling me now.

SPEAKER. The air is rich and soft, the air is mild and bland, her woods are tall and straight, grove rising over grove . . .

STAGE HAND. Yes, I know, but I don't know what I can do. You should have told me sooner. You see the shops is all shut now . . .

SPEAKER. And Sarah . . . Sarah Curran is gone too. Clear all this away!

72. **half two** two thirty

STAGE HAND. Ay, you can't touch that! That's wanted for the dancing class.

SPEAKER. Stop them! My play! Rathfarnham!

STAGE HAND. Ah you know I'm doing my best for you. But as a matter of fact I have to be off now.

SPEAKER. Off where?

STAGE HAND. I'm due at my Irish class this half hour.

SPEAKER. And what am I to do?

STAGE HAND. Ah sure aren't you doing well enough. You're very particular all of a sudden.

SPEAKER. Come back, damn you!

STAGE HAND. Ah, they won't know the difference. It's good enough for that gang. Ta-ta now or I'll be late.

SPEAKER. Stop! You must tell me . . .

STAGE HAND. You'll get a Rathfarnham bus over there at the corner. Goodbye-ee!

(He goes.)

SPEAKER. Here! Oh my head! At the corner where? Rathfarnham.

BUS MAN. Rathfarnham bus. No. 17 Rathfarnham. Step along now please.

SPEAKER. Are you going to Rathfarnham?

BUS MAN. This bus's full. Full, I tell ya. You'll have to wait for the next.

SPEAKER. Nonsense . . . there's lots of room. See . . .

BUS MAN. The bus's full. D'ye want to get me into trouble? Let go the bar now there's room for no more here. There'll be another along behind.

SPEAKER. I tell you there's nobody there.

(Ding Ding Ding.)

BUS MAN. Fares please.

(And he moves off mysteriously.)

SPEAKER. There's nobody there! Liar! Cheat! You're all a lot of . . . a lot of . . . I shall speak to the stage manager about . . . *(His voice breaks.)* Oh my head! I wish I wasn't so tired. I wish I wasn't so terribly tired!

(He sinks down upon something in the centre of the stage. The passers-by thin out and the noise dies away, first into a low hum and then into complete silence. There is nobody left but the figure of Grattan and an old tattered Flower Woman in a black straw hat who sits crouching at the base of the pedestal.)

SPEAKER *(mumbling)*. My bed was the ground—my way the greenwood above, and the wealth I sought . . . I sought . . . the wealth . . . Oh, what is it!

GRATTAN. How long, O Lord, how long?[73]

73. **How long, O Lord, how long?** curtain line from Shaw's *Saint Joan*

(Pause.)

SPEAKER *(without looking round)*. What was that?

GRATTAN. This place stifles me. The thick, sententious atmosphere of this little hell of babbling torment! Sometimes the very breath seems to congeal in my throat and I can scarce keep from choking.

SPEAKER *(nodding gravely)*. I might have known it.

WOMAN. Penny a bunch th' violets.

GRATTAN. God forgive me, but it is hard sometimes. Very hard.

SPEAKER. All the same I will not allow this. It is the voice of Major Sirr. It is not my part.

GRATTAN. Your part? Ah yes! More play-acting. Go on, go on.

SPEAKER. I am Robert Emmet and I . . .

GRATTAN. A young man playing Robert Emmet! Yes, yes, they all come here.

SPEAKER. I am Robert Emmet. I have written my name in letters of fire across the page of history. I have unfurled the green flag . . .

GRATTAN. Letters of fire?

SPEAKER. Their graves are red but their souls . . .

GRATTAN. Ah yes, the graves are red . . . the grave of one poor helpless old man, the justest judge in Ireland . . . dragged from his coach by the mob and slaughtered in the road.

SPEAKER. Kilwarden!

GRATTAN. Kilwarden's grave is red.

SPEAKER. Who said that? I did my best to save him, but the people were mad . . .

GRATTAN. "Let no man perish in consequence of my death," he cried, as his lifeblood stained the cobbles crimson . . .

SPEAKER. . . . maddened by long centuries of oppression and injustice. I did my best to save him. What more could I do?

GRATTAN. "Let no man perish, save by the regular operation of the laws." And with that, pierced by a dozen patriot pikes, he died, at the feet of his gallant countrymen.

SPEAKER. It was horrible. But it was war.

GRATTAN. Eighty tattered turncocks from the Coombe[74]; a plumed hat, and a silver sword. War, for the liberation of Erin!

WOMAN. Me four bewtyful gre-in fields. Me four bewtyful gre-in fields.

SPEAKER. Men of Eire, awake to be blest!

GRATTAN. The full long years of my life I gave for her, with the harness weighing on my shoulders and my heart bleeding for my country's woes.

SPEAKER. Rise, Arch of the Ocean!

GRATTAN. Full fifty years I worked and waited, only to see my country's

74. the Coombe poor inner-city Dublin district

new-found glory melt away at the bidding of the omniscient young Messiahs with neither the ability to work nor the courage to wait.

SPEAKER. I have the courage to go on.

GRATTAN. Oh, it is an easy thing to draw a sword and raise a barricade. It saves working, it saves waiting. It saves everything but blood! And blood is the cheapest thing the good God has made.

WOMAN. Two apples a penny. Penny a bunch th' gre-in fields.

SPEAKER. Listen! Something is telling me that I must go on. I must march proudly through to the final act. Look! *(Pointing.)* The people are waiting for me, watching me.

GRATTAN. Fool, fool, strutting upon the stage! Go out, into the cold night air, before you crucify yourself in the blind folly of your eternal play-acting.

SPEAKER *(to the audience)*. He is an old man. He does not understand the way we do. He can only doubt . . . while we believe . . . believe with heart and soul and every fibre of our tired bodies. Therefore I am not afraid to go on. I will kiss my wounds in the last act. I will march proudly through, head high, even if it must be to my grave. That is the only test.

GRATTAN. Ah, the love of death, creeping like a mist at the heels of my countrymen! Death is the only art in which we own no masters. Death is the only voice that can be heard in this distressful land where no man's word is taken, no man's message heeded, no man's prayer answered except it be his epitaph. Out into every quarter of the globe we go, seeking for a service in which to die: saving the world by dying for a good cause just as readily as we will damn it utterly by dying for a bad one. It is all the same to us. It is the only thing that we can understand.

(The Woman laughs shortly and shrilly and breaks into a wheezy cough.)

SPEAKER. What is that woman doing here?

WOMAN. God bless ye, lovely gentleman, spare a copper for a cuppa tea. Spare a copper for yer owin old lady, for when th' trouble is on me I must be talkin' te me friends.[75]

GRATTAN. A copper, lovely gentleman, for your own old lady.

SPEAKER. Go away! There is something horrible about your voice.

GRATTAN.

> Young she is, and fair she is
> And would be crowned a Queen.

SPEAKER. What can I do in this place? I can't even remember my lines!

WOMAN. Yer lines, ducky. Ay Jack, pull them up on ye!

SPEAKER. I must go back to Rathfarnham. They will understand there.

---

75. **I must be talkin' te me friends** Cathleen Ni Houlihan's words from the Yeats play of that name (1902)

GRATTAN. A shadowy land has appeared.

SPEAKER. Sally!

GRATTAN.

> Men thought it a region of Sunshine and Rest,
> And they called it "Rathfarnham," the Land of the Blest.

SPEAKER. Oh if the will had wings, how fast I'd fly to the home of my heart!

GRATTAN. Poor weary footsore fool. And we are all the same, every one of us, whether we look to the foreigner for our sovereign or for our salvation. All of us fit to lead, and none of us fit to serve.

SPEAKER.

> If wishes were power, if words were spells,
> I'd be this hour where my true love dwells!

GRATTAN. Driven blindly on by the fury of our spurious moral courage! Is there to be no rest for Ireland from her soul? What monstrous blasphemy has she committed to be condemned to drift for ever like the wandering Jew[76] after a Heaven that can never be?

WOMAN *(crooning softly to herself)*.

> She's a darlin', she's a daisy,
> She has all the neighbours crazy,
> And she's arrums an' legs upon her like a man.
> But no matter where she goes,
> Sure everybody knows
> That she's Mick Magilligan's daughter, Mary Ann.[77]

GRATTAN. In my day Dublin was the second city of a mighty Empire. What is she now?

SPEAKER. No! No!

GRATTAN *(with unutterable scorn)*. Free!

(He bursts into a wild peal of laughter.)

SPEAKER. You are lying! It is the voice of Major Sirr! You are trying to torment me . . . torture me . . . Ghosts out of Hell, that's what you are.

(The figures are blotted out by black curtains which sweep across behind the Speaker, entrapping him in their folds.)

SPEAKER. But I'm not afraid! Heads up! One allegiance only! Robert Emmet is not afraid! I know what I want and I'm going on. *(Feverishly fumbling with the folds.)*

---

76. **wandering Jew** figure of the proverbial Jewish outcast   77. **Mary Ann** "Mick Magilligan's Daughter, Mary Ann," anonymous popular bawdy Irish song about a masculine girl

God save Ireland cried the heroes,[78]
God save Ireland cry we all,
Whether on the scaffold high—
Whether on the scaffold high
The scaffold high . . .!

Come out! Come out! Where are you? Oh, where am I? Come out! I . . . can't . . . remember . . . my lines . . .!
(An old blind man, tap-tapping with his stick, passes slowly across the stage, a mug outstretched and a fiddle under his arm.)
SPEAKER. If only I could get through. Where's the way through?
(A Flapper[79] and a Trinity Medical[80] appear.)
FLAPPER. No, I don't like the floor there, the Metropole's[81] much better. As for that Buttery basement[82] up and down and down and up Grafton Street.[83] Tea for two and two for tea on one enchanted evening in the Dewdrop Inn.[84] Do you like my nails this shade? Heart's Despair it's called.
MEDICAL. Play wing three for Monkstown.[85] Four caps[86] in the last couple of seasons. Pity they've put those glass doors in the Capitol boxes.[87]
FLAPPER. Brown Thomas[88] for panty-bras and Elizabeth Arden[89] to rebuild drooping tissues. Max Factor, Chanel Number Five[90] and Mum's the Word.[91] Has your car got a strap round the bonnet?[92]
MEDICAL. Well let's go up to Mother Mason's and hold hands. She needs decarbonizing probably. Botany Bay,[93] you can be sure. Number twenty-one is my number.
SPEAKER. Can I get through here?
FLAPPER. Brittas Bay[94] in a yellow M.G.
SPEAKER. I beg your pardon.
MEDICAL. Would you like a part in the Trinity Players?[95]
SPEAKER. What?
FLAPPER. Tennis at Fitzwilliam[96] all through the summer. We all go to

78. **God save Ireland cried the heroes** popular patriotic ballad by T. D. Sullivan (1827–1914) commemorating the "Manchester Martyrs" of 1867 79. **Flapper** fashionable young woman of the 1920s 80. **Trinity Medical** a student at Trinity College school of medicine 81. **Metropole** a dance hall in central Dublin 82. **Buttery basement** in Trinity College 83. **Grafton Street** Dublin's premier shopping street 84. **Dewdrop Inn** bar in Kimmage, Dublin suburb 85. **Monkstown** a Dublin rugby football team 86. **Four caps** played four times for the Irish rugby team 87. **Capitol boxes** to prevent missiles from being thrown down from the theatre boxes 88. **Brown Thomas** fashionable department store 89. **Elizabeth Arden** brand name cosmetic 90. **Max Factor, Chanel Number Five** brand name cosmetics 91. **Mum's the Word** it's a secret 92. **bonnet** hood 93. **Botany Bay** courtyard in Trinity College 94. **Brittas Bay** beach in Co. Wicklow, forty miles south of Dublin 95. **Trinity Players** dramatic society at Trinity College 96. **Tennis at Fitzwilliam** exclusive tennis club

Alexandra where the Lady Ardilaun[97] lectures on Gilbert and Sullivan[98] are quite indescribable. See you at the Carrickmines Mixed Singles.[99] The Aga Khan[100] is playing.

MEDICAL. Tyson's[101] ties tie tightly. Going to crew next week for Dr. Snufflebottom. Coming in left, Wanderers.[102] Use your feet![103]

BOTH *(singing as they disappear)*.

> Kitty she was witty, Kitty she was pretty.
> Down in the valley where they tried to pull her leg.
> One of the committee thought he would be witty,
> So he hit her on the titty with a hard boiled egg.

SPEAKER. What was that?

(A Well-Dressed Woman and a Businessman appear.)

WELL-DRESSED WOMAN. This is the way to the Ringsend Baby Club. Double three Clubs. You are requested to attend a meeting of the Peamount[104] After-care Committee. Ballsbridge,[105] at 11:30 a.m.

(She yawns loudly.)

BUSINESSMAN. Dame Street to Clarinda Park East Kingstown not Dun Laoghaire. Second National Loan Deferred Preference is now at thirty under proof. And only last Saturday I went round the Island in twenty-five and a bisque. Service not self I always say. Telegrams: "Stability" Dublin. Have you got a *Herald*?"[106]

SPEAKER. Please . . . please! Can't you tell me the way out of here?

WELL-DRESSED WOMAN. Cover the milk. Do keep the milk covered, there's a good man.

(Goes.)

BUSINESSMAN *(making a secret sign)*. Past Grand High Deacon for the Fitzwilliam Lodge.[107] Honorary Treasurer of the Sandycove and District Philatelic Society. House Committee, Royal St George.[108] Assistant District Commissioner, South County Dublin Boy Scouts. Achievement.

(Goes.)

(Two Young Things from somewhere up Phibsboro'[109] way appear.)

---

97. **Lady Ardilaun** prominent socialite and patron of the arts   98. **Gilbert and Sullivan** Sir W. S. Gilbert and Sir Arthur Sullivan who collaborated on the comic operas (1875–1896)   99. **Carrick-mine's Mixed Singles** tennis tournament   100. **Aga Khan** Sultan Sir Mohammed Shah, imam of the Nizari Muslim sect   101. **Tyson's** brand name   102. **Wanderers** Dublin rugby club   103. **Use your feet!** tactical advice   104. **Peamount** sanitorium   105. **Ballsbridge** south city district in Dublin   106. ***Herald*** Dublin afternoon daily   107. **Fitzwilliam Lodge** Masonic   108. **Royal St George** yacht club in Dun Laoghaire   109. ***Phibsboro'*** working-class district in the north city

CARMEL. Down at the Girls' Club a Parnell Square.[110] Janey Mac,[111] such gas[112] as we had!

BERNADETTE. Ah God, if I'd only a known! I couldn't get out a Tuesday. Were the fellas in?

CARMEL. They were. The Grocers' and Vintners' Assistants Association.[113] D'ye know?

BERNADETTE. An' I suppose you had the Wet Dreams to play?

CARMEL. We had. The Gorgeous Wrecks were on in the Banba Hall.[114] But listen. D'ye know the fella out a Cusack's a Dorset Street?

BERNADETTE. Is it that awful-lookin' iabeck with the red hair?

CARMEL. He ain't an awful lookin' iabeck, Bernadette, an' his hair's auburrin.

BERNADETTE. Yer taste's in yer mouth, duckie. Anyway . . . eyes off. He's walkin' out[115] with Sarah Morrissy for I seen them meself last Sunday week a-clickin'[116] on the Cab-ar-a Road.

CARMEL. Well wait now till I tell ya. He asked me for an A.P.[117] at the Depot next Sunday an' he said to bring a pal an' he'll get her a fella, will ye come?

BERNADETTE. Will I come? Te th' Depot?[118] Looka Carmel, I'll be there in me best Viyella.[119]

CARMEL. Looka I'm off up to meet him a half five a Doyle's.[120] He said th' Phib,[121] but I think he has one eye on the Courtin' Park[122] if I know that laddo. Do ye know?

BERNADETTE (*giggling*). Ah such gas! Sarah'll be wild when I tell her.

CARMEL. That one! You'd think she was someone.

SPEAKER (*politely*). I beg your pardon.

(*Bernadette nudges Carmel.*)

SPEAKER. Did I hear you mention Sarah?

BERNADETTE. There's a fella tryin' to click.

CARMEL. Where? What sort of a fella?

BERNADETTE. Behind you. A queer-lookin' skin.

SPEAKER. If you would be so good? I'd be very much obliged.

(*Carmel queries Bernadette with her eyebrows. The latter thinks not.*)

BERNADETTE. Give him the back of yer hand, Carmel. I'm not on.

SPEAKER. Could you tell me . . . ?

---

110. **Girls' Club a Parnell Square** central northside   111. **Janey Mac** euphemized expression of surprise   112. **gas** fun   113. **Grocers' and Vintners' Assistants Asociation** shop assistants' union   114. **Banba Hall** dancehall on Parnell Square   115. **walkin' out** courting   116. **a-clickin'** kissing   117. **A. P.** appointment, date   118. **Depot** Garda Síochána (Police) Headquarters, Phoenix Park, a favorite meeting place for lovers   119. **Viyella** popular brand-name dress   120. **Doyle's** a northside bar   121. **Phib** Phibsborough   122. **Courtin' Park** a small park in Phibsborough

CARMEL *(turning with great dignity)*. Chase yerself Jiggs or I'll call the Guards.

SPEAKER. Please don't misunderstand me. I only want to make an inquiry.

(The two girls look knowingly at one another.)

BERNADETTE *(in a hoarse whisper)*. One of the Foresters.

CARMEL. Aw yes, well ye didn't meet me in Bray[123] last summer. So goodbye-ee.

SPEAKER. In Bray? I said . . .

(Bernadette giggles hysterically.)

CARMEL *(to Bernadette)*. That's th' stuff to give th' trupes. Well, I'll have to be off now or I'll be late. He'll be wild as it is. So long love.

BERNADETTE. Corner a Prussia Street a Sunday?

CARMEL. Mind yer there a half seven. Ta-ta so.

SPEAKER. Listen . . . I must speak. I will not have this!

CARMEL. Egs-scuse me! But may I ask who you're addressin' in that tone a voice?

BERNADETTE *(fluttering)*. Ay—ay!

SPEAKER. I can't have this.

(He tries to restrain her with a hand.)

BERNADETTE. Ay, give us a hand someone!

CARMEL. Oh ye can't have this so ye can't, then listen to me, me Mountjoy Masher, ye'll have the flat of me fist across yer puss if ye can't conduct yerself when addressin' a lady, an' I'll thank ye to take that big slab from fingerin' me bawneen[124] before I have ye run in the way God knows ye ought to be pesterin' an' pursuin' a pair a decent girls in th' public thoroughfare!

SPEAKER. Stop! For God's sake!

BERNADETTE. Ay-ay! Help! Help!

CARMEL. It's not safe for a respectable woman to leave th' shadda of her own door, so it's not, for the dirty gowgers[125] that would be after them like . . . *(He tries to place his hand over her mouth. She bites him. Bernadette screams.)* Looka, I suppose you think yer face is yer fortune, but God knows at that rate some of us should be on the dole![126]

VOICES. Ay, what's up? What's the matter?

CARMEL. I declare to God I'd be ashamed of meself. A big lowsey[127] yuck[128] the like of you, why can't ye get a job a honest work and not be annoyin' young girls in th' street. It's lucky for your skin me fella's[129] on th' far side of the Tolka River[130] this minnit d'ye hear that now!

---

123. **Bray** seaside resort ten miles south of Dublin   124. **bawneen** woolen sweater   125. **gowgers** swindlers, cheats   126. **dole** receiving unemployment assistance   127. **lowsey** dirty   128. **yuck** lout   129. **me fella** my boyfriend   130. **Tolka River** on Dublin's north side

VOICES.

What did he do?

Is that him?

What's up?

Ay, can't ye leave the girl alone?

(Rows of heads, hatted and becapped. The Curtains part again, disclosing a street.)

BERNADETTE *(breathlessly)*. Laida—laid aholt of us he did . . . an' says he, didn't I meet you in Bray last summer? says he, didn't I meet you in Bray? . . . An' then he takes her by the arms and says he . . .

SPEAKER. I did nothing of the sort!

VOICES.

Hold that fella.

Disgusting.

Put him out.

SPEAKER. I was only asking the way.

CARMEL *(choking)*. Askin' th' way! Now d'ye hear that? . . . only askin' th—looka what sort of a brass neck has that one got at all!

BERNADETTE. Look at what wants to ask th' way!

VOICES *(raucously—laughing)*. To ask the way! "Will any lady show a gentleman how who doesn't know the way?"

AN OLDER MAN. Ay, see here now. You ought to know better at your age. You'd better leave the girls alone or maybe some of these days you'll be finding your way where you least expect. This is a decent country.

VOICES.

Still dear. No longer dirty.[131]

Keep to the right.

Does your mother know yer out?

SPEAKER.

> How shall I reach the land that I love?
> Through the way of the wind, the high hills above?
> Down by the blue wide ways of the sea?

(Pause.)

OLDER MAN. What's that?

CARMEL. God blessus, he's up the spout!

SPEAKER. That this unsparing storm should wreak its wrath . . .

OLDER MAN. Ay, give over. What's up with ye?

CARMEL. Well ye won't see me in his bewty chorus!

(General laughter.)

---

131. **dear . . . dirty** from the popular phrase, "dear, dirty Dublin" (Lady Morgan, *Memoirs*)

OLDER MAN. Be quiet youse! I'm lookin' after this. What's yer name?

SPEAKER. I am Robert Emmet.

A VOICE. Robert Emmet?

A VOICE. Who?

A VOICE. Any relation to Paddy Emmet of Clonakilty?[132]

OLDER MAN. Ssssh!

VOICES. Ssssh!

SPEAKER. I could explain it all in a moment if only you thought it worth while to give me a chance.

OLDER MAN. Oh if you're Robert Emmet you'll get every chance you want here. This is a free country. Is this true what you say?

SPEAKER. It is.

BERNADETTE. Well, d'ye hear that?

CARMEL. Who did he say?

BERNADETTE. Emmet. D'ye know. That fella.

A VOICE *(as fingers point)*. That's Robert Emmet.

VOICES.

Emmet.

Emmet.

That's him.

Ay, d'ye know.

OLDER MAN. If yer Robert Emmet it must be all right.

SPEAKER. Won't you let me explain?

OLDER MAN. You can speak yer mind here without fear or favour.

VOICES.

Nor sex, nor creed, nor class.

One for all and all for one.

Can laws forbid the blades of grass

From growing as they grow?

That's right.

A free country.

Up freedom!

SPEAKER. I knew it would be all right when I told you. And it will be so much better for all of us.

OLDER MAN. Let him have his way. I'll see that justice is done.

VOICES.

Without fear or favour.

That's right.

It's Robert Emmet.

Fair play for all.

Let him have his way.

132. **Clonakilty** in south Co. Cork

He's all right.
Be reasonable.
Justice.
Free speech.
All right. All right.
OLDER MAN (*fussing round as if putting everybody into their seats*). Sit down now all. Be easy. I'll look after this. I'll see you through. Leave it all to me now an' we'll fix it all up for you in half a jiffy. Isn't that right?
(*General clapping. The Older Man assumes an air of platform importance, coughs, and comes forward to address the audience.*)
OLDER MAN. Ladies and gents . . . we are very fortunate . . . in having with us tonight . . . one, who . . . I am sure . . . will need no introduction from me to a Dublin audience . . . His fair fame . . . his manly bearing . . . his zeal in the cause of the Gael[133] . . . his upright character . . . his un-bounded enthusiasm for the old cause . . . whatever it may or may not have been . . . his Christian charity . . . his wide experience . . . his inde-fatigable courage . . . his spotless reputation . . . and his kindness to the poor of the city . . . have made his name a household word wherever th' ole flag flies.
CARMEL (*shrilly*). Who wounded Maud McCutcheon?
OLDER MAN (*tolerantly*). Now, now, we mustn't touch on controversial matters . . . In introducing him to you this evening . . . I can say with confidence . . . that you will one and all listen to what he has to say . . . whatever it may be . . . and I am sure we are all looking forward to it very much indeed . . . with the greatest interest and with the deepest respect . . . The views which he has at heart . . . are also very near to the hearts of every one of us in this hall . . . and before calling upon him to address you I would just like to say that the committee will be glad to see any or all of you at the Central Branch Whist Drive in Ierne Hall[134] next Friday and the treasurer will be waiting in the passage as you pass out for those members who have not yet paid their subs. Ladies and gents, Mr.—er—er–
A VOICE. Emmet.
OLDER MAN. Mr. Robert Ellis.
(*Applause.*)
SPEAKER. Don't gape at me like that. It is you who are confused—not I. It is only in this place that I am mocked. But I will carry you away to where the spirit is triumphant . . . where the streets have no terrors and the darkness no babbling torment of voices . . . where all will be plain . . . clear and simple . . . as God's sky above, and the chains will fall from your

---

133. **Gael** Irish people   134. **Whist Drive in Ierne Hall** card tournament at a hall on Parnell Square

souls at the first sound of her voice from the lighted window. Which of you would not be free?

BERNADETTE. Up the Repubbelick!

SPEAKER. We know only one definition of freedom. It is Tone's[135] definition; it is Mitchell's[136] definition; it is Rossa's definition. Let no man blaspheme the cause that the dead generations of Ireland served, by giving it any other name and definition than their name and their definition. Life springs from death, and from the graves of patriot men and women spring living nations.[137] Men and women of Eire, who is with me?

VOICES.

Up Emmet!

We are with you! Up the Partisans!

Fuck a bal la! Emmet leads!

SPEAKER. But hark, a voice in thunder spake! I knew it. Slaves and dastards, stand aside!

VOICES *(with great waving of arms)*. Rathfarnham! Rathfarnham! *(Singing.)*

> Yes, Ireland shall be free
> From the centre to the sea,
> Then hurrah for Liberty!
>   Says the Shan Van Vocht.

(Terrific enthusiasm. A queue forms.)

OLDER MAN *(ringing a hand-bell)*. Line up, line up, ladies and gents. This way for Rathfarnham. All aboard for the Priory. Leaving An Lar[138] every three minutes. Plenty of room on top. No waiting. This way ladies and gents. Seats for Rathfarnham.

TWO TOUTS *(distributing handbills)*. Next bus leaves in ten minutes. All aboard for Tir-na-n'Og.[139] Special reduced return fares at single and a third. The Radio Train for Hy Brasail.[140] No waits. No stops. Courtesy, efficiency and punctuality. Joneses Road, Walsh Road, Philipsburg Avenue, Clontarf, Clonturk, Curran's Cross[141] and the New Jerusalem.

OLDER MAN. Now then, quietly, quietly please. There is room for one and all. Step this way please. All those in favour will say "Taw."[142]

> Put your troubles on the shelf.
> Country life restores the health.

135. **Tone** Wolfe Tone (1763–1798), United Irishman and father of Irish Republicanism   136. **Mitchell** John Mitchel (1815–1875) patriot and founder of the *United Irishman*   137. **We know . . . living nations** from Pearse's Oration at the Grave of O'Donovan Rossa (1915)   138. **An Lar** the center of Dublin City   139. **Tir-na-n'Og** the legendary Land of Youth   140. **Hy Brasail** legendary island off Ireland's west coast   141. **Joneses Road . . . Curran's Cross** a list of north Dublin and provincial places   142. **Taw** Yes (Ir.)

(Many gentlemen and ladies shake hands with the Speaker as they file past.)

TWO TOUTS. Schoolchildren, under twelve half price. Senior Citizens free. Uniformed social workers will meet young girls travelling alone. Special Whit facilities when not on strike. Penalty for improper use, five pounds.[143] Empyrean Express, Park in Paradise. Hearts' Desire Non-stop picks up and sets down passengers only at the white pole. Please do not spit in or on the conductor.

HANDSHAKERS.
Proud to meet you, sir.
Look us up any time you're in Sandymount.[144]
Jacobs Vobiscuits.[145]
The country is with you.
My! how you've grown!
Remember me to the boys.
D'ye vanta vuya vatch?
Magnificent, sir!
Would you sign a snap?
Have ye e'er a Green Stamp?

TWO TOUTS. Excursions for schools and colleges. Boy Scouts and Girl Guides in uniform admitted free. Tea and boiled eggs may be had from the conductor. Special comfort facilities on all vehicles, except when standing in the station.

(The queue queues. Presently the Speaker finds himself shaking hands with the old Flower Woman. There is silence).

WOMAN. Wait, me love, an' I'll be with ye.

SPEAKER. You!

WOMAN. I thought I heard th' noise I used to hear when me friends come to visit me.

> Oh, she doesn't paint nor powdher,
> An' her figger-is-all-her-owin.
> Hoopsie-daisie! The walk of a Quee-in![146]

SPEAKER. Hurry on please.

WOMAN *(patting him roguishly on the shoulder)*. Ah, conduct yerself. We're all friends here. Have ye nothing for me, lovely gentleman?

SPEAKER. What do you want?

WOMAN. It's not food or drink that I want. It's not silver that I want. Ochone.[147]

---

143. **Penalty for improper use, five pounds** sign posted below the emergency cord in a train   144. **Sandymount** Dublin city neighborhood   145. **Jacobs Vobiscuits** conflation of "Jacobs' Biscuits" (Dublin cookie manufacturer) and *Dominus vobiscum* ("The Lord be with you") from the Catholic Mass: from Joyce's *Ulysses*, 473   146. **The walk of a Quee-in!** curtain phrase from Yeats's *Cathleen Ni Houlihan*   147. **Ochone** Alas! (Ir.)

SPEAKER. I have no time to waste talking to you.

WOMAN. What is it he called it? . . . the cheapest thing the good God has made . . . eh? He-he-he. That's all. For your own old lady.

SPEAKER. I've nothing for you.

WOMAN. Gimme me rights . . . me rights first!

SPEAKER. Go away!

WOMAN. Me rights! Me rights first . . . or I'll bloody well burst ye!

VOICES. Get on! Get on!

WOMAN (*turning on the crowd*). Aw ye have a brave haste about ye. Ye have a grand wild spirit to be up an' somewheres, haven't ye! Ye'll be off to a betther land will yez? Ye will . . . in me eye!

VOICES.

Ah, dry up!

What's she talking about?

Up Emmet!

WOMAN. An' a nice lot of bowsy scuts youse are, God knows!

Emmet! He-he-he! Up Emmet! Let me tell youse that fella's not all he says he is!

VOICES. What's that? Not Emmet?

WOMAN. Look at him, ye gawms! Use yer eyes an' ask him for yourselves.

A VOICE. But the costume?

WOMAN. Five bob a day from Ging.[148]

(*She disappears into the crowd, whispering and pointing.*)

SPEAKER. My friends . . .

OLDER MAN. Is this true?

SPEAKER. My friends . . . we must go on . . . at once.

OLDER MAN. I asked you a question.

VOICES.

Look at him.

Well, what about it?

Perhaps she's right.

SPEAKER. We can wait no longer.

VOICES. Can't you answer the gentleman's question?

OLDER MAN. Are these charges true?

SPEAKER. What are you talking about?

YOUNGER MAN (*in a beret*). What's all this?

OLDER MAN. This chap says he's Robert Emmet.

SPEAKER. I am.

OLDER MAN. Oh, you are, are you?

SPEAKER. I am.

148. **Ging** theatrical suppliers

OLDER MAN. Well answer me this then. *What's happened to your boots?*
VOICES.
Ah-ha!
Look!
What about his boots?
  SPEAKER. My boots!
  OLDER MAN. He comes here an' says he's Robert Emmet, and where
are his boots?
  VOICES.
That's right.
Such an idea.
He's an impostor.
Throw him out!
  SPEAKER. I don't know . . . I thought they were . . . I see your point
. . . I . . .
  VOICES. Well?
  SPEAKER. Perhaps I had better explain . . . You see . . . someone took
them from me when I was playing Robert Emmet and . . .
  OLDER MAN *(with heavy sarcasm)*. Oh so you were *playing* Robert
Emmet? A play-actor are you? Some of this high-brow stuff I suppose?
  SPEAKER. Oh no, not at all.
  VOICES. High-brow! Ha!
  OLDER MAN. I suppose you consider yourself a member of the so-
called Intelligentsia? One of the Smart Set.
  SPEAKER. Me?
  VOICES. Smart Set! Ha! Ha!
  OLDER MAN. A self-appointed judge of good taste, eh?
  SPEAKER. I don't want to judge anything.
  VOICES. Good taste. Ha! Ha! Ha!
  OLDER MAN. You want to pose before the world as representative of
the Irish people? Eh?
  SPEAKER. I only want to . . .
  VOICES. Representative. Ha! Ha! Ha! Ha!
  OLDER MAN. Tell me *(suddenly)* how much do you get for this?
  SPEAKER. That's none of your business!
  VOICES.
A job! A job!
He does it for a job!
He's related to someone!
And has a job!
  OLDER MAN. Honest friends and anti-jobbers! This so-called leader,
this self-appointed instructor of the Irish people, is owney linin' his pockets
at the expense of the poor. His downy couch, debauched with luxury is

watered with the sweat of the humble. A traitor's pillory in the hearts of his countrymen would be a proper reward for such an abattoir of licentiousness.

SPEAKER *(assuming a Parnellesque[149] attitude)*. Who is the master of this party?

OLDER MAN. Who is the mistress[150] of this party?

SPEAKER. Until the party deposes me I am leader.

A VOICE. You are not our leader. You are a dirty trickster.

A VOICE. Committee Room Fifteen!

SPEAKER. So you won't follow me any longer?

VOICES. No!

SPEAKER *(after a pause)*. Very well. I shall just have to go on by myself.

OLDER MAN. Oh no you don't. You're not going out of this.

SPEAKER. Who's going to stop me?

OLDER MAN. We are. You're not going to be allowed to hold up this country to disgrace and ridicule in the eyes of the world. Throwing mud and dirt at the Irish people.

VOICE. Give him a taste of backwoodsman's law.

SPEAKER *(to Younger Man)*. Tell him to get out of my way. You won't allow this.

YOUNGER MAN. It's nothing to do with me. The army has no interest in civilian affairs. All the same I don't like to see my country insulted by indecent plays.

OLDER MAN. That's right.

YOUNGER MAN. A high-spirited race resents being held up to scorn before the world, and it shows its resentment *(He takes out a revolver and hands it to the Older Man.)* in various ways. But as I say it has nothing to do with me.

(He walks away.)

OLDER MAN *(with revolver)*. Take off that uniform.

SPEAKER. Put up that revolver. I warn you, I am serious.

(He stretches out his hand and gently takes it from him. The crowd slowly closes in upon him with sheeplike heedlessness.)

SPEAKER. Stand back or I will have to shoot. I warn you I won't be interfered with, I am going on at all costs.

VOICES. Traitor. Spy. Cheat. Cur.

SPEAKER *(hidden in their midst)*. Back! Back! Slaves and dastards, stand aside! Back! Back! or I'll . . .

(The revolver emits a dull pop. The crowd melts away to the side and he is

149. **Parnellesque** of dignified command, after the manner of Charles Stewart Parnell (1846–1891), political leader   150. **mistress** reference to Kitty O'Shea, Parnell's mistress, a scandalous relationship

disclosed standing there alone with the smoking weapon still clenched in his fist. There is a deathlike silence.)

A VOICE. Oh, my God!

OLDER MAN *(very quietly)*. Now you've done it.

SPEAKER. Done what?

OLDER MAN. You've plugged somebody.

A VOICE. Oh, my God! My God!

SPEAKER. I've what?

A MAN *(looking out)*. It's Joe.

SECOND MAN. Joe?

FIRST MAN. He's got it in the breast.

YOUNGER MAN *(reappearing)*. Who fired that shot?

OLDER MAN. Joe's got it. Right through the left lung. He can't last long.

SECOND MAN. Christ!

FIRST MAN. It wasn't any of us, Tom. It was this chap.

SPEAKER. Stand back, stand back, I tell you. I'm fighting. This is war.

YOUNGER MAN *(quite unperturbed)*. There's a man out there. You've put a bullet through his breast.

OLDER MAN. God rest his soul!

SPEAKER. I warned you—I warned you all.

YOUNGER MAN. He's going to die. You did it. That's what comes of having guns.

VOICES.

He's going to die.

You did it.

You did it.

SPEAKER. I had to. It wasn't my gun.

(Two men appear bearing between them the body of another. The people take off their hats and stand mutely with bowed heads.)

JOE. It's welling out over me shirt, boys . . . Can't anybody stop . . . it?

YOUNGER MAN. A good man . . . a true man . . . That is what you did.

OLDER MAN. That is what he did.

VOICES.

You did.

He did.

Robert Emmet did.

Who did it?

He did it.

He there.

SPEAKER. I had to . . . *(All hands point.)*

JOE. Give me . . . me beads . . . before the life . . . has ebbed out of me . . . I can't breathe . . . oh, lads, I'm going . . .

SPEAKER. What could I do? I ask you, what could I do? It was war. I didn't mean to hurt him.

OLDER MAN. Joe, old scout. We're sorry . . . we're . . . O God!

JOE. God bless you boys . . . sure I know . . . I know well . . . it wasn't any of . . . you . . .

SPEAKER (*flinging down the revolver*). Shoot back then! It is war. Shoot! I can die too!

YOUNGER MAN. Will that give him back the warm blood you have stolen from him?

OLDER MAN. Ah, leave him alone, Tom, leave him alone.

VOICES (*whispering*).

Leave him alone.

He shot Joe.

Through the breast.

Poor Joe.

Leave him alone.

JOE (*as he is carried off, followed by the crowd*). O my God . . . I am heartily . . . sorry . . . for having offended . . . Thee . . . and . . . I . . .[151]

VOICES (*chanting*).

> Lacrymosa dies illa
> Qua resurget ex favilla
> Judicandus homo reus.
> Huic ergo parce Deus;
> Pie Jesu Domine
> Dona eis requiem
>   Amen.[152]

FLOWER WOMAN (*appearing in the shadows, but speaking with the voice of Sarah Curran*).

> Do not make a great keening
> When the graves have been dug tomorrow.
> Do not call the white-scarfed riders
> To the burying . . .

(*Hoarsely*). Ay misther—spare a copper for a cuppa tea—spare a copper for a poor old lady—a cuppa tea— (*Whisper.*) a copper for your own ole lady, lovely gentleman.

---

151. **O my God . . . and . . . I . . .** Act of perfect contrition from the Catholic prayerbook 152. **Dona eis requiem/Amen** conclusion of the hymn for the dead, the *Dies Irae*

(She fades away.)
SPEAKER. Sally! Sally!—where are you?—where are you? Sally!

THE CURTAIN FALLS

PART 2

Through the Curtain, amidst a hearty round of applause, comes the Minister's talented daughter, Maeve. She has on a nice white dress with a white bow to match in her long, loose, black hair which reaches quite to her waist. Around her neck on a simple gold chain hangs a religious medal. She curtsies in charming embarrassment and commences to recite.

MAEVE.[153]

>   Kingth Bweakfatht.[154]
>   The King athed de Queen
>   And de Queen athed de Dar-med
>   Could—I *(a little breathlessly)*—se—butter
>   For-de-roy——————thlaice—a—bwead?
>   Queen athed de Dar-med
>   De Dar-med thed Thertinley
>   Ah goan tell—Cow now
>   For he goeth tebed . . .

(She continues this amusing piece to the very end, when the Curtain parts amid general applause disclosing a fantastically respectable drawing-room loud with the clatter of tea things. A party is in progress under the aegis of the Minister for Arts and Crafts and his nice little Wife. The guests consist of one of the Redcoats, now a General in a green uniform, the Statue of Grattan, rather a nice woman called Lady Trimmer—one of those people whose expression of pleased expectancy never for a moment varies, the old Flower Woman who is seated unobtrusively in the background eating an orange, and a small but enthusiastic Chorus. Side by side upon the sofa reading from right to left are O'Cooney[155] the well-known dramatist, O'Mooney[156] the rising portrait painter, and O'Rooney[157] the famous novelist. O'Cooney wears a cloth cap, blue sweater and a tweed coat. O'Mooney has a red shirt and horn-rimmed spectacles, while O'Rooney is dressed in full saffron kilt together with Russian boots. The Minister himself bears a strange resemblance to the Stage Hand. It is all very nice indeed.)

153. **MAEVE** named after the mythological queen of Connacht   154. **Kingth Bweakfath** "King's Breakfast" by A. A. Milne (1882–1956)   155. **O'Cooney** based on Sean O'Casey   156. **O'Mooney** based on portrait artist Patrick Touhy   157. **O'Rooney** based on novelist Liam O'Flaherty (1896–1984)

CHORUS.

Oh very nice nice

Oh very nice nice nice

    How old how nice how very nice don't you think so

    Oh yes indeed yes very nice indeed I do think so indeed don't you indeed.

(Teaspoons clink.)

LADY TRIMMER. What was that one, my dear?

MAEVE. Kingth Bweakfatht pleathe.

LADY TRIMMER. Very nice indeed, Maeve. I must teach that one to my two chicks. Where do you learn, my dear?

MAEVE. The Banba Thcool of Acting, Lower Abbey Thweet.

CHORUS. The Banba School of Acting, Lower Abbey Street.

O'COONEY. Wasn't that bloody awful?

O'MOONEY. The question is, is she an aartist? A real aartist?

O'ROONEY. O'Mooney sounds better with his mouth shut.

WIFE. Of course, she hasn't been learning very long. But she has the language,[158] and that's half the battle these days. Show them, Maeve.

MAEVE. *Caed mile failte.*[159]

LADY TRIMMER. Oh very good indeed. But of course, she has her father's talent.

MINISTER. Ah, well, now . . .

WIFE *(pleased)*. Oh, Lady Trimmer!

MINISTER. Well, now, all the same I don't know about that. But mind you I do say this, Talent is what the country wants. Politics may be all O.K. in their way, but what I say to *An Taoischach*[160] is this, until we have Talent and Art in the country we have no National Dignity. We must have Talent and Art. Isn't that right?

CHORUS. We must have Art have Talent and Art.

LADY TRIMMER. Quite. And cultivated people of taste. You musn't forget them, Mr. Minister. Art cannot live you know by taking in its own washing—if I may put it that way.

O'COONEY. Aw Holy God!

O'MOONEY *(ruminatively)*. The reel aartist must be fundamental. Like Beethoven. Now, *I'm* fundamental.

O'ROONEY. Fundament, all right.

MINISTER. Now see here. I'm Minister for Arts and Crafts, you see. Well, a young fellow comes along to me and he says, Now look, Liam, here's some Art I'm after doing . . . it might be a book you see, or a

158. **the language** Irish Gaelic, the official language of the Irish Free State
159. *Caed mile failte* One hundred thousand welcomes (correctly *Céad,* Ir.): a cliché 160. *An Taoischach* the Prime Minister (correctly *Taoiseach,* Ir., "Chieftain")

drawing, or even a poem . . . and can you do anything for me, he says? Well, with that, I do . . . if he deserves it, mind you, only if he deserves it, under Section 15 of the Deserving Artists' (Support) Act, No. 65 of 1926. And there's none of this favouritism at all.

CHORUS. The State supports the Artist.

GRATTAN. And the Artist supports the State.

CHORUS. Very satisfactory for everybody and no favouritism at all.

MINISTER *(confidentially)*. And of course, then you see, it helps us to keep an eye on the sort of stuff that's turned out, you understand.

CHORUS. Clean and pure Art for clean and pure people.

LADY TRIMMER. What we need most is a small Salon.[161]

GENERAL. That's right. A small Art Saloon.

WIFE. We often have people in on Sunday evenings for music and things. Won't you sing something now, General?

GENERAL. Aw, I have no voice at all.

O'COONEY. He's bloody well right there.

O'MOONEY. The question is . . . Is he fundamental?

LADY TRIMMER. Just somewhere where the nicest people . . . the people one wants to meet . . . like Mr. O'Cooney and Mr. O'Mooney . . .

O'ROONEY *(suspiciously)*. And Mr. O'Rooney.

LADY TRIMMER. *And* Mr. O'Rooney, can get together quietly and discuss Art and common interests.

WIFE. Haven't you brought your music?

CHORUS. You must have brought your music.

GENERAL. Well now . . . if you insist. Maybe I might find something.

O'COONEY *(to O'Mooney)*. Ay, have *you* put my cap somewhere?

WIFE. Do, General.

GENERAL. I don't know for sure, mind you. I might . . . just happen to have something on me.

(He produces a roll of music from inside his tunic.)

CHORUS. The General's going to sing.

GENERAL. Ah, but . . . sure there's no one to play th' accompanyment.

WIFE. Maeve will play. Won't you, darling?

MAEVE. Yeth mammy.

(Signs of distress from the sofa.)

WIFE. Of course you will dear. Give her the music, General.

CHORUS. Sssh!

(The General gives her the music rather doubtfully and they are opening the performance, when there comes a loud, peremptory knock at the door. General surprise.)

WIFE *(bravely but apprehensively)*. What can that be?

161. **Salon** a meeting room for artists and intellectuals

LADY TRIMMER. Strange!

MINISTER. A knock at the door?

GENERAL. Ah now, isn't that too bad!

CARMEL *(entering)*. There's a gentleman at the door, ma'am, looking for the Rathfarnham bus.

WIFE. What kind of a gentleman, Carmel?

CARMEL. A gentleman in a uniform, ma'am.

MINISTER. A uniform? Tell me, does he look like the start of a Daring Outrage?

CHORUS. Possibly the Garda Síothchána.[162]

CARMEL. He has a sword, sir.

MINISTER. A sword?

CARMEL *(primly)*. And a pair of slippers.

WIFE. Slippers?

GENERAL. I don't think I know that unyform.

CHORUS. Can't be the Garda Síothchána after all.

WIFE. Did he give any name, Carmel?

CARMEL. Yes, ma'am. A Mr. Emmet.

LADY TRIMMER. Not *the* Mr. Emmet?

CARMEL. I don't know I'm sure, ma'am.

MINISTER. Ah, yes I remember. That's him all right.

GENERAL. Aw, the hard Emmet.

MINISTER. The old Scout.

WIFE. The gentleman who is far from the land. Show him up at once, Carmel.

CARMEL. Yes, ma'am. *(She goes, muttering.)* Doesn't look like a sailor to me.

LADY TRIMMER. How nice of him to call.

WIFE. Yes, indeed, but you know we can't be too careful since the Trouble.

MINISTER. Emmet's all right. I know him well. Used to work with him in the old days.

GENERAL. Aw, the rare old Emmet.

LADY TRIMMER. You know I've wanted to meet him for such a long time. My husband always says that we of the old regime ought to get in touch with those sort of people as much as possible. We can assist each other in so many ways.

MINISTER. That's right. We must all get together for the good of the country.

WIFE. I wonder has he brought his music too?

GRATTAN. I expect he has.

---

162. **Garda Síothchána** policeman "Guardian of the Peace"

(Carmel enters, cocking her head contemptuously towards the Speaker, who follows her with a strange, hunted look in his eye. He glances round apprehensively as though prepared for the worst and yet hoping against hope.)

CHORUS. Oh how do you how do you how do you how do you how . . .

WIFE. How do you do? Bring another cup, Carmel.

CARMEL. Yes, ma'am. *(She goes, muttering.)* I'll have to wash one first.

SPEAKER. Excuse . . . me.

WIFE. Come and sit down and let me introduce you to everybody. It was so nice of you to call. Liam has just been speaking about your work.

SPEAKER. I only came in to ask . . .

CHORUS. Have you brought your music?

WIFE. This is Lady Trimmer, Mr. Emmet.

CHORUS. Of the old regime.

LADY TRIMMER. Dee do.

SPEAKER *(after peering closely into her face)*. No, ah, no.

LADY TRIMMER. You must come and visit us too, Mr. Emmet. First Fridays.[163] Now promise.

WIFE. And General O'Gowna of the *Oglaigh na h-Eireann*.[164]

GENERAL *(affably)*. And many of them.

SPEAKER. It was you who hit me.

WIFE. And of course you know my husband, the Minister for Arts and Crafts.

CHORUS. Vote *Fianna na Poblacht*.[165]

MINISTER. *A chara*.[166]

(The Speaker tries to remonstrate but is hurried on.)

WIFE. And Mr. Grattan's statue from College Green.

GRATTAN. Welcome Don Quixote Alighieri. Did I speak the truth?

(The Speaker's head goes up.)

WIFE. And this is Mr. O'Cooney, the great dramatist.

SPEAKER. Cap?

WIFE. Oh, Mr. O'Cooney always wears his cap in the drawing-room.

O'COONEY. And why the bloody hell shouldn't I wear my cap in the drawing-room?

(General laughter.)

SPEAKER. I see.

O'MOONEY. Now me.

WIFE. This is Mr. O'Mooney, the artist, if you can remember everybody.

163. **First Fridays** when her salon meets   164. *Oglaigh na h-Eireann* Irish Volunteers founded in 1913 by Eoin MacNeill   165. *Fianna na Poblacht* "Warriors of the Republic." *Fianna Fáil* ("The Warriors of Destiny"), the Republican party, was founded in 1926.   166. *A chara* "Dear Friend": conventional formal address

O'MOONEY. The reel Aartist.

O'COONEY. The owl cod.

WIFE. Oh, please, Mr. O'Cooney!

CHORUS. I love the way he talks, don't you?

O'MOONEY. Oh, don't mind O'Cooney. He's a great friend of mine, really.

O'COONEY. He is not!

WIFE. And this is Mr. O'Rooney, the well-known novelist. Now I think you know everybody.

SPEAKER *(indicating the costume)*. You play the pipes?

(O'Mooney laughs shrilly.)

O'ROONEY. I do not. I do not believe in political Nationalism. Do you not see my Russian boots?

WIFE. Mr. O'Rooney believes in the workers.

O'ROONEY. I do not believe in the workers. Nor do I believe in the Upper Classes nor in the Bourgeoisie. It should be perfectly clear by now what I do not believe in, unless you wish me to go over it again?

LADY TRIMMER *(archly)*. Mr. O'Rooney, you dreadful man!

SPEAKER. I'm sorry.

WIFE. Sit down now and have a nice cup of tea.

(Carmel meanwhile has been back with a dirty cup.)

CHORUS. I do like a nice cup of tea.

SPEAKER. So she is here, too!

WIFE. What's that?

SPEAKER. That damned old flower woman who turned them all against me!

WOMAN. Ay, mister, have ye e'er an old hempen rope[167] for a neckcloth?

WIFE. You're joking, Mr. Emmet. There's no old flower woman.

SPEAKER. I mean . . . look there.

WIFE. Have some tea, Mr. Emmet. You're a little tired, no doubt.

SEMICHORUS. Delightful drink.

SEMICHORUS. Pity it tans the stomach.

WIFE. You'll feel much the better of it. And we'll have a little music afterwards. We often have music in the evenings.

MINISTER. Are you interested in Art, Mr. Emmet?

LADY TRIMMER. I suppose you're a member of the Nine Arts Club?

WIFE. And the Royal Automobile Academy?

CHORUS. Celebrity Concerts. The Literary Literaries.

SPEAKER. I don't feel very . . . Did you say that statue of Grattan was there?

WIFE. Oh yes, that's Mr. Grattan's statue from College Green. We

167. **hempen rope** hangman's noose

always have a few of the nicest statues in on Sunday evening. My husband is Minister for Arts and Crafts, you know.

LADY TRIMMER. Just to form a little group you know. A few people of taste.

WIFE. Of course we're only amateurs, but we're doing our best.

(Pause.)

SPEAKER *(suddenly)*. Let me be persuaded that my springing soul may meet the . . .

(Pause.)

LADY TRIMMER. I beg your pardon?

SPEAKER. Let me be per— *(He shakes his head hopelessly.)* I am Robert Emmet.

GRATTAN. You are not.

SPEAKER. Who are you to question me?

GRATTAN. You are only a play-actor.

SPEAKER. Look well to your own soul, Major Sirr!

GRATTAN. Have you found your Holy Curran, Galahad?[168]

WIFE. I always say to Liam, Liam you really *must* get a proper statue of Mr. Emmet. It's positively disgraceful that we haven't got a good one, don't you think?

MINISTER. Ah, well, dear, you know, expense, expense.

LADY TRIMMER. What a nice uniform! Tell me, do you admire the plays of Chekhov?[169]

WIFE. Perhaps he acts for the Civil Service Dramatics.[170]

SPEAKER. Act? . . . No. No cake, thank you.

CHORUS. Benevente Strindberg Toller Euripides Pirandello Tolstoy Calderon O'Neill.[171]

LADY TRIMMER. I'm sure you'd be good.

CHORUS. An annual subscription of one guinea admits a member to all productions and to all At Homes.[172]

MINISTER *(confidentially)*. Say the word and I'll get you into the Rathmines and Rathmines. I know the man below.

LADY TRIMMER. Now do tell us, Mr. Emmet, about your wonderful experiences in the Trouble.[173]

(The Speaker spills his tea and looks around wild-eyed.)

SPEAKER. What do you mean?

GRATTAN. Ah—ha!

WIFE. Never mind. It's quite all right. I'll pour you out another cup.

---

168. **your Holy Curran, Galahad** cf. Sir Galahad and the Holy Grail 169. **Chekhov** Anton Chekhov (1860–1904), Russian dramatist 170. **Civil Service Dramatics** amateur theater group 171. **Benevente . . . O'Neill** renowned dramatists 172. **At Homes** social gatherings 173. **Trouble** euphemism for armed insurrection

LADY TRIMMER (*hastily*). You must have had such interesting times all through the fighting.

SPEAKER. I shall never fight again!

(*He buries his face in his hands.*)

MINISTER. Oh come, Mr. Emmet! What's the matter?

WIFE. Are you not feeling well?

LADY TRIMMER (*aside*). Ssssh! Don't pay any attention. I understand. Do tell us about it, Mr. Emmet. Talk. Talk someone.

SPEAKER. God have pity on me.

CHORUS. Oh the fighting everyone talk don't pay any attention wonderful experiences those were the attention fighting days how wonderful do tell us about the fighting days interesting and wonderful.

SPEAKER. It was I who shot him and you all know it! You all know! Isn't it enough for you? Haven't I suffered enough?

CHORUS (*louder*). Oh tuttut poor man don't talk do talk as hard as you can fighting wonderful pay no attention shellshock probably to have seen it all wonderful is he better yet poor man everybody pretend not to fighting notice.

SPEAKER. They trapped me! A good man . . . a true man . . . and I did it!

WIFE. Well what if you did shoot somebody? Everybody's shot somebody nowadays. That'll soon be over.

LADY TRIMMER. Yes, yes; of course we didn't approve of it at the time, but it's all so interesting now.

SPEAKER. Interesting!

CHORUS. Perhaps we had better how is he change the subject change the subject getting on what's the wonderful experiences matter with him matter with him at all?

WIFE. How about a little song?

CHORUS. How about a little little song song song?

WIFE. Do you sing, Mr. Emmet?

SPEAKER. What do you all want with me?

LADY TRIMMER. Nothing, nothing at all, Mr. Emmet. Perhaps you'd like to act us a little snippet from your play?

WIFE. We often have plays on Sunday evenings. Poor man. There, there. We are all friends here.

LADY TRIMMER. The General has just obliged us.

GENERAL. I have not. I was interrupted before I got going.

WIFE. You're better now, I'm sure. Of course you are. Aren't you?

MINISTER. Well, I believe in supporting Art and acting's Art. So you have *my* consent anyhow.

WIFE. You'll act something for us, Mr. Emmet, won't you?

GRATTAN. Ah, leave him alone. Can't you see he's beaten.

SPEAKER. That voice! That voice!

GRATTAN. I said that you were beaten. You should have taken my advice from the first; but you would go on with your play-acting. Now, perhaps you know better. Rathfarnham! Ha! Sarah Curran! Ha-ha-ha!

SPEAKER *(slowly rising)*. I am not beaten. I still believe. I will go on.

CHORUS. Oh good, he's going to do something for us.

WIFE. Oh do, Mr. Emmet.

GENERAL. But look here . . .

GRATTAN. Don't be a fool. Do you imagine that they'll listen to you if you do?

MINISTER. Nothing political. That's barred of course.

O'COONEY. For God's sake make it short anyhow.

O'MOONEY. Nothing Iberian. There's no Iberian real Art.

O'ROONEY. See that it's not pompous. That would be an insult to the people of this country.

GENERAL. Hey, what about my song?

GRATTAN. Go on. Tell them all to go to hell.

SPEAKER. Please, please . . . if you want me to do it . . .

CHORUS. Oh yes yes, do Mr. Emmet.

Minister. I suppose it will be all right. I wouldn't like anything by somebody with the slave mind, you know.

SPEAKER. Nobody can object to my play.

MINISTER. Or calculated to excite you-know-what.

CHORUS. Emmet's play is all right.

GENERAL. Well you needn't expect me to sit down quietly under this sort of behaviour. When you ask a man to sing . . .

SPEAKER *(advancing towards the audience)*. It's very hard without Sally. It may seem a little strange here . . . but I'll do it.

GRATTAN. Very well. Have it your own way.

LADY TRIMMER. Did I hear him mention somebody called . . . er, Sally Somebody?

WIFE *(confidentially)*. I think it must be his young lady.

LADY TRIMMER. How charming.

GENERAL *(determinedly)*. One of Moore's Melodies entitled "She is Far from the Land."

(He bows.)

O'COONEY. Aw, this'll be bloody awful. *(Settles down.)* D'ye remember that night, Liam, when the two of us hid in the chimbley from the Tans?[174]

MINISTER. Will I ever forget it? Ah, those were the days, Seamus.

SPEAKER. I had got to the part where I am arrested, hadn't I? No. I think I was . . .

174. **Tans** the Black and Tans were a military force auxiliary to the police during the Irish War of Independence

WIFE. We always have music and things on Sunday evenings.

LADY TRIMMER. Just a nucleus. A few nice people.

GENERAL *(to Maeve)*. Have you got the place?

MAEVE. Mammy.

WIFE. Yes, dear?

MAEVE. Why ith that man wearing hith thlipperth in the dwawing woom?

WIFE. Hush, dear, you mustn't ask questions. You must be a good girl.

MAEVE *(plaintively)*. You never let me—

GENERAL. Ah, go on when I tell you!

(Maeve commences the introduction to "She is Far from the Land.")

SPEAKER.

> The air is rich and soft—the air is mild and bland.
> Her woods are tall and straight, grove rising over grove.
> Trees flourish in her glens below and on her heights above,
> Oh, the fair hills of Eire, oh.

O'ROONEY. Will you move up on the sofa and breathe into yourself.

O'MOONEY. We'd be better off if your hips were as soft as your head.

(Simultaneously.)

SPEAKER.	GENERAL *(singing)*.
Down from the high cliffs the rivulet is teeming	She is far from the land where her young hero sleeps
To wind around the willow banks that lure me from above;	And lovers around her are sighing:
Ah, where the woodbines with sleepy arms have wound me.	But coldly she turns from their gaze and weeps
	For her heart in his grave is lying.

MINISTER *(solo)*. And do you remember the day, Seamus, of the big round-up in Moore Street[175] when the "G" man[176] tried to plug me getting out of the skylight?

SPEAKER, GENERAL, *and* O'COONEY *(simultaneously)*.

SPEAKER *(louder)*.	GENERAL.
But there is lightning in my blood; red lightning tightening in my blood. Oh! if there was a sword in every Irish hand! If there was a flame in every Irish heart to put an	She sings the wild songs of her dear native plains, Every note which he loved awaking.

175. **Moore Street** central Dublin street, scene of fighting during the 1916 Rising   176. **"G" man** British government agent

end to slavery and shame! Oh, I would end these things!

Ah! little they think, who delight in her strains,
How the heart of the ministrel is breaking.

O'COONEY. Aw, Jesus, and the evenings down in the old I.R.B.[177] in Talbot Street, picking out the "Soldiers' Song"[178] on the blackboard.

SPEAKER, MINISTER, *and* GENERAL *(simultaneously)*.

I have written my name in letters of fire across the page of history. I have unfurled the green flag in the streets and cried aloud from the high places to the people of the Five Kingdoms: Men of Eire, awake to be blest! to be blest!

He had lived for his love, for his country he died,
They were all that to life had entwined him;
Nor soon shall the tears of his country be dried,
Nor long will his love stay behind him.

MINISTER. Sometimes I wish I was back again on the run with the old flying column[179] out by the Glen of Aherlow.[180]

(O'Mooney and O'Rooney join in in low undertones.)

O'ROONEY.

My good woman, I said, I'll tell you what's wrong with you. Virginity, my good woman, that's all. And believe me, its nothing to be proud of.

O'MOONEY.

Saint Peetric d'ye see because Saint Peter was the rock[181] and Saint Patrick was the seed. That makes Saint Peetric, d'ye see. For the rock is underneath and the seed lies above, so Saint Peter and Saint Patrick are Saint Peetric.

(At the same time.)

O'COONEY. And that night waiting up on the North Circular[182] for word of the executions. Ah, not for all the wealth of the world would I give up the maddenin' minglin' memories of the past . . .

SPEAKER.

Rise, Arch of the Ocean and Queen of the West! I have dared all for Ireland, I will dare all again for Sarah Curran. Their graves are red. O make her a maddening mingling glorious morrow . . .

GENERAL.

O! make her a grave where the sunbeams rest
When they promise a glorious morrow . . .

177. **the old I.R.B.** the Irish Republican Brotherhood, a revolutionary organization (1858–1924)   178. **"Soldiers' Song"** Ireland's national anthem   179. **flying column** small, mobile units of I.R.A. volunteers   180. **Glen of Aherlow** in Co. Wicklow   181. **Saint Peter was the Rock** . . . Matt. 16: 18   182. **North Circular** road in north Dublin city

(The black curtain closes behind the Speaker, blotting out the room, and the voices fade away. The Speaker himself has somehow chimed in upon the last few lines of the song, and is left singing it by himself.)

SPEAKER.

> They'll shine o'er her sleep like a smile from the west,
> From her own loved island of sorrow . . .

(The Blind Man comes tap-tapping with a fiddle under his arm and a tin mug in his hand. He bumps lightly into the Speaker.)

BLIND MAN *(feeling with his stick)*. Peek-a-boo! Peek-a-boo!

SPEAKER. Damn your eyes!

BLIND MAN *(looking up)*. That's right.

SPEAKER. You're . . . blind?

BLIND MAN *(with a chuckle)*. That's what they say.

SPEAKER. I didn't know. I didn't mean to hurt you.

BLIND MAN. Ah, not at all. I'm not so easily hurted.[183] *(Feeling him over.)* Oh, a grand man. A grand man. A grand man surely, from the feel of his coat.

SPEAKER. Do you know where I am?

BLIND MAN. Well, isn't that a rare notion now! Asking the way of an old dark fiddler, and him tip-tappin' over the cold sets day in and day out with never sight nor sign of the blessed sun above.

SPEAKER. I give it up.

BLIND MAN. And where might you be bound for, stranger?

SPEAKER. The Priory.

BLIND MAN *(with a start)*. Ah, so! So you're bound for them parts, are you, stranger dear?

SPEAKER. Yes.

BLIND MAN. Up the glen maybe as far as the edge of the white mist, and it hanging soft around the stones of Mount Venus, eh stranger? He-he-he!

SPEAKER. That's right.

BLIND MAN. Oh, I know you. I know you. Sure all the Queer Ones of the twelve counties[184] do be trysting around them hills beyond the Priory.

SPEAKER. The blessed hills!

BLIND MAN. It's sad I am, stranger, for my light words of greeting and the two of us meeting for the first time. Take my arm now, and walk with me for a while and I'll put you on your way. Come—take my arm!

---

183. **I'm not so easy hurted** . . . the Blind Man's language is a parody of the "sing-song" of J. M. Synge   184. **all the Queer Ones of the twelve counties** all the loose women of Leinster, Ireland's eastern province

Why should you not take my arm, stranger, for I'm telling you, my fathers are Kings in Thomond[185] so they are.

SPEAKER *(taking his arm gingerly)*. There.

BLIND MAN. That's better now. He-he-he. 'Tis proud I am to be walking arm in arm with the likes of you, stranger. Tell me now, or am I wrong? Would you by any chance be Mr. Robert Emmet?

SPEAKER. You know me?

BLIND MAN. Uh! I thought I recognized them words I heard you singing.

SPEAKER. Yes. I am Robert Emmet. He said that I wasn't. But I am. It was the voice of Major Sirr.

BLIND MAN. Ah, poor Bob Emmet. He died for Ireland. God rest his soul.

SPEAKER. He died. I died?

BLIND MAN. You did indeed. You remember the old song we used to sing?

(They sit down together.)

SPEAKER. You mean "The Struggle is Over."[186]

BLIND MAN. That's right. Ah, the rare old lilt of it. How does it go, now? *(He sings.)*

> The struggle is over, our boys are defeated,
> 　　And Erin surrounded with silence and gloom.
> We were betrayed and shamefully treated
> 　　And I, Robert Emmet, awaiting my doom.
> Hanged, drawn and quartered, sure that was my sentence,
> 　　But soon I will show them, no coward am I.
> My crime was the love of the land I was born in.
> 　　A hero I've lived and a hero I'll die.

BOTH.

> Bold Robert Emmet, the darling of Erin,
> Bold Robert Emmet will die with a smile.
> Farewell companions, both loyal and daring,
> I'll lay down my life for the Emerald Isle.

(Pause. From somewhere comes faint dance music.)

BLIND MAN. Ah, them are the songs. Them are the songs.

SPEAKER. He died for Ireland. I died. I?

BLIND MAN. High Kings in Thomond, my fathers are. Lords of the Gael. You'll know them stranger.

SPEAKER. How can I have died for Ireland? What is that I hear?

185. **Thomond** kingdom of the O'Briens, present-day Co. Clare　186. 'The **Struggle is Over'** "Bold Robert Emmet," song by Tom Maguire (1870–?)

BLIND MAN. Ah, never mind that. That's nothing. Nothing at all.

(A young man in evening dress and a pretty girl are walking out of the darkness into the edge of the light. It is the Trinity Medical and his friend, now a little older. They are smoking and laughing together.)

SPEAKER. Go away.

BLIND MAN. Never heed them stranger. That's nobody at all.

SPEAKER. And I am dead this hundred years and more?

BLIND MAN. What would the likes of you have to do with the likes of them? He-he-he.

HE. I remember when I was a kid in Clyde Road[187] how wonderful I thought a private dance was.

SHE. Now I suppose you've quite grown out of us all.

HE *(laughing)*. Oh, well, I wouldn't say that. But of course when one's lived abroad things do seem a little different, when you come back.

SHE. I suppose so.

HE. Small in a way and rather provincial. But that's to be expected.

SPEAKER. I wonder is Sally dead too?

BLIND MAN. Dust to dust and ashes to ashes.

HE. Of course, there have been a lot of improvements. But over there . . . well, after all, it takes over an hour and a half to get into the country.

SHE. And you like that?

HE. Well, you know how it is. It makes one feel one's sort of *in* the world. Everything seems more serious, somehow.

SHE. While we and the old days never seemed serious at all.

HE. Oh well, I didn't quite mean it that way.

SPEAKER. O God help me!

BLIND MAN. Coming and going on the mailboat. And they thinking themselves the real ones—the strong ones! I do have to laugh sometimes and I hearing the wings of the Queer Ones beating under the arch of the sky.

HE. Of course I liked the old days. We had some jolly good times together, didn't we?

SHE. I liked them too.

HE. I was crazy about you.

SHE. My eye and Betty Martin.[188]

HE. I was. I was, really. I often think about it all. It's a bit lonely sometimes over there, and often— Oh, I don't know. Do you ever think about me?

SHE. Sometimes.

HE. I hope you do. You know, Daphne, sometimes I wonder whether you and I oughtn't to have . . .

187. **Clyde Road** residential street in the south city   188. **My eye and Betty Martin** Nonsense!

SHE. Have what?

HE. I think we ought to have . . . maybe we still could . . .

(The music stops. There is a pause.)

HE. Hello. The music's stopped.

SHE. Yes. I suppose it has.

HE. Like to go in and have a drink?

SHE. I think we might as well.

HE *(briskly)*. Funny, you know, how the old place can get you for a bit. But after all, one can't get away from the fact that it's all so damned depressing— *(They vanish.)*

SPEAKER. O God, make speed to save us! I cannot tell what things are real and what are not!

BLIND MAN. Oh, but it is not myself that is dark at all, but them— blind and drunk with the brave sight of their own eyes. For why would they care that the winds is cold and the beds is hard and the sewers do be stinking and steaming under the stone sets of the streets, when they can see a bit of a rag floating in the wild wind, and they dancing their bloody Ceilidhes[189] over the lip of Hell! Oh, I have my own way of seeing surely. It takes a dark man to see the will-o'-the-wisps and the ghosts of the dead and the half dead and them that will never die while they can find lazy, idle hearts ready to keep their venom warm.

SPEAKER *(up)*. Out of the depths I have cried to Thee, O Lord: Lord, hear my voice![190]

BLIND MAN. In every dusty corner lurks the living word of some dead poet, and it waiting for to trap and to snare them. This is no City of the Living: but of the Dark and the Dead!

SPEAKER. I am mad—mad—mad! Sally!

(During his speech the stage darkens until both figures are blotted out and the Speaker is left groping in the dark.)

SARAH'S VOICE. Robert! Robert!

SPEAKER. What was that?

SARAH'S VOICE *(singing)*.

> She stretched forth her arms,
> Her mantle she flung to the wind,
> And swam o'er Loch Leane
> Her outlawed lover to find . . .

SPEAKER. Sally! Sally! Where are you?

SARAH'S VOICE. Why don't you come to me, Robert? I have been waiting for you so long.

---

189. **Ceilidhes** Irish dances (*céilí*, an evening musical entertainment)   190. **Out of the depths . . . voice!** Psalm 128: 1

SPEAKER. I have been searching for you so long.

SARAH'S VOICE. I thought you had forgotten me.

SPEAKER. Forgotten you! Forgotten you, Sally! Is that your hand, dear?
A cuisle geal mo chroidhe[191]— 'Tis you shall have a silver throne—Her sunny
mouth dimples with hope and joy: her dewy eyes are full of pity. It is you,
Sally—Deirdre[192] is mine: she is my Queen, and no man now can rob me!

*(The lights go up. He is in the dingy room of a tenement house. The plaster
is peeling off the walls. On a bed in the corner a young man with the face of
Joe is lying with an expression of serene contentment upon his pale, drawn
features. Two men—the Older and the Younger Man—are playing cards at a
table opposite, upon which stands a bottle with a candle perched rakishly in the
neck. The Speaker himself is affectionately clasping the arm of the old Flower
Woman. When he sees her he bursts into hysterical laughter.)*

WOMAN. Ah, me lovely gentleman, is it me yer calling?

SPEAKER. Well done! Well done! The joke is on me! Well done!

WOMAN. The Lord love ye, an' how's the poor head?

SPEAKER. Robert Emmet knows when the joke is on him! Kiss me,
lovely Sarah Curran!

WOMAN *(archly)*. Ah, go on owa that! D'jever hear the like!

OLDER MAN *(looking up from his game)*. Drunk.

YOUNGER MAN. Aw, disgustin'.

WOMAN. Sit down now. Ah, go along with ye! Sit down now there,
an' take no heed a them ignerant yucks . . . an' I'll get ye a small drop.

SPEAKER. My lovely Sarah Curran! Sweet Sally!

WOMAN *(aside to the Older Man)*. Ye bloody rip! I'll twist the tongue
of ye, that's what I will.

SPEAKER. Her sunny mouth dimples with hope and joy.

YOUNGER MAN. Ho, yes, you'll do the hell of a lot, ma . . . in me eye!

WOMAN. Don't heed them. Don't heed them at all mister. He's no son
of mine that has ne'er a soft word in his heart for th' old mudher that
reared him in sickness and in sorra te be a heart-scaldin' affliction an' a
theef a honest names.

OLDER MAN. Now ye can say what ye like, but there's a Man! There's
a Man! Drunk, an' it's hours after closin'! Drunk, an' in th' old green coat!
(Singing.) Oh, wrap the green flag round me, boys.[193]

SPEAKER *(joins in.)* Ta-ra-ra-ra-ra-ra, Ra! Ra!

WOMAN. Sure, he's not drunk are ye, gentleman, an' if he was itself
it's none a your concern. *(To Speaker.)* Isn't that right, son?

OLDER MAN. And why the hell shouldn't he be drunk? Tell me that.

---

191. *A cuisle geal mo chroidhe* "Bright pulse of my heart" (correctly: *chuisle,*
Ir.)   192. **Deirdre** fatal beauty of the Celtic Tale of the Sons of Uisneach
193. **Wrap the green flag round me, boys** patriotic song by J. K. O'Reilly

We're a Free State,[194] aren't we? Keep open the pubs. That's my motto. What man says we're not a Free State?

YOUNGER MAN. I say it, ye drunken bastard!

OLDER MAN. Drunken bastard . . . hell! I declare to God I'm sober'n you are, me bold, water-drinkin' Diehard.[195] God knows I'm cold an odd time, but sure a true Patriot is always drunk.

YOUNGER MAN. Have you no love for Ireland?

SPEAKER. God save Ireland!

OLDER MAN. Ho yes—"The Republic still lives."[196] Aw—go te hell!

YOUNGER MAN. I've been to hell all right, never fear. I went down into hell shouting "Up the living Republic," and I came up out of hell still shouting "Up the living Republic." Do you hear me? Up the Republic!

SPEAKER. Up the Priory!

OLDER MAN. Oh, I hear you well enough. But you'll not convince me for all your bridge blasting. Looka here, I stand for the status q-oh, and I'll not be intimidated by the gun.

WOMAN *(handing the Speaker a precious black bottle)*. Here, have another sup and never heed that old chat of them!

SPEAKER. A health, Sarah Curran! A toast to the woman with brave sons!

WOMAN. Aw God . . . If I was young again!

YOUNGER MAN. And who needs to convince you?

OLDER MAN. Oh, you needn't think . . .

YOUNGER MAN. Every day and every night while you were lying on your back snoring, wasn't I out in the streets shouting "Up the living Republic"?

OLDER MAN. Ah, don't we remember that too well.

SPEAKER. Up the living Departed!

YOUNGER MAN. Every morning and every night while you were sitting in the old snug, wasn't I out on the hills shouting "Up the living Republic"?

SPEAKER. Up the pole![197]

OLDER MAN. Well?

YOUNGER MAN. Every hour of the day that you spent filling your belly and gassing about your status q-oh, wasn't I crying "Republic, Republic, Republic"?

OLDER MAN. May God give ye a titther a sense some day.[198]

---

194. **Free State** the Irish Free State was established in 1922   195. **water-drinkin' Diehard** puritanical republican who rejected the Anglo-Irish Treaty of 1921   196. **"The Republic still lives"** slogan of the anti-treaty republicans   197. **Up the pole!** Mad!   198. **a titther a sense** curtain phrase in Act I of Sean O'Casey's *The Plough and the Stars* (1926)

SPEAKER. Up the blood-red Phlegethon! Up Cocytus,[199] frozen lake of Hell!

OLDER MAN *(turning for a moment)*. Aw, wouldn't that languidge disgust ye!

YOUNGER MAN. So one day, me laddo, you woke up and found that the Republic did live after all. And would you like to know why?

OLDER MAN. "Tell me not in mournful numbers" . . .

YOUNGER MAN. Just because I and my like had said so, and said so again, while you were too drunk and too lazy and too thick in the head to say anything at all. That's why. And then, with the rest of your kidney you hunched your shoulders, spat on your hands, and went back to your bed mumbling "Up the Status q-oh." So why the hell should I try to convince you?

SPEAKER. A long speech. A strong speech. A toast to the son that speaks. A toast to the son that swills!

OLDER MAN. Aw, that's all words. Nothing but bloody words. You can't change the world by words.

YOUNGER MAN. That's where you fool yourself! What other way can you change it? I tell you, we can make this country—this world—whatever we want it to be by saying so, and saying so again. I tell you it is the knowledge of this that is the genius and glory of the Gael!

SPEAKER. Up the Primum Mobile![200] Up the graters of verdigreece. Up the Apes Pater Noster.

JOE.

> Cupping the crystal jewel-drops
> Girdling the singing of the silver stream . . .
> *(He tries to scribble on the wall.)*
>
> What was it? . . . the singing of the silver stream.
> Damp acid-cups of meadowsweet . . .

SPEAKER. Hello! There's the fellow I shot. Is he not gone yet? A toast to the son that dies!

WOMAN. Ay . . . are ye lookin' for a bit of sport tonight?

SPEAKER. I have had brave sport this night!

WOMAN. Aw, mister . . . have a heart!

SPEAKER *(flaring up)*. A heart!

(Joe gives a short, contented laugh.)

SPEAKER. Do not do that. That is not the way to laugh.

YOUNGER MAN. I tell you, what the likes of me are saying tonight, the likes of you will be saying tomorrow.

199. **Phlegethon . . . Cocytus** mythic rivers surrounding Hades   200. **Primum Mobile!** "The First Mover"

OLDER MAN. Is that a fact? And may I be so bold as to in-quire what awtority you have for makin' that observation?

YOUNGER MAN. Because we're the lads that make the world.

OLDER MAN. You don't say!

SPEAKER (*passionately*). Then why have you made it as it is? Then will you stand before the Throne and justify your handiwork? Then will you answer to me for what I am?

YOUNGER MAN. What are *you* talking about? You're only a bloody play-actor. If you were a man and not satisfied with the state of things, you'd alter them for yourself.

OLDER MAN (*holding out a bottle*). Aw, have a sup and dry up for God's sake!

(*Joe laughs again.*)

SPEAKER. That blasphemous laugh! Do you not know you're going to die?

JOE (*laughing again*).

> Soft radiance of the shy new moon
> Above the green gold cap of Kilmashogue
> Where . . .

SPEAKER. Kilmashogue!

JOE.

> Where of a summer's evening I have danced
> A saraband.

SPEAKER. What of Kilmashogue? Look around you. Here! Don't you know me? I shot you.

JOE. Well, please don't interrupt. (*He coughs.*)

WOMAN. It's the cough that shivers ye, isn't it, son? Me poor lamb, will ye tell the gentleman . . . (*She goes as if to touch him.*)

JOE (*through his teeth*). Strumpet! Strumpet!

WOMAN. Blast ye! ye'd use that word t'yer own mudher, would ye! God, I'll throttle ye with me own two hands for the dirty scut ye are!

SPEAKER. Go back!

YOUNGER MAN (*seizing her from behind and flinging her away*). Away to hell, ye old trollop!

OLDER MAN. Ah, leave her alone.

WOMAN. Awlright, awlright! Yer all agin me. But it won't be th' cough will have th' stiffenin' of him not if I lay me hands on his dirty puss before he's gone. When I get a holt a ye I'll leave me mark on ye never fear.

YOUNGER MAN. Aw, shut yer mouth, ma!

JOE. I'd like to do it all again . . . That's right . . . Again . . . It's good . . . to feel the wind . . . in your hair . . .

(He laughs weakly.)

SPEAKER. Don't! Don't do that I tell you!

JOE.

> Stench of the nut-brown clay
> Piled high around the headstones and the yews,
> My fingers clotted with the crusted clay,
> My heart is singing . . . in the skies . . .

(He coughs again. The Blind Fiddler enters slowly through the door.)

OLDER MAN. You know, some of that stuff is very hard to follow. I'd sooner have the old stuff any day.

> "Oh I met with Napper Tandy[201]
> An' he took me by the hand."

SPEAKER. Sssssh!

YOUNGER MAN. What do you want here?

BLIND MAN. Wouldn't I have a right to pay my respects to one, and he passin' into the ranks of the Government? Isn't it a comely thing for me to be hopin' that he'll remember a poor old dark man an' he sittin' in the seats of the mighty in his kingdom out beyond?

JOE *(very soft)*. Well . . . so long, lads. It was . . . a grand life . . . so long, lad . . . that plugged me . . . So long . . . *(He dies.)*

WOMAN. Burn ye! Burn ye!

BLIND MAN. Be silent now, and a new shadow after being born! Do you not know, woman, that this land belongs not to them that are on it, but to them that are under it.

YOUNGER MAN. He's gone. Stiffening already, poor chap. Hats off, lads.

SPEAKER. Gone! And I am only a play-actor—unless I dare to contradict the dead! Must I do that?

BLIND MAN. Let them build their capitols on Leinster Lawn.[202] Let them march their green battalions out by the Park Gate.[203] Out by Glasnevin[204] there's a rattle of bones and a bit of a laugh where the presidents and senators of Ireland are dancing hand in hand, with no one to see them but meself an' I with the stick an' the fiddle under me arm.

OLDER MAN. Well . . . a wake's[205] a wake, anyhow. So pass over the bottle and give us a tune on the ole instrument.

BLIND MAN *(tuning up)*. It's many's the year an' I fiddled at a wake.

---

201. **Napper Tandy** political ballad, "The Wearin' of the Green"   202. **Leinster Lawn** site of Irish Free State *Dáil* (Parliament)   203. **Park Gate** of Dublin's Phoenix Park   204. **Glasnevin** Dublin's largest cemetery   205. **wake** traditional ritual celebration the night before a funeral

WOMAN. One son with th' divil in hell, an' two more with th' divils on earth. *(She spits.)* God forgive me for weanin' a brood a sorry scuts!

(The Speaker is seated silently at the foot of the bed, staring at the body with his back to the audience. There is a knock at the door.)

WOMAN. Wha's that?

(The Younger Man goes to the door, pauses, and flings it open. On the threshold stands Maeve.)

MAEVE. My mammy thez . . .

WOMAN. Ah love, is it yerself?

MAEVE. My mammy thez I'm to play the accompaniment of "The Thruggle Ith Over."

WOMAN. Come on in, duckie. God love ye an' welcome. The ole pianner's waiting for ye, love.

MAEVE. Yeth pleathe. My mammy . . .

(She comes in and, catching sight of the Speaker, she points, and bursts into tears.)

WOMAN. There, there! What's the matter, lamb? Ah God help her! What ails ye at all?

MAEVE *(gulping)*. Thlipperth . . .

WOMAN. There, there now . . .

OLDER MAN. Aw, will ye dry up?

WOMAN *(with an impatient flap of the hand)*. There's the pianner, so do what yer mammy says before I slaughter ye.

BLIND MAN. Play on now, young one. And when you've played, 'tis meself will fiddle for the shadows and they dancing at the wake.

MAEVE *(sniffling)*. My mammy thez . . .

(Maeve sits at an old cracked piano, upon which presently she commences to thump out carefully "The Struggle Is Over.")

WOMAN. There now. Ah God, hasn't she the gorgus touch on th' ole instrument!

(Another knock at the door. The Younger Man opens it. The Minister for Arts and Crafts is on the threshold in top hat, frock coat, and carrying one of those hemispherical glass cases full of white flowers.)

MINISTER. Deep concern—Government grieved to learn—struck down in prime—Requieum Mass[206]—life for Erin—send a gunboat[207]—bitter loss—token of our regard. *(He presents the case.)*

WOMAN *(very unctuous)*. Ah, aren't ye the kind-hearted Government, and isn't them th' gorgus flowers. God will reward ye, sir; He will indeed at the next election, for th' blessed pity ye've shown to a poor woman in her sorra.

---

206. **Requiem Mass** Catholic ceremony for the dead   207. **send a gunboat** for a ceremonial escort

(Another knock at the door. The Younger Man opens it. Lady Trimmer, dressed in widow's weeds, enters.)

LADY TRIMMER. So sad! So sad indeed! I can't simply say how sad it is. Quite a poet, too, I hear. Can any of his books be purchased?

WOMAN. At Hodges an' Figgis[208] ma'am. Be sure ye get the name right. Come in, come in!

(Before the Younger Man has the door properly closed there comes another knock. He abandons it, leaving it open. The Statue of Grattan is on the threshold.)

GRATTAN. A word-spinner dying gracefully, with a cliché on his lips. The symbol of Ireland's genius. Never mind. He passed on magnificently. He knew how to do that.

WOMAN *(her head quite turned)*. An' he was me favrit', too lady ... never a bitter word ... never a hard glance. Sure, it's them we love th' best is took th' first, God help us. Ullagone! Ullagone! Ochone-a-ree!

(Enter the General with crape upon his arm.)

GENERAL. ....a grand song called "Home to Our Mountains."[209] No. 17 bus passes the door or a bus to Ballyboden,[210] whenever the road's not up.[211] But of course if you don't want me to sing, I won't force myself on you. Won't I?

WOMAN.

> Low lie your heads this day
> My sons! My sons!
> The strong in their pride go by me
> Saying, "Where are thy sons?"

(O'Cooney, O'Mooney and O'Rooney enter, all in black gloves and top hats.)

ALL THREE. Who's a twister? I'm a twister? You're a twister? He's taken a header into the Land of Youth. Anyhow, he was a damn sight better man than some I could name, and there's no blottin' it out.

LADY TRIMMER. So yellow-haired Donough is dead! Dear, dear!

(A few more stray figures crush in, chattering and pressing forward in file before the body.)

WOMAN.

> Gall to our heart! Oh, gall to our heart!
> Ullagone! Ochone-a-ree!
> A lost dream to us now in our home!

MAEVE *(stopping her playing)*. Will that do, Daddy?

208. **Hodges an' Figgis** literary bookseller   209. **"Home to Our Mountains"** song by Charles Jeffreys   210. **Ballyboden** in South Co. Dublin   211. **up** under repair

BLIND MAN *(mounting upon a chair)*. The shadows are gathering, gathering. They're coming to dance at a wake. An' I playin' for them on the gut box.[212] Are yez ready all?

(He tunes up. The lights in front have dimmed, leaving a great sheet of brightness flooding from the sides upon the back-cloth. The walls of the room seem to fade apart while the crowd draws aside and seats itself upon the floor and upon all sides of the stage. The Speaker has vanished.)

THE VOICES OF THE CROWD. The Shadows are gathering, gathering: he says they must dance at a wake. Seats for the Shadows the gathering Shadows . . . The Shadows that dance at a wake.

(The Blind Man commences to fiddle a jig in the whole-tone scale.)

THE VOICES.
Overture started
Seats for the Shadows
Gathering, gathering
Dance at a wake
Loosen his collar
Basin of water
Dance Shadows
Oooooooh!

(Upon the back-cloth two great Shadows appear gesturing and posturing in time with the music.)

THE FIRST SHADOW *(stopping his dance and striking an attitude)*.

> Come clear of the nets of wrong and right;
> Laugh, heart, again in the grey twilight,
> Sigh, heart, again in the dew of the morn.
> Your Mother Eire is always young . . .[213]

(Hand clapping. The Second Shadow jostles the First aside and points one long arm vaguely in the direction of the Flower Woman.)

THE SECOND SHADOW. Stone traps of dead builders. Warrens of weasel rats! How serene does she now arise! Queen among the Pleiades, in the penultimate antelucan hour: shod in sandals of bright gold: coifed with a veil of gossamer.[214]

(Applause. Amidst shrieks of laughter the Flower Woman rises, curtsies and dances hilariously once round the foreground. Two more Shadows have elbowed the first pair aside and are now dancing to the music.)

THE VOICES.
Dance! Dance!
Speak, Shadows, speak!

212. **gut box** fiddle   213. **Come clear . . . young** W. B. Yeats, "Into the Twilight"   214. **How serene . . . gossamer** James Joyce, *Ulysses,* 414

THE THIRD SHADOW. It is difficult not to be unjust to what one loves. Is not He who made misery wiser than thou?[215]

(Applause, mingled with some booing. The Third Shadow throws up its arms and flees.)

THE FOURTH SHADOW. Every dream is a prophecy: every jest an earnest in the womb of time.[216]

(Shouts of laughter and applause. The Shadows change into a tumbling mass of blackness.)

THE VOICES.

Dance! Dance!

Speak, Shadows, speak!

A VOICE. There are no Shadows left to speak.

BLIND MAN. Speak, great Shadow! Shadow of Ireland's Heart.

VOICES *(whispering)*. We see him. He is here.

(The shadow of the Speaker precedes him as he comes slowly in from the back.)

BLIND MAN. Speak, shadow of Robert Emmet.

SPEAKER. I know whom you are calling. I am ready.

BLIND MAN. The eyes of the people are fixed on your face.

VOICES. Justify! Justify! Shadow of the Speaker, speak!

VOICES. Sssh!

SPEAKER. The souls in the seven circles of Purgatory cry out, Deliver us O Lord from the mouth of the Lion[217] that Hell may not swallow us up. The Word Made Flesh shall break the chains that bind me. Three armies may be robbed of their leader—no wretch can be robbed of his will.

Yes, there is darkness now, but I can create light. I can separate the waters of the deep, and a new world will be born out of the void. A challenge, Norns! A gage flung down before you! Justify! Justify!

VOICES. Justify! Justify!

(The Speaker continues to address the audience.)

SPEAKER *(continues)*. Race of men with dogs' heads! Panniers filled with tripes and guts! Thelemites! Cenobites! Flimflams of the law! Away! while Niobe[218] still weeps over her dead children. I have heard the angels chanting the Beatitudes to the souls in Malebolge, and I have done with you.

I do not fear to approach the Omnipotent Judge to answer for the conduct of my short life and am I to stand appalled here before this mere remnant of mortality? I do not imagine that Your Lordships will give credit to what I utter. I have no hopes that I can anchor my character in

215. **It is difficult ... thou?** Oscar Wilde, "De Profundis"   216. **Every dream ... time** G. B. Shaw, *John Bull's Other Island*   217. **mouth of the Lion ...** Cf. Peter I, 5: 8   218. **Niobe** mythological daughter of Tantalus

the breast of this court. I only wish Your Lordships may suffer it to float down your memories until it has found some more hospitable harbour to shelter it.

(Voices, shuffling, applause.)

SPEAKER *(continues)*. For now is the axe put to the root of the tree. My fan is in my hand, and I will burn the chaff with unquenchable fire.

VOICES.

Up Emmet!

Up Rathfarnham!

Up the Up that won't be Down!

(He draws his sword and turns upon them all. During the following commination the Voices give the responses in unison and the Figures in turn fling up their arms and take flight before him. The light fades, gradually blotting out all vestiges of the room.)

SPEAKER. Cursed be he who values the life above the dream.

VOICES. Amen.

SPEAKER. Cursed be he who builds but does not destroy.

VOICES. Amen.

SPEAKER. Cursed be he who honours the wisdom of the wise.

VOICES. Amen.

SPEAKER. Cursed be the ear that heeds the prayer of the dead.

VOICES. Amen.

SPEAKER. Cursed be the eye that sees the heart of a foe.

VOICES. Amen.

SPEAKER. Cursed be prayers that plough not, praises that reap not, joys that laugh not, sorrows that weep not.

VOICES *(dying away)*. Amen. Amen. Ah—men.[219]

(The last of the Figures fling up their arms and vanish. As the Speaker comes down stage they come creeping back again, crouching in the darkness and watching him with many eyes. It is dark.)

SPEAKER. I will take this earth in both my hands and batter it into the semblance of my heart's desire! See, there by the trees is reared the gable of the house where sleeps my dear one. Under my feet the grass is growing, soft and subtle, in the evening dew. The cool, clean wind is blowing down from Killakee, kissing my hair and dancing with the flowers that fill the garden all around me. And Sarah . . . Sarah Curran . . . you are there . . . waiting for Robert Emmet.

I know this garden well for I have called it into being with the Credo of the Invincibles:[220] I believe in the might of Creation, the majesty of the Will, the resurrection of the Word, and Birth Everlasting.

219. **Cursed be . . . Ah—men** parody of the Anglican Ash Wednesday Commination Service   220. **Invincibles** terrorist group responsible for the assassination of Lord Frederick Cavendish and Thomas Burke in the Phoenix Park in 1882

(He flings aside his sword and looks around him in triumph. It is very dark, so dark that for all we know perhaps it may be the garden of the first scene. Perhaps those may be the trees and the mountains beyond the Priory. For a moment we hear the tramp of feet and the distant sound of the Shan Van Vocht. His voice falters and he staggers wearily.)

SPEAKER. My ministry is now ended. Shall we sit down together for a while?[221] Here on the hillside . . . where we can look down over the city, and watch the lights twinkle and wink to each other . . . Our city . . . our willful, wicked old city . . .

(The gauze curtains close slowly behind him.)

I think . . . I would like to sleep . . . What? . . . On your shoulder? . . . Ah, I was so right to go on!

(His head sinks drowsily and his eyes stare out into the auditorium. He is lying just where the Doctor left him some time ago.)

> Strumpet city in the sunset
> Suckling the bastard brats of Scots, of Englishry, or Huguenot.
> Brave sons breaking from the womb, wild sons fleeing from
>   their Mother.
> Wilful city of savage dreamers,
> So old, so sick with memories!
> Old Mother
> Some they say are damned,
> But you, I know, will walk the streets of Paradise
> Head high, and unashamed.

(His eyes close. He speaks very softly.)

There now. Let my epitaph be written.

(There is silence for a moment and then the Doctor speaks off.)

DOCTOR. . . .do, fine.

(He appears bearing a large and gaudy rug. He looks towards the audience, places one finger to his lips, and makes a sign for the front curtains to be drawn. When last we see him he is covering the unconscious Speaker with his rug. That is the end of this play.)

Bloomsbury, 1926–Dalkey, 1976

221. **Shall we sit down together for a while?** Cf. Matt. 26: 36

AUSTIN CLARKE
1896 – 1974

Austin (Augustine Joseph) Clarke was born into a middle-class Catholic family in Dublin on May 9, 1896. His father, whom he described as generous and easy-going, was an official of the Dublin Corporation; his mother, a woman of "obstinacy, . . . coldness and reserve" (which Clarke felt he shared), had such dogmatic religious convictions that she burnt some "heretical books" he acquired during his university studies. When he was seven, Clarke was sent to Belvedere College, the Jesuit school whose visions of hellfire Joyce later presented so vividly in *A Portrait of the Artist As a Young Man*. He went on to study with Douglas Hyde and Thomas MacDonagh at University College Dublin, where he immersed himself in Irish language and culture and began to read (and to meet) the major figures of the Irish literary renaissance; also at this time he began to attend the Abbey Theatre's productions and saw most of Yeats's plays.

In 1916 and 1917 Clarke received his B.A. and M.A. with first class honors in English, and was launched on his literary career (which he signaled by wearing an extravagant green and gold bow tie, in imitation of Yeats's black one) with the acclaimed publication of his first long poem, *The Vengeance of Fionn* (1917). He was appointed Assistant Lecturer in English at U.C.D. to replace Thomas MacDonagh, who had been executed for his part in the Easter Rising. But the post did not last long. In December, 1910, Clarke married Lia Cummins in the Dublin Registry Office. It was a disastrous marriage, lasting only ten days, and the immediate consequence of the civil wedding was Clark's dismissal from his lectureship. Between 1922 and 1937 he lived in voluntary exile in England, supporting himself mainly by journalism, and writing poetry, two novels, and verse plays. His first play, *The Son of Learning,* was rejected by Yeats for the Abbey but was produced at the Cambridge Festival Theatre in 1927.

Clarke married Nora Walker in 1930, and in 1937 the family moved back to Dublin and he began a period of intense public literary activity, founding his own small press, the Bridge Press; broadcasting poetry on Radio Éireann; holding Sunday-evening literary gatherings at home; and most important, promoting the cause of verse drama, a form which had been generally neglected in Ireland apart from the writings of Yeats. "It was clear," Clarke observed, "that the imaginative aims of the dramatic movement were in danger of being forgotten." In 1940, therefore, he and Robert Farren founded the Dublin Verse-Speaking Society to train actors to speak poetry, and to encourage public appreciation of verse performance. The society broadcast dramatic poetry and radio plays over Radio Éireann. Along with its later outgrowth, the Lyric Theatre Company, which until the 1951 fire staged verse dramas in the Abbey Theatre, it stimulated a revival of the writing of verse plays by Irish authors including F. R. Higgins, Robert Farren, Louis MacNeice, Donagh MacDonagh, Padraic Fallon, and Clarke himself.

Between 1938 and 1955, Clarke published no poetry, but produced nine verse dramas and his third and last novel, *The Sun Dances at Easter* (which, like his first two, was banned in Ireland). For the last two decades of his life, his interests once again shifted back to poetry, and he published some eight books of poems, including some of his finest work, as well as two books of memoirs and his *Collected Plays*. He was awarded the Gregory Medal, the Irish Academy of Letters' highest literary award, was nominated by Irish PEN for the Nobel Prize, and completed the revisions for his *Collected Poems* in 1974, shortly before his death.

Although Clarke is known today primarily for his lyric poetry, he was also a gifted dramatist and wrote some seventeen verse plays. Prosodically and thematically, the poetry and the plays have much in common. Clarke's distinctive poetic voice owes much to Irish Gaelic prosody. His marvelous free translation of the Irish poem *Binn sin, a luin Doire in Chairn,* incorporated into *As the Crow Flies* ("Stop, stop and listen," page 421 below), shows both his intimate knowledge of the Irish tradition and his skilled imitation of its complexly patterned poetic devices: syllabic meter (each line has nine syllables), alliteration (*b*ough *t*op:*b*righ*t*er), internal rhyme (song:thong), harmonic rhyme (cash*el*:hand*bell*), rhyme on and off the accent (*morn*ing:haw*thorn*), assonance (sh*ou*ts:c*ou*nted:cl*ou*d), consonance (ba*ck*:be*ak*). (Of Clarke's poem Robert Farren commented that "every vowel, and every rest fit into place . . . like pieces of stained-glass, and . . . the thought and feeling come through like sunlight to make all the colours glow.")

The subject matter of Irish tradition also attracted Clarke. Some of his earliest poetry (including *The Vengeance of Fionn,* a version of the story of Diarmuid and Gráinne) was based on the epic and mythological narratives that had inspired the founders of the literary revival. By the 1920s, however, his interests had shifted to the Irish medieval period, and particularly to legends about Irish kings and clerics. *The Son of Learning* (1927) is a rendering of the same medieval anticlerical satire, *Aislinge Meic Conglinne,* that later provided Padraic Fallon's source for *The Vision of Mac Conglinne* (in this volume). Through the story's conflict between poet-scholar and monks, Clarke creates a brilliant satirical statement about one of his major themes: the conflict between faith and intellect, Church dogma and human freedom.

Although it was the drama of W. B. Yeats, and Yeats's ideals for the Irish theater, that first inspired Clarke to devote himself to verse drama, the younger man never imitated Yeats very closely. His plays are distinct from Yeats's in theme and tone: less ritualistic and symbolic, more concerned with individual human characters than with archetypes, and vastly more comic in situation and verbally witty. Some of his most successful plays are broadly humorous: the farcical *Black Fast* (1941), about a debate between an ancient Ulster king and his Munster queen over the celebration of Easter; the masque-like *The Kiss* (1942) and *The Second Kiss* (1946); and the romantic quasi-Shakespearean comedy, *The Plot Succeeds* (1950). But Clarke's drama is never far from a serious moral center; his recurrent concerns are problems of guilt and sinfulness, clerical repression of sexuality, and the need for spiritual freedom and intellectual courage.

Clarke's strongest verse play is probably *As the Crow Flies,* which was broadcast over Radio Éireann by the Dublin Verse-Speaking Society in February, 1942. The plot is derived from "The Adventures of Léithin," a medieval legend translated and published by Douglas Hyde in *Legends of Saints and Sinners* (Dublin: Talbot Press, 1915). A violent storm interrupts the rush-gathering of three monks from Clonmacnoise, who take shelter in a cave overnight; they overhear and variously understand a drama taking place among legendary creatures from the pagan past, and in the morning they witness its tragic conclusion, as an eagle, grieving at the murder of her nestlings by the malevolent old Crow of Achill, dashes herself in a frenzy against the cliff face. The terrifying noise of the storm (vivid in the broadcast) reinforces the message of the old Salmon of Assaroe about the irrational violence of the universe and the "unchanging misery of mankind":

> We are unseasoned,
> Unsensed, unearthed, riddle-diddled
> By what is hidden from the reason.
> How can the forethought of defilement
> Be reconciled with any faith
> That teaches mortals to be mild?

SELECT BIBLIOGRAPHY

Publications

Collected Plays. Dublin: Dolmen Press, 1963.
Two Interludes, Adapted from Cervantes. Dublin: Dolmen Press, 1968. (Plays)
The Impuritans. Dublin: Dolmen Press, 1973. (Play)
The Third Kiss. Dublin: Dolmen Press, 1976. (Play)
Liberty Lane, A Ballad Play of Dublin. Dublin: Dolmen Press, 1978. (Play)
Collected Poems. Dublin: Dolmen Press, 1974.

"Verse-speaking and Verse Drama." *The Dublin Magazine* 12,4 (Oct.–Dec. 1937): 9–17.

Biography and Criticism

Farren, Robert. *The Course of Irish Verse in English,* pp. 150–165. London: Sheed and Ward, 1948.

Halpern, Susan. *Austin Clarke, His Life and Works.* Dublin: Dolmen Press, 1975.

Irish University Review 4 (Spring 1974). (Special Clarke issue, edited by Maurice Harmon)

Mercier, Vivian. "Austin Clarke—The Poet in the Theatre." *Chimera* 5 (Spring 1947): 25–36.

———. "The Verse Plays of Austin Clarke." *The Dublin Magazine* 19,2 (April–June, 1944): 39–47.

Schirmer, Gregory A. *The Poetry of Austin Clarke.* Notre Dame: University of Notre Dame Press/Mountrath: Dolmen Press, 1983.

Tapping, G. Craig. *Austin Clarke: A Study of His Writings.* Dublin: Academy Press, 1981.

As the Crow Flies

*A Lyric Play
for the Air*

DRAMATIS PERSONAE

FATHER VIRGILIUS
BROTHER MANUS
BROTHER AENGUS
THE EAGLE OF KNOCK
HER EAGLETS
THE CROW OF ACHILL
THE STAG OF LEITERLONE
THE BLACKBIRD OF DERRYCAIRN
THE SALMON OF ASSAROE

SCENE 1

*An evening in late summer, on the Shannon,[1] in the seventh century. A boat,
in which there are two monks, is moored in a creek.*

MANUS *(softly)*.
    Father Virgilius . . .
                Father
    Virgilius . . .
VIRGILIUS *(waking)*.
    God bless us all. I must
    Have nodded again. My head was in the sun . . .
    My eyes are gilded by it.
(happily)
                Brother Manus
    The best of spirits came upon this journey
    With us to-day.
MANUS.
           Father, I am uneasy
    Now. We've been resting on our oars too long
    And Brother Aengus is still away.

1. **Shannon** the major river of western Ireland

409

VIRGILIUS.
                                        We've time
        Enough upon our hands. We can be back
        At Clonmacnoise² before the midnight bell rings.
MANUS.
        But you don't know the Shannon, Father. This
            boat-load
        Of rushes will be heavier than our faults
        The more we pull against it. Brother Aengus
        Should never have gone into the forest
        Alone.
VIRGILIUS.
            God will protect him.
MANUS *(obstinately)*.
        But why did you let him go?
VIRGILIUS.
                                Because he is young.
        And the young see but the eye in every bolt
        That keeps them from the meaning of Creation.
        Yes, they want all that breathing space
        Before bird, beast or reptile had been named
        And pain started the first rib.
MANUS.
                                But, Father . . .
VIRGILIUS *(good-humouredly)*.
        I know too well what you are going to say,
        Manus. For twenty years you've chased the raindrops
        From Clonmacnoise with crossbeam, patches, gluepot.
        Whenever we dare to sneeze, you give a nail
        Another rap and heal us with your hammer;
        And if our old bones creak too much in church,
        You hurry up the rungs to mend a joint
        Or clap a comfortable cap of stone
        About our chilling pates.
MANUS *(pleased, puzzled)*.
                                That's true.
        But why did Father Abbot send me out
        To cut him rushes³ in the wilderness?

2. **Clonmacnoise** important early Christian monastic foundation, located on
the Shannon about five miles south of Athlone   3. **to cut him rushes** for rush-
lights, rushes peeled, dried, and dipped in tallow, put in a pincers-like stand and lit
for evening illumination; also, green rushes and reeds were often used for floor
mats

VIRGILIUS *(quietly)*.
> Perhaps he sent you here
> To learn the mercy of the elements.

MANUS.
> Well, maybe so.

VIRGILIUS.
> > > Do take
> Another look at those gigantic reeds.
> Whoever saw green toppings half their size
> On any roof ? They might have been cut down
> To floor the heel of Finn.[4] The very Salmon
> Of Knowledge[5] mentioned by the storytellers
> Could scarcely jump their height.

MANUS.
> > > > > I do not like
> The look of them. They are unlucky, Father.

VIRGILIUS.
> Well, then, we'll bless them in the shed
> And sacristan will dip a few for me
> When he has fired our own fasciculi.[6]
> Good soul, he hates to see me annotating
> A manuscript at night. But they will strengthen
> My hand and dry my ageing eyes . . .

MANUS.
> > > > > Pardon
> Me, Father. I see big clouds upon the hob.[7]
> We should be gone.

VIRGILIUS.
> > > Call Aengus. He is sure
> To hear you from that rock there.

MANUS.
> > > > I will.

(at a distance)
> > > Aengus!
> Aengus!
> > > There's no reply.

VIRGILIUS.
> > > > Call, call again.

4. **Finn** Finn mac Cumhaill, legendary pre-Christian Irish hero, often portrayed in folklore as gigantic   5. **Salmon of Knowledge** in early Irish tradition, a salmon living in a pool in (or a well by) the Boyne River, who brings wisdom to poets; also associated with Finn's acquisition of superhuman knowledge   6. **fasciculi** physically separate parts (gatherings of pages) of a written work   7. **hob** horizon

MANUS.

>Aengus!

>>Aengus!

(a far shout)

MANUS *(coming back)*.

>>>Thank Heaven he is safe.

>>But why is he waving to us? Something

>>Has happened.

(running steps)

>>>What is it, Aengus?

AENGUS *(breathlessly)*.

>>>>The cave, Father

>>Virgilius, the cave!

MANUS *(impatiently)*.

>>>What cave?

VIRGILIUS.

>>>>Brother

>>Has been uneasy at your absence.

AENGUS.

>>>>Forgive

>>Me, Father, if I have been late.

>>>>The forest

>>Was dark as Doom. I groped from age to age,

>>Among the knottings of each century;

>>And then my eyes were opened

>>So suddenly by Heaven, it seemed their dust

>>Had risen and this everlasting body

>>Was glorified. Humbly I prayed, I ran . . .

>>My habit tripped me on a chiselled step

>>Beneath a cliff . . . and I saw the cave.

>>Father, a hermit must have lived there all

>>His life, it was so full of thought.

>>I could not catch up on my breath again

>>Because I was too happy with my spirit

>>In that heart-beaten solitude.

MANUS *(drily)*.

>>>>You heard

>>No stir of beetle, bird or beast?

AENGUS.

>>>>No stir.

>>No stir.

MANUS.

>>>I told you, Father. Every creature

>>Is hiding from the sky.

VIRGILIUS.

Brother

Is troubled, Aengus . . . fears a storm. So let

Us go.

(They get into the boat.)

AENGUS.

I'll take the other oar.

MANUS.

We must be cautious with that heavy load

Of cuttings.

Are you ready?

AENGUS.

Yes, yes. I

Am ready.

MANUS.

Pull now . . .

One . . two

One . . two

One . . two.

(The voices and splash of oars recede and only the quiet river is heard.

Gradually the dipping of the oars is heard again, then stops suddenly.)

MANUS.

Listen! Listen!

VIRGILIUS.

What is it?

MANUS.

The wilderness

Is stirring.

(A faint sound of wind.)

AENGUS.

And look, look at the forest.

MANUS.

We must turn back before the furrl[8] squall

Strikes down.

(The wind rises.)

There, there it is!

VIRGILIUS.

What shall we do?

AENGUS.

I know, I know, Father Virgilius.

Take shelter in the holy cave.

(Their voices are swept away by the sudden storm which rages with ever-

increasing fury.)

8. **furrl** gathered, rolled up

SCENE 2

Inside the cave.

AENGUS *(from the cave)*.
                              Father, can you hear
        Me?
VIRGILIUS *(below)*.
        Yes.
AENGUS.
                Give me your hand. I'll help you up
        Into the cave.
VIRGILIUS *(panting)*.
                              Bless you, my pupil. That climb
        Was heavier than my years. Heaven be thanked
        That we are safe at last.
(anxiously)
                              But where is Manus?
MANUS.
        Beside you, snug as your own Latin books
        At Clonmacnoise.
VIRGILIUS.
                              God sent us to this cave.
AENGUS.
        And Father, the rock is dry.
MANUS.
                              A bad night, surely
        For lath and latch. Can you remember, Father,
        So sudden a storm?
VIRGILIUS.
                              I can remember the Night
        Of the Big Wind and that was fifty years
        Ago, the very week that I had passed
        My first examination. The Shannon rose
        Three times and locked us in the chapel. Blocks
        Of mortar fell and the foundations moved
        Beneath our knees. Those hours come back to me
        Again. We prayed together, sang in turn
        The greater psalms and all that night in dread
        We heard the roar of waters multiplying
        As if God called His creatures from the deep.
        But in the morning, happy youngsters paddled[9]

9. **paddled** played with

The trout, indoors, with dish or pannikin, caught
Our dinner in the refectory and went
To class by boat. Thanksgiving services
Were held at ebb. But never have I known
So bad a night as this.

A VOICE *(outside)*.
                                    *Never have
I known so bad a night.*

MANUS *(alarmed)*.
                                    What's that? Who spoke?

VIRGILIUS.
        Nobody.

MANUS.
                Listen. Listen!

ANOTHER VOICE.
                            *Never have
I known so bad a night.*

MANUS.
                                I hear the voices
Of demons talking.

OTHER VOICES.
                        *Never have we known
So bad a night.*
(peal of thunder.)

AENGUS.
                            Father, are you near me?

VIRGILIUS.
        Yes, yes.

AENGUS.
                I crouched behind a chink of rock,
And clearly in that flash of lightning saw
A demon bird with eyes of glassy fire.

VIRGILIUS
        Where?

MANUS.
            Where?

AENGUS.
                    Sitting upon the cliff top.

MANUS.
                                            We
Are lost.

AENGUS.
                Father, Father, I am afraid.

VIRGILIUS *(calmly)*.

                                              And yet
        Aengus, you want to be a hermit.
                                              God
        Has let us hear the voices of the fallen.
        His pleasure is revealed by miracle.
        Kneel down, kneel down. The three of us will pray
        Together.
(They murmur in prayer as the storm rises again.)

                            SCENE 3

In the eagle's nest.

EAGLETS.
        Mother, mother, something wicked,
        Something cold is in our nest.
        Catch it and kill it, kill it quickly!
EAGLE.
        Come under my wing and try to rest.
EAGLETS.
        Mother, mother, can you hear us?
EAGLE.
        Yes, yes, my children.
EAGLETS.
                            Are you near us?
EAGLE.
        What is it children?
EAGLETS.
                            Something wicked,
        Something cold is in our nest.
        Catch it and kill it, kill it quickly!
EAGLE.
        Rain is drenching every stick
        And stone we own. Keep close together
        With every feather.
EAGLETS.
                            But the thing
        That freezes underneath your wing
        Is shivering. It must be sick.
        Catch and kill it!

AN EAGLET.
                    Kill it quick!
CROW.
          Don't be frightened, little chick,
          Because your mother doesn't know.
(Chuckling)
          I am a crow, a poor old crow.
EAGLE.
          What do you want?
CROW.
                              You are annoyed,
          Eagle. But feel me, now! Destroyed[10]
          I am this night, blown helterskelter.
          Give me an inch, a pinch of shelter.
          I am so weak, I can hardly speak,
          So very cold, I cannot build
          A nest: and this big wind that filled
          My wingbones blew me into the trees,
          For the first time in centuries.
EAGLE.
          Where do you live?
CROW.
                              I hop and pop
          Into a hole before I drop,
          As best I can on my bad leg.
          And I am baldy as the egg
          That hatched me out, so long ago
          I cannot count.
EAGLETS.
                              But has she known
          So bad a night, mother, so bad
          A night as this one?
CROW.
                              Clouds that shadow
          The Shannon dripped into the nest
          I used to have. The sudden west
          Would come at day with flap of waters.
          But I was strong as my own daughters,
          Though they were greedy of claw and craw.
          I kept the air. One time I saw
          The tree-tops bending back to snap

10. **Destroyed** worn out, exhausted

Their joints below. From pit and trap
The wild pigs came up with a bound,
Then hurried, grunting, underground
Again. Eels glided on the flood
With grassgreen skin through every wood.
The holy man who lived alone
Upon an island, threw no stone
At birds but fed them every morning,
Was carried off without a warning.

EAGLE.
    What did he do?

CROW.
                      He gave a screech,
Clutching at reeds beyond his reach
And vanished down a mighty hole
Among the waters. Salmon pole
And netting took the river races
And after, came pale floating faces
And painted timber, cattle trussed
In their own muscles.
                    Another night
When no house in the glen had light
But hers, I flew from salt and shingle
And foam to see the Hag of Dingle.[11]

EAGLE.
    For what?

CROW.
                    I was her messenger
That time. Every two-hundredth year
In storm, she casts another skin.
I saw her do it as I came in,
Step out of it on younger toes,
Quickly as someone changing clothes;
And brighter than a brand-new pin,
She shone from nape to slender shin,
Naked and shameless as a sin.
That night, there was no mortal caller
To see that woman stand there, taller
Than any man. Well might she stoop
To hoop the silk into a loop
And rummage in her box of treasure

11. **Hag of Dingle** in the folklore of southwestern Ireland, a powerful supernatural hag in the Dingle Peninsula known especially for her great age

Till she had found an old tape measure;
And as I nodded on a rafter
I heard her quiet, sinful laughter.

EAGLE.

Why does she change her old skin?

EAGLETS.

Tell
Us why she does it, dearest Crow?

EAGLE.

Yes, tell us.

CROW.

I know what I know.
But ask some hermit in his cell
How thought can keep his body warm.
I'll only say that this bad storm
Has come that she may change her form
Once more.

EAGLE.

You have experienced much.
But can you not remember such
A night?

CROW.

Eagle, I never knew
So bad a night since I first flew.
But I grow sleepy.
Ask the stag
Of Leiterlone.[12] He saw the hag
When she was young before that.

EAGLETS.

Mother,
Dear mother, ask the stag.

EAGLE.

Don't bother
Us.
Where is he, Crow?

CROW.

Beneath that jag
Of rock and furzebush.

EAGLETS.

Has he seen
So bad a storm?

---

12. **stag of Leiterlone** stag of legendary age in Irish folklore, usually associated with Ben Bulben in Co. Sligo

EAGLE.

                        Keep quiet!
                                    Stag
        Of Leiterlone, beneath my crag
        And furzebush, have you ever been
        In such a downpour?

STAG.

                            'Twas I who warned
        Diarmuid and Grainne,[13] night and morning.
        I knew the larger winds that roar
        At daybreak, saw them butting shoreward,
        Shadowing Shannon, clapping horns
        Of ice, but I was never cornered:
        For when they came before the winter
        They blew my scent away through mint
        And garlic. Over pebble and tussock,
        Deer leaped along the summer rock,
        But in bad weather, wandered freely
        Feeding beneath the forest trees,
        Before the Fianna[14] could fire
        The cooking pits they hid in briar
        And ash. I led my herd of does
        To quiet glens beneath the snows.
        But men were ever on our track;
        And when the thawing pools were blacker,
        One time, I ran their mighty dogs
        A fortnight through the rainy bogland,
        Never snapped a fallen branch
        Or struck the brown leaf with my antler
        As I went past it. Caoilte[15] swore
        To pull me down when I had worn out
        The heart of Bran,[16] seethe me for supper
        And fling my humbles[17] to his pups,
        But I got wind of him. At dawn, once,
        The woman who became a fawn
        Fled with me to the grassy lairs
        And heather tops. Though I was wary
        And in my prime, it was her son

---

13. **Diarmuid and Grainne** Diarmuid eloped with Finn's betrothed, Gráinne; the story of the legendary lovers recounts their flight, pursued by Finn, across Ireland   14. **Fianna** a pre-Christian band of roving warriors, the most famous of which was led by Finn mac Cumhaill   15. **Caoilte** a member of Finn's Fianna famous for his speed in running   16. **Bran** Finn's hound   17. **humbles** innards

Who wounded me with woman's cunning.
Where are the proud that never brandished
A head like mine? And where is Flann
Or Bran? Many a time they started
The chase and yet I broke their hearts.
Believe me I have seen the Christians
When they were ambushed in a mist
At Tara[18] change into a herd
Of deer—and yet they have not spared me.
By night and day, I am pursued
With pain and terror in the wood.

EAGLE.
But, Runner, have you ever heard
So loud a deluge?

STAG.
                              Ask the Blackbird
Of Derrycairn for it is perched
Upon my antler.

CROW.
                              Live and learn!

EAGLE *(imperiously)*.
A song!—
                              Blackbird of Derrycairn!

BLACKBIRD.
Stop, stop and listen[19] for the bough top
Is whistling and the sun is brighter
Than God's own shadow in the cup now!
Forget the hour-bell. Mournful matins
Will sound, Patric,[20] as well at nightfall.

Faintly through mist of broken water
Fionn[21] heard my melody in Norway.
He found the forest track, he brought back

---

18. **Tara** in Co. Meath, the site of the ancient kingship of Ireland; the allusion here is to an early story that St. Patrick and his clerics, ambushed by the pagan king Loegaire son of Niall, escaped by miraculously appearing to be a herd of deer.   19. **Stop, stop and listen . . .** This poem, reprinted by Clarke in *Ancient Lights* (1955), is an adaptation of the beautiful Fenian poem *Binn sin, a luin Doire an Chairn* ("That is sweet, Blackbird of Derrycairn"), recited to St. Patrick by Oisín, Finn's son, who on his return to earth from a 300-year stay in the Land of Youth finds the Fianna gone and Ireland taken over by the Christian clerics, to whom he tries to explain the joys of his former life in the pagan, natural world.   20. **Patric** St. Patrick, fifth-century missionary to Ireland   21. **Fionn** Finn (Modern Irish spelling, pronounced, in one syllable, "fyun")

This beak to gild the branch and tell, there,
Why men must welcome in the daylight.

He loved the breeze that warns the black grouse,
The shouts of gillies[22] in the morning
When packs are counted and the swans cloud
Loch Erne,[23] but more than all those voices
My throat rejoicing from the hawthorn.

In little cells behind a cashel,[24]
Patric, no handbell gives a glad sound.
But knowledge is found among the branches.
Listen! The song that shakes my feathers
Will thong the leather of your satchels.

EAGLE.

But have your ever known a night
As bad, Blackbird, in all your life?

BLACKBIRD.

Stop, stop and listen for the bough top
Is whistling and the sun is whiter
Than God's own shoulder in the cup now!
Forget the hour-bell . . .

CROW.

                                    O that bird
Will drive me foolish. Late and soon
More grace notes but the self-same tune!

EAGLE.

We *must* find out.

CROW.

                              I am disturbed
But let me think . . . Hm! Hm!
                                        There is another
Yes . . . he will know.

EAGLETS.

                              Then ask him, mother,
This very minute.

CROW.

                        Go and visit
His Home.

EAGLE.

            Where is it?

22. **gillies** servant lads   23. **Loch Erne** a lake system in the River Erne, in Co.
Fermanagh, in northwestern Ireland   24. **cashel** a walled stone fortification

EAGLETS.
                                    O where is it?
CROW.
          Under the falls of Assaroe.[25]
          The ancient salmon there will know
          The answer rightly if you call him
          For he is wiser than us all.
EAGLE.
          How can I go on such a night
          And leave my children?
EAGLETS.
                              Race the lightning,
          Dear Mother.
CROW *(eagerly)*.
                          Do. Now I am warm
          I'll tuck them in despite the storm.
EAGLETS.
          And be our grannie.
CROW.
                              Yes, dears.
EAGLETS.
                                    Hurry
          Now, mother, hurry. No need to worry.
EAGLE.
          The north is dangerous and darker.
EAGLETS.
          You will be back before the lark-cry
          Has made us hungry.
EAGLE *(doubtfully)*.
                              Can I peer
          Into the foam of the salmon-weir?
CROW.
          Fly down, fly down, but do not look.
          His name is stronger than the hook
          Men use.
(chuckling)
                    It broils him like an ember.
          Call Fintan.[26]

---

25. **Assaroe** waterfall near Ballyshannon, Co. Donegal, near the mouth of the River Erne   26. **Fintan** Fintan son of Bochra, in the medieval *Lebor Gabála Érenn* ("Book of the Taking of Ireland") the survivor of a group of settlers who arrived in Ireland before the Biblical Flood

EAGLE.
                    Fintan?
CROW.
                              Yes.
(calling after eagle)
                              Remember
          The name is . . .
EAGLE *(faintly far away in storm)*.
          Fintan.

                    SCENE 4

Inside the cave.

AENGUS *(softly)*.
          Father, are you awake?
VIRGILIUS.
          Yes, Aengus, I am still awake like you.
          Only the young and old are troubled at night.
          God has been merciful to Manus. He
          Is fast asleep.
AENGUS.
                         But were they really there?
          The voices, Father, that we seemed to hear
          Despite the storm.
VIRGILIUS.
                              I am inclined to think
          They were delusions of the senses,
          Secular follies of the mind.
AENGUS.
                              If so,
          What is their meaning?
VIRGILIUS.
                         They were sent to try
          Our faith to-night.
AENGUS *(in fear)*.
                         But that name, Father, that name.
VIRGILIUS.
          Come close. Why do you tremble at a name,
          My son?

AENGUS.
                    I heard that name before.
VIRGILIUS *(alarmed)*.
                                        But where?
AENGUS.
          In class . . . Our teacher quickly turned the page.
          Father . . .
(slowly)
                              Is Fintan still alive?
VIRGILIUS.
                                        Of course not.
          He went to Limbo.
(gravely)
                              Knowledge is old, my son,
          Older than us and there are thoughts men suffer
          Which are not fit for books. But try to go
          Asleep now.
AENGUS.
                    Father, I will try to.
(Silence.)
(softly)
          Archangels, pray for me to-night that I
          May sleep like Manus on this pillow of rock.
          Let me not dream of evils that afflict
          The young, and by your intercession, save me
          From the dreadful voice beneath the waters.
(The storm rages more shrilly through space now. Gradually it deepens again and far below is heard the thunder of a waterfall.)

SCENE 5

The Falls of Assaroe.

EAGLE *(above)*.
          Fintan . .
                    Fintan . .
                              Fintan.
SALMON *(below)*.
                                        I
          Am here.

EAGLE.
                    Where?
                              Where?
SALMON.
                         Beneath the Falls.
          Who is it calling from the sky?
          What spirit cries my name?
EAGLE.
                                        Eagle I
          Of Knock.
                         Through leagues I fought, I dared
          Unearthly waters flooding the air,
          To find your home beneath the foam-pit.
SALMON.
          Why have you come?
EAGLE.
                                   To ask a question.
SALMON.
          What is it?
EAGLE.
                         Tell me of a tempest
          At any time, as sudden, dreadful
          As this?
SALMON.
                         I knew the muddy beds
          Beneath the Bann, the Suck, the Barrow,[27]
          Leaped up the narrows where Shannon topples
          In miles of thunder, by torch-lit caves
          Of Cong,[28] half choking in the sunlight
          And bellied by the Atlantic waves
          Plunged down . .
                         down . .
                                   sank into the deeps
          Of darkness to a primal sleep.
          I dreamed of horrors that had shrieked
          Before creation. There the sightless
          And deafened creatures grope to life
          With deathly gulp: the giant claw
          Searching the forest of the fronds.

27. **the Bann, the Suck, the Barrow** major rivers in northeastern, western, and southeastern Ireland, respectively   28. **Cong** in Co. Mayo in western Ireland, between Lough Corrib and Lough Mask

In pulps of sperm, the shapeless maw
Swam slowly past me and mute monsters
Uncoupled one another's armour
Though they were blind.

EAGLE.

                                    I kill at sight,
For I am fearless.

SALMON.

                              How can you guess,
Poor bird, dressing your carrion meat
With highflown feet, that every creature
We know is eaten by disease
Or violent blow! We are unseasoned,
Unsensed, unearthed, riddle-diddled
By what is hidden from the reason.
How can the forethought of defilement
Be reconciled with any faith
That teaches mortals to be mild?
A thousand years, I waited, prayed
And all my fears were only answered
By agony of ignorance.
How must reality be named
If carnal being is so shamed?
From this humiliating body
And brutal brain, these loathsome scales
Itching with lice that no salt water
Can purify, I cry to God
To pity my madness.

EAGLE.

                          What are you?

(Pause.)

                                    Answer,
Great Salmon.

SALMON.

                          I am a man.

EAGLE.

                              A man?

SALMON.

      A man . . .
(kindly)

                    your enemy, poor bird.
The selfsame instinct that has stirred
Your wing is stronger than our will.

Innocent infants trying to kill
A bot[29] or housefly know as much
As their own father.

EAGLE (*from storm*).

Icicles clutch
My pins. Shout, shout, for I am hurled
Down gaps of hail.

SALMON.

I saw a deluge
Destroy in rage the ancient world
And millions perish in the surge
Hugeing above each mountain refuge.
I could not keep my subterfuge
By mortal shape. Yet I escaped
Into another consciousness
That did not know me. I lived on.
Men called me blessed. In the west
I prophesied to Partholan,[30]
Divined the arts but knew no rest.
The very plague-pit in my breast
Widened my time. How can I find
In all the ages I have known
The dreadful thought that slowly brought
My consciousness beneath these waters
Where memory unrolls the mind
In chronicles of war, greed, slaughter—
Unchanging misery of mankind!

EAGLE (*joyfully*).

The night of the Great Flood! I know
the answer now.

SALMON.

Before you go
One word.
How did you bait the hook
That I must bite, if pious monk
Pumice my name[31] from lessonbook?

EAGLE.

A scaldcrow told me.

SALMON.

Was she shrunk
And old?

---

29. **bot** maggot or fly   30. **Partholan** in *Lebor Gabála Érenn,* leader of the first legendary settlers of Ireland after the Flood   31. **pumice my name** erase by rubbing ink off vellum with pumice stone

EAGLE.
                    Yes.
SALMON.
          Baldy as the egg
      You lay?
EAGLE.
                    Yes, yes.
SALMON.
              And did she beg
                          For shelter?
EAGLE.
                  True.
SALMON.
                          That was the Crow
Of Achill[32] and well I know her ways.
Mummified fingers of the plaything
She gave her children with the great ring
Carbuncled by the jewellers
of Egypt—that was the hand of Nuadha.[33]
Aye, at Moytura,[34] she despoiled
Many a hero. In his boyhood
Cuchullin[35] was her friend. She croaked
Three times upon the pillarstone
Before he died. She was alone
With him in his last moment. Mist
Of blood had hid her from his fist.
She ripped the lashes from each lid
And blinded him.
                          Homeless with age,
Her food has changed but not her guile.
On stormy nights when she has crept
Upon her belly like a reptile
Into a nest and the frightened chicks
Cry out that some thing cold and wicked
Is sticking to their mother's wing,
(Eagle cries out.)

32. **Crow of Achill** cruel oldest animal in western Irish folk tradition, connected with Achill Island, Co. Mayo   33. **Nuadha** king of the pre-Christian Irish gods, the Tuatha Dé Danann, who in the mythical Battle of Moytura lost his hand, and because of his deformity was deposed   34. **Moytura** near Cong, Co. Mayo; site of mythical battle among the Irish gods   35. **Cuchullin** In the tale of his death, Cú Chulainn, the epic hero of Ulster, straps himself to a pillar stone so that he will die standing; when a raven alights on his shoulder, those watching realize that the hero has died.

She tells her story, makes excuses
(if they are very small and juicy)
To send their parent far away,
That she may overlay and kill them.
(The eagle cries out again.)
What is it, Eagle?
EAGLE *(far away in storm)*.
O my children,
My little children!

SCENE 6

*Early morning: the monks are rowing up the Shannon. They pause
to rest and look round them.*

VIRGILIUS.
Who would have thought there was a storm last evening.
The gravels run so softly.
MANUS.
When we are safe
At Clonmacnoise, I will be more myself.
This wilderness is not for journeyman
Or scholar.
VIRGILIUS.
How can we convert you, Manus?
Look at that wild-thorn on your left. I hear
An early blackbird in it praising Heaven
Above.
(as if despite himself)
Stop, stop and listen for the bough top
Is whistling . . .
MANUS *(alarmed)*.
Father.
VIRGILIUS.
What did I say just now?
Illusions of the night are still upon us.
(half to himself)
But why should they conspire against the east?
Well might the ancients warn the fortunate:
"Cave cavernam!"[36]

36. Cave cavernam! "Beware of the cave!"

AENGUS *(excitedly)*.
> No, Father, you were right.

VIRGILIUS.
> What do you mean?

AENGUS.
>   Look . . . Look . . . that speck within
> The sky.

VIRGILIUS.
>   Where?

AENGUS.
>   Coming swiftly from the north.

VIRGILIUS.
> I cannot see it.

AENGUS.
>   Now a cloud
> Has hidden it.
>   There, there it is again.
> It is the eagle.

MANUS.
>   Aengus is right. It is
> An eagle. Never have I seen so fast
> A goer.

VIRGILIUS.
>   I can see her now above
> Us.

MANUS.
>   She is turning.
>   She is striking from
> The air.

AENGUS.
>   No, she is swooping to the cliff
> Above the cave-mouth.

VIRGILIUS *(uneasily)*.
>   This is very strange.
> But why is she hovering so heavily?
> Why does she dash her wings against the rock
> Like that?

MANUS.
>   She must be wounded in the breast.

AENGUS.
> I know. I know.

VIRGILIUS.
>   What are you saying, Aengus?

AENGUS.
> I've known it all the time.
> > > > She is too late.
> Her little ones are dead.

VIRGILIUS.
> > > What do you mean,
> My son? Why is your habit shivering?
> Why are you frightened?

AENGUS.
> > > Father, Father, I know
> The ancient thought that men endure at night.
> What wall or cave can hide us from that
> > knowledge? . . .

(The voices are fading in the distance.)

THE END

M. J. MOLLOY

1917 −

M. J. Molloy was born on March 3, 1917, in Milltown, Co. Galway. After attending the National School in Milltown and St. Jarlath's College, he studied for the priesthood until illness forced him to leave the seminary. He has spent most of his life working a thirty-six-acre farm next door to his birthplace.

Molloy's plays are set in the rural west that he is himself a part of; they are what he terms "folk-plays," in which situations are viewed mainly through the eyes of the country people themselves. Noting that the country dialect spoken by his characters is accurate, rich, and easy for actors to speak, Robert Hogan has called him "a more authentic Synge."

Most of Molloy's plays are historical, presenting the peasant Ireland of the penal days and the nineteenth century: the "feudal mentality" of tenant farmers under the landlords; their reliance on folk healers and priests; their many stratagems to survive famine and exploitation; their drive to emigrate; their joy in old-fashioned amusements and storytelling. The plays tend to focus on moments of crisis and change in the old order.

Molloy's first play, *The Old Road* (produced at the Abbey Theatre in 1943), deals with the theme of emigration. *The Visiting House* (Abbey, 1946) takes as its subject the last years of an important institution in the Irish countryside, the local farmhouse where folk entertainment—storytelling, debate, music, dancing—took place in the evenings. His best-known play, *The King of Friday's Men* (Abbey, 1948), concerns an eighteenth-century landlord's kidnapping of a girl to be his new "tallywoman" (peasant concubine), against a background of the violent faction-fighting of pre-Famine Ireland; the play vividly dramatizes the "feudal mentality" Molloy speaks of, in the unquestioning loyalty of the landlord's retainers and in their support of his ancient *droit du seigneur,* his right to have sexual relations with the wives and daughters of his tenants.

The Wood of the Whispering (Abbey, January, 1953) is that improbable drama, a gentle comedy about the present-day depopulation of rural Ireland, its characters eccentric bachelors and frightened or disenchanted women. In a more recent play, *Petticoat Loose* (Abbey, 1979), set in 1822, a suspended priest struggles to counteract the sinister hold of the local fairy doctor, Biddy the Tosser, upon the superstitious minds of the country people. Many of the characters and events in Molloy's plays are drawn from real life.

Molloy has commented on the difficulty of presenting his plays in urban professional theaters, since they "may dramatize aspects, or periods of folk-life, of which city people have never heard before, and which they may find hard to believe, and worse still do not want to believe"; he cites in particular the example of the landlords' *droit du seigneur*. D. E. S. Maxwell, who like most critics considers Molloy in the dramatic lineage of Synge and Fitzmaurice, also sees him as more stubbornly local than these, "least exportable." Taken in their broadest significance, however, his themes are far from local or provincial. "The modern plays," writes Robert Hogan, "show characters fighting to stave off the death of a culture, and the historical plays show characters fighting to stave off the literal and metaphorical deaths that the culture caused."

The Paddy Pedlar, a masterful one-act play, was produced at the Abbey Theatre on September 5, 1953. It is a comedy with an ominous background: set in 1840, a year of partial failure of the potato crop, the play foreshadows in the desperate poverty of its characters the looming Great Famine of 1845–47. The rogue Ooshla apes the gentry (hence his nickname, from Irish *uaisle,* "nobility"), but the humor of his parody is undercut by the image of the real gentry: Sibby's landlord, Captain Blake of Lowberry, whom Ooshla pronounces "a thorough-bred gentleman, and from the real old stock"—and willing to let tenant children starve to death.

Molloy has written, too modestly, that "if *The Paddy Pedlar* has a theme, it is the old Irish proverb and belief that any son who looks after his mother will be lucky, and vice versa." We may also see several other themes, including reflections on the nature of true roguery, gentility, and generosity; in addition, the play demonstrates Molloy's fine ability to balance extravagant humor, violence, and sentimentality. The germ of the plot came from a story Molloy heard in a local visiting house; as for the title, he writes that it "had nothing to do with the itinerant's wares. The term was used, I think, simply because of the attractiveness of the alliteration and the fact that Irishmen were called paddies by both themselves and the English."

SELECT BIBLIOGRAPHY

Publications

The King of Friday's Men. Dublin: James Duffy, 1953.
The Paddy Pedlar. Dublin: James Duffy, 1954.
Old Road. Dublin: Progress House, 1961.
The Wood of the Whispering. Dublin: Progress House, 1961.
Daughter from Over the Water. Dublin: Progress House, 1963.
The Bitter Pill. In *Prizewinning Plays of 1964.* Dublin: Progress House, 1965.
The Visiting House in *Seven Irish Plays, 1946–1964.* Minneapolis: University of Minnesota Press, 1967.

Three Plays by M. J. Molloy. Newark, DE: Proscenium, 1975. (*The King of Friday's Men, The Paddy Pedlar, The Wood of the Whispering*)

Petticoat Loose. Newark, DE: Proscenium, 1982.

The Will and the Way. Dublin: P. J. Bourke, n.d.

"The Making of Folk Plays." In *Literature and Folk Culture: Ireland and Folk Culture.* Ed. Alison Feder and Bernice Schrank. St. John's, Newfoundland: Memorial University of Newfoundland, 1977, pp. 58–80.

Biography and Criticism

Hogan, Robert. "Michael Molloy's Dying Ireland." *After the Irish Renaissance.* London: Macmillan, 1968, pp. 86–98.

See also discussions in Maxwell, *Modern Irish Drama*; Hogan, *Dictionary of Irish Literature*; and Fitz-Simon, *The Irish Theatre.*

The Paddy Pedlar

In One Act

To the memory of Gerard Molloy
who directed the Ballina Players
in this play's first production in 1952

PRODUCTION NOTE

Don't let any part of the "contents" of the pedlar's sack be seen by the audience; the "contents" are best left entirely to their imagination. The sack itself should never be let stand on its end, or held in any way likely to outline its "contents."

The play is most successful when produced at a good fast pace, and should not take more than 45 to 50 minutes.

The scene is the kitchen of a small straw-thatched cottage on the outskirts of a peasant village, in an out-of-the-way hilly part of the Galway-Mayo border country. The time is the autumn of the year 1840 during Ireland's Famine decade.

The furniture is rudimentary. There are no chairs, only a few rough home-made wooden stools. There is no table, and the dresser is small and empty save for one wooden mug with a wooden porridge spoon laid across it, one large knife, and a few eggshells arranged in order. On the right hand wall hangs a smoke-blackened cross consisting merely of two sticks nailed together. The dresser stands against the back wall, on the right from the actor's point of view. On the left end of the back wall is the door opening on to the road. In this wall also is the usual small window. Some sheaves of straw stand in a corner. The fireplace is in the right hand wall, and doors in the right hand and left hand walls lead to the two bedrooms.

Ooshla Clancy lies fully dressed on his back on the floor, with one leg across one of the stools, from which he had fallen in drunken slumber. A small whiskey jar stands at his elbow on another stool.

After the curtain goes up there is stillness for a few moments, then a horseman can be heard riding by and driving a herd of cattle, cracking his whip, and shouting at both cattle and dog as he does so. "S-go on there! S-go on there!" *(Loudly.)* "Turn them out, dog! Get before them! Easy there." *And so, with much barking from the dog, they move on out of earshot.*

But the noise has awakened Ooshla, and he shifts uneasily, and finally sits up. He clutches at his head, and groans.

OOSHLA. Oh, murther! My head is ruined for life and for ever! My curse on the poteen,[1] and the curse of the Seven Ganders that plucked the grass off Solomon's grave! *(He turns over, sees the jar at his elbow, growls in hatred.)* There you are still, and may the Divil fly away with you! *(He hesitates a few moments, weakening at every moment; then with a cry.)* 'Tis kill or cure, and better be dead than the state I'm in. *(He grasps the jar in both hands and takes a mighty swig. He rises, and sets out for the door, a little shakily at first, but is soon himself again. He is a well built man of fifty with the alert eye and quick speech of the man who has contrived to live for many years on his wits and by roguery. But there is nothing low, or mean looking, about him. On the contrary there is a curious air of the gentleman; and it appears in his seriousness, in his impressive gestures and walk and carriage, in his clear cut speech, and in the way he waxes his moustache ends. His clothes he contrives to wear with an air, although they are old cast-offs. Yet all this seems to proceed not from affectation, but from some kind of inner conviction. He unbolts and opens the door, and looks upon the sunset for a few moments. Suddenly he starts, closes the door hastily, puts the poteen jar on the dresser and has just time to stretch on the hearth simulating sleep when Thady and Honor come in.*

(Honor is about twenty, tall, slow moving and quiet, and good-looking, too, in an unsophisticated country way. She is serious and silent, and her look is abstracted. She seems a kind, sincere type of girl.)

(Thady is a big, easy-going, good-humoured fellow in the late twenties. His voice is very soft and low for so big a man. Before speaking to, or replying to, anyone, he looks upon him a moment or two, and then addresses him directly and confidentially as if there was no one else in the room. His shrewd and tolerant eyes look around upon all the world good-humouredly. He wears a hat and he carries a stout blackthorn stick.)

1. **poteen** illicitly distilled whiskey

HONOR. He's sleeping yet. In the daytime he do sleep mostly, on account the dark night is his safest time for stealing.

THADY. And is this all the bed he has?

HONOR. Not it. He has a fine feather bed back in the room. He must be as drunk as a stick, or he'd not fall-off asleep here. *(She sets to work to light the fire. Thady espies the jar of poteen on the dresser, and duly sniffs at, and tastes it.)*

THADY. Prime poteen he has. D'ye think did he steal it the same as he steals all his wants of spuds and oatmeal?

HONOR. Ooshla steals only spuds and oatmeal, enough to keep the breath in him. A well-wisher gave him the poteen likely.

THADY *(looking into the bedroom on the right)*. 'Tis a fine lump of a house, and as clean as a leaf. We wouldn't call the Queen our Aunt if we were married in here.

HONOR. He's sure and certain to let us live here. He'd never have squandered my fortune[2] only his wife was after dying,[3] and he had no family, and he honestly meant to leave me his house and land that'd be worth more than my twenty guineas fortune.

THADY *(crossing to look into the other room)*. Your father behaved as silly as a duck to go giving Ooshla your fortune. Didn't he know well that money is tempting?

HONOR. Sure my father was failing fast with the fever himself, so he had to trust it to someone until I grew up. He knew my mother was lighthearted, and sure to spend it. *(Pulling a loose stone out of the wall.)* In here Ooshla had the guineas sleeping before the Divil coaxed him to start spending them at last.

THADY. Maybe he hasn't it all spent yet. If I left my thumb on his throat a while, maybe he'd own up to a few guineas saved. *(He kneels beside Ooshla, and begins to push back his sleeves.)*

HONOR. He hasn't a brass farthing left. Once he commenced spending he was a year taking his ease and pleasuring, and then he had to go stealing for a living, for he had the habit of work lost.

THADY. To go robbing a young orphan's fortune was a dirty turn. Rouse up, Ooshla Clancy, till we see will you act manful, and make the loss good. *(He pokes him in the ribs good-humouredly.)*

OOSHLA. Did I hear a stir? *(Sees Honor.)* Honor, is that yourself? *(Sees Thady.)* And who is the young man? *(He is affable; but serious and gentlemanly as usual.)*

HONOR *(between whom and Ooshla there seems to be a strong bond of affection)*. Thady Durkin my bachelor[4] that I was telling you about. Let ye

---

2. **fortune** the money set aside for Honor's dowry   3. **was after dying** had just died   4. **bachelor** fiancé

be talking, and I'll ready your breakfast first, and join in the talk further on.

(She is busy for some time now. She finds a dozen or so of warm roasted potatoes in the ashes, and places them upon a stool. She puts beside it a mug of water taken from a wooden bucket near the door. She finds a large piece of oaten cake in the dresser, and slices it up with the big knife displayed on the dresser. This also she leaves beside the potatoes. From time to time she pauses and watches the pair, listening in her silent way.)

OOSHLA *(quickly and anxiously)*. Tell me did you win your fight against your young brother?

THADY *(cheerfully)*. Not me; I'm no match for him at either the shillelagh,[5] or the thumps. There was more flour in the spuds[6] the year he was born.

OOSHLA *(very disappointed)*. Well that's dull news! So your father'll leave him the farm?

THADY. He will. Evermore in our family the farm is left to the best fighter. So herself and myself must go foreign[7] in search of a living.

OOSHLA. But did you not tell him, Honor, that ye can marry in here, and have my land.

HONOR. I told him all.

THADY. We are very thankful to you, Ooshla, but the way it is our people bore an honest name evermore, and how then could we go living with a rogue?

OOSHLA *(rising in dignified reproach)*. Is it me to be a rogue? Thady Durkin, blow that from your mind. *(He crosses to dresser, and takes up the poteen jar.)* My course of life was that I passed a year one time spending her money, and lost the habit of work, so I had to have the other tenant farmers do the work for me the same as they do for the gentlemen, their landlords. But I couldn't take their crops openly the same as the landlords do. All I could do was take enough to keep me living of spuds and oatmeal in the midnight, when the world is in bed. *(He comes from the dresser with the jar, and two eggshells. He fills one eggshell, and gives it to Thady. Honor takes the turf creel,[8] and goes out the front door.)*

THADY. But, Ooshla, 'tis God's law that all should work, but the gentlemen.

OOSHLA *(quickly and solemnly)*. That's it, work for all but the gentlemen, so no work for Ooshla, because God appointed Ooshla to be a gentleman too. *(He sits down, and pours out an eggshellful for himself.)*

---

5. **shillelagh** a blackthorn or oak cudgel, named after a village and barony in Co. Wicklow 6. **flour in the spuds** nutrition in the potatoes (the staple of the Irish diet at this period) 7. **go foreign** emigrate 8. **turf creel** basket for carrying turf (dried peat) for fuel

THADY (*chuckling*). How could God appoint you for a gentleman when He gave you no riches?

OOSHLA. He overlooked the riches some way or other; still He appointed Ooshla to be a gentleman.

THADY. He did! Give me the ins and outs of that, Ooshla.

OOSHLA. When men that aren't gentlemen get riches, they go ahead with the work, more or less of it; they wouldn't be content unless they were doing something. But from the first minute I had money to spend, I took to idleness as ready and easy as a woman takes to scolding. I didn't care if I never left hand, foot, or toe on a piece of work again.

THADY. At that gait of going every idler in the country was appointed to be a gentleman; every idler and lazy old scratch that does no work only lying across the hearth like a pig that'd be full up. (*Honor enters with a creel of turf.*)

OOSHLA (*rising indignantly*). Thady Durkin, is every drone in the country the same as me? Can they set their words out on their edges one after another the same as me? (*Taking up an impressive stance.*) Can they stand like gentlemen with their toes out and as straight as whipping posts the same as me? Can they step out like gentlemen the same as me? Steady your sight now. (*He walks up and down the kitchen a couple of times in imposing style.*)

THADY (*admiringly*). No lie, you can show your boot soles as good as any gentleman.

OOSHLA. Wait a minute. You didn't see the half of me yet. (*He goes into the bedroom peeling off his jacket as he goes.*)

THADY. The divil a such a man ever I clapped an eye on! Honor, 'tis time you went outside to see is the sky inclined to fall. In a minute he'll be back with nothing covering him only his spine.

HONOR (*smiling, for she knows Ooshla of old*). When you see him next, he'll surprise you.

(*Ooshla comes out dressed as before except for the important additions of a top-hat and dress coat, both more or less damaged cast-offs. He swings an ashplant peeled so as to resemble a cane. He crosses the stage, comes back, and confronts Thady triumphantly.*)

OOSHLA. Is it any wonder all call me Ooshla, meaning "The Gentleman"! Haven't I the cut of a gentleman every way you take me?

THADY. I give in you have. But still you're not entitled to go taking your needs from the poor people, and give them no return. The landlord gentlemen take a share of their crops, but they give them the use of their land.

OOSHLA (*vigorously*). But amn't I giving my cleverness free to the poor of this country? Here they are lowing with the hunger, and rackrented[9]

9. **rackrented** charged unbearably high rents

and robbed and threatened by rogue landlords, and rogue Bailiffs and rogue Attorneys. Whenever a poor man can see no way out, he'll come to me, and say: "Ooshla, I'm an honest man, and no match for these rogues; but you're the cleverest rogue since the Gobawn,[10] and maybe you could save me." So Ooshla makes a little thought, and in a minute has a trick made that'll bring that man safe. Isn't that so, Honor?

HONOR. No lie at all: the poor people are swarming like bees to Ooshla for help. Ooshla has as many tricks as the cat, and one more than him.

THADY. Still and all, Ooshla, if we went living with you, the rogue's brand'd be on all ever we'd have, or spend, or buy. The backbiting lot'd say all, and our daughters' fortunes as well, were saved up out of your rogueries.

HONOR. That's the hobble[11] we're in, Ooshla, so we must go foreign, unless you'll give up the roguery, and earn your living with the spade any more.

OOSHLA. But the digging'd dull my brain again, and I'd not be clever enough to help the poor against the rogue Bailiffs and the rogue landlords. 'Twould be the greatest sin in the world for me to go digging again.

HONOR (*sympathetically*). Never mind so, Ooshla, we'll go foreign to America; and in no time we'll be at the top of Fortune's wheel in it.

(*She rises to go.*)

OOSHLA (*genuinely concerned*). But I hear tell there's a bad time out there lately, with a power of[12] Banks failing, the foreign men begging for want of work, and the foreign girls having to earn their daily bread by night.

THADY. Still they reckon the American country is so wide and the people so few, that the dog never barks at a stranger in it. So there'll be land in plenty smiling at us to take it.

(*He goes to the door.*)

HONOR. We'll be all right, Ooshla. Thady is coming up now to meet my mother and my brother.

(*She goes to the door.*)

OOSHLA. I'll be up to ye the minute I have my supper down; and maybe I'll save ye yet from going foreign.

HONOR. Let you not be troubling your mind about that at all, Ooshla.

(*She goes. Thady turns in the doorway, and addresses Ooshla cheerfully.*)

THADY. Ooshla, you have yourself believing you're entitled to be a rogue; but you're as soft as a penny book[13] to believe the like of that. You're not entitled to make a living by roguery; 'tis oul' Nick himself is making a fool of you. But we're greatly obliged to you, whatever.

10. **Gobawn** the Gobán Saor, legendary contriver and builder in Irish folk tradition 11. **hobble** predicament 12. **a power of** many 13. **as soft as a penny book** gullible

(He goes. Ooshla looks downcast and doubtful for a moment or two; then as if to restore his confidence he rises, and does another superbly gentlemanlike walk around the kitchen. He takes off the tall hat, brushes a speck of dust from it, and goes into the room. He is back in a moment wearing his old jacket and minus the tall hat. He settles down to his breakfast. Sibby comes in, and makes her way up to him. She is haggard and listless with hunger and worry.)

SIBBY. Sir, aren't you Ooshla Clancy, the rogue of Killeenreevagh?

OOSHLA *(with dignity)*. I'm Ooshla Clancy, the friend of the poor!

SIBBY *(sitting down and looking into the fire listlessly)*. Last year the spuds failed on us greatly. Seven children we have, and you wouldn't know which of them is the biggest or the smallest with the hunger. Five of them maybe'll be able to stop[14] in our house, but the other two'll be gone to their graves before the new spuds are grown.

OOSHLA. Who is your landlord?

SIBBY. Captain Blake of Lowberry, Sir.

OOSHLA. The Captain is a thorough-bred gentleman, and from the real old stock; still he'll give ye no help.

SIBBY *(unemotionally)*. He won't, sir. He has two dogs as big as asses for tearing down poor people that'd come annoying him for help.

OOSHLA. To be sure he has. If a gentleman gave food to one poor person, he'd be swarmed out with people asking. A poor person'll get no help from them unless he'll trick them some way.

SIBBY. All tell me so, and all tell me you're the best hand at tricks on account you're a rogue.

OOSHLA *(impressively in his best professional style)*. Sit over there out of my view, while I'm reckoning up a remedy for your hobble.

SIBBY. God spare you the health, sir. God spare you the health.

(She takes up the stool, crosses to the back wall, and sits there watching Ooshla anxiously, blessing herself and praying hard.)

OOSHLA *(after eating away for a few moments)*. Likely the Captain steps out viewing his estate middling often?

SIBBY. Every morning after breakfast he walks out, but he'll give no hearing to any poor person that'll come looking for help.

OOSHLA. If you ask him for help, your case is lost. Instead, when he's coming the way, let you pass him out, and you driving the ass and baskets with a child in each basket. Let you be looking very wild, and be crying like the Banshee;[15] then he'll halt you and ask you where you're off to. Tell him you're bringing the children to the lake to drown them; that you couldn't be looking at them starving. For that he'll blacken your body with his walking stick; but you'll see he'll put you under keen commands to

14. **to stop** to stay   15. **the Banshee** Irish *bean sí*, the fairy woman whose cries announce impending death

send the children down to his kitchen door every day till the new spuds are grown.[16]

SIBBY (*jumping to her feet, and wild with relief and excitement*). Ooshla Clancy, you have my lot saved! And, if you're a rogue itself, you're the best friend the poor ever had!

OOSHLA (*confidentially*). Maybe now you could tell me of some well-doing farmer in yere country that has more than his needs of spuds and oatmeal, and that wouldn't suffer if Ooshla fetched away a few hatfuls in the midnight.

SIBBY. Ooshla, I'll give you tidings of where a clever rogue such as you can win riches and valuables.

OOSHLA. You can! Where?

SIBBY. There's a Paddy Pedlar on the roadside below, and several have offered him a night's shelter, but he's refusing them all. So some reckon he must have stolen valuables in his bag, and he's afeard any man'd go looking in the bag, while he'd be sleeping.

OOSHLA. No Paddy Pedlar ever refused a night's shelter before, so he must have more in his bag than the feathers and horsehair and spuds the Paddy Pedlars do be gathering. And, if 'tis stolen valuables he has, they aren't his by right, and isn't Ooshla as much entitled to a share of them?

SIBBY. I have no learning about the right and wrongs of roguery. 'Tis yourself can set the water running clear about that point.

(*She moves to the door.*)

OOSHLA. Tell him there's a lone blind man in this house. Then he'll not be afeard that I'd look in the bag. I'll only take what'll buy a strip of land for a young couple that must go foreign without it.

SIBBY. I'll tell him you're blind no matter if it withers my blood. My seven can stop in my house thanks to you . . .

(*She goes. Ooshla takes a couple of sheaves of straw from the corner, and makes a bed near the hearth. From the room on the right he brings out a blanket, which he spreads over the straw. He brings his stick from the corner. He sits on the blanket with his back to the door, takes off his jacket, then his shoes. He is thus engaged when Matthias Duggan appears. He is a huge powerful fierce-looking man of forty-five or so; and he carries a murderous looking shillelagh. He looks at Ooshla for a moment, advances upon him silently, takes him by the back of the collar, and throws him full length on the floor.*)

MATTHIAS (*roaring ferociously*). You limb of the divil up from Hell! You robber and thief and murderer!

OOSHILA (*gasping*). Matthias Duggan!

---

16. **till the new spuds are grown** According to Molloy, "that trick was successfully played on a local landlord named Birmingham by a starving tenant. Birmingham was born about 1810 and died in 1881."

MATTHIAS. Say your last prayers quick before Matthias puts you into eternity.

(He draws back shillelagh for a finishing blow.)

OOSHLA. Matthias, what did I do on you?

MATTHIAS. Last night you fetched away my spade, and sold it to Toby Kelly for a jar of his poteen.

OOSHLA *(desperately)*. Matthias, I'm as innocent of that as of burning myself in the fire. I never steal anything only enough spuds and oatmeal to keep me living.

MATTHIAS. Didn't my own neighbour see the spade in Kelly's kitchen with my mark upon it, and wasn't it he told for true you sold it last night for poteen? My spade that was my only way of living, and now the hunger'll bring my ghost up in no time. You murderer and rogue; you'll rogue and murder no more. Say your last prayers directly; then I'll clout your two temples together, and kill you.

OOSHLA. But, Matthias, if I die without paying you back for your spade, my prayers'll be worth no more than the braying of an ass, and I'll be scorching in Purgatory for maybe ten years. Give me a small while to gather up the costs for a new spade. Then you can thrash my soul out to your heart's content.

MATTHIAS *(suspiciously)*. And where would you get the costs for a new spade?

OOSHLA *(quickly)*. There's a Paddy Pedlar on the road below, and he's coming lodging here for the night. In his bag he has stolen valuables, and in the midnight when he's asleep, I'll steal enough that'll buy you the finest spade in the Barony.

MATTHIAS. D'ye want to make me as black a rogue as yourself?

OOSHLA. What roguery is in it? They're stolen valuables, so they aren't the pedlar's by right, and we're as much entitled to them.

MATTHIAS. But what about the gentleman that owned them?

OOSHLA. Sure he's unknown, and the pedlar'll never tell who he is. And anyway, how do the gentlemen get the costs for their valuables? By rackrenting their poor tenants till they're lowing with the hunger.

MATTHIAS *(in a fury)*. They took the last crop I had left in the year of the floods, and the wife and children sickened and died on me. But she didn't die till she cursed the gentlemen with a curse that'll wear them from the earth at last. And now they have the rent raised on me again, so I can afford no pinch of salt with my spuds, nor a sup of milk ever! For every meal of the year I have nothing only potatoes and spits!

OOSHLA. You'll want to go, or he'll be afeard to come in. I sent him word there was a lone blind man in this house, and the like couldn't look in his bag.

MATTHIAS. I'll lie ahiding in the furze until the Paddy Pedlar is sleeping.

(He goes to door.)

OOSHLA. Tap at the window here after about an hour of the night.

MATTHIAS. Here he's coming with his basket and his bag!

OOSHLA. Creep away in the shadow of the wall.

(Matthias goes. Ooshla slips back to the straw bed, and is kneeling down smoothing out the straw and the blanket when the Pedlar comes into the doorway. On his left arm the Pedlar carries the long rectangular shallow basket containing pins and needles, combs, brooches, laces, etc., each in its separate department, and separated from its neighbours by a wicker-work partition. In his right hand he carries a home-made walking-stick. On his back he carries the large bag in which the pedlars usually carried the feathers and horsehair and rags with which many country people paid for their purchases. The bag is hung upon his back in the traditional manner. Two potatoes are stuck in the two bottom corners of the bag, and, around the base of the bulges which these potatoes make, two straw ropes are tied, the ropes coming up around the chest and shoulders, where they are tied to the top corners of the bag. A third straw rope tied around the middle of the bag and around his chest keeps the other ropes from slipping off his shoulders. The Pedlar is middle-aged, insignificant looking, and stupefied by extreme physical exhaustion. Dogged devoted will-power keeps him going; but every time he relaxes he seems to crumble up both mentally and physically. He is a sad and lonely-looking figure, and remarkably timid. He peeps in first, and takes stock of Ooshla, and of everything. He works his way stealthily until he is close to Ooshla. Ooshla is kneeling down facing him, and talking to himself, rubbing his back painfully as he does so.)

OOSHLA. You had the pains as bad before, still God Almighty picked you up again, and you know well He can do as much for you this time, too. Evermore you're complaining about the pains in your back, and the darkness in your eyes; but wouldn't you be a score of times worse off, if you were an unbeliever, or a murderer, or a rogue? And when you see Heaven at last, won't it be twice more wonderful, because you seen nothing at all when you were living in this world?

(After peering into Ooshla's eyes at close range, the Pedlar seems to be satisfied, so he withdraws a little, and then speaks.)

PEDLAR *(timidly)*. God save you, sir.

OOSHLA *(his gaze falling well wide of the Pedlar)*. God and Mary save you, whoever you are. Your voice is strange to me.

PEDLAR. I'm a pedlar, sir.

OOSHLA. A paddy pedlar is it? Draw down to the fire, Paddy, and take your ease.

PEDLAR. I'm thankful to you, sir.

(He sits on the stool to the left of Ooshla.)

OOSHLA. And very apt, Paddy, you'd like a night's shelter. Between rain and hailstones 'tis nicer weather for looking out than for looking in.

PEDLAR *(anxiously)*. But will there be any in the house besides ourselves two, sir?

OOSHLA *(gravely)*. No living person, Paddy; but on account I haven't the sight, I couldn't say whether my people that are dead and gone, come back ever in the midnight. They say no word, Paddy, whatever.

PEDLAR. I'll stop so, sir, till morning at the first light, sir; and I'm thankful to you, sir.

(He loosens the straw rope tied around his chest.)

OOSHLA. And, Paddy, have you any wife, or Christian that'd like shelter too?

PEDLAR. I had no wife ever, sir; and I'm thinned out of the last of my friends. All dead and gone, sir.

OOSHLA *(rising with his stick, and tapping his way to the door, which he bolts)*. Still you're luckier than myself that is without sight or friends, and as bad as Ossian[17] that was blinded and withered by the first sting of Ireland's ground when he ventured back after three hundred years in the Land of Youth. *(From the dresser he takes the poteen jar and two eggshells.)* The poor fellow—was it any wonder he soaked three towels every day with tears for his lost sight, and for the Land of Youth, and for his Queen Niamh of the Golden Hair?

(All this talk is to keep the Pedlar from suspecting the fact that Ooshla is watching his movements out of the corner of his eye. For the moment Ooshla moved to the door, the Pedlar pulls himself together, slips off his shoes, and carries the bag stealthily into the room on left, handling it with extraordinary care, as if it contained something very valuable and fragile. He slips back to the stool, and puts on his shoes again.)

OOSHLA. Fine floury spuds are roasted in the ashes there, Paddy, and let you be making free with them.

(He comes back to his stool with the jar and the eggshells.)

PEDLAR. 'Tisn't long since I had a good bite, sir; and I don't be inclined for eating in a house, sir, on account I'm eating in the wind evermore.

OOSHLA. Well, you'll down a jorum[18] of poteen. Long travelling'll have you burning for a drink.

(He pours out an eggshellful.)

PEDLAR *(taking the eggshell)*. I'm very thankful to you, sir.

(He drinks it.)

17. **Ossian** son of Finn mac Cumhaill (Angl. "mac Cool") who followed the fairy woman Niamh to the Land of Youth, spent 300 years there, then returned to Ireland, withering into age as soon as he touched Irish soil 18. **jorum** a large drinking vessel (ironic here)

OOSHLA. Are you a well-doing man at the peddling, Paddy?

PEDLAR. Middling only, sir. I never was able enough, or severe enough at the bargaining; and the times are going worse, too, sir.

(Again and again his gaze returns uneasily to the main object of his thoughts—the bag in the room.)

OOSHLA. That's true, Paddy; but did you hear Dan O'Connell[19] is to get a better Act of Parliament passed that'll make everyone well-to-do?

PEDLAR *(sadly)*. Every year, sir, that is foretold, and every year Dan has great actions done for Ireland, and great speeches made; but still and all every year the poor are poorer.

OOSHLA. The gentlemen are rackrenting their poor tenants, Paddy.

PEDLAR. The gentlemen are taking more than they're entitled to, sir.

(Again he looks around uneasily in the direction of the bag.)

OOSHLA. In the olden times Spain and Ireland had the same king; and 'tis foretold that the same will come again. Maybe there will be fair play and plenty for all when that time comes.

PEDLAR. Maybe in God, sir.

OOSHLA *(transferring to straw bed)*. Myself must go sleeping now, Paddy, on account the pains kept tickling me every hour of last night. The turf for raking the fire you'll find in the room beyond . . . Do you see where I'm pointing, Paddy?

PEDLAR *(rousing himself)*. I do, sir; I'll rake the fire directly, sir.

(He goes into the room on left. He comes out carrying an armful of turf.)

OOSHLA. Myself must sleep anear the heat of the fire for fear the pains'd come back. You can sleep in my bed in the room there, Paddy.

(Indicating the room on right.)

PEDLAR *(stopping in his tracks)*. Is it sleep in the room beyond, sir?

(He looks towards it, and then back to the room where the bag is, with obvious dismay.)

OOSHLA. A fine bed you'll have, Paddy. A goose-feather mattress and bolster and all. 'Twould delight you to look at it, not to mind sleeping in it.

PEDLAR *(sorely tempted)*. A feather bed, sir! Never in my lifetime did I get sleeping in the like.

OOSHLA. One night's rest in it, Paddy, and you'll be five years a younger man.

PEDLAR. No lie, sir, 'twould do me great good, for too long carrying

---

19. **Dan O'Connell** Daniel O'Connell (1775–1847), Irish political leader whose abilities at organizing the Irish peasantry won Catholic emancipation for Ireland in 1829, and very nearly brought about the repeal of the Act of Union with England and restoration of a representative Irish parliament in the 1840s. Popularly known as the "Liberator," O'Connell is famous in Irish folklore for his clever legal stratagems.

and trouble, sir, have me made dizzy, like a goose that'd be struck on the back of the head, sir.

(He is still hesitating.)

OOSHLA. Good night, Paddy.

(He rolls over, and settles down to sleep.)

PEDLAR. Good night, sir.

(The Pedlar "rakes" the fire by covering some live coals and fresh sods with ashes. Then he comes around, and peers into Ooshla's face, whispering, "Sir, sir" softly. But there is no reply, and, the Pedlar, satisfied at last that Ooshla is asleep, crosses to the room on left where the bag is, looks in a moment, hesitates again, then comes over to the hearth, and places his pedlar's basket on a stool right beside Ooshla, so that he is bound to feel it the moment he stirs. Then he takes the candle, and goes into the bedroom on the right. A few moments after he has gone, closing the door behind him, a tapping is heard at the kitchen window. Ooshla jumps up and runs to the window.)

OOSHLA. Go easy, you divil, he's hardly in his bed at all yet.

(He hurries to the door, and admits Matthias.)

MATTHIAS. The bag. Where is it?

OOSHLA. Wait till I light a candle.

(He lights a rush candle[20] at the fire.)

MATTHIAS. D'ye think he has valuables in the bag?

OOSHLA. From his carry-on I'd take my book oath he has valuables in it. 'Tis in the room beyond. Carry it easy now for fear you'd hurt any of the valuables.

(Matthias goes into the room ahead of him, while Ooshla stands in the doorway holding aloft the candle.)

OOSHLA. There it is above in the far corner. Go easy with it, man; go easy.

(Matthias comes out, and places the bag on the floor.)

MATTHIAS. 'Tis as heavy as the Hill of the Heads. He must have half the gentlemen of Ireland robbed, and the Divil mend them.

(He is opening the bag.)

OOSHLA. Go easy, or you'll rouse him.

(Matthias opens the bag, and pokes his head into it in his eagerness. Instantly a smothered cry is heard from him, and he pulls out his head as if it had been bitten.)

MATTHIAS *(in horror putting his hands to his eyes)*. Thunder and fire! My sight is scattered! God's Curse has struck me for my league with a rogue!

OOSHLA. Go easy will you! What's in the bag?

MATTHIAS. A fearful thing, or my eyes are false and my friends no more!

---

20. **rush candle** a rush that has been peeled, dried, and soaked in tallow

(He is screwing his eyes, and blinking, as if testing them.)

OOSHLA *(incredulous)*. 'Tis the truth what they say that you don't be yourself half the time. *(He looks into the sack, and gasps.)* By the kingdom of O'Neill! . . . A woman's body and she killed and cold!

MATTHIAS *(bounding to his feet in a fury)*. The blackhearted son of the Earl of Hell! He smothered her life out for her gold!

OOSHLA. She hasn't the looks of money. 'Tis poor clothes that's on her body.

MATTHIAS. Sure isn't it the likes of her that'd have the money. A miser that never let a penny go for clothes, or anything.

OOSHLA *(closing the bag thoughtfully)*. Maybe that was it; or maybe 'twas for her body he killed her.

MATTHIAS. For her body, Clancy?

OOSHLA. Yes, to sell it to the doctors. Up the country the high doctors are paying a wonderful great price for bodies for the apprentice doctors to be practising how to cut the insides out of people.

MATTHIAS. One thing is sure, he banished her life someway; and, if we let him go ahead, he'll do the same to many a poor person more. Come in, and we'll take him by the legs, and keep pelting him into the lake until he dies.

(He sets out for the bedroom brandishing his shillelagh.)

OOSHLA *(urgently)*. Matthias, wait a minute.

MATTHIAS *(impatiently)*. What's it?

OOSHLA. We'll make a prisoner of him first. Then we'll call in the neighbours to hear his case and judge him. No man should be put to death without a hearing.

MATTHIAS. Very well so. Bring the ropes, you.

(They creep into the bedroom, Matthias going first and Ooshla following with the candle, and the two straw ropes. In a moment the smothered cries of the Pedlar are heard, and over all the bull-throated roars of Matthias: "Stop quiet, or we'll kill you." "Hold him down." "Tie him to the bedpost." "That's it." "Be saying your last prayers now." "Short till you'll be on trial before your God." They come out, Ooshla carrying the candle.)

OOSHLA. Let you ring the word out around the village, and bring down a big flock of men to judge him.

MATTHIAS. I will that; and let you stand here in garrison over him; and if he ventures on more villainy, dash his brains against the gable.

(Matthias goes, and Ooshla closes the door. He hauls the bag containing the dead woman back into the room again. He comes out, and considers for a few moments, then he takes a large knife from the dresser, feels the edge and the point of it, takes the candle in his left hand, and goes into the room. He comes out leading the Pedlar by the cut end of the straw rope which had bound him to the bedpost. His hands are still bound with the straw-rope. He does not seem

to be frightened or trembling, perhaps he is too tired for that; but he does seem to be downcast and worried.)

OOSHLA *(motioning him to a stool near the hearth)*. Take your ease there till my comrade comes back.

(He swings out the fire-crane, and ties the loose end of the rope to it.)

PEDLAR *(with humble matter-of-factness)*. Is it to cut my neck ye mean, sir?

OOSHLA *(gravely)*. My comrade turned very wild and savage ever since the wife and children were starved on him. Wait till I see now . . . Tell him he'll be fattening Hell, if he kills you this minute, without first giving you time and chance to get the Holy Sacraments from the priest.

PEDLAR. 'Tis little money I have, sir, but ye're welcome to the lot, sir, if ye'll free me out, and not cut my neck, sir.

OOSHLA *(pouring the last of the poteen into an eggshell)*. You'll be wanting extra courage soon, Paddy, so here's what the cobbler gave his wife—the last.

PEDLAR *(taking the eggshell resignedly)*. I'm thankful to you, sir.

OOSHLA *(gravely)*. Myself is a rogue, too, Paddy. I was stealing enough spuds and oatmeal to keep me living until at last the roguery made its home the same as if it was a maggot in my brain. Then last night I was troubled over the girl going foreign, and the next thing the maggot twisted, and I stole a poor man's spade, and sold it for poteen to banish my trouble. The dirtiest turn ever I done; and was it the same way the roguery kept ever growing till it made a ruffian of you?

PEDLAR. I was no rogue, ever, sir, nor anybody belonging to me.

OOSHLA *(jumping up)*. You were no rogue ever? Your impudence is enough to make a dog beat his father. *(He strides into the room, and drags out the bag.)* Didn't you rob this poor old woman of her life?

(On the instance the Pedlar springs to his feet in a state of intense agitation.)

PEDLAR. Mamma! Mamma! *(He pronounces it M'ma in the western fashion.)* What are you doing to Mamma? *(He runs towards her blindly, but is stopped by the rope tying him to the crane.)* God and Mary and Patrick help me!—help me! *(Struggling like a madman he breaks the rope, and running forward drops on his knees beside the body.)* Mamma! Mamma! did he bruise you? He threw you down, and bruised you; and 'twas my fault, Mamma: for a feather bed I left you. Mamma, Mamma, down on your back he flung you, and injured you sore.

OOSHLA *(mildly)*. Paddy, how could we injure her? She was dead when we opened the bag?

PEDLAR. Two days she's dead, sir. My heart could never bear to see her harmed any way at all, sir. *(With feverish haste, and as skillfully as his bound hands will allow he is laying her out in the bag. Then he turns to Ooshla in passionate pleading, pointing to his own throat.)* Let ye cut my neck if ye like, sir, but in the honour of God, sir, let ye not harm Mamma, sir.

OOSHLA. We'll not harm either of ye, but tell me, Paddy, why have you her in the bag?

PEDLAR. When she was dying in Clanrickard's country,[21] sir, she asked me to bury her with my father in the north in Lord Leitrim's country,[22] sir.

OOSHLA. And we judged 'twas some old woman you robbed and killed. I'll get the knife and free your hands out.

PEDLAR. Then I'll be able to lay her out nice and decent. God bless you, sir.

OOSHLA *(taking the knife from the dresser)*. She must have a great wish for your father, Paddy, when she asked you to carry her that length.

PEDLAR. He cared for whiskey, only, sir. He'd make her go begging money for whiskey, and, if she wouldn't bring back enough, he'd give her blood to drink, sir.

OOSHLA *(feeling edge of the knife)*. Blood! What blood, Paddy?

PEDLAR. Blood from her lips and teeth, sir, from fisting her down on the mouth, sir. I had to be ever watching and ever-fighting him, sir; and that's what has myself left without marriage or a son that'd lift me out of the dust, or the mud, when the age sets me tumbling at last, sir. *(Holding up his bound wrists pleadingly.)* In the honour of God, sir.

OOSHLA *(approaching)*. But, Paddy, if he was that cruel to her, why would she ask to be buried with him?

PEDLAR. She well knew, sir, there wouldn't be one in the world wide only herself to say a good word for him on the Judgment Day; so she'd like to rise near him that day. He was good to her in his younger days before the drink made him ravenous.

OOSHLA. I understand all now, Paddy, and I'll free your hands out.

PEDLAR *(holding up his wrists, his eyes shining with eager joy)*. God be good to you, sir. I'll be every day asking God to be good to you, sir.

(The moment the rope joining his wrists is cut, he whips a long bladed knife from some kind of hidden sheath in his belt, and leaps to his feet brandishing it fiercely, while Ooshla backs away in the utmost dismay.)

PEDLAR. Hullabaloo! Hullabaloo! *(Twice he leaps into the air with that hiss of savage joy; drawing back the knife each time as if about to charge at Ooshla. But instead he leaps again, and cries aloud in triumph.)* Now, Mamma! Timmy has his knife! Timmy has his knife! No one'll dare harm you no more!

OOSHLA. Why should I want to harm her, Paddy?

(But the Pedlar does not hear him. He is standing still, and looking down at his mother, and the life has gone out of him.)

---

21. **Clanrickard's country** the old earldom of Clanricarde Burke in southern Connacht, roughly the eastern half of present-day Co. Galway   22. **Lord Leitrim's country** roughly, present-day Co. Leitrim

PEDLAR *(numbly)*. She never looked! She heard no word! She'll hear no more till we meet on God's floor.

(He sinks on his knees beside her, and puts the knife back into his belt.)

OOSHLA. Was she very old, Paddy?

PEDLAR. She wasn't too old, sir. She was young enough and she dying to have sense and reason to talk to God and His Son and the Blessed Virgin.

OOSHLA. You'll be very lonesome after her, Paddy?

PEDLAR. She had the priest in time, sir, and a happy death, so I'm happy since, but lonesome.

OOSHLA. And you're mortal tired too, Paddy?

PEDLAR *(his eyes never leave her face)*. Two days I'm walking, sir, every hour that the clock struck. I must have her in her grave soon, before the death alters her, sir.

OOSHLA. Well, if you're only fit to carry her half a mile itself, you should do that, Paddy, for my comrade was never safe since the wife and children were starved on him. He mightn't believe she was your mother, and he might go against your knife, and in the fighting she might take harm.

PEDLAR *(rising quickly)*. I'll fetch her away directly, but two of my ropes are spoiled, sir. Have you two idle, sir, that you'd swap for your needs from the basket beyond.

OOSHLA. I have two fine ropes idle in the barn, and you're heartily welcome to them.

(He hurries out. The Pedlar droops a little, and sinks on his knees beside the body again. He murmurs to himself drowsily, and half dazedly.)

PEDLAR. He's proving a decent man at last, Mamma, still we'll trust no other house till you're safe for ever from the badness of the world. *(Exhaustion seems to overwhelm him for a few moments, but, with a great effort, he pulls himself together, and speaks to her mildly, as if in reply to a comment by her.)* Sure I'm not denying it, Mamma, I am tired. *(Then pressing his hands to his head dazedly.)* My mind is very near off its firmness I'm that tired. I'm not safe carrying you I'm that tired . . . *(His eyes wander about a little desperately, and suddenly light up as they see the crude wooden cross on the dresser. He whispers to her excitedly.)* Wait, Mamma. *(He rises, and crosses slowly towards the Cross on the right hand wall. He does not come too near. He speaks with quiet, tired, matter-of-factness.)* They do say Yourself was mortal tired, too, that day, and stumbled greatly while You were carrying it. Just the same way myself is now, my two shoulders cut and scalded with the ropes, and my two feet gripping the ground they're that tired. 'Tis an old saying we have that God is strong, and His Mother is kind, and let the two of Ye help me out this night, so as I won't injure Mamma with stumbles . . . I'll be thankful to Ye evermore; and I'll send no complaint over no more against the hunger or the cramp, or the rain every day rotting my clothes, or the snow and hailstones blinding my eyes; or against the want of a son or a daughter that'd keep the rats from my head when I'll be getting death at last. Let ye brace me up till I have Mamma safe in her grave, and after that please Yereselves about me. *(He is on his way back when he turns suddenly.)* And let Ye mind the darkness too. Yereselves will well remember of how awkward the darkness is when the paths are crooked, and rough. *(He comes back to the body, drops on his knees beside it, glances in the direction of the Cross as if to make sure he is not being overheard, and whispers.)* You'll see, Mamma; They'll be with us at every turn and twist.

OOSHLA *(hurrying in with two stout straw ropes)*. Here are two good hardy lads that'll carry her till ye come to the mountains whatever.

PEDLAR. Take your needs from the basket here, sir.

(He rolls up the two straw ropes, puts them into the basket.)

OOSHLA. I'm in want of nothing, Paddy. *(He wanders off to the fireplace thinking hard, makes up his mind, and exclaims aloud.)* Well here! Hit or miss! *(He takes a stool, and sits down at the centre of the kitchen, facing the Pedlar.)* I'm after making a little thought, Paddy; and I'd reckon I'd be a good man to carry a bag, and a good help at bargaining, too, for I had a quick tongue ever, and it got great practise while I was a gentleman. Maybe 'twould suit you if I went peddling with you through Ireland for evermore.

PEDLAR. Is it to go leaving your home and land, sir?

OOSHLA. I was believing I was entitled to take my needs from the tenants the same as the gentlemen; but it appears now that that was the Divil's notion; for last night the roguery betrayed me all out, and I sold a poor man's spade for poteen, and to-day he found out, so I'm disgraced for life and for ever in this barony; and my life'll be in danger from him too. So 'tis God's Will for me to leave this country, and the roguery.

PEDLAR. But who'll have your house and land, sir?

OOSHLA. That was pledged to a young girl nearby, and 'tis God's Will, too, she to get it, and be saved from going foreign.

PEDLAR *(earnestly looking at corpse)*. In three days I'll have no comrade no more, and I'm falling to age, moreover; so 'twould suit me greatly you to come with me. But she was evermore happy when she'd hear good praise of me, and she'd be shamed now when she'd hear I had a rogue for comrade.

OOSHLA *(rising vigorously)*. Sure to shake off the roguery is what I want, Paddy; for 'twas commencing to make a mean man of me altogether. With you I'll be in honest company, and you'll help me against the roguery.

(He is getting together the dress coat, top-hat, and cane and some food from the dresser for the journey.)

PEDLAR *(eagerly)*. Maybe I could cure you, sir, the way I cured my father out of hurting Mamma, sir?

OOSHLA *(with enthusiasm)*. What way did you cure him, Paddy?

PEDLAR *(taking out knife gravely)*. Every time he'd set into lashing her I'd give him a dart of this, sir. I could give you a dart, too, sir, every time you'd commit a roguery.

OOSHLA. Oh, murther! And would it be a deep prod, Paddy?

PEDLAR *(earnestly)*. Sure if it wasn't, sir, 'twould do you no good, sir.

OOSHLA *(with a shudder)*. But if it was too deep, 'twould do me no good either.

PEDLAR. I'd make sure not to give you a dart in the killing places, sir.

OOSHLA. Oh, murther! Oh, murther! . . . Still you'll cure me. The divil a bit of roguery'll stop long more in me.

(They are busy readying. Thady and Honor enter.)

THADY *(excitedly)*. Matthias Duggan is up and down telling that you went robbing another rogue for the price of a farm for us.

OOSHLA. Ye're just in time! I'm going peddling for a living with Paddy here, so ye can have this place all to yereselves.

THADY. You're going living in the wind so as you can leave us your place!

HONOR. Ooshla, we'd give ourselves up to the Divil before we'd send you living in the wind—at your age and all!

OOSHLA. But I must leave this country whether or no. Last night I stole a poor man's spade!

HONOR. You did!

THADY. Thunder and turf!

OOSHLA. I did, and by to-morrow all the country'll know.

(He gets his stick from a corner.)

THADY. 'Tis as well for you to go so before the roguery gets the better of you altogether.

HONOR. Yes, Ooshla, 'tis time for you to go.

(She goes to the hearth, and seems shocked and depressed.)

OOSHLA *(vigorously)*. Never fret, girl. Paddy here has a wonderful great cure for the roguery. Soon he'll have me as honest as a Bishop. *(He turns to Thady.)* Out of your sailing money that you won't need now, give two shillings to Silke the Smith, and he'll sledge out a new spade for Matthias.

(He puts on his dress coat.)

THADY. I'll not fail you in that, Ooshla.

OOSHLA *(turning to Pedlar who is on his way to the door with bag on his back)*. Timmy! Timmy! They do call me Ooshla. I'm fresh. Let me carry the bag for to-night.

PEDLAR *(quickly, the wild look coming back into his eyes)*. You will not! You might shake or jolt Mamma! Let you carry the basket. *(He opens the door, and looks out anxiously. He draws his knife, holds it at the ready. He speaks with his humble matter-of-factness, never taking his eyes off the dangerous darkness outside.)* If he crosses me, 'twill be me or him, and if 'tis me, let ye put me down along with Mamma in whatever graveyard is nearby, and we'll be very thankful to ye.

(He goes.)

HONOR. Did you see the knife! Is he safe at all?

OOSHLA. 'Tis only how he's afeard anything might happen the mother. It appears he was very good to her while she was living, and her dying wish was he to bury her with his father in Lord Leitrim's country.

THADY. Well, when he was that good to the mother, there's no badness in him.

HONOR *(as Ooshla goes to the door)*. Ooshla, as soon as you're middling honest at all, draw back to us before the hardship breaks you down.

OOSHLA *(in the best of spirits)*. What hardship? Carrying a basket or a bag? What is that only walking? And buying and selling? What is that only talking? Walking and talking isn't that how the gentlemen pass the time? So isn't God good that's after rummaging out a way I can live like a gentleman, and be no rogue? *(At the door he claps the tall hat on his head.)* Ooshla'll be the gentleman-pedlar, keeping only the best, he'll say, and entitled to charge twice more than the rest. When Ooshla comes the way again, he'll be a well-doing man, with a white waistcoat fastened, and a watch chain slinging, and gold guineas sounding and all. Till that day God be good to ye.

(He goes.)

THADY. Good luck, Ooshla.

HONOR *(at the door waving after him)*. God be with you, Ooshla.

THADY *(returning to the fire)*. Ooshla'll be all right. He's in lucky company whatever. The Pedlar was very good to his mother while she lived, and the like do be lucky, they reckon.

(He takes out the clay pipe.)

HONOR *(turning excitedly)*. Right enough, Thady: the like do be lucky, all reckon.

THADY *(filling his pipe)*. And they say the mother doesn't be slow about sending the luck either.

HONOR *(coming back to fire)*. As sure as the day Ooshla himself is the first good luck she sent the Pedlar, for Ooshla should make an able Pedlar, and a hearty comrade for the road!

(She sits beside him.)

THADY *(taking her hand in his, and smiling wisely)*. She sent her son a comrade, and she sent Ooshla an honest way of living, and she sent you and me our own fireside. She has good fortune won for everyone, so she must be well thought of where she is.

CURTAIN

PADRAIC FALLON
1905 — 1974

Padraic Fallon was born in Athenry, Co. Galway, on January 3, 1905, and was educated at St. Joseph's College, Roscrea. He spent forty years as an Irish Customs and Excise official, first, briefly, in Dublin, and then in Wexford in the southeast; he also worked a small farm near Wexford. He married in 1930, and had six sons. For a biographical note in Devin A. Garrity's *New Irish Poets* anthology (1948), he supplied the information that "aside from poetry" he was "interested in pantheistic philosophy and folklore, sailing a small boat, and in starting a verse magazine."

Fallon is known primarily as a poet—indeed, a very good one, adept in the imitation of Gaelic prosody in English—but his work has not had the reputation it deserves because of its publishing history. His poetry began to appear in periodicals in the early 1930s, but no separate volume was published until 1974 (*Poems,* Dolmen Press), just after his death. He also wrote plays, two of which were published: *The Fallen Saint* (1936) and *Dialogue between Raftery and Death* (1952). Two other stage plays saw production: *The Seventh Step* (1954) and *Sweet Love Till Morn* (Abbey, 1971).

There is little argument, however, that Fallon's most significant work lay elsewhere. Fallon was one of the writers stimulated to create verse plays for the radio by Austin Clarke's and Robert Farren's Dublin Verse-Speaking Society. He wrote three fine plays—all of them, until now, unpublished—which were produced by Micheál Ó hAodha for broadcast on Radio Éireann: *Diarmuid and Gráinne* (1950), *The Vision of Mac Conglinne* (1953), and *The Wooing of Étáin* (1955). There were some later performances on the BBC Third Programme, and broadcasts in translation in Germany and the Netherlands.

These plays present complicated, resonant, and delightful reworkings of stories from early Irish literature and mythology. Writing for radio broadcast clearly freed Fallon to develop some aspects of medieval Irish storytelling often played down in theatrical adaptations. Drawing on the visual imagination of his listeners, Fallon endows his heroes with supernatural gifts and maneuvers. In *Diarmuid and Gráinne* we "see" Diarmuid enter the skin of the Quicken-Tree Giant and squeeze him out. The mysterious nature of the warrior Fionn (Finn mac Cumhaill) can be visualized:

He climbs the earthworks. He leaps, floating like a bird, to the ground forty feet below. He walks to a stone-bound well and drinks. He squats on his heels like a great bird and stares wide-lidded into the half-dark that is Ireland. He is an eagle, he is darkness, he is an aging soldier of fortune, his hair is spindrift for whiteness, he is a winter morning.

The plays are conducted by narrators who, like storytellers, compress time to magnify effects, transport the scene from one end of Ireland to the other instantaneously, and control and interpret the course of the action. In these radio plays, of course, the language *is* action. Fallon has chosen to use the mixed forms typical of medieval Irish narrative: prose to carry the action, lyric verse for moments of intense feeling or dialogue. He wields a flexible diction, at one moment whimsical or broadly humorous (as in some deliberately anachronistic uses of Irish regional dialects), at another taut with excitement, at another, lyrical, as in this introduction of the young Gráinne (pronounced "grawnya"):

How can I define her?
A girl? A burst of sunlight in a room?
First breath of the apple tree? Or the first dawn
In the first garden pausing between two yews?
Or the virgin moment before strings are struck?

But those are the statements of innocence: and there is no
      innocence.
Who knows what lusts in the leaf and craves right-of-way through
      the bud?
Can sap be simple that is so old? Or innocent
The girl on her way to womanhood?
No, says the storyteller, blood is too old.

So hold the strings; they are too young for her.
She makes her own music standing up between
Two yew trees, still as the dawn, a listener
Like Eve in that first garden, a design
In breasts and light between two sombre angels.

Diarmuid and Gráinne is a reworking of the medieval Irish story of the seduction of Fionn's young lieutenant Diarmuid by the girl Gráinne, after she has been betrothed to the elderly warrior. Most of the story depicts the adventures of the young couple as Fionn pursues them vengefully around Ireland; finally they marry, and Diarmuid and Fionn are ostensibly reconciled, but when Diarmuid is mortally wounded on a boar hunt, Fionn's anger prevents him from bringing the magic water that would save the young man. As in the medieval tale, Fallon's version stresses the poignancy of the self-exiled Diarmuid's longing for Fionn:

A sweet comrade is Fionn.
He is sleepy stalls. The byres are full.

Corn is hived: and over the empty pastures
Comes the cooking-smoke from houses. A rich warm smell.

The psychological complexity of Diarmuid's death symbolizes the dilemma
of his life—the conflict between his devotion to Fionn and his magical
bondage to the willful and sensual Gráinne. He and the fateful Boar of
Ben Bulben are doubles, "the two shadows of the one person"; as they
exchange echoing poetry, Diarmuid recognizes in the boar "the dark that
grimaced beyond my lamp, . . . the corruption in me when I was born."
Micheál Ó hAodha whimsically caught the essence of the manifold richness
of the work: "It is not set in pre-Christian Ireland nor in an Irish otherworld of pagan belief but in a mythopoeic universe where Orpheus, Jung,
Frazer, Adonis, Robert Graves, Demeter, Freud and Dionysus can wander
at will."

The rollicking medieval anticlerical satire *Aislinge Meic Conglinne* has
had two major modern adaptations: Austin Clarke's witty verse play *The
Son of Learning* (1927), and Fallon's more extravagant and earthy *The Vision
of Mac Conglinne* (pronounced "mak con-glinnuh"), whose typescript is
dated July 11–21, 1951. Fallon has played down the social and ecclesiastical
satire of the *Aislinge,* which poked fun at both court poetry and the
monastic church, and he has set aside the original political satire, which
ridiculed southern Irish claims to the kingship of Ireland through the
portrayal of Cathal mac Finguine (a genuinely powerful and threatening
king of Munster who died in 742 A.D.) ludicrously in thrall to a hunger
demon.

The relationship between man and woman, between the poet Mac Conglinne and Ligach, the Queen, dominates the action of Fallon's play. (In
the *Aislinge* Ligach—sister, not wife, to the northern King Fergal—func-
tions only to send her tainted gifts to Cathal, then disappears from the
plot.) Connected from the first moments of the play with willfulness,
famine, and primitive religious power, Ligach, like Gráinne, is an object
of desire and fear. "Weary of the litany" of lovers' words, she demands of
the poets "a new language," and "every carolling boy of them [lays] down
his metres like carpets before her so that she may pace down in a stately
progress through the ages." Her sexual power is dangerous and fascinating.
"As a queen you shine / Like a stone after rain," Fergal tells her; "What
an offering to the eyes. . . . But none dares break the stone, your queenly
covering, / Lest you vault naked, arched, arrowy and cold, / Into the world,
each breast a thunderbolt."

At the end of the medieval *Aislinge,* Mac Conglinne is strong and triumphant, victor over the hunger demon through his poetic powers of vision
and language; at the end of Fallon's *Vision,* he is a pretentious old man,
shorn of innocence, tormented and burnt out in the service of woman.
And Ligach, indefatigable, carries on as she pleases.

SELECT BIBLIOGRAPHY

Publications

The Fallen Saint. The Dublin Magazine (1936). (Play)
Dialogue between Raftery and Death. The Dublin Magazine (1952). (Play)
Lighting-Up Time. Dublin: Orwell, 1938. (Story)
Poems. Dublin: Dolmen Press, 1974.

Biography and Criticism

See discussions in Robert Hogan, *After the Irish Renaissance* and *Dictionary of Irish Literature,* and Micheál Ó hAodha, *Theatre in Ireland.*
Meyer, Kuno, ed. and trans. *Aislinge Meic Conglinne: The Vision of MacConglinne, A Middle-Irish Wonder Tale*. London: David Nutt, 1892.

The Vision of Mac Conglinne

CHARACTERS

STORYTELLER
ANIER MAC CONGLINNE, *a young poet and scholar*
LIGACH, *Fergal's queen*
FERGAL, *King of Ailech*
CAHAL, *King of Cashel*
MUINCHEN, *Abbot of Cork*
PICHAN, *a Munster king*
HUNGER DEMON
CAPTAIN OF FERGAL'S BORDER GUARD
OTHER OFFICERS AND SOLDIERS OF FERGAL
CHIEF DOORKEEPER TO FERGAL
WAITING WOMAN
FISHERMAN
WOMAN
FIRST CRANE
SECOND CRANE
THIRD CRANE
YEWTREE
ABBOT OF LITTLE IRELAND
MONK OF LITTLE IRELAND
MAN
HERALD OF KING CAHAL
MONKS OF CORK
SCHOOLMASTER
RAVEN
AIDAN, *the youngest monk of Cork*
THE GOD OF MAC CONGLINNE
VOICES

PART 1

STORYTELLER. My story tonight is a story of Ireland, of two Kings and a treacherous beautiful woman.
(Strings)

O woman. She is everywhere.
An element.
Behind each quarrel; at the back of every sermon;
At the bottom of every bad debt.

And yet I hail her.
How can I help it? She
Who divides herself around me like a calendar,
Who is my twelve climates of feeling,
Who musters me
So many shapes I live like the sun,
A god within my year.

The woman is Ligach, the stepdaughter of Maelduin in the north, King of Ailech.[1] The kings are Fergal, son of Maelduin; and Cahal mac Finguine, King of Cashel in the south, two mighty men who can wax and wane, as equal as the north is to the south, as equal as the two parts of a foot rule, as one half of the year is to the other. And the woman stands with one foot upon each, and when she is a while with one she feels a desire for the company of the other; and the one from whom she is absent is nothing but a great hunger for her, a hunger that travels round him like a famine on circuit.

(Strings)

O never will I love a woman.
Give me a cat to nurse or a dog to pat;
Give me a stone to kneel on. I
Will be no woman's alphabet.

Look at her now. Her sun-room in Ailech is big and bright. In the green of the garden her fifty of maidens are merry. They are wheeling and laughing. A gold ball goes from one to the other. But the game cannot end, for the lovely queen-pin is absent, the queen does not play any more, she broods in the frozen sunlight of the window.

(A soft trumpet.)
WAITING WOMAN. Queen. O my queen.
LIGACH. I hear you.
WAITING WOMAN. It is the King again. Fergal demands an audience.
LIGACH. I have pleaded sleep.
WAITING WOMAN. He carries a cure for sleepiness.

---

1. **Ailech** Greenan Elly, an iron-age fortification situated on the neck of the Inishowen peninsula in Donegal, about seven miles northwest of Derry; historic capital of the Cenél nEogáin of the Northern Uí Néill dynasty, of which Fergal was king

LIGACH. I have pleaded weariness.

WAITING WOMAN. He answers he will cure that, too.

LIGACH. I have pleaded melancholy.

WAITING WOMAN. A sorrow shared is a sorrow halved, he says.

LIGACH. I have pleaded coldness.

WAITING WOMAN. He answers that his presence is warmth itself.
(Sudden trumpet)
He is here, now.

FERGAL. Ligach.

LIGACH. This is the queen's room, O King.

FERGAL. Ligach, wherever the queen is, that is the queen's room.

LIGACH. You have no rights of entry to my room.

FERGAL. Wherever you are, there my heart is. May I not enter my own heart, since my heart is your sun-room?

LIGACH. I am tired of the words of love.

FERGAL. That is not true.

LIGACH. Weary of the litany.
(Strings)

> Words stand around me
> Like old and obsolete soldiers pensioned to sentry-go;
> They bow me this way, that way,
> Obsequiously on the paths I know.
>
> They are afflicted with a palsy,
> Their points are blunted, they are too old for my age;
> What can they in their rusted armour tell
> To one so young, whose needs are a new language?

I repeat; I am tired of the words of love.

FERGAL. And I repeat you lie to me. You are not tired of the speech but of the speaker; not so much tired of love as of the lover. Ho, there. You, the doormen;
(Ringing gong)
Bring in those men.
(Echo of steps etc.)

CHIEF DOORKEEPER. Softly, now, Bigfoot. Fat buttocks, you, walk easy. Soles must be silent here. O heavy heel, a strop on your backside for this. . . . Majesties, the men. *(Whispers)* Laggards, to the earth, you! Rub your nostrils in it. Make proper obeisance.

FERGAL. You know those men, my queen.

LIGACH. They are mine.

FERGAL. You have not seen them for some time.

LIGACH. Not for some time.

FERGAL. You did not miss them?

LIGACH. I did not miss them.

FERGAL. Did you send them on a mission?

LIGACH. Have you questioned them?

FERGAL. Have I questioned them? I have more than questioned them. I have scourged them.

LIGACH. And they did not answer you? Why then do you expect an answer from their mistress?

FERGAL. I demand it. I do not expect it.

LIGACH. I keep my rights to be silent. And my men have my rights to be silent. In whipping them, you exceeded your rights of kingship.

FERGAL. Sometimes the man must overlap the king. You refuse to speak?

LIGACH. I will speak as a queen.

FERGAL. It is an aspect of you I would willingly leave to my people, to the gapers at the door, to the loungers at the crossroads, to the lads at the corner.

(Strings)

> As a queen you shine
> Like a stone after rain; and every man's prayer
> Though you have nothing for any man
> Gives you the face that he would sculpture.
>
> The long and lingering white thighs,
> I see them, and the birds below
> Your delicate shanks. What an offering to the eyes.
> Each man uncovers you in that stone.
>
> Each man makes you with a look.
> But none dares break the stone, your queenly covering,
> Lest you vault naked, arched, arrowy and cold,
> Into the world, each breast a thunderbolt.

Be a queen to the people, wife, but to me you must be a woman. You refuse to tell me to whom you sent those messengers?

LIGACH. I think that you know already.

FERGAL. I have followed a little chain of reasoning. Shall I wag it for you? Call me that border captain.

(Gong etc.)

CAPTAIN. My lord, I am here.

FERGAL. Your duties are?

CAPTAIN. One week in two I keep the watchman's ford in Slieve Fuat. I question, I pass, I detain, I admit, I turn back.

FERGAL. You detailed those men? Why?

CAPTAIN. At my lord's order. And following out that order I had them searched. I list my findings. Item, an oaken apple; item, a white cloak, with six undercloaks to match; item, a brooch of gold for those cloaks; item, a bag of seed wheat; item, a queen bee in a stone jar; item, the half of a queen's shift; item, the half of a queen's head-dress; item, a sword of war. That is my enumeration.

FERGAL. You have done well. Shall I read the story, Queen? Shall I decipher this cypher of apples and bees and cloaks?

LIGACH. Could I stop my lord?

FERGAL. Certainly. No man can speak if a woman's mouth is on his mouth, or find zest for speech if her breast is on his breast.

LIGACH. I will leave you the faculty of speech.

FERGAL. Ah. Then, all that is left to me is to withdraw into my king-ship. I speak henceforth as the law speaks. I will assemble the court. I will accuse you of holding commerce with my enemy and the enemy of Ulster, Cahal of Munster, but the penalty I can already whisper in your ear.

LIGACH. Banishment?

FERGAL. Certainly not. And have you within a month inside the crook of his arm. Are you curious about your punishment?

LIGACH. You will tell me as you will.

FERGAL. I will tell you now, my love. Deposition. Deprivation of queenly rights. Deprivation of the rights of a citizen. As a person of no rights you will be a slave, and as a slave I will purchase you from the commonwealth and enroll you among my body-servants.

LIGACH. You will not dare.

FERGAL. Then, my queen, you will not close your doors against me and refuse me audience.

STORYTELLER. I end this scene thoughtfully among the clamour of gongs.

(Gongs and music)

I open the next scene on a sight that gives pleasure to my soul. It is the throne room of Ailech. The king is carved in colours on high. Sea-greens and the acid blues predominate. Below him, the assembled court is a multicolour like bedded flowers. Those are the lawmen, the laymen, the white clerics, the holymen, the wisemen, the heroes, the schools, and immediately under the great Kingseat, where his two tanists[2] support the sacred heel of the king, is the assembled college of the poets. On a lower throne of ivory and blue sits the queen. She is faintly smiling. Her eyes have caught up the stare of the poets and you can see every carolling boy of them laying down his metres like carpets before her so that she may pace down in a stately progress through the ages, and every bald and bawdy

2. **tanists** heirs apparent

ancient of them arranging her in their eyes like an image in a bed. I dare not look on her any longer. Her glance is a crepitation up my backbone. The Lord save us. I could leap nine cubits for her. I will do the chariot trick for her. I will do the dangerous sword trick. I will do the wild feat of the spear and balance my bulk upon the point—

(Gongs)

Hush, it is the King speaking.

(Fergal's voice comes forward from background)

FERGAL. The oak apple is a greeting from royalty to royalty and has the double meaning that the days of love will come again. You agree?

MANY SOFT VOICES. We agree, Lord.

FERGAL. The white cloak, the six subcloaks, the golden brooch, all symbols of kingship. Why do they go from north to south, from Fergal's country to Cahal's country from the queen? It is evident she offers him kingship over her.

SOFT VOICES. It is evident, Lord.

FERGAL. The bag of seed. My reading is: I offer my lands to your sowing.

VOICES SOFTLY. That is our reading.

FERGAL. The queen bee reads: I am ready to leave the hive.

VOICES. We agree with that reading.

FERGAL. The half of a queen's shift, the half of a queen's crown. I have left a king's bed. I seek the other half of my crown in the bed of another king.

VOICES SOFTLY. That is our reading.

FERGAL. You will agree, then, that the queen has been making overtures to Cahal mac Finguine of Cashel, my hereditary enemy?

SOFT VOICES. We agree, Lord.

FERGAL. Then, it remains only to name the punishment. You agree?

SOFT VOICES. We agree.

YOUNG POET. I do not agree, my lord.

FERGAL. You are a young poet. Have you orders of merit that give you a right to be heard?

YOUNG POET. My Lord, at this moment I am endowed with grace and dowered with the loveliness of all the world, for I sit within sight of the queen's face. This gives my small years a right to be heard greatly.

FERGAL. I give you permission to speak. Your name?

YOUNG POET. Anier the son of Conglinne, my Lord, a master of the alphabets, of no country but the sea, one who has rolled from one seatop to another and got drunk with gravity in all the great houses of this world.

FERGAL. Say your say.

MAC CONGLINNE. The queen is saying it for me, Lord. Very silently, but her soft thunder is all around her and the earth is speaking for her.

The different trees are singing in one still voice that this queen is not of the kind that accepts a judgement she does not give. She is law and lawgiving. She is that that she is.

FERGAL. She is the queen of Ulster, Mac Conglinne, and my queen. As such she is not the law but amenable to the law.

MAC CONGLINNE. King, she is a woman and her throne is her own will.

FERGAL. Not so, Poet.

MAC CONGLINNE. By my hand, I assert it, for she is the business of the poets and our vision of life. In the wayward will of woman we live and love and die. She bears us and buries us. She is our year of life.

(Strings)

On her changing levels
She demands of me more than one body;
So I invent myself
Everyday anew till there is enough of me.

I am my father and my son.
I am a town. I am a country. I establish her.
But she is flown, she is gone
When the time comes for me to inhabit her.

She is my labour and my law. She lures me,
Loves me, lives with me, loathes me, leaves me, that is her way;
Yet when I take at last the grave she offers me,
What a large legacy I leave in clay,
I who have lived like a god the livelong day.

(End of music)

King, it is the business of a woman to bear man, rear man, and love man. But it is also the business of the woman in the woman to tempt him beyond himself so that he spends himself in extending the ways of life and the breadth of life. She is the spark in his inertia, the little white ewe of the new year that tempts the drowsy ram till his horns run gold and his stamping wakens the whole of the heavens. It is even her business to deceive him so that his anger and horror and hate make him welcome his inevitable end and the peace that the grave offers.

FERGAL. I think you invert wisdom, Mac Conglinne. Do the Ulster poets agree with you?

SOFT VOICES. We do not.

MAC CONGLINNE. I am not disconcerted. Do I not agree with myself among the confluence of my selves? I lay down this lady as a law and I challenge the poets of Ulster to contradict me if I assert that they have behaved at this trial as the King's bondmen, and that they have left empty the seat under the Willow, the tree of the Goddess, where the poet is both votary and king.

SOFT VOICES. This stranger is insulting, King.

FERGAL. I agree with you. Yourselves can name his punishment.

SOFT VOICES. Banishment from Ulster.

FERGAL. I have good rodmen. If I suggested whipping?

SOFT VOICES. His art exempts him.

FERGAL. Let it be banishment in that case.

MAC CONGLINNE. I take it as an honour to be barred from Ulster. But I crave a boon before I leave.

FERGAL. Is there good reason for this?

MAC CONGLINNE. Is there a greater reason than justice?

FERGAL. There is no greater reason than justice.

MAC CONGLINNE. I demand that this assembly listen to the queen, if the queen should wish to speak.

FERGAL. She has our permission. The queen may speak.

MAC CONGLINNE. King, you use a churl's speech where the occasion asks for bended knees.

FERGAL. Now, by my royalty, Mac Conglinne, you have offended a king.

MAC CONGLINNE. By your lack of it, O Royalty, you offend a queen and the order of poets to which I belong.

FERGAL. I am entitled to have you whipped for lack of reverence.

MAC CONGLINNE. I am entitled to lampoon you for lack of true majesty.

(Gong. Then clamour. Gong again)

FERGAL. Mac Conglinne, your peers can name the number of strokes you will have.

MAC CONGLINNE. King, I have no peers in this assembly. I will allow the assembled poets, however, to name the number of stanzas in which I may satirize you, pulverize you, blister you and flay you.

FERGAL. Will the assembled poets allow me to name the number of this man's strokes?

SOFT VOICES. You have our permission, King.

FERGAL. How many stanzas will you use to lampoon the King, Mac Conglinne?

MAC CONGLINNE. I will number them by the strokes, O King.

FERGAL. I do not think you will live that long, Mac Conglinne. I order you five strokes for every consonant and ten for every vowel in the alphabet.

MAC CONGLINNE. Calculate that, O King, in one number.

FERGAL. Thirteen at five is three score and a quarter, five at ten is two score and a half. I add those and get five score and three-quarters of a score. Does the total satisfy you?

MAC CONGLINNE. I asked that I might display to the court your ignorance of learning. Wise men will know from now that I am being punished by an ignorant churl of a provincial nobody of a king who is so backward that the true alphabet has not yet reached him through his learned men. I will have great pleasure in composing five score and three-quarters of a score of stanzas on the King's ignorance and churlishness, on his lack of majesty and variety—

FERGAL. Variety?

MAC CONGLINNE. That he cannot be thirteen men in one and keep his queen interested.

(Laughing strings as the Queen laughs)

MAC CONGLINNE. I have amused the queen.

QUEEN. You have pleased me, Mac Conglinne.

MAC CONGLINNE. It is my hard fate not to have been born a king. It is my hard fate.

(Strings)

> I have many mirrors for a woman.
> O the delight of the long glass;
> And the little glass that nurses one blue eye;
> And the silver one that fills with a red mouth.
> I have two long shafts of light for the rich thigh.
>
> I hold a running glass like water
> When hair comes tumbling from the pin
> Of a May morning to stream down the shoulder
> In waves of sunlight over the white skin.
> You will stand there like a swimmer.
>
> But for the secret night,
> There is plain gold in the room that will take a candle
> And make it seven; while I lean from the shadows
> With a peacock's feather in my hand,
> All eyes, all bright and foreign eyes.

FERGAL. Now, by all the Gods, Mac Conglinne.

MAC CONGLINNE. It is my regret, Queen, that I was not born a king.

QUEEN. I could almost regret my royalty, Mac Conglinne.

FERGAL. Take this poet away. Rope him to the pillar stone on the green and give him the number of strokes he has been adjudged. After that, turn him loose in a wicker boat on the Foyle that he may float out to the wastes of the seas where he belongs.

MAC CONGLINNE. I bow to the queen.

QUEEN. You are pleasant company, Mac Conglinne. If I remember you tomorrow I will be sorry for you.

MAC CONGLINNE. That saying will warm me, O Queen, when I sit before a big bonfire. I leave my farewells with you, as I will leave the skin of my back on this pillar stone of the King's green.

(Trampling sound. Arms)

ULSTER VOICE. Come gently, Poet. Take his arm, there. No trouble, now. Move on, clappertongue, lively, bigmouth. We are only going to flay you alive.

(Trampling dies out.)

FERGAL. That is that. Now, where were we, gentlemen? Yes. The queen was about to speak. Were you not, my love?

QUEEN. I do not think so, my Lord.

FERGAL. You will not defend yourself?

QUEEN. It is not necessary. That poet has spoken for me the words I bade him speak.

FERGAL. You know this poet, then?

QUEEN. For some minutes only. His mind was open to me and I entered him. There is one thing, my Lord, I did not ask him to mention for it is my wish always to play in my own drama and bring myself to a crisis.

FERGAL. What thing is that?

QUEEN. I would wish that captain who arrested my messengers to be brought before me.

FERGAL. It is done. Bring the captain of the Ford.

(Gong)

CAPTAIN *(Ulster accent)*. I am here, Lady.

QUEEN. King, bid him eat the oak apple that he seized, the apple that he pawed, the apple that he stuffed in a common pocket among shreds of tobacco and bits of string. It was a message from one throne to another. Now, it is soiled and it must to a garbage can.

CAPTAIN. I did but the King's will, Lady, and a soldier's duty. But I will eat the apple.

FERGAL. Give him the apple.

CAPTAIN. I have no taste for such greenery as is not boiled with old bacon, but I will eat it. By god, it is a heavy apple.

(Sound of a lump of iron hitting the ground)

My good big toe. Is the bloody thing made of bronze? Excuse the soldier's tongue, my Lady.

QUEEN. Eat it.

CAPTAIN. I eat it.

(Sound of a monstrous crunching)

Is this quartz?

(Bray of music)

Is this limestone?

(Bray of music)
Is this the great rock of time?
(Bray of music)
Those tooth-noises I am making, by God, you must excuse me, Lords
and Lady. Such mouth-music I never made nor heard before.
(Bray of music)
This is the first subsoil of all the world.
(Bray of music)
And here I come to the core. I have eaten the earth, Lady.

QUEEN. You have also eaten something that is less pleasant. You have
eaten poison, good Captain. Now you must die. But don't hurry yourself.
It does not cause me too much inconverience.

CAPTAIN. I have not deserved this.

QUEEN. Why not? The good soldier is promoted and his trade is to
die.

(Sound of falling body. Crash of music)
VOICES. He is dead. He is dead.

FERGAL. He is dead. And Cahal of Munster would have died likewise.

QUEEN. I have given you a proof by demonstration.

FERGAL. We record that. It is not a pleasant way of stating evidence.

QUEEN. I have also taken a revenge on you which was due to me for
the whipping of my seven messengers.

FERGAL. I would prefer law and not revenge.

QUEEN. I would point out, too, that it is now time for you to ask
pardon of me before the court for this public humiliation of a queen.

FERGAL. I must do that.

QUEEN. Further, you will agree before sureties to certain demands I
will make on you as to our future relations. This must be your reparation.

FERGAL. Name your demands.

QUEEN. Ensurance of my privacy. Freedom from the demands of a
husband unless I will it otherwise—

FERGAL. WHAT?

QUEEN. Rights of my personal freedom in travel and entertainment.
Indulgence of my fancies.

FERGAL. By my oath, no.

QUEEN. Equal rights of sovereignty. Separate establishments in the
same establishment.

FERGAL. Am I a king or a cuckold?

QUEEN. I demand these as my rights, for they were a queen's rights
of old. I will put it to the assembled court, now, as is my prerogative.

FERGAL. By my soul, you won't. You will get back to your carpet and
play kitten. You will toss the ball among the girls and make eyes at the
guards. You will regard your reflection in your polished nails and bore

yourself to death; but what man has won from woman, what rights he has beaten from her throughout the ages, you will not obtain from Fergal, the High King of Ulster, by leading him into a little trap. Bow to the court and run to the women's quarters.

(Raucous music. Then tripping music as if women were running)

STORYTELLER. Phew, I end this scene with my handkerchief. For things are very hot here.

(Music. There are hints of the sounds of a man being scourged.)

STORYTELLER. I open this scene with a scourging. The poor poet is strapped against the tall pillar-stone on the king's green and the soldiers are gathered round him.

(The soldiers all speak in Ulster accents.)

CAPTAIN. Lieutenant, begin the alphabet.

LIEUTENANT. Beth, luis, beth, luis, luis, nion[3]—Sergeant, begin the alphabet.

SERGEANT. Certainly, sir. Beth, luis, nion, beth, luis, nion—

CAPTAIN. Corporal!

CORPORAL. Present, sir.

SERGEANT. Begin the bleeding alphabet.

CORPORAL. Beth, luis, er, aliph—

SERGEANT. Aliph's a bleeding vowel.

CORPORAL. Sorry, sir. I only knows my pees and cues.

CAPTAIN. Lieutenant, the alphabet I said.

LIEUTENANT. Yes, sir. Sergeant, the alphabet!

SERGEANT. Yes, sir. Corporal, the alphabet. You son of a stunned pimp, you brothel of a boy, you stuffed and stifled grandson of a Munster woolmerchant, how did you get your stripes? Have you been to school to any master except the paymaster?

CORPORAL. The alphabet it is, sir. *(Whispers)* Any of you lousers who've lain and lazed your life away at school remember your bleeding letters?

SOLDIER. Beth, luis, nion, fearn, sáille etc.

SERGEANT. Enough. Stand by the Captain and call out the trees. Corporal, call the tally. All ready, sir. We begin with consonant Beth, the good birch tree, and very apt if I may say so, sir.

CAPTAIN. Is the scholar ready?

MAC CONGLINNE. I am ready.

(Strings)

---

3. **beth, luis . . . nion** "birch, rowan-tree, ash," signifying by their initials the first letters (B, L, N) of the early Irish Ogham alphabet, in which nearly all of the letters are named after trees

I am learning my letters
The painful way.
Not by attention, not by the rote of my fingers,
But by rough strokes from the hand of a tree.

Scholars, come to me.
The consonants are mine, the vowels bleed on my side.
Put up your slates, schoolmasters, all the world
May cypher the alphabet on my backside.

The lovely grove of trees
The learned planted will leave scars on me.
But my seat will be a seat of learning
When I reach the last black vowel, the tall and hissing Yewtree.

SOLDIERS. Hahaha. Hahaha. Hahaha.
(A hissing music. Raucous laughter. Sounds of the whipping)
(Short interlude of this music becoming raucous and jerky, ending in a violence. Sudden silence)
SOLDIER. And wham. By God, I buried that black vowel in his bum.
CAPTAIN. Well struck. And how is our scholar now?
MAC CONGLINNE. Bumptious.
LIEUTENANT. By God, he speaks.
MAC CONGLINNE *(roaring)*. Speaks? I can bawl, I can bellow like a bull, I can bell like the brute-throated bigmouth of the pack. O, you men of Ulster, you have struck blows today that will resound in many hedge-schools.[4] While you beat me, I lost myself in many stanzas, a stanza for every blow, and they will be rods upon your backs till the day of doom.
(Resonance of music)

> In Ulster a sour and sacred king
> Had a bad wife. But he was worse.
> And worse than he were the bonded people.
> Here on all of them is the poet's curse.

CAPTAIN. Shut him up, shut him up. Bawl, shout, cry.
MAC CONGLINNE. I can outbawl you. My God is the God of Eloquence.

> That king was never a king in bed
> For the queen she was never there
> But walking up walls with a pain in her head—

CAPTAIN. Wrap this shirt round his mouth.

---

4. **hedgeschools** rural Irish schools of the eighteenth and early nineteenth centuries, run by traveling schoolmasters known for their pretentious and polysyllabic learning and their harsh physical punishment of pupils

MAC CONGLINNE. —Or tempting a guardsman by the pillar.

(In music the sounds of struggle)

CORPORAL. Cripes, that man has strength.

SERGEANT. He is quiet enough, now. The half of his teeth are down in his jersey.

CAPTAIN. Lieutenant. Have a chariot prepared. He must to the river, now. And immediately. We have listened to a blasphemy that might cost us our heads.

LIEUTENANT. Sergeant.

SERGEANT. Sir.

LIEUTENANT. A chariot at once. Detail two men. Detail two more to follow me to the kitchens. We will ration up and leave for the Foyle River at once.

SERGEANT. Two of youse. At the double. After me. Quick march.

CAPTAIN. I need a drink. Call to the mess before you leave.

LIEUTENANT. Am I going?

CAPTAIN. Do you think I am? The nastier jobs fall to the lowest in rank. Quite properly.

LIEUTENANT. Is the poet to be left alone?

CAPTAIN. What can he do? Steal the pillar stone? See you for a drink before you leave.

LIEUTENANT. The scholar has fainted.

CAPTAIN. It may be a trick. They are full of tricks, those scholars. A minor poet stole my wife for a week one time on the pretence of teaching her something. He sent her back because she knew more than he bargained for. Well, he seems safe enough. We can be off.

(Music. Quiet. Dreamy)

MAC CONGLINNE. There is someone in the middle of my pains.

QUEEN. It is I, Mac Conglinne.

MAC CONGLINNE. The bad queen.

QUEEN. Not so, Mac Conglinne. A queen needs to be royal, not good. You will agree with me in that?

MAC CONGLINNE. More thoroughly if I had not been beaten for it. You must want something from me if you break the tabus to look upon a naked and beaten man.

QUEEN. I speak from inside you.

MAC CONGLINNE. No use in that case to ask you to touch me and let my head fall upon your breast.

QUEEN. You are there, now, Mac Conglinne. My child, my boy, my man.

MAC CONGLINNE. I think you are my lady of the Willow Tree.

QUEEN. I am your lady and still I am not your lady. I am a queen, Mac Conglinne. My favours are a commonwealth.

MAC CONGLINNE. I sigh on that account, but I must agree with you.

QUEEN. Your pains have gone.

MAC CONGLINNE. Why, yes, and that is a wonder. I think that my red alphabet has healed.

QUEEN. Pain is but a thought. I have given you another thought.

MAC CONGLINNE. That is right. I can think, now, of nothing but you.

QUEEN. You are my favorite among the poets.

MAC CONGLINNE. I thank you. And now I know, indeed, that you have come to ask me for something.

QUEEN. You sing of woman. It is always one woman who is no woman but all women. You sing of me.

MAC CONGLINNE. I sing of you.

QUEEN. So, you must serve me.

MAC CONGLINNE. So, I will serve you. You will bring me beatings and contumely, you will bring me hunger and thirst. You will leave me wifeless and houseless, but I will serve you. Have you not ordained me under the willow tree?

QUEEN. You have my thanks, you have my love, you have my art. You will be taken from here to the banks of the Bann.[5] They will put you in a wicker boat. When they do, you must ask for clothing. A woman standing by will take off her cloak and give it to you. It will be folded and you must not open it. You will travel far but you must not open it. Where you will land, in that place you must call for the king, and you will fast on him till he comes. The king will be Cahal of Munster. You will give him the folded cloak. But in the midwinter to come you must be in Cork. In the midwinter to come you must be in Cork. I kiss you now—from the outside. You are my beloved.

MAC CONGLINNE. Queen, I tremble. This is my initiation. Forgive me if I tremble.

(Rumbling music of a chariot. Stops. Sound of voices. Steps)

LIEUTENANT. Is there life in that hulk, Sergeant?

SERGEANT. Corporal, does that corpse kick?

CORPORAL. Soldiers, listen to that stiff 's ticker.

SOLDIER. There is a faint pulse. In some hole and corner of him there is a spark of life. What will I do with the Captain's shirt? A breath tighter and it would have noosed him.

CORPORAL. Softly, fool. Give me that shirt.

SERGEANT. Now, hang me for a pissabed rogue. The captain's shirt. Is not that a sergeant's prerogative?

CORPORAL. Allow me, sergeant. The Sergeant's prerogative is the corporal's perquisite in certain circumstances. Article Beth-Luis-Nion 143 states—

LIEUTENANT. What are you two quarrelling about? There are leagues

5. **the Bann** major river in northeastern Ireland

of country before us tonight and not a star—the Captain's shirt. Give me that shirt, pickpockets. I will dye it in saffron—

SOLDIER. This poet is alive, nobles.

SERGEANT. So much the worse for him.

SOLDIER. He is talking about the queen.

LIEUTENANT. Lord, must the shirt go back upon his mouth? Sergeant, boot him one in the belly. Put out that little spark.

SERGEANT. Corporal.

(Sudden strings)

MAC CONGLINNE.

A marvel has happened to the scholar.
His books light up.
The birds and beasts he has inked in manycolour
On the white margin speak to his fingertip.

They are praising a queen.
The Bull, the Lion, the serpent on the branch
Of the tall and tinted tree,
And the griffoned eagle are singing, praise to the queen of all lands.

LIEUTENANT. Sergeant, did you hear what I heard?

SERGEANT. Corporal, did you—why, yes, sir. The fellow has changed his tune.

LIEUTENANT. We will not need the shirt. Hoist up the carcase and let us be shortening the road.

STORYTELLER. I end this scene with the grunt of straining men.

(Interval of music)

I open this scene in darkness and torches.

ULSTER VOICE. King or no King, I'll no' give my coracle without payment on the nail.

LIEUTENANT. Knock him on the head, Sergeant.

ULSTER VOICE. Ye'll no' do that, master. Hola, my sons. Neighbours. Ye see, sogers, we're clannish hereabouts. And we keep a guard on the village, if ye'll mind. We put our trust in the king all right, and we drink the goodman's health of a feasting day, but we keep an eye on him at the same time.

LIEUTENANT. What do you want for the coracle?

ULSTER VOICE. Well, a coracle's an expensive piece of manufacturing these times. Have you tokens or kind?

LIEUTENANT. What do you think? Do you expect me to carry a bull or a bloody ram lamb about with me on the King's business—

ULSTER VOICE. Moderate your language, Master. We're all Kirk[6] here. You will give me ten tokens for the coracle.

6. **Kirk** Church of Scotland (anachronism)

LIEUTENANT. I will. Ten bleats from my Daddy's goat. I'll give you two tokens.

ULSTER VOICE. Do you want a good coracle or no'?

LIEUTENANT. No. The very worst will do.

ULSTER VOICE *(ominously)*. You said the very worst?

LIEUTENANT. The very worst.

ULSTER VOICE. Lads, he said the very worst.

VOICES. He said the very worst.

ULSTER VOICE. Light all the torches to Bran's causeway. Spread the nets along the path. Touch the bonfire. And bring the beer down to the river's brink.

LIEUTENANT. Fishermen, if you are considering a quarrel, I would advise you to the contrary. I will give you ten tokens—

ULSTER VOICE. Noble, we give you a coracle without charge. We did not understand the king on whose business you move, the king who owns all coracles, but sacrifices one to his mother the great White One, when it is the time and number. We are ignorant people and we beg your pardon.

(A wild music in the distance)

They are ready below. Let us go down, now, with your holy burden.

LIEUTENANT. Sergeant, you hear what I hear?

SERGEANT. Sir, there was one word struck pleasantly on my two ears. The word was beer. If you will verify my hearing on that word I offer it as my opinion that we are in for a pleasurable night in the way of business, for I remember, now, that those sea people hold an Autumn festival that is different from ours.

LIEUTENANT. Carry the poet down.

SERGEANT. Corporal, bring the body.

CORPORAL. You stiffs, shoulder the dead one here. Right. Ready. Beat, beat, beat—

(Distant drums take up the corporal's rhythm. Through it the storyteller speaks.)

STORYTELLER. Fires have been lit on a small green above the river Bann where there is a hut or two, a pillar stone, and a tiny jetty of alder. The seapeople are making something of a ceremony in their reception of the poet's body. Three women take it from the soldiers, the only women on the green. They wash him and tend to his hair, they rub his cheeks with a limewash, a coracle is taken from the causeway, it is lined with ivy leaves, and the poet is placed in it. It is quite a ceremony, this. We seem to have struck on some old relic of Dionysian[7] days—

(Suddenly a bitter wailing, then a quiet.)

---

7. **Dionysian** alluding to the orgiastic ancient Greek festivals celebrating the god Dionysus

FISHERMAN. Nobles, he is to be divided, now. The head we set adrift on the river that it may prophesy to us. The rest we keep.

LIEUTENANT. Not so, Fisherman. The king's order is that the unmaimed body be set adrift.

FISHERMAN. The king is ignorant.

LIEUTENANT. The king is a king. Lift up that coracle, now, upon your shoulders, men.

FISHERMAN. It is an imperfect sacrifice.

LIEUTENANT. It is warranted by the king of this land.

FISHERMAN. That is a good point. I will make it clear to my brothers. Wait for me. We will move in procession.

LIEUTENANT. Sergeant. Sergeant.

SERGEANT *(drunk)*. What's the bloody row about? And where are the women? Time we saw a good round dance.

LIEUTENANT. You're drunk.

SERGEANT. 'Course I'm drunk. That's why I'm a soldier, so I can get drunk oftener than the landtillers and the turfcutters and the foresters who can manage it only at Christmas. 'TENTION. You there, who gave you permission to lift that body? Not the ivy-ale. Wait for orders! Lieutenant.

LIEUTENANT. The body may be removed, Sergeant.

SOLDIER. Corporal, there is a little life in this body still.

CORPORAL. Lift it. Ready, lads. Steady.

(A wailing small music begins.)

(The drums keep rhythm.)

CORPORAL. A beat, a beat, a beat. Halt. To the ground, now. And, now, gently, into the water. Easy, now, the bloody ozier in this basket is rotten. There. Why, look, look. The water has revived him.

(An awe of music)

SOLDIER. I said he was not dead. He's sitting up.

(Crash of cymbals)

MAC CONGLINNE. I am cold. I was told to ask for a cloak.

SERGEANT. Won't you have a jacket of water soon enough? You're a troublesome bloody man.

MAC CONGLINNE. I must have a cloak.

SERGEANT. It's wilful waste, that's what it is.

MAC CONGLINNE. I will not leave without a cloak. I will leave a curse on the black police of Ulster if I am not provided with a cloak. Am I to go to hell naked and indecent? Is there a tall woman near me?

SERGEANT. Now, by the Gods, that's too much from you. First, a cloak, and then, a woman. What will you ask for next?

WOMAN. I am a woman, and I will provide a cloak.

SERGEANT. By God, woman, it would be better if you gave that cloak to a man who could use it.

VOICES. O, what a cloak. O, what a cloak.
(*Strings*)

> My curse on poets.
> They are more wayward than women. They gad
> From word to word. They have many Gods.
> They are quite mad.

> They undermine kings.
> They upset queens. You will find them in a bed
> Sacred to a priest or in the straw of a harlot.
> They have no stability. They are quite mad.

Say goodbye to Ireland, bigmouth. And say your prayers. What the hell is wrong with those people behind us, Corporal?

CORPORAL. They are expecting the poet to sing a prophecy, Sergeant. It is an old custom that the head should sing.[8] And look at him. Has he lighted a torch in the boat, that he should blaze so brightly?

VOICES. Vo. Vo.

(*Soft music. Trumpets inset giving hints of the last post*)

MAC CONGLINNE.

> I go on a journey
> To which there is no ending.
> I move without mourning
> Into the beautiful heart of a woman.
> I am now a story

> I will not be lost;
> For the footprints of tall ones go before me
> From God to God! I will recover my ghost.
> I will recover a country.
> In the green of Cork I will be a story.

(*His voice is growing distant as he ends*)

VOICES. Vo. Evoe.

SERGEANT. The devil's cure to him. There goes a lovely cloak. Corporal.

CORPORAL. Here.

SERGEANT. Hail me that woman that bestowed the cloak. She may have something else of note?

CORPORAL. I thought of that myself, but she's disappeared.

SERGEANT. Nothing left us, so, but the ivy ale.

STORYTELLER. I end this scene with a wish for the ivy ale. For one

---

8. **the head should sing** In early Irish literature there are several episodes in which the severed head of a poet sings or recites.

would need to be drunk, indeed, to follow the poor poet in his coracle of ozier. The night plucks him to the seaboard. He disappears out of ken. But there are mariners' stories coming into this port and that port of a golden head that floats and sings upon the wastes of the waters in the Irish sea. But you know what sailors' stories are. You can divide them by a woman into half, and then by another woman into half again. But one delicate morning in October, when the skies were watercolours of hazy blues and early sun-rays, on the bar of Wexford[9] where a few mild monks of Ibar's community[10] were knotting a torn herring-net, a salt-white coracle of ozier wattles moved towards them on the tide from around the Raven Point.[11] It was the wonderful golden head of the poet they noticed first. Then, as slowly he whorled past them, they saw he was green ivy to the chin, that his face was moulded like a mask of molten gold, and that he lived. Past them he went on the stream, with three curious young seals hangdogging him, and around the muddy swirl of the holy Island where the tall yewtree quivered slightly and whispered to the three cranes that stood on sentry by Ibar's painted house. The coracle brought him to the wooden landing and the cranes hissed. The three cranes hissed and the first of them stepped forward.

(Music. Croak)

FIRST CRANE. Do not enter.

SECOND CRANE. Pass on your way.

THIRD CRANE. Goodbye.

(Strings)

MAC CONGLINNE.

> Good birds, you slight me. You threaten me.
> You speak short to Mac Conglinne
> Who knows you, who has picked your brain
> For the pattern of your living.

FIRST CRANE. Do not enter.

SECOND CRANE. Keep away.

THIRD CRANE. Goodbye.

(Strings)

MAC CONGLINNE.

> You fish from one leg,
> And the fish you catch you lay them round in a wheel.

9. **Wexford** coastal town in southeastern Ireland (anachronistic here, since the town was founded by Vikings some 100 years after the play's action takes place)   10. **Ibar's community** the monastery of Becc Ériu ("Little Ireland"), on Beggery Island in Wexford Harbor   11. **Raven Point** the northern point of land at the entrance to Wexford Harbor

Do not be proud of your knowledge.
I know all the delicate steps of your dance-reel.

FIRST CRANE. Do not enter.
SECOND CRANE. Keep away.
THIRD CRANE. Goodbye.
(Strings)
MAC CONGLINNE.

I know what you spell
By wheel and dance. It is my command
You waken the voice of the Yewtree to welcome
Mac Conglinne to his own land.

(Hissing music. An old, cold, measured voice from a height)
YEWTREE. This land is everybody's land and nobody's land.
MAC CONGLINNE. Yewtree, it is Ireland.
YEWTREE. It is not Ireland, but little Ireland.
FIRST CRANE. Do not enter.
SECOND CRANE. Keep away.
THIRD CRANE. Goodbye.
MAC CONGLINNE. Yewtree, I think you know me.
YEWTREE. I will know everybody by the end of time. The knowledge
is of small advantage to me. Have you anything to give me?
MAC CONGLINNE. Only a lesson in manners. Only to tell you that you
are but the part of a pattern, that there is life as well as death, and that
the lady who supports your right side is about to get annoyed with your
churlishness in receiving me. She will let you topple in a moment, and
you will have a large accounting to make to your peers.
YEWTREE. I see you have a right to come to land.
MAC CONGLINNE. I have. And also a right to leave.
YEWTREE. You may land so.
FIRST CRANE. You may enter.
SECOND CRANE. Do not keep away.
THIRD CRANE. Welcome.
(Music)
STORYTELLER. The poet lands. And in a moment the island changes.
The great Yew becomes formalised as a tall and painted sculpture. Two
marvellous goats support it in the rampant way of heraldry and one has a
crescent moon in her horns, the other a wane. And from wooden houses
all around a closecropped green quiet monks emerge to welcome the poet
as if he were an ordinary pilgrim. And, indeed, he is, and very much too
ordinary, for he is, of a sudden, mother naked, unwashed, and hungry.
The ivy and the gold are gone and his salt white face is peeling off skins
of sun. He is drunk from the motion of the sea, he is a worn-out, ship-

wrecked, battered mariner, and the monks wash him and put milkdrinks before him, but before he can touch the tableware he is asleep. He has not forgotten the folded cloak, however. It sleeps with him. It is a light in the dim dormitory. It is a crepitation of the sun. It is rushlight in glimmering candlesticks of gold, and the monks, amazed and wondering, have brought the ancient Abbot to view it, and the Abbot, amazed and wondering, has sent runners to the king, and the king is Cahal of Cashel whose royal household is a hundred and fifty miles away, and the runners are there before Mac Conglinne opens an eye. When he does, the Abbot, folded in a musty old mantle, has gone asleep at the end of his bed.

(Chirpy morning music)

MAC CONGLINNE. Priest, does your brotherhood never wash? I can count and distinguish seven different stinks upon your person.

ABBOT. Eh?

MAC CONGLINNE. Remove your seven odours from the bones of my ankles.

ABBOT. Speak louder, son of the Cloak.

MAC CONGLINNE. Do you mean to carry those to heaven? If so, speak, that I may go the other way. *(Loudly)* Look, find some other place of rest.

ABBOT. Plaice for breakfast? No, No, son of the Cloak. It is not the season for plaice. Herring you shall have, goat's milk, cheese, bread panned and mixed from unblackened wheat. And stirabout, the lucky caul of spring oats.

MAC CONGLINNE. Do I hear you mention food?

ABBOT. Yes, indeed, God is good . . .

MAC CONGLINNE. Is there no person in this establishment with two good ears? Do I see a gong? Strike it.

ABBOT. Indeed, breakfast will not be long, now, and you may bite it. But you must be careful. Long fast has given you the narrow belly of a knitting needle and the more fanciful of my brothers asserts that the music you made coming up Hantoon was caused when you struck your ribs like harpstrings.

(Strings)

MAC CONGLINNE.

> In the mad months
> The Jackass stamps the hill till grass goes mad.
> The dog unloops himself
> From the doorstep, his face one wrinkled snarl.
>
> But the Jackass has long ears
> And the dog will hear me if I call.
> I would wish this Abbot had the donkey's ears,
> And I dog-madness so that I could howl.

MONK. Master of the Cloak, we apologize for our aged Abbot. He is deaf, but kind; he is old, but wise; he is failing, but the God is still within him. Speak to him with your fingertips.

MAC CONGLINNE. I was impertinent, and I offer you my regrets, brother. Can you tell me where I am, and the manner in which I came here?

MONK. You do not know?

MAC CONGLINNE. Would I ask otherwise?

MONK. You fell into our quiet like a spark, master of the cloak. *(Strings)*

> The brothers who haul the herring,
> The cotmen, the netmen, met you at sunrise there
> At the point of the Raven,
> You and the sun together.
>
> Twinbrother of the sun,
> O Hazel one, ivy had twined you to the throat;
> Your mouth was a song
> Without sorrow or anguish or threat.
>
> You arrived among the reeds
> Of our holy and restful island without a sound.
> And we found you worn and torn,
> Wearied and many-scarred, dead like a man long drowned.
>
> In your weedy coracle
> Barnacle and shell had a long sea-lease;
> But your cloak was new, your cloak was a miracle,
> A golden tabernacle by your knees.

MAC CONGLINNE. This is the cloak. By God, I remember something about this cloak. And still I remember nothing.

MONK. You do remember whence you came?

MAC CONGLINNE. I do not. But there is something about that cloak that sticks in the thick of my gullet. How did Mac Conglinne arrive at a wonder like this? Look, look, this cloak is the worth of a kingdom.

MONK. It is a heavenly cloak. We have not dared to touch it. Even as we washed you, your hands guarded it.

ABBOT. Son of the Cloak, if you could get up, now, we could break our fasts together, and you could tell me your story if you have it in mind to tell me.

MONK. And the cloak seemed to evade us, it avoided our fingers, it shifted, it changed its place. Our Abbot said a wonder of this kind did not fall to be dealt with by a single shrine-keeper, so he sent word of it to King Cahal of Cashel—

MAC CONGLINNE. That is it. You have taken my tongue from my mouth and spoken for me. That cloak is the king's.

MONK. The king's? You could not have stolen that cloak from the king.

MAC CONGLINNE. Have I thief signs on my forehead?

MONK. You have not. You have the signs of the tall poet, you have the swagger of the Hazel-man.

MAC CONGLINNE. I am Mac Conglinne. I do not know how that cloak was given to me, but I know that I am under bonds to present it to Cahal of Cashel.

MONK. It is a present worthy of him. It is a god's raiment. You will break your fast, now.

MAC CONGLINNE. I have lost the gift of hunger.

MONK. You must eat to travel. And Cashel is a long way.

MONK. I will munch on the road. No. There is something else comes back to me. I am to stay where I land till the king comes.

MONK. Your cloak expects a large and kingly condescension, it requires a mighty obeisance from the king if he has to travel so far for it.

MAC CONGLINNE. I remember that as a condition.

MONK. I respect your memory.

MAC CONGLINNE. I am also to fast till the king comes. And now, O Lord, because of this obligation on me, hunger is gnawing at my every gut.

ABBOT. Will the son of the Cloak breakfast with me, now? I am old and morning hunger is not good for me.

MAC CONGLINNE. O, my lord!!!

ABBOT. There is herring on the grill, butter that has talked with salt and raspberry, bread from a horsemill, white and brown, buttermilk, sweet milk with a hot lacing from a jar—

MAC CONGLINNE. If you hear thunder, it is my gums falling one on the other. Bring this Abbot to a pot and boil him.

MONK. I will take him to his table.

MAC CONGLINNE. Why does he stink this way?

MONK. He bears the odours of his office, Mac Conglinne; the smells of mortality. This is the sign of the Yewtree. The tree of death. Sleep, now, since you cannot eat.

MAC CONGLINNE. How can I sleep and this demon in my belly?

MONK. I will ask the Abbot to lay his hands on you. I could give you sleep, but it is his privilege.

ABBOT. What does he want to go asleep for and breakfast waiting us? The young waste too much time on sleep. What? Fast till the king comes? But the king will not come here. Our oratory is not a place he wishes to patronize. Well, well. If he wishes to sleep, let it be so. Lift my right arm. Leave your eyes to my eyes, son of the Cloak. You see into my look. You see the pool. You see the Salmon. The pool sleeps, the salmon sleeps. The son of the Cloak sleeps—now. You will sleep till the king comes. But if he never comes, what then, son of the Cloak? I cannot wait breakfast until then.

(Music)

STORYTELLER. But the king does come. With round cursing and martial threats, he takes the green route by Fethard[12] and Ross-bercon,[13]

(Martial music with a hint of fun)

takes a dipping, chariot and all, at the old bridge of Ross where the barrels hold up the bridges—

(Squawk of music)

arrives hot tempered at Wexford where there is wattle and mound, a multitude of wild geese, and a couple of boys bobbing for eels. All the menfolk, as usual, are out beyond the bar fishing the famous herring that cannot be smoked and all the women are in each others' houses playing some card game or other with fireirons. But the Custom-house is very busy. There are ten carracks loading great barrels of yew and twenty Customs men in charge of them. Cahal halts in his tracks.

(Blare of music)

CAHAL. What have those men in those barrels?

A MAN. Wine of the country, Lord, a bishop's brew.

CAHAL. Let it be a brew for the king. Tip me a barrel. Stave in the head, Crowfingers. Your king is thirsty.

(Crashing wooden music)

CAHAL. Good. Good. I will hold it myself, I will tilt it.

(Gulping music)

By the gods, it is rich. Let the stream from which that liquid is drawn be called the King's River. Tilt me another.

A MAN. My lord, another will bring pimples, a red nose and the yellow trembling.

CAHAL. That is for little bellies, good man. For Wexford bellies. From henceforth, they shall be called yellowbellies, those little bellies of Wexford. Where is this Ibar fellow's island. Yonder? Now, how may a chariot skim that meadow of waste water?

A MAN. By the ferry, Lord. A scant furlong to the north there.

CAHAL. Away, then. Away. Is a king to be delayed by every man who offers him a barrel?

(Hurry of music)

STORYTELLER. The hasty king is ferried over the wide Slaney,[14] and he

---

12. **Fethard** in Co. Tipperary, southeast of Cashel   13. **Ross-bercon** Rosbercon, in Co. Kilkenny just across the River Barrow from New Ross   14. **Slaney** the river that empties into Wexford Harbor

rumbles over the ruts of Ardcavan[15] where slow streams wind like heavy cattle through the reed country. The reed is the second last tree of the consonants in the alphabet.

He comes to the wood causeway. It resounds.

(Trumpets)

MONK. My father, the Abbot.

ABBOT. No need for the finger-spelling, my son. I know the king is here.

(Strings)

> I have heard wheels
> In Ross. The waters of the Barrow broke
> In a drift of steam. There are feathers on his heels.
> The tall tree croaked.
>
> The black bird has his bright eyes.
> I am his speechman. I quote what he says to me.
> I am at the end of his promises.
> I look two ways over his country.

Bid the son of the Cloak waken. He has been a long time waiting for his breakfast. Tell them in the kitchens. Send him the smells of good food cooking, woodcock and snipe on the spit, and the great arctic bird; have sauces in cup and soup in tureen, milk, buttermilk and mead, large bread and smallbread and sweetbread, bullmeat and pigmeat, the white chicken and the smoked haunch of the little bonave.[16]

MONK. This is a feast.

ABBOT. It is a feast of smells, the delicate odours from the brazing charcoal. I do not think we will eat this feast. But if not, we can eat of another.

MONK. You are in the mood to prophesy.

ABBOT. I have said my say for the moment. Do as I have bid. I will meet the king at my treeseat.

(Trumpets. Trumpets. Trumpets)

HERALD. The King. Spread the wool, unroll the rug, uncoil the round carpet.

(Trumpets)

The King.

ABBOT. My Lord is welcome. May all trees smile on him. May all trees blossom through him. May he live in the fruit of all.

CAHAL. After the welcome is accepted, after the compliments are returned, show me this blazing cloak that I have travelled leagues to see.

---

15. **Ardcavan** parish at the end of a peninsula jutting into Wexford Harbor, opposite the town   16. **bonave** piglet (Irish *banbh*)

ABBOT. You have been told the story.

CAHAL. It is now the property of every subcourt in my portion of Ireland. And I think I will have trouble with that Corkman, Muinchen. He has laid claim to that cloak already. It is the cloak of his God, he asserts, the lad of the vine, the body who drinks ten tubs at a sitting and then warbles a stave or two. O, glory be to God, I really must put law on the pantheon. Can we not supply the home market ourselves? We import more than we export and our theogany is lopsided. One day I will declare myself high king of all the heavens and deport everybody found with a crown in their possession. Do I wait much longer to see this cloak?

MONK. The son of the Cloak approaches, my Lord.

CAHAL. I can see that. And I notice that the measure of light increases accordingly.

(Faint trumpeting music in the background)

I begin to think my journey was worthwhile. Who is the lad that carries it?

MONK. He has a name, my Lord, but is nameless among nobles. You will not have heard of him.

(Music comes forward. Final blast)

CAHAL. Bearer of the cloak, lay it softly on the carpet. Unfold it.

MAC CONGLINNE. I will lay it down, King, but I will not unfold it. My errand ends when you accept the cloak from my hands.

CAHAL. The cloak is then a present to me. By my hand, it is a royal gift. You will tell me who sent it?

MAC CONGLINNE. My errand was determined for me, King, and limited to this act of handing you the cloak in person. I do not know who gave me the cloak, I do not know where I come from. Is the cloak itself no hint of the giver?

CAHAL. I will open the cloak.

(Music. A few short raps of excitement. A general gasp. A hurryscurry of excitement and amazement)

VOICES. Oh. Oh.

Now, by my hand.

CAHAL. It is, indeed, a cloak.

(Strings)

> It is the living skin of a god.
> It stands, it flies, it lies down,
> It breathes, it grows, it spreads over the sod
> In greenery, in flower; it is softer than swansdown.
>
> It is speaking throughout a country
> And its words are gifts of the air; the tillage acres
> Welcome it, it clothes each tree,
> And talks in sap to the wide pastures.

Scholar, there is something hiding in it. What is it?

MAC CONGLINNE. King, I do not know. My errand is ended, and I smell the marvellous smells of good food cooking. Without disrespect, my Lord, my nose quivers, my gums drip, my teeth are ajar, my mouth grinds, my gullet is wide open and my belly is crying out for that food that is on spit and table.

MONK. The scholar has fasted for a time that no one knows, King.

CAHAL. I am nosing that feast, too. Let the scholar wait till this small packet can be opened.

MAC CONGLINNE. O King, I am one leaping mad mass of appetite. If it is permitted I will dip with scullion and horseboy, cook, server, and tableboy while you examine that package.

CAHAL. Certainly not. You shall sit at my right hand. It is an honour I owe to the giver of this cloak. Why, what's here? Another cloak with its seven subcloaks, fit for a king. And an oaken apple, greeting from royalty with the double meaning that the days of love are not over; a bag of seed, a woman offers me lands for sowing; a queen bee in a stone jar, a queen is ready to leave the hive for me; a queen's nightgown and the half of her crown—it is the half of the nightgown too. Ha. And Ha again. The message is too plain. It comes from a great white bitch with whom I will have nothing more to do. Lead me to the feasting chamber, good Abbot.

MONK. We will pack the cloak, Lord.

CAHAL. Give it to the bearers. It is kingly. It will cause admiration in Cashel. So she has tired of her Northman.

(Strings)

> O Scholar
> Bend to your book when a woman passes,
> Or your adventure
> Will exceed all your wildest guesses.
>
> If she is beautiful,
> Read your book. Histories
> Have no more terrible
> Story than the woman to whom you lift your eyes.
>
> If she be ugly,
> Still she is a woman. That is enough.
> Read your book, my boy,
> And stay with the simple stuff.

MAC CONGLINNE. King, at this moment I would eat a woman if she were broiled, boiled, boned or on the fillet; if she were baked, brawned, browned, underdone, overdone, or a mere juice in the black bottom of a country skillet; and I would eat her family after and then begin upon her family tree. I tell you, King, I will eat your royalty if I am not served at once, for a greater hunger there was never in the world since the word uttered itself than there is at this moment howling and yowling in the snarling pit of my bowels.

CAHAL. By the gods, that is a great hunger, Scholar. It is a notable hunger, but I will see to it that it is royally satisfied. You will sit at my right hand, and every second bit will be your bit.

MAC CONGLINNE. King, I will want all the bits that will be on this table.

(Music imitates howl of a wolf)

CAHAL. By my hand, that is indeed the true howl of hunger. Monks, platter the table there, lay on the big meats and the small meats, the glutinous gravy, the luscious soup, bread in portion.

(Music, Mac Conglinne howling)

Gently now, Scholar. Here are the servers. Indeed, those smells give myself an appetite. Sit this scholar beside me. We will talk of women. I have great wisdom on that subject. I will teach the scholar.

MAC CONGLINNE. King, you have an oaken apple in your hand.

CAHAL. That, Scholar, is a greeting from one Royalty to another.

MAC CONGLINNE. Give it to me. It whets my front tooth, it frets my back one. Give it to me, King.

CAHAL. By my soul, I cannot. It is tabu. I could eat it, but you would die.

MAC CONGLINNE. I will die, but I will eat it.

CAHAL. Then I must eat it myself to save you.

MAC CONGLINNE. No. Leave it to me. You are eating it, you are munching it. You shall not rob me. I will follow it down your throttle. I go after it.

(Prolonged howl of music)

CAHAL. Something has jumped from your mouth into mine, Scholar. By the Gods, it could be your hunger that jumped from you to me. I am starving.

MAC CONGLINNE. And I am no longer hungry. I think there was a demon in me and he is now in you.

CAHAL. O, wise demon. He knows that kings will provide what scholars cannot. Welcome, demon. O, when have I felt such a wonderful hunger. To the carving, monks, to the knife and the tall fork. Now, great bird. That leg of mutton, now. That leg of mutton, now. That pot of broth. You are nibbling my piece of bread, scholar. Back to your books.

I will clear this table and look for more. O lovely appetite. Away, all of you. Back. The king dines. That ham, O mast[17] and barley-fed beauty of

---

17. **mast** fruit of the beech, oak, chestnut, and other trees, used to feed swine

the pigstye, my little bit of bacon. Snipe, woodcock, tastes for a small tooth. Have I cleared the table? Is there no more?

(The foregoing has a background of music. Ends in a wolf-howl)

Is there no more? Where are your pantries, monks? Where are your storehouses, your kitchens and back-kitchens? Bring in the bacon, the stirabout, the birds, the fresh fish, the salt fish, the crayfish, the oysterfish. No. I will visit them in person. The king will make a royal progress through your foodstuffs. Lead on, lead on.

(A royal howling of hunger)

STORYTELLER. Only Mac Conglinne and the old Abbot are left at the table. The table is a curious sight. Every platter is bone bright with unused cleanliness, but there is not a pick of food on any of them, all signs of food have vanished into the king's mouth. What a royal digestion that man must have!

MAC CONGLINNE. It seems to me, Abbot, that I have started something.

ABBOT. I would say that you have begun a season of dearth in the South, Scholar. I would say that many great houses will feel the winter and the small ones suffer accordingly.

MAC CONGLINNE. Can I have a drop of milk?

ABBOT. Certainly, you are not guilty.

MAC CONGLINNE. I said MILK. Here, I will name it on my fingertips for you. M. I. L. K.

ABBOT. Milk. I fear you will have to go to the goats for it.

MAC CONGLINNE. I fear so, too.

ABBOT. They are in a pound beyond the causeway.

MAC CONGLINNE. I will do without.

(Music returning)

The royal hunger is returning. He would drink it anyway.

CAHAL *(booming)*. Where is that scholar? I must thank him for my hunger. But bring wine, bring mead, bring buttermilk. We will talk of women. I will tell him of that great bitch, Ligach, who wants me to love her once more. Scholar.

MAC CONGLINNE. I am here, King.

CAHAL. Never mind the women, Scholar. A good belly-hunger is much better than a queen. Its demands are less and can be always satisfied. I will now proceed to tell you the tale of Ligach. You know why she left me? She wanted to have all my king's rights. She wanted to be queen and king at once. By the Gods, I feel a nibble of hunger again. O lovely appetite. Is there any chicken in this house? Is there any roast beef? Or mutton broiled? Is there a salty hard piece of a pig? Is there anything at all?

(Music)

STORYTELLER. I end this scene with a great hunger.
(Music)

END OF PART I

PART 2

STORYTELLER. I open this scene with a madness of feasting. Cahal is delighted with his appetite at first. He displays it to ten chieftains on his way home to Cashel. They are not as pleased as he is, for he eats them out of house and home. He eats them to the scullery, he eats them to the piggery, he lays bare the fowl run and then climbs to the pigeon-cote. He walks into the stubble-field and gnaws the sheaf in the pointed stook. He is forever nibbling. He picks the leaves from the trees as his chariot passes beneath them, he catches at the tops of the grasses. His face is green from grass-juice, greasy from fat bacon, grey with dust, and he is anything but royal as the gates of his city open to him and he climbs up the great rock of Cashel.
(Trumpets. Sounds of a kingly progress)
HERALD. Welcome to Cahal. Welcome to the son of the Bright One.
VOICES. He is welcome to his own place.
(Trumpets)
CAHAL. The welcome is accepted, the compliments are returned, we will take the ceremony as completed. But where are the boiling pots, and the bright braziers with their pleasant grills and their delightful wholesome smells? Is there no food in Cashel, no green food, red food, brown food, no beasts in pens, no bulls on the hoof, no birds in the run? Have I no cooks, no potboys, no scullions? Have I no kingdom, no revenues, no servitors? Does Cahal's household sleep when he goes on a journey? Ring bells, gongs, bring whips and scourging staffs. I am insulted, I am demeaned, I am hungry . . .
(Wild music of hurrying servitors, tableware. Clash of silver, murmur of voices)
STORYTELLER. He eats Cashel down to the last pantry. He licks every plate. He devours the substance of his nearer neighbours. He makes excuses to visit his sub-kings and strips their households, too. The country groans under his vast appetite. The monasteries murmur, for even in those days there were monasteries and religious settlements all over Ireland, some of them with the hue of Christ *r.1* them covering an older image, as in Muinchen's establishment at Cork where the traffic of the sea-people had touched the Bible story somewhere and resolved it in their own way. Muinchen was a Briton, as we learn in the tale of the TWO SWINE-HERDS,[18] a righteous monk who would bow to nothing but his own

18. *Two Swineherds* since this relates to Munster, probably a reference

God; a clever man, too, and a headstrong, who put his own establishment before all the other establishments of Ireland and was ever a-tiptoe to glorify it. When he heard of the great cloak in the King's possession, he set off for Cashel to lay claim to it. It was a curious procession, Muinchen, alone, at the head of it, in a wine-painted chariot drawn by two milk-white asses, whose bridles are the bright findrinny,[19] whose trappings are of red leather. The monk himself has the formality of a wine-god. Behind him, his monks sing gentle hymns. He arrives in Cashel and is welcomed by the King.

CAHAL. I know what you are after, Briton, and you can whistle for it at full moon. The cloak is mine and I retain it.

MUINCHEN. The cloak is the cloak of our God, King, and I must demand it of you.

CAHAL. You are entitled to demand. I am entitled to refuse. Off with you, now, back to the hungry sides of the Lee[20] river.

MUINCHEN. I will fast on you[21] for that cloak, King.

CAHAL. You will fast anyway, for I have no food to spare for you. And don't you turn your donkeys into my stables. I have cattle fattening and I can spare you no hay, no straw, and no grain at all of any description. And nobody in this neighbourhood can spare them either. I have engaged them all to fatten stock and birds for me. I have a royal hunger for such things since the day I got that cloak.

MUINCHEN. I notice you have not been to Cork lately.

CAHAL. I knew you would notice that. I did not want to trouble you, for I guessed that you would trouble me about this cloak.

MUINCHEN. Cork is the only place I have seen thriving since I set out upon my journey. The rest of the county has been harrowed by your hunger.

(Strings)

> Field and byre are swept clean;
> The rich dung of the beast is gone from the farmyard;
> The churns of yew are empty.
> There is no soft lowing from any barn.

> Cahal's hunger is great.
> It has the magnificence of a season of winter.
> There is a great cold after his great heat.
> The king has emptied field and byre.

---

to the medieval *Senchas Fagbála Caisil,* "The Story of the Finding of Cashel," which involves two swineherds and tells of the establishment of the Eoganacht kingship of Munster at Cashel; however, Muinchen does not appear in the tale.

19. **findrinny** *findruine,* an alloy of precious metals often mentioned in early Irish sagas, valued between gold and bronze   20. **Lee** the River Lee, which flows eastward to Cork Harbor   21. **fast on you** an early Irish legal tactic of public fasting to force a powerful person to comply with a law or contract

But in Cork of the Lee,
In the harbourage of my bells, the season is full of flavour,
We sweat sweet oils, our girths are easy;
We fill our cloaks with the warmth of good eating.

CAHAL. It would seem that you invite me to Cork, Monk.

MUINCHEN. That is not my intention, King. We are a free settlement who owe you no rights but a yearly tribute. But I think that in all Ireland it is the only place at this moment where you could eat your fill of the ripe things of the world.

(Strings)

The spits are laden and drip gravy;
The cow misses her fat calf;
The bell-wether is troubled about the tally;
But the spit drips gravy, it roasts a lamb.

The appled orchards, the quince, the pear,
The plum is in the jar. We are fat and happy
In Cork of the Lee this year.
Cahal leaves us alone; so the spit drips gravy.

CAHAL. What I want to come at is this: do you challenge me to a feast or a battle?

MUINCHEN. Neither, King. But for that cloak, I would offer you seven days of rich feasts, seven nights of dancing, seven serving-maids for your night-guard, seven vats to be on hand for your drinking; and for your occasional picking, a large fat county of arable households.

(A wolf-howl of hunger from Cahal)

CAHAL. My hunger has spoken for me. You are cheating me by temptation. You can have your blazing cloak and may it burn you to the bottom. When do I progress to this feasting?

MUINCHEN. It will be ready when the sun falls to the lowest rung. That is the time of our feasting.

CAHAL. Now, hurry that sun. I famish. I famish. You will earn that cloak, Monk. You will pay for it. I will eat you out of Cork, and out of the surroundings of Cork, I will eat you out of the sea and out of your colonies. I will eat you down to the very sandals of your season. Give me bonds for that cloak and that feasting. Hurry, hurry.

(Wolf howl of hunger)

STORYTELLER. Muinchen returns to Cork. He is received with acclamation in the monkhouses and with wonder in the farmhouses. He has struck a mighty bargain. All agree with that. All the same, the sly farmers are already removing their stock into Kerry and to the summer booleys[22]

22. **booleys** Ir. *buaile* (pl. *buailte*), milking places in summer pastures

in the hills. And larders go underground. In west Cork, indeed, there is a rioting when Muinchen's tall fellows are seen upon the roads and some hardy spirits engage them from ambush, as is the traditional way of the west Cork people. Muinchen is hard put to it to keep his word. But in the end he is ready for Cahal. The stores groan, the piggeries squeak, the sheepfolds bleat, the byres and paddocks bellow, the butchers' shops are a-ring with cold iron, there is a great scraping of pots and pans in a hundred kitchens, the charcoal-burners and the furzemen men are up and down with their donkey-loads. Then, two days before his time, the King arrives.

(Music in kind for above)

He is hasty, avid, ravenous. His progress is a rhythm of wolf-howls. The country yields before him as to a wolf-pack. He is mad, snarling, vicious. He is a mighty hunger.

(Trumpets. Trumpets, trumpets)

CAHAL. The mighty dinner, Monk. It is ready, it is boiled, it is broiled, it is baked, it is braised, it is browned—

MUINCHEN. There is nothing yet. It is not the time.

CAHAL. Time. My belly has changed time. It has issued edicts. It has proclaimed that day begins with my breakfast, that the sun must reach its zenith at the middle of my lunch, that it must decline into my dinner at afternoon, and go to sleep in my supper and be absent from the sky whiles I sleep. I offer you a new calendar, and it is your duty as my vassal to accept it.

MUINCHEN. I do not accept it.

(Strings)

> I take my time
> From the steps of God. I find Him
> In the divisions of the day in which he circles the womb.
> One year is his flow and his ebb. The year is his rhythm.

CAHAL. I want my feasting. I will have it, I will bolt it.

MUINCHEN. It is a time of annual feasting. It is a time of preparation. We are down on the Sun's ebb and we wear black. Can I break the heavenly order because a king is hungry?

(Wolf howl in music)

CAHAL.

> O, the lying Abbot of Cork.
> His promises are plenty. He gives bonds for a feast.
> But I find myself in a hungry country.
> I am offered a black fast.
>
> He is a holy man.
> He moves by order; his rota is axled on a year;

But for the king there is only a little can
Of holy water. He blesses hunger
And leads me to a table that is bare.

MUINCHEN. King, that satire is not a fair saying on the ways of a priest. I follow the law, but you would have the children of this town of Cork sing about me as if I had sinned in hospitality. I would ask you to withdraw it.

CAHAL. I will not withdraw it.

MUINCHEN. Then by example you will allow free tongue to every minor satirist, to every catchpenny quarreller, to every subversive talker inside the kingdom. That is an example which will rebound on you, for after the priest will come the king. One is not more sacred than the other.

CAHAL. I will withdraw it if the board is laid.

MUINCHEN. The board will not be laid till the proper time.

(Wolf howl in music)

CAHAL.

I must have food. I must have filling.
I must have swilling, I must have solids.
Lids must be off for me and tables laid.
The king's belly lays down that law.

MUINCHEN.

Small bread and wheywater
Is all men's lot in Cork for two days more.
No bright beef, no milk, no butter.
We fast by the law's letter.

(Wolf howl)

CAHAL. I will go out into your country. I will beggar farmers. I will strip chiefs, I will have every house boiling pots for me within the hour. There will be no law in the country of Cork but the king's hunger.

MUINCHEN. You will destroy festival, interfere with fertility, and enforce famine on the future. There is a demon in you.

(Wolf howl of music)

I know, now, there is a demon in you and if he is not exorcised you will eat up the country and your kingdom will be a kingdom of hunger. I will exorcise this demon.

(Savage music)

DEMON. You will not exorcise me, monk. I will break your bells.

(Clash of bells)

I will blast your holy water.

(Water music)

I will burn your books.
(Whirl of flame-music)
I have already done it. There is in Cork, now, not a bell nor a book
nor a drop of holy water. Come on, King, and let us eat.
(Flourish and crash of music)
MUINCHEN. God help us all.
(Flourish of music at a distance.
Another flourish
Another flourish
Another flourish)
FRIGHTENED MONK. Father Abbot, the buttery is gone.
MUINCHEN. God help us all.
ANOTHER MONK. Father Abbot, the kitchen is cleared. The king's
mouth is a demon's mouth.
MUINCHEN. God help us all.
(The flourishes are going into the distance.)
MUINCHEN.

> He is stripping this street, he is stripping that street.
> Every larder, every larder.
> There is no more grocery, no more sweet.
> The rich are lost, the poor are poorer.
>
> He will go into the country.
> His tongue will be in every house.
> From here to Doneraile[23] he will be eating
> Till he comes to Pichan's dwelling behind the mountain.
>
> There he will be stayed
> By a richness of victual, by such a hosting of food
> That even his appetite, enraged as it may be,
> Could not consume to the full moon.
>
> I will go there.
> I will wear this wonderful cloak I have.
> I will pluck this demon by the hair.
> I will bring him down to a grave.

Come with me to the oratory, my sons. We will pray and I will array
myself in this miracle of raiment. I will go to Pichan's dwelling and I will
lay this demon.
(Flourish of music)
STORYTELLER. I end this scene with a paternoster. King and demon
are ravaging the country toward Doneraile and rumours of the ravage travel

23. **Doneraile** about twenty miles north of Cork

before them from tongue to tongue. The rumours are faster and they go
farther. They range over Munster. They are over the Suir[24] and the Nore.[25]
They are up the Barrow. They shiver along the Slaney. And from every
little hill they leap to other hills. They reach Mac Conglinne at Elphin in
Roscommon,[26] where he has put himself to school to a very old master.
This teacher has divined the Reign of Christ in his numbering and Mac
Conglinne is mastering the attributes of His divinity and altering his poetic
psyche till it is in tune with his new beliefs. The news of Cahal's ravages
disturb him. His sudden problem makes him silent in the school, but
silences are accepted there as a mental process.

(Strings)

> The poet is quiet.
> Leave him. His leisures work for him.
> Behind his still eye
> His silences are busy, they gather him in rhythm.
>
> He works without end,
> Dependent on everything, yet dependent on
> One thing only, the self that has no end,
> The self he flies and follows, the self that is one.

At the hour of afternoon sleep, a raven perches on the top of the thatch
where the poet has tossed his cloak. The master sees it first.

MASTER. You have a visitor, Mac Conglinne. That bird wishes speech
with you.

MAC CONGLINNE. I suppose you know what the bird wants to say to
me.

MASTER. I can divine that. She says it is time you gathered up your
cloak and went down to Cork to cure the king. Raven, am I not right?

(Squawk of music)

RAVEN. You are right. But you might do me the honour of allowing
me to deliver my own messages.

MAC CONGLINNE. How am I to cure the king?

RAVEN. Let your wise master answer that.

MASTER. That is something I cannot answer.

RAVEN. I trust your ignorance will make you humble.

MASTER. Raven, I accept the rebuke.

RAVEN. That is well. Gird yourself up, Mac Conglinne. Take staff and
scrip. You can sell your books and buy bacon for the price you get, for

---

24. **Suir** river that flows eastward to Waterford in southeastern Ireland
25. **Nore** river flowing southeastward into the Barrow above New Ross, Co.
Wexford   26. **Elphin in Roscommon** the monastery of Ail-finn, about sixteen
miles north of the present town of Roscommon

you will need food in Munster where there is little enough since that demon in the king went on rampage.

MAC CONGLINNE. But how am I to cure the king?

RAVEN. That demon thinks more of herself than to bother with a poverty-stricken little man who hums a song now and again and thinks he overtops the world. Begone, now, and have no more talk out of you. It is time for you to remember that you made a promise to be in Cork the day the lynchpin falls out of the year. You have but the quarter of a day to go there and it is a good journey enough.

MAC CONGLINNE. I'd say it was a good journey. But I remember no promise and I do not know how to cure the king.

RAVEN. You made the promise, and you will know how to cure the king. Are you not a poet?

MAC CONGLINNE. I will take your word for it.

(Strings)

> Drink in fine houses and a rush chair
> Over the embers, people of quality
> In a ring around me, every face aware;
> That is to be a poet. But that is not a poet.
>
> For the hungry god in me
> Is wild when I waste myself on foolish faces.
> He would have me forever in the agony
> Of delivering him by wild guesses.
>
> I say my say once
> That others may say it after me.
> They have the credit, I have the pains,
> My god has the authority.
>
> I guess right, I guess wrong.
> But I know my wrongness, and the god knows it.
> I sacrifice myself in very song.
> Death on death is the hard way of a poet.

Master, will you give me a round of old bacon for my painted book, will you give me a piece of leather for two sandals?

MASTER. I will give you that. And you may keep your book.

RAVEN. He will need no book. He will invent a new book. Hurry, now, and put your bits together.

MAC CONGLINNE. I suppose you couldn't give me a lift on your back, Raven.

RAVEN. I am of the order of Ravens. If the Gods wished you a carrier, they would have sent you that litter-bird, the pigeon, the jade of the woods, the sounds of whose courting keeps half the world awake when the sun would have them sleep. I leave you my goodwill for your journey, Mac Conglinne. Go by Slieve Aughty[27] and Limerick,[28] thence to Fermoy,[29] and if you are not there before they close the guesthouse, you might as well stay at home.

MAC CONGLINNE. Goodbye, Omen. Farewell, squawk. I go to cut out sandals.

RAVEN. Good luck to the work.

(Strings)

MAC CONGLINNE.

> Now, poor shanks, you must be spindles
> And wind me a quick road to Cork.
> Bless you, big toe; and you, the tiny one,
> I trust you are up to heavy work.
>
> O, ball of the foot, I am no light-weight;
> Ankle, up-gatherer, you hold all the reins
> Of this five-horsed chariot of my foot,
> Keep the sweet instep arched upon its ways.
>
> And heel, O sacred and sunny heel, I know
> Something is happening you as I take the road.
> A wing lifts my foot from heel to toe,
> And I above it tread tall air like a god.

(A whirl of music as he soars)

MASTER *(going into distance)*. Farewell, Mac Conglinne. Lucky the road.

(A flying music with pleasant whirls)

STORYTELLER. Slieve Aughty and the waters of Loughrea.[30]

(Whirl of music)

The stones of Ennis.[31]

(Whirl of music)

The waters of Shannon.

(Whirl)

Cattle plains of Limerick.

(Whirl)

Blue mountains of Cork.

(Whirl)

The blue washing of the sea.

We will leave that poet to his running. We will go before him. For something has been happening in Cork. Something sad, sorrowful and

27. **Slieve Aughty** mountains in southern Co. Galway and adjacent Co. Clare 28. **Limerick** town at the eastern end of the Shannon River estuary 29. **Fermoy** about twenty miles northeast of Cork 30. **Loughrea** lake to the north of Slieve Aughty 31. **Ennis** site of a medieval monastery; in present Co. Clare about twenty miles northwest of Limerick

dreadful, something frightening. Muinchen has returned from exorcising the demon. He has returned without his cloak. He and his frightened community are gathered in the wooden oratory, Muinchen huddled and head-down in the great chair of the Abbot, his monks, ordained and lay, mouths to the floor upon the sacred cedar wood.

MUINCHEN. It could not be because I was afraid of IT.

MONKS *(as in a litany)*. You did not fear it, Father.

MUINCHEN. Did I not face it hardily?

MONKS. You faced it hardily, father.

MUINCHEN. I repeated the ordained words?

MONKS. You repeated them.

MUINCHEN. I did not fear to sprinkle the water.

MONKS. You sprinkled the water.

MUINCHEN. Then, it was the bell. I lacked a bell.

MONKS. It was the bell.

MUINCHEN. Why did my sons not provide a bell?

MONKS. There was no bell.

MUINCHEN. Yes, the demon broke all the bells.

MONKS. The demon broke all the bells. O father, what are we to do?

MUINCHEN. We will pray.

MONKS. Let us pray.

MUINCHEN. My sons, it has been a shame for me and it has abased me that a priest of my quality should have been subdued by a demon and robbed of the cloak that came to me out of the heart of the god. To you, now, I confess that it was pride before a fall. But there was also a thing that I had not taken into account, brothers. It was the position of the sun in the heavens. Our God is down upon his golden knees tonight. He is tired, grey, worn. His body is at the last. But in an hour or two there will be resurrection from the sea. The young one will come that is still the old one. Earth will tremble and turn upon the axle. The name of the tree will change, and another mighty digit will be added to our numbering. My sons, with the help of our young God, I will try again.

MONKS. The people are on the sea-shore. They are ready for him with welcomes, with psalms, with shouting. The ozier basket is ready in the reeds.

MUINCHEN. And the green is empty.

MONKS. No one is there on the green.

MUINCHEN. The guesthouse is ready.

MONKS. The door is open. Hinges squeak. Fleas abound. Coverings and beds are grey with dirt. Last night's wash is still in the foot-bath. The towels smell. The guesthouse is ready.

MUINCHEN. Then, we can begin. Who is the youngest brother this year?

AIDAN. Aidan, Reverence. And I am ready. I stand at the door. I have a wisp of the Barley-god in my hand and the two seeds of fire are beside me in my brazier. I am ready, Reverence. And when I hear the cry in the guesthouse, I will succour the marvellous child.

MUINCHEN. We will begin, then. Where is my bellringer?

MONK. Here, Worship.

MUINCHEN. Ring my bell.

MONK. Reverence, there is no bell.

MUINCHEN. Make a bell, some bell, any bell, dumbell. What do I say? I have not lost reverence, but my temper scatters. I lose my thread. We will do without a bell. Let us play.

MONKS. O. O.

MUINCHEN. My sons, it seems that I slip into unnatural errors of speech. I will withdraw for a time. The choirmaster will lead you. I am lost for the moment, I am cowed, I am cursed. And I know that my temper is swelling, is rising, is raging. If I remain, brothers, I feel that I will pull down the house in order to assert myself. And that would be bad example and unwarranted expense, I bow to you, and I retire. You will pray for me.

MONKS. We will pray for you.

(Music)

STORYTELLER. Muinchen retires to his dormitory. His defeat by the demon trembles in him in a terrible temper. His teeth gnash—

(Quirk of music)

his hair comes out in fistfuls.

(Quirk of music)

His nails rip sheet and covering.

(Quirk of music)

And outside in the dark, footsore, with a droop in every bone of his body, the student Mac Conglinne arrives in a town that is mysterious and deserted. It is a night of the three things; wind and snow and rain about the door, so that the wind left not a wisp of thatch, nor a speck of ashes that it did not sweep in one door and out through the other. And that was the way he found the guesthouse. The doors open and slapping, all winds and draughts loose in the place, the beds tumbled, the fleas hopping, and a mournful dead blackness over all things.

(Background music to go with above culminating in a kind of creaking gusty door banging climax)

MAC CONGLINNE. I suppose if I blessed this house, there is no one who would reply to me.

(A hiss of music)

Nor an answer from you, O west wind.

(Soft whispering music)

And you, O snow, may whisper elsewhere. From the three weathers, roof, I ask you to shelter me. Doors, do your duty and shut up. By my soul, if this is the far-famed hospitality of the clerics, I will pick up my living from profane houses. The wash-tub? It smells greasily. The towel? It stinks. The bed? Why, it is ready to go nightwalking all by itself. The flea is my guestmaster tonight.

(Strings)

> The flea is my guestmaster in Cork tonight.
> His arms are open to me.
> He welcomes me well; I know that
> He is glad of my company.
>
> He is red-mouthed as a woman
> And he lies as close to me.
> I would have chosen a different sort of lover.
> Yet I accept his hospitality.

No fire, no food, no master in the house. The taxpayers should learn of this, the farmers who salt pigs, the men who buy and sell, the tradesmen who ply this art and that art. By my soul, I will make a satire. I will tell them about it. I will publish it. They shall learn of this Cork cleric from Slieve Mish[32] to Rathlin Island.[33] My god is the god of eloquence. For once he shall do my bidding, and not I his.

THE GOD. I will do that, Mac Conglinne. Speak now and you shall be heard a mile away.

MAC CONGLINNE. Glory be to god. I never heard your voice before. It sounds very like my own.

THE GOD. It is your own. What other voice can I use except your voice, seeing that you were endowed with me at your birth and I with you? Not that I care for your voice very much. I keep on thinking how much better I could do on my own.

MAC CONGLINNE. I won't argue with you, for I am in a hurry to blast those monks of Cork. Are they at their prayers or in their sleep?

THE GOD. Never mind that. Let us say our say and I promise you we will make a sensation.

MAC CONGLINNE. Then, let us say our say.

(Strings)

MAC CONGLINNE. You have put me out, speaking to me out of the air like that. I can think of nothing.

THE GOD. I will say it for you.

(A major music)

---

32. **Slieve Mish** mountain in the Dingle Peninsula, southwest of Tralee   33. **Rathlin Island** in the far northeast of Ireland, off the coast of Co. Antrim

MAC CONGLINNE *(heard after a moment)*. That is a voice that will be heard. But I'm damned if I understand a word you are saying.

(Continue music. Stop on a jarring chord. A gentle knocking)

AIDAN. I am the youngest brother. I am Aidan. I come to welcome the occupant with fire and food. I hurry and I tremble and I worship and I fear, for this is the first time, Lord, such a mighty voice has resounded in Cork from such a frail if heavenly body. I will make the fire. Already the milk is warmed and the woman follows me.

MAC CONGLINNE. Well, you got results, queer fellow. But I can't say much more about your performance.

(Laugh of music)

But milk, old one. Can we thrive on that, we the viny lads who love the vat? You with the spark, you, O cowled one, I am not pleased with you, I do not love the service.

(Strings)

> A scum of water and a dirty towel
> Is my cleansing in Cork of the clerics;
> I, who have washed in the silver vowel of a spring,
> I am not pleased, O clerics, O Corkmen.

> A dark house is now welcome,
> For a house speaks from the hearth, the warm tongue
> Of fire is pleasant and the laden table.
> I did not find them here in Cork.

AIDAN. My Lord.

MAC CONGLINNE. I am no lord. I am a poet.

AIDAN. Grace be around me. A poet in the house on this night? On the God's night. O, my dear and sainted halo. There will be a riot in ritual, a clangour in commentaries, and a story in the holy water.

MAC CONGLINNE. I see you've had pleasant training in evasions. I see that you can beat the usual retreat behind the clerical wall. But I will accept no excuses. I am right. I am firm. I have been insulted by lack of welcome, by the meagreness of fire, by a weakness of cow's milk. And you, it seems, are insulted because I will not be a child and cry for its nanny. Let us, mutually, put the case into quatrains. The poets of Ireland will judge between us. Any little technical assistance I can give you, I will, since you do not appear much of a metre-man to me and your head is tonsured on that spot where the sun should spreadeagle wildly in your hair.

AIDAN. Do not make a satire on our establishment, O poet. Our reverend Abbot is in a temper already. He has failed to dislodge the demon from the king and he has lost his cloak and something of his mind. Do not do it, scholar. You will be disciplined if you do.

(Strings)
MAC CONGLINNE.

> I do not like big sticks.
> I carry the slender hazel wand,
> The long and lively tongue that never breaks,
> The elastic fellow who has no end.
>
> No end at all
> For he goes up to the nut and lives in it.
> He is the matter in a nutshell,
> A sweet voice and I deliver it.
>
> For I am the salmon in the pool.
> The hazel knows me. I am friend to a friend.
> Big sticks are the tools of the fool.
> I carry the tall and slender wand.

The little monk has gone.

STORYTELLER. Indeed, the little monk has gone. He is flying, he is rushing, he is tumbling over his habit and he is badly frightened. Bump, through one door; bash, through another; bish, through the third. And his reverend Abbot is glowering at him over a praying stool. He gathers his breath.

(Music to go with above)

AIDAN. O, father Abbot.

MUINCHEN. Brother, is excitement a part of the ritual?

AIDAN. O, father Abbot.

MUINCHEN. You are frightened, you are afraid. Brother, this is a simple, a reverend, and a yearly ritual. You need not be frightened or afraid. The child you have welcomed to the house need be no cause for fear. It is merely a symbol. It is human and ordinary. The woman will take it up. The woman will feed it, the woman will warm it. And the brothers will transform the house in a twinkling till it glitters and shines and welcomes.

AIDAN. O, father Abbot. It is not a child that has come. It is a poet.

MUINCHEN. Do I hear correctly? Does the demon still mock me? Am I out of my mind?

AIDAN. It is a poet.

(Strings)

> The house that has emptied itself,
> That is dead, that is a tomb
> Which must be refurnished by the One beyond wit
> Has given itself to a poet, to a coxcomb.
>
> He will speak loudly for a child.
> He will be heard outside the cradle, his bitter wit

Is not the comment of the humble and the mild.
God knows him. But he stands opposite.

The poet spoke to you, boy? What did he say?

AIDAN. He is making a satire upon the monks of Cork because he was not received and warmed as a guest.

MUINCHEN. That is the poets' way. He shall not make that satire except he speaks through scourges and rods. The brothers must out to him without delay. They will remove him to the green. They will knot him to the Pillar stone. They will scourge satire out of him until his flesh and skin break loose from his bones. But his bones must not be broken. And when that has been done, let him be dipped soundly into the river Lee, aye, without a stitch of clothing. And after that he may inhabit the guesthouse until morning, for it is now desecrated and the ritual of the year cannot be completed with regularity. His death must absolve us for that, death by crucifixion. To the guesthouse, now, to the guesthouse.

(Hurry of music ending with a recurrence of the phrases used in the first scourging at Grinnaun Ailech)

STORYTELLER. That is the poor poet learning his lessons over again.
(Strings)

A bitter thing it is
To be creature to a tongue, to a current of speech
That will carry you out of yourself
Beyond all reach.

What do you say, Tongue?
Have you so much to give
That I should die so many deaths
That my tongue may live?

They have flayed him to an empty skin. He is bloodless and breathless. But there's an undaunted devil in him somewhere. He is still mocking when they toss him over the long reeds into the sluggard riverwater.

(Splash, splash of music)
MONK. Mud to mud.
(Splash of music)
MONK. Mind to mind.
(Splash of music)
MONK. The stay of the river.
(Splash of music)
MONK. The blight of mankind.
(Splash of music)
MONK. Let him bide by his element for a while, the unstable man in the unstable water. Learn of mutability, Poet.

(Strings)
MAC CONGLINNE.

> I am among the reeds of the Lee and they talk to me
> As my peers, for the reed is royal.
> O tall sceptre, a starry man in Egypt
> Lifted you in jewels. He knows you for an equal.
>
> Flow on, lovely river. Do not mind me.
> I have friends in this court, stately and tufted Lords
> Who have sway over a country, who find me
> A mud-relation and understand my words.

MONKS. Have you had enough of water, Poet?
MAC CONGLINNE. I would like more land, Monk, if it weren't for the tithes you would grab from me.
MONK. Push him under a little more.
(Bubble of music)
MONK. I will repeat my question about water, Poet.
(Bubble. Bubble)
MONK. The scholar has the speech of water, now. He talks in bubbles. Pull him to the bank. I think he is senseless, or his tongue would be still wagging.
MONK. Up with him, brothers. Now, who will carry this oozy mass of the river Lee? God spare us. The vesper hour has come and gone. We have not sung, we have not prayed. The child has not come from the water as in every other year from time out of mind, and we have spent our hours in scourging a poet.
MONK. Lift this waterman. Holy father! What a weight. Certainly, if this man has divinity, it would weigh before the Lord.
MONK. At least something comes to us from the water. There is a symbol in that, if one could read. Ah, to be a wise man.
MONK. Better to be holy.
MONK. Better to be lucky; for to be lucky is to find the heaven that is at the end of holiness. Up, sweet brother of the Tongue, you have neither luck nor grace but certainly you smell to the highest of the heavens.
(Music flourish)
STORYTELLER. The unfortunate poet is lodged in the icy guesthouse for the long night. He gathers his own skin about him for warmth and sleeps in a palpitation of the flea-world. He does sleep. He has learned the secret of pain from somebody he cannot remember at the moment, some She that he has met at some time or other, but there have been so many Shes in his life he cannot distinguish his teacher. But she is warm inside him. She is a thought without a visual symbol and in thinking her out he

forgets that he ought to be in plaster and under a vegetable drug. The monks wake him in the morning. They come bearing gifts. The gifts are: sour faces, sour words, and sour judgements. They array themselves before his pallet and stand silently until the stately Abbot enters slowly. His every step is a pondering, his every look is a rendering. When he stops the world stops and he envelops the earth in a vast silence.

(*Appropriate music*)

MUINCHEN. He is awake?

MONKS. He is awake, father.

MUINCHEN. Let him stand. Let him bow.

MONKS. You must stand. You must bow.

(*Strings*)

MAC CONGLINNE.

> This Abbot, it seems,
> Demands largely like a king.
> Is he a tall tree among trees?
> What is his family? Does he hail from some royal thing?

MUINCHEN.

> I think largely. I believe profoundly,
> I live wisely. In that I am a king.
> God is my family tree,
> And tall enough to my thinking.

MAC CONGLINNE. I do not think I will stand and bow to you. Instead, I would ask you to make obeisance to me.

MONKS. Make obeisance to him?

MAC CONGLINNE.

> This Abbot is self-chosen.
> His qualities are worldly, his cloak too large for him.
> His signs are only the signs of a servant.
> Give him a mattock. Set him to till.

MONKS. O. O. O.

MUINCHEN. I suppose I must sit in judgement for this insult. I will do so with justice and calm, as might be expected of me. I think generally and not particularly when I condemn him to be crucified after the fashion of a malefactor.

MAC CONGLINNE. There was a certain malefactor whom you may not have heard of yet. He was condemned to a crucifixion, too, but his sin was Divine Justice. I will take it as an honour to suffer a death of that kind, for I am tired of the injustice of this world where a man is whipt clerically for no fault and half-drowned for no sin at all but for some mild objection to a failure in hospitality, a hospitality that is due to him under all the laws and which is well paid for by the community.

MUINCHEN. I tell the world there was no lack of hospitality on the part of the monks of Cork. You come to us on a night that is one night in the year for us, you take over a house that is prepared for another, and you lampoon holy men whose only business it is to serve God and deliver Him credibly to a world that is lost in all the sins.

MAC CONGLINNE. I would have begged pardon of the monks of Cork if I had known of this thing, but it was not explained to me. I was taken and flogged and half-drowned and not allowed to ask a thing or say a word. I have been evilly treated, for if I did evil it was unwittingly.

MUINCHEN. You have continued in your evil. You have insulted an Abbot. And in me all Abbots and Religious are offended. To condone that is to cheapen offence. And so, I will not remit my judgement.

MAC CONGLINNE. How can I expect justice? The face that I look on is not a just face.

(Strings)

> The heraldry of that white face
> Is that of the lawman who wins arguments.
> It is painted law but not justice.
> It is pride rampant. It lacks god-sense.

MONKS. O. O. O.

MUINCHEN. You see. You still follow the ways of pride. Will you die with some wild lampoon in your mouth?

MAC CONGLINNE. You see. You still follow the ways of pride. You will die with some wild opinion of your own worth.

MONKS. O. O. O.

MAC CONGLINNE. I charge you, now, with the murder of a body, my body.

MONKS. O. O. O.

MAC CONGLINNE. I charge you, too, with the murder of a soul, your soul.

MONKS. O. O. O.

MUINCHEN. You may take him away. He has earned so many deaths, he is lucky he can die but the one time.

MAC CONGLINNE. Cleric, there is something you have forgotten.

MUINCHEN. I have overlooked nothing.

MAC CONGLINNE. The law lays down the offences for which crucifixion is the legal punishment. How will you justify yourself to the King when the poet-schools of Ireland bring my death before him?

MUINCHEN. That need not trouble you. My conduct is impeccable. You have been adjudged guilty by a convocation of clergy, over which I presided. The sentence is a matter for me. Away with him, now.

MAC CONGLINNE. Not so fast, if you please. I have a right to ask a boon of you.

MUINCHEN. If it is to liberate you, scholar, you can shut your mouth.

MAC CONGLINNE. It is only a minor boon, a thing that is insignificant and small, but I warn you in advance that I will try to make more out of it.

MUINCHEN. Name it.

MAC CONGLINNE. I must have sureties,[34] first.

MUINCHEN. You may trust in my mercy.

MAC CONGLINNE. I will trust in my sureties, Monk, and in the bond of God I will put on them. That is not a right, but it is a custom.

MUINCHEN. Name your sureties.

MAC CONGLINNE. Ibar of Little Ireland, Cahal of Cashel, and all of your brotherhood that are present here at this moment shall take a pledge that I may have this boon.

MUINCHEN. My sons may do so.

MONKS. We take the pledge of fulfilment.

MUINCHEN. You can name your wish, now.

MAC CONGLINNE. Let my satchel be given to me. Let it be opened. It is my wish now to eat those two wheaten cakes that are in it and the round of old bacon. I believe in food for a journey, and by the signs of things I would seem to be going on a long one. I would eat my meal at the door, with a spark of the sun on my head, and the people of Cork watching me. I demand to be taken there.

MUINCHEN. You may be taken there.

(Music)

STORYTELLER. Poor Mac Conglinne. He is taken to the door from which the poor of Cork are fed every evening before the vesper bell, but around which they gather early, playing pitch-and-toss and the horseshoe game and the sly gamble of the shell-and-pea.

MAC CONGLINNE. I need a knife.

MUINCHEN. Let him have a knife.

MAC CONGLINNE. It is the law that the man who eats must give tithes to a man who is poorer than himself. I am cutting a just tenth of my mite and I will give it to anyone who can be found to be poorer than I am.

(Clamour of beggars. Music)

(Strings)

---

34. **sureties** in early Irish law, guarantors appointed to enforce the terms of a contract

MAC CONGLINNE.

> The beggars of Cork, the rough and tumble men,
> The lazy women who never delouse,
> The one-legged man, the blind stick-tapper, children
> On arm-crook and shawl, they are after me with their claws.

> I save myself from the outstretched fingers
> With difficulty. I would feed those poor
> If I had plenty; but this poet has hungers
> Inside himself that knock at every door.

Before God, you rag-and-bone people, it can never be known if any of you stands in greater need of those tithes than the man that has them in his hand; and since possession is nine points of any law, I propose with God's consent to put them into my own belly. For my journey yesterday was longer than any of yours. And my treatment in Cork was worse. I was received by curs and hounds and stripped and scourged and dowsed in the waters of the Lee. And in the presence of my Maker, O you evil monks of Cork, I say that it will not be charged to me by the fiend when I reach the Judgement that I gave you those tithes, for you deserve them not.

MUINCHEN. I did not bargain for this oration to the laity, Scholar.

MAC CONGLINNE. There will be still more, Monk, which you did not foresee. I suppose you will agree that a drinking goes with an eating. Take me now to the Lee, to the well that is ever-full.

MUINCHEN. I did not bargain for a drinking, Scholar.

MAC CONGLINNE. You can over-ride law but not custom, Monk. I put the case to your congregation.

MONKS. The scholar is right, Father.

MUINCHEN. Then, take him to his well. But I will wait here within my house. I will lose no dignity on him.

MAC CONGLINNE. That is a pity, for I have lessons for you still. Note that I have eaten enough for three days to come and that there is no time limit within which I must take the drink that goes with that meal. It is my intention, accordingly, O Monk, to fast for another three days, and then for three days more to be drinking water and doing penance for my sins. I think, O you bad Abbot, that I have obtained nine days of respite from you in spite of yourself.

MUINCHEN. I allow no trickery, scholar.

MAC CONGLINNE. The stretching of a custom is no trick.

MUINCHEN. I will ponder it. In the meantime, go to your drink. Get out of my presence, for neither your face nor your ways are a pleasure to me. Take him to this well and stick his head in it.

MAC CONGLINNE. Not so, Monk. I go to a drinking, not to a drowning, and I shall take my drink in my own way—

(Fading out)
There is a method in all things.
(Music)
STORYTELLER. And what a drinking, and what a method of drinking! The poet reaches the well, guarded by the monks, but accompanied by half the population of the town of Cork. On the flag before it, he halts, he loosens his cloak and the big brooch of his cloak with the long pin. He lays the cloak down upon the flag and lies down upon it, like a strong man about to perform the feat of the stone-sledging. His head is to the well.

CORK VOICE. What is he at, all, boy? Is it an acrobat the fellow is? What's he doing with the brooch?

MAC CONGLINNE. My method of drinking, people of Cork, is to dip the pin of this brooch over my head into the water. Watch me. You see I gather water on the pin, and when I lift it it runs down the pinhead into one drop. I hold the pin over my mouth and the drop falls into it.

(Laughter of the people in Cork in music)

It is somewhat laborious, people. It will take a long time to satisfy my thirst, my legal and proper thirst, but you must admit that I have a right to stay alive while my thirst is dissatisfied.

(Laughter in music)

Am I not making a fool of that abbot, that bad Abbot, Muinchen, O people of Cork?

(Laughter in music)

MONK. It was no part of our bargain, Scholar, that you should make the people laugh at us.

MAC CONGLINNE. It is a man's business to live while he may, Monk.

MONK. He must die when his death is ordained, Scholar.

MAC CONGLINNE. To give up life easily is to commit the sin of suicide.

MONK. Take this question to the Abbot, brother. You must run, for we are but objects of ridicule here before the people.

(Strings)

MAC CONGLINNE.

> The monk has a quandary.
> He follows a trodden path. He does not lift his eyes.
> He is nervous of the glory
> I catch. He fears my sunrise.
>
> The monk is right.
> But so am I. He finds in abstinence
> And knee-worship all the glories I
> Startle each moment out of every sense.

MONK. Brothers.

MONKS. We hear you, brother.

MONK. We cannot stay here much longer. We are becoming a mockery.

MONKS. Does that matter? We will sit here and be comfortable while the scholar is uncomfortable—

MAC CONGLINNE. Monks, I am always comfortable wherever I am. One of the lessons the poet learns is to feel in different parts of himself, so that he can unfold his own drama in one eye and regard it with the other.

(Strings)

> In Cork by the Lee
> I am married to the earth. We lie so lightly
> That the earth must think me
> Thin and warm as early sunlight.
>
> We are happy together.
> We are two in one. We are so young
> That our drink is one bright drop of water,
> One small golden egg that falls through our marriage ring.

(Heavy abbot music approaching)

MUINCHEN. I will not have this, Scholar.

MAC CONGLINNE. O, the bad Abbot.

MUINCHEN. I will not allow custom to be stretched till it becomes farce. You can stand up, now.

MAC CONGLINNE. I refuse to leave here till I have drunk my fill.

MUINCHEN. I allowed you to drink and the time to drink. If you have not drunken what you need, it is your own fault. Take him up, my sons.

MONKS. A boon from you, Father Abbot.

MUINCHEN. What boon do you want of me?

MONKS. Time has gone astray on us today. We have not offered Mass nor blessing, and it is now past the noon. Let us have a respite for this poet till those things have been done.

MUINCHEN. Afterwards you shall do them. The day of his transgression shall be the day of that man's punishment. You may rise up and take him to the wood of the foxes. Let him cut his own tree, let him carry it to the green, let him be crucified. I will not be mocked by a mocker, I will not be demeaned. *(Fading)* I will not be dishonoured in my community.

(Heavy abbot music recedes)

STORYTELLER. Ochone.[35] Poor Mac Conglinne is marched to the wood of the foxes. An axe is thrust into his hands and an elder tree pointed out to him on a ditch.

35. **Ochone** Alas (Irish *ochón*)

(Strings)
Mac Conglinne.

> Elder tree, I fear
> You are lucky for me. You will stretch
> My poor body on spokes of air
> Till nothing is beyond my reach.

> What will I be
> When bone and bone is racked around in a ring
> And I see the stars from the end of my heel,
> A sunwheel thundering?

Storyteller. But the winter day is short. When he labours back with his cross, the monks are tired and without food.

Monk. This scholar is a great trouble to us.

Monk. What brought you to Cork, wonderman? Could you not have holidayed somewhere else? B'l'ath Cliath[36] is a great place for the poetry and the drink. Or that fishtown[37] by Ibar's island.

Monk. Brothers, there is a void in me.

Monk. There is a void in us all.

Monk. I am never myself the day I do not spend the morning in my little chapel.

Monks. Nor I, nor I.

Monk. Nor I when I miss the morning's porridge.

Monk. Little time today we have had for praying. Let us in convocation pray the Abbot for a respite for this lost one until the morning.

Monks. That is a good thought.

Monk. That is a good thought. We will halt here, now, and I will call Muinchen. Stand here, now. You may halt, Scholar. Scholar, you may halt. He does not hear me. Scholar. Scholar.

(Heavy music of the abbot)

Muinchen. Another respite.

Monk. This time it is for us, father Abbot, for monks who have not said Mass, nor offered a prayer in the course of this day in our little chapel. We crave this benefit of clergy and we request it because it is our right.

Muinchen. Rights, rights, boons, boons, respites, respites. Am I to hear nothing all day but those words? A demon loose in the country, a poet loose in Cork, and my monks fail me and do my bidding slowly.

Monk. Not so, father. We have failed in no thing. It is your own power and your own insight and oversight that have failed you and allowed the demon to overcome you and the poet to delay you.

---

36. **B'l'ath Cliath** Dublin (Irish *Baile Átha Cliath,* pronounced "blah cleeah")
37. **that fishtown** Wexford

MUINCHEN. Which of you has spoken?

MONKS ALL. All of us have spoken, father Abbot.

MUINCHEN. I see. Many faggots make a bundle that cannot be broken. Let this poet have a respite till tomorrow morning. But let him be stripped, let him be bound to the stone, and let him have no food and no drink.

(Receding abbot music)

STORYTELLER. The unlucky poet is knotted once more to that tall stone. And the night comes down on him. He can hear the monks in the chapel, he can listen to the dogs barking on the horizon, he can feel the grass of the green thicken and crinkle with ice and he can count more comfort. But he falls asleep. He falls into the warm cloak of a thought. And the cloak is very like the cloak that he delivered to the king on Ibar's island. And there is somebody else inside the cloak. There is a tall and golden woman. There is a queen.

MAC CONGLINNE. There is someone in the middle of my pain.

QUEEN. It is I, Mac Conglinne.

MAC CONGLINNE. The bad queen.

QUEEN. Not so, Mac Conglinne. A queen needs to be royal, not good. You have agreed with me in that before.

MAC CONGLINNE. I did. And I don't know why. I carry a red alphabet for you on the backs of my buttocks, the mud of the Lee is in my gullet because of you, and before me there is a great stretching of arms and legs, the kind of a laying on of hands that I am not partial to. They call it a crucifixion.

QUEEN. I know that.

MAC CONGLINNE. I expect you do. And it is plain to me, now, that many have been crucified because of you. Do you speak outside or inside of me?

QUEEN. I speak from inside.

MAC CONGLINNE. No use in that case to ask you to touch me and let my head fall upon your breast.

QUEEN. You are there, now, Mac Conglinne. My child, my boy, my man.

MAC CONGLINNE. You are my lady of the Willow Tree.

QUEEN. That is one aspect of me.

MAC CONGLINNE. You are also a terrible nuisance to me.

QUEEN. That is another aspect of me. But it is my business to establish myself. I need your help for that.

MAC CONGLINNE. If you think to establish yourself with Cahal of Cashel, you can put it out of your head. He calls you a great bitch. Your name is farmyard muck to him, and all that goes with it.

QUEEN. I am aware of that. But it is not an expression I would wear to dinner. The king is necessary to me.

MAC CONGLINNE. Have you no pride to follow him this way?
QUEEN. I have proportion, I have business, I have being.
(Strings)

> I alternate,
> How can I help it? I
> Rise and fall with the spirit
> That moves me, that is me.

> Do not remark me.
> I am not remarkable. I am a country
> You know well.
> My demands are simple. My demands are me.

> I ask you to carry me.
> But I carry you, too, though you grow taller and taller
> And I the larger for you till the time
> Comes when you grow smaller.

You have this to do for me, now, my poet. I am the great hunger in Cahal of Cashel.
MAC CONGLINNE. You are that great demon?
QUEEN. It is another aspect of me. The most terrible. It is my requiem side. And the day has now come when I leave it aside. In the morning you will go to the king.
MAC CONGLINNE. If I go there it will be on one side of a cross. Tomorrow I will be a dead man.
QUEEN. I will have talk with the Abbot Muinchen.
MAC CONGLINNE. That's all the good that will be. You do not know this Abbot.
QUEEN. I do know him. He has his own dream of me. And he is steadfast to it.
(Strings)
MAC CONGLINNE.

> Do you tempt every bed,
> You, O long hair, O white one, are you
> A different woman in every head,
> A woman of thousands? And who will wear you?

> Who will wear you when time ends,
> You, O long hair, O white one, every man
> Carrying you in his head to heaven,
> When time ends, will you be the only woman?

QUEEN. I will be the only woman, Mac Conglinne.
MAC CONGLINNE. I know you, now, and I am lost. O Goddess, my

heart is in my mouth for you and it will talk love. When you were a queen, you were the profane thought in my mind, and you were a hope there, too, that some day I would come on you when you were not queenly. I am lost, now.

QUEEN. You are not lost. You will find me in every poem.

MAC CONGLINNE. Is that enough?

QUEEN. Nothing is ever enough in itself. I am not enough in myself. But everything has enough to go on with so that it can will and desire and change, so that it is ever in the process of creation. Is not that enough?

MAC CONGLINNE. Lady of the Willow Tree.

QUEEN. My child, my boy, my lover.

MAC CONGLINNE. How will I know the way to release you from the— kingly appetite?

QUEEN. I leave that to you. Are you not a poet and master of the arts? Are you not now in the visionary state in which things can happen? This Abbot, who is an ogre to you, has he not served you in that?

MAC CONGLINNE. It was harsh service.

QUEEN. His mission is to be hard. And I am afraid you will have some revenge on him tomorrow. You will be given his cloak.

MAC CONGLINNE. I do not want his cloak.

QUEEN. Tomorrow you will want it. It is the cloak of the delivery of a god, and in time you will become so proud of it that you will have to be removed from under it, for that is the way of things. You will become dry, arid, sterile and haughty, and you will misinterpret your god so much that he will find it necessary to remove you.

MAC CONGLINNE. If I wear this cloak, I will never be of that kind.

QUEEN. It is in the nature of things for you to be of that kind.

MAC CONGLINNE. I will leave the nature of things.

QUEEN. Then, you will cease to know me.

MAC CONGLINNE. I will take you along with me.

QUEEN. I am there before you. But what there is here of me remains till the fan is folded from before the face. I leave you, now. I kiss you, I love you, and I will receive you when the world has ended for you.

(Music of the queen's going)

STORYTELLER. I end this scene with a sigh. To the poet his vision, to the storyteller his hard work and little profit, to the Monk his Abbot, to the Abbot a matin bell that is cracked and newly made out of a kitchen skillet.

(Cracked skillet music. Sounds of rousing monks)

MONK. It is not a good omen, this cracked bell of the morning. Pax tecum, pax tecum.

MONK. Fresh holywater has been blessed.

MONK. My soul is cold. The Abbot must allow us mass this morning.

(Heavy music of the abbot)
MUINCHEN. My sons.
MONKS. Our father.
MUINCHEN. After matin, after mass, it is usual for us to have some collation. This morning you must fast with me, for last night I had most unseemly dreams of good food and I wakened this morning with an appetite that climbs to the devilish level of the king's.
MONKS *(softly)*. It is the demon, the demon of the king.
MUINCHEN. That is my dread, sons. It is yet a baby hunger to the king's hunger, but big things can begin small. Once the world was a tiny egg. You will fast with me this morning.
MUINCHEN. We will fast with you this morning.
MUINCHEN. We will pray, now.
MONKS. We will pray, now.
(Heavy abbot music recedes)
STORYTELLER. Prayers waken Mac Conglinne. He, too, feels a passion of hunger. He smacks his lips.
(Quirk of music)
His gums are saliva.
(Watery squish of music)
But his teeth are warriors in white armour who clash one on another.
(An iron music)
In the air by his head a hawk dives; no, it is that quarrelsome little bastard, the cock-robin. But what a robin. Has he borrowed feathers from the eagle? He plunges at a little wren, the tiny goldcrest, and by God, he's got him. And O what a ripping of small plumes. The sky wakens. Chimneys are smoking. Dogs are sniffing. Cats are mewing at kitchen windows. Milk pails are clinking and there are the tiny chimes of good delph[38] all along the streets. And O the smells. It is breakfast time in Cork. Mac Conglinne sniffs, sniffs, sniffs.
(Quirks of music)
And now, the Abbot Muichen begins a stately progress across the green.
(Heavy abbot music)
MUINCHEN. I smell good things.
MONKS. The earth is gracious.
MUINCHEN. It is the tables of the Corkmen I smell.
(Quirky sniff of music)
O muttons, pray with me.
MONKS. O. O. O.
MUINCHEN. O Lard look down on me. My tongue sniffs. I cannot say a bird right.

38. **delph** china

MONKS. The demon is in the Abbot.

MUINCHEN. It is the feast in me. Again, again. My tongue tripes at every curd. I cannot speak to this scholar with this hunger in my mouth. I will return and read in my little cook. O. O.

MONKS. O. O. O.

MAC CONGLINNE. What a lot of "Os" there are in Ireland this morning. What ails all the grand sons of this monk?

MUINCHEN. You are awake, you are bright, you are beaming early. I have no stomach for morning wit, please be gravy.

(Quirk of music)

MAC CONGLINNE. O weighty Abbot.

(Strings)

> O, weighty Abbot, how could you be light
> From such a family tree
> As yours? I saw it all last night.
> It was a vision that came to me.
>
> You are the son of honeybag and lard,
> Son of stirabout, son of butter,
> Son of a cow's cream, son of curd,
> Son of bacon-flitch, son of shoulder.
>
> Son of back, son of paunch,
> Son of leg and loin, son of kidney,
> Son of pig's head, son of haunch.
> Shall I go on? Do you forbid me?

MUINCHEN. You would not hurt me, Mac Conglinne, by finding my pedigree in food but for one thing; and that is that you should speak of it this morning when my tongue sloughs over. But you have said a trough, I mean, I mean. . . .

MONKS. O. O. O.

MAC CONGLINNE. Monk, there is a demon of food talking through you.

MUINCHEN. Not yet, not yet. It is a cream I had in sleep last night.

(Quirk of music)

MONKS. O. O. O.

MAC CONGLINNE. It is quite clear to me.

MUINCHEN. Your sight will not help you much. You will die even if I am beflitched.

(Quirk)

MONKS. O. O. O.

MAC CONGLINNE. Old bacon, I can cure you.

MUINCHEN. If you could, I would reward you.

MAC CONGLINNE. In what way would you reward me?

MUINCHEN. By allowing you to confess your sins and shriving you before death.

MAC CONGLINNE. By my soul there is a large sulk inside you. You will do much more for me, O Muinchen. You will also take my body into consideration. You will release me from all bonds. You will let me have the ownership of that great cloak that I presented to the king of Ibar's island.

MUINCHEN. It was you, then, who gave the king that cloak?

MAC CONGLINNE. It was I.

MUINCHEN. You are a power, then?

MONKS. O. O. O.

MAC CONGLINNE (imitating monks). O. O. O. You owe me so much, I should hang out the usurer's sign. I will add to my offer. When I have cured you, I will cure the king.

MONKS (softly). A marvel amongst us, a marvel amongst us.

MAC CONGLINNE. You are considering it.

MUINCHEN. I am crunchsidering it. That cloak, that cloak. O, Lard suck for me.

(Quirk of music)
(Strings)

> It is raiment. A cloak of every stew.
> It was Muinchen's. Now, a young roaster
> Because of an ignorance in Muinchen's belly will go
> In God's guise and eat above me.

You may cure me, Scholar.

MAC CONGLINNE. Sureties first, Monk. Name them.

MUINCHEN (breathlessly to music).

> Beef, mutton, lamb, a kid,
> Stewy smells that lift the lid.
> Tripe and sausage, wheat in milk—
> Stop me, I cannot help myself.
> Back rashers dripping smoke and fat,
> The brains of a pig, his little hat—
> O, help me brothers, bacon boiled,
> Slices roasted, then half broiled.
> Brothers, brothers, I am lost
> In food, I'm soup-and-gravy tossed—

(Blare of music. Sudden silence)

MAC CONGLINNE. You are cured, now.

MUINCHEN. What did you do to me?

MAC CONGLINNE. I allowed you to boil over. I have taken your hunger on myself.

MONKS. O. O. O.

MUINCHEN. You show no signs of my hunger.

MAC CONGLINNE. That is because I am much larger than you are.

MUINCHEN. I can see that, now.

MAC CONGLINNE. That surprises me. I thought you had one little eye and that it was eternally turned upon yourself in adoration. Loose me, now, for I have work to do.

MONKS. It is a marvel. It is a marvel. O. O. O.

(Music)

STORYTELLER. But Mac Conglinne is away to greater marvels, to the curing of Cahal of Cashel and the salvation of South Ireland. He lifts his five-folded, well-stropped cloak on to the slope of his shoulders, he ties his shirt around the rounds of his fork, and in a twinkling his heels are feathery with speed and he is striding over Raheen and Bealnablath and coming to the Dun of Coba,[39] the wide dwelling of Pichan. The crossroads are peopled with quiet men in their Mass-suits, men who say nothing but are waiting for something to happen. So, unchallenged by any doorkeeper, Mac Conglinne bursts into Pichan's enclosure where the soldiers are in chattering groups and the women gossiping and the children running around playing a new game that they call King and Demon. The king is abroad somewhere, somewhere unknown. And Pichan, his friend and warrior-mate, awaits him in the great hall of the Dun, the wide living room where walls are lined with sleeping places where soldiers lounge, where they sharpen weapons on the big stone, where they line the board at mealtimes, where they quarrel and take their turns in boasting according to their orders. Into the enclosure, turning cartwheels, and doing wild juggleries, comes this new and strange Mac Conglinne. He has been fasting, he has been beaten till his mind has left his skin, he has been drowned till all his life has gone inward, and now he is light, airy, and like a shaft of the sun for power. Pichan watches him out of a tired dream.

(A tired music)

MAC CONGLINNE. I do not make you merry, Pichan.

PICHAN. You do your best, Scholar, but your best is of little use against the king's worst.

(Strings)

> He is all my friends in one.
> I cannot deny him, he may have heart and all;

39. **over Raheen . . . to the Dun of Coba** traveling southwestward from Cork into Pichan's kingdom, Uí Echach Muman

But what I give is given to a demon.
A demon is eating my heart, he is eating Cahal.

If there was help from God
I would meet it on my four bones and crawl with it
From heaven to Corcalee;[40]
If my knees were to redden the earth, it is I would haul it here.

MAC CONGLINNE. Help has come, O Pichan.

PICHAN. I am not aware of it, Student. I only see a scholar before me who demeans a high art by the trumperies of jugglers and twopenny tumblers. I do not blame, you, Scholar; every man to his own image.

MAC CONGLINNE. Still, I bring help, Pichan. What will I receive from you if I keep the king from eating for one whole day?

PICHAN. A golden ring and a Welsh horse.

MAC CONGLINNE. I see you put me in the penny place. My demands are larger.

PICHAN. I can see that, now. I will give you, too, a white sheep from every house and fold from Carn to Cork.

MAC CONGLINNE. That is my due. Sureties, now, if you please.

> Kings and lords of the land,
> Poets and satirists must be pledged to me;
> Kings to enforce the dues, lords to spend
> On collectors, the poets to satirise me,
> Satirists to travel, to spread the abuse
> Of the poets. In that way I get my dues?

PICHAN. It is done.

MAC CONGLINNE. I will take that for a pledge.

PICHAN. And you may begin, now, for I hear the rush and the approach of my sick friend and king.

(*Appropriate music*)

STORYTELLER. It is the king, indeed, and a changed king. The demon is showing through his face. He is lean as a tapeworm. And he seems to have wings on his shoulders, but that is only the cloak of Muinchen that is awry and flying about his great hurry. From the serving quarters there is a rush of servants, gillies and maidservants, they have placed him on the top king-seat of the board, they are loosening his boots, they have the utensils of the wash, but he pulls the hide table-covering on to his lap and starts to munch the barrowload of apples that have been piled on it in section and order. O, what a munching.

40. **Corcalee** territory of the Corco Loígde tribe, west Kerry, around the Beare Peninsula

(Appropriate munch music)

O. O. but there is another munching, too, a tooth-on-edge kind of munching that draws all eyes, even the King's.

(Appropriate tooth-on-edge music)

Now, this is a strange sight. Mac Conglinne has taken the huge stone-block on which the soldiers sharpen their points and edges and is holding it with abnormal strength to his mouth. O what a horrible munching. The King stops to watch.

(Tooth-on-edge music which recedes)

CAHAL. What makes you mad, Son of Learning?[41]

MAC CONGLINNE. I grieve to see a King eating alone.

CAHAL. Small reason for grief in that. A King is always alone.

MAC CONGLINNE. A king is a kingdom. He is his people's honour. If there were a foreigner here, he would be entitled to scoff at our bad manners if my beard did not wag mutually in movement with yours.

CAHAL. That is a good point. I will give you an apple. This one is too large for you.

(Crunch crunch of music)

This is large, too.

(Crunch crunch)

So is this.

(Crunch)

This also.

(Tooth-racking music again)

MAC CONGLINNE. I still eat my stone, O King.

CAHAL. May you have good digestion. All those apples are too big to give away.

MAC CONGLINNE. And how that foreigner would laugh at us, at you.

CAHAL. True. I will give you an apple. This one, no, this, no. By God, you are a greedy man, Scholar. Is it necessary at all that I should give you an apple?

MAC CONGLINNE. For your own honour and the honour of your kingdom.

CAHAL. Here, before I change my mind. Catch, greedy one.

(Whizz of an apple thrown)

MAC CONGLINNE. I catch, but it was ungraciously given. I have one, but better two things than one in learning. One is that path for another, King.

CAHAL. Another. Am I made of apples?

MAC CONGLINNE. You are a great tree of apples.

CAHAL. O. O. Here, Scholar.

41. **Son of Learning** literal translation of Old Irish *mac léiginn,* clerical student

(Another whizz of music)

MAC CONGLINNE. I have only two. And the number of the Trinity is one more.

CAHAL. No.

MAC CONGLINNE. King, you dishonour the Trinity.

CAHAL. Do I do that? Here, then.

(Another whizz)

MAC CONGLINNE. The Gospel is in four books. That is one more.

CAHAL. I give you the four books of the Gospels. I cannot eat them.

MAC CONGLINNE. Then, the floor of your hall falls under you.

CAHAL. Here. Here.

(Another whizz)

MAC CONGLINNE. I have four. But there are five books of Moses.

CAHAL. Why should you count them in apples? Count them in spears or in buttons. Those I will give you.

MAC CONGLINNE. The apple is blessed.

CAHAL. Woe, woe.

(Another whizz)

MAC CONGLINNE. I have five. But there is a number which consists of its own parts and divisions. Its half is three, its third is two, and its sixth is one. Give me that lovely number.

CAHAL. You rob me, you reave me, you unrobe me.

MAC CONGLINNE. The sixth, King.

(Whizz)

I thank you. There were seven things prophesied of God on Earth, however—

CAHAL. Do you ask me for a seventh?

(Wolfish howl)

MAC CONGLINNE. I do. And an eighth for your own Royalty. And nine for the orders of heaven, and ten is the number of mankind. And the eleventh, King, is the imperfect number of the apostles after sin, twelve is the perfect number of the apostles after sin. And then, for the triumph of triumphs, Cahal, the number thirteen, the perfect number, Christ with his apostles.

(There is a whizz after each number above, but at thirteen there is a violence of whizzes.)

CAHAL. Take all, O devourer. Let me rise, let me reach for my anger. Let me rear and roar.

(Snarl of trumpets)

MAC CONGLINNE. This is not kingly. If you curse me, you cut me off from heaven. I remind you of the mercy you carry, for I stand in need of it. I have also something to say to you.

CAHAL. I will calm myself. I will listen. Be brief as my meal was brief.

MAC CONGLINNE. I must ask a boon first. I ask it of your kingship.

CAHAL. Are you entitled to that? Have you degrees, poet? Have you the signs of the houses on you?

MAC CONGLINNE. Pichan will witness for me.

PICHAN. I will bail him, Cashel.

CAHAL. Ask, then.

MAC CONGLINNE. Sureties, first, that my boon be granted?

CAHAL. My princely word on it.

MAC CONGLINNE. I will speak so. Because of you I came south to Cork. Because of you I transgressed in Cork. Because of you I was punished in Cork, and there is a curse on me still for my innocent transgression. It is in your power to release me from that curse, for you are an original brother.

CAHAL. But if I release you, I must do a fast for it. Do you ask me to do that?

MAC CONGLINNE. That is what I ask.

CAHAL. By my faith, you will carry your curse along with you to the end of time.

MAC CONGLINNE. King, your bond, your bails, your princeliness.

CAHAL. O. O. Student, ask me for a cow from every enclosure in Munster, ask me for an ounce from every householder, ask me for a cloak from every church, all to be levied by my steward, and yourself to stay feasting with me till the tax is heaped before you and the taxmen touching their caps.

MAC CONGLINNE. It would not be lawful. Is it lawful that I should feast my body and give my soul to eternal perdition? I hold you to your bails and your bonds and your sureties.

(Wolf howl of king)

CAHAL.

This sprig of learning,
With his satchel, with his wand, he walks
The roads and the delicate bye-paths of all things
Where the world is talking.
And where no world talks.

Learning is no load. He walks lightly
And so deceptively, five things are graces in him,
The solar month, the age of the moon, the seatide,
The calendar of the perfect deity
And the year in its rhythm.

He slips through me. He enters
From so many roads he is before me here
In the flash of my anger, and suddenly I see him

With my country in his power.
That is what learning has done for him. That is the way of learning.

I will fast with you, student. But I will hate you.
  (Wolf music)
  STORYTELLER.

  Cahal does fast, but if he sleeps, nobody else sleeps.
  He dreams of fat pots *(Quirk of music)*
  Poleaxed bullocks skin-stripped by the cooks. *(Quirk of music)*
  Fires under black vats. *(Quirk of music)*
  The kitchen turning, brown smells on the hooks. *(Quirk of music)*

  (Wolfish howls)

  The weighty belly of the table *(Quirk of music)*
  The crunch and munch of everything *(Quirk of music)*
  Food like a fable *(Quirk of music)*
  ENOUGH FOR A KING. *(Quirk of music)*

(Wolfish music)
CAHAL. Where is that student?
MAC CONGLINNE. I am here, nodding by the wall.
CAHAL. Release me from my bails, relieve me of my sureties.
MAC CONGLINNE. There will be no release, there will be no relieving.
CAHAL. It is too much.
MAC CONGLINNE. That is your story, Cahal. Too much.
CAHAL. I will halve my dinner with you. I will give you three parts of
my breakfast—
MAC CONGLINNE. Sleep, King.
(Strings)

  In little thatches
  Where men who work the fields are tired out
  Women sing sleepy snatches
  To the cradle by the fire. They stir with one bare foot.

  Let them sleep.
  They have the rights of labour. If a man
  Turns over there should be a warm meeting
  On the pillow-side, for winter is on the land.

  My words to great kings are:
  Justice; be gentle; start no great shows
  That the man and the woman together
  Sleep warm in the winter snows.

CAHAL. I will take that scholar by the throat. I will throttle him. I will bottle him, I will baste him, I will roast him, I will toast him, I will thrust him into the wild den of my mouth. I will be the first cannibal king of Ireland.

(Wolfish music)

STORYTELLER. But in the morning he is still under bails and bonds and his stomach is still a mighty emptiness. The daylight hours are all to pass. The student calls on the clergy. He puts them in pulpits and they preach to the king. They get on well enough till one of them tells the story of the ravens who fed some prophet or other, and then there is a commotion in the royal pew. Wood flies, timber skips, kneel-props whistle through the air. Towards evening, there is nobody in Pichan's world-wide dwelling who isn't tired, flat, flabby and flatulent with hunger, thirst, excitement and depression. At the supper-hour, the king is raving.

(Wolf music)

CAHAL. That scholar, that scholar. Let him release me, now, now, now.

MAC CONGLINNE. King, I am here. I bring you another request.

CAHAL. Bring me my supper.

MAC CONGLINNE. I would prefer to bring you salvation from your appetite.

CAHAL. Leave me my appetite. I shall dine on my salvation.

MAC CONGLINNE. Those are demon's words.

(Wolf music)

DEMON. They are demon's words, Mac Conglinne, for it is the demon who speaks to you, now. You had better leave me alone, or I will come out to you as I did to Muinchen of Cork. I took his cloak and I will take your skin, for you have little else that is yours.

MAC CONGLINNE. You will only come out to a good dinner, Demon. I know your nature. And when you come out I will be ready for you.

DEMON. I will be a blast in your mind.

MAC CONGLINNE. My mind is withdrawn.

DEMON. In your body a hunger.

MAC CONGLINNE. I have a greater hunger.

DEMON. Your soul shall not escape me.

MAC CONGLINNE. It has escaped you. It waits on a woman in heaven.

(Howling music)

You hear, King?

CAHAL. I hear nothing but my belly, Son of Learning. I ask you to release me this minute. Have the half of my house, the half of my authority, even the half of my dinner, but sit me down at a big table. Let me eat.

MAC CONGLINNE. Not yet. You have fasted for me, you have restrained your world-wide appetite for me, and you have given me that power over the demon that is in you. You have done that for me. Now, do it for yourself. Fast for one night for yourself.

CAHAL. I smell a mighty supper.

MAC CONGLINNE. The demon is in your nose.

CAHAL. I munch, I crunch. I will have that supper.

MAC CONGLINNE. King.

CAHAL. I do not hear you, Son of Learning.

MAC CONGLINNE. It is not yet suppertime. Nothing is ready, nothing is prepared, we all fast and we will fast with you.

CAHAL. Fasting is not food I like.

MAC CONGLINNE. If you sleep you will not dream of fasting. Sleep till supper.

CAHAL. No. You would trick me.

MAC CONGLINNE. King, fast for me till supper as you have bailed to do.

CAHAL. What else am I doing? But I ask you again to release me.

MAC CONGLINNE. Let me whisper in your ear.

CAHAL. Approach me and I will bite your nose.

MAC CONGLINNE. Still I will say my say.

(Strings)

> There is a secret in the king's hunger.
> The hunger is not for food, otherwise
> The king would be bird or boar,
> The wing-beast or the foot-beast. It is otherwise.
>
> There is a sweet mate somewhere.
> She calls to the king.
> This woman is the king's hunger;
> She is his hungering.

CAHAL. I think you are speaking of that great bitch, Ligach, Scholar. I remember you now. You are that castaway who brought me the cloak I gave and took from that ass-eared Muinchen. Have you a league with Ligach? By my soul, if you have, you can take three jumps out of here on the toe of a royal boot.

MAC CONGLINNE. King, I came to save you from her, to save you from that hunger for her that is in you.

CAHAL. You lie, Scholar. The hunger I have is for food. For Ligach I have nothing but a wish to turn my tail on her and run.

MAC CONGLINNE. King, take a scholar's oath. The desire for that woman is inside you. I will cure it. Fast one night for your own self and tomorrow, I will free you.

CAHAL. You assert that?

MAC CONGLINNE. Have my head otherwise.

DEMON. Have his head, now, Cahal of Cashel. Little curly Cahal, have this scholar's head.

CAHAL. By God, I recognise the turn of that phrase. Are you here within me, then, O you lovely dangerous bitch?

DEMON. Do not believe the scholar. I am a table-worshipper. Bid them lay a table for us, big, bright, groaning, bellyful, belching—

(Howl)

CAHAL. Scholar, I will fast tonight. I will purge this demon with prayer, I will fast till she bites her own nails, till she shrews her fingers, till she starts viciously to make a dinner out of her own skin.

(Wolf music)

Fast with me, all of you that are in Pichan's house tonight. Pray for me, priests; bishops, any preaching will please me; poets, pick your pearls for me; and you, Son of Learning, watch with me, watch with me, for there is no fasting, no praying that I must shirk tonight to kick that woman out of her place in my belly.

(Appropriate music)

STORYTELLER. So to the fast again. And if one night was bad, the second was a horror. Cahal was as loud as a den of animals. Where his tongue would pray, the demon substituted food words as in the case of Abbot Muinchen. He slept towards morning. And then Mac Conglinne rose up and went into the great kitchens where Pichan was lost in reverie before the cold fires.

PICHAN. What is to do, now, Son of Learning?

MAC CONGLINNE. This is cure day. I want, now, ash-billets for a large fire. I want four long, strong spits of hazelwood. I want four mighty pieces in slab of corned beef, red beef, wether mutton and a young ham. In addition, I must be supplied with twenty strong helpers of proved courage and with hammered cables of iron and there must be dug into the floor and outside the house, strong staples that will hold those chains.

DEMON. What to do, Son of Learning?

MAC CONGLINNE. To do a terrible thing, Master of the house, for which I must have your permission and your blessing. To take and bind the king, for that is necessary if he is to be cured.

PICHAN. If it is necessary, it must be done. I will get you what you wish.

MAC CONGLINNE. Softly as you may, O Pichan. We must be ready when he wakens up.

(Music)

STORYTELLER. Mac Conglinne makes his fire, four ridges in it, four apertures, of four-cleft ashwood. And he put a name into the fire that is hidden to this day. And on each side of it he clamped one spit and its sizzling burden. And from one to the other he skipped so that no drop fell but what he gathered, and indeed, in his linen cap and his linen apron of the purest white, he was the master of the world's cooks. But when the king awakes, the king is astounded, for while the most marvellous smells await his nostrils, he cannot stir hand nor foot for all the chains and the mighty cables in which he is cobbled.

CAHAL. Do they truss royalty in Pichan's house? Is this treason? Untie those things.

VOICES (softly). We have been ordered, King. We are advised it is necessary.

CAHAL. Oh, by the gods.

VOICES. It is for your cure, King. And the cure of your kingdom.

CAHAL. O, by the gods.

(Wolf howl)

I smell breakfast. Now, let me free before I chew chains, ropes, twine and tape, let me free to clear that table and I will forgive you of this crime of handling me.

CORK VOICE. O Lord, lads, are we wrong or right? Can he have law on us?

ANOTHER. Pichan, away here for a minute.

PICHAN. King, we regret this. But the scholar knows the thing to do.

CAHAL. The scholar will pay. You, Pichan, I will forgive, I will exonerate, I will absolve for one mouthful of that smell.

(Howl)

MAC CONGLINNE. Breakfast is ready, King. Come, now, and sit by this fire. But you must eat in chains and cables. There is a reason for that which will be shown to you.

CAHAL. I will eat in buckets and iron collars, I will be Billy the bowl, I will eat standing, walking, rolling, flying, I will eat standing on my head provided there is food brought to me. Scholar, you are a cook among cooks. Come to Cashel with me. I sniff—

(Quirk)

Dish up. Dish up. Wait, leave my hands free, boys, at least my hands.

MAC CONGLINNE. You must have no freedom, King. That is a condition you have accepted. Are the chains bedded in the ground without?

CORK VOICES (Softly). They are indeed, Scholar.

MAC CONGLINNE. Are they bedded within?

VOICES. They are, indeed, Scholar.

MAC CONGLINNE. And he is tightfast to wall and floor?

VOICES. He is, indeed, Scholar.

CAHAL. Begin, begin. I am a dearth among a plenty. I am a starvation in paradise, I am the sun that sees from afar the promised land of early summer. Begin.

MAC CONGLINNE. First, we will talk.

CAHAL. O God, this student. Will talk fill me? Can I chew it, chaff it, chaw it? Can I gobble it?

MAC CONGLINNE. I have a dream to tell you.

CAHAL. Keep it for some woman in the night.

MAC CONGLINNE. It is a dream about food, King, it is a prelude to a king's meal, it is sauce, it is savour.

CAHAL. I will give you ten beats of my pulse to tell me. After that, I will eat or I will pull down this house upon us all.

(Wolf howl)

DEMON. It is a trick, Cashel. Do not listen, little curly Cahal.

CAHAL. I recognize the turn of that phrase. I will abate hunger, I will starve it. I will listen to you, Scholar, for this bitch inside me bids otherwise.

MAC CONGLINNE. I will begin, so.

(Strings)

> I walked in sleep last night
> Into this vision. I was hungry too.
> I saw a tall well-filled house
> With great pantries of good food.

(Lupine howl)

> A pond of new milk
> In a plain that knows no cow's hoof.
> A mighty pat of yellow butter
> Thatched the roof.

(Howl)

> The doorposts were white custard
> Frozen till it stood,
> The windows were white wine,
> The doors were cheese, a lovely wood.

(Howl howl)

> The walls were smoked bacon.
> There was that and more
> In the naked cauldron
> That bubbled on the fire.

Shall I tell you more, King?

(Wolf howl)

CAHAL. Tell me more and I will go mad.

MAC CONGLINNE. I will give you the fable, then, in another way. It was in this country I met the wizard doctor who lives in the island of Eating. "Limp is the look on your face," says he. "The shine of good food is not around you like a bright corslet. You are sick, you are ill. Come with me."

I went with him. We came to a lake of beer in which was a coracle of hard lard waiting for us and we rowed over that lake to the wizard's dwelling. "I know what ails you," he says. "What is it?" says I. "You have a desire of eating," he says, "that cannot be satisfied. And you are a burden to yourself and a plague to others, since it is your desire to be first at a feast, to grudge a share to others, to gobble, to push, to scrape, to shoulder away, to gather all plates and platters, mugs, jugs, and bowls before you. But I will cure you," says he.

"What way will you cure me?" says I. "For, indeed, I would wish to be cured. I am built in a shameful way and I am in constant sorrow over my great and abnormal appetite."

"I will cure you this way," says he.

(Strings)

> Go tonight to the well. Wash head and hand.
> Then spread a calfskin by a fire of ash
> Ripped octagonally, and call the noble woman
> Of the fivefolded purple cloak. She is all men's wish.
>
> Active, sensible, whitehanded, witty, merry
> Is this woman. She is three tall graces in one.
> The three nurses of dignity are about her.
> Three joys are delicate colours in her skin.
>
> With a tree-swaying sauntering walk she will come to the door
> And wait like a stately avenue. Under her black brows
> Are calm blue eyes that will receive you
> Into her look as into a big house.
>
> She will move around you with a woman's music,
> The reed music of a riverside;
> But her laugh is lively, her red mouth is such
> It warms you with friendly humour that is fire and fireside.
>
> O, but you will go a long journey
> On her voice, man; you will go and come home
> To a woman whose hair is down upon her shoulders,
> To a shining eye and a lifted comb.

CAHAL. You are describing Ligach to me, Poet. You are describing that great bitch as she was to me one time.

MAC CONGLINNE. I am describing a process and a cure.

CAHAL. You are filling me with an old desire and a wish that has gone from me.

MAC CONGLINNE. I have not finished yet, King. Said the wizard doctor: "Let this maiden, who is without stain, give you three times nine morsels, each morsel the exact size of a heath-poult's egg. You will take those morsels into your mouth with a round swing, and while you are in the process of chewing them, your eyes must move sunwise round your skull." Now, we will proceed to give you your breakfast.

CAHAL. Ah, that is talk to a purpose.

MAC CONGLINNE. But, first—

CAHAL. Another "but." Are you a ram, Scholar, are you a bull-calf that you but me so much?

MAC CONGLINNE. First, that cloak. You gave it to Muinchen for a feast. Will you now bestow it on me for one mouthful?

CAHAL. ROBBER.

MAC CONGLINNE. It is a good large-smelling mouthful of roasted beef. I put it to your nostrils. Smell.

(Wolverine howl)

CAHAL. You may have my cloak.

MAC CONGLINNE. I will take it off so.

CAHAL. First, the mouthful.

MAC CONGLINNE. The cloak, first.

CAHAL. I will submit.

MAC CONGLINNE. I take the cloak, then. O mighty armful.

CAHAL. That mouthful, now.

MAC CONGLINNE. There is yet something else.

(Despairing howl)

It is not something for myself. It is for the kingdom and the natural order of things. A king must have a noble queen.

CAHAL. I knew you were in league with that Ligach.

MAC CONGLINNE. Is it Ligach that I talk of? I do not think so. I saw that queen once when I was in Grinnaun Ailech, but I remember her only as a distant, cold, and difficult queen.

CAHAL. She can be otherwise. O, she can be otherwise.

(Strings)

> She can call out of her hair
> So softly that one warm candle is her breath
> And all the shadowy air
> About each breast.
>
> I was her room. I know her
> For she filled me to curtain and window till my eyes
> Were my window-blinds at morning
> That stared inward on all beauties.
>
> Tell of her, now, and I will break
> Countries apart to find

That room inside me, and again, again
Draw down each window blind.

MAC CONGLINNE. A queen of that sort should have all the old pre-
rogatives of a queen, otherwise she is a slave lifted to throne-level, she is
a king's serf, his meaty bedfellow. You agree, King?
      CAHAL. I will agree to nothing but my breakfast, my mouthful of beef,
my ham, my wether-mutton.
      MAC CONGLINNE. That is coming. Look. The beef is bubbling, the
mutton sizzling, the ham is humming. About this queen. She has rights
that go back to the foundation of the world. She has queen's rights. Privacy
at will; freedom in travel and entertainment; indulgence of her fancies. A
separate establishment.
      (Lupine howl)
      CAHAL. I want my breakfast.
      MAC CONGLINNE. It is ready, it is ready. See it. O marvellous breakfast.
      (Howl)
King, for each of those rights that have been stolen from the woman,
for the return of them to the queen that you must take, I will give your
hunger one large mouthful.
      CAHAL. Robbery, larceny, treason, what is this crime you commit upon
the king?
      MAC CONGLINNE. I put it to your nostrils. Smell.
      (Howl)
      CAHAL. Whatever queen she is, she can have those rights.
      MAC CONGLINNE. There is yet something else.
      (Prolonged howling)
      CAHAL. There is nothing else in the world but food.
      MAC CONGLINNE. Rights of equal sovereignty for your queen.
      CAHAL. She can have them and roast. O Roast, roast, roast beef, mut-
ton, bacon.
      (Monstrous howling)
      MAC CONGLINNE. To the chains and cables, now, my men. All of you
outside. I will hang this cloak upon that warrior stone with this root of
the birchtree underneath. Pichan, your blessing now, for I will need it,
and have all the bishops pray for me and the priests down to the youngest
theological student in his first year; and whoever is within a mile of this
place, let him go on his knees. There must be no word out of anybody
but a prayer.
      PICHAN. I will see to that.
      MAC CONGLINNE. Empty the house till there is nothing living in it
but the king, the cloak, the fire and myself.
      PICHAN. I will see to that. I leave my good will with you, Poet.

MAC CONGLINNE. I will need it.

(Howling howling)

MAC CONGLINNE. King, I will sit by you, now. First, the mouthful I owe you for the cloak. I cut it. MMMM.

(Sniff of music)

I will give you an apple, a mouthful I mean. Do you remember refusing me an apple?

CAHAL. Give me to eat, student.

MAC CONGLINNE. MMMM. *(Sniff of music)* This is too large for you, I will eat this myself, but first you may smell it.

(A mighty sniff of music, then a vulpine howling)

CAHAL. Give me that mouthful.

MAC CONGLINNE. It is too large. I will eat it.

(Pleasant gulping music)

CAHAL. O. O. O.

DEMON. That was a wrestler's trick, Mac Conglinne. A dirty feint.

MAC CONGLINNE. Ha, Demon, have I got your nose out?

DEMON. I will be all out in a moment if I do not have food. Then, upon my words, we will have ructions.

MAC CONGLINNE. I do not think so. I am very swift. I go to cut another piece now. See, O delightful roasting chunk of the year-old heifer, O paunchy piece, how the poet's gullet goes for you. MMMM.

(Sniff of music)

You must smell this, demon. I will put it to the King's nose, and then I will race you for it to that pillar stone where the cloak is hanging. Are you ready?

DEMON. By my words, Mac Conglinne, you will run for that piece.

MAC CONGLINNE. I will beat you, demon, for this mass of roasting and spitting food at the fire will delay you. You will never jump that fire without laying your tongue on everything.

DEMON. I can still do that and beat you.

MAC CONGLINNE. Here, then. Sniff.

(Howl)

(Trumpets of music)

Sniff, I said. Now, run for it.

(A blast of things)

DISTANT VOICES.

> O, the world shakes.
> Our father who art in heaven.
> The great house is rocking.
> Hail Mary, hail Mary.
> The poet is gone. The king is gone.

MUINCHEN. And my cloak is gone, Muinchen's little cloak, my marvel, my love, my lifeblood.

STRONG VOICE. Not so, the house still stands. It wavers, it struggles, it recovers. It stands. O, the large foundations of this great house!

(Thrill of music)

STORYTELLER. I end this scene with a shiver of excitement. But where is the poet? The king is a huddle of chains and cables. He is knotted, twisted, curled bone on bone. One eye is sunken into his head till the long bill of a wading heron could not reach it. The other eye is eight inches out from his head.[42] But he is wild, he is angry, he is terrible.

CAHAL. Beggars, brawlers, bosthoons. How comes the king to lie here with such indignity? Release me. I will pull this house to pieces. I will stamp on the ruins.

(Majestic music)

STORYTELLER. Well, no lack of life in him. Outside, threading a way with a retinue through the bowed and frightened people comes the Queen, Queen Ligach who used to be of Ailech. Little trumpets go before her and the mass of people before the house of Pichan are even more silent as they lift their eyes to her beauty.

WHISPERS. It is the queen, it is the queen.

(Trumpets and herald)

HERALD. Make a path, make a path, make a path. The Queen Ligach to the owner of this house. To Pichan, the queen orders that she be taken into the presence of the King, Cahal of Cashel.

PICHAN. Pichan bows, queen. I bow to the ground.

QUEEN. Take me to Cashel, now.

PICHAN. Pichan bows, lady, but he regrets that—

(Rumble of music and falling debris)

VOICES.

> The sidewall of the house is gone.
> No. It is holding. It is holding.
> It is returning to its foundations again
> O mighty foundations.

QUEEN. What is happening this house?

PICHAN. Lady, the king is within, alone with a scholar and a demon.

QUEEN. Do you tell the queen that you have left the king alone with a demon and a scholar? Are you responsible for his safety, for his health, for his humour?

---

42. **One eye . . . from his head** an allusion to the famous description of the Irish epic hero Cú Chulainn going into his heroic distortion before he accomplished superhuman warrior feats

PICHAN. Lady, the king is my childhood's friend. I do the best for him according to my understanding.

QUEEN. You will account to me later. Lead me, now, to the great door and open it wide for me. I will enter first.

PICHAN. Lady.

QUEEN. At once!

(The king's hullaballoo in middle ground)

QUEEN. That is the king's voice.

(King to foreground)

CAHAL. I will pull this house to pieces. I will stamp on the ruins.

QUEEN. What have you done to the king? *(Very loudly)* What have you done to Cahal of Cashel? O, Cahal, O little curlyhead Cahal, what have they done to you?

CAHAL. O, Ligach, I am cabled, stapled and chained, I am handcuffed, I am nailed, I am stifled, I am exhausted—

QUEEN. Release the King.

VOICES. But the demon, the demon.

QUEEN. Release him. There will be a great accounting for this.

PICHAN. We will release him, Lady. But you do not understand. There was a demon of hunger in the king—

QUEEN. A demon of hunger? I do not believe it. Why, my poor Cahal never ate more then tidbits. Cahal, are you hungry, my love?

CAHAL. Hungry. I would not call this minute if I never saw pick nor plate again.

QUEEN. You see.

PICHAN. Then the king is cured. The king is cured. MY PEOPLE, THE KING IS CURED.

(Clamour in music)

PICHAN. Hush, now. This is a miracle. Release the king with gentle hands. Take him to the woman's sun-room.

QUEEN. This is my business, Pichan. I will order things.

PICHAN. No, Lady. When the king is hale, you may have him. My women shall wait on him.

QUEEN. I will wait on him.

PICHAN. No, lady. Four of you to that litter, the gold litter. Light a fire of octagonal ash in that room, four-apertured, and with four ridges, and before this fire lay the king on a soft calfskin when he has been washed and combed.

(Appropriate music)

STORYTELLER. But where is Mac Conglinne? Pichan, busy with the King, remembers him suddenly—

(Loud chord)

PICHAN. That student? That noble scholar? Has he been seen?

VOICE. Pichan, there is no sign of that scholar anywhere. We have searched and searched, for we were anxious to look upon a wonder.

ANOTHER. He is not within this house, Pichan.

PICHAN. Look for him, look for him. We owe him a country and a king. He must be found, I say, he must be found.

WOMAN'S VOICE. The king is wakening, O Pichan.

CAHAL. Who must be found? Who is lost that he must be found?

PICHAN. The poet who cured you of the demon, King.

CAHAL. I will take your word that I had a demon, but upon my own word I can remember nothing at all about him. Indeed, there is so much that is unkingly about the whole thing that you must take it as an edict that it is not to be mentioned again in my presence. Am I washed enough to please you, or is the skin to be scrubbed off my poor but responsible back?

PICHAN. Still, that poet must be found. We are in his debt. Find him, find him.

VOICES. He is nowhere to be found.

PICHAN. I will look for him myself.

VOICE. The holy Abbot Muinchen is asking to see the king.

PICHAN. He wishes to pray over him and to ask for his cloak back.

PICHAN. It is his cloak no longer. It was given to that noble young scholar.

(Heavy abbot music)

MUINCHEN. It is my cloak, Pichan, and it was taken from me by a trick of the demon.

PICHAN. The cloak was yours while you could hold it.

MUINCHEN. Possession is nine points of law. I see it on that pillar and I will have it.

PICHAN. Four of you. Guard this cloak from this abbot.

MUINCHEN. I will put a curse on the man who stops me.

CORK VOICE. Abbot, we will not worry much about that. We saw how little the demon cared for your curse. By God, boys, there is something inside this cloak.

VOICES. There is, there is.

VOICE. Pichan, there is somebody inside this holy cloak. Could it be the scholar?

PICHAN. Perhaps it is that scholar, that noble young man. Let me look.

(Blast of music)

This is an old man. He is asleep or he has fainted.

VOICE. Pichan, he has the face of that young scholar, even if he is old.

PICHAN. By my hand, that is true. I will waken him.

(Three drum taps)

You are awake.

MAC CONGLINNE. I am awake. I see, by the happy hand of my God, I have reached the cloak in safety. Have I cured the king?

PICHAN. The king is cured.

MAC CONGLINNE. Honour and glory to me then.

PICHAN. But are you the man who cured the king? That man was young, he was a student, his face was bright, his head was a glory.

MAC CONGLINNE. Am I otherwise? Or is Pichan seeking to evade our bargain?

PICHAN. Give this man a mirror. Put it in his hand.

(Pale and wondering music)

(Strings)

MAC CONGLINNE.

> This is an old face.
> It is a ruin. Some big fire
> Has burned me out of my self. There is no place
> Left in this countenance that will flare again.
>
> Some sad agony has wrung me dry.
> I am a willow tree without water. My song is sung.
> No queen will love me again for my poetry.
> I am old, I am wiser. But my song is sung.

(Music)

STORYTELLER. I end this scene sadly. The poet is washed and combed as the king was washed and combed. Pichan is tender, Pichan is loving. The poet is soothed, he is richly dressed, he waxes in importance in a matter of seconds; for poetry he substitutes pride; for inspiration, self-will; for delight in argument, he substitutes haughtiness. He has arrived and paid all the usual fees for his transportation. Meanwhile, there is some matter to be solved between the king and the queen. The king is in the women's sun-room on a calfskin before the fire. He is morose, weary and utterly without appetite. To him comes a harassed Pichan.

(A small trumpet)

PICHAN. King, O my king.

CAHAL. I hear you.

PICHAN. It is your queen again.

CAHAL. I have pleaded sleep.

PICHAN. She carries a cure for sleepiness.

CAHAL. I have pleaded weariness.

PICHAN. She answers she will cure that, too.

CAHAL. I have pleaded melancholy.

PICHAN. A sorrow shared is a sorrow halved, she says.

CAHAL. Plead coldness.

PICHAN. She answers that her presence is warmth in itself.
(Trumpets. Trumpets. Trumpets)
LIGACH. O Cashel.
CAHAL. This is the king's room, lady.
LIGACH. Wherever the king is, that is the king's room. And wherever
the king is, there my heart is too.
CAHAL. Was I ever in Ulster? Was I ever in Grinnaun Ailech?
LIGACH. I think you were, my king. I think you are everywhere I go.
I think you are a kind of self of me I am always losing and finding again.
CAHAL. I am tired of being lost and found.
LIGACH. O, but the joy of the finding.
CAHAL. O, but the lostness of being lost. Why must you leave me?
Why must you halve my heart yearly into an Ulster and a Munster? Why
am I half a king for half a year, and only a bright and brilliant nonentity
for the other half, a suck-a-thumb lover, an apron-string husband?
LIGACH. You are my king, O, you are my king.
CAHAL. You are my queen, O, you are my queen.
QUEEN. I have brought you food by the hands of my own women.
CAHAL. I do not want food.
QUEEN. It is only a little food, three times nine morsels, each the size
of a heath-poult's egg. Little curlyhead Cahal. I will feed you myself.
CAHAL. You are a bad woman, but you make me happy.
(Appropriate music)
STORYTELLER. We leave them to it.
(Strings)

> O Woman. She is everywhere.
> An element.
> Behind each quarrel; at the back of every sermon;
> At the bottom of every bad debt.
>
> And yet I hail her.
> How can I help it? She
> Who divides herself around me like a calendar,
> Who is my twelve climates of feeling,
> Who musters me
> So many shapes I live like the sun,
> A god within my year.

FINIS

GLORY BE GOD

July 11–21, 1951

BRENDAN BEHAN
1923 – 1964

To Londoners, 1956 was the year of the Suez Crisis, John Osborne's *Look Back in Anger,* and Brendan Behan's *The Quare Fellow.* No Irish play since O'Casey's *The Plough and the Stars* had caused such a sensation. Reviewing *The Quare Fellow* for *The Observor,* Kenneth Tynan was moved to hyperbole: "The English hoard words like misers; the Irish spend them like sailors; and in Brendan Behan's tremendous new play language is out on a spree, ribald, dauntless and spoiling for a fight.... It is Ireland's sacred duty to send over, every few years, a playwright to save the English theatre from inarticulate glumness." Meanwhile *The Tablet* (Alex Matheson Cain) cut coolly to the heart of the matter: "To live in close contact with sudden, premeditated death, to make it one's business—what effect does this have on a community of men?" In *The Quare Fellow,* Brendan Behan had indeed struck a masterful consonance between his robust jocularity and the theme which dogged his short, tragic life.

Brendan Francis Behan was born into a Dublin working-class family on February 9, 1923. Both sides of his family were committed Irish Republicans, and as a very young man he became active in the Irish Republican Army. His illegal activities under these auspices led to a series of prison sentences in Britain and Ireland, so that eight of his forty-one years were spent within prison walls as a political prisoner. This experience was fundamental to his world view, since it confirmed him in the outlook inculcated by his family background, made more complex his feeling for Irish Republicanism, and provided an approximate equivalent for the formal education he never got.

His literary career began with contributions of poetry and prose to the magazine *Fianna: The Voice of Young Ireland,* the organ of the junior branch of the IRA. Acting on the sentiments expressed in these patriotic juvenilia, Behan undertook a solo bombing mission to England in November, 1939, which resulted in his arrest and sentence to three years in Borstal, the detention center for juvenile offenders. Shortly after his release, he found himself again behind bars, this time in Ireland, serving five of the fourteen years to which he was sentenced for attacking an Irish detective at a political funeral. During these years (he was released in 1945), when many of the prison population were Irish Republicans, he enlarged his appreciation of the native culture of Ireland through a wide reading of its literature. Moreover, through daily conversations with Seán Ó Briain, a native speaker of Irish from Kerry, he became a fluent Irish speaker himself. Out of these experiences grew the conviction that through writing in Irish, his political commitments and his literary ambitions could be simultaneously realized. Consequently, he wrote some poetry in Irish, and a play, *Casadh Súgáin Eile* (*The Twisting of Another Rope*) about hanging as seen from inside the prison. It was the beginning of *The Quare Fellow*.

Meanwhile, he was supporting himself by housepainting, occasional journalism, and radio spots. In the early 1950s he published some short stories, two short plays for radio, and a crime series for *The Irish Times* which eventually became *The Scarperer* (1964). Translated and revised, *Casadh Súgáin Eile* became *The Quare Fellow*; and it got its premier production by Alan Simpson at the Pike Theatre, Dublin in 1954. Two years later, Joan Littlewood's production at the Theatre Workshop in London, gained for this play and its author a reputation outside of Ireland. In 1957 he wrote two plays under commission: *The Big House* for the BBC, and for the Damer, Dublin's Irish language theatre, *An Giall*. But it was not until his text was translated (as *The Hostage*) and adapted according to the spontaneous, group principles of the Theatre Workshop (1958) that the full theatrical potential of Behan's text was realized. His apparently effortless, nonstop supply of dialogue, jokes and songs complemented her company's sense of what worked in the theatre. The result was the transformation of a relatively spare tragedy into a farcical musical entertainment laced with social commentary. Behan's *annus mirabilis* was completed with the appearance of *Borstal Boy,* his autobiographical account of his teenage years in detention. Beneath this apparent exposé of the British prison system is an artfully contrived portrait of his own coming of age; it is perhaps his most successful work.

Within a couple of years, Behan had been transformed from a Dublin working-class "character" into an international literary celebrity. But he was unable to handle the attention, and underlying insecurities concerning his own creative capacities began to take greater toll, and express themselves in bouts of public drunkenness and exhibitionism. The result was that he became increasingly dependent on alcohol and media attention, and his last literary efforts were fitful drafts or transcriptions of his humorous anecdotes.

A series of hospital stays ended on March 20, 1964, when he died in Dublin from complications arising from alcoholism and diabetes. He had the largest funeral of any literary figure in Ireland, although its size had as much to do with his notoriety and the personal affection felt for him by the common people of inner-city Dublin as with his literary success. He was given a soldier's funeral by the Irish Republican Army.

The prime of Behan's creative career was confined to four years—1954 to 1958, the first few years of his marriage to Beatrice ffrench-Salkeld. During this time, his two full-length plays, *The Quare Fellow* and *The*

Hostage, brought fresh energy into Irish theatre. Their distinct qualities were his humorous use of ordinary Dublin speech, iconoclastic social comment, and free use of music hall songs and gags, all woven around political themes. It is clear that Joan Littlewood contributed much to the shaping of these plays as we have them today, but all the materials are unquestionably Behan's own.

In the case of *The Quare Fellow,* the subject derives from the execution of one Bernard Kirwan, who was hanged for the gruesome murder of his own brother. Behan was in Mountjoy Jail at the time, knew the prisoner, and had himself been close to death on a number of occasions. So while his play is primarily an attack on capital punishment, it has a wider social relevance in criticizing all those who are complicit in the deed—the executioner, warders, governor, the public at large, and indeed the other prisoners—all those who for motives of self-interest work within the system.

The endless round of wise talk, underworld jargon, the scheming and subterfuge, the deals and talks of deals, show the cast of characters, jailers and prisoners alike, to be a hardbitten lot, aware of no more than the short-term, individual advantages of their transactions. Only two characters are seen in a sympathetic light: Warder Regan and Prisoner C. Each represents an aspect of Behan's own moral and social conscience: the one a thoughtful and sensitive member of the established social system, the other the pure soul of Gaelic Ireland (with his tragic love song delivered in the traditional *sean nós* style). And behind all of this busy foreground sits the invisible, silent protagonist whose last day it is. The cacophony of black humor, the pious, officious and craven language, the rank-pulling and deal-making comprise a metaphor for the meretricious chaos of life. The climax of this design comes at daybreak, in the scene corresponding to the offstage execution: the clatter of a hundred tin mugs, the momentary silence, the running commentary delivered in Mícheál Ó hEithir's breathless, ringing tenor style, fading out on the poignant, risqué ballad. The dramatic effect is electric. In this way, the play is not simply a propagandist diatribe against capital punishment; it is a brilliantly effective dramatic metaphor for the moral jungle of modern civilized society. In *The Quare Fellow,* Behan transcended the seductive appreciation of the barroom crowd and the condescending appreciation of those to whom he played the time-worn role of drunken, roistering stage Irishman.

SELECT BIBLIOGRAPHY

Publications

Brendan Behan: *The Complete Plays.* Intro. Alan Simpson. London: Eyre Methuen/ New York: Grove Press, 1978. (*The Quare Fellow, The Hostage, Richard's Cork Leg, Moving Out, A Garden Party, The Big House*)

Borstal Boy. London: Methuen, 1958; New York: Knopf, 1959.
Poems and Stories. Dublin: Liffey Press, 1978.

Biography and Criticism

Behan, Beatrice. *My Life with Brendan.* With Des Hickey and Gus Smith. London: Leslie Frewin; Los Angeles, Nash, 1973.

Boyle, Ted E. *Brendan Behan.* New York: Twayne, 1969.

Cronin, Anthony. *Dead as Doornails; A Chronicle of Life.* Dublin: Dolmen Press/ London: Calder and Boyars, 1976.

Kearney, Colbert. *The Writings of Brendan Behan.* Dublin: Gill and Macmillan, 1977.

McCann, Sean, ed. *The World of Brendan Behan.* London: New English Library, 1965.

McMahon, Sean. "The Quare Fellow," *Éire-Ireland* 4 (Winter 1969): 143–57.

Mikhail, E. H., ed. *The Art of Brendan Behan.* New York: Barnes and Noble, 1979.

———. *Brendan Behan: An Annotated Bibliography of Criticism.* Totowa, NJ: Barnes and Noble, 1980.

O'Connor, Ulick. *Brendan Behan.* London: Hamish Hamilton/Englewood Cliffs, NJ: Prentice-Hall, 1970.

See also discussions in Hogan, *After the Irish Renaissance,* Krause, *Profane Book,* and Simpson, *Beckett and Behan.*

The Quare[1] Fellow

A Comedy-Drama

ACT 1

(A prisoner sings: he is in one of the punishment cells.)

> A hungry feeling came o'er me stealing
> And the mice were squealing in my prison cell,
> And that old triangle[2]
> Went jingle jangle,
> Along the banks of the Royal Canal.[3]

THE CURTAIN RISES

The scene is the bottom floor or landing of a wing in a city prison, "B1." The cell doors are of metal with a card giving the name, age and religion of the occupant. Two of the cells have no cards. The left of the stage leads to the circle, the administrative heart of the prison, and on the right, in the wall and at right angles to the audience, is a window, from which a view may be had of the laundry yard of the women's prison. On the wall and facing the audience is printed in large block shaded Victorian lettering the word "SILENCE."

PRISONER.

> To begin the morning
> The warder bawling
> Get out of bed and clean up your cell,
> And that old triangle
> Went jingle jangle,
> Along the banks of the Royal Canal.

(A triangle is beaten, loudly and raucously. A Warder comes briskly and, swinging a bunch of keys, goes to the vacant cells, looks in the spyholes, takes two white cards from his pocket, and puts one on each door. Then he goes to the other doors, looks in the spyholes and unlocks them.)

(Meanwhile the singer in the base punishment cells in on his third verse:)

---

1. **Quare** strange, odd, notorious   2. **triangle** the prison schedule signal   3. **Royal Canal** Mountjoy jail, on Dublin's North Side, is adjacent to this canal

The screw[4] was peeping
And the lag was weeping . . .

(But this only gets as far as the second line, for the warder leans over the stairs and shouts down . . .)

WARDER. The screw is listening as well as peeping, and you'll be bloody well weeping if you don't give over your moaning. We might go down there and give you something to moan about. *(The singing stops and he turns and shouts up and down the landing.)* B Wings: two, three and one. Stand to your doors. Come on, clean up your cells there. *(He goes off Right.)*

(Prisoners A and B come out of their cells, collect buckets and brushes, and start the morning's chores. A is a man of 40, he has done two "laggings," a sentence of five years or more, and some preventive detention. B is a gentle-looking man and easy-going.)

PRISONER A. Nice day for the races.

PRISONER B. Don't think I can make it today. Too much to do in the office. Did you hear the commotion last night round in D Wing? A reprieve must have come through.

PRISONER A. Aye, but there's two for a haircut and shave, I wonder which one's been chucked?[5]

PRISONER B. Dunlavin might know; give him a call there.

PRISONER A. Dunlavin!

VOICE *(from cell)*.

There are hands that will welcome you in[6]
There are lips that I am burning to kiss
There are two eyes that shine . . .

PRISONER A. Hey, Dunlavin, are you going to scrub that place of yours away?

VOICE.

Far away where the blue shadows fall
I will come to contentment and rest,
And the toils of the day
Will be all charmed away . . .

PRISONER A. Hey, Dunlavin.

(Dunlavin appears in the door of the cell polishing a large enamel chamber pot with a cloth. An old man, he has spent most of his life in jail. Unlike most old lags he has not become absolutely dulled from imprisonment.)

4. **screw** prison officer 5. **chucked** hanged 6. **There are hands that will welcome you in** "The Little Grey Home in the West," sentimental song (1911) by Wilmot D. Eardley and Hermann Lohr

DUNLAVIN. . . . In my little grey home in the West.

PRISONER A. What do you think that is you're polishing—the Railway Cup?[7]

DUNLAVIN. I'm shining this up for a special visitor. Healey of the Department of Justice is coming up today to inspect the cells.

PRISONER A. Will he be round again so soon?

DUNLAVIN. He's always round the day before an execution. I think he must be in the hanging and flogging section.

PRISONER B. Dunlavin, there you are, at the corner of the wing, with the joints in the hot-water pipes bringing you news from every art and part, any time you put your ear to it.

DUNLAVIN. Well? Well?

PRISONER B. Well, what was the commotion last night round in D Wing? Did the quare fellow get a reprieve?

DUNLAVIN. Just a minute till I put back me little bit of china, and I'll return and tell all. Now which quare fellow do you mean? The fellow beat his wife to death with the silver-topped cane, that was a presentation to him from the Combined Staffs, Excess and Refunds branch of the late Great Southern Railways,[8] was reprieved, though why him any more than the other fellow is more nor[9] I can tell.

PRISONER A. Well, I suppose they looked at it, he only killed her and left it at that. He didn't cut the corpse up afterwards with a butcher's knife.

DUNLAVIN. Yes, and then of course the other fellow used a meat-chopper. Real bog-man[10] act. Nearly as bad as a shotgun, or getting the weed-killer mixed up in the stirabout. But a man with a silver-topped cane, that's a man that's a cut above meat-choppers whichever way you look at it.

PRISONER A. Well, I suppose we can expect Silver-top round soon to start his life.

PRISONER B. Aye, we've a couple of vacancies.

DUNLAVIN. I declare to God you're right. *(Goes to read one of the cards.)* It's not him at all, it's another fellow, doing two year, for . . . oh, the dirty beast, look what the dirty man-beast is in for. 'Clare to God, putting the likes of that beside me. They must think this is the bloody sloblands.

PRISONER B. There's another fellow here.

DUNLAVIN. I hope it's not another of that persuasion. *(Reads the card.)* Ah, no, it's only the murderer, thanks be to God.

(The others have a read of the card and skip back to their own cells.)

DUNLAVIN. You wouldn't mind old Silver-top. Killing your wife is a

7. **Railway Cup** interprovincial Gaelic sports trophy   8. **Great Southern Railways** Irish regional rail system   9. **nor** than   10. **bog-man** barbaric, country fellow

natural class of a thing could happen to the best of us. But this other dirty animal on me left . . .

PRISONER B. Ah well, now he's here he'll just have to do his birdlime[11] like anyone else.

DUNLAVIN. That doesn't say that he should do it in the next flowery dell to me. Robbers, thieves and murderers I can abide, but when it comes to that class of carry-on—Good night, Joe Doyle.[12]

PRISONER A *(indicates 22)*. This fellow was dead lucky.

PRISONER B. Live lucky.

PRISONER A. Two fellows waiting to be topped[13] and he's the one that gets away. As a general rule they don't like reprieving one and topping the other.

DUNLAVIN. So as to be on the safe side, and not to be making fish of one and flesh of the other, they usually top both. Then, of course, the Minister might have said, enough is as good as a feast.

(They rest on their brooms.)

PRISONER B. It must be a great thing to be told at the last minute that you're not going to be topped after all. To be lying there sweating and watching. The two screws for the death watch coming on at twelve o'clock and the two going off shaking hands with you, and you go to bed, and stare up at the ceiling.

DUNLAVIN. And the two screws nod to each other across the fire to make a sup of tea, but to do it easy in case they wake you, and you turn round in the bed towards the fire and you say "I'll take a sup[14] as you're at it" and one of the screws says "Ah, so you're awake, Mick. We were just wetting[15] it; isn't it a good job you spoke up in time."

PRISONER A. And after that, the tea is drunk and they offer you cigarettes, though the mouth is burned off you from smoking and anyway you've more than they have, you've got that many you'll be leaving them after you, and you lie down and get up, and get up and lie down, and the two screws not letting on to be minding you and not taking their eyes off you for one half-minute, and you walk up and down a little bit more . . .

PRISONER B. And they ask you would you like another game of draughts[16] or would you sooner write a letter, and getting on to morning you hear a bell out in the city, and you ask them the time, but they won't tell you.

DUNLAVIN. But they put a good face on it, and one says "There's that old watch stopped again" and he says to the other screw "Have you your watch, Jack?" and the other fellow makes a great joke of it, "I'll have to

11. **birdlime** time, jail sentence   12. **Good night, Joe Doyle** an expression of disdain   13. **topped** executed by hanging   14. **sup** small drink   15. **wetting** brewing, drawing   16. **draughts** checkers

take a run up as far as the North City Pawn shop and ask them to let me
have a look at it." And then the door is unlocked and everyone sweats
blood, and they come in and ask your man to stand up a minute, that's if
he's able, while they read him something: "I am instructed to inform you
that the Minister has, he hasn't, he has, he hasn't recommended to the
President, that . . ."

PRISONER A. And the quare fellow says "Did you say 'has recommended or has not recommended. . . .?' I didn't quite catch that."

DUNLAVIN. My bloody oath but he catches it. Although I remember
once in a case like now when there were two fellows to be topped over
two different jobs, didn't the bloody fellow from the Prison Board, as it
was then, in old Max Greeb's time, didn't he tell the wrong man he was
reprieved? Your man was delighted for a few hours and then they had to
go back and tell him "Sorry, my mistake, but you're to be topped after
all"?

PRISONER B. And the fellow that was reprieved, I bet he was glad.

DUNLAVIN. Of course he was glad, anyone that says that a condemned
man would be better off hung than doing life, let them leave it to his own
discretion. Do you know who feels it worse going out to be topped?

PRISONER A. Corkmen and Northerners[17] . . . they've such bloody
hard necks.

DUNLAVIN. I have to do me funny half-hour[18] for Holy Healey. I'm
talking serious now.

PRISONER A. All right, come on, let's have it—

DUNLAVIN. The man that feels it worst, going into that little house
with the red door and the silver painted gates at the bottom of D Wing,
is a man that has been in the nick before, when some other merchant[19]
was topped; or he's heard screws or old lags in the bag shop[20] or at exercise
talking about it. A new chap that's never done anything but murder, and
that only once, is usually a respectable man, such as this Silver-top here.
He knows nothing about it, except the few lines that he'd see in the papers.
"Condemned man entered the hang-house at seven fifty-nine. At eight
three the doctor pronounced life extinct."

PRISONER B. That's a lot of mullarkey.[21] In the first place the doctor
has his back turned after the trap goes down, and doesn't turn and face it
until a screw has caught the rope and stopped it wriggling. Then they go
out and lock up the shop and have their breakfast and don't come back
for an hour. Then they cut your man down and the doctor slits the back
of his neck to see if the bones are broken. Who's to know what happens

17. **Corkmen and Northerners** proverbially tough provincials   18. **funny half-
hour** unsavory duty   19. **merchant** fellow   20. **bag shop** workshop for making
mailbags   21. **mullarkey** nonsense

in the hour your man is swinging there, maybe wriggling to himself in the pit.

PRISONER A. You're right there. When I was in the nick in England, there was a screw doing time, he'd been smuggling out medical reports on hangings and selling them to the Sunday papers, and he told me that one bloke had lived seventeen minutes at the end of a rope.

DUNLAVIN. I don't believe that! Seventeen minutes is a bloody long time to be hanging on the end of a rope.

PRISONER A. It was their own medical report.

PRISONER B. I'll lay odds to a make that Silver-top isn't half charmed with himself he's not going with the meat-chopper in the morning.

DUNLAVIN. You could sing that if you had an air to it.

PRISONER A. They'll have him down to reception, changed into Fry's[22] and over here any time now.

DUNLAVIN. Him and this other jewel[23] here. Bad an' all as Silver-top was to beat his wife's brains out, I'd as lief[24] have him near to me as this article.[25] Dirty beast! I won't have an hour's luck for the rest of me six months, and me hoping to touch Uncle Healey today for a letter to the Room-Keepers[26] for when I'd go out.

PRISONER B. Eh, Dunlavin, is the Department trying to reform, reconstruct and rehabilitate you in your old age?

DUNLAVIN. Ah now, it's nothing to do with the Department. Outside his job in the Department, Uncle Healey's in some holy crowd, that does good be stealth. They never let the right hand know what the left hand doeth, as the man said. Of course they never put either hand in their pocket, so you'd never get money off them, but they can give letters to the Prisoners' Aid[27] and the Room-Keepers. Mind you. Healey's not here today as a holy man. He'll just be fixing up the man that's getting hung in the morning, but if I can get on the right side of him, he might mix business with pleasure and give me a letter for when I get out.

PRISONER B. Now we know the cause of all the spring-cleaning.

DUNLAVIN. And a fellow in the kitchen told us they're doing a special dinner for us on account of Uncle Healey's visit.

PRISONER A. Do you mean we're getting food with our meals today?

DUNLAVIN. That's right, and I can't be standing yapping to youse. I've to hang up my holy pictures and think up a few funny remarks for him. God, what Jimmie O'Dea[28] is getting thousands for I've to do for a pair of old socks and a ticket for the Prisoners' Aid.

---

22. **Fry's** ironic reference to prison garb   23. **jewel** good fellow   24. **as lief** prefer to   25. **article** person (derogatory)   26. **Room-Keepers** charitable association to help house the homeless   27. **Prisoners' Aid** charitable organization to rehabilitate ex-convicts   28. **Jimmie O'Dea** Dublin comedian popular in the 1940s and 1950s

(Dunlavin goes into his cell. Two Young Prisoners aged about seventeen go past with sweeping brushes in front of them, singing softly and in unison.)
YOUNG PRISONERS.

> Only one more cell inspection
> We go out next Saturday,
> Only one more cell inspection
> And we go far, far away.

PRISONER A. What brings you fellows round here this morning?

YOUNG PRISONER 1. Our screw told us to sweep all round the Juvenile Wing and then to come round here and give it a bit of a going over.

PRISONER B. And have you your own wing done?

YOUNG PRISONER 2. No, but if we did our wing first, we'd miss the mots[29] hanging out the laundry. You can't see them from our wing.

PRISONER A. Just as well, maybe; you're bad enough as it is.

YOUNG PRISONER 1. But I tell you what you will see from our wing this morning. It's the carpenter bringing up the coffin for the quare fellow and leaving it over in the mortuary to have it handy for the morning. There's two orderlies besides us over in the Juveniles, and we were going to toss up who'd come over here, but they're country fellows and they'd said they'd sooner see the coffin. I'd sooner a pike at a good-looking mot than the best coffin in Ireland, wouldn't you, Shaybo?

YOUNG PRISONER 2. Certainly I would, and outside that, when you're over here, there's always a chance of getting a bit of education about screwing jobs, and suchlike, from experienced men. Do you think Triplex or celluloid is the best for Yale locks, sir?

YOUNG PRISONER 1. Do you carry the stick all the time, sir?

PRISONER A. If I had a stick I'd know where to put it, across your bloody . . .

YOUNG PRISONER 2. Scholara, get sweeping, here's the screw.

(They drift off sweeping and singing softly.)

PRISONER B. He's bringing one of 'em. Is it Silver-top or the other fellow?

PRISONER A. Silver-top. I remember him being half carried into the circle[30] the night he was sentenced to death.

PRISONER B. He has a right spring in his step this morning then.

PRISONER A. He's not looking all that happy. Still, I suppose he hasn't got over the shock yet.

(Warder and a Prisoner come on Left. The Prisoner is in early middle age; when he speaks he has a "good accent." He is carrying a pillow slip which contains his sheets and other kit. The Warder halts him.)

29. **mots** girls   30. **circle** exercise yard

WARDER REGAN. Stand by the door with your name on it. Later on when you've seen the doctor these fellows will show you how to lay your kit. Stand there now, till the doctor is ready to see you. *(He goes. There is a pause, while the Prisoners survey the newcomer.)*

PRISONER B. He'll bloody well cheer the place up, won't he?

LIFER. Have any of you got a cigarette?

PRISONER A. That's a good one. You're not in the condemned cell now, you know. No snout[31] allowed here.

PRISONER B. Unless you manage to scrounge a dog-end[32] off the remands.[33]

PRISONER A. Or pick one up in the exercise yard after a man the like of yourself that's allowed them as a special concession. Not, by God, that we picked up much after you. What did you do with your dog-ends?

LIFER. Threw them in the fire.

PRISONER B. You what!

PRISONER A. How was it the other poor bastard, that's got no reprieve and is to be topped in the morning—how was it he was always able to leave a trail of butts behind him when he went off exercise?

LIFER. I've never been in prison before; how was I to know?

PRISONER A. You're a curse of God liar, my friend, you did know; for it was whispered to him by the fellows from the hospital bringing over the grub to the condemned cell. He never gave them as much as a match! And he couldn't even bring his dog-ends to the exercise yard and drop them behind for us to pick up when we came out later.

PRISONER B. I bet you're charmed with yourself that you're not going through the iron door tomorrow morning.

(The Lifer doesn't speak, but looks down at his suit.)

PRISONER A. Aye, you're better off in that old suit, bad as it is, than the wooden overcoat[34] the quare fellow is going to get tomorrow morning.

PRISONER B. The longest you could do would be twenty years. More than likely you'll get out in half of that. Last man to finish up in the Bog,[35] he done eleven.

LIFER. Eleven. How do you live through it?

PRISONER A. A minute at a time.

PRISONER B. You haven't got a bit of snout for him, have you? *(Prisoner A shakes his head.)* Maybe Dunlavin has. Hey, Dunlavin, have you e'er a smoke you'd give this chap? Hey, Dunlavin.

DUNLAVIN *(coming from his cell)*. Yes, what is it? Anyone there the name of headache?

---

31. **snout** tobacco   32. **dog-end** cigarette butt   33. **remands** detainees   34. **wooden overcoat** coffin   35. **Bog** Portlaoise Prison, in the Irish midlands, for long-term sentences

PRISONER B. Could you manage to give this chap something to smoke? E'er a bit of snout at all.

DUNLAVIN. There's only one brand of tobacco allowed here—"Three Nuns." None today, none tomorrow, and none the day after.

(He goes back into his cell.)

PRISONER B. Eh, Dunlavin, come back to hell out of that.

DUNLAVIN. Well, what?

PRISONER B. This poor chap after being smoking about sixty a day . . .

DUNLAVIN. Where?

PRISONER B. In the condemned cell—where else?

DUNLAVIN. Now I have you. Sure I thought you were the other fellow, and you're not, you're only the murderer. God comfort you. *(Shakes hands.)* Certainly so. *(Takes off his jacket, looks up and down the wing, undoes his trousers and from the depths of his combinations he produces a cigarette end, and a match, and presents them to the Lifer.)* Reprieved in the small hours of this morning. Certainly so. The dead arose and appeared to many,[36] as the man said, but you'll be getting yourself a bad name standing near that other fellow's door. This is your flowery dell, see? It has your name there on that little card. And all your particulars. Age forty-three. Religion R.C.

LIFER *(reads)*. Life.

DUNLAVIN. And a bloody sight better than death any day of the week.

PRISONER B. It always says that. The Governor will explain it all to you later this morning.

DUNLAVIN. Or maybe they'll get holy Uncle Healey to do it.

PRISONER B. Go into your cell and have a smoke for yourself. Bring in your kit bag. *(Passes in kit to Lifer.)* Have a quiet burn there before the screw comes round; we'll keep nick.[37]

(Lifer closes the door of his cell.)

DUNLAVIN. God knows I got the pick of good neighbours. Lovely people. Give me a decent murderer though, rather than the likes of this other fellow. Well, I'll go into me little place and get on with me bit of dobying[38] so as to have it all nice for Healey when he comes round.

(He goes back to his cell.)

PRISONER B *(to Lifer)*. Don't light up yet! Here's the screw coming.

PRISONER A. With the other fellow.

(Warder Regan and another prisoner, "the Other Fellow," an anxious-faced man, wearing prison clothes and carrying a kit bag, come on Left.)

WARDER REGAN. Yes, this is your flowery dell. Leave in your kitbag and stand at your door and wait for the doctor. These other fellows will show you where to go when he comes.

---

36. **The dead arose and appeared to many** Matt. 27: 53   37. **nick** watch, lookout   38. **dobying** washing

OTHER FELLOW. Right, sir. Very good, sir.

(Warder Regan goes, the Other Fellow has a look round.)

PRISONER B. There's a bloke in the end cell getting himself a quiet burn. Why don't you join him before the screws get back?

(The Other Fellow notices the card on Lifer's cell.)

OTHER FELLOW. My God! Is this what I've come to, mixing with murderers? I'd rather not, thank you, though I could do with a smoke. I'll have to spend long months here, even if I get my remission, with murderers and thieves and God knows what! You're not all murderers are you? You haven't killed anyone, have you?

PRISONER B. Not for a while, I haven't.

OTHER FELLOW. I can't imagine any worse crime than taking a life, can you?

PRISONER B. It'd depend whose life.

OTHER FELLOW. Of course. I mean, a murderer would be justified in taking his own life, wouldn't he? "We send him forth" says Carlisle[39]—you've heard of Carlisle haven't you?—"We send him forth, back to the void, back to the darkness, far out beyond the stars. Let him go from us."

DUNLAVIN *(head out of door of cell)*. Oh. *(Looks at Other Fellow.)* I thought it was Healey from the Department or someone giving it out of them.

PRISONER A. Looks like this man is a bit of an intellectual.

DUNLAVIN. Is that what they call it now?

LIFER. Thanks for the smoke, Mr. Dunlavin.

DUNLAVIN. Not at all, sure, you're welcome, call again when you're passing. But remember the next wife you kill and you getting forty fags a day in the condemned cell, think of them as is not so fortunate as yourself and leave a few dog-ends around the exercise yard after you. Here's these noisy little gets[40] again.

(The two Young Prisoners come round from the left, their sweeping brushes in front of them and singing their song. The Other Fellow stands quite still at his door.)

YOUNG PRISONERS.

> Only one more cell inspection
> We go out next Saturday
> Only one more cell inspection
> Then we go far far away.

(They are sweeping near the Lifer.)

> Only one more cell inspection
> We go out next Saturday
> Only one more cell . . .

39. **Carlisle** Thomas Carlyle (1795–1881)   40. **gets** children

LIFER. For God's sake shut up that squeaking . . .

YOUNG PRISONER 1. We've as much right to open our mouth as what you have, and you only a wet day in the place.

PRISONER B. Leave the kids alone. You don't own the place, you know. They're doing no harm. *(To the Young Prisoners.)* You want to sweep this bit of floor away?

DUNLAVIN. What brings you round here so often? If you went over to the remand wings you might pick up a bit of snout or a look at the paper.

YOUNG PRISONER 1. We get a smoke and the *Mail*[41] every day off a limey[42] on our road that's on remand. He's in over the car smuggling. But round here this morning you can see the mots from the laundry over on the female side hanging out the washing in the exercise yard. Do youse look at them? I suppose when you get old, though, you don't much bother about women.

PRISONER B. I'm thirty-six, mac.

YOUNG PRISONER 1. Ah, I thought that. Don't suppose you care if you never see a mot. There's Shaybo there and he never thinks of anything else. Do you think of anything else but women, Shaybo?

YOUNG PRISONER 2. Yes. Robbing and stealing, Scholara. You go to the window and keep an eye out for them and I'll sweep on round here till you give us a call.

YOUNG PRISONER 1. Right, Shaybo, they should be nearly out now. *(Goes out and stands by window.)*

PRISONER B. I forgot about the women.

DUNLAVIN. I didn't. It's a great bit of a treat today—that and having me leg rubbed. Neighbour and I wait in for it.

YOUNG PRISONER 1 *(from the window, in a coarse whisper)*. Shaybo, you can see them now.

YOUNG PRISONER 2. The blondy one from North Crumlin?[43]

YOUNG PRISONER 1. Yes, and there's another one with her. I don't know her.

YOUNG PRISONER 2. Must be a country mot. Scholara doesn't know her. Women.

DUNLAVIN. Women.

PRISONER A. I see the blondy one waving.

YOUNG PRISONER 1. If it's all the one to you, I'd like you to know that's my mot and it's me she's waving at.

PRISONER A. I'll wave you a thick ear.

DUNLAVIN. Hey, Neighbour! Where the hell is he this morning? Neighbour!

41. *Mail The Evening Mail,* a Dublin afternoon newspaper   42. **limey** Englishman   43. **North Crumlin** working class district of Dublin City

AN OLD MAN'S CREAKING VOICE. Here I am, Neighbour, here I am.
(Neighbour, a bent old man, comes on from Left hobbling as quickly as he can on a stick.)
DUNLAVIN. Ah, you lost mass.[44]
NEIGHBOUR. What, are they gone in already?
DUNLAVIN. No, but they're finished hanging up the top row of clothes. There'll be no stretching or reaching off chairs.
NEIGHBOUR. Still, thanks be to God for small mercies. They'll be out again this day week.
PRISONER A. If you lives to see it.
NEIGHBOUR. Why wouldn't I live to see it as well as what you would? This is not the nearest I was to fine women, nor are they the first good-looking ones I saw.
PRISONER A. With that old cough of yours they could easy be the last.
NEIGHBOUR. God, you're a desperate old gas bag.[45] We remember better-looking women than ever they were, don't we, Dunlavin? Meena La Bloom, do you remember her?
DUNLAVIN. Indeed and I do; many's the seaman myself and Meena gave the hey and a do, and Mickey Finn to.[46]
NEIGHBOUR. And poor May Oblong.
DUNLAVIN. Ah, where do you leave poor May? The Lord have mercy on her, wasn't I with her one night in the digs, and there was a Member of Parliament[47] there, and May after locking him in the back room and taking away his trousers, with him going over the north wall that morning to vote for Home Rule.[48] "For the love of your country and mine," he shouts under the door to May, "give me back me trousers." "So I will," says May, "if you shove a fiver out under the door."
NEIGHBOUR. He had the wad hid? Dirty suspicious old beast.
DUNLAVIN. That's right. He was cute enough to hide his wad somewhere, drunk and all as he was the previous night. All we got in his trousers was a locket of hair of the patriotic plumber of Dolphin's Barn[49] that swore to let his hair grow till Ireland was free.
NEIGHBOUR. Ah, poor May, God help her, she was the heart of the roll.[50]
DUNLAVIN. And when she was arrested for carrying on after the curfew, the time of the trouble,[51] she was fined for having concealed about

44. **you lost mass** you are a worthless fool 45. **gas bag** frivolous talker
46. **gave the hey and a do, and Mickey Finn to** greeted and drugged
47. **Parliament** Westminster 48. **Home Rule** Irish autonomy within the United Kingdom 49. **Dolphin's Barn** working class district of Dublin 50. **the heart of the roll** the best, the hard center of a wad of chewing tobacco 51. **time of the trouble** Irish War of Independence and Civil War (1919–23)

her person two Thompson submachine guns, 1921 pattern, three Mills bombs, and a stick of dynamite.

NEIGHBOUR. And will you ever forget poor Lottie L'Estrange, that got had up for pushing the soldier into Spencer Dock?

DUNLAVIN. Ah, God be with the youth of us.

NEIGHBOUR. And Cork Annie, and Lady Limerick.

DUNLAVIN. And Julia Rice and the Goofy One.

NEIGHBOUR *(turns towards window)*. Hey, you, move out of the way there and give us a look. Dunlavin, come up here before they go, and have a look at the blondy one.

YOUNG PRISONER 1. Go 'long, you dirty old dog. That's my mot you're speaking about. *(Shoves Neighbour.)* You old heap of dirt, to wave at a decent girl.

PRISONER A. Hey, snots, d'you think you own the bloody place?

YOUNG PRISONER 1. Would you like it, to have that dirty old eyebox looking at your mot?

PRISONER B. He's not going to eat her.

DUNLAVIN *(from behind)*. No, but he'd like to.

YOUNG PRISONER 2. That's right, and Scholara is nearly married to her. At least she had a squealer[52] for him and he has to pay her money every week. Any week he's outside like, to give it, or her to get it.

YOUNG PRISONER 1 *(blows a kiss)*. That's right, and I have him putting his rotten old eye on her.

OTHER FELLOW *(at his doorway)*. God preserve us.

PRISONER A. Well, you don't own the bloody window. *(Shoves Young Prisoner 1 out of way and brings over Neighbour.)* Come on, you, if you want to see the May procession.

NEIGHBOUR. Ah, thanks, butty,[53] your blood's worth bottling.[54]

PRISONER A. I didn't do it on account of you, but if you let them young pups get away with too much they'd be running the place.

YOUNG PRISONER 2. Come on, Scholara, we'll mosey back. The screw will think we're lost.

(They go back down the stairs, pick up their brushes, and start sweeping again and singing . . .)

YOUNG PRISONER 1.

> Only one more cell inspection
> We go out next Saturday.

YOUNG PRISONER 2.

> Only one more cell inspection . . .

52. **squealer** child   53. **butty** friend   54. **your blood's worth bottling** jocular compliment

LIFER. Shut your bloody row, can't you?

DUNLAVIN. Shut up yourself; you're making more noise than any of them.

YOUNG PRISONER 1. Don't tell us to shut up, you bastard.

PRISONER B. Ah leave him alone; he started life this morning.

YOUNG PRISONER 1. Ah we're sorry, mister, ain't we, Shaybo?

YOUNG PRISONER 2. God, we are. Go over and take a pike[55] at the female yard. They hang up the clothes now and Scholara's mot is over there. You can have a look at her. Scholara won't mind, will you, Schol?

YOUNG PRISONER 1. Certainly and I won't. Not with you going to the Bog to start life in a couple of days, where you won't see a woman.

YOUNG PRISONER 2. A child.

YOUNG PRISONER 1. A dog.

YOUNG PRISONER 2. A fire.

PRISONER A. Get to hell out of that round to your own wing. Wouldn't you think a man would know all that forbye[56] you telling it to him?

YOUNG PRISONER 2. We were going anyway. We've seen all we wanted to see. It wasn't to look at a lot of old men we came here, but to see mots hanging out the washing.

YOUNG PRISONER 1. And either ways, we'll be a lot nearer the women than you'll be next Saturday night. Think of us when you're sitting locked up in the old flowery,[57] studying the Bible, Chapter i, verse 2, and we trucking round in chase of charver.[58]

(They samba out with their brushes for partners, humming the Wedding Samba.)

PRISONER A. Them young gets have too much old gab[59] out of them altogether. I was a Y.P.[60] in Walton[61] before the war and I can tell you they'd be quiet boys if they got the larrying[62] we used to get.

OTHER FELLOW. And talking so disrespectfully about the Bible.

NEIGHBOUR. Be God and they needn't; many's the time the Bible was a consolation to a fellow all alone in the old cell. The lovely thin paper with a bit of mattress coir[63] in it, if you could get a match or a bit of tinder or any class of light, was as good a smoke as ever I tasted. Am I right, Dunlavin?

DUNLAVIN. Damn the lie, Neighbour. The first twelve months I done, I smoked my way half-way through the book of Genesis and three inches of my mattress. When the Free State[64] came in we were afraid of our life

55. **pike** look   56. **forbye** without   57. **old flowery** prison cell   58. **in chase of charver** good-time girls   59. **old gab** backtalk   60. **Y.P.** Young Prisoner   61. **Walton** British holdover prison   62. **larrying** thrashing   63. **coir** coconut fiber   64. **When the Free State came in** after 1922

they were going to change the mattresses for feather beds. And you couldn't smoke feathers, not, be God, if they were rolled in the Song of Solomon itself. But sure, thanks to God, the Free State didn't change anything more than the badge on the warders' caps.

OTHER FELLOW. Can I be into my cell for a while?

PRISONER B. Until the doctor calls you.

(Goes into his cell.)

PRISONER A. Well, I'm going to have a rest. It's hard work doing a lagging.

LIFER. A lagging? That's penal servitude, isn't it?

DUNLAVIN. Three years or anything over.

LIFER. Three years is a long time.

DUNLAVIN. I wouldn't like to be that long hanging.

NEIGHBOUR. Is he the . . .

DUNLAVIN *(sotto voce)*. Silver-top! *(Aloud.)* Started life this morning.

NEIGHBOUR. So they're not going to top you after all? Well, you're a lucky man. I worked one time in the hospital, helping the screw there, and the morning of the execution he gave me two bottles of stout[65] to take the hood off the fellow was after being topped. I wouldn't have done it a second time for two glasses of malt,[66] no, nor a bottle of it. I cut the hood away; his head was all twisted and his face black, but the two eyes were the worst; like a rabbit's; it was fear that had done it.

LIFER. Perhaps he didn't feel anything. How do you know?

NEIGHBOUR. I only seen him. I never had a chance of asking him. *(Neighbour goes to the murderer's door.)* Date of expiration of sentence, life. In some ways I wouldn't mind if that was my lot. What do you say?

DUNLAVIN. I don't know; it's true we're too old and bet[67] for lobbywatching[68] and shaking down[69] anywhere, so that you'd fall down and sleep on the pavement of a winter's night and not know but you were lying snug and comfortable in the Shelbourne.[70]

NEIGHBOUR. Only then to wake up on some lobby and the hard floorboards under you, and a lump of hard filth for your pillow, and the cold and the drink shaking you, wishing it was morning for the market pubs to open, where if you had the price of a drink you could sit in the warm anyway. Except, God look down on you, if it was Sunday.

DUNLAVIN. Ah, there's the agony. No pub open, but the bells battering your bared nerves and all you could do with the cold and the sickness was to lean over on your side and wish that God would call you.

---

65. **stout** dark beer 66. **malt** whiskey 67. **bet** beaten 68. **lobbywatching** staking out 69. **shaking down** extortion 70. **Shelbourne** premier Dublin City hotel

LIFER. If I was outside my life wouldn't be like that.

NEIGHBOUR. No, but ours would.

DUNLAVIN (*quietly*). See, we're selfish, mister, like everyone else.

WARDER (*shouts off*). Medical applications and receptions. Fall in for the doctor. (*Lifer looks lost.*)

DUNLAVIN. Yes, that's you. Go up there to the top of the wing and wait there till the screw tells you to go in. Neighbour, call them other fellows.

(*Exit Lifer.*)

NEIGHBOUR. Come on—the vet's here.

DUNLAVIN (*calling in to the Other Fellow*). Hey, come out and get gelded.

(*Other Fellow and Prisoners A and B come out of cells.*)

NEIGHBOUR. You're for the doctor. Go on up there with the rest of them. Me and Dunlavin don't go up. We only wait to be rubbed.

DUNLAVIN. Don't have any chat at all with that fellow. D'you see what he's in for?

(*Neighbour goes and looks. Exit Other Fellow and Prisoners A and B.*)

NEIGHBOUR. What the hell does that mean?

DUNLAVIN. A bloody sex mechanic.[71]

NEIGHBOUR. I didn't know.

DUNLAVIN. Well, you know now. I'll go in and get me chair. You can sit on it after me. It'll save you bringing yours out.

NEIGHBOUR. Well, if you go first and you have a chance of a go at the spirit bottle, don't swig the bloody lot. Remember I'm for treatment too.

DUNLAVIN. Don't be such an old begrudger. He'll bring a quart bottle of it, and who could swallow that much methylated spirit[72] in the few drops you'd get at it?

NEIGHBOUR. You could, or a bucket of it, if it was lying anywhere handy. I seen you do it, bluestone[73] and all, only buns to a bear as far as you were concerned.

DUNLAVIN. Do you remember the old doctor they had here years ago?

NEIGHBOUR. The one they used to call Crippen.

DUNLAVIN. The very man. There was one day I was brought in for drinking the chat[74] and I went to court that morning and was here in the afternoon still as drunk as Pontius Pilate. Crippen was examining me. "When I put me hand there you cough," and all to that effect. "Did you ever have V.D.[75]?" says he. "I haven't got your habits," says I to him. These fellows weren't long.

71. **mechanic** maniac   72. **methylated spirit** a mixture of ethyl alcohol and methyl alcohol   73. **bluestone** inferior gin or whiskey resembling vitriol   74. **drinking the chat** getting drunk   75. **V.D.** venereal disease

(Re-enter Prisoners A and B.)

NEIGHBOUR. What did he give youse?

PRISONER B *(passing into cell)*. Extra six ounces of bread. Says we're undernourished.

PRISONER A. Is the bar open yet?

NEIGHBOUR. Never you mind the bar. I've cruel pains in my leg that I want rubbed to take out the rheumatics, not to be jeered at, and I've had them genuine since the war.

PRISONER A. What war? The economic war?[76]

NEIGHBOUR. Ah, you maggot. It's all your fault, Dunlavin, telling them fellows we do get an odd sup out of the spirit bottle. Letting everyone know our business.

(Prisoners A and B go into cells and shut the doors.)

DUNLAVIN. No sign of Holy Healey yet.

NEIGHBOUR. You're wasting your time chasing after old Healey. He told me here one day, and I trying to get myself an old overcoat out of him, that he was here only as a head man of the Department of Justice, and he couldn't do other business of any other sort or size whatever, good, bad or indifferent. It's my opinion that old Healey does be half-jarred[77] a deal of the time anyway.

DUNLAVIN. The likes of Healey would take a sup all right, but being a high-up civil servant, he wouldn't drink under his own name. You'd see the likes of Healey nourishing themselves with balls of malt,[78] at eleven in the morning, in little back snugs[79] round Merrion Row.[80] The barman would lose his job if he so much as breathed their name. It'd be "Mr. H. wants a drop of water but not too much." "Yes, Mr. O." "No, sir, Mr. Mac wasn't in this morning." "Yes, Mr. D. Fine morning; it will be a lovely day if it doesn't snow." Educated drinking, you know. Even a bit of chat about God at an odd time, so as you'd think God was in another department, but not long off the Bog, and they was doing Him a good turn to be talking well about Him.

NEIGHBOUR. Here's the other two back. The M.O.[81] will be down to us soon.

(Lifer and Other Fellow go into cells and shut the doors.)

DUNLAVIN. That other fellow's not looking as if this place is agreeing with him.

NEIGHBOUR. You told me a minute ago that I wasn't even to speak to him.

DUNLAVIN. Ah, when all is said and done, he's someone's rearing after

76. **economic war** the imposition of mutual tariffs on trade between the Irish Free State and Britain (1932–38)   77. **half-jarred** half-drunk   78. **balls of malt** shots of whiskey   79. **snugs** private drinking booths in bars   80. **Merrion Row** in central Dublin, upperclass   81. **M.O.** medical officer

all, he could be worse, he could be a screw or an official from the Department.

(Warder Regan comes on with a bottle marked "methylated spirit.")

WARDER REGAN. You're the two for rubs, for your rheumatism.

DUNLAVIN. That's right, Mr. Regan sir, old and bet, sir, that's us. And the old pains is very bad with us these times, sir.

WARDER REGAN. Not so much lip, and sit down whoever is first for treatment.

DUNLAVIN. That's me, sir. Age before ignorance, as the man said. *(Sits in the chair.)*

WARDER REGAN. Rise the leg of your trousers. Which leg is it?

DUNLAVIN. The left, sir.

WARDER REGAN. That's the right leg you're showing me.

DUNLAVIN. That's what I was saying, sir. The left is worst one day and the right is bad the next. To be on the safe side, you'd have to do two of them. It's only the mercy of God I'm not a centipede, sir, with the weather that's in it.

WARDER REGAN. Is that where the pain is?

DUNLAVIN. *(bending down slowly towards the bottle).* A little lower down, sir, if you please. *(Grabs the bottle and raises it to his mouth.)* Just a little lower down, sir, if it's all equal to you.

(Regan rubs, head well bent, and Dunlavin drinks long and deeply and as quickly lowers the bottle on to the floor again, wiping his mouth and making the most frightful grimaces, for the stuff doesn't go down easy at first. He goes through the pantomime of being burnt inside for Neighbour's benefit and rubs his mouth with the back of his hand.)

DUNLAVIN. Ah, that's massive,[82] sir. 'Tis you that has the healing hand. You must have desperate luck at the horses;[83] I'd only love to be with you copying your dockets.[84] *(Regan turns and pours more spirit on his hands.)* Ah, that's it, sir, well into me I can feel it going. *(Reaches forward towards the bottle again, drinks.)* Ah, that's it, I can feel it going right into me. And doing me all the good in the world. *(Regan reaches and puts more spirit on his hand and sets to rubbing again.)* That's it, sir, thorough does it; if you're going to do a thing at all you might as well do it well. *(Reaches forward for the bottle again and raises it. Neighbour looks across in piteous appeal to him not to drink so much, but he merely waves the bottle in elegant salute, as if to wish him good health, and takes another drink.)* May God reward you, sir, you must be the seventh son of the seventh son or one of the Lees from Limerick[85] on your mother's side maybe. *(Drinks again.)* Ah, that's the cure for the cold of the wind and the world's neglectment.

82. massive very satisfying   83. desperate luck at the horses great luck in betting   84. copying your dockets stealing a look at your bets   85. seventh son of the seventh son or one of the Lees from Limerick reputedly endowed with special gifts

WARDER REGAN. Right, now you.

(Neighbour comes forward.)

WARDER DONELLY *(offstage)*. All present and correct, Mr. Healey, sir.

DUNLAVIN. Holy Healey!

(Enter Warder Donelly.)

WARDER DONELLY. This way, Mr. Healey.

WARDER REAGAN. Attention! Stand by your doors.

DUNLAVIN. By the left, laugh.

WARDER DONELLY. This way.

(Enter Mr. Healey, an elegantly dressed gentleman.)

HEALEY. Good morning.

WARDER DONELLY. Any complaints?

PRISONER A. No, sir.

HEALEY. Good morning!

WARDER DONELLY. Any complaints?

OTHER FELLOW.
PRISONER B.   } No, sir.

HEALEY. Good morning all! Well, now, I'm here representing the Department of Justice, if there are any complaints now is the time to make them.

SEVERAL PRISONERS. No complaints, sir.

WARDER REGAN. All correct, sir. Two receiving medical treatment here, sir.

DUNLAVIN. Just getting the old leg rubbed, sir, Mr. Healey.

HEALEY. Well, well, it almost smells like a bar.

DUNLAVIN. I'm near drunk myself on the smell of it, sir.

HEALEY. Don't let me interrupt the good work.

DUNLAVIN. Ah, the old legs. It's being out in all weathers that does it, sir. Of course we don't have that to contend with while we're here, sir.

HEALEY. Out in all weathers, I should think not indeed. Well, my man, I will be inspecting your cell amongst others in due course.

DUNLAVIN. Yes, sir.

HEALEY. It's always a credit to you, I must say that. *(He turns to Regan.)* Incorrigible, some of these old fellows, but rather amusing.

WARDER REGAN. Yes, sir.

HEALEY. It's Regan, isn't it?

WARDER REGAN. Yes, sir.

HEALEY. Ah yes, you're helping the Canon at the execution tomorrow morning, I understand.

WARDER REGAN. Well, I shall be with the condemned man sir, seeing that he doesn't do away with himself during the night and that he goes down the hole with his neck properly broken in the morning, without making too much fuss about it.

HEALEY. A sad duty.

WARDER REGAN. Neck breaking and throttling, sir? *(Healey gives him a sharp look.)* You must excuse me, sir. I've seen rather a lot of it. They say familiarity breeds contempt.

HEALEY. Well, we have one consolation, Regan, the condemned man gets the priest and the sacraments, more than his victim got maybe. I venture to suggest that some of them die holier deaths than if they had finished their natural span.

WARDER REGAN. We can't advertise "Commit a murder and die a happy death," sir. We'd have them all at it. They take religion very seriously in this country.

HEALEY. Quite, quite so! Now, I understand you have the reprieved man over here, Regan.

WARDER REGAN. Number twenty-six, sir.

DUNLAVIN. Just beside me, sir.

HEALEY. Ah, yes! So here we are! Here's the lucky man, eh? Well, now the Governor will explain your position to you later in the day. Your case will be examined every five years. Meanwhile I thought you might like a holy picture to hang up in your cell. Keep a cheerful countenance, my friend. God gave you back your life and the least you can do is to thank him with every breath you draw! Right? Well, be of good heart. I will call in and see you again, that is, if duty permits.

(He moves to Dunlavin's cell.)

HEALEY *(at Dunlavin's cell).* Very creditable. Hm.

DUNLAVIN. Well, to tell you the truth, sir, it's a bit extra special today. You see, we heard you was here.

HEALEY. Very nice.

DUNLAVIN. Of course I do like to keep my little place as homely as I can with the little holy pictures you gave me of Blessed Martin,[86] sir.

HEALEY. I see you don't recognize the colour bar.[87]

DUNLAVIN. The only bar I recognize, sir, is the Bridge Bar or the Beamish House the corner of Thomas Street.

HEALEY. Well, I must be off now, and I'm glad to see you're being well looked after.

DUNLAVIN. It's neither this nor that, but if you could spare a minute, sir?

HEALEY. Yes, what is it? But hurry; remember I've a lot to do today.

DUNLAVIN. It's like this, sir. I won't always be here, sir, having me leg rubbed and me bit of grub brought to me. As it says in the Bible, sir, have

86. **Blessed Martin** de Porres, Peruvian saint of mixed race (1579–1639), canonized 1962   87. **colour bar** racial discrimination

it yourself or be without it and put ye by for the rainy day, for thou knowest not the night thou mayest be sleeping in a lobby.[88]

HEALEY. Yes, yes, but what is it you want?

DUNLAVIN. I've the chance of a little room up round Buckingham Street,[89] sir, if you could only give me a letter to the Room-Keepers after I go out, for a bit of help with the rent.

HEALEY. Well, you know, when I visit the prison, I'm not here as a member of any outside organization of which I may be a member but simply as an official of the Department of Justice.

DUNLAVIN. Yes, but where else would I be likely to meet you, sir? I'd hardly bump into you in the Bridge Bar when I'd be outside, would I, sir?

HEALEY. No, no, certainly not. But you know the Society offices in the Square. See me there any Friday night, between eight and nine.

DUNLAVIN. Thank you, sir, and a bed in heaven to you, sir.

HEALEY. And the same to you.

(Goes to next cell.)

DUNLAVIN. And many of them, and I hope we're all here this time next year *(venomously after Mr. Healey)* that it may choke you.

(Warder Donelly bangs on Lifer's closed door, then looks in.)

WARDER DONELLY. Jesus Christ, sir. He's put the sheet up![90] Quick.

(Regan and Donelly go into Lifer's cell. He is hanging. They cut him down.)

WARDER REGAN. Gently does it.

(They lay him down in the passage and try to restore him.)

HEALEY. What a dreadful business, and with this other coming off tomorrow.

(The Prisoners crowd out of line.)

WARDER DONELLY. Get back to your cells!

HEALEY. Is he still with us?

WARDER REGAN. He'll be all right in an hour or two. Better get the M.O., Mr. Donelly.

(The triangle sounds.)

WARDER DONELLY. B Wing, two, three and one. Stand by your doors. Right, lead on. Now come on, come on, this is no holiday. Right sir, over to you. Lead on, B1.

(Warder Regan and Healey are left with the unconscious Lifer.)

HEALEY. Dear, dear. The Canon will be very upset about this.

WARDER REGAN. There's not much harm done, thank God. They don't have to put a death certificate against the receipt for his live body.

HEALEY. That doesn't seem a very nice way of looking at it, Regan.

WARDER REGAN. A lot of people mightn't consider ours a very nice job, sir.

88. **As is says in the Bible . . . lobby** travesty of Matt. 25: 13   89. **Buckingham Street** inner city Dublin   90. **put the sheet up** as cover

HEALEY. Ours?

WARDER REGAN. Yes, ours, sir. Mine, the Canon's, the hangman's, and if you don't mind my saying so, yours, sir.

HEALEY. Society cannot exist without prisons, Regan. My job is to bring what help and comfort I can to these unfortunates. Really, a man with your outlook, I cannot see why you stay in the service.

WARDER REGAN. It's a soft job, sir, between hangings.

(The triangle is heard. The M.O. comes on with two stretcher-bearers.)

THE CURTAIN FALLS

ACT 2

THE CURTAIN RISES

The prison yard, a fine evening.

VOICE OF PRISONER *(off-stage, singing)*.

A hungry feeling came o'er me stealing
And the mice were squealing in my prison cell
And the old triangle
Went jingle jangle
Along the banks of the Royal Canal.

WARDER DONELLY. B1, B2, B3. Head on for exercise, right! Lead on, B1. All one, away to exercise.

(The prisoners file out, Warder Donelly with them.)

On a fine spring evening,
The lag lay dreaming
The seagulls wheeling high above the wall,
And the old triangle
Went jingle jangle
Along the banks of the Royal Canal.
The screw was peeping
The lag was sleeping,

(The prisoners wander where they will; most go and take a glance at the half-dug grave.)

While he lay weeping for the girl Sal,

WARDER DONELLY. Who's the bloody baritone? Shut up that noise, you. Where do you think you are?

NEIGHBOUR. It's not up here, sir; it's one of the fellows in the base-ment, sir, in the solitary.

WARDER DONELLY. He must be getting birdseed with his bread and water. I'll bloody well show him he's not in a singing house. *(Song is still going on.)* Hey, shut up that noise! Shut up there or I'll leave you weeping. Where do you think you are? *(Song stops.)* You can get sitting down any of you that wants it.

(Dunlavin sits.)

NEIGHBOUR *(at the grave)*. They'll have to bottom out another couple of feet before morning.

PRISONER B. They! Us you mean; they've got four of us in a working party after tea.

NEIGHBOUR. You want to get that clay nice and neat for filling in.

(He spits and wanders away.)

PRISONER B. We'll get a couple of smokes for the job at least.

(They wander.)

NEIGHBOUR. How are you, Neighbour?

DUNLAVIN. Dying.

NEIGHBOUR. If you are itself, it's greed that's killing you. I only got a sup of what was left.

DUNLAVIN. I saved your life then; it was very bad meths.

PRISONER B. What did Regan say when he caught youse lying in the cell?

NEIGHBOUR. He wanted to take us up for drinking it on him, but Dunlavin said we were distracted with the events of the morning and didn't know what we were doing. So he just told us to get to hell out of it and he hoped it would destroy us for life.

DUNLAVIN. May God forgive him.

NEIGHBOUR. I thought it was as good a drop of meths as ever I tasted. It would never come up to the pre-war article, but between the spring-time and the warmth of it, it would put new life into you. Oh, it's a grand evening and another day's work behind us.

PRISONER B. With the winter over, Neighbour, I suppose you don't feel a day over ninety.

NEIGHBOUR. If you'd have done all the time I have you wouldn't look so young.

PRISONER A. What time? Sure, you never done a lagging in your life. A month here and a week there for lifting the collection box out of a chapel[91] or running out of a chemist's[92] with a bottle of cheap wine. Any-thing over six months would be the death of you.

NEIGHBOUR. Oh, you're the hard chaw.[93]

91. **lifting the collection box out of a chapel** stealing the poorbox from a Catholic church   92. **chemist's** drugstore   93. **hard chaw** tough guy

PRISONER A. Two laggings, I've done. Five year and seven, and a bit of Preventive Detention,[94] on the Moor and at Parkhurst.[95]

NEIGHBOUR. What for? Ferocious begging?[96]

PRISONER A. I've never been a grasshopper[97] or a nark[98] for the screws anyway, wherever I was; and if you were in a lagging station I know what they'd give you, shopping[99] the poor bastard that was singing in the chokey.[100] He was only trying to be company for himself down there all alone and not knowing whether it was day or night.

NEIGHBOUR. I only did it for his own good. If the screw hadn't checked him the Principal might have been coming out and giving him an extra few days down there.

DUNLAVIN. Will youse give over the pair of youse for God's sake. The noise of youse battering me bared nerves is unhuman. Begod, an Englishman would have more nature[101] to a fellow lying with a sick head. A methylated martyr, that's what I am.

NEIGHBOUR *(to Prisoner A)*. Meself and that man sitting there, we done time before you came up. In Kilmainham,[102] and that's where you never were. First fourteen days without a mattress, skilly[103] three times a day. None of your sitting out in the yard like nowadays. I got my toe amputated by one of the old lags so I could get into hospital for a feed.[104]

DUNLAVIN *(looks up and feebly moans)*. A pity you didn't get your head amputated as you were at it. It would have kept you quiet for a bit.

NEIGHBOUR. I got me mouth to talk, the same as the next man. Maybe we're not all that well up, that we get up at the Christmas concert and do the electrocutionist[105] performance, like some I could mention.

DUNLAVIN. It's neither this nor that, Neighbour, but if you would only give over arguing the toss[106] about nothing and change over to a friendly subject of mutual interest—like the quare fellow that's to be topped in the morning.

NEIGHBOUR. True, true, Dunlavin, and a comfortable old flowery dell he'll have down there. *(He prods the grave with his stick.)* We'll be eating the cabbages off that one in a month or two.

PRISONER A. You're in a terrible hurry to get the poor scut[107] under the cabbages. How do you know he won't get a reprieve, like old Silvertop?

LIFER. Jesus, Mary and Joseph, you'd like to see me in there, wouldn't you!

94. **Prevention Detention** precautionary imprisonment   95. **Moor and Parkhurst** (Dartmoor): British prisons   96. **Ferocious begging** robbery   97. **grasshopper** informer   98. **nark** informer   99. **shopping** betraying   100. **chokey** punishment cells   101. **nature** sympathy   102. **Kilmainham** Dublin prison   103. **skilly** porridge   104. **feed** a big meal   105. **electrocutionist** elocutionist   106. **the toss** of a coin   107. **scut** little chap

(He moves violently away from them.)

NEIGHBOUR. Your man doesn't like any talk about hanging.

PRISONER A. No more would you, if you'd tried to top yourself this morning.

NEIGHBOUR. Anyway he's gone now and we can have a chat about it in peace. Sure we must be saying something and it's better than scandalizing our neighbours.

PRISONER B. You never know what might happen to the quare fellow. God is good.

PRISONER C. And has a good mother.[108]

(They look in surprise at the young person who has quietly joined them.)

DUNLAVIN. No, no, it's too late now for him to be chucked.

PRISONER A. It has been known, a last-minute reprieve, you know.

NEIGHBOUR. He bled his brother into a crock,[109] didn't he, that had been set aside for the pig-slaughtering and mangled the remains beyond all hope of identification.

PRISONER C. Go bfóiridh Dia 'rainn.[110]

NEIGHBOUR. He hasn't got a chance, never in a race of cats.[111] He'll be hung as high as Guilderoy.[112]

PRISONER A. You're the life of the party, aren't you? You put me in mind of the little girl who was sent in to cheer her father up. She was so good at it that he cut his throat.

PRISONER E. Ah, sure he was only computing the odds to it. He'll be topped.

NEIGHBOUR. I'd lay me Sunday bacon[113] on it if anyone would be idiot enough to take me up.

(Prisoner E, a bookie, has been listening.)

PRISONER E. I wouldn't take your bacon, but I'll lay it off for you if you like.

(Another prisoner watches for the screws. Prisoner E acts as if he were a tick-tack man at the races.)

PRISONER E. The old firm. Here we are again. Neighbour lays his Sunday bacon the quare fellow will be topped tomorrow morning. Any takers?

PRISONER D. Five snout.

PRISONER E. Away home to your mother.

MICKSER. Half a bacon.

PRISONER E. Half a . . .

---

108. **God is good. And has a good mother** saw from Ir.   109. **crock** large bowl   110. **Go bfóiridh Dia 'rainn** God have mercy on us (Ir.)   111. **race of cats** at any odds   112. **as high as Guilderoy** Guilderoy, a famous Scottish highwayman, was hanged in Edinburgh in 1636.   113. **Sunday bacon** extra treat for Sunday breakfast

NEIGHBOUR. Even bacons.

PRISONER E. Even bacons. Even bacons any takers? Yourself, sir, come on now, you look like a sportsman.

PRISONER A. I wouldn't eat anything after he'd touched it, not if I were starving.

NEIGHBOUR. Is that so . . .

PRISONER E. Now, now, now, don't interrupt the betting. Any takers?

DUNLAVIN. I'll take him up if only to shut his greedy gob.

NEIGHBOUR. You won't! You're having me on!

DUNLAVIN. No, I'll bet you my Sunday bacon that a reprieve will come through before morning. I feel it in my bones.

NEIGHBOUR. That's the rheumatics.

PRISONER E. Is he on, Neighbour?

NEIGHBOUR. He is.

PRISONER E. Shake on it, the two of youse!

DUNLAVIN. How d'ye do, Lord Lonsdale![114]

NEIGHBOUR. Never mind all that. The minute the trap goes down tomorrow morning your Sunday bacon is mine.

PRISONER A. God leave you health to enjoy it.

NEIGHBOUR. He'll be topped all right.

PRISONER A. And if he isn't, I'm the very man will tell him you bet your bacon on his life.

NEIGHBOUR. You never would.

PRISONER A. Wouldn't I?

NEIGHBOUR. You'd never be bad enough.

PRISONER A. And what would be bad about it?

NEIGHBOUR. Causing a dissension and a disturbance.

(The two Young Prisoners enter.)

PRISONER A. You mean he mightn't take it for a joke.

PRISONER B. Here's them two young prisoners; they've the life of Reilly,[115] rambling round the place. Where youse wandering off to now?

SCHOLARA. We came over here to see a chiner[116] of ours. He turned twenty the day before yesterday, so they shifted him away from the Juveniles to here. *(He sees Prisoner C.)* Ah, there you are. We were over in the hospital being examined for going out on Saturday and we had a bit of snout to give you. *(Takes out a Woodbine package, extracts a cigarette from it and gives it to Prisoner C, who shyly stands and takes it.)*

PRISONER C *(quietly)*. Thanks.

SCHOLARA. Gurra morra gut,[117] you mean.

114. **Lord Lonsdale** President of the National Sporting Club, London, and originator (1909) of the boxing award "The Lonsdale Belt" 115. **the life of Reilly** a high time 116. **chiner** pal 117. **Gurra morra gut** *Go raibh maith agat* "Thank you" (crude Ir. pronunciation)

PRISONER C (*smiles faintly*). Go raibh maith agat.

SCHOLARA (*grandly*). Ná bac leis.[118] (*To the other prisoners.*) Talks Irish to beat the band.[119] Comes from an island between here and America.[120] And Shaybo will give you a couple of strikers.

SHAYBO (*reaches in the seams of his coat and takes out a match which he presents to Prisoner C.*) Here you are. It's a bloody shame to shove you over here among all these old men even if you are twenty itself, but maybe you won't be long after us, and you going home.

PRISONER C (*Kerry accent*). I will, please God. It will be summer-time and where I come from is lovely when the sun is shining.

(*They stand there, looking embarrassed for a moment.*)

DUNLAVIN. Go on, why don't you kiss him good-bye.

SHAYBO. Eh, Schol, let's have a pike at the grave before the screw comes out.

SCHOLARA. Ah, yes, we must have a look at the grave.

(*They dive into the grave, the old men shout at them, but Warder Donelly comes to the door of the hospital.*)

WARDER DONELLY. Get up to hell out of that and back to your own wing, youse two. (*Shouts to the warders in the prison wing.*) Two on you there, pass them fellows into the Juveniles. Get to hell out of that!

(*Scholara and Shaybo samba off, give the so-called V-sign,[121] slap the right biceps with the left palm, and turning lightly, run in through the door.*)

NEIGHBOUR. Aren't they the impudent pups? Too easy a time they have of it. I'd tan their pink backsides for them. That'd leave them fresh and easy. Impudent young curs is going these days. No respect for God nor man, pinch anything that wasn't nailed down.

PRISONER B. Neighbour, the meths is rising in you.

DUNLAVIN. He might as well rave there as in bed.

ENGLISH VOICE (*from one of the cell windows*). I say, I say, down there in the yard.

DUNLAVIN. The voice of the Lord!

PRISONER A. That's the geezer[122] from London that's in over the car smuggling.

ENGLISH VOICE. I say, down there.

PRISONER B. Hello, up there.

NEIGHBOUR. How are you fixed for fillet?[123]

PRISONER B. Shut up a minute. Wait till we hear what is it he wants.

ENGLISH VOICE. Is there any bloke down there going out this week?

---

118. **Na bac leis** Don't pay any attention to him (Ir.) 119. **to beat the band** to the limit, without limit 120. **an island between here and America** off Ireland's west coast, a Gaeltacht area 121. **V-sign** victory 122. **geezer** fellow, guy 123. **How are you fixed for fillet** how are you doing?

PRISONER B. Mickser is going out tomorrow. He's on this exercise. *(Shouts.)* Hold on a minute. *(Looks round.)* Hey, Mickser.

MICKSER. What's up?

PRISONER B. That English fellow that's on remand over the cars, he wants to know if there's anyone going out this week. You're going out tomorrow, ain't you?

MICKSER. Yes, I am. I'm going out in the morning. *(To English Prisoner.)* What do you want?

ENGLISH VOICE. I want you to go up and contact my mate. He's in Dublin. It's about bail for me. I can write his name and address here and let it down to you on my string. I didn't want the law to get his address in Dublin, so I can't write to him. I got a quid[124] in with me, without the screw finding it, and I'll let it down with the address if you'll do it.

MICKSER. Good enough. Let down the address and the quid.

ENGLISH VOICE. My mate will give you some more when you see him.

MICKSER. That's all right. Let the quid down now and the address before the screw comes out of the hospital. I'm going out tomorrow and I'll see him for you, soon as we get out of the market pubs at half two.

PRISONER B. He's letting it down now.

MICKSER. There's the quid anyway. *(Reading the note. Neighbour gets to his feet and goes behind and peers over his shoulder. Mickser sees him.)* Get to hell out of it, you.

NEIGHBOUR. I only just wanted to have a look at what he wrote.

MICKSER. And have his mate in the Bridewell,[125] before the day was out. I know you, you bloody old stag.[126]

NEIGHBOUR. I saw the day you wouldn't say the like of that.

MICKSER *(proffering him the pound)*. Here, get a mass said for yourself.

NEIGHBOUR. It wouldn't do you much harm to put yourself under the hand of a priest either.

MICKSER *(laughs at him)*. That's for sinners. Only dirty people has to wash.

NEIGHBOUR. A man of your talent and wasting your time here.

MICKSER *(going back to walk with the prisoners behind)*. Good luck now, Neighbour. I'll call up and see you in the hospice for the dying.

NEIGHBOUR *(stands and calls loudly after him)*. You watch yourself. I saw the quare fellow in here a couple of years ago. He was a young hard chaw like you in all the pride of his strength and impudence. He was kicking a ball about over in A yard and I was walking around with poor old Mockridge, neither of us minding no one. All of a sudden I gets such a wallop on the head it knocks the legs from under me and very nigh cuts

124. **quid** pound sterling   125. **Bridewell** Dublin jail   126. **stag** informer

off my ear. "You headed that well," says he, and I deaf for three days after it! Who's got the best of it now, young as he is and strong as he is? How will his own ear feel tomorrow morning, with the washer under it, and whose legs will be the weakest when the trap goes down and he's slung into the pit? And what use is the young heart?

(Some of the prisoners walking round stop and listen to him, but Mickser gives him a contemptuous look and walks on, shouting at him in passing.)

MICKSER. Get along with you, you dirty half animal.

(A Warder passes, sounds of the town heard, factory sirens, distant ships. Some of the prisoners pace up and down like caged animals.)

NEIGHBOUR. Dunlavin, have you the loan of a pencil for a minute?

DUNLAVIN. What do you want it for?

NEIGHBOUR. I just want to write something to that English fellow about his bail.

DUNLAVIN. You'd better hurry, before the screw comes back out.

(Neighbour writes.)

NEIGHBOUR. Hey, you up there that's looking for the bail.

ENGLISH VOICE. Hello, you got the quid and the address?

PRISONER A. What's the old dog up to?

DUNLAVIN. Ah, leave him alone. He's a bit hasty, but poor old Neighbour has good turns in him.

PRISONER A. So has a corkscrew.

NEIGHBOUR. Let down your string and I'll send you up this bit of a message.

ENGLISH VOICE *(his hands can be seen at the window holding the note)*. "Get a bucket and bail yourself out." *(Shouts in rage.)* You dirty bastard bleeder[127] to take my quid and I'll tell the bloody screw I will; I'll shop you, you bleeding . . .

MICKSER. What's up with you?

NEIGHBOUR. Get a bucket and bail yourself out. *(Laughing an old man's cackle.)*

ENGLISH VOICE. You told me to get a bucket and bail my bleeding self out, but I'll tell the screw; I'll shop you about that quid.

MICKSER *(shouts up to the window)*. Shut your bloody big mouth for a minute. I told you nothing.

PRISONER A. It was this old get here.

MICKSER. I sent you no message; it was this old pox bottle.[128]

NEIGHBOUR *(ceases to laugh, is alarmed at the approach of Mickser)*. Now, now, Mickser, take a joke, can't you, it was only a bit of gas.

MICKSER *(advancing)*. I'll give you gas.

(Mickser advances on Neighbour. The lags stop and look—suddenly Mickser

127. **bleeder** blackguard 128. **pox bottle** syphilis carrier

seizes the old man and, yelling with delight, carries Neighbour over to the grave and thrusts him into it. The prisoners all crowd around kicking dirt on to the old man and shouting "Get a bucket and bail yourself out.")

PRISONER B. Nick, Mickser, nick, nick, here's the screw.

PRISONER A. It's only the cook with the quare fellow's tea.

(A Prisoner comes through the hospital gate and down the steps. He wears a white apron, carries a tray and is surrounded by an interested band, except for the Lifer, who stands apart, and Dunlavin, who lies prone on the front asleep. From the prisoners around the food rises an excited chorus:)

PRISONER A. Rashers[129] and eggs.

PRISONER B. He got that last night.

MICKSER. Chicken.

NEIGHBOUR. He had that for dinner.

PRISONER B. Sweet cake.

PRISONER A. It's getting hung he is, not married.

NEIGHBOUR. Steak and onions.

MICKSER. Sausages and bacon.

PRISONER B. And liver.

PRISONER A. Pork chops.

PRISONER B. Pig's feet.

PRISONER A. Salmon.

NEIGHBOUR. Fish and chips.

MICKSER. Jelly and custard.

NEIGHBOUR. Roast lamb.

PRISONER A. Plum pudding.

PRISONER B. Turkey.

NEIGHBOUR. Goose.

PRISONERS A, B, AND NEIGHBOUR. Rashers and eggs.

ALL. Rashers and eggs, rashers and eggs, and eggs and rashers and eggs and rashers it is.

COOK *(desperate)*. Ah, here, lads.

PRISONERS. Here, give us a look, lift up the lid, eh, here, I never seen it.

(The Cook struggles to protect his cargo, the Prisoners mill round in a loose scrum of excitement and greed, their nostrils mad almost to the point of snatching a bit. There is a roar from the gate.)

WARDER DONELLY *(from inside the hospital gate)*. Get to hell out of that. What do youse think you are on?

(The Prisoners scatter in a rush.)

(The Cook with great dignity carries on.)

NEIGHBOUR *(sitting down)*. Oh, the two eggs, the yolk in the middle

---

129. **rashers** sliced bacon

like . . . a bride's eye under a pink veil, and the grease of the rashers . . . pale and pure like melted gold.

DUNLAVIN. Oh, may God forgive you, as if a body wasn't sick enough as it is.

NEIGHBOUR. And the two big back[130] rashers.

PRISONER A. Go along, you begrudging old dog. Maybe when you go back the standard of living in your town residence, No. 1 St. James Street,[131] might be gone up. And they'll be serving rashers and eggs. You'd do a lot for them, when you'd begrudge them to a man for his last meal on this earth.

NEIGHBOUR. Well, it's not his last meal if you want to know. He'll get a supper tonight and a breakfast in the morning, and I don't begrudge him the little he'll eat of that, seeing the rope stew to follow, and lever pudding and trap door doddle[132] for desert. And anyway didn't you run over the same as the rest of us to see what he was getting?

PRISONER A. And if I did, it wasn't to begrudge it to the man.

PRISONER B. Sure we all ran over, anything to break the monotony in a kip like this.

(The triangle is heard.)

PRISONER A *(gloomily)*. I suppose you're right. In Strangeways, Manchester, and I in it during the war, we used to wish for an air-raid. We had one and we were left locked up in our cells. We stood up on our tables and took the blackouts off the windows and had a grand-stand view of the whole city burning away under us. The screws were running round shouting in the spy-holes at us to get down from the windows, but they soon ran off down the shelters. We had a great view of the whole thing till a bomb landed on the Assize Court next door, and the blast killed twenty of the lags. They were left standing on their tables without a mark on them, stone dead. Sure anyway, we all agreed it broke the monotony.

(Enter Warder Donelly.)

WARDER DONELLY. Right, fall in there!

PRISONER B. Don't forget the bet, Neighbour.

WARDER DONELLY. Come on, get in line there.

PRISONER A. And don't forget what I'm going to tell the quare fellow.

WARDER DONELLY. Silence there. *(Search begins.)* What's this you've got in your pocket? A file? Scissors out of the bag shop? No? A bit of rope? Oh, your handkerchief, so it is. *(Searching next Prisoner.)* You here, what's this? A bit of wax end, you forgot to leave in the bag shop? Well, don't forget the next time. What's this? *(Man takes out two inches of rope.)* What's this for? You were roping mail bags today, and after all they don't rope themselves. Ah, you forgot to leave it behind? Well, go easy, save as

130. **back** premier cut 131. **No. 1 St. James Street** poorhouse 132. **doddle** amble

much as that each time and in five years' time you'd have enough to make a rope ladder. Oh, you're only doing six months? Well maybe you want to save the taxpayers a few quid and hang yourself. Sorrow the loss if you did, but they'd want to know where you got the rope from. *(Prisoners laugh as they are expected to do.)* Come on, next man. *(He hurries along now.)* Come along now, no mailbags, scissors, needles, knives, razor blades, guns, hatchets or empty porter bottles. No? *(To the last Prisoner.)* Well, will you buy a ticket to the Police Ball?

(Prisoners laugh dutifully.)

WARDER REGAN *(voice from prison wing)*. All done, sir?

PRISONER A. Don't forget, Neighbour.

WARDER DONELLY. Right, sir, on to you, sir. *(Gate swings open.)* Right, lead on, B1.

NEIGHBOUR. Anyway, his grave's dug and the hangman's on his way.

PRISONER A. That doesn't mean a thing, they always dig the grave, just to put the wind up them—

WARDER DONELLY. Silence!

(The prisoners march, the gate clangs behind them; the tramp of their feet is heard as they mark time inside.)

WARDER REGAN *(voice from the prison wing)*. Right, B Wing, bang out your doors. B1, get in off your steps and bang out your doors, into your cells and bang out your doors. Get locked up. BANG THEM DOORS! GET INSIDE AND BANG OUT THEM DOORS!

(The last door bangs lonely on its own and then there is silence.)

VOICE FROM BELOW *(singing)*.

> The wind was rising,
> And the day declining
> As I lay pining in my prison cell
> And that old triangle
> Went jingle jangle

(The triangle is beaten, the gate of the prison wing opens and the Chief and Warder Donelly come down the steps and approach the grave.)

> Along the banks of the Royal Canal.

CHIEF *(resplendent in silver braid)*. Who's that singing?

WARDER DONELLY. I think it's one of the prisoners in the chokey, sir.

CHIEF. Where?

WARDER DONELLY. In the punishment cells, sir.

CHIEF. That's more like it. Well, tell him to cut it out.

SONG.

> In the female prison
> There are seventy women . . .

WARDER DONELLY *(goes down to the area and leans and shouts)*. Hey, you down there, cut it out, or I'll give you jingle jangle.

(The song stops. Warder Donelly walks back.)

CHIEF. Is the quare fellow finished his tea?

WARDER DONELLY. He is. He is just ready to come out for exercise, now. The wings are all clear. They're locked up having their tea. He'll be along any minute.

CHIEF. He's coming out here?

WARDER DONELLY. Yes, sir.

CHIEF *(exasperated)*. Do you want him to see his grave, bloody well half dug? Run in quick and tell those bloody idiots to take him out the side door, and exercise him over the far side of the stokehold,[133] and tell them to keep him well into the wall where he'll be out of sight of the cell windows. Hurry and don't let him hear you. Let on it's something about another duty. Warders! You'd get better in Woolworths.[134]

(He goes to the area and shouts down.)

Hey, you down there. You in the cell under the steps. You do be singing there to keep yourself company? You needn't be afraid, it's only the Chief. How long you doing down there? Seven days Number 1 and twenty-one days Number 2. God bless us and love us, you must have done something desperate. I may be able to do something for you, though God knows you needn't count on it, I don't own the place. You what? With who? Ah sure, I often have a bit of a tiff[135] with the same man myself. We'll see what we can do for you. It's a long time to be stuck down there, no matter who you had the tiff with.

(Enter Warder Donelly.)

CHIEF. Well?

WARDER DONELLY. It's all right, they've brought him out the other way.

(They look out beyond the stage.)

CHIEF. Looks as if they're arguing the toss about something.

WARDER DONELLY. Football.

CHIEF. Begod, look at them stopping while the quare fellow hammers his point home.

WARDER DONELLY. I was down in the condemned cell while he was getting his tea. I asked him if it was all right. He said it was, and "Aren't the evenings getting a grand stretch?" he says.

CHIEF. Look at him now, putting his nose to the air.

WARDER DONELLY. He's a grand evening for his last.

CHIEF. I took the name of the fellow giving the concert in the pun-

133. **stokehold** furnace area   134. **Woolworths** synonymous with cheap goods   135. **tiff** argument

ishment cells. In the morning when we get this over, see he's shifted to Hell's gates over the far side. He can serenade the stokehold wall for a change if he's light enough to make out his music.

(Warder Donelly copies the name and number.)

CHIEF. I have to attend to every mortal thing in this place. None of youse seem to want to do a hand's turn, bar draw your money—you're quick enough at that. Well, come on, let's get down to business.

(Warder Donelly goes and uncovers the grave.)

CHIEF *(looking off)*. Just a minute. It's all right. They've taken him round the back of the stokehold. *(Looking at the grave.)* Not so bad, another couple of feet out of the bottom and we're elected.[136] Regan should be down with the working party any minute, as soon as the quare fellow's finished his exercise.

WARDER DONELLY. There, he's away in now, sir. See him looking at the sky?

CHIEF. You'd think he was trying to kiss it good-bye. Well, that's the last he'll see of it.

WARDER DONELLY. No chance of a reprieve, sir?

CHIEF. Not a chance. Healey never even mentioned fixing up a line with the Post Office. If there'd been any chance of developments he'd have asked us to put a man on all night. All he said was "The Governor will get the last word before the night's out." That means only one thing. Go ahead.

(Warders Regan and Crimmin come out with Prisoners A B C and D.)

WARDER REGAN. Working party all correct, sir. Come on, get those boards off. Bottom out a couple more feet and leave the clay at the top, nice and neat.

CHIEF. Oh, Mr. Regan.

WARDER REGAN. Take over, Mr. Crimmin.

CHIEF. Mr. Regan. All I was going to say was—why don't you take yourself a bit of a rest while these fellows are at work on the grave. It's a long old pull till eight tomorrow morning.

WARDER REGAN. Thank you, sir.

CHIEF. Don't mention it. I'll see you before you go down to the cell. Get yourself a bit of a smoke, in the hospital. Don't forget now.

(He and Warder Donelly go back in.)

WARDER REGAN. Mr. Crimmin. The Chief, a decent man, he's after giving us his kind permission to go into hospital and have a sit down and a smoke for ourselves when these fellows have the work started. He knew we'd go in anyway, so he saw the chance of being floochalach,[137] at no

---

136. **elected** home free, finished, successful   137. **floochalach** generous (Ir. *flaithiúlach*)

expense to the management. Here *(takes out a packet of cigarettes, and takes some from it)*, here's a few fags for the lads.

CRIMMIN. I'll give them some of mine too.

WARDER REGAN. Don't do anything of the sort. One each is enough, you can slip them a couple when they're going to be locked up, if you like, but if these fellows had two fags each, they'd not work at all but spend the time out here blowing smoke rings in the evening air like lords. I'll slip in now, you come in after me. Tell them not to have them in their mouths if the Chief or the Governor comes out.

(He goes up the steps to the hospital.)

CRIMMIN *(calls Prisoner C)*. Hey!

PRISONER C *(comes to him)*. Seadh a Thomáis?[138]

CRIMMIN *(gives him cigarettes and matches)*. Seo, cúpla toitín. Táim fhéin is an screw eile ag dul isteach chuig an oispeadéal, nóiméat. Roinn amach na toitíní siúd, is glacfhaidh sibh gal. Má thagann an Governor nó'n Chief nó an Principal, ná bíodh in bhur mbéil agaibh iad. A' tuigeann tú?[139]

PRISONER C. Tuigim, a Thomáis, go raibh maith agat.[140]

CRIMMIN *(officially)*. Right, now get back to your work.

PRISONER C. Yes, sir.

(Crimmin goes up the hospital steps.)

PRISONER C. He gave me some cigarettes.

(Prisoner D has gone straight to the grave, Prisoner B is near it.)

PRISONER A. May I never dig a grave for less! You two get on and do a bit of digging while we have a quiet burn, then we'll take over.

PRISONER C. He said to watch out for the chief and them.

PRISONER B. Pass down a light to your man. He says he'd enjoy it better down there, where he can't be seen! Decent of him and Regan wasn't it?

PRISONER A. They'd have you dead from decency. That same Regan was like a savage in the bag shop today, you couldn't get a word to the fellow next to you.

PRISONER C. I never saw him like that before.

PRISONER B. He's always the same at a time like this, hanging seems to get on his nerves.

PRISONER A. Why should he worry, he won't feel it.

---

138. **Seadh a Thomáis** Yes, Thomas? (Ir.) 139. **Seo, cúpla toitín . . . tuigeann tú?** Here, a couple of cigarettes. Myself and the other screw are going in to the hospital for a minute. Divide out these cigarettes, and you will have a smoke. If the Governor or the Principal arrives, let you not have them in your mouths. Do you understand? (Ir.) 140. **Tuigim, a Thomáis, go raibh maith agat** I understand, Thomas, thanks. (Ir.)

PRISONER B. He's on the last watch. Twelve till eight.

PRISONER A. Till death do us part.

PRISONER C. The quare fellow asked for him, didn't he?

PRISONER A. They all do.

PRISONER C. He asked to have Mr. Crimmin too.

PRISONER A. It'll break that young screw up, and him only a wet day in the place.

PRISONER B. Funny the way they all ask for Regan. Perhaps they think he'll bring them good luck, him being good living.

PRISONER A. Good living! Whoever heard of a good living screw? Did you never hear of the screw, married the prostitute?

PRISONER B. No, what happened to him?

PRISONER A. He dragged her down to his own level.

PRISONER B. He told me once that if I kept off the beer I need never come back here. I asked him what about himself, and he told me he was terrible hardened to it and would I pray for him.

PRISONER C. When I was over in the Juveniles he used to talk like that to us. He said that the Blessed Virgin knew us better than the police or the judges—or ourselves even. We might think we were terrible sinners but she knew we were good boys only a bit wild . . .

PRISONER A. Bloody mad he is.

PRISONER C. And that we were doing penance here for the men who took us up, especially the judges, they being mostly rich old men with great opportunity for vice.

(Prisoner D appears from the grave.)

PRISONER A. The dead arose and appeared to many.

(Prisoner A goes and rearranges the work which Prisoner D has upset.)

PRISONER B. What's brought you out of your fox hole?[141]

PRISONER D. I thought it more discreet to remain in concealment while I smoked but I could not stop down there listening to talk like that, as a ratepayer, I couldn't stand for it, especially those libellous remarks about the judiciary.

(He looks accusingly at the boy.)

PRISONER C. I was only repeating what Mr. Regan said, sir.

PRISONER D. He could be taken up[142] for it. According to that man, there should be no such thing as law and order. We could all be murdered in our beds, the innocent prey of every ruffian that took it into his head to appropriate our goods, our lives even. Property must have security! What do you think society would come to without police and judges and suitable punishments? Chaos! In my opinion hanging's too good for 'em.

141. **fox hole** protective hole in the ground (military) 142. **taken up** arrested

PRISONER C. Oh, Mr. Regan doesn't believe in capital punishment, sir.

PRISONER D. My God, the man's an atheist! He should be dismissed from the public service. I shall take it up with the Minister when I get out of here. I went to school with his cousin.

PRISONER A. Who the hell does he think he is, a bloody high court judge?

PRISONER D. Chaos!

PRISONER B. He's in for embezzlement, there were two suicides and a bye-election[143] over him.

PRISONER D. There are still a few of us who care about the state of the country, you know. My family's national tradition goes back to the Land War.[144] Grandfather did four weeks for incitement to mutiny[145]— and we've never looked back since. One of my young nephews, as a matter of fact, has just gone over to Sandhurst.[146]

PRISONER B. Isn't that where you done your four years?

PRISONER A. No, that was Parkhurst.

PRISONER C *(to others)*. A college educated man in here, funny, isn't it?

PRISONER D. I shall certainly bring all my influence to bear to settle this Regan fellow.

PRISONER C. You must be a very important man, sir.

PRISONER D. I am one of the Cashel Carrolls, my boy, related on my mother's side to the Killens of Killcock.[147]

PRISONER B. Used to wash for our family.

PRISONER C. Go bhfóiridh Dia 'rainn.

PRISONER D. Irish speaking?

PRISONER C. Yes, sir.

PRISONER D. Then it might interest you to know that I took my gold medal[148] in Irish.

PRISONER C. Does that mean he speaks Irish?

PRISONER D. Of course.

PRISONER C. Oh sir. Tá Gaeilge go leor agamsa. Ó'n gcliabháin amach, sir.[149]

PRISONER B. That's fixed you.

PRISONER D. Quite. Tuigim tú.[150]

143. **bye-election** single-constituency election   144. **Land War** in the 1880s, the struggle between the Land League and the landlords for agrarian reform   145. **incitement to mutiny** apparently an officer in the British Army with Irish nationalist sympathies   146. **Sandhurst** Royal Military College   147. **Cashel Carrolls . . . Killens of Killcock** absurdly pretentious pedigree   148. **gold medal** university award   149. **Tá Gaeilge go leor agamsa. Ó'n gliabháin amach** I have Irish galore. From the cradle up. (Ir.)   150. **Tuigim tú** I understand you. (Ir.)

PRISONER B. The young lad's from Kerry,[151] from an island where they don't speak much else.

PRISONER D. Kerry? Well of course you speak with a different dialect to the one I was taught.

PRISONER B. The young screw Crimmin's from the same place. He sneaks up to the landing sometimes when the other screws aren't watching and there they are for hours talking through the spy hole, all in Irish.

PRISONER D. Most irregular.

PRISONER B. There's not much harm in it.

PRISONER D. How can there be proper discipline between warder and prisoner with that kind of familiarity?

PRISONER C. He does only be giving me the news from home and who's gone to America or England; he's not long up here and neither am I . . . the two of us do each be as lonely as the other.

PRISONER B. The lad here sings an old song sometimes. It's very nice. It makes the night less lonely, each man alone and sad maybe in the old cell. The quare fellow heard him singing and after he was sentenced to death he sent over word he'd be listening every night around midnight for him.

PRISONER A. You'd better make a big effort tonight, kid, for his last concert.

PRISONER C. Ah, God help him! Sure, you'd pity him all the same. It must be awful to die at the end of a swinging rope and a black hood over his poor face.

PRISONER A. Begod, he's not being topped for nothing—to cut his own brother up and butcher him like a pig.

PRISONER D. I must heartily agree with you sir, a barbarian if ever there was one.

PRISONER C. Maybe he did those things, but God help him this minute and he knowing this night his last on earth. Waiting over there he is, to be shaken out of his sleep and rushed to the rope.

PRISONER A. What sleep will he take? They won't have to set the alarm clock for a quarter to eight, you can bet your life on that.

PRISONER C. May he find peace on the other side.

PRISONER A. Or his brother waiting to have a word with him about being quartered in such an unmannerly fashion.

PRISONER C. None of us can know for certain.

PRISONER D. It was proved in a court of law that this man had experience as a pork butcher and put his expert knowledge to use by killing his brother with an axe and dismembering the body, the better to dispose of it.

151. **Kerry** county in the extreme southwest

PRISONER C. Go bfóiridh. Dia 'rainn.

PRISONER A. I wouldn't put much to the court of law part of it, but I heard about it myself from a fellow in from his part of the country. He said he had the brother strung up in an outhouse like a pig.

PRISONER D. Actually he was bleeding him into a farmhouse vessel according to the evidence. He should be hung three or four times over.

PRISONER A. Seeing your uncle was at school with the President's granny, perhaps he could fix it up for you.

PRISONER C. I don't believe he is a bad man. When I was on remand he used to walk around with me at exercise every day and he was sad when I told him about my brother, who died in the Yank's army, and my father, who was buried alive at the demolition of Manchester.[152] . . . He was great company for me who knew no one, only jackeens[153] would be making game of[154] me, and I'm sorry for him.

PRISONER A. Sure, it's a terrible pity about you and him. Maybe the jackeens should spread out the red carpet for you and every other bog barbarian that comes into the place.

(He moves away irritably.)

Let's get a bit more off this bloody hole.

PRISONER B. Nick. Nick.

WARDER REGAN *(entering with Crimmin)*. I've been watching you for the last ten minutes and damn the thing you've done except yap, yap, yap the whole time. The Chief or the Governor or any of them could have been watching you. They'd have thought it was a bloody mothers' meeting. What with you and my other bald mahogany gas pipe here.

PRISONER D. We were merely exchanging a few comments, sir.

WARDER REGAN. That's a lie and it's not worth a lie.

PRISONER A. All right! So we were caught talking at labour. I didn't ask to be an undertaker's assistant. Go on, bang me inside and case me in the morning! Let the Governor give me three days of Number 1.

WARDER REGAN. Much that'd worry you.

PRISONER A. You're dead right.

WARDER REGAN. Don't be such a bloody big baby. We all know you're a hard case. Where did you do your lagging? On the bog?

PRISONER A. I did not. Two laggings I done! At Parkhurst and on the Moor.

WARDER REGAN. There's the national inferiority complex for you. Our own Irish cat-o'-nine-tails[155] and the batons of the warders loaded with lead from Carrick mines aren't good enough for him. He has to go Dart-

---

152. **the demolition of Manchester** in World War II bombing 153. **jackeens** Dublin city slickers 154. **making game of** mocking 155. **cat-o'-nine-tails** lash used to flog prisoners

mooring and Parkhursting it. It's a wonder you didn't go further while you were at it, to Sing Sing[156] or Devil's Island.[157]

PRISONER A *(stung)*. I'm not here to be made a mock of, whether I done a lagging in England or not.

WARDER REGAN. Who said a word about it, only yourself—doing the returned Yank in front of these other fellows? Look, the quare fellow's got to be buried in the morning, whether we like it or not, so cut the mullarkey and get back to work.

PRISONER A. I don't let anyone make game of me!

WARDER REGAN. Well, what are you going to do about it? Complain to Holy Healey's department? He's a fine bloody imposter, isn't he? Like an old I.R.A.[158] man with a good agency in the Sweep[159] now. Recommend me to the respectable people! Drop it for Christ's sake, man. It's a bad night for all of us. Fine job, isn't it, for a young fellow like him, fresh from his mother's apron strings. You haven't forgotten what it's like to come from a decent home, have you, with the family rosary[160] said every night?

PRISONER A. I haven't any time for that kind of gab. I never saw religion do anything but back up the screws. I was in Walton last Christmas Eve, when the clergyman came to visit a young lad that had been given eighteen strokes of the cat that morning. When the kid stopped moaning long enough to hear what he had to say, he was told to think on the Lord's sufferings, then the cell door closed with a bang, leaving a smell of booze that would have tripped you up.

(He takes a look at the quare fellow's side of the stage and, muttering to himself, goes back to work.)

WARDER REGAN. You should pray for a man hardened in drink. Get back to it, all of you, and get that work a bit more advanced. Myself and Crimmin here have a long night ahead of us; we don't want to be finishing off your jobs for you.

(They get into the grave.)

PRISONER A. I never seen a screw like that before.

PRISONER B. Neither did anyone else.

(They work.)

CRIMMIN. What time is it, sir?

WARDER REGAN. Ten to seven.

CRIMMIN. Is himself[161] here yet?

WARDER REGAN. Yes, he came by last night's boat.[162] He's nervous of

---

156. **Sing Sing** New York prison   157. **Devil's Island** penal settlement in French Guiana   158. **old I.R.A.** veteran of Irish War of Independence   159. **agency in the Sweep** position in the Irish national lottery   160. **family rosary** traditional family prayer consisting of a circuit of sixty Hail Marys and other prayers   161. **himself** the hangman   162. **night's boat** from England

the 'plane, says it isn't natural. He'll be about soon. He's been having a sleep after the trip. We'll have to wait till he's measured the quare fellow for the drop, then we can go off till twelve.

CRIMMIN. Good.

WARDER REGAN. And for Christ's sake try to look a bit more cheerful when you come back on.

CRIMMIN. I've never seen anyone die, Mr. Regan.

WARDER REGAN. Of course, I'm a callous savage that's used to it.

CRIMMIN. I didn't mean that.

WARDER REGAN. I don't like it now any more than I did the first time.

CRIMMIN. No sir.

WARDER REGAN. It was a little Protestant lad, the first time; he asked if he could be walked backwards into the hanghouse so as he wouldn't see the rope.

CRIMMIN. God forgive them.

WARDER REGAN. May He forgive us all. The young clergyman that was on asked if the prison chaplain could accompany him; it was his first hanging too. I went to the Canon to ask him, a fine big man he was. "Regan," he says, "I thought I was going to escape it this time, but you never escape. I don't suppose neither of us ever will. Ah well," he says, "maybe being hung twenty times will get me out of purgatory[163] a minute or two sooner."

CRIMMIN. Amen, a Thighearna Dhia.[164]

WARDER REGAN. The young clergyman was great; he read a bit of the Bible to the little Protestant lad while they waited and he came in with him, holding his hand and telling him, in their way, to lean on God's mercy that was stronger than the power of men. I walked beside them and guided the boy on to the trap and under the beam. The rope was put round him and the washer under his ear and the hood pulled over his face. And still the young clergyman called out to him, in a grand steady voice, in through the hood: "I declare to you, my living Christ this night . . ." and he stroked his head till he went down. Then he fainted; the Canon and myself had to carry him out to the Governor's office.

(A pause. We are aware of the men working at the grave.)

WARDER REGAN. The quare fellow asked for you especially, Crimmin; he wanted you because you're a young lad, not yet practised in badness. You'll be a consolation to him in the morning when he's surrounded by a crowd of bigger bloody ruffians than himself, if the truth were but told. He's depending on you, and you're going to do your best for him.

CRIMMIN. Yes, Mr. Regan.

(Regan walks to the grave.)

163. **purgatory** place of temporary punishment in the afterlife   164. **a Thighearna Dhia** O Lord God (Ir.)

WARDER REGAN. How's it going?

PRISONER A. Just about done, sir.

WARDER REGAN. All right, you can leave it.

(They get up.)

WARDER REGAN. Leave your shovels; you'll be wanting them in the morning. Go and tell the warder they've finished, Mr. Crimmin. I'll turn them over.

(He searches the Prisoners, finds a cigarette end on A and sniffs it.)

Coffin nail. Most appropriate. *(He goes towards exit and calls.)* You needn't bother searching them, sir. I've turned them over.

PRISONER A *(aside)*. He's as mad as a coot.[165]

PRISONER C. But charitable.

WARDER REGAN. Right, lead on there!

PRISONER D. This is no place for charity, on the taxpayers' money.

PRISONER A. Take it up with your uncle when you get back into your stockbroker's trousers.

WARDER REGAN. Silence. Right, sir, working party off.

(As the Prisoners march off, the Hangman comes slowly down the steps.)

CRIMMIN. Is this . . .

WARDER REGAN. Himself.

HANGMAN. It's Mr. Regan, isn't it? Well, as the girl said to the soldier "Here we are again."

WARDER REGAN. Nice evening. I hope you had a good crossing.

HANGMAN. Not bad. It's nice to get over to old Ireland you know, a nice bit of steak and a couple of pints as soon as you get off the boat. Well, you'll be wanting to knock off, won't you? I'll just pop down and have a look, then you can knock off.

WARDER REGAN. We were just waiting for you.

HANGMAN. This young man coming with us in the morning?

CRIMMIN. Yes, sir.

HANGMAN. Lend us your cap a minute, lad.

CRIMMIN. I don't think it would fit you, sir.

HANGMAN. We don't have to be so particular. Mr. Regan's will do. It ought to fit me by this time, and he won't catch cold the time I'll be away.

(He goes out.)

CRIMMIN. What does he want the cap for?

WARDER REGAN. He gets the quare fellow's weight from the doctor so as he'll know what drop to give him, but he likes to have a look at him as well, to see what build he is, how thick his neck is, and so on. He says he can judge better with the eye. If he gave him too much one way he'd strangle him instead of breaking his neck, and too much the other way he'd pull the head clean off his shoulders.

---

165. **coot** a diving bird with apparently erratic movements

CRIMMIN. Go bhfóiridh Dia 'rainn.

WARDER REGAN. You should have lent him your cap. When he lifts the corner of the spy-hole all the quare fellow can see is the peak of a warder's cap. It could be you or me or anyone looking at him. Himself has no more to do with it than you or I or the people that pay us, and that's every man or woman that pays taxes or votes in elections. If they don't like it, they needn't have it.

(The Hangman comes back.)

HANGMAN. Well set up lad. Twelve stone,[166] fine pair of shoulders on him. Well, I expect you'll give us a call this evening over at the hospital. I'm in my usual apartment. This young man is very welcome, too, if he wants to join the company.

WARDER REGAN. Right, sir.

HANGMAN. See you later.

(He goes out.)

WARDER REGAN. Right, Crimmin. Twelve o'clock and look lively. The quare fellow's got enough on his plate without putting him in the blue jigs altogether. As the old Home Office memorandum says "An air of cheerful decorum is indicated, as a readiness to play such games as draughts, ludo, or snakes and ladders;[167] a readiness to enter into conversations on sporting topics will also be appreciated."

CRIMMIN. Yes, sir.

WARDER REGAN *(as they go)*. And, Crimmin, . . .

CRIMMIN. Yes, sir?

WARDER REGAN. Take off your watch.

(They go out.)

NEIGHBOUR *(from his cell)*. Hey, Dunlavin. Don't forget that Sunday bacon. The bet stands. They're after being at the grave. I just heard them. Dunlavin, do you hear me?

PRISONER A. Get down on your bed, you old Anti-Christ. You sound like something in a week-end pass out of Hell.

ENGLISH PRISONER. Hey, you bloke that's going out in the morning. Don't forget to see my chiner and get him to bail me out.

NEIGHBOUR. Get a bucket and bail yourself out.

SONG.

> The day was dying and the wind was sighing,
> As I lay crying in my prison cell,
> And the old triangle
> Went jingle jangle
> Along the banks of the Royal Canal.

THE CURTAIN FALLS

166. **stone** fourteen pounds   167. **ludo, or snakes and ladders** parlor games of chance

ACT 3

SCENE I

Later the same night. Cell windows lit. A blue lamp in the courtyard. A faint tapping is heard intermittently.

(As the curtain rises, two Warders are seen. One is Donelly, the other a fellow new to the job.)

WARDER 1. Watch the match.

WARDER 2. Sorry.

WARDER 1. We're all right for a couple of minutes, the Chief 'll have plenty to worry him tonight; he's not likely to be prowling about.

WARDER 2. Hell of a job, night patrol, at any time.

WARDER 1. We're supposed to pass each cell every half-hour tonight, but what's the use? Listen to 'em.

(The tapping can be distinctly heard.)

WARDER 2. Yap, yap, yap. It's a wonder the bloody old hot-water pipes aren't worn through.

(Tapping.)

WARDER 1. Damn it all, they've been yapping in association since seven o'clock.

(Tapping.)

WARDER 2. Will I go round the landings[168] and see who it is?

WARDER 1. See who it is? Listen!

WARDER 2. Do you think I should go?

WARDER 1. Stay where you are and get yourself a bit of a burn. Devil a bit of use it'd be anyway. As soon as you lifted the first spy-hole, the next fellow would have heard you and passed it on to the whole landing. Mind the cigarette, keep it covered. Have you ever been in one of these before?

WARDER 2. No.

WARDER 1. They'll be at it from six o'clock tomorrow morning, and when it comes a quarter to eight it'll be like a running commentary in the Grand National.[169]

(Tapping.)

WARDER 1 *(quietly)*. Shut your bloody row! And then the screeches and roars of them when his time comes. They say it's the last thing the fellow hears.

168. **landings** platforms between flights of stairs   169. **Grand National** annual British horserace

(Tapping dies down.)

WARDER 2. Talk about something else.

(Tapping.)

WARDER 1. They're quietening down a bit. You'd think they'd be in the humour for a read or a sleep, wouldn't you?

WARDER 2. It's a hell of a job.

WARDER 1. We're in it for the three P's, boy, pay, promotion and pension, that's all that should bother civil servants like us.

WARDER 2. You're quite right.

WARDER 1. And without doing the sergeant major on you, I'm senior man of us two, isn't that right, now?

WARDER 2. I know what you mean.

WARDER 1. Well, neither bragging nor boasting—God gives us the brains and no credit to ourselves—I think I might speak to you as a senior man, if you didn't mind.

WARDER 2. Not at all. Any tip you could give me I'd be only too grateful for it. Sure it'd only be a thick wouldn't improve his knowledge when an older man would be willing to tell him something that would be of benefit to him in his career.

WARDER 1. Well now, would I be right in saying that you've no landing of your own?

WARDER 2. Quite right, quite right. I'm only on here, there or any old where when you or any other senior man is wanting me.

WARDER 1. Well, facts is facts and must be faced. We must all creep before we can walk, as the man said; but I may as well tell you straight, what I told the Principal about you.

WARDER 2. Tell me face to face. If it's fault you found in me I'd as lief hear it from me friend as from me enemy.

WARDER 1. It was no fault I found in you. If I couldn't do a man a good turn—I'd be sorry to do him a bad one.

WARDER 2. Ah, sure I know that.

WARDER 1. What I said to the Principal about you was: that you could easily handle a landing of your own. If it happened that one was left vacant. And I don't think I'm giving official information away, when I say that such a vacancy may occur in the near future. Before the month is out. Have you me?

WARDER 2. I have you, and I'm more than grateful to you. But sure I'd expect no less from you. You're all nature.

WARDER 1. It might happen that our Principal was going to the Bog on promotion, and it might happen that a certain senior officer would be promoted in his place.

WARDER 2. Ah, no.

WARDER 1. But ah, yes.

WARDER 2. But there's no one in the prison but'd be delighted to serve under you. You've such a way with you. Even with the prisoners.

WARDER 1. Well, I hope I can do my best by me fellow men, and that's the most any can hope to do, barring a double-dyed bloody hypocrite like a certain party we needn't mention. Well, him and me have equal service and it's only the one of us can be made Principal, and I'm damn sure they're not going to appoint a half-lunatic that goes round asking murderers to pray for him.

WARDER 2. Certainly they're not, unless they're bloody-well half-mad themselves.

WARDER 1. And I think they know him as well as we do.

WARDER 2. Except the Canon, poor man; he has him well recommended.

WARDER 1. You can leave out the "poor man" part of it. God forgive me and I renounce the sin of it, the Lord says "touch not my anointed," but the Canon is a bloody sight worse than himself, if you knew only the half of it.

WARDER 2. Go to God.

WARDER 1. Right, I'll tell you now. He was silenced[170] for something before he came here and this is the *only* job he can get. Something terrible he did, though God forgive us, maybe it's not right to talk of it.

WARDER 2. You might sing it.

WARDER 1. I hear it was the way that he made the housekeeper take a girl into the house, the priest's house, to have a baby, an illegitimate!

WARDER 2. And could a man like that be fit to be a priest!

WARDER 1. He'd hardly be fit to be a prison chaplain, even. Here's the Chief or one of them coming. Get inside quick and let on you're looking for them fellows talking on the hot-water pipes, and not a word about what I said. That's between ourselves.

WARDER 2. Ah sure I know that's under foot.[171] Thanks anyway.

WARDER 1. You're more than welcome. Don't be surprised if you get your landing sooner than you expected. Thirty cells all to yourself before you're fifty.

WARDER 2. I'll have the sister's children pray for you.

(Enter Chief Warder.)

WARDER 1. All correct, sir.

CHIEF. What the hell do you mean, "All correct, sir"? I've been watching you this half-hour yapping away to that other fellow.

WARDER 1. There were men communicating on the hot-water pipes, sir, and I told him ten times if I told him once to go inside the landing and see who it was; it's my opinion, sir, the man is a bit thick.

---

170. **silenced** forbidden to preach publicly   171. **under foot** going on

CHIEF. It's your opinion. Well, you're that thick yourself you ought to be a fair judge. And who the bloody hell are you to tell anyone to do anything? You're on night patrol the same as what he is.

WARDER 1. I thought, sir, on account of the night that's in it.

CHIEF. Why, is it Christmas? Listen here, that there is an execution in the morning is nothing to do with you. It's not your job to care, and a good job too, or you'd probably trip over the rope and fall through the bloody trap. What business have you out here, anyway?

WARDER 1. I thought I had to patrol by the grave, sir.

CHIEF. Afraid somebody might pinch it? True enough, this place is that full of thieves, you can leave nothing out of your hand. Get inside and resume your patrol. If you weren't one of the old hands I'd report you to the Governor. Get along with you and we'll forget about it.

WARDER 1. Very good, sir, and thank you, sir.

(Tapping.)

CHIEF. And stop that tapping on the pipes.

WARDER 1. I will, sir, and thanks again, sir.

(First Warder salutes, goes up the steps to the prison gates, which open. The Governor comes in in evening dress. The First Warder comes sharply to attention, salutes and goes off. The Governor continues down the steps and over to the Chief Warder.)

CHIEF. All correct, sir.

GOVERNOR. Good. We had final word about the reprieve this afternoon. But you know how these things are, Chief, hoping for last-minute developments. I must say I should have been more than surprised had the Minister made a recommendation. I'll go down and see him before the Canon comes in. It makes them more settled for confession when they know there is absolutely no hope. How is he?

CHIEF. Very well, sir. Sitting by the fire and chatting to the warders. He says he might go to bed after he sees the priest.

GOVERNOR. You'll see that there's a good breakfast for himself and the two assistants?

CHIEF. Oh, yes, sir, he's very particular about having two rashers and eggs. Last time they were here, some hungry pig ate half his breakfast and he kicked up murder.

GOVERNOR. See it doesn't happen this time.

CHIEF. No indeed. There's a fellow under sentence of death next week in the Crumlin;[172] we don't want him going up to Belfast and saying we starved him.

GOVERNOR. Have they come back from town yet?

CHIEF *(looks at his watch)*. It's after closing time. I don't expect they'll

172. **the Crumlin** Crumlin Road Gaol, Belfast

be long now. I put Clancy on the side gate to let them in. After he took the quare fellow's measurements he went over to the place he drinks in. Some pub at the top of Grafton Street. I believe he's the life of the bar there, sir; the customers think he's an English traveller. The publican knows who he is, but then they're both in the pub business, and sure that's as tight a trade as hanging.

GOVERNOR. I suppose his work here makes him philosophical, and they say that drink is the comfort of the philosophers.

CHIEF. I wouldn't doubt but you'd be right there, sir. But he told me himself he only takes a drink when he's on a job. The rest of the time he's serving behind his own bar.

GOVERNOR. Is Jenkinson with him?

CHIEF. Yes, sir. He likes to have him with him, in case he gets a bit jarred. Once he went straight from the boat to the pubs and spent the day in them, and when he got here wasn't he after leaving the black box with his rope and his washers and his other little odds and ends behind him in a pub and forgot which one it was he left them in.

GOVERNOR. Really.

CHIEF. You could sing it. You were in Limerick at the time, sir, but here we were, in a desperate state. An execution coming off in the morning and we without the black box that had all his tools in it. The Governor we had then, he promised a novena to St. Anthony[173] and two insertions in the *Messenger*[174] if they were found in time. And sure enough after squad cars were all over in the city, the box was got in a pub down the North Wall,[175] the first one he went into. It shows you the power of prayer, sir.

GOVERNOR. Yes, I see what you mean.

CHIEF. So now he always brings Jenkinson with him. You see, Jenkinson takes nothing, being very good living. A street preacher he is, for the Methodists or something. Himself prefers T.T.s.[176] He had an Irishman from Clare helping one time, but he sacked him over the drink. In this Circus, he said, there's only one allowed to drink and that's the Ringmaster.

GOVERNOR. We advertised for a native hangman during the Economic War. Must be fluent Irish speaker. Cailíoctaí de réir Meamram V. aSeacht.[177] There were no suitable applicants.

CHIEF. By the way, sir, I must tell you that the warders on night patrol were out here conversing, instead of going round the landings.

GOVERNOR. Remind me to make a note of it tomorrow.

173. **a novena to St. Anthony** a campaign of prayer to the patron of lost objects 174. **insertions in the *Messenger*** notices of thanksgiving in *The Sacred Heart Messenger,* a pious periodical 175. **North Wall** in Dublin's dockland 176. **T.T.s** teetotalers 177. **Cailíoctaí de réir Meamram V. a Seacht** Qualifications in accordance with Memorandum Seven (Ir.)

CHIEF. I will, sir, and I think I ought to tell you that I heard the principal warder make a joke about the execution.

GOVERNOR. Good God, this sort of thing is getting out of hand. I was at my School Union[178] this evening. I had to leave in sheer embarrassment; supposedly witty remarks made to me at my own table. My eldest son was furious with me for going at all. He was at a table with a crowd from the University. They were even worse. One young pup went so far as to ask him if he thought I would oblige with a rendering of "The night before Larry was stretched."[179] I shall certainly tell the Principal that there's at least one place in this city where an execution is taken very seriously indeed. Good night to you.

CHIEF. Good night, sir.

(Tapping. The Chief Warder walks up and down. Regan enters.)

Ah, Mr. Regan, the other man coming along?

WARDER REGAN. He'll be along in a minute.

CHIEF. I don't know what we'd do without you, Regan, on these jobs. Is there anything the Governor or I could do to make things easier?

WARDER REGAN. You could say a decade of the rosary.

CHIEF. I could hardly ask the Governor to do that.

WARDER REGAN. His prayers would be as good as anyone else's.

CHIEF. Is there anything on the practical side we could send down?

WARDER REGAN. A bottle of malt.

CHIEF. Do you think he'd drink it?

WARDER REGAN. No, but I would.

CHIEF. Regan, I'm surprised at you.

WARDER REGAN. I was reared among people that drank at a death or prayed. Some did both. You think the law makes this man's death someway different, not like anyone else's. Your own, for instance.

CHIEF. I wasn't found guilty of murder.

WARDER REGAN. No, nor no one is going to jump on you in the morning and throttle the life out of you, but it's not him I'm thinking of. It's myself. And you're not going to give me that stuff about just shoving over the lever and bob's your uncle.[180] You forget the times the fellow gets caught and has to be kicked off the edge of the trap hole. You never heard of the warders down below swinging on his legs the better to break his neck, or jumping on his back when the drop was too short.

CHIEF. Mr. Regan, I'm surprised at you.

WARDER REGAN. That's the second time tonight.

(Tapping. Enter Crimmin.)

---

178. **School Union** alumni association dinner   179. **"The night before Larry was stretched"** eighteenth-century Dublin streetsong on the subject of hanging   180. **bob's your uncle** you're a winner

CRIMMIN. All correct, sir.

CHIEF. Regan, I hope you'll forget those things you mentioned just now. If talk the like of that got outside the prison . . .

WARDER REGAN (*almost shouts*). I think the whole show should be put on in Croke Park;[181] after all, it's at the public expense and they let it go on. They should have something more for their money than a bit of paper stuck up on the gate.

CHIEF. Good night, Regan. If I didn't know you, I'd report what you said to the Governor.

WARDER REGAN. You will anyway.

WARDER REGAN (*to Crimmin*). Crimmin, there you are. I'm going into the hospital to fix up some supper for us. An empty sack won't stand, as the man said, nor a full one won't bend.

(*He goes. Crimmin strolls. Traffic is heard in the distance, drowning the tapping. A drunken crowd are heard singing. Donelly and the New Warder appear in the darkness.*)

WARDER 1. Is that young Mr. Crimmin?

CRIMMIN. Yes, it's me.

WARDER 1. You've a desperate job for a young warder this night. But I'll tell you one thing, you've a great man with you. Myself and this other man here are only after being talking about him.

WARDER 2. That's right, so we were. A grand man and very good living.

WARDER 1. There's someone coming. Too fine a night to be indoors. Goodnight, Mr. Crimmin.

CRIMMIN. Good night, sir.

WARDER 1 (*as they go off*). Come on, let's get a sup of tea.

(*Crimmin waits. Tapping heard. Warder Regan reenters.*)

WARDER REGAN. Supper's fixed. It's a fine clear night. Do you hear the buses? Fellows leaving their mot's home, after the pictures or coming from dances, and a few old fellows well jarred but half sober for fear of what herself will say when they get in the door. Only a hundred yards up there on the bridge, and it might as well be a hundred miles away. Here they are back from the pub.

(*Voices are heard in the dark approaching. Enter Hangman and Jenkinson.*)

HANGMAN (*sings*).

> She was lovely and fair like the rose of the summer,
> Though 'twas not her beauty alone that won me,
> Oh, no, 'twas the truth in her eyes ever shining,
> That made me love Mary the Rose of Tralee.[182]

181. **Croke Park** Gaelic athletic stadium   182. **"Rose of Tralee"** sentimental Irish love song

Don't see any signs of Regan.

JENKINSON. He's probably had to go on duty. You've left it too late.

HANGMAN. Well, if the mountain won't come to M'ammed then the M'ammed must go to the mountain.

WARDER REGAN (*from the darkness*). As the girl said to the soldier.

HANGMAN. As the girl said to the soldier. Oh, it's you, Regan. Will you have a drink?

WARDER REGAN. I'm afraid we've got to be off now.

HANGMAN. Never mind off now. Have one with me. It's a pleasure to see you again. We meet all too seldom. You have one with me. Adam, give him a bottle of stout.

(*He sings again.*)

> Oh, no, 'twas the truth in her eyes ever shining,
> That made me love Mary the Rose of Tralee.

Not bad for an old 'un. Lovely song, isn't it? Very religious though. "The Poor Christian Fountain."[183] I'm very fond of the old Irish songs; we get a lot of Irish in our place on a Saturday night, you know.

WARDER REGAN. Is it what they call a sporting pub?[184]

HANGMAN. That's just what it is, and an old sport behind the bar counter an' all. All the Irish come in, don't they, Adam?

JENKINSON (*gloomily*). Reckon they do. Perhaps because no one else would go in it.

HANGMAN. What do you mean? It's best beer in the district. Not that you could tell the difference.

WARDER REGAN. Good health.

HANGMAN. May we never do worse. (*To Jenkinson.*) You're in a right cut, aren't you, making out there's nobody but Irish coming into my pub? I've never wanted for friends. Do you know why? Because I'd go a 'undred mile to do a man a good turn. I've always tried to do my duty.

JENKINSON. And so have I.

HANGMAN. Do you remember the time I got out from a sickbed to 'ang a soldier at Strangeways,[185] when I thought you and Christmas 'adn't had enough experience?

JENKINSON. Aye, that's right enough.

HANGMAN. I'm not going to quarrel with you. Here, go and fetch your concertina[186] and sing 'em that hymn you composed.

(*Jenkinson hesitates.*)

HANGMAN. Go on. It's a grand tune, a real credit to you. Go on, lad.

---

183. **"The Poor Christian Fountain"** travesty of "pure crystal fountain" from "The Rose of Tralee"   184. **sporting pub** pub for the racing set   185. **Strangeways** in Lancashire   186. **concertina** small hexagonal reed instrument

JENKINSON. Well, only for the hymn, mind.

(He goes off to fetch it.)

WARDER REGAN. Sure, that's right.

HANGMAN. 'E's a good lad is our Adam, but 'e's down in the dumps at the moment. 'Im and Christmas, they used to sing on street corners with the Band of Holy Joy,[187] every Saturday night, concertina and all. But some of the lads found out who they were and started putting bits of rope in collection boxes; it's put them off outdoor testimony. But this 'ymn's very moving about hanging and mercy and so forth. Brings tears to your eyes to 'ear Adam and Christmas singing it.

(Jenkinson returns.)

JENKINSON. Right?

HANGMAN. Right.

JENKINSON *(sings)*.

> My brother, sit and think.
> While yet some time is left to thee
> Kneel to thy God who from thee does not shrink
> And lay thy sins on Him who died for thee.

HANGMAN. Take a fourteen-stone man as a basis and giving him a drop of eight foot . . .

JENKINSON.

> Men shrink from thee but not I,
> Come close to me I love my erring sheep.
> My blood can cleanse thy sins of blackest dye,
> I understand if thou canst only weep.

HANGMAN. Every half-stone lighter would require a two-inch longer drop, so for weight thirteen and a half stone—drop eight feet two inches, and for weight thirteen stone—drop eight feet four inches.

JENKINSON.

> Though thou hast grieved me sore,
> My arms of mercy are open wide,
> I still hold open Heaven's shining door
> Come then, take refuge in my wounded side.

HANGMAN. Now he's only twelve stone so he should have eight foot eight, but he's got a thick neck on him so I'd better give him another couple of inches. Yes, eight foot ten.

JENKINSON.

> Come now, the time is short.
> Longing to pardon and bless I wait.

187. **Band of Holy Joy** Salvation Army

Look up to me, my sheep so dearly bought
And say, forgive me, ere it is too late.

HANGMAN. Divide 412 by the weight of the body in stones, multiply
by two gives the length of the drop in inches. *(He looks up and seems
sobered.)* 'E's an R.C., I suppose, Mr. Regan? *(Puts book in his pocket.)*
WARDER REGAN. That's right.
HANGMAN. That's all, then. Good night.
JENKINSON. Good night.
WARDER REGAN. Good night. *(The Hangman and Jenkinson go off.)*
Thanks for the hymn. Great night for stars. If there's life on any of them,
I wonder do the same things happen up there? Maybe some warders on
a planet are walking across a prison yard this minute and some fellow up
there waiting on the rope in the morning, and looking out through the
bars, for a last look at our earth and the moon for the last time. Though
I never saw them to bother much about things like that. It's nearly always
letters to their wives or mothers, and then we don't send them—only
throw them into the grave after them. What'd be the sense of broadcasting
such distressful rubbish?
PRISONER C *(sings from his cell window)*. Is é fáth mo bhuartha na
bhfhaghaim cead chuarta.[188]
WARDER REGAN. Regular choir practice going on round here tonight.
CRIMMIN. He's singing for . . . for . . .
WARDER REGAN. For the quare fellow.
CRIMMIN. Yes. Why did the Englishman ask if he was a Catholic?
WARDER REGAN. So as they'd know to have the hood slit to anoint
him on the rope, and so as the fellows below would know to take off his
boots and socks for the holy oil on his feet[189] when he goes down.
PRISONER C *(sings)*. Níl gaoth adthuaidh ann. Níl sneachta cruaidh
ann[190] . . .
WARDER REGAN. We'd better be getting in. The other screws will be
hopping mad to get out; they've been there since four o'clock today.
PRISONER C *(sings)*. Mo mhúirnín bhán . . .[191]
(His song dies away and the empty stage is gradually lightened for)

SCENE 2

(The prison yard. It is morning.)
WARDER 1. How's the time?

188. **Is é fáth . . . chuarta** It is the cause of my sorrow that I have not permission
to visit (Ir. lovesong) 189. **holy oil on his feet** for the last rites 190. **Níl gaoth
adthuaidh ann. Níl sneachta cruaidh ann.** There is no north wind there. There
is no hard snow there. (Ir.) 191. **Mo mhúirnín bhán** My dear white darling (Ir.)

WARDER 2. Seven minutes.

WARDER 1. As soon as it goes five to eight they'll start. You'd think they were working with stop watches. I wish I was at home having my breakfast. How's the time?

WARDER 2. Just past six minutes.

MICKSER'S VOICE. Bail ó Dhia oraibh go léir a cháirde.[192]

WARDER 1. I knew it. That's that bloody Mickser. I'll fix him this time.

MICKSER'S VOICE. And we take you to the bottom of D Wing.

WARDER 1. You bastard, I'll give you D Wing.

MICKSER'S VOICE. We're ready for the start, and in good time, and who do I see lined up for the off but the High Sheriff of this ancient city of ours, famous in song and story as the place where the pig ate the whitewash brushes[193] and— *(The Warders remove their caps.)* We're off, in this order: the Governor, the Chief, two screws Regan and Crimmin, the quare fellow between them, two more screws and three runners from across the Channel, getting well in front, now the Canon. He's making a big effort for the last two furlongs. He's got the white pudding bag[194] on his head, just a short distance to go. He's in. *(A clock begins to chime the hour. Each quarter sounds louder.)* His feet to the chalk line. He'll be pinioned, his feet together. The bag will be pulled down over his face. The screws come off the trap and steady him. Himself goes to the lever and . . .

(The hour strikes. The Warders cross themselves and put on their caps. From the Prisoners comes a ferocious howling.)

PRISONERS. One off, one away, one off, one away.

WARDER 1. Shut up there.

WARDER 2. Shut up, shut up.

WARDER 1. I know your windows, I'll get you. Shut up.

(The noise dies down and at last ceases altogether.)

Now we'll go in and get that Mickser. *(Grimly.)* I'll soften his cough. Come on . . .

(Warder Regan comes out.)

WARDER REGAN. Give us a hand with this fellow.

WARDER 1. We're going after that Mickser.

WARDER REGAN. Never mind that now, give us a hand. He fainted when the trap was sprung.

WARDER 1. These young screws, not worth a light.

(They carry Crimmin across the yard.)

NEIGHBOUR'S VOICE. Dunlavin, that's a Sunday bacon you owe me. Your man was topped, wasn't he?

192. **Bail ó Dhia oraibh go léir a cháird** The blessing of God on all of you, my friends (Ir.)   193. **where the pig ate the whitewash brushes** a place of no consequence   194. **white pudding bag** a cloth bag used to package blood sausages

PRISONER A's VOICE. You won't be long after him.

DUNLAVIN'S VOICE. Don't mind him, Neighbour.

NEIGHBOUR'S VOICE. Don't you forget that bacon, Dunlavin.

DUNLAVIN'S VOICE. I forgot to tell you, Neighbour.

NEIGHBOUR'S VOICE. What did you forget to tell me?

ENGLISH VOICE. Where's the bloke what's going out this morning?

NEIGHBOUR'S VOICE. He's up in Nelly's room behind the clock. What about that bacon, Dunlavin?

ENGLISH VOICE. You bloke that's going out this morning, remember to see my chiner and tell him to 'ave me bailed out.

NEIGHBOUR'S VOICE. Get a bucket and bail yourself out. What about me bacon, Dunlavin?

ENGLISH VOICE. Sod[195] you and your bleeding bacon.

DUNLAVIN'S VOICE. Shut up a minute about your bail, till I tell Neighbour about his bet.

NEIGHBOUR'S VOICE. You lost it, that's all I know.

DUNLAVIN'S VOICE. Yes, but the doctor told me that me stomach was out of order; he's put me on a milk diet.

CHIEF *(comes through prison gates and looks up)*. Get down from those windows. Get down at once. *(He beckons inside and Prisoners A, B, C and D file past him and go down on the steps. Prisoner B is carrying a cold hammer and chisel.)* Hey, you there in front, have you the cold chisel and hammer?

PRISONER B. Yes, sir.

CHIEF. You other three, the shovels are where you left them; get to work there and clear the top and have it ready for filling it.

(They go on to the canvas, take up the shovels from behind and begin work. Prisoner B stands on the foot of the steps with his cold chisel while the Chief studies his paper to give final instructions.)

CHIEF. Yes, that's it. You're to carve E777. Got that?

PRISONER B. Yes, sir. E777.

CHIEF. That's it. It should be E779 according to the book, but a "7" is easier for you to do than a "9." Right, the stone in the wall that's nearest to the spot. Go ahead now. *(Raising his voice.)* There's the usual two bottles of stout a man, but only if you work fast.

WARDER 1. I know the worst fellow was making this noise, sir. It was Mickser, sir. I'm going in to case[196] him now. I'll take an hour's overtime to do it, sir.

CHIEF. You're a bit late. He was going out this morning and had his civilian clothing on in the cell. We were only waiting for this to be over to let him out.

195. **Sod** expletive   196. **case** to remove all furniture from cell and put on bread and water diet

WARDER 1. But . . . Sir, he was the whole cause.

CHIEF. Well, what do you want me to do, run down the Circular Road after him? He went out on remission. We could have stopped him. But you were too bloody slow for that.

WARDER 1. I was helping to carry . . .

CHIEF. You were helping to carry . . . Warders! I'd get better in Woolworths.

WARDER 2. To think of that dirty savage getting away like that. Shouting and a man going to his God.

WARDER 1. Never mind that part of it. He gave me lip in the woodyard[197] in '42, and I couldn't do anything because he was only on remand. I've been waiting years to get that fellow.

WARDER 2. Ah, well, you've one consolation. He'll be back.

(At the grave Prisoner A is the only one visible over the canvas.)

PRISONER B. Would you say that this was the stone in the wall nearest to it?

PRISONER A. It'll do well enough. It's only for the records. They're not likely to be digging him up to canonize him.

PRISONER B. Fair enough. E777.

(Regan drops the letters into the grave, and goes.)

PRISONER A. Give us them bloody letters. They're worth money to one of the Sunday papers.

PRISONER B. So I understood you to say yesterday.

PRISONER B. Well, give us them.

PRISONER D. They're not exclusively your property any more than anyone else's.

PRISONER B. There's no need to have a battle over them. Divide them. Anyone that likes can have my share and I suppose the same goes for the kid.

PRISONER D. Yes, we can act like businessmen. There are three. One each and toss for the third. I'm a businessman.

PRISONER A. Fair enough. Amn't I a businessman myself? For what's a crook, only a businessman without a shop.

PRISONER D. What side are you on? The blank side or the side with the address?

VOICE OF PRISONER BELOW *(singing).*

> In the female prison
> There are seventy women
> I wish it was with them that I did dwell,

197. **the woodyard** exercise or work area

Then that old triangle
Could jingle jangle
Along the banks of the Royal Canal.

THE CURTAIN FALLS

SAMUEL BECKETT

1906 –

When Samuel Beckett was awarded the Nobel Prize for Literature in 1969, the committee praised "a body of work that, in new forms of fiction and the theatre, has transmuted the destitution of modern man into his exaltation." His major original contribution to modern drama is his bold forging of a unity between the medium, the method, and the meaning of each work. Beckett has a disciplined, subtle and educated imagination, which takes a radical view of the relationship between the sounds, gestures and symbols of drama. Beckett's art arises out of the conflict between the prospect of metaphysical nihilism and the refusal to be dumbfounded: his successive works continue to generate provisional meaning out of experience which is at bottom absurd. In this way, despite the grim spiritual suffering which is its constant subject, Beckett's work—for its brilliance, its intellectuality, its humor, and its utter sincerity—is a defiant vindication of the human soul.

Samuel Barclay Beckett was born in Foxrock, Dublin, on Good Friday, April 13, 1906. From a financially secure professional family of Huguenot descent, he was educated at Portora Royal School and Trinity College, and graduated with distinction in French in 1927. Most of his life thereafter was spent in Paris, beginning as a *lecteur* at the École Normale Supérieure in 1928, continuing during the thirties as a bohemian poet, translator, and sometime assistant to James Joyce, and finally as a permanent resident in 1937. Apart from a brief period (1930–32) as a lecturer in French at Trinity College, his contact with Ireland has not exceeded occasional visits. During the occupation of France, Beckett was active in the Resistance, barely escaping into the countryside from a Gestapo dragnet. In the wake of D-Day, he served with the Irish Red Cross. For his valor, he was awarded the *Croix de Guerre*. Today, he lives quietly in Paris.

Beckett the writer was relatively unknown until the sensational *Waiting for Godot* was first produced in its original French, *En attendant Godot,* in January 1953. Ironically, when Beckett undertook it (at the end of 1948), he considered it a diversion from the more serious work of writing fiction. Before that, he had undertaken two plays—*Johnson Fantasy* and *Éleuthéria*—which so dissatisfied him that he abandoned them. But he had published a critical study of Proust (1931), a collection of short fiction, *More Pricks Than Kicks* (1934), and three novels, *Murphy* (1938), *Molloy* (1951), and *Malone meurt* (1951).

Since *Waiting for Godot,* Beckett has written numerous dramatic texts for stage, radio and screen, and fictional works of progressive conciseness. Throughout his creative career, Beckett chose to write many of his works in French, preferring the detachment and spareness it gave him over the emotional top-heaviness of his native English. These works reflect his wide reading in Western philosophy, religion and literature—Dante, Descartes, Geulincx, Schopenhauer, Jung—as well as his affinities with modern film and theatre—Chaplin, Artaud, and the anti-commercial French art theatre. Beckett's plays, in turn, have had wide influence on the serious drama of postwar Europe, in the existential "theatre of the absurd." Beckett's drama has several distinct features: limited action, sparse dialogue, reduction of interest in individual human character, the absence of conventional problem and resolution, a strong sense of the ritual origins of drama, and an awareness of the nature and conventions of drama itself. A meticulous craftsman, he has taken a direct hand in the production of many of his plays.

In *Waiting for Godot,* the most influential play since the second world war, every detail of the action, every word and gesture, is existentially weighted and has a place in its grand symmetry. *All That Fall* is similarly designed, so that the more limited resources of sound, voice and silence bear the same dismal freight; in Beckett's words, "*All That Fall* is specifically a radio play, or rather a radio text, for voices, not bodies . . . [whose quality] depends on the whole thing's coming out of the dark." For all that, it is one of Beckett's most recognizably Irish plays.

All That Fall was written at the suggestion of the BBC during the summer months of 1956. Under the direction of Donal McWhinnie, it was first broadcast January 13, 1957, on the Third Programme. It was immediately praised as a radio classic, although some critics were puzzled by the ending. This does not disconcert Hugh Kenner, who keeps his eye on the essentials, observing that "in a radio play there is nothing to see, an elementary fact which not all radio dramatists are willing to accept. Much radio drama fights this limitation, looking for ways to offer us mental pictures. Beckett instead made a play about a blind man, and toyed with the odd fact that in a drama exclusively auditory the unheard, unspoken, is the non-existent." Beckett thus turns the limitations of the radio medium—its confinement to sounds and silence—to advantage. The radio listeners' functional blindness in respect to the action conveys, in itself, the idea that existence is arbitrary and metaphysically uncertain.

On the naturalistic level, this play has a lot of Irish flavor. Boghill is Beckett's native Foxrock, with its suburban railway station and Leopardstown Race Course. The outlook of Dublin middle-class Protestants is reflected in the mental habits of the Rooneys and the unconscious bigotry of Miss Fitt. The bawdy and black humor, the extravagant language, the cheery mix of references to weather, sports, religion, and the contemptuous familiarity of village life all add up to a humorous impression of an Irish scene. In these respects, *All That Fall* is less austere than Beckett's other plays, such as *Waiting for Godot* and *Endgame*.

Despite all of this local color, *All That Fall* is designed so as to take its listeners beyond naturalism. The directions, for instance, indicate that the various animal sounds do not precede but follow Maddy's comments on them—thus implying that the Rooneys' universe is an enclosure of their own making. At the same time, the play itself bears the marks of its author's controlling hand: the careful listeners are reminded that they are experiencing an artful illusion. Thus, the leitmotifs of modes of travel, of rising and falling, of sterility and desire, and of debility and death are woven in rhythmic patterns into a three-part sonata structure. Yet despite these structural constraints, the play has a measure of conventional suspense, rising to a final crescendo.

The tone of the play modulates from pure comedy to bitter pathos, as its bleak existential theme comes more clearly to the surface. Simultaneously, despite her bawdy humor, Maddy Rooney becomes a more sympathetic character. Thus the bitter laughter at the promises of religion does not obscure our feeling for her suffering. Moreover, by the conclusion, her emotional isolation has become an existential metaphor. At this point, we realize that the play cries out against the silence of God: His refusal to claim or disclaim His existence.

Finally, *All That Fall,* in its mix of comedy and tragedy, its significant humor, its colloquial yet exact language, may be recognized as a descendant of O'Casey's *Juno and the Paycock.* Maddy Rooney's reflections on the mess around her re-echoes Captain Boyle's summary motto that "th' whole worl's in a terrible state o' chassis!"

SELECT BIBLIOGRAPHY

Publications

Waiting for Godot. (Originally *En attendant Godot,* 1952) New York: Grove Press, 1954; London: Calder and Boyars, 1975.

Endgame, Followed by Act Without Words [I]. (Originally *Fin de partie, suivi de Acte sans paroles*) New York: Grove Press/London: Faber and Faber, 1958.

Happy Days. New York: Grove Press, 1961; London: Faber and Faber, 1962.

Three Novels. New York: Grove Press, 1965. (*Molloy, Malone Dies, The Unnamable*)

I Can't Go On, I'll Go On: A Selection from Samuel Beckett's Work. Ed. Richard W. Weaver. New York: Grove Press, 1976.

Collected Shorter Plays of Samuel Beckett. London: Faber and Faber/New York: Grove Press, 1984.

Biography and Criticism

Andonian, Cathleen Culotta. *Samuel Beckett: A Reference Guide*. Boston, MA: G. K. Hall, 1989.

Bair, Deirdre. *Samuel Beckett*. New York: Harcourt Brace Jovanovich, 1978.

Cohn, Ruby. *Samuel Beckett: The Comic Gamut*. New Brunswick, NJ: Rutgers University Press, 1962.

Fletcher, John. *Samuel Beckett's Art*. London: Chatto and Windus, 1967.

———, and John Spurling. *Beckett: A Study of His Plays*. New York: Hill and Wang, 1972.

Kenner, Hugh. *A Reader's Guide to Samuel Beckett*. New York: Farrar, Straus and Giroux, 1973.

Zilliacus, Clas. *Beckett and Broadcasting*. Turku, Finland: Acta Academie Aboensis, 1976.

See also discussions in Deane, *Celtic Revivals*; Krause, *Profane Book*; Maxwell, *Modern Irish Drama*; and Simpson, *Beckett and Behan*.

All That Fall

A Play for Radio

CHARACTERS

MRS. ROONEY (MADDY), *a lady in her seventies*
CHRISTY, *a carter*
MR. TYLER, *a retired bill-broker*[1]
MR. SLOCUM, *Clerk of the Racecourse*
TOMMY, *a porter*
MR. BARRELL, *a station-master*
MISS FITT, *a lady in her thirties*
A FEMALE VOICE
DOLLY, *a small girl*
MR. ROONEY (DAN), *husband of Mrs. Rooney, blind*
JERRY, *a small boy*

(Rural sounds. Sheep, bird, cow, cock, severally, then together. Silence. Mrs. Rooney advances along country road towards railway station. Sound of her dragging feet. Music faint from house by way. "Death and the Maiden."[2] The steps slow down, stop.)

MRS. ROONEY. Poor woman. All alone in that ruinous old house.

(Music louder. Silence but for music playing. The steps resume. Music dies. Mrs. Rooney murmurs, melody. Her murmur dies. Sound of approaching cartwheels. The cart stops. The steps slow down, stop.)

MRS. ROONEY. Is that you, Christy?

CHRISTY. It is, Ma'am.

MRS. ROONEY. I thought the hinny[3] was familiar. How is your poor wife?

CHRISTY. No better, Ma'am.

MRS. ROONEY. Your daughter then?

CHRISTY. No worse, Ma'am.

(Silence.)

MRS. ROONEY. Why do you halt? *(Pause.)* But why do I halt?

---

1. **bill-broker** stock exchange broker   2. **"Death and the Maiden"** Song and String Quartet by Franz Schubert based on the poem by Matthias Claudius in which a young woman pleads with Death for her life, in vain   3. **hinny** hybrid offspring of she-ass and stallion

(Silence.)

CHRISTY. Nice day for the races,[4] Ma'am.

MRS. ROONEY. No doubt it is. *(Pause.)* But will it hold up?[5] *(Pause. With emotion.)* Will it hold up?

(Silence.)

CHRISTY. I suppose you wouldn't—

MRS. ROONEY. Hist! *(Pause.)* Surely to goodness that cannot be the up mail[6] I hear already.

(Silence. The hinny neighs. Silence)

CHRISTY. Damn the mail.

MRS. ROONEY. Oh thank God for that! I could have sworn I heard it, thundering up the track in the far distance. *(Pause.)* So hinnies whinny. Well, it is not surprising.

CHRISTY. I suppose you wouldn't be in need of a small load of dung?

MRS. ROONEY. Dung? What class of dung?

CHRISTY. Stydung.[7]

MRS. ROONEY. Stydung . . . I like your frankness, Christy. *(Pause.)* I'll ask the master. *(Pause.)* Christy.

CHRISTY. Yes, Ma'am.

MRS. ROONEY. Do you find anything . . . bizarre about my way of speaking? *(Pause.)* I do not mean the voice. *(Pause.)* No, I mean the words. *(Pause. More to herself.)* I use none but the simplest words, I hope, and yet I sometimes find my way of speaking very . . . bizarre. *(Pause.)* Mercy! What was that?

CHRISTY. Never mind her, Ma'am, she's very fresh in herself[8] today.

(Silence.)

MRS. ROONEY. Dung? What would we want with dung, at our time of life? *(Pause.)* Why are you on your feet down on the road? Why do you not climb up on the crest of your manure and let yourself be carried along? Is it that you have no head for heights?

(Silence.)

CHRISTY *(to the hinny)*. Yep! *(Pause. Louder.)* Yep wiyya to hell owwa that!⁹

(Silence.)

MRS. ROONEY. She does not move a muscle. *(Pause.)* I too should be getting along, if I do not wish to arrive late at the station. *(Pause.)* But a moment ago she neighed and pawed the ground. And now she refuses to advance. Give her a good welt on the rump. *(Sound of welt. Pause.)* Harder! *(Sound of welt. Pause.)* Well! If someone were to do that for me I should

---

4. **races** Leopardstown horse races   5. **it hold up** the weather stay dry   6. **up mail** the mailtrain towards the city   7. **Stydung** pig manure   8. **she's very fresh in herself** forward, frisky   9. **Yep wiyya to hell owwa that!** Up with you to hell out of that!

not dally. *(Pause.)* How she gazes at me to be sure, with her great moist cleg-tormented[10] eyes! Perhaps if I were to move on, down the road, out of her field of vision. . . . *(Sound of welt.)* No, no, enough! Take her by the snaffle[11] and pull her eyes away from me. Oh this is awful! *(She moves on. Sound of her dragging feet.)* What have I done to deserve all this, what, what? *(Dragging feet.)* So long ago. . . . No! No! *(Dragging feet. Quotes.)* "Sigh out a something something tale of things, Done long ago and ill done."[12] *(She halts.)* How can I go on, I cannot. Oh let me just flop down flat on the road like a big fat jelly out of a bowl and never move again! A great big slop thick with grit and dust and flies, they would have to scoop me up with a shovel. *(Pause.)* Heavens, there is that up mail again, what will become of me! *(The dragging steps resume.)* Oh I am just a hysterical old hag, I know, destroyed with sorrow and pining and gentility and church-going and fat and rheumatism and childlessness. *(Pause. Brokenly.)* Minnie! Little Minnie! *(Pause.)* Love, that is all I asked, a little love, daily, twice daily, fifty years of twice daily love like a Paris horse-butcher's regular, what normal woman wants affection? A peck on the jaw at morning, near the ear, and another at evening, peck, peck, till you grow whiskers on you. There is that lovely laburnum again.

(Dragging feet. Sound of bicycle-bell. It is old Mr. Tyler coming up behind her on his bicycle, on his way to the station. Squeak of brakes. He slows down and rides abreast of her.)

MR. TYLER. Mrs. Rooney! Pardon me if I do not doff my cap, I'd fall off. Divine day[13] for the meeting.

MRS. ROONEY. Oh, Mr. Tyler, you startled the life out of me stealing up behind me like that like a deer-stalker! Oh!

MR. TYLER *(playfully).* I rang my bell, Mrs. Rooney, the moment I sighted you I started tinkling my bell, now don't you deny it.

MRS. ROONEY. Your bell is one thing, Mr. Tyler, and you are another. What news of your poor daughter?

MR. TYLER. Fair, fair. They removed everything, you know, the whole . . . er . . . bag of tricks.[14] Now I am grandchildless.

(Dragging feet.)

MRS. ROONEY. Gracious how you wobble! Dismount, for mercy's sake, or ride on.

MR. TYLER. Perhaps if I were to lay my hands lightly on your shoulder, Mrs. Rooney, how would that be? *(Pause.)* Would you permit that?

MRS. ROONEY. No, Mr. Rooney, Mr. Tyler I mean, I am tired of light old hands on my shoulders and other senseless places, sick and tired of

---

10. **cleg** horsefly   11. **snaffle** horse's bit   12. **"Sigh out a something something tale of things, Done long ago and ill done"** the words of Meleander from John Ford's *The Lover's Melancholy*, IV, ii: for "something something" read "lamentable"   13. **Divine day** lovely day   14. **whole . . . bag of tricks** hysterectomy

them. Heavens, here comes Connolly's van! *(She halts. Sound of motor-van. It approaches, passes with thunderous rattle, recedes.)* Are you all right, Mr. Tyler? *(Pause.)* Where is he? *(Pause.)* Ah there you are! *(The dragging steps resume.)* That was a narrow squeak.

MR. TYLER. I alit in the nick of time.

MRS. ROONEY. It is suicide to be abroad.[15] But what is it to be at home, Mr. Tyler, what is it to be at home? A lingering dissolution. Now we are white with dust from head to foot. I beg your pardon?

MR. TYLER. Nothing, Mrs. Rooney, nothing, I was merely cursing, under my breath, God and man, under my breath, and the wet Saturday afternoon of my conception. My back tire has gone down again. I pumped it hard as iron before I set out. And now I am on the rim.

MRS. ROONEY. Oh what a shame!

MR. TYLER. Now if it were the front I should not so much mind. But the back. The back! The chain! The oil! The grease! The hub! The brakes! The gear! No! It is too much!

(Dragging steps.)

MRS. ROONEY. Are we very late, Mr. Tyler? I have not the courage to look at my watch.

MR. TYLER *(bitterly)*. Late! I on my bicycle as I bowled along was already late. Now therefore we are doubly late, trebly, quadrupedly late. Would I had shot by you, without a word.

(Dragging feet.)

MRS. ROONEY. Whom are you meeting, Mr. Tyler?

MR. TYLER. Hardy. *(Pause.)* We used to climb together. *(Pause.)* I saved his life once. *(Pause.)* I have not forgotten it.

(Dragging feet. They stop.)

MRS. ROONEY. Let us halt a moment and let this vile dust fall back upon the viler worms.

(Silence. Rural sounds.)

MR. TYLER. What sky! What light! Ah in spite of all it is a blessed thing to be alive in such weather, and out of hospital.

MRS. ROONEY. Alive?

MR. TYLER. Well half alive shall we say?

MRS. ROONEY. Speak for yourself, Mr. Tyler. I am not half alive nor anything approaching it. *(Pause.)* What are we standing here for? This dust will not settle in our time. And when it does some great roaring machine will come and whirl it all skyhigh again.

MR. TYLER. Well, shall we be getting along in that case?

MRS. ROONEY. No.

MR. TYLER. Come, Mrs. Rooney—

15. **abroad** outdoors

MRS. ROONEY. Go, Mr. Tyler, go on and leave me, listening to the cooing of the ring-doves. *(Cooing.)* If you see my poor blind Dan tell him I was on my way to meet him when it all came over me again, like a flood. Say to him, Your poor wife, she told me to tell you it all came flooding over her again and . . . *(the voice breaks)* . . . she simply went back home . . . straight back home . . .

MR. TYLER. Come, Mrs. Rooney, come, the mail has not yet gone up, just take my free arm and we'll be there with time and to spare.

MRS. ROONEY *(sobbing)*. What? What's all this now? *(Calmer.)* Can't you see I'm in trouble? *(With anger.)* Have you no respect for misery? *(Sobbing.)* Minnie! Little Minnie!

MR. TYLER. Come, Mrs. Rooney, come, the mail has not yet gone up, just take my free arm and we'll be there with time and to spare.

MRS. ROONEY *(brokenly)*. In her forties now she'd be, I don't know, fifty, girding up her lovely little loins, getting ready for the change[16] . . .

MR. TYLER. Come, Mrs. Rooney, come, the mail—

MRS. ROONEY *(exploding)*. Will you get along with you, Mr. Rooney, Mr. Tyler I mean, will you get along with you now and cease molesting me? What kind of a country is this where a woman can't weep her heart out on the highways and byways without being tormented by retired bill-brokers! *(Mr. Tyler prepares to mount his bicycle.)* Heavens you're not going to ride her flat! *(Mr. Tyler mounts.)* You'll tear your tube to ribbons! *(Mr. Tyler rides off. Receding sound of bumping bicycle. Silence. Cooing.)* Venus birds![17] Billing in the woods all the long summer long. *(Pause.)* Oh cursed corset! If I could let it out, without indecent exposure. Mr. Tyler! Mr. Tyler! Come back and unlace me behind the hedge! *(She laughs wildly, ceases.)* What's wrong with me, what's wrong with me, never tranquil, seething out of my dirty old pelt, out of my skull, oh to be in atoms, in atoms! *(Frenziedly.)* ATOMS! *(Silence. Cooing. Faintly.)* Jesus! *(Pause.)* Jesus!

(Sound of car coming up behind her. It slows down and draws up beside her, engine running. It is Mr. Slocum, the Clerk of the Racecourse.)

MR. SLOCUM. Is anything wrong, Mrs. Rooney? You are bent all double. Have you a pain in the stomach?

(Silence. Mrs. Rooney laughs wildly. Finally.)

MRS. ROONEY. Well if it isn't my old admirer the Clerk of the Course, in his limousine.

MR. SLOCUM. Are you going in my direction?

MRS. ROONEY. I am, Mr. Slocum, we all are. *(Pause.)* How is your poor mother?

MR. SLOCUM. Thank you, she is fairly comfortable. We manage to keep her out of pain. That is the great thing, Mrs. Rooney, is it not?

16. **the change** menopause   17. **Venus birds** love birds

MRS. ROONEY. Yes, indeed, Mr. Slocum, that is the great thing, I don't know how you do it. *(Pause. She slaps her cheek violently.)* Ah, these wasps!

MR. SLOCUM *(coolly)*. May I then offer you a seat, Madam?

MRS. ROONEY *(with exaggerated enthusiasm)*. Oh that would be heavenly, Mr. Slocum, just simply heavenly. *(Dubiously.)* But would I ever get in, you look very high off the ground today, these new balloon tires[18] I presume. *(Sound of door opening and Mrs. Rooney trying to get in.)* Does this roof never come off? No? *(Efforts of Mrs. Rooney.)* No . . . I'll never do it . . . you'll have to get down, Mr. Slocum, and help me from the rear. *(Pause.)* What was that? *(Pause. Aggrieved.)* This is all your suggestion, Mr. Slocum, not mine. Drive on, Sir, drive on.

MR. SLOCUM *(switching off the engine)*. I'm coming, Mrs. Rooney, I'm coming, give me time, I'm as stiff as yourself.

(Sound of Mr. Slocum extracting himself from driver's seat.)

MRS. ROONEY. Stiff! Well I like that! And me heaving all over back and front. *(To herself.)* The dry old reprobate!

MR. SLOCUM *(in position behind her)*. Now, Mrs. Rooney, how shall we do this?

MRS. ROONEY. As if I were a bale, Mr. Slocum, don't be afraid. *(Pause. Sounds of effort.)* That's the way! *(Effort.)* Lower! *(Effort.)* Wait! *(Pause.)* No, don't let go! *(Pause.)* Suppose I do get up, will I ever get down?

MR. SLOCUM *(breathing hard)*. You'll get down, Mrs. Rooney, you'll get down. We may not get you up, but I warrant you we'll get you down.

(He resumes his efforts. Sound of these.)

MRS. ROONEY. Oh! . . . Lower! . . . Don't be afraid! . . . We're past the age when . . . There! . . . Now! . . . Get your shoulder under it . . . Oh! . . . *(Giggles.)* Oh glory! . . . Up! Up! . . . Ah! . . . I'm in! *(Panting of Mr. Slocum. He slams the door. In a scream.)* My frock! You've nipped my frock! *(Mr. Slocum opens the door. Mrs. Rooney frees her frock. Mr. Slocum slams the door. His violent unintelligible muttering as he walks round to the other door. Tearfully.)* My nice frock! Look what you've done to my nice frock! *(Mr. Slocum gets into his seat, slams the driver's door, presses starter. The engine does not start. He releases the starter.)* What will Dan say when he sees me?

MR. SLOCUM. Has he then recovered his sight?

MRS. ROONEY. No, I mean when he knows, what will he say when he feels the hole? *(Mr. Slocum presses starter. As before. Silence.)* What are you doing, Mr. Slocum?

MR. SLOCUM. Gazing straight before me, Mrs. Rooney, through the windscreen, into the void.

18. **balloon tires** in the mid-1930s these low-pressure tires replaced an earlier patent

MRS. ROONEY. Start her up, I beseech you, and let us be off. This is awful!

MR. SLOCUM *(dreamily)*. All morning she went like a dream and now she is dead. That is what you get for a good deed. *(Pause. Hopefully.)* Perhaps if I were to choke her. *(He does so, presses the starter. The engine roars. Roaring to make himself heard.)* She was getting too much air!

(He throttles down, grinds in his first gear, moves off, changes up in a grinding of gears.)

MRS. ROONEY (in anguish). Mind the hen! *(Scream of brakes. Squawk of hen.)* Oh, mother, you have squashed her, drive on, drive on! *(The car accelerates. Pause.)* What a death! One minute picking happy at the dung, on the road, in the sun, with now and then a dust bath, and then—bang!— all her troubles over. *(Pause.)* All the laying and the hatching. *(Pause.)* Just one great squawk and then . . . peace. *(Pause.)* They would have slit her weasand[19] in any case. *(Pause.)* Here we are, let me down. *(The car slows down, stops, engine running. Mr. Slocum blows his horn. Pause. Louder. Pause.)* What are you up to now, Mr. Slocum? We are at a standstill, all danger is past and you blow your horn. Now if instead of blowing it now you had blown it at that unfortunate—

(Horn violently. Tommy the porter appears at the top of station steps.)

MR. SLOCUM *(calling)*. Will you come down, Tommy, and help this lady out, she's stuck. *(Tommy descends the steps.)* Open the door, Tommy, and ease her out.

(Tommy opens the door.)

TOMMY. Certainly, sir. Nice day for the races, sir. What would you fancy for—

MRS. ROONEY. Don't mind me. Don't take any notice of me. I do not exist. The fact is well known.

MR. SLOCUM. Do as you're asked, Tommy, for the love of God.

TOMMY. Yessir. Now, Mrs. Rooney.

(He starts pulling her out.)

MRS. ROONEY. Wait, Tommy, wait now, don't bustle me, just let me wheel round and get my feet to the ground. *(Her efforts to achieve this.)* Now.

TOMMY *(pulling her out)*. Mind your feather, Ma'am. *(Sounds of effort.)* Easy now, easy.

MRS. ROONEY. Wait, for God's sake, you'll have me beheaded.

TOMMY. Crouch down, Mrs. Rooney, crouch down, and get your head in the open.

MRS. ROONEY. Crouch down! At my time of life! This is lunacy!

TOMMY. Press her down, sir.

19. **weasand** throat

(Sounds of combined efforts.)

MRS. ROONEY. Pity!

TOMMY. Now! She's coming! Straighten up, Ma'am! There!

(Mr. Slocum slams the door.)

MRS. ROONEY. Am I out?

(The voice of Mr. Barrell, the station-master, raised in anger.)

MR. BARRELL. Tommy! Tommy! Where the hell is he?

(Mr. Slocum grinds in his gear.)

TOMMY *(hurriedly)*. You wouldn't have something for the Ladies Plate,[20] sir. I was given[21] Flash Harry.

MR. SLOCUM *(scornfully)*. Flash Harry! That carthorse!

MR. BARRELL *(at top of steps, roaring)*. Tommy! Blast your bleeding bloody—*(He sees Mrs. Rooney)*. Oh, Mrs. Rooney. . . . *(Mr. Slocum drives away in a grinding of gears.)* Who's that crucifying his gearbox, Tommy?

TOMMY. Old Cissy Slocum.

MRS. ROONEY. Cissy Slocum! That's a nice way to refer to your betters. Cissy Slocum! And you an orphan!

MR. BARRELL *(angrily to Tommy)*. What are you doing stravaging[22] down here on the public road? This is no place for you at all! Nip up there on the platform now and whip out the truck! Won't the twelve-thirty be on top of us before we can turn round?

TOMMY *(bitterly)*. And that's the thanks you get for a Christian act.

MR. BARRELL *(violently)*. Get on with you now before I report you! *(Slow feet of Tommy climbing steps.)* Do you want me to come down to you with the shovel? *(The feet quicken, recede, cease.)* Ah God forgive me, it's a hard life. *(Pause.)* Well, Mrs. Rooney, it's nice to see you up and about again. You were laid up[23] there a long time.

MRS. ROONEY. Not long enough, Mr. Barrell. *(Pause.)* Would I were still in bed, Mr. Barrell *(pause)*. Would I were lying stretched out in my comfortable bed, Mr. Barrell, just wasting slowly, painlessly away, keeping up my strength with arrowroot[24] and calves-foot jelly,[25] till in the end you wouldn't see me under the blankets any more than a board. *(Pause.)* Oh no coughing or spitting or bleeding or vomiting, just drifting gently down into the higher life, and remembering, remembering . . . *(the voice breaks)* . . . all the silly unhappiness . . . as though . . . it had never happened . . . What did I do with that handkerchief? *(Sound of handkerchief loudly applied.)* How long have you been master of this station now, Mr. Barrell?

MR. BARRELL. Don't ask me, Mrs. Rooney, don't ask me.

MRS. ROONEY. You stepped into your father's shoes, I believe, when he took them off.

20. **Ladies Plate** a particular race   21. **given** tipped to win   22. **stravaging** wandering about aimlessly   23. **laid up** ill in bed   24. **arrowroot** light starch biscuits or cookies   25. **calves-foot jelly** a delicate food for convalescents

MR. BARRELL. Poor Pappy! *(Reverent pause.)* He didn't live long to enjoy his ease.

MRS. ROONEY. I remember him clearly. A small ferrety purple-faced widower, deaf as a doornail, very testy and snappy. *(Pause.)* I suppose you'll be retiring soon yourself, Mr. Barrell, and growing your roses. *(Pause.)* Did I understand you to say the twelve-thirty would soon be upon us?

MR. BARRELL. Those were my words.

MRS. ROONEY. But according to my watch which is more or less right—or was—by the eight o'clock news the time is now coming up to twelve . . . *(pause as she consults her watch)* . . . thirty-six. *(Pause.)* And yet upon the other hand the up mail has not yet gone through. *(Pause.)* Or has it sped by unbeknown to me? *(Pause.)* For there was a moment there, I remember now, I was so plunged in sorrow I wouldn't have heard a steam roller go over me. *(Pause. Mr. Barrell turns to go.)* Don't go, Mr. Barrell! *(Mr. Barrell goes. Loud.)* Mr. Barrell! *(Pause. Louder.)* Mr. Barrell! *(Mr. Barrell comes back.)*

MR. BARRELL *(testily)*. What is it, Mrs. Rooney, I have my work to do. *(Silence. Sound of wind.)*

MRS. ROONEY. The wind is getting up. *(Pause. Wind.)* The best of the day is over. *(Pause. Wind. Dreamily.)* Soon the rain will begin to fall and go on falling, all afternoon. *(Mrs. Barrell goes.)* Then at evening the clouds will part, the setting sun will shine an instant, then sink, behind the hills. *(She realizes Mr. Barrell has gone.)* Mr. Barrell! Mr. Barrell! *(Silence.)* I estrange them all. They come towards me, uninvited, bygones bygones, full of kindness, anxious to help . . . *(the voice breaks)* . . . genuinely pleased . . . to see me again . . . looking so well. . . . *(Handkerchief.)* A few simple words . . . from my heart . . . and I am all alone . . . once more. . . . *(Handkerchief. Vehemently.)* I should not be out at all. I should never leave the grounds! *(Pause.)* Oh there is that Fitt woman, I wonder will she bow to me. *(Sound of Miss Fitt approaching, humming a hymn. She starts climbing the steps.)* Miss Fitt! *(Miss Fitt halts, stops humming.)* Am I then invisible, Miss Fitt? Is this cretonne so becoming to me that I merge into the masonry? *(Miss Fitt descends a step.)* That is right, Miss Fitt, look closely and you will finally distinguish a once female shape.

MISS FITT. Mrs Rooney! I saw you, but I did not know you.

MRS. ROONEY. Last Sunday we worshipped together. We knelt side by side at the same altar. We drank from the same chalice. Have I so changed since then?

MISS FITT *(shocked)*. Oh but in church, Mrs. Rooney, in church I am alone with my Maker. Are not you? *(Pause.)* Why even the sexton himself, you know, when he takes up the collection, knows it is useless to pause before me. I simply do not see the plate, or bag, whatever it is they use, how could I? *(Pause.)* Why even when all is over and I go out into the sweet fresh air, why even then for the first furlong or so I stumble in a kind of daze as you might say, oblivious to my co-religionists. And they are very kind I must admit—the vast majority—very kind and understanding. There she goes, they say, there goes the dark Miss Fitt, alone with her Maker, take no notice of her. And they step down off the path to avoid my running into them. *(Pause.)* Ah yes, I am distray,[26] very distray, even on week-days. Ask Mother, if you do not believe me. Hetty, she says, when I start eating my doily instead of the thin bread and butter, Hetty, how can you be so distray? *(Sighs.)* I suppose the truth is I am not there, Mrs. Rooney, just not really there at all. I see, hear, smell, and so on, I go through the usual motions, but my heart is not in it, Mrs. Rooney, but heart is in none of it. Left to myself, with no one to check me, I would soon be flown . . . home. *(Pause.)* So if you think I cut you just now, Mrs. Rooney, you do me an injustice. All I saw was a big pale blur, just another big pale blur. *(Pause.)* Is anything amiss, Mrs. Rooney, you do not look normal somehow. So bowed and bent.

MRS. ROONEY *(ruefully)*. Maddy Rooney, née Dunne, the big pale blur. *(Pause.)* You have piercing sight, Miss Fitt, if you only knew it, literally piercing.

(Pause.)

MISS FITT. Well . . . is there anything I can do, now that I am here?

MRS. ROONEY. If you would help me up the face of this cliff, Miss Fitt, I have little doubt your Maker would require[27] you, if no one else.

MISS FITT. Now, now, Mrs. Rooney, don't put your teeth in me. Require! I make these sacrifices for nothing—or not at all. *(Pause. Sound of her descending steps.)* I take it you want to lean on me, Mrs. Rooney.

MRS. ROONEY. I asked Mr. Barrell to give me his arm, just give me his arm. *(Pause.)* He turned on his heel and strode away.

MISS FITT. Is it my arm you want then? *(Pause. Impatiently.)* Is it my arm you want, Mrs. Rooney, or what is it?

MRS. ROONEY *(exploding)*. Your arm! Any arm! A helping hand! For five seconds! Christ what a planet!

MISS FITT. Really. . . . Do you know what it is, Mrs. Rooney, I do not think it is wise of you to be going about at all.

MRS. ROONEY *(violently)*. Come down here, Miss Fitt, and give me your arm, before I scream down the parish!

(Pause. Wind. Sound of Miss Fitt descending last steps.)

MISS FITT *(resignedly)*. Well, I suppose it is the Protestant thing to do.

MRS. ROONEY. Pismires[28] do it for one another. *(Pause.)* I have seen slugs do it. *(Miss Fitt proffers her arm)*. No, the other side, my dear, if it's

26. **distray** absent-minded   27. **requite** repay   28. **Pismires** ants

all the same to you, I'm left-handed on top of everything else. *(She takes Miss Fitt's right arm.)* Heavens, child, you're just a bag of bones, you need building up. *(Sound of her toiling up steps on Miss Fitt's arm.)* This is worse than the Matterhorn,[29] were you ever up the Matterhorn, Miss Fitt, great honeymoon resort. *(Sound of toiling.)* Why don't they have a handrail? *(Panting.)* Wait till I get some air. *(Pause.)* Don't let me go! *(Miss Fitt hums her hymn.[30] After a moment Mrs. Rooney joins in with the words.)* . . . the encircling gloo-oom . . . *(Miss Fitt stops humming.)* . . . tum tum me on. *(Forte.)* The night is dark and I am far from ho-ome, tum tum—

MISS FITT *(hysterically)*. Stop it, Mrs. Rooney, stop it, or I'll drop you!

MRS. ROONEY. Wasn't it that they sung on the *Lusitania*?[31] Or Rock of Ages?[32] Most touching it must have been. Or was it the *Titanic*?[33]

(Attracted by the noise a group, including Mr. Tyler, Mr. Barrell, and Tommy, gathers at top of steps.)

MR. BARRELL. What the—

MR. TYLER. Lovely day for the fixture.[34]

(Loud titter from Tommy cut short by Mr. Barrell with back-handed blow in the stomach. Appropriate noise from Tommy.)

FEMALE VOICE *(shrill)*. O look, Dolly, look!

DOLLY. What, Mamma?

FEMALE VOICE. They are stuck! *(Cackling laugh.)* They are stuck!

MRS. ROONEY. Now we are the laughing-stock of the twenty-six counties. Or is it thirty-six?[35]

MR. TYLER. That is a nice way to treat your defenseless subordinates, Mr. Barrell, hitting them without warning in the pit of the stomach.

MISS FITT. Has anybody seen my mother?

MR. BARRELL. Who is that?

TOMMY. The dark Miss Fitt.

MR. BARRELL. Where is her face?

MRS. ROONEY. Now, deary, I am ready if you are. *(They toil up remaining steps.)* Stand back, you cads!

(Shuffle of feet)

FEMALE VOICE. Mind yourself, Dolly!

MRS. ROONEY. Thank you, Miss Fitt, thank you, that will do, just prop me up against the wall like a roll of tarpaulin and that will be all, for the moment. *(Pause.)* I am sorry for all this ramdam,[36] Miss Fitt, had I

---

29. **Matterhorn** a precipitous Alpine peak 30. **hymn** from "Lead, Kindly Light," by John Henry Cardinal Newman 31. *Lusitania* transatlantic liner sunk by Germany off the Irish coast, May 7, 1915, with the loss of 1,198 lives 32. **Rock of Ages** popular Protestant hymn by R. Redhead (1853) 33. *Titanic* transatlantic liner built in Belfast, sunk on her maiden voyage, April 14–15, 1912, with the loss of 1,513 lives 34. **fixture** horseraces 35. **twenty-six counties . . . thirty-six?** the Irish Free State's 26 of Ireland's 32 counties 36. **ramdam** rumpus

known you were looking for your mother I should not have importuned you, I know what it is.

MR. TYLER *(in marvelling aside).* Ramdam!

FEMALE VOICE. Come, Dolly darling, let us take up our stand before the first class smokers. Give me your hand and hold me tight, one can be sucked under.

MR. TYLER. You have lost your mother, Miss Fitt?

MISS FITT. Good morning, Mr. Tyler.

MR. TYLER. Good morning, Miss Fitt.

MR. BARRELL. Good morning, Miss Fitt.

MISS FITT. Good morning, Mr. Barrell.

MR. TYLER. You have lost your mother, Miss Fitt?

MISS FITT. She said she would be on the last train.

MRS. ROONEY. Do not imagine, because I am silent, that I am not present, and alive, to all that is going on.

MR. TYLER *(to Miss Fitt).* When you say the last train—

MRS. ROONEY. Do not flatter yourselves for one moment, because I hold aloof, that my sufferings have ceased. No. The entire scene, the hills, the plain, the racecourse with its miles and miles of white rails and three red stands, the pretty little wayside station, even you yourselves, yes, I mean it, and over all the clouding blue, I see it all, I stand here and see it all with eyes . . . *(the voice breaks)* . . . through eyes . . . oh if you had my eyes . . . you would understand . . . the things they have seen . . . and not looked away . . . this is nothing . . . nothing . . . what did I do with the handkerchief?

(Pause.)

MR. TYLER *(to Miss Fitt).* When you say the last train—*(Mrs. Rooney blows her nose violently and long)*—when you say the last train, Miss Fitt, I take it you mean the twelve-thirty.

MISS FITT. What else could I mean, Mr. Tyler, what else could I *conceivably* mean?

MR. TYLER. Then you have no cause for anxiety, Miss Fitt, for the twelve-thirty has not yet arrived. Look *(Miss Fitt looks.)* No, up the line *(Miss Fitt looks. Patiently.)* No, Miss Fitt, follow the direction of my index. *(Miss Fitt looks.)* There. You see now. The signal. At the bawdy hour of nine. *(In rueful afterthought.)* Or three alas! *(Mr. Barrell stifles a guffaw.)* Thank you, Mr. Barrell.

MISS FITT. But the time is now getting on for—

MR. TYLER *(patiently).* We all know, Miss Fitt, we all know only too well what the time is now getting on for, and yet the cruel fact remains that the twelve-thirty has not yet arrived.

MISS FITT. Not an accident, I trust! *(Pause.)* Do not tell me she has left the track! *(Pause.)* Oh darling mother! With the fresh sole for lunch! *(Loud titter from Tommy, checked as before by Mr. Barrell.)*

MR. BARRELL. That's enough old guff out of you. Nip up to the box now and see has Mr. Case anything for me.

(Tommy goes.)

MRS. ROONEY. Poor Dan!

MISS FITT *(in anguish)*. What terrible thing has happened?

MR. TYLER. Now now, Miss Fitt, do not—

MRS. ROONEY *(with vehement sadness)*. Poor Dan!

MR. TYLER. Now now, Miss Fitt, do not give way . . . to despair, all will come right . . . in the end. *(Aside to Mr. Barrell.)* What *is* the situation, Mr. Barrell? Not a collision surely?

MRS. ROONEY *(enthusiastically)*. A collision! Oh that would be wonderful!

MISS FITT *(horrified)*. A collision! I knew it!

MR. TYLER. Come, Miss Fitt, let us move a little up the platform.

MRS. ROONEY. Yes, let us all do that. *(Pause.)* No? *(Pause.)* You have changed your mind? *(Pause.)* I quite agree, we are better here, in the shadow of the waiting-room.

MR. BARRELL. Excuse me a moment.

MRS. ROONEY. Before you slink away, Mr. Barrell, please, a statement of some kind, I insist. Even the slowest train on this brief line is not ten minutes and more behind its scheduled time without good cause, one imagines. *(Pause.)* We all know your station is the best kept of the entire network, but there are times when that is not enough, just not enough. *(Pause.)* Now, Mr. Barrell, leave off chewing your whiskers, we are waiting to hear from you—we the unfortunate ticket-holders' nearest if not dearest.

(Pause.)

MR. TYLER *(reasonably)*. I do think we are owed some kind of explanation, Mr. Barrell, if only to set our minds at rest.

MR. BARRELL. I know nothing. All I know is there has been a hitch. All traffic is retarded.

MRS. ROONEY *(derisively)*. Retarded! A hitch! Ah these celibates! Here we are eating our hearts out with anxiety for our loved ones and he calls that a hitch! Those of us like myself with heart and kidney trouble may collapse at any moment and he calls that a hitch! In our ovens the Saturday roast is burning to a shrivel and he calls that—

MR. TYLER. Here comes Tommy, running! I am glad I have been spared to see this.

TOMMY *(excitedly, in the distance)*. She's coming. *(Pause. Nearer.)* She's at the level-crossing!

(Immediately exaggerated station sounds. Falling signals. Bells. Whistles. Crescendo of train whistle approaching. Sound of train rushing through station.)

MRS. ROONEY *(above rush of train)*. The up mail! The up mail! *(The up mail recedes, the down train approaches, enters the station, pulls up with great hissing of steam and clashing of couplings. Noise of passengers descending, doors banging. Mr. Barrell shouting "Boghill! Boghill!," etc. Piercingly.)* Dan! . . . Are you all right? . . . Where is he? . . . Dan! Did you see my husband? . . . Dan! . . . *(Noise of station emptying. Guard's whistle. Train departing, receding. Silence.)* He isn't on it! The misery I have endured, to get here, and he isn't on it! . . . Mr. Barrell! . . . Was he not on it? *(Pause.)* Is anything the matter, you look as if you had seen a ghost. *(Pause.)* Tommy! . . . *Did you see the master?*

TOMMY. He'll be along, Ma'am, Jerry is minding him.

(Mr. Rooney suddenly appears on platform, advancing on small boy Jerry's arm. He is blind, thumps the ground with his stick and pants incessantly.)

MRS. ROONEY. Oh, Dan! There you are! *(Her dragging feet as she hastens towards him. She reaches him. They halt.)* Where in the world were you?

MR. ROONEY *(coolly)*. Maddy.

MRS. ROONEY. Where were you all this time?

MR. ROONEY. In the men's.

MRS. ROONEY. Kiss me!

MR. ROONEY. Kiss you? In public? On the platform? Before the boy? Have you taken leave of your senses?

MRS. ROONEY. Jerry wouldn't mind. Would you, Jerry?

JERRY. No Ma'am.

MRS. ROONEY. How is your poor father?

JERRY. They took him away, Ma'am.

MRS. ROONEY. Then you are all alone?

JERRY. Yes, Ma'am.

MR. ROONEY. Why are you here? You did not notify me.

MRS. ROONEY. I wanted to give you a surprise. For your birthday.

MR. ROONEY. My birthday?

MRS. ROONEY. Don't you remember? I wished you your happy returns in the bathroom.

MR. ROONEY. I did not hear you.

MRS. ROONEY. But I gave you a tie! You have it on!

(Pause.)

MR. ROONEY. How old am I now?

MRS. ROONEY. Now never mind about that. Come.

MR. ROONEY. Why did you not cancel the boy? Now we shall have to give him a penny.

MRS. ROONEY *(miserably)*. I forgot! I had such a time getting here! Such horrid nasty people! *(Pause. Pleading.)* Be nice to me, Dan, be nice to me today!

MR. ROONEY. Give the boy a penny.

MRS. ROONEY. Here are two halfpennies, Jerry. Run along now and buy yourself a nice gobstopper.[37]

37. **gobstopper** large round hard candy

JERRY. Yes, Ma'am.

MR. ROONEY. Come for me on Monday, if I am still alive.

JERRY. Yessir.

(He runs off.)

MR. ROONEY. We could have saved sixpence. We have saved fivepence. *(Pause.)* But at what cost?

(They move off along platform arm in arm. Dragging feet, panting, thudding stick.)

MRS. ROONEY. Are you not well?

(They halt, on Mr. Rooney's initiative.)

MR. ROONEY. Once and for all, do not ask me to speak and move at the same time. I shall not say this in this life again.

(They move off. Dragging feet, etc. They halt at top of steps.)

MRS. ROONEY. Are you not—

MR. ROONEY. Let us get this precipice over.

MRS. ROONEY. Put your arm around me.

MR. ROONEY. Have you been drinking again? *(Pause.)* You are quivering like a blanc-mange. *(Pause.)* Are you in a condition to lead me? *(Pause.)* We shall fall into the ditch.

MRS. ROONEY. Oh, Dan! It will be like old times!

MR. ROONEY. Pull yourself together or I shall send Tommy for the cab. Then instead of having saved sixpence, no, fivepence, we shall have lost . . . *(calculating mumble)* . . . two and three less six one and no plus one one and no plus three one and nine and one ten and three two and one . . . *(normal voice)* two and one, we shall be the poorer to the tune of two and one.[38] *(Pause.)* Curse that sun, it has gone in. What is the day doing?

(Wind.)

MRS. ROONEY. Shrouding, shrouding, the best of it is past. *(Pause.)* Soon the first great drops will fall splashing in the dust.

MR. ROONEY. And yet the glass was firm. *(Pause.)* Let us hasten home and sit before the fire. We shall draw the blinds. You will read to me. I think Effie is going to commit adultery with the Major.[39] *(Brief drag of feet.)* Wait! *(Feet cease. Stick tapping at steps.)* I have been up and down these steps five thousand times and still I do not know how many there are. When I think there are six there are four or five or seven or eight and when I remember there are five there are three or four or six or seven and when finally I realize there are seven there are five or six or eight or nine. Sometimes I wonder if they do not change them in the night. *(Pause. Irritably.)* Well? How many do you make them today?

---

38. **two and one** two shillings and one penny   39. **Effie is going to commit adultery with the Major** the protagonist of Theodor Fontane's novel *Effi Briest* (1895)

MRS. ROONEY. Do not ask me to count, Dan, not now.

MR. ROONEY. Not count! One of the few satisfactions in life!

MRS. ROONEY. Not steps, Dan, please, I always get them wrong. Then you might fall on your wound and I would have that on my manure-heap on top of everything else. No, just cling to me and all will be well.

(Confused noise of their descent. Panting, stumbling, ejaculations, curses. Silence.)

MR. ROONEY. Well! That is what you call well!

MRS. ROONEY. We are down. And little the worse. *(Silence. A donkey brays. Silence.)* That was a true donkey. Its father and mother were donkeys. *(Silence.)*

MR. ROONEY. Do you know what it is, I think I shall retire.

MRS. ROONEY *(appalled)*. Retire! And live at home? On your grant!

MR. ROONEY. Never tread these cursed steps again. Trudge this hellish road for the last time. Sit at home on the remnants of my bottom counting the hours—till the next meal. *(Pause.)* The very thought puts life in me! Forward, before it dies!

(They move on. Dragging feet, panting, thudding stick.)

MRS. ROONEY. Now mind, here is the path . . . Up! . . . Well done! Now we are in safety and a straight run home.

MR. ROONEY *(without halting, between gasps)*. A straight . . . run! . . . She calls that . . . a straight . . . run! . . .

MRS. ROONEY. Hush! Do not speak as you go along, you know it is not good for your coronary. *(Dragging steps, etc.)* Just concentrate on putting one foot before the next or whatever the expression is. *(Dragging feet, etc.)* That is the way, now we are doing nicely. *(Dragging feet, etc. They suddenly halt, on Mrs. Rooney's initiative.)* Heavens! I knew there was something! With all the excitement! I forgot!

MR. ROONEY *(quietly)*. Good God.

MRS. ROONEY. But you must know, Dan, of course, you were on it. Whatever happened? Tell me!

MR. ROONEY. I have never known anything to happen.

MRS. ROONEY. But you must—

MR. ROONEY *(violently)*. All this stopping and starting again is devilish, devilish! I get a little way on me and begin to be carried along when suddenly you stop dead! Two hundred pounds of unhealthy fat! What possessed you to come out at all? Let go of me!

MRS. ROONEY *(in great agitation)*. No, I must know, we won't stir from here till you tell me. Fifteen minutes late! On a thirty-minute run! It's unheard of!

MR. ROONEY. I know nothing. Let go of me before I shake you off.

MRS. ROONEY. But you must know! You were on it! Was it at the terminus? Did you leave on time? Or was it on the line? *(Pause.)* Did something happen on the line? *(Pause.)* Dan! *(Brokenly.)* Why won't you tell me!

(Silence. They move off. Dragging feet, etc. They halt. Pause.)

MR. ROONEY. Poor Maddy! *(Pause. Children's cries.)* What was that? *(Pause for Mrs. Rooney to ascertain.)*

MRS. ROONEY. The Lynch twins jeering at us.

(Cries.)

MR. ROONEY. Will they pelt us with mud today, do you suppose? *(Cries.)*

MRS. ROONEY. Let us turn and face them. *(Cries. They turn. Silence.)* Threaten them with your stick. *(Silence.)* They have run away.

(Pause.)

MR. ROONEY. Did you ever wish to kill a child? *(Pause.)* Nip some young doom in the bud. *(Pause.)* Many a time at night, in winter, on the black road home, I nearly attacked the boy. *(Pause.)* Poor Jerry! *(Pause.)* What restrained me then? *(Pause.)* Not fear of man. *(Pause.)* Shall we go on backwards now a little?

MRS. ROONEY. Backwards?

MR. ROONEY. Yes. Or you forwards and I backwards. The perfect pair. Like Dante's damned, with their faces arsy-versy.[40] Our tears will water our bottoms.

MRS. ROONEY. What is the matter, Dan? Are you not well?

MR. ROONEY. Well! Did you ever know me to be well? The day you met me I should have been in bed. The day you proposed to me the doctors gave me up. You knew that, did you not? The night you married me they came for me with an ambulance. You have not forgotten that, I suppose? *(Pause.)* No, I cannot be said to be well. But I am no worse. Indeed I am better than I was. The loss of my sight was a great fillip. If I could go deaf and dumb I think I might pant on to be a hundred. Or have I done so? *(Pause.)* Was I a hundred today? *(Pause.)* Am I a hundred, Maddy?

(Silence.)

MRS. ROONEY. All is still. No living soul in sight. There is no one to ask. The world is feeding. The wind—*(brief wind)*—scarcely stirs the leaves and the birds—*(brief chirp)*—are tired singing. The cows—*(brief moo)*—and sheep—*(brief baa)*—ruminate[41] in silence. The dogs—*(brief bark)*—are hushed and the hens—*(brief cackle)*—sprawl torpid in the dust. We are alone. There is no one to ask.

(Silence.)

MR. ROONEY *(clearing his throat, narrative tone)*. We drew out on the tick of time, I can vouch for that. I was—

40. **Dante's damned, with their faces arsy-versy** In the *Inferno* (Canto XX), those who attempted to foresee the future are punished by having their heads turned backwards, their eyes blinded by tears   41. **ruminate** chew the cud or meditate

MRS. ROONEY. How can you vouch for it?

MR. ROONEY *(normal tone, angrily)*. I can vouch for it, I tell you! Do you want my relation or don't you? *(Pause. Narrative tone.)* On the tick of time. I had the compartment[42] to myself, as usual. At least I hope so, for I made no attempt to restrain myself. My mind—*(Normal tone.)* But why do we not sit down somewhere? Are we afraid we should never rise again?

MRS. ROONEY. Sit down on what?

MR. ROONEY. On a bench, for example.

MRS. ROONEY. There is no bench.

MR. ROONEY. Then on a bank, let us sink down upon a bank.

MRS. ROONEY. There is no bank.

MR. ROONEY. Then we cannot. *(Pause.)* I dream of other roads, in other lands. Of another home, another—*(he hesitates)*—another home. *(Pause.)* What was I trying to say?

MRS. ROONEY. Something about your mind.

MR. ROONEY *(startled)*. My mind? Are you sure? *(Pause. Incredulous.)* My mind? . . . *(Pause.)* Ah yes. *(Narrative tone.)* Alone in the compartment my mind began to work, as so often after office hours, on the way home, in the train, to the lilt of the bogeys.[43] Your season-ticket, I said, costs you twelve pounds a year and you earn, on an average, seven and six a day, that is to say barely enough to keep you alive and twitching with the help of food, drink, tobacco and periodicals until you finally reach home and fall into bed. Add to this—or subtract from it—rent, stationery, various subscriptions, tramfares to and fro, light and heat, permits and licences, hairtrims and shaves, tips to escorts, upkeep of premises and appearances, and a thousand unspecifiable sundries, and it is clear that by lying at home in bed, day and night, winter and summer, with a change of pyjamas once a fortnight, you would add very considerably to your income. Business, I said—*(A cry. Pause. Again. Normal tone.)* Did I hear a cry?

MRS. ROONEY. Mrs. Tully I fancy. Her poor husband is in constant pain and beats her unmercifully.

(Silence.)

MR. ROONEY. That was a short knock. *(Pause.)* What was I trying to get at?

MRS. ROONEY. Business.

MR. ROONEY. Ah yes, business. *(Narrative tone.)* Business, old man, I said, retire from business, it has retired from you. *(Normal tone.)* One has these moments of lucidity.

MRS. ROONEY. I feel very cold and weak.

MR. ROONEY *(narrative tone)*. On the other hand, I said, there are the

42. **compartment** Carriages on Irish trains are partitioned into sections
43. **bogeys** revolving undercarriages of a train

horrors of home life, the dusting, sweeping, airing, scrubbing, waxing, waning, washing, mangling,[44] drying, mowing, clipping, raking, rolling, scuffling,[45] shovelling, grinding, tearing, pounding, banging and slamming. And the brats, the happy little healthy little howling neighbour's brats. Of all this and much more the week-end, the Saturday intermission and then the day of rest, have given you some idea. But what must it be like on a working-day? A Wednesday? A Friday! What must it be like on a Friday! And I fell to thinking of my silent, backstreet, basement office, with its obliterated plate, rest-couch and velvet hangings, and what it means to be buried there alive, if only from ten to five, with convenient to the one hand a bottle of light pale ale and to the other a long ice-cold fillet of hake. Nothing, I said, not even fully certified death, can ever take the place of that. It was then I noticed we were at a standstill. *(Pause. Normal tone. Irritably.)* Why are you hanging out of me like that? Have you swooned away?

MRS. ROONEY. I feel very cold and faint. The wind—*(whistling wind)*—is whistling through my summer frock as if I had nothing on over my bloomers. I have had no solid food since my elevenses.[46]

MR. ROONEY. You have ceased to care. I speak—and you listen to the wind.

MRS. ROONEY. No no, I am agog, tell me all, we shall press on and never pause, never pause, till we come safe to haven.

(Pause.)

MR. ROONEY. Never pause . . . safe to haven. . . . Do you know, Maddy, sometimes one would think you were struggling with a dead language.

MRS. ROONEY. Yes indeed, Dan, I know full well what you mean, I often have that feeling, it is unspeakably excruciating.

MR. ROONEY. I confess I have it sometimes myself, when I happen to overhear what I am saying.

MRS. ROONEY. Well, you know, it will be dead in time, just like our own poor dear Gaelic,[47] there is that to be said.

(Urgent baa.)

MR. ROONEY *(startled)*. Good God!

MRS. ROONEY. Oh the pretty little woolly lamb, crying to suck its mother! Theirs has not changed, since Arcady.

(Pause.)

MR. ROONEY. Where was I in my composition?

MRS. ROONEY. At a standstill.

44. **mangling** clothes wringing   45. **scuffling** stirring with a hoe   46. **elevenses** mid-morning (11 a.m.) tea break   47. **like our own poor dear Gaelic** the numbers of native Irish Gaelic language speakers has declined precipitously since the early nineteenth century

MR. ROONEY. Ah yes. *(Clears his throat. Narrative tone.)* I concluded naturally that we had entered a station and would soon be on our way again, and I sat on, without misgiving. Not a sound. Things are very dull today, I said, nobody getting down, nobody getting on. Then as time flew by and nothing happened I realized my error. We had not entered a station.

MRS. ROONEY. Did you not spring up and poke your head out of the window?

MR. ROONEY. What good would that have done me?

MRS. ROONEY. Why to call out to be told what was amiss.

MR. ROONEY. I did not care what was amiss. No, I just sat on, saying, If this train were never to move again I should not greatly mind. Then gradually a—how shall I say—a growing desire to—er—you know— welled up within me. Nervous probably. In fact now I am sure. You know, the feeling of being confined.

MRS. ROONEY. Yes yes, I have been through that.

MR. ROONEY. If we sit here much longer, I said, I really do not know what I shall do. I got up and paced to and fro between the seats, like a caged beast.

MRS. ROONEY. That is a help sometimes.

MR. ROONEY. After what seemed an eternity we simply moved off. And the next thing was Barrell bawling the abhorred name. I got down and Jerry led me to the men's, or Fir[48] as they call it now, from Vir Viris I suppose, the V becoming F, in accordance with Grimm's Law[49] *(Pause.)* The rest you know. *(Pause.)* You say nothing? *(Pause.)* Say something, Maddy. Say you believe me.

MRS. ROONEY. I remember once attending a lecture by one of these new mind doctors,[50] I forget what you call them. He spoke—

MR. ROONEY. A lunatic specialist?

MRS. ROONEY. No, no, just the troubled mind. I was hoping he might shed a little light on my lifelong preoccupation with horses' buttocks.

MR. ROONEY. A neurologist.

MRS. ROONEY. No no, just mental distress, the name will come back to me in the night. I remember his telling us the story of a little girl, very strange and unhappy in her ways, and how he treated her unsuccessfully over a period of years and was finally obliged to give up the case. He could find nothing wrong with her, he said. The only thing wrong with her as far as he could see was that she was dying. And she did in fact die, shortly after he washed his hands of her.

48. **Fir** Men (Irish Gaelic) in the official language of the Irish Free State   49. **Grimm's Law** formula describing the changes undergone by Indo-European stop consonants as represented in Germanic, developed by German philologist Jakob Grimm (1785–1863)   50. **one of these new mind doctors** C. G. Jung, whom Beckett heard lecture in 1935. See Bair, *Samuel Beckett,* pp. 208–10.

MR. ROONEY. Well? What is there so wonderful about that?

MRS. ROONEY. No, it was just something he said, and the way he said it, that have haunted me ever since.

MR. ROONEY. You lie awake at night, tossing to and fro and brooding on it.

MRS. ROONEY. On it and other . . . wretchedness. *(Pause.)* When he had done with the little girl he stood there motionless for some time, quite two minutes I should say, looking down at his table. Then he suddenly raised his head and exclaimed, as if he had had a revelation, The trouble with her was she had never been really born! *(Pause.)* He spoke throughout without notes. *(Pause.)* I left before the end.

MR. ROONEY. Nothing about your buttocks? *(Mrs. Rooney weeps. In affectionate remonstrance.)* Maddy!

MRS. ROONEY. There is nothing to be done for those people!

MR. ROONEY. For which is there? *(Pause.)* That does not sound right somehow. *(Pause.)* What way am I facing?

MRS. ROONEY. What?

MR. ROONEY. I have forgotten what way I am facing.

MRS. ROONEY. You have turned aside and are bowed down over the ditch.

MR. ROONEY. There is a dead dog down there.

MRS. ROONEY. No no, just the rotting leaves.

MR. ROONEY. In June? Rotting leaves in June?

MRS. ROONEY. Yes, dear, from last year, and from the year before last, and from the year before that again. *(Silence. Rainy wind. They move on. Dragging steps, etc.)* There is that lovely laburnum again. Poor thing, it is losing all its tassels. *(Dragging steps, etc.)* There are the first drops. *(Rain. Dragging feet, etc.)* Golden drizzle.[51] *(Dragging steps, etc.)* Do not mind me, dear, I am just talking to myself. *(Rain heavier. Dragging steps, etc.)* Can hinnies procreate, I wonder?

(They halt.)

MR. ROONEY. Say that again.

MRS. ROONEY. Come on, dear, don't mind me, we are getting drenched.

MR. ROONEY *(forcibly).* Can what what?

MRS. ROONEY. Hinnies procreate. *(Silence.)* You know, hinnies, or jinnies, aren't they barren, or sterile, or whatever it is? *(Pause.)* It wasn't an ass's colt[52] at all, you know, I asked the Regius Professor.[53]

(Pause.)

51. **Golden drizzle** fireworks; cf. Zeus's fathering of Perseus in a shower of gold 52. **ass's colt** on which Jesus rode into Jerusalem on Palm Sunday, see Matt. 21: 2–8 53. **Regius Professor** holding a professorship established by royal decree at an established British university

MR. ROONEY. He should know.

MRS. ROONEY. Yes, it was a hinny, he rode into Jerusalem or whatever it was on a hinny. *(Pause.)* That must mean something. *(Pause.)* It's like the sparrows,[54] than many of which we are of more value, they weren't sparrows at all.

MR. ROONEY. Than many of which! . . . You exaggerate, Maddy.

MRS. ROONEY *(with emotion)*. They weren't sparrows at all!

MR. ROONEY. Does that put our price up?

(Silence. They move on. Wind and rain. Dragging feet, etc. They halt.)

MRS. ROONEY. Do you want some dung? *(Silence. They move on. Wind and rain, etc. They halt.)* Why do you stop? Do you want to say something?

MR. ROONEY. No.

MRS. ROONEY. Then why do you stop?

MR. ROONEY. It is easier.

MRS. ROONEY. Are you very wet?

MR. ROONEY. To the buff.[55]

MRS. ROONEY. The buff?

MR. ROONEY. The buff. From buffalo.

MRS. ROONEY. We shall hang up all our things in the hot-cupboard and get into our dressing gowns. *(Pause.)* Put your arm round me. *(Pause.)* Be nice to me! *(Pause. Gratefully.)* Ah, Dan! *(They move on. Wind and rain. Dragging feet, etc. Faintly same music as before. They halt. Music clearer. Silence but for music playing. Music dies.)* All day the same old record. All alone in that great empty house. She must be a very old woman now.

MR. ROONEY *(indistinctly)*. Death and the Maiden.

(Silence.)

MRS. ROONEY. You are crying. *(Pause.)* Are you crying?

MR. ROONEY *(violently)*. Yes! *(They move on. Wind and rain. Dragging feet, etc. They halt. They move on. Wind and rain. Dragging feet, etc. They halt.)* Who is the preacher tomorrow? The incumbent?

MRS. ROONEY. No.

MR. ROONEY. Thank God for that. Who?

MRS. ROONEY. Hardy.[56]

MR. ROONEY. "How to be Happy though Married"?[57]

MRS. ROONEY. No no, he died, you remember. No connexion.

MR. ROONEY. Has he announced his text?

MRS. ROONEY. "The Lord upholdeth all that fall and raiseth up all those that be bowed down."[58] *(Silence. They join in wild laughter. They move*

---

54. **than many of which we are of more value** "Fear yet no therefore, ye are of more value than many sparrows" Matt. 10: 31   55. **buff** skin   56. **Hardy** Rev. Edward John Hardy (1849–1920), bestselling author   57. **"How to be Happy though Married"** London, 1885   58. **"The Lord upholdeth . . . bowed down"** Psalm 145: 14

on. Wind and rain. Dragging feet, etc.) Hold me tighter, Dan! *(Pause.)* Oh yes!

(They halt.)

MR. ROONEY. I hear something behind us.

(Pause.)

MRS. ROONEY. It looks like Jerry. *(Pause.)* It is Jerry.

(Sound of Jerry's running steps approaching. He halts beside them, panting.)

JERRY *(panting).* You dropped—

MRS. ROONEY. Take your time, my little man, you will burst a blood-vessel.

JERRY *(panting).* You dropped something, sir. Mr. Barrell told me to run after you.

MRS. ROONEY. Show. *(She takes the object.)* What is it? *(She examines it.)* What is this thing, Dan?

MR. ROONEY. Perhaps it is not mine at all.

JERRY. Mr. Barrell said it was, sir.

MRS. ROONEY. It looks like a kind of ball. And yet it is not a ball.

MR. ROONEY. Give it to me.

MRS. ROONEY *(giving it).* What *is* it, Dan?

MR. ROONEY. It is a thing I carry about with me.

MRS. ROONEY. Yes, but what—

MR. ROONEY *(violently).* It is a thing I carry about with me!

(Silence. Mrs. Rooney looks for a penny.)

MRS. ROONEY. I have no small money. Have you?

MR. ROONEY. I have none of any kind.

MRS. ROONEY. We are out of change, Jerry. Remind Mr. Rooney on Monday and he will give you a penny for your pains.

JERRY. Yes, Ma'am.

MR. ROONEY. If I am alive.

JERRY. Yessir.

(Jerry starts running back towards the station.)

MRS. ROONEY. Jerry! *(Jerry halts.)* Did you hear what the hitch was? *(Pause.)* Did you hear what kept the train so late?

MR. ROONEY. How would he have heard? Come on.

MRS. ROONEY. What was it, Jerry?

JERRY. It was a—

MR. ROONEY. Leave the boy alone, he knows nothing! Come on!

MRS. ROONEY. What was it, Jerry?

JERRY. It was a little child, Ma'am.

(Mr. Rooney groans.)

MRS. ROONEY. What do you mean, it was a little child?

JERRY. It was a little child fell out of the carriage, Ma'am. *(Pause.)* On to the line, Ma'am. *(Pause.)* Under the wheels, Ma'am.

(Silence. Jerry runs off. His steps die away. Tempest of wind and rain. It abates. They move on. Dragging steps, etc. They halt. Tempest of wind and rain.)

END

HUGH LEONARD
(JOHN KEYES BYRNE)
1926 –

In his early reminiscences, *Home Before Night* (1979), Hugh Leonard recounts the traumas and deprivations of his own childhood, and the romantic ambitions of his adolescence brought to ground by a stultifying clerkship in the Irish civil service. Towards the end of that account, he tells of his first visit to a theater, where he experienced an epiphany of the theatrical potential of ordinary life around him. It was an Abbey production of O'Casey's *The Plough and the Stars,* starring F. J. McCormick and Cyril Cusack. "But it was more than the acting that made Jack stand outside the theatre afterwards, looking towards the roof tops for the red glow of Dublin burning that he had seen through the window of Bessie Burgess's attic room. The life that roared through the play itself had spilled over from the stage, sweeping him with it so that he knew he would never again be content just to sit and watch and applaud with the rest of them." So began the creative career of one of the most productive and renowned Irish dramatists.

John Byrne was the adopted son of a working-class couple named Keyes. He grew up in the picturesque south County Dublin village of Dalkey, and attended the secondary school run by the Presentation Brothers in nearby Glasthule. In 1945 he joined the Land Commission, where he clerked for fourteen years. During this time, he became involved in amateur theater as an actor, writer, and critic. His second play, *The Big Birthday,* submitted under the pseudonym "Hugh Leonard," was accepted by the Abbey in 1956, and after two more of his plays, *A Leap in the Dark* (1957) and *Madigan's Lock* (1958), were produced in Dublin, he abandoned his desk job to become a professional writer.

This decision quickly took him from scriptwriting for Irish radio (the popular serial *The Kennedys of Castleross*) to Granada Television in Manchester and thence to London in 1963 as a freelance writer. From these beginnings, he developed a highly professional and productive commercial and artistic career. He wrote film scripts, and adapted novels and plays for television. Among his work in this genre were: the screenplays for *Great Catherine* (1968), *Our Miss Fred* (1972) and *Da* (1987); the television serials *The Hound of the Baskervilles* (1968), *Nicholas Nickleby* (1969), and *A Sentimental Education* (1970); and the television play *Silent Song,* which won the Italia Award in 1967.

But he also maintained contacts with Dublin and with serious theater through a continuous association with the Dublin Theatre Festival, at which a work of his has been produced almost every year since 1960. His *Stephen D,* an adaptation of James Joyce's *A Portrait of the Artist as a Young Man* and *Stephen Hero,* presented at the 1962 festival, won him an immediate reputation for his stagecraft. Since then, his work for stage has included a number of similar adaptations, including *When the Saints Go Cycling In* (1964) from Flann O'Brien's novel *The Dalkey Archive* and *Liam Liar* (1976) from Keith Waterhouse and Willis Hall's *Billy Liar.* But it is on his original work for stage—now some two dozen plays—that his claim to our attention rests.

Since 1970, he has been living with his wife and daughter in his home village of Dalkey, now an upscale suburb of Dublin City. He is a well-known figure in Irish life, writing weekly humorous and satirical columns for various newspapers. In these essays he writes with scathing wit, denouncing political violence, extreme nationalism, provinciality, inefficiency, and the mores of Irish suburban social climbers. This journalism has made Leonard's name synonymous with acid, hilarious caricature, a feature of most of his work for stage. When this barbed wit is shaped by the technical experience he has gained from his work for the media, satirical stage comedy emerges as his *métier.* Perhaps the best example of a typical Leonard comedy is *The Patrick Pearse Motel* (1971). A bedroom farce after the fashion of Georges Feydeau, and set in Dublin's suburbia, it lampoons the vulgarity of Ireland's middle class who commercialize their own tragic past. Leonard handles the absurd complications with brilliant dexterity, his script sparkles with wisecracks, all moving with breakneck speed through a series of uproarious situations. A polished dinner theater entertainment, although it may suffer from a deficit in feeling, it has pace, control, and a sharp satirical bite.

It is a tribute to Leonard's maturity as a writer that for all his success in this vein he has used his talents to more serious purpose. He told Ned Chaillet: "I am conscious that my main faults are cleverness (in the structural sense) . . . and at times irresponsible sense of comedy, which is not so much out of place as inclined to give my work an unintended lightness. These faults at least I know and can guard against. I regard myself as an optimist, and the theme that emerges from my plays is that life is good if it is not misused. . . ." His more reflective, autobiographical plays—*Da* and *A Life*—act on these observations.

Da is Leonard's finest achievement to date, winning numerous theater awards, including a Tony in 1978. Conceived and first produced at Olney Theatre, near Washington, D.C., 1972–73, it is a memory play in tribute to the author's adoptive father. It has much of the humor of Leonard's comedies, but here the humor contributes to the mellow, nostalgic feeling of the play, saving it from overt sentimentality. The theatrical device of having two actors play Charlie Now and Charlie Then is exploited to complex purposes, so that the humorous illumination shines in both directions. Charlie's relationship with his father is developed with an affection that does not wink at the striking differences of temperament, intelligence, and social values between them. The image of Da modifies Leonard's normally cynical humor. The use of stage space is similarly dexterous, allowing for complex shifts backwards and forwards in time. The interweaving of images from the present and various stages of the past is skillfully devised, and with increasing virtuosity as the play progresses in a design that provides for a moving dramatic cumulation. All of these devices effectively fuse past and present, and reconcile the modern, sophisticated Charlie to his socially humble past: he is finally able to rediscover and articulate for himself the reality of love behind the distorted masks of life.

Historically and socially, with its references to popular culture and political and social attitudes in the neutral Irish Free State, the play is an accurate evocation of the atmosphere of Ireland during World War II. The clichés of Irish republicanism don't affect Da's own self-image as a servant of the Quality. More poignantly, the images of romance and heroism that Young Charlie derives from the movies serve a central purpose in setting off Da's servility, loneliness, reticence, and self-limitation.

Other aspects of the play deserve consideration: the interaction of the several dialects of class, age, and time; the Joycean themes of the artist's ironic view of his own adolescence, and of reconciliation with the father who is the source of his *daimon*; and the manner in which the pain of illegitimacy is shown to be a driving force in the play, a source of its bitter energy, scarcely annealed by the final leavetaking.

Speaking of this play to *The New York Times,* Leonard said: "*Da* set out to be a monument to my father. I wrote the play to pay off a debt to my father. But the play made me successful as a writer and since I couldn't have written it without my father, the debt's now greater than ever."

SELECT BIBLIOGRAPHY

Publications

Stephen D. London: Evans, 1962.
The Poker Session. London: Evans, 1963.
The Patrick Pearse Motel. London: Samuel French, 1971.
The Au Pair Man. New York: Samuel French, 1974.
Da. Newark, DE: Proscenium Press, 1973; rev. ed., London: Samuel French, 1978.
Leonard's Last Book. Enniskerry, Ireland: Egotist Press, 1978. (Essays)
Home Before Night. London: Deutsch, 1979; New York: Atheneum, 1980. (Autobiography)

A Peculiar People and Other Foibles. Enniskerry, Ireland: Tansy Books, 1979. (Occasional essays)
Summer. London: Samuel French, 1979.
Time Was. London: Samuel French, 1980.
Da, Time Was, and *A Life.* Harmondsworth, U.K.: Penguin, 1981.
Madigan's Lock & Pizzazz. Dublin: Brophy Books, 1987.
The Mask of Moriarty. Dublin: Brophy Books, 1987.

Biography and Criticism

Griffin, Christopher. "Hugh Leonard." *Critical Survey of Drama: Supplementary Volume.* Pasadena, CA: Salem Press, 1987: 226–34.
Hickey, Des, and Gus Smith. *A Paler Shade of Green.* London: Leslie Frewin, 1972, pp. 191–201.
Kosok, Heinz. "Hugh Leonard." *Dictionary of Literary Biography* 13: 284–91.

See also discussions in Hogan, *After the Irish Renaissance,* and Krause, *Profane Book.*

Da

A Comedy
in Two Acts

THE CAST

CHARLIE NOW
OLIVER
DA
MOTHER
CHARLIE THEN
DRUMM
THE YELLOW PERIL
MRS. PRYNNE

THE PLACE
A kitchen and, later, places remembered.

THE TIME
May 1968 and, later, times remembered.

THE SET

*There are several playing areas. The main one is the kitchen. This is the kitchen–
living room plus small hallway of a corporation house. An exit at the rear to
the scullery. A hint of stairs running up from the hall. There are two areas at
either side of the kitchen and a series of connecting steps and ramps which climb
up and over, behind the kitchen. One of the two areas is the seafront . . . it
includes a park bench. Behind the seafront, on the rising platforms, is the hilltop.
On the other side of the stage is a neutral area, defined by lighting. This can
be a number of locales as the script requires. (In the Second Act there is an
ornamental bench there; the park bench is removed.) The kitchen, however, is
the womb of the play.*

ACT 1

*(Charlie, overcoat on, is at the kitchen table, sorting letters, family papers, old
photos, etc., into two piles. He finds one paper of interest and puts on his glasses
to examine it. He then goes to the range and pours boiling water from the kettle
into a teapot. He then picks up the teapot as Oliver comes to the door.*

He is Charlie's age—early 40s. His clothes are too neat for him to be prosperous; youthful bouncy step, handkerchief exploding from his breast pocket. He sees that the door is ajar. He knocks all the same.)

CHARLIE. Yes? *(Oliver is about to come in, but stops to remove a crepe bow from the door.)* Yes, who is it? *(Oliver steps into the hall and coughs. Half to himself.)* I didn't ask how you are, but who you are. *(Then, seeing him.)* Oliver!

OLIVER. Instant recognition. Oh-yes, full marks.

CHARLIE. You . . . good God.

OLIVER *(careful speech, equal emphasis on each syllable.)* Well, I'm still a native-you-know. Not a globe-trotter like some. *(Almost wagging a finger.)* Oh, yes.

CHARLIE. Well, today's the day for it.

OLIVER. Par-don me?

CHARLIE. Old faces. They've turned up like bills you thought you'd never have to pay. I'm on my own . . . come in. *(He puts the teapot down on the table.)*

OLIVER. Won't intrude. Thought I'd offer my . . .

CHARLIE. Sure.

OLIVER. For your trouble. *(Holding up the wreath.)* I took the liberty.

CHARLIE. That's damn nice of you, Oliver. Thank you.

OLIVER. It was . . .

CHARLIE. He would have liked that.

OLIVER. It's from the door.

CHARLIE. From . . . ? *(A loud laugh.)* I thought it was a . . . gift-wrapped Mass card.[1] I mean, Masses in English, the priest facing you across the altar like a chef at a buffet luncheon . . . I thought it was one more innovation.[2] *(Taking it purposefully.)* Yes, by all means. *(He drops it into the range.)*

OLIVER. Gwendolyn—the wife-you-know—saw the notice in the "Press." I would have gone to the funeral—

CHARLIE. What for!

OLIVER. But business-you-know.

CHARLIE. It's nice to see you. It must be ten . . . I don't know, fifteen years? Sit down . . . the mourners left a soldier or two standing. *(He takes a bottle of stout[3] out of a crate.)*

OLIVER. It's seldom I take a drink.

CHARLIE. I've made tea for myself, do you mind? I never drink in this house. Every Christmas the Da would say: "Will you have a bottle of stout, son?" Couldn't. It was the stricken look I know would come on my moth-

---

1. **Mass card** offering a requiem mass   2. **innovation** the Roman Catholic Church reformed many rituals in the late 1960s   3. **stout** strong, very dark beer brewed in Ireland

er's face, as if I'd appeared in my first pair of trousers or put my hand on a girl's tit in her presence.

OLIVER *(dutifully)*. Ho-ho-ho.

CHARLIE. So I . . . *(Blankly.)* What?

OLIVER. Joll-y good.

CHARLIE. My God, Oliver, you still think saying "tit" is the height of depravity. You must find married life unbearably exciting.

OLIVER *(beaming.)* Haven't changed, haven't changed!

CHARLIE *(pouring the stout.)* Anyway, I kept meaning to take that Christmas drink and send her upstairs in tears with a frenzied petition to St. Ann.[4] Next thing I knew, there I was aged thirty-nine, the year she died, a child on my lap who was capable of consuming the dregs of everyone else's tawny port to wild grandparental applause, and my wife sitting where you are, looking with disbelieving nausea at the man she had half-carried home the previous night, as he shook his greying head virtuously and said: "No, thanks, Da, I still don't." *(He hands the stout to Oliver.)* After she died, the not altogether frivolous thought occurred to me that the man who will deliberately not cause pain to his mother must be something of a sadist. I suppose I could have had a drink since then, but why spoil a perfect . . . *(Looking down at Oliver.)* You've got a bald spot.

OLIVER. Me? No . . . ha-ha, it's the wind. *(Producing a comb.)* Breezy out. No, no: fine head of hair still-you-know. *(Charlie smiles and pours his tea, using a pot-holder. As he combs.)* Warm for a coat, but.

CHARLIE. Yes.

OLIVER. Month of May-you-know.

CHARLIE *(an evasion).* I was halfway out the door when I remembered this lot. Rubbish mostly. HP agreements,[5] rent books, insurance, broken pipe . . . *(He moves them to the bureau.)*

OLIVER. Now!

CHARLIE. What?

OLIVER *(bowing his head for inspection.)* Look. You see . . . see?

CHARLIE. Mm . . . you were right and I was wrong. Hair care is not an idle dream.

OLIVER. The old massage-you-know.

CHARLIE. Ah-hah.

OLIVER *(firmly).* Oh, yes. *(Stroking his hair, he picks up his glass and drinks.)*

CHARLIE. Have you children? *(Drinking, Oliver holds up four fingers.)* Ah? *(Oliver jabs a finger towards Charlie.)* Um? *(Takes a sip of tea. Charlie points interrogatively towards himself and raises one finger.)*

---

4. **St. Ann** mother of the Blessed Virgin, patroness of Christian marriage
5. **HP agreements** purchase on credit

OLIVER. Ah.

CHARLIE. What else?

OLIVER. What?

CHARLIE. Is new.

OLIVER. Oh, now.

CHARLIE. Long time. So?

OLIVER. Oh, now. *(He thinks. Pause. Charlie waits, then is about to go back to his sorting.)* Yes, by Jove, knew I had something to tell you. Six years ago . . .

CHARLIE. Yes?

OLIVER. I finally got the theme music from "King's Row."[6]

CHARLIE. Is that so?

OLIVER. Only electronically-simulated stereo-you-know. But still . . .

CHARLIE. Still . . .

OLIVER. That was a good fillum.[7]

CHARLIE. Wasn't it.

OLIVER. I got billy-ho[8] for going with you to that fillum. My mother wouldn't let me play with you over that fillum.

CHARLIE. Why?

OLIVER. Oh, pretend he doesn't know!

CHARLIE. Remind me.

OLIVER. You made me miss my elocution class.

CHARLIE *(remembering)*. So I did.

OLIVER. Ah, sappy days. Do you remember that expression we had, ah, sappy days? I was glad I kept up with the old elocution-you-know. A great stand-by. Always pronounce properly and look after your appearance: that's how you get on.

CHARLIE. *Did* you get on?

OLIVER. Oh-well-you-know.

CHARLIE. How fantastic.

OLIVER. No harm being ready and waiting.

CHARLIE. None.

OLIVER. That's why I was always smart in myself.

CHARLIE. And got all the best girls.

OLIVER. I did, though, did-n't I?

CHARLIE. Betty Brady . . .

OLIVER. Oh, now.

CHARLIE. And that one who lived in the maze of buildings behind Cross Avenue. What was it we called her?

---

6. **"King's Row"** Hollywood film (1941) on the theme of cruelty and madness behind a facade of pleasantry in smalltown America   7. **fillum** film   8. **billy-ho** chastisement

OLIVER. The Casbah.[9]

CHARLIE. The Casbah. And Maureen O'Reilly.

OLIVER. Maureen . . . oh, don't-be-talking. There was a girl who took pride in her appearance. With the big—well, it was-you-know—chest.

CHARLIE. Tits.

OLIVER *(as before)*. Ho-ho-ho.

CHARLIE. She once told me . . . she said: "Oliver is going to be a great man." Believed it. *(Oliver's smile crumples; it is as if his face had collapsed from inside.)* Mad about you. They all were. What's up? *(Oliver shakes his head. He affects to peer closely at a wall picture.)* All I ever seemed to get was the kind of girl who had a special dispensation from Rome to wear the thickest part of her legs below the knees.[10] *(Looking for reaction.)* Yes?

OLIVER *(face unseen.)* Oh, now.

CHARLIE. Modelled yourself on Tyrone Power,[11] right? I favoured Gary Cooper[12] myself, but somehow I always came across as Akim Tamiroff.[13] Jesus, Oliver, us in those days! We even thought Gene Autry[14] could act.

CHARLIE *(turning)*. He could sing "Mexicali Rose,"[15] still and all.

CHARLIE. Least he could do.

OLIVER. Your drawback was you didn't take the Dale Carnegie course[16] like I done.

CHARLIE. Too lazy.

OLIVER. Very worthwhile-you-know. Then, after you went over the Pond,[17] as they say, I joined the Rosicrucians.[18] That was a great comfort to me the time the mother died. It's all about the soul surviving-you-know in the Universal Consciousness. Do you think I should keep on with it?

CHARLIE. Of course, if it helps.

OLIVER. Your da-you-know came to the mother's funeral. I never forgot that to him.

CHARLIE. Well, he was always fond of you. *(Da comes in from the scullery and looks at Oliver.)*

DA. Fond of him? Fond of that one? Jesus, will you give over, my grave's too narrow to turn in. *(He goes out again. Charlie, in whose mind this has happened, winces.)*

---

9. **Casbah** native section of a North African city, containing nightclubs and houses of prostitution   10. **dispensation . . . knees** nineteenth-century Anglo-Irish joke about the reputedly thick-ankled Irish Catholic girls   11. **Tyrone Power** Babyfaced American film actor (1914–58), at the height of his career, 1939–41   12. **Gary Cooper** American film actor (1901–61) cast in heroic roles   13. **Akim Tamiroff** Russian-born Hollywood actor (1899–1972) usually cast as a villain with a foreign accent   14. **Gene Autry** Hollywood actor (b. 1907), singing cowboy, especially in the 1930s and 1940s   15. **"Mexicali Rose"** song in Hollywood film of same name (1939) starring Gene Autry   16. **Dale Carnegie course** for the development of speech and personality   17. **over the Pond** to England   18. **Rosicrucians** a mystical sect devoted to the application of esoteric religious doctrine to ordinary life

CHARLIE. In his way.

OLIVER. In the end, was it . . . 'em, if you don't mind me asking . . . ?

CHARLIE. No, it wasn't sudden. He got these silent strokes,[19] they're called. Old age. What I mean is, it wasn't unexpected. He *went* suddenly.

OLIVER *(still delicately)*. You weren't, em . . .

CHARLIE. I was in London: flew over yesterday, off tonight. Well, my middle-aged friend, now we're both parentless. We've gone to the head of the queue.[20]

OLIVER. Queue for what? Oh, now. Long way to go yet, only getting started. *(He bounces to his feet.)* Well!

CHARLIE. Don't go. Finish your drink.

OLIVER. The wife-you-know.

CHARLIE. Let me finish here and I'll run you home.

OLIVER. No, must be riding the trail to the old hacienda.[21]

CHARLIE *(a hint of urgency)*. Ten minutes.

OLIVER. The little woman . . . *(Oliver moves to the door, takes gloves from his jacket pocket.)* Queer-you-know how a house looks empty after a funeral. What will happen to it now, do you think?

CHARLIE. This place? It'll be re-let,[22] I suppose.

OLIVER. I wondered—what was it I wondered?—do you happen to know anybody in the Corporation?[23]

CHARLIE. Me?

OLIVER. Well, I hear you got on, so they tell me. Gwendolyn and me are on the list[24] for a house this long time. If you had a bit of pull-you-know.

CHARLIE *(his manner cooling)*. No, I haven't. Sorry.

OLIVER. Oh, now. Man who's up in the world . . .

CHARLIE. I haven't.

OLIVER. Oh. Well, ask not and you receive not.

CHARLIE. Dale Carnegie.

OLIVER. Ho-ho. Oh, now. Well, see you next time you're over. Sorry for the trouble. Sappy days, eh?

CHARLIE. Sappy days. *(Oliver goes. Charlie closes the door.)* Fucking vulture. *(He faces the empty room. He returns the teapot to the range with Oliver's unfinished tumbler of stout. He looks briefly at Da's chair and then goes to the bureau and begins to sort papers. He finds a wallet and puts on his glasses to examine a photograph in it. Da comes in. He wears workingman's clothes: Sunday best. Refusing to look at him.)* Hoosh. Scat. Out.

DA. That wasn't too bad a day.

---

19. **silent strokes** mild strokes   20. **queue** waiting line   21. **hacienda** ranch or ranchhouse (southwestern U.S. and Mexico)   22. **re-let** leased or rented out again   23. **Corporation** Dun Laoghaire municipal government   24. **on the list** waiting for public housing

CHARLIE. Piss off.[25] *(Da sits in his chair, Charlie looks at him.)* Sit there, then! No one is minding you.

DA. I knew it would hold up for you. You were lucky with the weather when you came over at Christmas, too. *(Charlie ignores him and returns the papers to the table and goes on sorting them.)* Mind, I wouldn't give much for tomorrow. When you can see the Mountains of Mourne,[26] that's a sure sign it'll rain. Yis, the angels'll be having a pee.

CHARLIE *(whirling on him)*. Now that will do!

DA. That's a good expression. Did you ever hear that expression?

CHARLIE. Did I? Thanks to you, until I was twelve years of age every time the rain came down I had a mental picture of a group of winged figures standing around a hole in the clouds relieving themselves. Go away; I'm working, I'm clearing up. *(Working, half to himself.)* Oh, yes, that was him. A gardener all his life, intimately associated with rainfall: i.e., the atmospheric condensation of warm air which, when large enough to fall perceptibly to the ground, constitutes precipitation. Hot air rises, the rain falls; but as far as he was concerned that kind of elementary phenomenon was . . .

DA. Codology.[27]

CHARLIE. Codology. No, it was easier and funnier and more theologically oriented to say that the angels were having a pee. *(He goes to the range and drops a large pile of papers in.)*

DA. You ought to put that down in one of your plays.

CHARLIE. I'll die first. *(Da rises and, without moving more than a step or two, takes a look at Charlie's teacup, then turns towards the range.)* What are you doing?

DA. Sitting there without a cup of tea in your hand.

CHARLIE. I've a cupful.

DA. It's empty.

CHARLIE. It's full.

DA *(dismissively)*. G'way out that.

CHARLIE. Now don't touch that teapot. Do you hear me? For forty-two years I've been through this, you and that bloody teapot, and I know what's going to happen. So don't touch it!

DA. Not a drop of tea in his cup . . . no wonder he's delicate.

CHARLIE. Look, will you— *(He watches dumbly, almost tearfully, as Da picks up the teapot and starts with it across the room. Halfway across he sets the teapot down on the floor.)*

DA *(agonized)*. Jesus, Mary and Joseph. *(He hugs his hand.)*

CHARLIE. I knew it.

25. **Piss off** Get lost   26. **Mountains of Mourne** in County Down, sixty miles north   27. **Codology** nonsense

DA, CHARLIE *(together)*. That's hot.

CHARLIE. Too damn headstrong. Couldn't you have waited until my ma came in and let her— *(Softly.)* Jesus. *(Da begins to stalk the teapot.)*

DA. Bad cess[28] to it for an anti-Christ of a teapot. The handle must be hollow. Whisht, now . . . say nothing. *(He takes Charlie's cup from the table and looks contemptuously into it.)* Empty! *(He pours the contents—it is three-quarters full—into a scuttle, then kneels down, placing the cup in front of the teapot. He holds the handle of the pot between fingers and thumb, using the end of his necktie as a potholder, and pours the tea. Wincing.)* The devil's cure[29] to it, but it's hot. *(Rising.)* Oh, be the hokey. *(He sets the cup before Charlie.)* There you are, son.

CHARLIE *(controlling himself.)* Thanks.

DA *(hovering)*. That'll put the red neck on you.[30]

CHARLIE. Right!

DA. Where's the sugar?

CHARLIE. I have it. *(Beating him to the sugar and milk.)*

DA. Is there milk?

CHARLIE. Yes!

DA. If you don't want tea I'll draw you a bottle of stout.

CHARLIE. No! *(More composed.)* You know I never . . . *(Correcting himself.)* I don't want a bottle of stout. Now sit.

DA. Sure there's no shaggin'[31] nourishment in tea. *(Returning to his chair. He is brought up short by the sight of the teapot.)* How the hell are we going to shift it? Hoh? If herself walks in on us and sees that on the floor there'll be desolation.[32] The gee-gees[33] let her down today, and if the pictures in the Picture House[34] was a washout[35] as well she'll come home ready to eat us. That's a right conundrum, hoh?

CHARLIE *(coldly)*. Cover it with a bucket.

DA. That handle is hot for the night. *(A solution.)* Don't stir. Keep your ear cocked for the squeak of the gate.

CHARLIE. Why? What . . . *(Da goes to the range, picks up a long rusting pair of tongs and starts to use them to lift the teapot.)* Oh, God. *(Charlie rushes over, grabs the teapot and puts it back on the range. Da drops the tongs. He sucks his scorched hand.)* Now will you get out and leave me be. You're dead. You're in Dean's Grange,[36] in a box, six feet under . . . with her. I carried you . . . it's over, you're gone, so get out of my head. *(Da sits in the armchair, unperturbed, filling his pipe with tobacco.)* Or at least stay quiet. Eighty miserable years of you is in this drawer, and as soon as I've sorted out the odds and ends, I'm slamming that front door and th⌐t's *it*. Your

---

28. **Bad cess** bad luck   29. **devil's cure** devil's curse   30. **put the red neck on you** make you healthy   31. **shaggin'** an all-purpose mild obscenity   32. **desolation** great trouble   33. **gee-gees** racehorses   34. **Picture House** movie theatre in Dun Laoghaire   35. **washout** disappointment   36. **Dean's Grange** Dublin cemetery

nephew Paddy got the TV set, I gave the radio to Maureen and Tom, and Mrs. Dunne next door got my sincere thanks for her many kindnesses and in consequence thereof has said she'll never talk to me again. The junkman can have the rest, because I've got what *I* want. An hour from now that fire will go out and there'll be no one here to light it. I'll get rid of you. I'm sweating here because I couldn't wait to put my coat on and be off. So what do you say to that?

DA *(amiably)*. Begod, son, you're getting as grey as a badger.

CHARLIE. Old Drumm was right about you. The day he came here to give me the reference.

DA. Drumm is not the worst of them.

CHARLIE. He had *you* taped.[37]

DA. Was he here today?

CHARLIE. He was at the Mass . . . next to the pulpit.

DA. Was that him? I wouldn't recognize him. God, he's failed[38] greatly.

CHARLIE. You can talk.

DA. Decent poor bugger, but.

CHARLIE. Do you know what he called you? The enemy.

MOTHER *(off)*. Charlie, will you come down when I tell you.

CHARLIE. Who's that?

MOTHER *(off)*. Charlie! *(She comes in from the scullery. At this time she is in her late '50s; Da is four years older. Looking towards the ceiling.)* Do you want me to come up to you?

CHARLIE. I'd forgotten what she looked like.

MOTHER *(to Da)*. Will you get off your behind and call him. He's in the lavatory with his curse-o'-God books again.

DA *(galvanized into action, yelling)*. Do you hear your mother? Come down out of there. You pup, come when you're called. If I put my hand to you . . .

MOTHER. That will do.

DA *(now wound up)*. Slouching around . . . skipping and jumping and acting the go-boy. Mr. Drumm is halfway up the path!

MOTHER. I said that will do. Read your paper.

DA *(a grotesque imitation of a boy leaping about)*. With your hopping and-and-and leppin' and your playing cowboys on the Green Bank.[39] Buck Jones.[40]

CHARLIE. You were always behind the times. I hadn't played cowboys in five years.

---

37. **taped** sized up   38. **failed** aged   39. **Green Bank** an outcrop of jagged rocks along Ulverton Road, Dalkey   40. **Buck Jones** Hollywood actor (1889–1942); cowboy star in the 1920s and 1930s

DA. Hoot-shaggin'-Gibson,[41] Tim McCoy[42] and Randoloph Scott.[43]

MOTHER. You'd give a body a headache.

DA *(subsiding)*. And-and-and-and Jeanie Autry.

MOTHER. When Mr. Drumm comes in this house you're not to say yes, aye or no to him, do you hear me?

DA. Sure *I* know Drumm. Who was it pruned his rose-trees?

MOTHER. No passing remarks. *(She picks up the teapot.)*

DA. Mag, that teapot is . . .

MOTHER. Say nothing. *(She takes the teapot into the scullery.)*

CHARLIE. I never knew how she did it.

DA. "Tynan," says he to me, "'clare to God, I never seen the beating of you for roses." That's as true as you're standing there, Mag. Never seen the beating of me. *(Ruddy with pleasure.)* Hoh?

CHARLIE. Throw you a crumb and you'd call it a banquet.

DA. "I hear," says he to me, "you're a great man for the whist drives."[44] Do you know, I nearly fell out of my standing. "Who told you that?" says I, looking at him. "Sure," says he, "there's not a dog or divil in the town doesn't know you!" *(He laughs. Young Charlie comes downstairs. He is 17, shabbily dressed. He carries a book. To Young Charlie.)* Charlie, I was saying, sure I know old Drumm these donkey's years.[45]

CHARLIE. Oh, God: not that little prick. *(Young Charlie looks at him, smarting at the insult. Their contempt is mutual.)* You were, you know.

YOUNG CHARLIE. And what are you, only a big—

CHARLIE. Careful, that could lead to a compliment. *(Young Charlie sits at the table and opens his book.)*

DA. Oh, Drumm will give you a grand reference. *(Mother returns with the teapot and pours boiling water into it.)* And if he didn't itself, what odds? Aren't we all grand and comfortable, owing nothing to no one, and haven't we got our health and strength and isn't that the main thing?

CHARLIE. Eat your heart out, Oscar Wilde.[46]

MOTHER *(to Young Charlie)*. Don't lie over the table . . . You'll get a hump-back like old Totterdel.

DA. Old Totterdel was a decent man.

CHARLIE. What's the book?

YOUNG CHARLIE *(surly)*. "Story of San Michele."[47] *(He pronounces it "Michelle" as in French.)*

---

41. **Hoot-shaggin'-Gibson** Edmund Gibson (1892–1962); comic cowboy actor from the 1920s to the early 1940s 42. **Tim McCoy** Hollywood cowboy actor (1891–1978); teamed up with Buck Jones on "Rough Rider" westerns 1940–42 43. **Randolph Scott** prototypical Hollywood actor, playing romantic and cowboy roles between 1929 and 1962 44. **whist drives** card parties 45. **donkey's years** a long time 46. **Oscar Wilde** Irish wit, dramatist, and *bon vivant* 47. **"Story of San Michele"** Axel Munthe's best-selling account (1929) of a doctor's life

CHARLIE *(Italian)*. Michele, you thick.

MOTHER. The state of that shirt. I'll give you a fresh one.

YOUNG CHARLIE. It's only Tuesday.

MOTHER. Take it off.

YOUNG CHARLIE. How am I to wear one shirt all week?

MOTHER. You can go easy on it, can't you? Do as you're told. *(Going into the scullery.)* More you do for them, the less thanks you get. *(Young Charlie removes his shirt: under it is a singlet.)*

DA. You could plant seed potatoes on that shirt, son.

YOUNG CHARLIE *(muffled, the shirt over his head)*. Ah, dry up.

DA *(singing to himself: the tune is "The Girl I Left Behind Me")*.[48]

> "Oh, says your oul' wan to my oul' wan,[49]
> 'Will you come to the Waxie Dargle?'
> And says my oul' wan to your oul' wan,
> 'Sure I haven't a farthin'.'"[50]

The Waxies were tailors and the Waxie Dargle was a fair they used to have beyant in Bray in old God's time.[51] You never knew that. Hoh? *(Young Charlie, shivering, ignores him.)*

CHARLIE *(glaring)*. Answer him.

YOUNG CHARLIE *(to Da)*. Yeah, you told me. *(To Charlie.)* You're a nice one to talk about being polite to him.

CHARLIE. Privilege of age, boy.

DA *(pinching Young Charlie's arm)*. Begod, son, there's not a pick on you. "I'm thin," the fella says, "and you're thin"; but says he: "Y'r man is thinner than the pair of us put together!" *(Mother has returned with the shirt.)*

MOTHER. This is newly-ironed. Put it on. *(She holds it for him. It has been lengthened by the addition of ill-matching pieces from another shirt to the tail and sleeves.)*

YOUNG CHARLIE. What's that?

MOTHER. Put it on you.

YOUNG CHARLIE. Look at it.

MOTHER. There's not a brack[52] on that shirt, only it's gone a bit small for you. There's many a poor person 'ud be glad of it.

YOUNG CHARLIE. Then give it to them.

MOTHER. You cur.

YOUNG CHARLIE. God, look at the tail.

MOTHER. Who's going to see it?

---

in Paris and on Capri   48. **"The Girl I Left Behind Me"** popular Irish street ballad   49. **my oul' wan** my mother (derogatory)   50. **farthin'** a quarter penny, the smallest coin   51. **old God's time** long ago   52. **brack** spot

YOUNG CHARLIE. I'm not wearing it.

MOTHER *(flinging the shirt down)*. Leave it there, then. Don't. *(Picking it up at once.)* Put that shirt on you.

YOUNG CHARLIE. I won't.

MOTHER *(turning to Da)*. Nick . . .

DA *(a half-feigned, half-real, rather frightened anger)*. Do like the woman tells you. Can we not have a bit of peace and quiet in the house the one day of the week? Jasus Christ tonight, do you want old Drumm to walk in on top of you?

MOTHER *(quietly)*. That will do you with your Sacred Name. *(To Young Charlie.)* Lift your arms.

YOUNG CHARLIE *(already beaten)*. I'm not wearing that— *(She slaps his face briskly and, almost in the same movement, thrusts the shirt over his head. She pulls his arms into the sleeves, jerks him to her and fastens the buttons.)*

DA *(relieved)*. That's the boy. Herself cut up one of my old shirts for that, son: didn't you, Mag?

CHARLIE. You were always there with the good news.

MOTHER *(coldly, wanting to hurt back)*. The day you bring money in, you can start being particular. Time enough then for you to act the gentleman. You can do the big fellow in here then, as well as on the sea front.[53] Oh, it's an old saying and a true one: the more you do for them . . .

DA. Sure that looks grand.

MOTHER. How bad he is . . . And at the end of it they'd hang you. *(Young Charlie puts his jacket on. He sits and picks up his book.)*

CHARLIE. You always gave in. Too soft to stand up to them. No guts. *(Mother is at the door looking out.)* It could have been worse. Like the time you had the date with Ita Byrne and you asked her (Mother) to press your navy-blue trousers: told her it was for the altar boys' outing. She'd never pressed a pair of trousers in her life, and she put the creases down the side. And every little gurrier in the town followed you and Ita that night singing "Anchors Aweigh." Remember?

YOUNG CHARLIE *(now grinning)*. Sappy days.

(The gate squeaks.)

MOTHER. There he is now. *(To Young Charlie, fearfully, the quarrel forgotten.)* God and his holy Mother send he'll find you something. *(Da starts towards the door. She yanks him back.)* Will you wait till he knocks.

DA *(almost an incantation)*. Sure I know old Drumm.

MOTHER. And keep that mouth of yours shut. Have manners.

YOUNG CHARLIE. He's only a clerk, you know. *(She looks at him venomously. Drumm comes into view: he is in his mid-50s, thin, acerbic. He knocks. Mother and Da go to the door. The greetings are mimed.)*

53. **sea front** promenade, boardwalk

DA. He was a chief clerk. (*Young Charlie looks towards the door, anguish on his face, fists clenched.*) Five-fifty a year . . . not bad for nineteen-forty . . . what?

YOUNG CHARLIE. Four . . . November.

CHARLIE. What's up?

YOUNG CHARLIE. Nothing.

CHARLIE. Don't be proud with me, boy.

YOUNG CHARLIE. Listen to them: they always *crawl.*

CHARLIE. Blessed are the meek: they shall inherit the dirt.[54] The shame of being ashamed of them was the worst part, wasn't it? What are you afraid of?

YOUNG CHARLIE. Tell us . . . That day.

CHARLIE. When?

YOUNG CHARLIE. Then. Now. Today. Did they . . . say anything to him?

CHARLIE. About what? (*Drumm is shown in.*)

MOTHER. Still, we're terrible, dragging you out of your way.

DRUMM. Is this the young man? (*Shaking hands.*) How do you do?

DA (*belatedly*). Shake hands, son.

DRUMM. A bookworm like myself, I see.

MOTHER (*to Da*). Move out and let the man sit down.

DA (*offering his chair, saluting with one finger*). Here you are, sir!

CHARLIE (*angry*). Don't call him sir.

MOTHER. Now you'll sit there and have a cup of tea in your hand. (*She sets about pouring the tea.*)

DRUMM (*quite sternly*). No, I will not.

DA (*aggressive*). Don't mind him. Yes, he will. You will!

DRUMM. You're a foolish woman. In these times we may take hospitality for granted. A ration of a half-ounce of tea per person per week doesn't go far.

MOTHER (*serving him*). Now it won't poison you.

DA. And them's not your tea-leaves that are used and dried out and used again, sir. Get that down you. There's your milk and there's your sugar.

DRUMM. Look here, my dear man, will you sit. I'm not helpless.

MOTHER. Nick . . .

DA. Sure what the hell else have we only for the cup of tea? Damn all . . . amn't I right?

DRUMM (*ignoring him, to Young Charlie*). Your name is . . . ?

MOTHER. Charles Patrick.

54. **inherit the dirt** travesty of Jesus' words (Matt. 5: 3)

DRUMM. And you've done with school?

MOTHER. He's got a scholarship to the Presentation Brothers.[55] There was many a one got it and took the money; but no, we said, let him have the education, because it'll stand to him when we're gone.

DA. Oh, Charlie's the boy with the brains.

DRUMM. Bright are you? Who's your favourite author?

YOUNG CHARLIE. Shakespeare.

CHARLIE. You liar.

DRUMM. And where do your talents lie?

YOUNG CHARLIE. Dunno.

DRUMM. An authority on Shakespeare shouldn't mumble. I asked, what kind of post do you want?

MOTHER. He'll take what he's offered. He's six months idle since he left school. He won't pick and choose.

DA. And if there's nothing for him, sure he can wait. There'll be any amount of jobs once the war's over.

DRUMM. Past history says otherwise. There's usually a depression.

DA. Not at all.

DRUMM. You're an expert, are you?

DA *(a stock phrase)*. What are you talking about, or do you know what you're talking about? The Germans know the Irish are their friends,[56] and sign's on it,[57] when the good jobs are handed out in England they'll give us the first preference.

DRUMM. Who will?

DA. The Jerries, amn't I telling you . . . when they win.

DRUMM. You support the Germans, do you?

CHARLIE *(to Da)*. Shut up. *(To Young Charlie.)* Don't go red. Smile. *(Young Charlie summons up an unnatural grin. He laughs. At once Drumm looks at him bad-temperedly.)*

DRUMM. Is something amusing you?

YOUNG CHARLIE. No.

DA. Hitler's the man that's well able for them. He'll give them lackery, the same as *we* done.[58] Sure isn't he the greatest man under the sun, himself and De Valera?[59]

MOTHER *(not looking at him)*. Now that will do . . .

DA. What the hell luck could the English have? Didn't they come into

55. **Presentation Brothers** Presentation College, Glasthule, a boy's secondary school run by a Catholic religious community of teachers 56. **The Germans know the Irish are their friends** the Irish Free State was neutral during World War II 57. **sign's on it** all indications are 58. **lackery, same as we done** give them a beating as the I.R.A. did (the Irish War of Independence, 1919–21) 59. **De Valera** Eamon De Valera (1882–1975), Irish *taoiseach* (prime minister) during World War II

the town here and shoot decent people in their beds?[60] But they won't see the day when they can crow it over Heil Hitler. He druv them back into the sea in 1940,[61] and he'll do it again now. Sure what's Churchill anyway, bad scran to him,[62] only a yahoo,[63] with the cigar stuck in his fat gob and the face on him like a boiled shite. *(Pause. Drumm just looks at him.)*

MOTHER. There's plenty more tea in the—

DRUMM. No, I must be going.

MOTHER *(with a false smile)*. You oughtn't to mind him.

DRUMM. I don't at all. I thought the boy might walk with me, and I could ask him what it is I need to know.

MOTHER. Charlie, do you hear? Go and comb your hair and give your face a rub. *(Young Charlie goes upstairs, glad to get away.)* I know you'll do your best for him. You will.

DRUMM. It would be a poor best. There's nothing here for anyone. Have you thought of letting him go to England?

DA. England!

DRUMM. There's work there.

MOTHER. Ah, no.

DRUMM. It might be for his good.

MOTHER. No, we'd think bad of losing him.

DA. There's good jobs going here if you keep an eye out. I'm gardening above in Jacob's[64] these forty-six years, since I was a young lad . . . would you credit[65] that?

DRUMM. Yes, I would.

MOTHER. What is there in England only bombs and getting into bad health? No, he'll stay where he's well looked after. Sure, Mr. Drumm, we're all he has. His own didn't want him.

DRUMM. His own?

MOTHER *(bitterly)*. Whoever she was.

DRUMM. Do you mean the boy is adopted?

(Young Charlie comes downstairs at a run, anxious to be off. He hears what Drumm has said and hangs back on the stairs.)

MOTHER *(purely as punctuation)*. Ah, don't talk to me.

CHARLIE. And I listened, faint with shame, while you delivered your party-piece.

MOTHER. I took him out of Holles Street Hospital[66] when he was ten days old, and he's never wanted for anything since. My mother that's dead and gone, the Lord have mercy on her, said to me: "Mag, he's a nurse-

---

60. **shoot decent people in their beds** British military repression was notorious   61. **He druv them back into the sea in 1940** British evacuation of Dunkirk   62. **bad scran** bad luck   63. **yahoo** lout   64. **Jacob's** W & R Jacob, biscuit (cookie) manufacturers, Quakers   65. **credit** believe   66. **Holles Street Hospital** Dublin's Catholic maternity hospital

child.[67] You don't know where he was got or how he was got, and you'll rue the day. He'll turn on you."

DA *(a growl)*. Not at all, woman.·

MOTHER. Amn't I saying! *(To Drumm.)* You try rearing a child on thirty shillings a week then and two pounds ten now after forty years of slaving, and see where it leaves you.

CHARLIE. Stand by. Finale coming up.

MOTHER. And a child that was delicate. She tried to get rid of him.

DRUMM. Get rid?

CHARLIE. Roll of drums, *and* . . . !

MOTHER. Before he was born. Whatever kind of rotten poison she took. Dr. Enright told me; he said, "You won't rear that child, ma'am, he'll never make old bones."[68] But I did rear him, and he's a credit to us.

CHARLIE. Band-chord. Final curtain. Speech!

MOTHER. He's more to us than our own, so he is.

CHARLIE. Thunderous applause. *(To Drumm.)* Hand her up the bouquet.

DRUMM. You're a woman out of the ordinary. The boy has cause to be grateful.

CHARLIE. Well done. House-lights. *(Young Charlie, his lips pressed tight together to suppress a howl, emits a high-pitched half-whimper, half-squeal, and flees into the garden.)* And the scream seemed to come through my eyes.

MOTHER. Charlie?

DRUMM *(looking out)*. I see he's leading the way. Goodbye, Mrs. Tynan: I'll do what little I can.

MOTHER. Sure I know. God never let me down yet.

DRUMM *(he looks at Da and then at Mother)*. You surprise me.

MOTHER. Nick, say goodbye.

DA. Are you off ? Good luck, now. *(Giving a Nazi salute.)* We shall rise again. Begod, we will.

DRUMM. You're an ignorant man. *(He nods to Mother and goes out. Da laughs softly and shakes his head, as if he had been complimented. Off.)* Young man, come here.

DA *(as Mother comes in from hall)*. There's worse going than old Drumm. A decent man. "I never seen the beating of you," says he, "for roses." *(She glares at him, too angry to speak, and takes Drumm's teacup out to the scullery.)*

CHARLIE *(to Da)*. You could have stopped her. You could have tried. You never said a word.

DA *(calling to Mother)*. I think I'll do me feet tonight, Mag. I have a welt on me that's a bugger.

CHARLIE. All those years you sat and looked into the fire, what went

---

67. **nurse-child** foster-child   68. **make old bones** grow to full manhood

through your head? What did you think of ? What thoughts? I never knew
you to have a hope or a dream or say a half-wise thing.

DA *(rubbing his foot)*. Aye, rain tomorrow.

CHARLIE. Whist drive on Wednesday, the Picture House on Sundays
and the Wicklow regatta every first Monday in August. Bendigo plug-
tobacco and "Up Dev"[69] and "God bless all here when I get in meself."[70]
You worked for fifty-eight years, nine hours a day, in a garden so steep a
horse couldn't climb it, and when they got rid of you with a pension of
ten shillings a week you did hand-springs for joy because it came from the
Quality.[71] You spent your life sitting on brambles, and wouldn't move in
case someone took your seat.

DA *(softly)*. You're a comical boy.

CHARLIE *(almost an appeal)*. You could have stopped her.

(Mother comes in.)

MOTHER. Ignorant, he said you were, and that's the word for you.

DA *(taken aback)*. What?

MOTHER. With your "Up Hitler" in front of him and your dirty expressions. Ignorant.

DA. What are you giving out about?

MOTHER. You. You sticking your prate in[72] where it's not wanted, so's
a body wouldn't know where to look. I said to you: "Keep that mouth of
yours shut," I said. But no . . . it'd kill you.

DA. Sure I never said a word to the man, good, bad or indifferent.

MOTHER. You're not fit to be let loose with respectable people. I don't
wonder at Charlie running out of the house.

DA. What? Who did?

MOTHER. It wouldn't be the first time you made a show of him and
it won't be the last. God help the boy if he has you to depend on.

DA *(upset)*. Ah now, Mag, go easy. No . . . sure Charlie and me is—

MOTHER. *Anyone* would be ashamed of you.

DA. No, him and me is—

MOTHER. He's done with you now. Done with you. *(She goes out.)*

CHARLIE. Serves you right. You could have stopped her.

*(The lights go down on the kitchen and come up on the promenade. The
sound of seagulls. Drumm and Young Charlie appear. They stand in front of
a bench.)*

DRUMM. The wind has moved to the east. Do you take a drink?

YOUNG CHARLIE. Not yet.

DRUMM. You will, please God. Do you chase girls?

69. **"Up Dev"** election slogan in support of De Valera's republican party, Fianna
Fáil 70. **"God bless all here when I get in meself"** a supposedly humorous way
of entering a house 71. **the Quality** the Anglo-Irish aristocracy 72. **sticking
your prate in** intruding, interrupting

YOUNG CHARLIE. Pardon?

DRUMM. Female persons. Do you indulge?

YOUNG CHARLIE. The odd time.

DRUMM. As a diversion I don't condemn it. Henry Vaughan, an otherwise unremarkable poet of the seventeenth century, summed it up happily when he wrote "How brave a prospect is a bright backside."[73] Do you know Vaughan?

YOUNG CHARLIE. "They are all gone into the world of light."[74]

DRUMM. So you do read poetry! Listen to me, my friend: if you and I are to have dealings you had better know that I do not tolerate liars. Don't try it on with me ever again.

YOUNG CHARLIE. I didn't . . .

DRUMM *(firmly)*. Shakespeare is nobody's favourite author. *(He gives Young Charlie a searching look.)* We'll say no more about it. Yes, chase away by all means and give them a damn good squeeze if you catch them, but be slow to marry. The maximum of loneliness and the minimum of privacy.[75] I have two daughters myself . . . no boys.

YOUNG CHARLIE. I know your daughters.

DRUMM. Oh?

YOUNG CHARLIE. To see. Not to talk to.

DRUMM. I would describe them as . . . bird-like.

YOUNG CHARLIE *(trying to say the right thing)*. Yes, I suppose they—

DRUMM. Rhode Island Reds.[76] You may laugh . . .

YOUNG CHARLIE. I wouldn't.

DRUMM. I say you may. *I* do. No . . . no boys. *(He sits on the bench and motions for Young Charlie to sit beside him.)* There will be a vacancy in my office for a filing clerk. I don't recommend it to you: jobs are like lobster pots, harder to get out of than into, and you seem to me to be not cut out for clerking. But if you want to sell your soul for forty-five shillings a week I daresay my conscience won't keep me awake at nights.

YOUNG CHARLIE. Do you mean I can have it?

DRUMM. If you're fool enough. My advice—

YOUNG CHARLIE. A job. A job in an office, in out of the cold. Oh, Janey, I think I'll go mad. *(He jumps up.)* Yeow! *(Drumm taps the umbrella on the ground.)* God, I think I'll split in two. I'm a millionaire, Mr. Drumm . . . any time, if there's e'er an oul' favour[77] I can do for you over this—

73. **"How brave a prospect is a bright backside"** adolescent travesty 74. **"They are all gone into the world of light"** opening line of "They are All Gone," by Henry Vaughan (1622–95) 75. **The maximum of loneliness and the minimum of privacy** after "Marriage is popular because it combines the maximum of temptation with the maximum of opportunity" (Shaw) 76. **Rhode Island Reds** red-plumaged poultry breed 77. **if there's e'er an oul' favour** if there is ever a favor

DRUMM. You can speak correct English.

YOUNG CHARLIE. Honest to God, Mr. Drumm, I'm so delighted, if you asked me to I'd speak Swahili. A job!

DRUMM *(sourly)*. And this is how we throw our lives away.

YOUNG CHARLIE *(grins, then)*. Beg your pardon?

DRUMM. You'll amount to nothing until you learn to say no. No to jobs, no to girls, no to money. Otherwise, by the time you've learned to say no to life you'll find you've swallowed half of it.

YOUNG CHARLIE. I've been looking for a job since school, Mr. Drumm. I couldn't refuse it.

DRUMM. To be sure.

YOUNG CHARLIE. I mean, I'm the only one at home . . .

DRUMM. I'm aware of that. *(Considered it settled.)* So be it. There's a grey look about your face: I suggest you begin to wash yourself properly. And I'll need a copy of your birth certificate. What's your name?

YOUNG CHARLIE *(surprised)*. Tynan.

DRUMM. I mean your real name. You overheard what your foster-mother told me, didn't you? That you're illegitimate. Don't give me that woe-begone look. It's a fact, you're going to have to live with it and you may as well make a start. Bastardy is more ignominious in a small town than in a large one, but please God it may light a fire under you. Do your friends know? *(Young Charlie shakes his head.)* Probably they do. So don't tell them: they won't thank you for spiking their guns. What ails you? Look here, my friend: tears will get no sympathy from me. I said we'll have done with it . . . people will take me for a pederast. Your nose is running: wipe it.

YOUNG CHARLIE. I haven't got a handkerchief.

DRUMM. Well, you can't have mine. Use something . . . the tail of your shirt. *(Young Charlie is about to comply when he remembers.)* Well?

YOUNG CHARLIE. I won't.

DRUMM *(bristling)*. Won't?

YOUNG CHARLIE *(loftily)*. It's a disgusting thing to do.

DRUMM. You think so? *(They outglare each other. Young Charlie sniffs deeply. Brass band music is heard in the distance.)* Well, perhaps there's hope for you yet.

YOUNG CHARLIE. There's a band on the pier.

DRUMM *(rising to look)*. Hm? Yes, the Artana Boys from the orphan-age,[78] by the sound of them. *(Young Charlie whips out his shirttail, wipes his nose and readjusts his dress as Drumm turns to face him.)* Your . . . mother, shall we call her? . . . is a fine woman.

---

78. **Artane Boys from the orphanage** Dublin orphanage with a famous marching band

YOUNG CHARLIE. Yeah. Except she tells everyone.

DRUMM. About you?

YOUNG CHARLIE. All the old ones. Then they say to her: isn't she great and how I ought to go down on my bended knees. Even the odd time I do something right, it's not enough . . . it's always the least I could do. Me da is different: if you ran into him with a motor car he'd thank you for the lift.

DRUMM. I'm fond of him.

YOUNG CHARLIE *(disbelieving)*. Of me da?

DRUMM. I can afford that luxury: I'm not obliged to live with him. You are. That's why he's the enemy.

YOUNG CHARLIE. The what?

DRUMM. Your enemy.

YOUNG CHARLIE *(straight-faced, trying not to laugh)*. I see.

DRUMM. Don't be polite with me, my friend, or you'll be out of that job before you're into it. Once at a whist drive I heard him say that the world would end in 1940. It was a superstition that had a fashionable currency at one time among the credulous. Well, 1940 came and went, as you may have noticed, and finding myself and the county of Dublin unscathed, I tackled him on the subject. He was unruffled. He informed me that the world hadn't ended because the German bombs had upset the weather. *(Young Charlie laughs boisterously. He bangs his fists on his knees. Da enters the neutral area and rings a doorbell.)* Yes, the dangerous ones are those who amuse us. *(The bell is rung again. Da puts his pipe in his pocket and waits.)* There are millions like him: inoffensive, stupid, and not a damn bit of good. They've never said no in their lives or to their lives, and they'd cheerfully see the rest of us buried. If you have any sense, you'll learn to be frightened of him. *(A light is flashed on Da's face as if a door had been opened.)*

DA *(saluting)*. That's a hash[79] oul' day, ma'am. Certainly you know me . . . Tynan, of Begnet's Villas, sure I'm as well known as a begging ass.[80] And do you know what I'm going to tell you? . . . that back field of yours, the meadow: if you was to clear that field of the rocks that's in it and the stumps of trees and had it dug up with a good spreading of manure on the top of it, begod, you wouldn't know yourself. There's bugger-all[81] you couldn't grow in it.

DRUMM. From people too ignorant to feel pain, may the good God deliver us!

DA. The young lad, do you see, he's starting work. Oh, a toppin' job: running an office, sure he's made for life. And the way it is, I'd think bad

79. **hash** harsh   80. **begging ass** a wandering ass that comes to doors wanting to be fed   81. **bugger all** nothing

of him starting off without a decent suit on his back or the couple of good shirts. Sure you couldn't let him mix with high-up people and the arse out of his trousers. Have you me?

DRUMM. I'm advising you to live in your own world, not with one foot in his.

DA. I'll come to you so on Sundays and do the field . . . sure it won't take a feather out of me. *(Embarrassed by mention of money.)* Very good, yis . . . I'll leave that to yourself: sure whatever you think. *(Saluting.)* Thanks very much, more power. *(He starts off, then bobs back again.)* More power, says oul' Power when young Power was born,[82] wha'? *(The doorlight snaps off. As he moves away, the lights on the neutral area go down.)*

DRUMM. Are we still on speaking terms?

YOUNG CHARLIE *(hating him)*. Yes!

DRUMM. You aren't angry?

YOUNG CHARLIE. No!

DRUMM. Indeed, why should you be! Shall we stroll down and listen to the Artane Boys? *(They walk off. Lights come up quickly on Charlie and Da in the kitchen as before.)*

CHARLIE. And I went off with him like a trollop.

DA. Drumm is a decent skin. Came in here once to see how I was managing after herself died. Three years ago this month, yis. Gev me a packet of cigarettes. "No," says I, "I won't. You will," says he; "take them when you're told to." So I did. Wait now till I see where I have them.

CHARLIE. We listened to the band and I even made excuses for you. Told him about your grandfather and two uncles starving to death in the Famine.[83]

DA. Oh, aye. Them was hard times. They died in the ditches.

CHARLIE. What ditches? I made it up!

DA. Fierce times they were. Where the hell did I put them? You can smoke them in the aeroplane. *(Going to the dresser.)*

CHARLIE. I don't want them.

DA *(searching)*. Yes, you do.

CHARLIE. Don't make a— *(He takes a packet of "Player's"[84] from his pocket.)* It's all right . . . look, I found them.

DA. Hoh?

CHARLIE. Look.

DA. Good lad. Yis, it was in the month of— *(He breaks off.)* Drumm smoked "Sweet Aftons"[85] . . . that's not them. *(He resumes the search.)*

CHARLIE. Messer![86]

82. **More power says oul' Power when young Power was born** popular Irish inanity   83. **Famine** Irish potato famine (1845–48)   84. **"Players"** popular cigarette by Player & Wills   85. **"Sweet Aftons"** popular cigarette by P. J. Carroll   86. **Messer!** bungler

DA. It was in the month of May herself died, and it was in the month of May I went. Would you credit that? *(He climbs on a chair.)*

CHARLIE. Congratulations. I should have stuck up for you and told him to keep his job. Then I could have hated you instead of myself. Because he was dead on: he described you to a— *(Seeing him.)* Oh, get down. *(Da finds the cigarettes on top of the dresser. He begins to climb down.)* You destroyed me, you know that? Long after I'd quit the job and seen the last of Drumm, I was dining out in London: black dickie-bow,[87] oak paneling, picture of Sarah Bernhardt[88] at nine o'clock: the sort of place where you have to remember not to say thanks to the waiters. I had just propelled an erudite remark across the table and was about to shoot my cuffs, lose my head and chance another one, when I felt a sudden tug as if I was on a dog-lead. I looked, and there were you at the other end of it. Paring your corns, informing me that bejasus the weather would hold up if it didn't rain, and sprinkling sugar on my bread when Ma's back was turned. *(Da gives him the cigarettes as if he was passing on contraband.)*

DA. Say nothing. Put this in your pocket.

CHARLIE. So how could I belong there if I belonged here?

DA. "Take them," says Drumm to me, "when you're told to."

CHARLIE. And it was more than a memory. She was dead then, and at that moment I knew you were sitting here on your own while the daylight went. Did you think bad of me? I wish I were a fly inside your head, like you're a wasp inside of mine. Why wouldn't you come and live with us in London when we asked you?

DA. What would I do that for?

CHARLIE. You were eighty-one.

DA. Sure I was a marvel. "Begod, Tynan," says Father Kearney to me, "we'll have to shoot you in the wind-up."[89] What a fool I'd be to leave herself 's bits and pieces here where any dog or divil could steal them. And for what? To go to England and maybe land meself in an early grave with the food they serve up to you.

CHARLIE. No, you'd rather stay here instead, like a maggot in a cabbage, and die of neglect.

DA. I fended for meself. No better man.

CHARLIE. Out of sight, you were a millstone. You couldn't even let me lose my virginity in peace.

DA. Lose your what?

CHARLIE. Nothing. It's a slang word, now obsolete.

(Mary Tate walks on. She is 25, a loner.)

DA. Who's that? That's a fine figure of a girl. What's she doing around here?

---

87. **dickie-bow** bowtie   88. **Sarah Bernhardt** French stage actress (1844–1923)   89. **wind-up** finish

CHARLIE. She's not here: she's on the sea-front. And she wasn't a fine girl. She was known locally as the Yellow Peril.[90] *(Young Charlie and Oliver—younger now—are lounging in the neutral area. Mary walks by. They pay her no obvious attention.)*

YOUNG CHARLIE *(suddenly, singing)*.

"Underneath the lamplight . . ."[91]

OLIVER.

"By the barracks gate . . ."

YOUNG CHARLIE.

"Darling, I remember . . ."

OLIVER.

"The way you used to wait."

YOUNG CHARLIE, OLIVER *(together)*.

"I heard you walking in the street,
I smelt your feet,[92]
But could not meet,
My lily of the lamplight,
My own Lily Marlene."

(Mary's step falters as she hears the lyrics. She continues on to the bench, where she sits and opens a copy of "Modern Screen." The two youths go on singing—quietly now and to themselves. Young Charlie looks covertly at her once or twice.)

CHARLIE *(to Da)*. We all dreamed, privately and sweatily, about committing dark deeds with the Yellow Peril. Dark was the word, for if you were seen with her, nice girls would shun you and tell their mothers, and their mothers would tell yours: the Yellow Peril was the enemy of mothers. And the fellows would jeer at you for your beggarman's lust—you with your fine words at settling for nothing less than Veronica Lake.[93] We always kept our sexual sights impossibly high: it preserved us from the stigma of attempt and failure on the one hand, and success and mortal sin on the other. The Yellow Peril never winked, smiled or flirted: the sure sign of an activist. We avoided her, and yet she was a comfort to us. It was like

90. **Yellow Peril** the supposed danger that yellow races will take over the world   91. **"Underneath the lamplight"** "Lily Marlene," German sentimental song (1939) universally popular during the war   92. **I smelt your feet** adolescent travesty   93. **Veronica Lake** Hollywood actress (1919–73), blonde glamor girl of the 1940s

having a trusty flintlock handy in case of necessity. *(Young Charlie and Oliver both look at Mary.)*

YOUNG CHARLIE. They say she's mustard.

OLIVER. Oh, yes. Red-hot-you-know.

YOUNG CHARLIE. And she has a fine-looking pair.

OLIVER. Of legs-you-mean?

YOUNG CHARLIE. Well, yeah: them, too.

OLIVER. Oh, Ho-ho-ho. Oh, now. Joll-y good. *(Mary looks up from her book as Oliver raises his voice: a calm direct look, neither friendly nor hostile.)*

YOUNG CHARLIE. She's looking. *(To Mary, bravely.)* 'Evening.

OLIVER *(embarrassed)*. Don't.

YOUNG CHARLIE. Why?

OLIVER. We'll get ourselves a bad name. Where was I? Yes . . . I was telling you about Maria Montez in "Cobra Woman."[94] Now there's a fine figure of a—

YOUNG CHARLIE. They say she'd let you. All you have to do is ask.

OLIVER. Maria Montez? Is that a fact?

YOUNG CHARLIE *(pointing)*. Her.

OLIVER. Ah, yes: but who is that hard up for it?

CHARLIE. I was.

OLIVER. I mean, who wants to demean himself?

CHARLIE. I did.

YOUNG CHARLIE. God, I wouldn't touch her in a fit. I'm only—

OLIVER. And she would make a holy show of you,[95] you know, like she done with the man who tried to interfere with[96] her in the Picture House.

YOUNG CHARLIE. When?

OLIVER. I think it was a Bette Davis.[97] The man sat down next to her and as soon as the big picture came on the screen he started tampering with her in some way. And she never said a word, only got up and dragged him to the manager by his wigger-wagger.

YOUNG CHARLIE *(stunned)*. She never.

OLIVER. True as God. He felt very small. I can tell you.

YOUNG CHARLIE. Still, if she minded she can't be all that fast.

OLIVER. Oh-I-don't-know. If she wasn't fast she'd have dragged him by something else.

(Young Charlie looks at Mary in awe.)

CHARLIE. Lust tied granny-knots[98] in my insides. I wanted the Yellow

94. **Maria Montez in "Cobra Woman"** exotic beauty from the Dominican Republic (1920–51); *Cobra Woman* (1944) featured this "Queen of Technicolor" 95. **make a holy show of you** greatly embarrass 96. **interfere with** sexually harass 97. **a Bette Davis** film starring this American actress (1908–1989) 98. **granny-knots** badly tied knots

Peril like I wanted no girl before or no woman since. What was worse, I was wearing my new suit for the first time and I had to do it now, now or never, before the newness wore off.

OLIVER *(who has been talking)*. So will we trot up to the billiard hall?

YOUNG CHARLIE. You go.

OLIVER. Me?

YOUNG CHARLIE. I'll follow you. *(He looks almost tragically at Oliver. Pause. Then Oliver stares from him to Mary.)*

OLIVER. Her?

YOUNG CHARLIE *(agonised)*. Go on.

OLIVER. Ho-ho-ho-ho. Oh, now. *(Dismay.)* You wouldn't.

YOUNG CHARLIE. Olly . . . fizz off.

OLIVER. But you don't want to chance your arm with her; she'd let you. *(Then.)* Where will you take her?

YOUNG CHARLIE. I dunno; down the back.

OLIVER. I'll see you, then.

YOUNG CHARLIE. Yeah.

OLIVER. I suppose you know you'll destroy your good suit.

YOUNG CHARLIE. Will you go on. See you. *(Oliver does not move. Hostility forms on his face.)*

OLIVER. I was the one you came out with-you-know. *(Young Charlie waits for him to go.)* They say it's very disappointing-you-know, very overrated. *(Pause. Angrily.)* Well, don't salute me in the town when you see me, because you won't be saluted back. *(He goes. Young Charlie goes towards the bench. He stops, suddenly panic-stricken. Charlie has by now moved out of the kitchen area.)*

CHARLIE. Do you want a hand? *(Still looking at Mary, Young Charlie motions to him to be quiet.)* If they think you're afraid of them they attack you. You said yourself, all you have to do is ask.

YOUNG CHARLIE. Dry up, will you. *(Mary looks at him.)*

CHARLIE. Now . . . quick!

YOUNG CHARLIE. 'Evening.

MARY. You said that.

CHARLIE. Sit. *(Young Charlie sits beside her. What follows is ritual, laconic and fast.)*

MARY. Didn't ask you to sit down.

YOUNG CHARLIE. Free country.

MARY. Nothing doing for you here.

YOUNG CHARLIE. Never said there was.

MARY. Ought to have gone off with that friend of yours.

YOUNG CHARLIE. Who ought?

MARY. You ought.

YOUNG CHARLIE. What for?

MARY. Nothing doing for you here.

YOUNG CHARLIE. Never said there was.

(Pause. Phase Two in conversation.)

MARY. What's your name, anyway?

YOUNG CHARLIE. Bruce.

MARY *(a sceptical grin)*. Yeah?

YOUNG CHARLIE. It is. *(He crosses his eyes and thums his nose at Charlie by way of defiance.)*

MARY. Bruce?

YOUNG CHARLIE. Mm.

MARY. Nice name.

YOUNG CHARLIE *(pointing off)*. He's Oliver.

MARY. That so?

YOUNG CHARLIE. He's from the town.

MARY. Where *you* from?

YOUNG CHARLIE. Trinity College.[99]

MARY. That right?

YOUNG CHARLIE. English Literature.

MARY. Must be hard.

YOUNG CHARLIE. Bits of it.

(She goes back to her reading. A lull. End of Phase Two.)

CHARLIE. Ask her.

YOUNG CHARLIE. She's not on.

CHARLIE. Ask. *(Instead, Young Charlie clamps his arm heavily around Mary. She does not look up from her magazine during the following.)*

MARY. Wouldn't Edward G. Robinson[100] put you in mind of a monkey?

YOUNG CHARLIE. Let's see. Do you know, he does.

MARY. One of them baboons.

YOUNG CHARLIE. Yes. Yes, yes, yes, yes. *(At each "yes" he slaps her vigorously on the knee. She stares as if mesmerized at his hand as it bounces up and down and finally comes to rest on her knee in an iron grip. As she returns to her magazine he begins to massage her kneecap.)*

CHARLIE *(staring)*. You insidious devil, you.

MARY. It doesn't screw off.

YOUNG CHARLIE. What?

MARY. Me leg. *(His other hand now slides under her armpit, intent on touching her breast. He is unaware that he is kneading and pinching her handbag, which is tucked under her arm. She watches this hand, fascinated.)*

CHARLIE. I think you're getting her money all excited.

99. **Trinity College** Protestant university in Dublin   100. **Edward G. Robinson** a much-caricatured, Romanian-born Hollywood character actor (1893–1973)

MARY *(having returned to her reading)*. You needn't think there's anything doing for you here.

YOUNG CHARLIE. I don't.

MARY. Dunno what you take me for . . . sort of person who'd sit here and be felt with people passing. If you won't stop I'll have to go down the back. *(She looks at him directly for the first time.)* If you won't stop.

YOUNG CHARLIE *(not stopping; hoarsely)*. All right.

MARY *(looking off)*. Wait till that old fella goes past.

YOUNG CHARLIE. Who?

MARY. Him. *(Fondling his knee.)* Not that you're getting anything.

YOUNG CHARLIE *(dazed with lust)*. I know.

CHARLIE. My silver-tongued eloquence had claimed its helpless victim. Defloration stared me in the face. My virginhood swung by a frayed thread. Then . . . !

DA *(off)*.

> "Oh, says your oul' one to my oul' one:
> Will you come to the Waxie Dargle?
> And says my oul' one to your oul' one:
> Sure I haven't got a farthing."

(Young Charlie's kneading and rubbing comes to a halt. As Da walks on at a good stiff pace, he tries to extract his hand from under Mary's armpit but she holds it fast. Passing.) More power. *(He walks a few more paces, stops, turns and stares.)* Jesus, Mary and Joseph.

YOUNG CHARLIE *(his voice cracking)*. Hello.

MARY. Don't talk to him. *(Da looks at Mary's hand on Young Charlie's knee. Young Charlie removes her hand; she replaces it.)*

DA. Sure the whole world is going mad.

MARY. Don't answer him. *(Da sits next to her.)*

DA. The whist drive was cancelled, bad scran to it. Only four tables. Says I: "I'm at the loss of me tram fare down, but I won't be at the loss of it back, for I'll walk." *(He looks at Young Charlie's hand flapping helplessly.)* I dunno. I dunno what to say.

MARY. He'll go away. Don't mind him.

CHARLIE. If my hand was free I'd have slashed my wrists.

DA. Oh, the young ones that's going nowadays would eat you. I dunno.

MARY. He doesn't know much.

DA. He knows too shaggin' much. *(To Young Charlie.)* If your mother was here and seen the antrumartins[101] of you, there'd be blood spilt.

MARY. Much she'd care.

DA. Much who'd care.

---

101. **antrumartins** antics, derived from "Andrew Martin"

MARY. Me ma.

YOUNG CHARLIE. He's talking to me.

DA. Certainly I'm talking to him, who else? That's my young lad you're trick-acting with.

MARY *(to Young Charlie)*. Is he your—

DA. Oh, that's Charlie.

MARY. Who?

YOUNG CHARLIE. Bruce is me middle name.

DA. That's Charles Patrick.

YOUNG CHARLIE. Oh, thanks.

DA *(to Mary)*. You mind me, now. What is it they call you?

MARY *(a little cowed)*. Mary Tate.

YOUNG CHARLIE. Leave her alone.

DA. You hold your interference. From where?

MARY. Glasthule . . . the Dwellin's.[102] *(Da makes a violent gesture, gets up, walks away, turns and points at her dramatically.)*

DA. Your mother was one of the Hannigans of Sallynoggin. Did you know that?

MARY. Yes.

DA. And your uncle Dinny and me was comrades the time of the Troubles.[103] And you had a sister that died of consumption[104] above in Loughlinstown.[105]

MARY. Me sister Peg.

DA. And another one in England.

MARY. Josie.

DA. Don't I know the whole seed and breed of yous! *(To Young Charlie.)* Sure this is a grand girl. *(He nudges Young Charlie off the bench and sits down next to Mary.)* Tell me, child, is there news of your father itself?

MARY *(her face clouding)*. No.

DA. That's hard lines.

MARY *(bitterly)*. We don't *want* news of him. Let him stay wherever he is—we can manage without him. He didn't give a curse about us then, and we don't give a curse about him now.

DA. There's some queer people walking the ways of the world.

MARY. Blast him. *(Da talks to her. She listens, nods, wipes her eyes.)*

CHARLIE. And before my eyes you turned the Yellow Peril into Mary Tate of Glasthule, with a father who had sailed off to look for work in Scotland five years before, and had there decided that one could live more cheaply than seven. The last thing I'd wanted that evening was a person. *(Da rises, about to go.)*

102. **Dwellin's** name of local slum   103. **Troubles** Irish Civil War (1922–23)   104. **consumption** tuberculosis   105. **Loughlinstown** sanitorium, now general hospital

DA *(to Young Charlie)*. You mind your manners and treat her right, do you hear me. *(To Mary.)* Don't take any impudence from him. Home by eleven, Charlie.

YOUNG CHARLIE. Yes, da.

DA. 'Bye-'bye, so. Mind yourselves.

MARY. 'Bye . . . *(They watch until he is out of sight.)* Your old fellow is great gas.[106]

YOUNG CHARLIE *(sourly)*. Oh, yeah. A whole bloody gasometer.

MARY *(pause, then)*. Well, will we go down the back?

YOUNG CHARLIE. Uh . . . down the back . . . yeah.

MARY. He's gone, he won't see us. *(Affectionately, mocking.)* Bruce!

YOUNG CHARLIE. The thing is, I promised Oliver I'd see him in the billiard hall.

MARY. Oh, yeah?

YOUNG CHARLIE. Maybe some evening next week, if you're around, we can—

MARY. Mm . . . sure.

YOUNG CHARLIE. Oliver's holding a table for us. Got to run. Well . . . see you.

MARY. Suppose you will. *(As he goes.)* Y'ought to wrap yourself in cotton wool.[107] *(Chanting.)* Daddy's little baby! . . . Daddy's little b— *(She stops and begins to cry, then goes off.)*

CHARLIE. I stayed away from the sea front for a long time after that. *(He finds an object on the table in front of him.)* Is this yours? *(He sees that he is alone. He looks at it more closely.)* Tug-o-war medal. Nineteen . . . God almighty, nineteen-twelve. It was different then. It was even different when . . . when? When I was seven. You were an Einstein in those days. *(Da comes in from the scullery. He is 30 years younger; in his prime.)*

DA *(A roar.)* Hup out of that! Put up your homework, get off your backside, and we'll take the dog for a run around the Vico.[108]

CHARLIE *(happily)*. Yes, da.

DA *(summoning the dog)*. Come on, Blackie . . . who's a good dog? That's the fella . . . hup, hup! *(He crouches as if holding a dog by the forepaws, and allows his face to be licked.)* Give us the paw . . . give. Look at that . . . begod, wouldn't he near talk to you? Get down. Are you right, son? *(He extends his hand. Charlie takes it. Mother comes in from the scullery with a woollen scarf.)*

MOTHER. No, he's not right. *(She puts the scarf around Charlie's neck, tucking it in tightly.)* You have as much sense in you as a don't-what-what. Dragging him out with his chest exposed. Do you want to get him into bad health?

---

106. **gas** fun   107. **cotton wool** absorbent cotton   108. **Vico** picturesque coast road in Killiney

CHARLIE. Ah, ma . . .

MOTHER. Ah, ma! Go on. Bless yourselves going out, the pair of you. *(Charlie and Da go into the hall. Da dips his fingers into a holy-water font and flicks the water at Charlie.)*

DA *(opening the front door: to the dog, stumbling).* Blast you, don't trip me up . . . hoosh owa that! *(They stop on the doorstep, Da looking at the sky. During this scene, Charlie does not attempt to imitate a child. He is an adult re-enacting a memory. Trust is evident in his attitude towards Da.)* That's a fine mackerel sky. Sure isn't it the best bloody country in the world!

CHARLIE. Da, say it.

DA. Say what?

CHARLIE. What you always say. Ah, you know . . . what the country mug in the army said. Say it.

DA *(feigning innocence).* What did he say?

CHARLIE. Ah, do . . .

DA. Yis, well, he joins up. And he sits down to his dinner the first night, and says he . . .

CHARLIE. Yeah, yeah!

DA. Says he: "Yes, sir; no, sir; sir, if you please. Is it up the duck's arse that I shove the green peas?" *(Charlie laughs delightedly. They walk hand in hand up and around the stage, both singing "Waxie Dargle." Lights go down on the kitchen. They stop at an upper level. Da reaches back to help Charlie up.)* Come on, now . . . big step.

CHARLIE. I can't, da.

DA. Yes, you can.

CHARLIE. I'll fall.

DA. You won't fall. Catch a hold of me hand. That's the lad . . . and there you go! Looka that, looka them mountains. There's a view, if you were rich enough you couldn't buy it. Do you know what I'm going to tell you? . . . there's them that says that view is better nor the Bay of Naples.

CHARLIE. Where's Naples, da?

DA. Ah, it's in Italy.

CHARLIE. What's Italy like, da?

DA *(pause, then gravely).* Sticky, son . . . sticky.

CHARLIE. Da . . .

DA. What?

CHARLIE. Will I go to Italy when I grow up?

DA *(comforting).* Not a fear of it . . . we wouldn't let you.

CHARLIE *(looking out and down).* There's a ship. Is that it, da? . . . is that our ship coming in?

DA. Where? No . . . no, son, that one's going out.

CHARLIE. Will ours come in tomorrow, da?

DA. Begod now it might.

CHARLIE. We'll be on the pig's back[109] then, da, won't we? When we're rich.

DA. We won't be far off it.

CHARLIE. And what'll we do?

DA. Do?

CHARLIE. When we win the Sweep.[110]

DA *(the standard answer)*. We won't do a shaggin' hand's turn.

CHARLIE *(awe and delight)*. Gawny![111]

DA *(deadpan)*. Sure the girl drew out me ticket the last time, and bad cess to her, didn't she drop it.

CHARLIE *(dismay)*. She didn't?

DA. She did.

CHARLIE. The bloomin' bitch.

DA. The what? Where did you hear that expression?

CHARLIE. I dunno, da.

DA. Don't ever again let me hear you saying the like of that. That's a corner-boy expression.

CHARLIE. Sorry, da.

DA. Women is different from you and me: y'ought to grow up to have respect for them. No, never call a woman a name like that, son, not even if she was a right ou'l whoor.[112] *(Pause.)* Do you know where we are now?

CHARLIE. Dalkey Hill,[113] da.

DA. Not at all. In my day this was called Higgin's Hill, and oul' Higgins used to chase us off it and him up on a white horse. He never set foot in church, chapel or meeting,[114] and sign's on it when he died no one would have him, and *(Pointing off.)* that's where he's buried, under that stump of what's left of a cross after it was struck be lightnin'. Sure they say he sold his soul to the Oul' Fella[115] himself.

CHARLIE. What oul' fella?

DA *(pointing down)*. Your man. Isn't the mark of his hoof on the wall below on Ardbrugh Road[116] where he tripped running down to the mailboat to go back to England.

CHARLIE. Da, let's go home.

DA. What ails you?

CHARLIE. I'm afraid of old Higgins.

DA. Are you coddin' me?

CHARLIE. And it's getting dark. I want to go home.

DA. Sure ghosts won't mind you if you don't mind them.

CHARLIE. Da . . . *(Reaching for his hand.)*

109. **on the pig's back** in luck   110. **Sweep** Irish national lottery   111. **Gawny!** golly   112. **whoor** whore   113. **Dalkey Hill** highest point in Dalkey   114. **church, chapel or meeting** religious observance of any sect   115. **Oul' Fella** the devil   116. **Ardbrugh Road** Dalkey

DA. Wait now till I light me pipe and then we'll go.

CHARLIE. Da, you know the thing I'm worst afraid of?

DA. What's that?

CHARLIE. Well, you know me mother? . . . not Ma: me real one.

DA. What about her?

CHARLIE. Me Aunt Bridgie says when it gets dark she comes and looks in at me through the window.

DA. Looks in at you?

CHARLIE. And she says she's tall and with a white face and a black coat, and she comes out from Dublin on the tram, and she wants me back.

DA. Is that a fact?

CHARLIE. And me Aunt Bridgie says it wasn't true what you told me when I was small, about me mother being on Lambay Island[117] where she wasn't able to get hold of me, and living on pollack[118] and Horny Cobblers.[119]

DA. Not true? Did I ever tell you a word of a lie?

CHARLIE. I don't believe she's on Lambay Island.

DA. No. No, she's not there. That wasn't a lie, son: it was . . . a makeup. Because you were too young, do you follow me . . . you wouldn't have understood.

CHARLIE *(apprehensively).* Understood what? Why, where is she? *(Da looks impassively out to sea.)* Da, tell us.

DA *(seeming to change the subject).* Do you see that flashing light?

CHARLIE. That's the Kish[120] lightship.

DA. Well, that's where she is.

CHARLIE *(stunned).* On the Kish?

DA. God help her.

CHARLIE. What's she doing on the Kish?

DA. She . . . she cooks.

CHARLIE. For the lightshipmen?

DA. Yis.

CHARLIE. What does she cook?

DA. Ah, pollack, son, and Horny Cobblers. *(Charlie gives him a suspicious look, then peers out to sea.)*

CHARLIE. Gawny.

DA. So now you know.

CHARLIE. Da . . . what if she got off the Kish? What if she's at home now before us and looking through the window?

DA. Well, if she is, I'll tell you what we'll do. I'll come up behind her and I'll give her the biggest root up in the arse a woman ever got.

117. **Lambay Island** small island north of Dublin Bay 118. **pollack** common food fish found in Dublin Bay 119. **Horny Cobblers** inedible fish 120. **Kish** lightship seven miles out in Dublin Bay, now a lighthouse

CHARLIE (*pleased*). Will you, da?

DA. I will. And bejasus[121] it'll be nothing compared to the root I'll give your Aunt Bridgie. (*Rising, brushing his trousers-seat.*) Now where the hell is that whelp of a dog?

CHARLIE. Da, I love you.

DA (*staring at him in puzzlement.*) Certainly you do. Why wouldn't you? (*Moving away.*) Blackie, come here to me! (*Da's reply has the effect of causing Charlie to revert to his present-day self.*)

CHARLIE (*fuming*). Why wouldn't I? I'll tell you why bloody wouldn't I. Because you were an old thick, a zombie, a mastodon. My God . . . my mother living on a lightship, trimming the wick and filleting Horn Cobblers. What a blazing, ever-fertile imagination you had—Cobblers aren't even edible!

DA (*whistles*). Blackie!

CHARLIE. And pollacks!

DA. You're right son, bolloxed[122] that's what he is.

CHARLIE. The black dog was the only intelligent member of the family. He died a few years later. He was poisoned and no one will convince me it wasn't suicide. God knows how Ma ever came to marry you. (*Lights come up in the kitchen. Mother looks on while Young Charlie is writing a letter.*) Oh, I know how, sort of . . . she told me. I mean why.

MOTHER. He was called Ernie Moore. He used to be on the boats . . . the B and I.[123] The "Lady Hudson-Kinahan" it was. I was very great[124] with him for a while. Then himself came to the house one day and said how he had the job above in Jacob's and he wanted to marry me. So that was that.

YOUNG CHARLIE. How?

MOTHER. It was fixed.

YOUNG CHARLIE. How fixed?

MOTHER. My father told him I would, so it was fixed. Things was arranged in them days.

YOUNG CHARLIE. Did you want to?

MOTHER. I had no say in it.

YOUNG CHARLIE. How well did you know him?

MOTHER. Well enough to bid the time of day to.

YOUNG CHARLIE. That was handy.

MOTHER. A body's not put into this world to pick and choose and be particular. I was seventeen, I done what I was told to.

YOUNG CHARLIE. What about Popeye the Sailor?

121. **bejasus** by Jesus   122. **bolloxed** ruined, destroyed   123. **the B and I** British & Irish Steampacket Co. Ltd., sailing between Dublin and Liverpool   124. **very great with** in love with

MOTHER. Who?

YOUNG CHARLIE. The other one.

MOTHER. Mr. Moore in your mouth. When your time comes and you have to answer to God in the next world it makes no differ who you married and who you didn't marry. That's when everything will be made up to us.

YOUNG CHARLIE. You mean they hand out free sailors?

MOTHER. What? You little jeer, you. *(She aims a blow at him which he wards off.)* Well, God send[125] that you never have to get married young for fear that if you stayed at home you might die, like many another died, of consumption for want of proper nourishment. *(Young Charlie affects to ignore her. He resumes writing and sings "Popeye the Sailorman" under his breath in derisive counterpoint.)* Waited on hand and foot, never wanting for nothing. Well, when you do get married, to whatever rip[126] will have you, I only hope you'll be half the provider for her as himself has been for me. Is that letter done?

YOUNG CHARLIE. Yeah.

MOTHER. Read it out.

YOUNG CHARLIE. The Jacobs don't care whether I get a job or not.

MOTHER. It's manners to tell them, they ask after you. Go on.

YOUNG CHARLIE. "Dear Nelson and Jeanette . . ." *(She gives him a look. He amends.)* "Dear Mr. and Mrs. Jacob: My father has told me how often you have been so good as to enquire as to whether I have yet found employment. I am grateful for your interest and am glad to say that I have now been given a clerical position. So, happily, I am no longer like Mr. Micawber, constantly expecting something to turn up. Thanking you for your—"

MOTHER. What sort of codology is that?

YOUNG CHARLIE. What?

MOTHER. You're no longer like who?

YOUNG CHARLIE. It's an expression out of a book.[127]

MOTHER. Write it out again and do it proper.

YOUNG CHARLIE. What for?

MOTHER. Because you're told to.

YOUNG CHARLIE. Look, there's this character in a book. He's always hard up, but he's an optimist. He—

MOTHER. Do as you're bid.

YOUNG CHARLIE. There's nothing wrong with it. Maybe you don't understand it, but the Jacobs will. It's meant to be funny, they'll laugh when they read it.

125. **God send** God grant   126. **rip** reprobate   127. **book** Dickens's *David Copperfield*

MOTHER. Aye, to be sure they will. At you, for setting yourself up to be something you're not.

YOUNG CHARLIE. It's my letter. You're not writing it: I am.

MOTHER. Then write it proper.

YOUNG CHARLIE. Proper-*ly!*

MOTHER. Don't you pull *me* up. Don't act the high-up lord with *me,* not in this house. They said I'd rue the day, and the gawm[128] I was, I didn't believe them. He'll turn on you, they said. My own mother, me good neighbours, they all—

YOUNG CHARLIE. Oh, play another record.

MOTHER. Don't you back-answer me, you cur.

YOUNG CHARLIE. Whatever it is, if you don't understand it, it's rubbish. To hell with Charles Dickens and the rest of them: Zane Grey[129] and Ruby M. Ayres[130] made the world.

MOTHER. Are you going to write that out again, yes or no?

YOUNG CHARLIE. No, because there's nothing the—

MOTHER. Are you not! *(She looks up at Da, who with Charlie is still standing in the hill area.)* Nick . . .

DA. Ah, son, write it out the way she want you to.

MOTHER. Don't beg him: tell him.

DA *(violently).* Will you do as you're bloody well told and not be putting the woman into a passion! Can we not have a solitary minute's peace in the house with you and your curse-o'-God Jack-acting?

MOTHER. Do that letter again.

YOUNG CHARLIE *(in a rage).* All right, all right! I'll do it. *(He crumples up the letter, takes the notepad and writes furiously.)* "Dear Mr. and Mrs. Jacob . . . I am very well. My parents hope you are well, too, as it leaves them. I have a j-o-b now. I do not know myself, I am that delighted. Thanking you and oblige . . ." *(He signs it.)* Now are you happy?

MOTHER. Hand it here. I wouldn't trust you to post it. *(She takes the letter and puts it into an envelope. He cannot quite believe that she is taking it seriously.)*

YOUNG CHARLIE. You're not going to send—

DA *(turning to Charlie).* Begod, son, you always made a great fist of writing a letter.

YOUNG CHARLIE *(barely in control).* I'm going to the billiard hall.

MOTHER. Go wherever you like.

(Young Charlie storms out, loudly singing "Popeye the Sailorman." He emits a last mocking "Boop-boop!" as he vanishes. We hear the far-off barking of a dog.)

---

128. **gawm** fool   129. **Zane Grey** best-selling American author of sixty melodramatic westerns (1892–1939)   130. **Ruby M. Ayres** British author (1883–1955) of popular romances

CHARLIE. It was a long time before I realized that love turned upside down is love for all that.

DA. There's the whoorin' dog gone down ahead of us in the finish. And the lights is on in the town. *(Pointing.)* That's the Ulverton Road,[131] son, where we frightened the shite out of the Black-and-Tans.[132] And the lamp is lit in your uncle Paddy's window.

CHARLIE. If it is, he didn't light it: he's dead these donkey's years. Uncle Paddy, Kruger Doyle, Gunjer Hammond, Oats Nolan—all your cronies—and old Bonk-a-bonk with his banjo and Mammy Reilly in her madhouse of a shop, with her money, so they said, all in sovereigns, wrapped up inside her wig. All dead. Like yourself . . . and, trust you, last as usual.

DA. That's a hash old wind starting up. We'll need a couple of extra coats on the bed tonight, son.

CHARLIE. We will.

DA. Mind your step now. If you slip and cut yourself she'll ate the pair of us. Give me your hand. Let the light from the Kish show you where the steps are.

CHARLIE. That's it, mother: light us home. Least you can do.

CURTAIN

ACT 2

Charlie and Young Charlie appear, walking towards the front door. There is a slightly exaggerated vivacity in Charlie's manner: the result of having had a few drinks.

CHARLIE. Ikey Meh?[133] I remember the *name* . . .

YOUNG CHARLIE. The tram conductor. We used to yell Ikey Meh at him when the tram went past, and he'd pull the emergency stop and lep off after us—

CHARLIE. *Leap* off.

YOUNG CHARLIE. . . . And leave the passengers sitting high and dry. God, he could run.

CHARLIE. Of course: yes! Ikey Meh. *("Meh" is drawn out in imitation of a goat.)* He— *(He catches sight of Da, who is trailing behind them.)* I told you to stop following me. Now go away.

131. **Ulverton Road** Cf. *Home Before Night*, 45–47   132. **Black-and-Tans** British force mobilized from World War I veterans to help contain the I.R.A., 1919–21   133. **Ikey Meh** nonsense nickname

YOUNG CHARLIE. Leave him alone.

CHARLIE. I go out for a bite to eat and a quiet jar, to get away from him, and what happens? He's in the pub ahead of me. Fizz off.

(Da hangs back and lurks in the shadows.)

YOUNG CHARLIE. You might be civil to him. I mean, it's his day.

CHARLIE. It was. The funeral's over.

YOUNG CHARLIE *(coldly)*. Oh, that's exquisite. You're a gem, you are.

CHARLIE. Don't get uppish with me, sonny Jim: you're as dead as he is. Come in and keep me company while I finish up.

YOUNG CHARLIE. I think I'll hump off.

CHARLIE *(aggressively)*. You'll hump nowhere. You'll stay in my head until I choose to chase you out of it.

YOUNG CHARLIE. Oh, will I?

CHARLIE. There's only room for one of you at a time, and if I let you leave he'll come back like a yo-yo. Look at him, lurking. Get in there when you're told to. *(He has opened the front door with a key and pushes Young Charlie in ahead of him.)*

YOUNG CHARLIE. Mind who you're shaggin' pushin'.

CHARLIE. Shagging. Pushing. Get in. *(Da comes up to the door, moving fast.)* Oh, no you don't. Out, and stay out. *(He shuts the door. Da promptly walks through the fourth wall and sits in his armchair filling his pipe.)*

YOUNG CHARLIE. Someone to see you.

CHARLIE. Who? *(He stares angrily at Da.)*

DA. God, they done wonders with that public house, son. I wouldn't recognise it. All the metally bits and the red lights . . . it'd put you in mind of a whoorhouse.

YOUNG CHARLIE. When were you ever in a—

CHARLIE. Say nothing. Ignore him. *(He searches through the bureau drawers.)*

DA. That pub used to be called Larkin's . . . you didn't know that. *(Charlie fetches a jug from the dresser and empties it. It is filled with old keys, bits of yarn and thread, receipts, newspaper clippings, odds and ends.)*

YOUNG CHARLIE. If you hadn't gone out out you could have been finished and away by now. But no, you couldn't wait to get maggoty[134] drunk.

CHARLIE. Maggoty? On three small ones?

DA. I never seen you take a drink before, son. But sure what odds? Aren't you old enough?

YOUNG CHARLIE *(primly)*. I never needed artificial stimulets.

CHARLIE. Stimulants.

YOUNG CHARLIE. Booze. Look at you.

---

134. **maggoty** very drunk

DA *(placidly)*. The way you swally-ed them. Begod, says I to meself, that fellow would drink Lough Erin[135] dry.

CHARLIE. Shut up. *(To Young Charlie.)* What's wrong with me?

YOUNG CHARLIE. Well, you're a bit of a disappointment.

CHARLIE. Oh, yes?

YOUNG CHARLIE. I mean, I'd hoped to do better for meself.

CHARLIE. What had you in mind?

YOUNG CHARLIE. Don't get huffy. It's not that I amn't glad to see you: at least it means I'll live till I'm forty: that's something.

CHARLIE. Thanks.

YOUNG CHARLIE *(looking at Charlie's wrist)*. And I like the watch.

CHARLIE. Oh, good.

YOUNG CHARLIE. I suppose I could have done worse: but you can't deny you're a bit ordinary. It gives a fellow the creeps, seeing himself at your age: everything behind him and nothing to look forward to.

CHARLIE. I get the old-age pension next year: there's that.

YOUNG CHARLIE. Yesterday I was thinking: I'm only eighteen, anything can happen to me . . . anything. I mean, maybe a smashing girl will go mad for me. Now I dunno. *(Charlie puts on his glasses to read a receipt. Young Charlie looks at him.)* Ah, God.

CHARLIE. What?

YOUNG CHARLIE. Glasses. I'm blind as well.

CHARLIE. I'm sorry about that. The time I was castrated in a car crash, it affected my eyesight.

YOUNG CHARLIE *(horrified)*. You weren't. *(Then.)* You're so damn smart.

DA. Oh, them motor cars is dangerous.

YOUNG CHARLIE. Everything's a laugh, isn't it? Anyone I see who's your age . . . same thing. All lah-de-dah and make a joke of it. God, if something good happens to me, I jump in the air, I let out a yell, I run. Your sort just sits there.

CHARLIE. Arthritis.

YOUNG CHARLIE. You're dried up. Dead.

CHARLIE. I'm a seething torrent inside.

YOUNG CHARLIE. You? You're jizzless.

CHARLIE. I'm what?

YOUNG CHARLIE. There's no jizz in you. The fun's gone out of you. What's worse, you're no good . . . wouldn't even take him with you to London when me Ma died.

CHARLIE. I asked him.

YOUNG CHARLIE. Instead of forcing him.

135. **Lough Erin** Lough Erne, Co. Fermanagh, is one of Ireland's largest lakes

CHARLIE. Him? Who could force him to do anything?

YOUNG CHARLIE. Did you try?

CHARLIE. Don't you get righteous with me, my pasty-faced little friend. It doesn't become you. Were *you* any good? Who was it once gave him a packet of six razor blades for Christmas.

YOUNG CHARLIE. I was broke.

CHARLIE. Yeah, and why? Because you'd bought a pair of nylons for that typist from Cappoquin[136] who let you grope her up against the railings of the Custom House.[137] Six Gillette blades!

DA. Oh, there was great shaving in them blades.

YOUNG CHARLIE. You weren't even here when he died.

CHARLIE. It was sudden.

DA *(rising)*. I think I have one of them still. Hold on.

CHARLIE, YOUNG CHARLIE *(together)*. Sit down.

CHARLIE. It was sudden. I'm not clairvoyant.

YOUNG CHARLIE. You were glad it was sudden, though, weren't you?

CHARLIE. Why not? It's the best way. No pain . . .

YOUNG CHARLIE. No pain for you, you mean. No having to go to him and wait and watch him and say things. All the dirty bits over with when you got here.

CHARLIE. Do you think I planned it?

YOUNG CHARLIE. No, but it suited you. Didn't it?

CHARLIE. I was . . .

YOUNG CHARLIE. Relieved.

CHARLIE *(nodding)*. Mm.

YOUNG CHARLIE. Look at me, you with your lousy watch. I haven't got a tosser,[138] but at least I've got a few principles. Where's yours?

CHARLIE. Principles? You mean like when you took that job Drumm offered you?

YOUNG CHARLIE. That's a stop-gap.

CHARLIE. I see.

YOUNG CHARLIE. I'll be out of it in a month and doing what I want to.

CHARLIE. A month?

YOUNG CHARLIE. A month!

(Drumm appears in the neutral area, a letter in his hand.)

DRUMM. My friend . . . *(As Young Charlie looks around.)* Come in here.

YOUNG CHARLIE. Now what? *(He leaves the kitchen through the fourth wall and goes over to Drumm.)* Yes, Mr. Drumm?

DRUMM. How long have you been employed here?

136. **Cappoquin** market town in Co. Waterford   137. **railings of the Custom House** in Dublin's dockland   138. **tosser** penny

YOUNG CHARLIE. Thirteen years, Mr. Drumm.

DRUMM. In those thirteen years it may not have escaped your notice that there is one filing drawer for names with the initial letter "M," and another for those which are adorned with the prefix "Mac," whether written M-a-c, M-c or M-apostrophe. This letter pertains to one James Maguire. I found it, after a forty-minute search, in the "Mac" drawer. Spell "Maguire," would you?

CHARLIE, YOUNG CHARLIE *(together)*. M-a-g-u-i-r-e.

DRUMM *(slowly, as if it were a death sentence)*. M-a-g.

YOUNG CHARLIE. I must have—

DRUMM. M-a-g.

YOUNG CHARLIE. Yes.

DRUMM. You will concede that this was incorrectly filed?

YOUNG CHARLIE. Technically, yes . . .

DRUMM *(with venom)*. Don't use words you don't know the meaning of. A barely literate child could have filed this letter where it belongs. But not, apparently, a man thirty years of age, with a wife, the beginnings of a family and pretensions towards intellectual superiority.

YOUNG CHARLIE. That has nothing to do with— *(He stops.)*

DRUMM *(dangerously)*. With whom? *(He nods towards the other, unseen members of the staff.)* Get on with your work. *(To Young Charlie.)* With whom?

YOUNG CHARLIE *(a retreat)*. With this place. *(Drumm smiles at him scornfully.)*

DRUMM. File this where it—

YOUNG CHARLIE. Or with you either, Mr. Drumm.

DRUMM. Don't get insolent with me, my friend. If you don't like it here, be off with you. No one is holding you. But while you remain you will stay awake and do your work. Accurately. Do you understand? *(Young Charlie holds out his hand for the letter.)* I asked if you understood.

YOUNG CHARLIE. Yes. *(He takes the letter.)*

DRUMM. We all know that you think your position here is beneath you. But you must try and put up with it and with us, Mr. Tynan. Or whatever your name is. *(Young Charlie looks at him, then goes. Drumm remains standing during the following.)*

DA. Oh, old Drumm is a decent man.

CHARLIE. For years he'd taken me in hand like a Victorian father. He taught me, not by his enthusiasms—he had none—but by his dislikes.

DRUMM. Women, Mr. Tynan, should be given a damn good squeeze at the earliest opportunity, and thereafter avoided.

CHARLIE. Perhaps he wanted a son or a fondness for strays. He made me his confidant.

DRUMM. That man Kelly is known to be a pervert. Shun him. What's more, he spits as he talks. I move away from him, and he follows me and spits on me again.

CHARLIE. One evening, I was in a hurry somewhere—to meet a girl, go to a film: I don't know. I saw him coming towards me. I didn't want to stop and talk, so I crossed over. He'd seen me avoid him. It was that simple. Except at work, he never spoke to me again.

(The light fades on Drumm. Da gets the razor blade from the bureau.)

DA. Ah.

CHARLIE. What?

DA. I dunno is this one of the blades you gev me, son.

CHARLIE. Show. *(He sniffs at it.)* A Gillette, definitely. Sheffield, I'd say . . . nineteen-forty-three. An impudent blade, sharpish after-taste . . . precocious, but not presumptuous. Damn it, I bet this *is* one of them. Anything I ever gave you, you took and wouldn't use. Wouldn't be under a compliment to me. *(Da slips the blade into Charlie's pocket.)*

DA. Say nothing . . . take them home with you.

CHARLIE. It's a wonder you cashed the cheques I sent you for tobacco.

DA. Certainly I cashed them. Wasn't that how I got thrun out[139] of that home you put me into last January.

CHARLIE. Home? Blast your impudence, that was a private hotel.

DA. Whatever it was.

CHARLIE. I'm telling you what it was. An hotel.

DA *(carelessly)*. Yis.

CHARLIE. Because you'd gone dotty.[140] Shouting out to Ma, who was two years dead. Going around to my cousin Rosie for your Christmas dinner at two in the morning. Do you know how hard it was to get you into that hotel?

DA. Hotel me arse. Sure they wouldn't let me go up to the bank to cash that cheque you sent me. But begod, says I, I'll bate them yet. Do you know what I done?

CHARLIE. I heard.

DA. I got out over the shaggin' wall. And these two big impudent straps of country ones cem after me. "Come back," says they. "Leave go of me," says I; "The divil's cure to the pair of yiz." Then doesn't one of them put her mawsy[141] red hands on me be the collar. "Be a good boy," says she to me. Well . . . *(He laughs fondly.)* I drew out with me fist and I gev her a poke for herself in the stomach.

CHARLIE. They told me it was on the breast.

DA. It was in the pit of the stomach . . . I wouldn't poke a woman in the breast. Yis, I drew out with me fist . . . ! That wasn't bad for eighty-three, wha'?

---

139. **thrun out** thrown out   140. **dotty** mad   141. **mawsy** clumsy

CHARLIE. So they threw you out.

DA. And after that you had me put into the Union.

CHARLIE. Into the what?

DA *(ashamed to say it)*. You know . . . the . . . the . . . the poorhouse.

CHARLIE. Oh, you malignant, lop-sided old liar. It was a private room in a psychiatric hospital.

DA. I know, I know.

CHARLIE. A hospital.

DA. Yis.

CHARLIE *(incredulous)*. Poorhouse!

DA. Sure it's greatly improved since I was a young lad. You wouldn't know a bit of it.

CHARLIE *(beginning to shout)*. It was not the p—

DA. I amn't saying a word again' it. Sure hadn't I the best of everything, and wasn't I better off there than I was where you put me before that— in the home?

CHARLIE *(giving up)*. Jesus.

DA. Do you know what I'm going to tell you? If the oul' heart hadn't gone on me the evenin' before last, I'd be alive today.

CHARLIE. Is that so?

DA. It is.

CHARLIE. There are no shallows to which you won't sink, are there?

DA *(proudly)*. There aren't! *(Reminiscent.)* I drew out with me fist and I give her a poke. You never seen me when I was riz, did you, son?

CHARLIE. No. *(Then.)* Yes . . . once.

DA. You did not.

CHARLIE. Nineteen-fifty-one. You were sixty-seven . . . She was sixty-three then, and I still don't believe I saw it happen.

(There is a squeak of the gate and Mother appears. She is carrying a shopping bag.)

DA *(looking out)*. There she is at long last. It's gone half-past six; I thought she was run over. *(He opens the door. Mother comes in. She is in a good mood, humming to herself.)* I say, we thought you were under the wheels of a bus. Where were you at all? The boy is home before you, with his stomach roaring for his tea.

MOTHER *(unruffled)*. He'll get it when it's put in front of him, not before. *(She takes off her coat and hangs it up, then puts on her apron.)*

DA *(grumbling)*. We didn't know *what* happened to you. Was the picture any good itself?

MOTHER. It was an old love thing, all divorces and codology. A body couldn't make head or tail of it. Charlie, clear that rubbidge[142] off the table

142. **rubbidge** rubbish

and be a bit of help to me. *(Charlie puts the odds and ends back in the jug. Mother begins to lay the table.)*

DA. It's seldom we hear a song out of you.

MOTHER. I ought to cry to suit you.

DA. I'm only saying, any other time the picture is a washout you come home to us raging. *(Pause.)* And your horse finished down the field today as well.

MOTHER. Did it? *(Nodding, not caring.)* The going was too soft. *(She goes on with her work, still humming. Charlie and Da exchange puzzled looks.)*

DA *(curious, fishing)*. I suppose Dun Laoghaire was packed.

MOTHER. Crowds.

DA. Nothing strange or startling, so?

MOTHER *(almost coyly)*. Mm . . .

DA. Well, tell us or don't tell us, one or the other. *(Mother turns. She cannot keep her adventure to herself.)*

MOTHER. I was treated to a glass of port in the Royal Marine Hotel.[143]

DA. You were what?

MOTHER. Someone I met in Lipton's.[144]

CHARLIE. The grandeur of you!

DA *(laughing)*. Was he good-looking itself?

MOTHER. It wasn't a "him" at all—don't be such a jeer. This woman comes up to me. "Excuse me," says she, "for asking. Are you not Margaret Tynan . . . Maggie Doyle, that was?" "I am," says I; "Do I know you?" "You do," says she.

DA *(in disgust)*. Ah!

MOTHER. Well, to cut a long story, who was she but Gretta Moore out of the Tivoli in Glasthule.

DA. I never heard tell of her.

MOTHER. Ah, Gretta Nolan that married Ernie Moore off of the B and I.

CHARLIE *(remembering)*. Who?

MOTHER. He's retired these two years.

CHARLIE *(it comes to him; singing)*. "I'm . . . Popeye the sailorman!"

MOTHER. Hold your tongue. *(Da is staring at her, numbed.)* So in with the pair of us into the Royal Marine Hotel. Says she to me: "Sure we're as good as the best of them." And the style of all the old ones[145] there, with their dyed hair and the fur coats on them. Tea, they were all having, and sweet cake. "Sure," says Gretta, "we can have *that* at home in the house." *(To Charlie.)* So this waiter comes up in a swalla-tail coat.[146] Oh, she was well able for him. "We want two large glasses of port wine," says she, and off he went like a hare to get them!

143. **Royal Marine Hotel** upscale hotel in Dun Laoghaire   144. **Lipton's** grocery chain   145. **old ones** elderly women   146. **swalla-tail coat** dress coat

DA. Making a show of yourself.

CHARLIE. What show?

DA. High-up people looking at you.

MOTHER *(loftily)*. Pity about them!

DA. The whole town'll have it tomorrow.

CHARLIE *(to Mother)*. Then what?

MOTHER. Three shillings for two glasses of port wine you'd be hard put to it to wet your lips with . . . and sixpence on top of that for the waiter. Oh, it was scandalous. Says I to her—

DA. Sure Ernie Moore is dead these donkey's years.

MOTHER. What?

DA *(dogged)*. I know he's dead.

MOTHER. How do you know?

DA. I know.

MOTHER. The man's wife says different.

DA. Oh aye, ask me brother am I a liar! Oh, she must be a right good thing. And you're worse. Pouring drink into you in the Royal Marine Hotel, and the crowds of the world looking at you and . . . and . . . laughing.

CHARLIE. What crowds?

MOTHER. Don't mind him.

DA. And I say he's dead and long dead.

MOTHER. Is he? Well, I'll soon tell you next Thursday whether he's dead or no.

DA. What's next Thursday.

MOTHER *(almost coquettishly)*. I'm invited down for me tea.

DA. Down where, for your tea?

MOTHER. To the Tivoli.[147] *(To Charlie.)* Gretta was telling me her eldest is beyant[148] in Canada, and she has a grandson nearly your age, and—

DA. Well, you'll go there by yourself if you go, because I'm staying where I am.

MOTHER. You can stay wherever you like, for you weren't invited.

DA. Am I not!

MOTHER. Your own tea will be left here ready for you.

DA. Well, it needn't be, because you're not going.

MOTHER. Why amn't I?

DA. You aren't setting foot outside of here.

MOTHER. You won't stop me.

DA. Will I not!

MOTHER *(her fury mounting)*. You were always the same and you always will be the same. The one time I'm invited to a person's house, you be-

147. **Tivoli** slum in Glasthule   148. **beyant** beyond

grudge it to me. *(Beginning to shout.)* Well, I'll go *wherever* I like and see *whoever* I like.

DA. Do, and you'll go out of this. I'm the boss in this house and I'll stay the boss in it.

CHARLIE. She's only going for a cup of tea.

DA *(wildly)*. Oh', aye . . . aye, that's what she'd like us to think. But it's to see him . . . *him.*

MOTHER. To see who?

DA. You faggot,[149] you: don't let on you don't know. It's Ernie . . . Ernie . . . curse-o'-God Ernie! *(His fist crashes on the table.)* May he die roaring for a priest . . . curse-o'-God Ernie! *(Even Mother who knows him, is alarmed by the violence of his rage. She stares at him. He strikes the table again.)*

CHARLIE *(remembering)*. And the floorboards barked like dogs, and the cups went mad on their hooks.

DA. You set one foot in the Tivoli, you look crossways at a whoor-master the like of him, and be Jesus, I'll get jail for you, do you hear me? I won't leave a stick or a stone standing in the kip.

MOTHER *(recovering, still a little afraid)*. Look at you . . . look at the yellow old face of you.

DA *(savagely, almost skipping with rage)*. With your . . . your port wine, and your sweet cake, and your Royal Marine Hotel.

MOTHER. The whole town knows you for a madman . . . aye, and all belonging to you.

DA. Ernie . . . Ernie! You'll stay clear of him, Thursday and every other day.

MOTHER. Because you know I preferred him over you, and that's what you can't stand. Because I never went with you. Because you know if it wasn't for me father, God forgive him, telling me to— *(Da makes a violent rush at her, his fist raised.)*

CHARLIE. Hey . . . *(Da's fist comes down and stops almost touching her face, where it stays, trembling, threatening.)*

MOTHER *(quietly)*. Go on. Go on, do it. And that'll be the first time and the last. I'll leave here if I was to sleep on the footpath. *(Pause. Da starts past her towards the scullery. Half to herself.)* You went behind my back to him because you knew I wouldn't have you. *(Da runs to the table and raises a cup as if to dash it to pieces. Instead, he takes his pipe from the table and throws it on the ground. It breaks. He goes into the scullery. Charlie stoops to pick up the pieces of the pipe as Mother faces away from him to wipe her eyes.)*

CHARLIE *(still stooping)*. Will you go? On Thursday? *(She faces him. Although tears are coming, there is a wry, almost mocking attempt at a smile.)*

149. **faggot** a "baggage," applied to a woman

MOTHER. The jealous old bags.[150]

(The lights fade. Then we see a woman enter and sit on a rustic seat in the neutral area. She is Mrs. Prynne, 50, Anglo-Irish accent, dressed for the country.)

YOUNG CHARLIE *(off, singing: the tune is "Blaze Away")*[151]

"Tight as a drum,
Never been done,
Queen of all the fairies!"

(Mrs. Prynne opens her eyes. Through the following, Young Charlie comes on carrying two quart cans.)

"Bollicky Biddy had only one diddy[152]
To feed the baby on.
Poor little fucker had only one sucker
To grind his teeth up . . ."

(He stops on seeing Mrs. Prynne.)

MRS. PRYNNE. Good evening. Do you know where Tynan is? The gardener.

YOUNG CHARLIE. He's in the greenhouse. Will I tell him you want him?

MRS. PRYNNE. If you would.

YOUNG CHARLIE. Sure. *(He goes across the stage.)* Da! Hey . . . *(Da appears, carrying a basket of tomatoes.)* You're wanted.

DA. Who wants me?

YOUNG CHARLIE. I dunno. Posh-looking old one.

DA *(a mild panic)*. It's the mistress. Hold this for me . . . will you hold it! *(He thrusts the basket at Young Charlie and getting his coat from Offstage struggles to put it on.)*

YOUNG CHARLIE. Easy . . . she's not on fire, you know. *(Helping him.)* How much do you think?

DA. How much what?

YOUNG CHARLIE. Money.

DA *(confidently)*. I'll get me due. Pour oul' Jacob wouldn't see me stuck, Lord ha' mercy on him . . . no, nor none of us. Says he many's the time: "Yous'll all be provided for." The parlourmaid and Cook got their envelopes this morning. *(A sob in his throat.)* A decent poor man.

YOUNG CHARLIE. Don't start the waterworks, will you?

DA *(voice breaking)*. God be good to him.

YOUNG CHARLIE. Hey, is it true they bury Quakers standing up?

---

150. **bags** affectionate but dismissive epithet   151. **"Blaze Away"** popular march (1901) by Abe Holzmann (1874–1939)   152. **diddy** pap

DA. Jasus, you don't think they do it sitting down, do you? Where's the mistress?

YOUNG CHARLIE. Yours or mine? *(As Da looks at him.)* By the tennis court. *(He calls after him.)* Da . . . how much was the cook left?

DA. A hundred.

YOUNG CHARLIE. Pounds? *(He emits a quiet "Yeoww!" of pleasure. Exits. Da makes his way painfully, carrying the basket of tomatoes. He salutes Mrs. Prynne.)*

MRS. PRYNNE. Oh, Tynan, isn't this garden beautiful? Mr. Prynne and I shall hate not to see it again. I'm sure you'll miss it too. Sit down, Tynan: next to me. *(Da salutes and sits beside her.)* We loathe selling "Enderley," but with my dear father gone and the family with homes of their own, there's no one left to live in it.

DA. I picked you the best of the tomatoes, ma'am.

MRS. PRYNNE. Aren't you the great man. We'll take them back to Mountmellick[153] with us in the morning. And the rose-trees.

DA *(authoritative, tapping her knee)*. Yis . . . now don't forget: a good pruning as soon as you plant them. Cut the hybrids—the Peer Gynts, the Blue Moons and the Brasilias—cut them well back to two buds from the bottom, and the floribundas to five buds.

MRS. PRYNNE. The floribundas to five buds.

DA. The harder you cut, the better the bloom: only don't cut into a stem that's more than a year old.

MRS. PRYNNE *(attentive)*. I'll remember.

DA *(slapping her knee)*. I'll make a rose-grower out of you yet, so I will. And feed the buggers well in July, do you hear, if you want a good second bush.

MRS. PRYNNE. I do hope they take: my father loved the Enderley roses. Did you hear we have a buyer for the house, Tynan? A schoolteacher and his wife. She owns a fashion business in the city . . . I daresay that's where their money is. Catholics, I believe.

DA *(contemptuous)*. Huh!

MRS. PRYNNE. I'm sure they'll want a gardener.

DA. Let them. Catholics with money, letting on they're the Quality: sure they're the worst there is. No, I wouldn't work for me own: they'd skin you. The way it is, the legs is gone stiff on me, and the missus says it's time I gev meself a rest.

MRS. PRYNNE. What age are you now, Tynan?

DA. I'm sixty-eight, and I'm here since I was fourteen.

MRS. PRYNNE. Fifty-four years?

DA. The day yourself was born, the boss called me in. Nineteen-

153. **Mountmellick** market town in the Irish midlands

hundred-and-three, it was. "Take this in your hand, Tynan," he says to me, "and drink it." Begod, I never seen a tumbler of whiskey the size of it. "And now," says he, "go off to hell home for the rest of the day."

MRS. PRYNNE. The world is changing, Tynan, and not for the better. People are growing hard; my father's generation is out of fashion. *(Da's eyes are moist again. She takes an envelope from her handbag. Da gets to his feet.)* In his will he asked that Mr. Prynne and I should attend to the staff. We think you should have a pension, Tynan: you're entitled to it. We thought twenty-six pounds per annum, payable quarterly.

DA *(saluting automatically)*. Thanks, ma'am; thanks very much.

MRS. PRYNNE. Nonsense, you've earned it. Now, the lump sum. Poor Cook is getting on and will have to find a home of her own, so we've treated her as a special case. But I'm sure you and Mrs. Tynan won't say no to twenty-five pounds, with our best wishes and compliments. *(Da takes the envelope and again salutes automatically. He looks at it dumbly.)* You're a great man for the work, and whatever you may say, we know you wouldn't give it up for diamonds. And there's that boy of yours. Once he leaves school he'll be a great help to you. You did well to adopt him.

DA. The way it is, do you see, the young lad is saving up to get married . . .

MRS. PRYNNE. Married?

DA. So we'd think bad of asking him to—

MRS. PRYNNE. How old is he?

DA. Sure didn't yourself send him up to get me.

MRS. PRYNNE. Was that he? But he's a young man.

DA *(calling)*. Charlie! Come here to me. *(To Mrs. Prynne.)* Sure he's working these six years. Only every shilling he earns, do you see, has to be put by. So herself and me, we couldn't ask him to—

MRS. PRYNNE. You mustn't encourage him to be selfish. Young people can live on next to nothing. *(As Young Charlie arrives.)* Hello. How d'you do?

YOUNG CHARLIE. 'Evening.

DA. Shake hands now, son. *(To Mrs. Prynne.)* He cem to pick the loganberries. Sure we couldn't leave them to go rotten.

MRS. PRYNNE. You are thoughtful. I'll ask Cook to make jam and send it to us in Mountmellick. *(To Young Charlie.)* I hear you're getting married!

YOUNG CHARLIE. I hope so.

MRS. PRYNNE. Well done. But you must look after this old man. Remember how much you owe him, so be good to him, and generous. *(She looks in her handbag and finds a five-pound note.)* Mr. Prynne and I would like you to have this. A wedding gift. Perhaps you'll buy something for your new home.

YOUNG CHARLIE. No . . . thank you. I—

DA. Yes, he will. Take it.

YOUNG CHARLIE. Well . . . *(Taking it.)* I'm sure we could do with a Sacred Heart picture for over the bed.

DA *(missing the sarcasm)*. That's the boy!

MRS. PRYNNE. I see you've reared an art-lover, Tynan. And now the most important thing. I know my father would want you to have a keep-sake . . . one of his treasures. *(She picks up a loosely-wrapped package from the seat. Da and Young Charlie are intrigued. To Young Charlie.)* Have you travelled?

YOUNG CHARLIE. Not much.

MRS. PRYNNE. You must. In these days of aeroplanes, young people have no excuse. When my father was your age he'd been around the world. In nineteen-hundred-and-six he was in San Francisco at the time of the earthquake. That's on the west coast of America, you know.

YOUNG CHARLIE. Yes, I saw the film.[154]

MRS. PRYNNE. After the great fire, he was passing a gutted jewelry shop when he saw this, lying on the ground for the taking. A find in a thousand, Tynan. *(She reverently lifts the paper, unveiling a mass of tangled bits of wire mounted on a metal base.)* What do you think of that? Thirty or more pairs of spectacles, fused together by the heat of the fire. *(Pause.)* My father had them mounted.

DA. Sure, what else would he do with them?

MRS. PRYNNE. Extraordinary, yes?

DA. That's worth having.

MRS. PRYNNE. It is, and there you are. *(She gives it to him; then shaking hands.)* Goodbye, Tynan. Take care of yourself and we'll call to see you when we're in town. *(To Young Charlie.)* See that he doesn't overdo things, won't you? Goodbye . . . our best to your intended. *(She goes off, taking the various cans with her. Da salutes her, tears in his eyes.)*

YOUNG CHARLIE. It's a miracle she didn't take the bench. When she said he found it in the ruins of a jeweller's shop, I thought for sure it was the Star of India.[155] Thirty pairs of spectacles.

DA. You hold them: me hands is dirty. Don't drop them.

YOUNG CHARLIE. Don't what?

DA. They're worth money.

YOUNG CHARLIE *(irate)*. Ah, for—What are you bawling for?

DA. A great man, she said I was. Sure I am, too.

YOUNG CHARLIE. How much did you get?

DA. Fifty-four years in one place. I laid that tennis court . . . aye, and rolled it, too.

---

154. **the film** *San Francisco* (1936) starring Clark Gable   155. **Star of India** star sapphire (536 carats) discovered in Sri Lanka

Young Charlie. I don't care if you knitted the net. How much?

Da *(looking up)*. And I planted them trees.

Young Charlie *(realising)*. You've been diddled.[156]

Da. What diddled? Sure she needn't have gev me anything. The work I done, wasn't I paid for it . . . every Friday like clockwork. I got me week off in the summer . . .

Young Charlie. Give me that. *(He takes the envelope and opens it.)*

Da *(unheeding, ranting away)*. And me two days at Christmas, with an extra pound note put into me fist, and the sup[157] of whiskey poured and waiting for me in the pantry. Wasn't I—

Young Charlie *(looking at the cheque)*. Twenty-five?

Da *(snatching it back)*. Don't go tricking with that.

Young Charlie. Is that *it*?

Da. Isn't it money for doing bugger-all?[158] And sure haven't I the offer of work from the people that's bought the house.

Young Charlie. What work? You're giving it up.

Da. Ah, time enough to give it up when I'm going downhill. Catholics, yis. They own a dress shop. Sure if your own won't look after you, who will?

Young Charlie. My God, she'll kill you.

Da. Who will?

Young Charlie. *She* will, when you bring that home to her. *(Meaning the cheque.)* Here, put this with it. *(He offers him the five-pound note.)*

Da. What for?

Young Charlie. It'll save you a couple of curses.

Da. Go 'long out of that . . . that's for yourself and Polly, to buy the holy picture with. Are you off into town to see her?

Young Charlie. Well, I'm not going home, that's for sure. Blast her anyway, and her twenty-five quid and her Californian wire puzzle.

Da. Sure the Quakers was the only ones that was good to us the time of the Famine.[159] Oh, the mistress is a decent skin.[160] *(He laughs.)* "Tynan," says she to me, "aren't you the greatest man that ever trod shoeleather!" And I planted them hyacinths, too. *(Young Charlie has gone off, taking the parcel with him. Da goes into the house.)* Mag . . . Mag. Do you know what the mistress said to me?

(Lights up. Charlie, his glasses on, is writing. The jug, with its contents, is back on the table.)

Charlie. Twenty-five pounds divided by fifty-four. I make that your gratuity worked out at nine shillings and three pence per year of service. No wonder she didn't talk to you for a week.

---

156. **diddled** cheated 157. **sup** small drink 158. **bugger-all** none 159. **Famine** The Quakers were the first to open soup kitchens during the Famine; official government relief was notoriously belated. 160. **skin** person (familiar)

DA. Who didn't?

CHARLIE. She didn't.

DA. Are you mad? In fifty-nine years there was never a cross word between us.

CHARLIE. Oh, dear God.

DA. There was not.

CHARLIE. "Ernie, Ernie, curse-o'-God Ernie!"

DA. Sure I was only letting on I was vexed with her. *(With relish.)* Oh, I put a stop to her gallop, her and her . . . high tea![161] Son, do you remember them spectacles from San Francisco?

CHARLIE. Do I?

DA. Herself took them down to the pawn office. "How much will you give me on these?" says she. "I'll give you nothing at all on them, ma'am," says he, "for they're too valuable for me to keep under this roof." And you saying I was diddled: you thick, you!

CHARLIE. Where are they?

DA. What?

CHARLIE. The spectacles.

DA *(shiftily)*. I musta lost them.

CHARLIE. Liar. *(Searching.)* They're in this house, and if I find them I'll pulp them and bury them. You ignorant, wet, forelock-tugging[162] old crawler. *(Mimicking him.)* "Begod, ma'am, sure after fifty-four years all I needed to be set up for life was a parcel of barbed wire." And then you put in another four years, toiling for the Catholic but somewhat less than Christian Diors of Grafton Street.[163]

DA. "Tynan," says that bitch's ghost to me, and him only a school-master, "I want more honest endeavor from you and less excuses." "Do you see this fist?" says I to him—

CHARLIE *(still searching)*. I asked you where they were.

DA. I disrecall.[164]

CHARLIE. You probably had them buried with you. I can hear St. Peter now— "Hey God, there's an old gobshite[165] at the tradesmen's entrance with thirty pairs of spectacle-frames from the San Francisco earthquake. What'll I tell him?" *(God's voice, with a Jewish accent.)* "Tell him we don't want any." *(He scoops up the contents of the jug and moves to dump them in the range.)* Mind up: this is the last.

DA *(seizing on an article)*. That pipe is worth keeping.

CHARLIE. It's in bits. You broke it.

DA. Sure a piece of insulating tape would—

---

161. **high tea** large supper with meat or eggs   162. **forelock-tugging** groveling   163. **Grafton Street** Dublin's fashionable shopping street   164. **disrecall** forget   165. **gobshite** fool

CHARLIE. No. Move. *(He goes past Da and drops the lot in the range.)*

DA. You could have smoked that, and you'll folly a crow for it yet. What else did you throw out? *(He opens Charlie's dispatch case and goes through the papers.)*

CHARLIE. At the funeral this morning I heard one of your old cronies muttering what a great character you were and how I'll never be the man me da was.

DA. Don't belittle yourself: yes, you will. What's this?

CHARLIE. Death certificate. Tell me, what was it like?

DA. What?

CHARLIE. Dying.

DA *(offhand)*. Ah, I didn't care for it. *(Peering at a document.)* Eighteen-hundred-and—

CHARLIE. . . . Eighty-four. Birth certificate.

DA *(annoyed)*. You kept nothing worth keeping at all. There was more to me than this rubbidge. Where's me old IRA service certificate?[166] And the photograph of the tug-o'-war team? I still have the mark under me oxter where the rope sawed into it. And the photo herself and meself had took in the Vale of Avoca.[167]

CHARLIE. I threw them out.

DA. And yourself the day of your first Communion with me beside you.

CHARLIE. I burned them. I don't want them around. *(Da stares blankly at him. Charlie waits, almost daring him to be angry.)*

DA. You wha'?

CHARLIE. I got rid of them. You're gone, now they're gone. So?

DA *(nodding)*. Ah, sure what the hell good were they anyway.

CHARLIE. Eh?

DA. Bits of paper. Sure they only gather dust.

CHARLIE. I burned all that was left of you and you can't even get angry. You were a sheep when you lived: you're still a sheep. "Yes, sir; no, sir; sir, if you please—"

DA *(chuckling)*. "Is it up the duck's arse that I shove the green peas?" Oh, that was a good poem.

(Singing.)

"Is it up the—"

CHARLIE. Where's my coat? I'm going to the airport.

DA. Yis. *(Calling.)* Mag . . . Mag, the lad is off.

CHARLIE. She won't answer you. Goodbye. *(Mother comes in quickly from the scullery. She pays Charlie no attention.)*

---

166. **old IRA service certificate** scroll in recognition of military service
167. **Vale of Avoca** beauty spot in Co. Wicklow, thirty miles south of Dalkey

MOTHER *(briskly)*. Where is he? *(Calling upstairs.)* Charlie, you'll be late. *(To Da.)* Call him.

DA *(yelling)*. You pup, will you come down before the shaggin' aeroplane is off up into the air and you're left standin'!

MOTHER. Charlie!

DA. If he misses that aeroplane there'll be no whoorin' weddin'. Then he'll be nicely destroyed. Jasus, come when you're called! *(Young Charlie, carrying a suitcase, is on the stairs, followed by Oliver.)*

MOTHER. That will do. He won't miss it.

YOUNG CHARLIE *(coming in)*. Will you quit roaring. I'm not deaf.

MOTHER. It's the last time you'll have to put up with it, so hold your tongue. Have you everything?

YOUNG CHARLIE. Yes.

MOTHER. Smarten yourself. Anyone'd think it was Oliver that was getting married.

OLIVER. Oh, now. Ho-ho. Oh, now.

YOUNG CHARLIE. I left Oliver's wedding present upstairs. Will you keep it for me?

OLIVER. It's just a bowl to float rose-petals in-you-know. Maybe your da will give you some of his roses.

DA. I only grow the shaggers. I don't learn[168] 'em to swim.

MOTHER. You're to mind yourself in that aeroplane and bless yourself when it starts.

YOUNG CHARLIE. Yes.

DA. Oh, Charlie won't crash.

MOTHER *(half-snapping)*. No one is saying to the contrary.

DA. Divil a fear[169] of him.

MOTHER *(aggrieved)*. Going off to the other side of the world to get married.

YOUNG CHARLIE. Five hundred miles . . .!

MOTHER. It's far enough. Too far.

YOUNG CHARLIE. It's where she lives.

DA. Oh, Belgium is a great country.

MOTHER. It's little you or I will ever see of it. No matter.

YOUNG CHARLIE *(angrily)*. Don't start. You were both invited—

MOTHER. Oh, aye. Aye, I'm sure we were.

YOUNG CHARLIE *(to Oliver)*. They damn well were. But no, it's too far, it's too foreign, his legs won't let him . . .

MOTHER. I said it's no matter. *(Young Charlie gives her a hostile look.)*

OLIVER. When he gets time during the honeymoon, Charlie is going to drop you a line and give me all the details. *(As they look at him.)* About

168. **learn** teach   169. **Divil a fear** no fear

going in an aeroplane-you-know. *(Pause. Young Charlie is chafing to be off and trying to conceal it. Charlie moves to be near him.)*

MOTHER. You may as well be off, so. There's nothing to keep you.

YOUNG CHARLIE *(protesting)*. I'll be back in a fortnight. *(She nods, upset.)*

MOTHER. Please God.

CHARLIE. Now. Goodbye, and out.

YOUNG CHARLIE. Yeah, well, mind yourselves.

MOTHER. You mind yourself. *(She reaches for him blindly. He half-resists the kiss, half-accepts it. She steps back and looks at him, eyes large. He reaches for his case as Da comes forward, hand extended.)*

CHARLIE. Hang on . . . one to go.

DA *(shaking hands)*. Good luck now, son. Sure you'll get there in great style. Oh, aeroplanes is all the go these days.

YOUNG CHARLIE. Yeah. 'Bye, now.

DA *(not letting go)*. Have you your tickets?

YOUNG CHARLIE. Yes.

CHARLIE *(to Da)*. Let go.

DA. Have you your passport?

YOUNG CHARLIE. Yes.

CHARLIE. It's the Beast with Five Fingers.[170]

DA. Have you your—

YOUNG CHARLIE. I've got to go. *(He pries his hand free and starts out.)*

MOTHER. Bless yourself! *(He dips his fingers in the holywater font and hurries out. Mother and Da come to the door. Oliver is caught behind them. He coughs.)*

OLIVER. I'm going with him. As far as the bus-you-know.

YOUNG CHARLIE *(agonised, waiting for him)*. For God's sake.

OLIVER. Well, 'bye-'bye now and sappy days. That's an expression him and me have-you-know. Oh, yes.

YOUNG CHARLIE *(half to himself)*. Oliver!

OLIVER *(turning to wave)*. Cheerio, now.

CHARLIE *(from the house)*. Well, at least wave to them. *(Young Charlie raises a hand without turning and climbs across to an upper level where he rests, waiting for Oliver.)*

OLIVER. That went well, I thought. I mean, they can get very senti-mental-you-know. Often with my mother I can't feel anything because I'm trying to stop *her* from feeling anything. How do *you* feel? *(Young Charlie makes a huge gesture of relief.)* They're all the same-you-know. I dread the roars of my mother when I get married. She cries even if I go to a late-night dance.

170. **Beast with Five Fingers** 1946 horror film starring Peter Lorre

YOUNG CHARLIE. Come on before we meet someone.

OLIVER. Oh-ho. Off to the altar. Can't wait.

YOUNG CHARLIE. Dry up.

OLIVER. The eager bridegroom. Oh, yes.

YOUNG CHARLIE. Well, it's the beginning, isn't it? *(They go off.)*

MOTHER. Well, that's the end of him. *(She and Da return to the kitchen.)*

DA. Still and all, mebbe we ought to have gone, Mag, when we were asked. *(She gives him a sour look.)* Sure it'd have been a . . . a . . . a change for us.

MOTHER. I never hindered him. I wasn't going to start now.

DA. What hinderment? Weren't we asked?

MOTHER *(it is not a disparagement, but evasion)*. You'd be a nice article to bring to a foreign country. *(Then.)* I think I'll make his bed now and have done with it. *(She goes upstairs. She is in view during part of the following.)*

DA *(laughing, watching her)*. Oh, a comical woman.

CHARLIE. She died an Irishwoman's death, drinking tea.

DA. Do you want a cup?

CHARLIE. No! Two years afterwards, I told a doctor in London about you, on your own and getting senile. I said you'd have to be made to come and live with us. He said: "Oh, yes. Then he can die among strangers in a hospital in Putney or Wandsworth,[171] with nothing Irish around him except the nurses." But with your luck you'd probably have got Jamaicans. It's always pleasant to be told what you half-want to hear. So when I came to see you—the last time—there was no talk of your going to London. I was solicitous: asked you how you were managing, were you eating regularly . . . *(Da is in his 80s, stooped and deaf. Charlie's attitude is paternal.)*

DA. Hoh?

CHARLIE. I said are you eating regularly?

DA. Sure I'm getting fat. I go to Rosie for me tea and Mrs. Dunne next door cooks me me dinner. Are *you* eating regular.

CHARLIE. She's a widow. I'd watch her.

DA. Hoh?

CHARLIE. I say I'd watch her.

DA. I do.

CHARLIE. You reprobate. Do you need extra cash, for whist drives?

DA. I gave up going. Me hands is too stiff to sort the cards into suits. The last time I went, oul' Drumm was there. Do you remember oul' Drumm?

CHARLIE. Yes.

DA. He accused me of renagin'.[172] "Why don't you," says he, "join the

171. **Putney or Wandsworth** boroughs of southwest London   172. **renagin'** reneging: failing to follow suit at cards

Old People's club and play there?" Says I to him back: "I would," says I, "only I'm too shaggin' old for them!" *(He laughs.)*

CHARLIE. That was good.

DA. Sure I have the garden to do . . . fine heads of cabbage that a dog from Dublin never pissed on. I'm kept going. I say I blacked the range yesterday.

CHARLIE. You're a marvel.

DA. I am. How's all the care.

CHARLIE. They're great. Send their love.

DA *(rising)*. I was meaning to ask you . . .

CHARLIE. What?

DA *(saluting him)*. I do often see your young one in the town.

CHARLIE. What young one?

DA. Her . . . Maggie. Your eldest. 'Clare to God, Mr. Doyle, I never seen such shiny bright hair on a girl. *(Charlie stares at him. [Note: this is not a flashback to Da as a young man; it is Da in his 80s, his mind wandering.])* Sure she's like a young one out of the story books. The way it is, Mr. Doyle, I'm above at Jacob's these six years, since I was fourteen. I have a pound a week and the promise of one of the new dwellin's in the square. I'd think well of marrying her, so I would.

CHARLIE. Da, no, she's—

DA. You can ask anyone in the town about me. And, and, and she wouldn't want for an'thing. The job is safe, we won't go short. I'm learning roses, do you see. To grow them. Oh, yis: Polyanthas and Belles de Crecys and Cornelias and Tuscanys and Amy Robsarts and Janet's Prides and—

CHARLIE. Da, stop.

DA. And, and, and Portlands and Captain John Ingrams and Heidlebergs and Munsters and Shepherdesses and Golden Jewels and Buccaneers and New Dawns and King's Ransoms and—

CHARLIE. Jesus Christ, will you stop. *(In despair.)* You old get, what am I going to do with you?

DA. A rainbow of roses. I never seen a young one like her . . . so I know you'd think bad of refusing me. *(Looking at Charlie.)* But sure you wouldn't.

CHARLIE. No.

DA. And you'll put in a good word for me? She wouldn't go again' you.

CHARLIE. I'll talk to her.

DA *(happy now)*. I'm on the pig's back, so. On it for life. Oh, she won't be sorry. *(Looking up at the ceiling.)* Mag! Mag, are you up there?

CHARLIE. Da, sh. *(He seats Da.)*

DA *(begins to sing aimlessly)*.

"I've just been down to Monto Town
To see the bould McArdle,
But he wouldn't give me half a crown
To go to the Waxy—"

CHARLIE. Stop it: it's not then any more, it's now. *(Picking up a paper.)* See that? Death certificate . . . yours. *(Da nods and straightens up, returning to the present. Charlie puts the papers back into his dispatch case and closes it.)*

DA. I never carried on the like of that.

CHARLIE. How?

DA. Astray in the head. Thinking it was old God's time and you were herself 's da.

CHARLIE. Oh, didn't you!

DA. And you're not a bit like him. Begod, I don't wonder at you putting me into the poorhouse.

CHARLIE *(getting annoyed again)*. You useless old man.

(The gate squeaks.)

DA. Sure it must have gev you a laugh, anyway. *(Charlie is too angry to speak. He picks up his overcoat. Da moves to assist him. Drumm appears outside the house carrying a briefcase. He is now 70, still erect.)* Are you off, so? Well, God send you good weather, son. Tell them I was asking for them. *(Drumm knocks at the front door.)* That must be another Mass card. Do you know, I have enough of them to play whist with. *(As Charlie goes to the door.)* Did you see the flowers on me coffin? . . . shaggin' weeds, the half of them. *(He sits. Charlie opens the door.)*

CHARLIE *(surprised)*. Mr. Drumm . . .

DRUMM. I'm glad I caught you. Might I have a word?

CHARLIE. Of course . . . come in. *(They go into the kitchen.)*

DA. Oh, old Drumm is not the worst of them.

DRUMM. It's been many years. Will you agree to shake hands? . . . it's a bad day for grievances. *(They do so.)* There, that's done . . . I'm obliged. Mind, I won't say it's generous of you: *I* was the wounded party.

CHARLIE. It was a long time ago.

DRUMM *(good-humored)*. Don't play word-games with me, my friend. Time doesn't mitigate an injury; it only helps one to overlook it. *(Indicating a chair.)* May I?

CHARLIE. Please.

DRUMM *(sitting)*. Years ago I made a choice. I could have indiscriminate friendships or I could have standards. I chose standards. It's my own misfortune that so few people have come up to them.

CHARLIE. Including me.

DRUMM. You tried. You had your work cut out.

CHARLIE. I had.

DRUMM *(being fair)*. I daresay I was difficult.

CHARLIE. Impossible.

DRUMM *(bridling)*. And you've become impudent.

CHARLIE *(unruffled)*. Yes.

DRUMM. A beggar on horseback.

CHARLIE. It's better than walking.

DA. There was a young fella went to confession. "Father," says he, "I rode[173] a girl from Cork." "Yerra, boy," says the priest, "sure 'twas better than walking." *(Charlie's face twitches. Drumm glares at him.)*

CHARLIE. I hope you're well.

DRUMM. Your hopes are unfounded.

CHARLIE. Oh?

DA. Didn't I tell you he was sick? Sure he has a face on him like a boiled—

CHARLIE *(hastily)*. It's hard to believe. You look well. *(Drumm chuckles to himself as if at a private joke. He leans confidentially towards Charlie.)*

DRUMM. I have this . . . tummy trouble. I told a certain person—I don't know why, out of mischief, it isn't like me—I told him cancer was suspected. Quite untrue. Of course he told others, and since then my popularity has soared. I said to one man: "I know you for a rogue and a blackguard." Was he offended? "You're right,' he said; "Come and have a drink." *(With defiant pleasure.)* I did.

CHARLIE. There'll be ructions[174] when you don't die.

DRUMM. There will.

CHARLIE. False pretences.

DRUMM. Pity about them.

CHARLIE. Still . . .

DRUMM. They shun a man because he's intelligent, but get maudlin over a few supposedly malignant body-cells. I'm as bad. Ten years ago I wouldn't have given one of them the time of day, still less have taken pleasure in their approbation.

CHARLIE. Do you?

DRUMM. People like them, like the old man—your foster-father they thank God for a fine day and stay diplomatically silent when it rains. They deride whatever is beyond them with a laugh, a platitude and a spit. They say: "How could he be a dental surgeon?—his father was warned by the police for molesting women."

DA. Who would that be? Old Martin Conheedy used to tamper with women. Is his son a dentist now?

DRUMM *(answering Charlie's question)*. They . . . amuse me.

DA *(derisive)*. Who'd trust that fella to pull a tooth?

173. **rode** had sexual intercourse with   174. **ructions** disturbances

DRUMM *(picking up his briefcase).* When the old man was in hospital he sent word that he wanted to see me.

CHARLIE. My father?

DRUMM. Who lived here.

CHARLIE *(persisting).* My father.

DRUMM *(letting it pass).* He asked my advice. I told him that not being related by blood you would have no natural claim on his estate.

CHARLIE. What estate? He had nothing.

DRUMM. At his request I wrote out a will for him then and there. He signed it and I had it witnessed. *(He takes an envelope and hands it to Charlie.)* It'll stand up with the best of them.

CHARLIE. But he had bugger-all.

DRUMM. There was also the matter of an heirloom which he gave into my keeping.

CHARLIE. Heirloom? *(Drumm dips into his briefcase and takes out a familiar-looking brown-paper parcel.)*

DA *(jovially).* There now's a surprise for you.

CHARLIE *(staring at the parcel).* No . . .

DA *(crowing).* You won't guess what's in that!

DRUMM. He said it was valuable, so I asked my bank manager to keep it in his vault.

CHARLIE *(under stress).* *That* was in a bank vault?

DRUMM. I can see that the value was also sentimental. *(Rising.)* Well, I'm glad to have discharged my trust.

CHARLIE. Thank you. *(Looking at the parcel.)* His estate.

DRUMM. Oh, no. Whatever that is, it has nothing to do with what's in the will. And I'd be careful with that envelope. There's money involved!

CHARLIE. Money?

DRUMM. He mentioned the sum of a hundred and thirty-five pounds, with more to come.

CHARLIE. He never had that much in his life.

DRUMM. He thought otherwise.

CHARLIE. He was raving. I *know.* All he had was his pension and the cheques I sent him for— *(He breaks off and looks around at Da.)*

DA *(strategically).* That dog from next door is in the garden. Hoosh . . . hoosh, you bastard. *(Charlie watches him murderously as he beats a retreat into the scullery.)*

DRUMM *(waiting for Charlie to finish).* Yes?

CHARLIE. I was wrong. I've remembered where it came from.

DRUMM. The money?

CHARLIE. Yes.

DRUMM. I imagined it was hard-earned.

CHARLIE *(grimly).* It was.

DRUMM *(sternly)*. Now, my friend, no caterwauling.[175] To whom else could he leave it? I once called him an ignorant man. I still do. And yet he may have been better off. Everything I once thought I knew for certain I have seen inverted, revised, disproved, or discredited. Shall I tell you something? In seventy years the one surviving fragment of my knowledge, the only indisputable poor particle of certainty in my entire life, is that in a public house lavatory incoming traffic has the right of way. *(Acidly.)* It isn't much to take with one, is it?

CHARLIE *(smiling)*. Well, now *I* know something.

DRUMM. I have always avoided him and his kind, and yet in the end we fetch up against the self-same door. I find that aggravating. *(Moving towards the door.)* The old couple, had they children of their own?

CHARLIE. I was told once there were several. All still-born.

DRUMM. He didn't even create life—at least I have the edge on him there.

CHARLIE. How are the two Rhode Island Reds?

DRUMM. Moulting. *(He offers his hand.)* It was pleasant to see you. I enjoyed it. Goodbye.

CHARLIE. Mr. Drumm, he never took anything from me, he wouldn't let me help him, what I offered him he kept and wouldn't use. Why?

DRUMM. Don't you know?

CHARLIE. Do *you?*

DRUMM. The Irish national disease.

CHARLIE. Bad manners?

DRUMM. Worse, no manners. *(He holds out his hand, inspecting the sky for rain, then goes. Charlie closes the door, returns to the kitchen.)*

CHARLIE. Where are you? *(Yelling.)* Come . . . in . . . here!

(Da comes in.)

DA. Do you want a cup of tea?

CHARLIE. You old shite. You wouldn't even use the money.

DA. I did.

CHARLIE. How?

DA. Wasn't it something to leave you?

CHARLIE. I'll never forgive you for this.

DA *(not worried)*. Ah, you will.

CHARLIE. Since I was born. "Here's sixpence for the chairoplanes, a shilling for the pictures, a new suit for the job. Here's a life." When did I ever get a chance to pay it back, to get out from under, to be quit of you? You wouldn't come to us in London; you'd rather be the brave old warrior, soldiering on.

DA. And wasn't I?

175. **caterwauling** wailing

CHARLIE. While I was the ingrate. The only currency you'd take, you knew I wouldn't pay. Well, I've news for you, mate. You had your chance. The debt is cancelled, welshed on. *(Tapping his head.)* I'm turfing you out. Of here. See that? *(He tears the black armband from his overcoat and drops it in the range.)* And this? *(He holds up the parcel containing the spectacle frames.)*

DA. You wouldn't. Not at all.

CHARLIE. Wouldn't I? You think not? *(He bends and crushes the frames through the paper with increasing violence.)*

DA. Ah, son . . .

CHARLIE. San Francisco earthquake!

DA. You'd want to mind your hand with them—

CHARLIE *(cutting his finger).* Shit.

DA. I told you you'd cut yourself. *(Charlie gives him a malevolent look and very deliberately shoves the parcel into the range. He sucks his hand.)*

CHARLIE. Now wouldn't I?

DA. Is it deep? That's the kind of cut 'ud give you lock-jaw. I'd mind[176] that.

CHARLIE. Gone . . . and you with it.

DA. Yis. *(Taking out a dirty handkerchief.)* Here, tie this around it.

CHARLIE. Get away from me. Ignorant man, ignorant life!

DA. What are you talking about, or do you know what you're talking about? Sure I enjoyed meself. And in the windup I didn't die with the arse out of me trousers like the rest of them—I left money!

CHARLIE. *My* money.

DA. Jasus, didn't you get it back? And looka . . . if I wouldn't go to England with you before, sure I'll make it up to you. I will now.

CHARLIE. You what? Like hell you will.

DA. Sure you can't get rid of a bad thing.

CHARLIE. Can't I? You watch me. You watch! *(He picks up his case, walks out of the house and closes the front door. He locks the door and hurls the key from him. A sigh of relief. He turns to go, to find Da has walked out through the fourth wall.)*

DA. Are we off, so? It's starting to rain. The angels must be peein' again.

CHARLIE. Don't you dare follow me. You're dead . . . get off.

DA. Sure Noah's flood was only a shower. *(Following him.)* Left . . . left . . . I had a good job and I left, right, left!

CHARLIE. Hump off. Get away. Shoo. I don't want you. *(He goes to the upper level. Da follows, lagging behind.)*

DA. Go on, on on. I'll keep up with you. *(Charlie stops at the top level.)*

---

176. **mind** take care of

CHARLIE. Leave me alone. *(Charlie slowly walks down as Da follows, singing:)*

DA *(singing)*.

> "Oh, says your oul' one to my oul' one:
> 'Will you come to the Waxy Dargle?'
> And says my oul' one to your oul' one:
> 'Sure I haven't got a farthin'.'"

CURTAIN

BRIAN FRIEL

1929 −

Brian Friel was born in Omagh, Co. Tyrone, in Northern Ireland. He was educated at St. Columb's College, Derry City, the Catholic seminary in Maynooth, and St. Joseph's Teacher Training College, Belfast. He taught primary and intermediate school in Derry for ten years (1950–60), during which time he wrote some radio plays and short stories. He was persuaded to risk a full-time professional writing career after *The New Yorker* published a few of these stories. Of his early plays, *The Enemy Within* (1962), a study of St. Columcille, patron of Derry, made a mark in Ireland. But it was not until his introduction to Tyrone Guthrie that he realized his potential as a playwright.

He spent several months of 1963 at the Tyrone Guthrie Theatre in Minneapolis, Minnesota, and the next year, *Philadelphia, Here I Come* was the hit of the Dublin Theatre Festival. This "memory play" on the conflicts in a young man's mind and spirit on the eve of his emigration employs the device of having two actors play the public and private sides of Gar O'Donnell. It exposes the religious and sexual repression of rural Ireland, the lack of emotional and intellectual stimulation, and the yearning for fuller self-realization; yet the Philadelphia of Gar's future offers no more than a physical escape from Gar's spiritual purgatory. On Broadway it had the longest run of any Irish play, and was subsequently made into a film (1970).

The Ballybeg of this play represents the geographic and spiritual territory that has been Friel's chosen estate in most of his work, fictional and dramatic. Geographically, it is the northwest quarter of Ireland, between the River Bann and the Atlantic Ocean, centered on the Foyle Valley and Derry City, and comprising the counties of Donegal, Tyrone and Londonderry (its colonial name). Politically, the region is bisected by the western segment of the border dividing Northern Ireland from the Republic. It is a socially and economically depressed area, in which high unemployment and emigration are endemic. Within the borders of Northern Ireland, these features are exacerbated for the Catholic community by seventy years of discrimination and political repression, which has resulted in political turmoil since 1969. Spiritually, Ballybeg is a small, rural community, with a strong sense of having been under pressure for a long time, and of its traditions being eroded by political and cultural imperialism. Strongly marked by the fervent, pious, and conservative mores of Irish

Catholicism, it has learned to live with a profound sense of historic injustice, which has included the loss of its native institutions, its language, and most of its self-respect. With no immediate prospect of reversing these trends from within, the only apparent solutions are escape, self-delusion, personal or political violence, or talk.

A major theme in Friel's work, then, has been a community in the process of dissolution. In *The Freedom of the City* (1973), his most acclaimed work between *Philadelphia* and *Translations,* he catches this process at one of its political flashpoints. Yet, while his concerns are constant, there is no really typical "Friel play." The blandishments of commerce have never drawn him into formula writing: his pride in craftsmanship has continuously moved him to seek new forms.

Translations is the result of his search for an original dramatic technique to express a familiar theme. It was written for Field Day, a theatre project undertaken in collaboration with actor Stephen Rea, poets Tom Paulin, Seamus Heaney and Seamus Deane, and David Hammond, broadcaster and musician. As the inaugural production of this company's agenda to provide politically informed literature and cultural criticism, it was first produced in Derry City's Guildhall in 1980. When it moved to London, it was greeted enthusiastically by the critics and public alike for the originality of its approach to historical, political, and linguistic issues. His characters are enfolded in conflicts central to the Irish experience. This play is imbued with a profound sympathy for the privations and graces of rural Irish life, and out of the apparently amorphous processes of history, it shapes a powerfully persuasive dramatic symbol.

The best introduction to the play is Friel's own. His diary for the summer and fall of 1979 records the gestation of the play. He introduces a few extracts from this log:

> I was working on a play that came to be called *Translations. Translations* is set in a hedge-school in Ballybeg, County Donegal. The year is 1833. The British army is engaged in mapping the whole of Ireland, a process which involves the renaming of every place name in the country. It is a time of great upheaval for the people of Ballybeg: the hedge-school is to be replaced by one of the new national schools; there is recurring potato blight; they have to acquire a new language (English); and because their townland is being renamed, everything that was familiar is becoming strange.
>
> 14 MAY. Went to Urris today, the setting of the hedge-school in the play-in-the-head. No response to the place apart from some sense of how the ordinary British sappers might have reacted to this remote, bleak, desolate strip of land attenuated between mountain and sea. And perhaps in an attempt to commit myself to the material I bought a first edition of Colonel Colby's *Memoir of the City and North Western Liberties of Londonderry.*

The people from Urris/Ballybeg would have been Irish-speaking in 1833. So a theatrical conceit will have to be devised by which—even though the actors speak English—the audience will assume or accept that they are speaking Irish. Could that work?

15 MAY. I keep returning to the same texts: the letters of John O'Donovan, Colby's *Memoir, A Paper Landscape* by John Andrews, *The Hedge-Schools of Ireland* by [P. J.] Dowling, [George] Steiner's *After Babel*.

And at each rereading I get interested in some trivial detail or subside beneath the tedium of the whole idea. For some reason the material resists the intense and necessary fusion of its disparate parts into one whole, and the intense and necessary mental heat that accomplishes that. One aspect that keeps eluding me: the wholeness, the integrity, of that Gaelic past. Maybe because I don't believe in it.

16 MAY. I can envisage a few scenes: the hedge-school classroom; the love scene between lovers who have no common language; the actual task of places being named. Nothing more.

23 MAY. I believe that I am reluctant even to name the characters, maybe because the naming-taming process is what the play is about.

29 MAY. I don't want to write a play about Irish peasants being suppressed by English sappers.

I don't want to write a threnody on the death of the Irish language.

I don't want to write a play about land-surveying. Indeed I don't want to write a play about naming places. And yet portions of all these are relevant. Each is part of the atmosphere in which the real play lurks.

1 JUNE. What worries me about the play—if there is a play—are the necessary peculiarities, especially the political elements. Because the play has to do with language and only language. And if it becomes overwhelmed by that political element, it is lost.

18 JUNE. In Ballybeg, at the point when the play begins, the cultural climate is a dying climate—no longer quickened by its past, about to be plunged almost overnight into an alien future. The victims of this situation are the transitional generation. The old can retreat into and find new cultural implements. The in-between ages become lost, wandering around in a strange land. Strays.

6 JULY. One of the mistakes of the direction in which the play is presently pulling is the almost wholly *public* concern of the theme: how does the eradication of the Irish language and the substitution of English affect this particular *society*? How long can a *society* live without its tongue? Public questions; issues for politicians; and that's what is wrong with the play now. The play must concern itself only with the exploration of the dark and private places of individual souls.

9 OCTOBER. Persistent, nose-to-the-desk, 9:30 a.m.–5:30 p.m., grinding work . . . I'm not sure what has been achieved.
5 NOVEMBER. The play, named *Translations*, completed.

SELECT BIBLIOGRAPHY

Publications

Selected Plays of Brian Friel, introduced by Seamus Deane. London: Faber and Faber/Washington, DC: The Catholic University of America Press, 1984. (*Philadelphia, Here I Come, The Freedom of the City, Living Quarters, Aristocrats, Faith Healer, Translations*, 1980)

The Loves of Cass Maguire. London: Faber and Faber/New York: Farrar, Straus and Giroux, 1967.

Lovers. New York: Farrar, Straus and Giroux, 1968; London: Faber and Faber, 1969.

Two Plays: Crystal and Fox and The Mundy Scheme. London: Faber and Faber/New York: Farrar, Straus and Giroux, 1970.

Volunteers. London: Faber and Faber, 1979.

Selected Stories. Dublin: Gallery Press, 1979.

The Communication Cord. London: Faber and Faber, 1983.

Making History. London: Faber and Faber, 1988.

Biography and Criticism

Andrews, John, Kevin Barry, and Brian Friel. "*Translations* and a Paper Landscape: Between Fiction and History." *The Crane Bag* 7,2 (1983), pp. 118–24.

Dantanus, Ulf. *Brian Friel. A Study*. London: Faber and Faber, 1988.

Frield, Brian. "Extracts from a Sporadic Diary." In *Ireland and the Arts*, ed. Tim Pat Coogan. London: Quartet, n.d., pp. 56–61.

Maxwell, D. E. S. *Brian Friel*. Lewisburg, PA: Bucknell University Press, 1973.

O'Brien, George. *Brian Friel*. Boston, MA: Twayne/Dublin: Gill and Macmillan, 1989.

See also discussions in Deane, *Celtic Revivals*, and Maxwell, *Modern Irish Drama*.

Translations

for Stephen Rea

CHARACTERS

MANUS
SARAH
JIMMY JACK
MAIRE
DOALTY
BRIDGET
HUGH
OWEN
CAPTAIN LANCEY
LIEUTENANT YOLLAND

The action takes place in a hedge-school in the townland of Baile Beag/
Ballybeg,[1] an Irish-speaking community in County Donegal.

Act 1.   An afternoon in late August 1833.[2]
Act 2.   A few days later.
Act 3.   The evening of the following day.
One interval—between the two scenes in Act 2.

ACT 1

Narr y setting.
? descript, war

*The hedge-school[3] is held in a disused barn or hay-shed or byre. Along the back
wall are the remains of five or six stalls—wooden posts and chains—where cows
were once milked and bedded. A double door left, large enough to allow a cart
to enter. A window right. A wooden stairway without a banister leads to the
upstairs living-quarters (off) of the schoolmaster and his son. Around the room
are broken and forgotten implements: a cart-wheel, some lobster-pots, farming
tools, a bottle of hay,[4] a churn,[5] etc. There are also the stools and bench-seats*

Detailed Rep /Real (inverse in) v. Setting

1. **Baile Beag/Ballybeg** small town   2. **1833** The Ordnance Survey of Ireland is
in its tenth year, and the national schools system has been enabled by the 1831
act.   3. **hedge-school** unofficial school, managed and taught by an independent
teacher/scholar, the "master"   4. **bottle** bundle   5. **churn** barrel-like implement
for making butter

which the pupils use and a table and chair for the master. At the door a pail
of water and a soiled towel. The room is comfortless and dusty and functional—
there is no trace of a woman's hand.

When the play opens, Manus is teaching Sarah to speak. He kneels beside
her. She is sitting on a low stool, her head down, very tense, clutching a slate
on her knees. He is coaxing her gently and firmly and—as with everything he
does—with a kind of zeal.

Manus is in his late twenties/early thirties; the master's older son. He is pale-
faced, lightly built, intense, and works as an unpaid assistant—a monitor—to
his father. His clothes are shabby; and when he moves we see that he is lame.

Sarah's speech defect is so bad that all her life she has been considered locally
to be dumb and she has accepted this: when she wishes to communicate, she
grunts and makes unintelligible nasal sounds. She has a waiflike appearance
and could be any age from seventeen to thirty-five.

Jimmy Jack Cassie—known as the Infant Prodigy—sits by himself, content-
edly reading Homer in Greek and smiling to himself. He is a bachelor in his
sixties, lives alone, and comes to these evening classes partly for the company and
partly for the intellectual stimulation. He is fluent in Latin and Greek but is
in no way pedantic—to him it is perfectly normal to speak these tongues. He
never washes. His clothes—heavy top coat, hat, mittens, which he wears now—
are filthy and he lives in them summer and winter, day and night. He now
reads in a quiet voice and smiles in profound satisfaction. For Jimmy the world
of the god and the ancient myths is as real and as immediate as everyday life
in the townland of Baile Beag.

Manus holds Sarah's hands in his and he articulates slowly and distinctly
into her face.

MANUS. We're doing very well. And we're going to try it once more—
just once more. Now—relax and breathe in . . . deep . . . and out . . . in
. . . and out . . .
(Sarah shakes her head vigorously and stubbornly.)
MANUS. Come on, Sarah. This is our secret.
(Again vigorous and stubborn shaking of Sarah's head.)
MANUS. Nobody's listening. Nobody hears you.
JIMMY. *Ton d'emeibet epeita thea glaukopis Athene*[6] . . ."
MANUS. Get your tongue and your lips working. "My name—" Come
on. One more try. "My name is—" Good girl.
SARAH. My . . .
MANUS. Great. "My name—"

6. *Ton . . . glaukopis Athene* Τὸν δ' ἠμείβετ' ἔπειτα θεὰ γλαυκῶπις' Αθήνη
(Homer, *Odyssey*, XIII, 420): "But the grey-eyed goddess Athene then replied to
him" (Brian Friel)

SARAH. My . . . my . . .

MANUS. Raise your head. Shout it out. Nobody's listening.

JIMMY. ". . . *alla hekelos estai en Atreidao domois*[7] . . ."

MANUS. Jimmy, please! Once more—just once more—"My name—"
Good girl. Come on now. Head up. Mouth open.

SARAH. My . . .

MANUS. Good.

SARAH. My . . .

MANUS. Great.

SARAH. My name . . .

MANUS. Yes?

SARAH. My name is . . .

MANUS. Yes?

(Sarah pauses. Then in a rush.)

SARAH. My name is Sarah.

MANUS. Marvellous! Bloody marvellous!

(Manus hugs Sarah. She smiles in shy, embarrassed pleasure.)
Did you hear that, Jimmy?—"My name is Sarah"—clear as a bell. *(To
Sarah)* The Infant Prodigy doesn't know what we're at. *(Sarah laughs at
this. Manus hugs her again and stands up.)* Now we're really started! Nothing'll stop us now! Nothing in the wide world!

(Jimmy, chuckling at his text, comes over to them.)

JIMMY. Listen to this, Manus.

MANUS. Soon you'll be telling me all the secrets that have been in that
head of yours all these years. Certainly, James—what is it? *(To Sarah)*
Maybe you'd set out the stools?

(Manus runs up the stairs.)

JIMMY. Wait till you hear this, Manus.

MANUS. Go ahead. I'll be straight down.

JIMMY. "*Hos ara min phamene rabdo epemassat Athene*[8]—" "After Athene had said this, she touched Ulysses with her wand. She withered the
fair skin of his supple limbs and destroyed the flaxen hair from off his head
and about his limbs she put the skin of an old man . . ."! The divil! The
divil!

(Manus has emerged again with a bowl of milk and a piece of bread.)

JIMMY. And wait till you hear! She's not finished with him yet!

(As Manus descends the stairs he toasts Sarah with his bowl.)

7. . . . *alla hekelos . . . domois* ἀλλὰ ἔκηλος ἧσται ἐν Ἀτρείδαο δόμοις (Homer, *Odyssey*, XIII, 423–4): ". . . but he sits at ease in the halls of the Sons of
Athens . . ." (BF)   8. *Hos ara . . . Athene* Ὡς ἄρα μιν φαμένη ῥάβδῳ ἐπεμάσσατ'
Ἀθήνη (Homer, *Odyssey*, XIII, 429): "As she spoke Athene touched him with her
wand" (BF)

JIMMY. *"Knuzosen de oi osse—"*[9] "She dimmed his two eyes that were so beautiful and clothed him in a vile ragged cloak begrimed with filthy smoke . . ."! D'you see! Smoke! Smoke! D'you see! Sure look at what the same turf[10]-smoke has done to myself! *(He rapidly removes his hat to display his bald head.)* Would you call that flaxen hair?

MANUS. Of course I would.

JIMMY. "And about him she cast the great skin of a filthy hind, stripped of the hair, and into his hand she thrust a staff and a wallet"! Ha-ha-ha! Athene did that to Ulysses! Made him into a tramp! Isn't she the tight one?

MANUS. You couldn't watch her, Jimmy.

JIMMY. You know what they call her?

MANUS. *"Glaukopis Athene."*[11]

JIMMY. That's it! The flashing-eyed Athene! By God, Manus, sir, if you had a woman like that about the house, it's not stripping a turf-bank[12] you'd be thinking about—eh?

MANUS. She was a goddess, Jimmy.

JIMMY. Better still. Sure isn't our own Grania[13] a class of a goddess and—

MANUS. Who?

JIMMY. Grania—Grania—Diarmuid's Grania.

MANUS. Ah.

JIMMY. And sure she can't get her fill of men.

MANUS. Jimmy, you're impossible.

JIMMY. I was just thinking to myself last night: if you had the choosing between Athene and Artemis and Helen of Troy—all three of them Zeus's girls[14]—imagine three powerful-looking daughters like that all in the one parish of Athens!—now, if you had the picking between them, which would you take?

MANUS *(to Sarah).* Which should I take, Sarah?

JIMMY. No harm[15] to Helen; and no harm to Artemis; and indeed no harm to our own Grania, Manus. But I think I've no choice but to go bull-straight for Athene. By God, sir, them flashing eyes would fair keep a man jigged up constant![16]

(Suddenly and momentarily, as if in spasm, Jimmy stands to attention and

---

9. *Knuzosen de oi osse* κνύζωσεν δέ οἱ ὄσσε (Homer, *Odyssey*, XIII, 433): "She dimmed his eyes" (BF) 10. **turf** peat used as fuel 11. *Glaukopis Athene* Γλαυκῶπις 'Αθήνη: flashing-eye Athene (BF) 12. **stripping a turf-bank** removing the top layer of vegetation and sod from a section of bog to prepare it for harvesting 13. **our own Grania** in Celtic legend, the lover of Dermot, who fled with him from her fiancé, Finn Mac Cool (mac Cumhaill) 14. **choosing between . . . Zeus's girls** Paris was given this task 15. **harm** offense 16. **jigged up constant** continuously excited

salutes, his face raised in pained ecstasy. Manus laughs. So does Sarah. Jimmy
goes back to his seat, and his reading.)

MANUS. You're a dangerous bloody man, Jimmy Jack.

JIMMY. "Flashing-eyed"! Hah! Sure Homer knows it all, boy. Homer
knows it all.

(Manus goes to the window and looks out.)

MANUS. Where the hell has he got to?

(Sarah goes to Manus and touches his elbow. She mimes rocking a baby.)

MANUS. Yes, I know he's at the christening; but it doesn't take them
all day to put a name on a baby, does it?

(Sarah mimes pouring drinks and tossing them back quickly.)

MANUS. You may be sure. Which pub?

(Sarah indicates.)

MANUS. Gracie's?

(No. Further away.)

MANUS. Con Connie Tim's?[17]

(No. To the right of there.)

MANUS. Anna na mBreag's?[18]

(Yes. That's it.)

MANUS. Great. She'll fill him up. I suppose I may take the class then.

(Manus begins to distribute some books, slates and chalk, texts, etc., beside
the seats. Sarah goes over to the straw and produces a bunch of flowers she has
hidden there. During this:)

JIMMY. "*Autar o ek limenos prosebe*"[19]—"But Ulysses went forth from
the harbour and through the woodland to the place where Athene had
shown him he could find the good swineherd who"—"*o oi biotoio malista*
kedeto"[20]—what's that, Manus?

MANUS. "Who cared most for his substance."

JIMMY. That's it! "The good swineherd who cared most for his substance above all the slaves that Ulysses possessed . . ."

(Sarah presents the flowers to Manus.)

MANUS. Those are lovely, Sarah.

(But Sarah has fled in embarrassment to her seat and has her head buried
in a book. Manus goes to her.)

MANUS. Flow-ers.

(Pause. Sarah does not look up.)

MANUS. Say the word: flow-ers. Come on—flow-ers.

SARAH. Flowers.

17. **Con Connie Tim's** the pub belonging to Con, son of Connie, grandson of
Tim 18. **Anna na mBreag** Anna of the Lies 19. *Autar o ek limenos prosebe*
Αὐτὰρ ὁ ἐκ λιμένος προσέβη (Homer, *Odyssey*, XIV, 1): "But he went forth from
the harbour . . ." (BF) 20. *o oi boitoio malista kedeto* ὅ οἱ βιότοιο μάλιστα (Homer, *Odyssey*, XIV, 3–4): ". . . he cared very much for his substance . . ." (BF)

MANUS. You see?—you're off!

(Manus leans down and kisses the top of Sarah's head.)

MANUS. And they're beautiful flowers. Thank you.

(Maire enters, a strong-minded, strong-bodied woman, in her twenties with a head of curly hair. She is carrying a small can of milk.)

MAIRE. Is this all's here? Is there no school this evening?

MANUS. If my father's not back, I'll take it.

(Manus stands awkwardly, having been caught kissing Sarah and with the flowers almost formally at his chest.)

MAIRE. Well now, isn't that a pretty sight. There's your milk. How's Sarah?

(Sarah grunts a reply.)

MANUS. I saw you out at the hay.

(Maire ignores this and goes to Jimmy.)

MAIRE. And how's Jimmy Jack Cassie?

JIMMY. Sit down beside me, Maire.

MAIRE. Would I be safe?

JIMMY. No safer man in Donegal.

(Maire flops on a stool beside Jimmy.)

MAIRE. Ooooh. The best harvest in living memory, they say; but I don't want to see another like it. *(Showing Jimmy her hands.)* Look at the blisters.

JIMMY. *Esne fatigata?*[21]

MAIRE. *Sum fatigatissima.*[22]

JIMMY. *Bene! Optime!*[23]

MAIRE. That's the height of my Latin. Fit me better if I had even that much English.

JIMMY. English? I thought you had some English?

MAIRE. Three words. Wait—there was a spake[24] I used to have off by heart. What's this it was? *(Her accent is strange because she is speaking a foreign language and because she does not understand what she is saying.)* "In Norfolk[25] we besport[26] ourselves around the maypoll." What about that!

MANUS. Maypole.[27]

(Again Maire ignores Manus.)

MAIRE. God have mercy on my Aunt Mary—she taught me that when I was about four, whatever it means. Do you know what it means, Jimmy?

JIMMY. Sure you know I have only Irish like yourself.

MAIRE. And Latin. And Greek.

JIMMY. I'm telling you a lie: I know one English word.

21. *Esne fatigata?* Are you tired? (BF)   22. *Sum fatigatissima* I am very tired (BF)   23. *Bene! Optime!* Good! Excellent! (BF)   24. **spake** speech   25. **Norfolk** eastern English county   26. **besport** East Anglian reflexive usage   27. **Maypole** pole decorated with streamers that May Day celebrants hold while dancing

MAIRE. What?

JIMMY. Bo-som.

MAIRE. What's a bo-som?

JIMMY. You know—(*He illustrates with his hands*)—bo-som—bo-som—you know—Diana, the huntress, she has two powerful bosom.

MAIRE. You may be sure that's the one English word you would know. (*Rises.*) Is there a drop of water about?

(*Manus gives Maire his bowl of milk.*)

MANUS. I'm sorry I couldn't get up last night.

MAIRE. Doesn't matter.

MANUS. Biddy Hanna sent for me to write a letter to her sister in Nova Scotia. All the gossip of the parish. "I brought the cow to the bull three times last week but no good. There's nothing for it now but Big Ned Frank."

MAIRE (*Drinking*). That's better.

MANUS. And she got so engrossed in it that she forgot who she was dictating to: "The aul drunken schoolmaster and that lame son of his are still footering[28] about in the hedge-school, wasting people's good time and money."

(*Maire has to laugh at this.*)

MAIRE. She did not!

MANUS. And me taking it all down. "Thank God one of them new national schools is being built above at Poll na gCaorach."[29] It was after midnight by the time I got back.

MAIRE. Great to be a busy man.

(*Maire moves away. Manus follows.*)

MANUS. I could hear music on my way past but I thought it was too late to call.

MAIRE (*to Sarah*). Wasn't your father in great voice last night?

(*Sarah nods and smiles.*)

MAIRE. It must have been near three o'clock by the time you got home?

(*Sarah holds up four fingers.*)

MAIRE. Was it four? No wonder we're in pieces.

MANUS. I can give you a hand at the hay tomorrow.

MAIRE. That's the name of a hornpipe, isn't it?—"The Scholar In The Hayfield"—or is it a reel?[30]

MANUS. If the day's good.

MAIRE. Suit yourself. The English soldiers below in the tents, them sapper[31] fellas, they're coming up to give us a hand. I don't know a word they're saying, nor they me; but sure that doesn't matter, does it?

28. **footering** fooling   29. **Poll na gCaorach** the Hole of the Sheep   30. **hornpipe . . . reel** two types of Irish dance tune   31. **sapper** military engineer

MANUS. What the hell are you so crabbed[32] about?!

(Doalty and Bridget enter noisily. Both are in their twenties. Doalty is brandishing a surveyor's pole. He is an open-minded, open-hearted, generous and slightly thick young man. Bridget is a plump, fresh young girl, ready to laugh, vain, and with a countrywoman's instinctive cunning. Doalty enters doing his imitation of the master.)

DOALTY. Vesperal salutations[33] to you all.

BRIDGET. He's coming down past Carraig na Ri[34] and he's as full as a pig!

DOALTY. *Ignari, stulti, rustici*[35]—pot-boys and peasant whelps—semi-literates and illegitimates.

BRIDGET. He's been on the batter[36] since this morning; he sent the wee[37] ones home at eleven o'clock.

DOALTY. Three questions. Question A—Am I drunk? Question B—Am I sober? *(Into Maire's face) Responde—responde!*[38]

BRIDGET. Question C, Master—When were you last sober?

MAIRE. What's the weapon, Doalty?

BRIDGET. I warned him. He'll be arrested one of these days.

DOALTY. Up in the bog with Bridget and her aul fella,[39] and the Red Coats were just across at the foot of Croc na Mona,[40] dragging them aul chains and peeping through that big machine they lug about everywhere with them—you know the name of it, Manus?

MAIRE. Theodolite.[41]

BRIDGET. How you do you kow?

MAIRE. They leave it in our byre[42] at night sometimes if it's raining.

JIMMY. Theodolite—what's the etymology of that word, Manus?

MANUS. No idea.

BRIDGET. Get on with the story.

JIMMY. *Theo—theos*[43]—something to do with a god. Maybe *thea*—a goddess![44] What shape's the yoke?[45]

DOALTY. "Shape!" Will you shut up, you aul eejit you! Anyway, every time they'd stick one of these poles into the ground and move across the bog, I'd creep up and shift it twenty or thirty paces to the side.

BRIDGET. God!

DOALTY. Then they'd come back and stare at it and look at their calculations and stare at it again and scratch their heads. And cripes,[46] d'you know what they ended up doing?

32. **crabbed** ill-tempered 33. **Vesperal salutations** good evening 34. **Carraig na Ri** Rock of the Kings 35. *Ignari, stulti, rustici* Ignoramuses, fools, peasants (BF) 36. **on the batter** drinking 37. **wee** little 38. *Responde—responde!* Answer—answer! (BF) 39. **aul fella** father 40. **Croc na Mona** Hill of the Turf 41. **Theodolite** a surveying instrument with built-in telescope 42. **byre** cowshed or barn 43. *theos* θέος: a god (BF) 44. *thea* θέα: a goddess (BF) 45. **yoke** thing 46. **cripes** euphemism for "Christ"

BRIDGET. Wait till you hear!

DOALTY. They took the bloody machine apart!

(And immediately he speaks in gibberish—an imitation of two very agitated and confused sappers in rapid conversation.)

BRIDGET. That's the image of them!

MAIRE. You must be proud of yourself, Doalty.

DOALTY. What d'you mean?

MAIRE. That was a very clever piece of work.

MANUS. It was a gesture.

MAIRE. What sort of gesture?

MANUS. Just to indicate . . . a presence.

MAIRE. Hah!

BRIDGET. I'm telling you—you'll be arrested.

(When Doalty is embarrassed—or pleased—he reacts physically. He now grabs Bridget around the waist.)

DOALTY. What d'you make of that for an implement, Bridget? Wouldn't that make a great aul shaft for your churn?

BRIDGET. Let go of me, you dirty brute! I've a headline to do before Big Hughie comes.

MANUS. I don't think we'll wait for him. Let's get started.

(Slowly, reluctantly they begin to move to their seats and specific tasks. Doalty goes to the bucket of water at the door and washes his hands. Bridget sets up a hand-mirror and combs her hair.)

BRIDGET. Nellie Ruadh's[47] baby was to be christened this morning. Did any of yous hear what she called it? Did you, Sarah?

(Sarah grunts: No.)

BRIDGET. Did you, Maire?

MAIRE. No.

BRIDGET. Our Seamus says she was threatening she was going to call it after its father.

DOALTY. Who's the father?

BRIDGET. That's the point, you donkey you!

DOALTY. Ah.

BRIDGET. So there's a lot of uneasy bucks about Baile Beag this day.

DOALTY. She told me last Sunday she was going to call it Jimmy.

BRIDGET. You're a liar, Doalty.

DOALTY. Would I tell you a lie? Hi, Jimmy, Nellie Ruadh's aul fella's looking for you.

JIMMY. For me?

MAIRE. Come on, Doalty.

DOALTY. Someone told him . . .

47. **Ruadh** Red

MAIRE. Doalty!

DOALTY. He heard you know the first book of the Satires of Horace[48] off by heart . . .

JIMMY. That's true.

DOALTY. . . . and he wants you to recite it for him.

JIMMY. I'll do that for him certainly, certainly.

DOALTY. He's busting to hear it.

(Jimmy fumbles in his pockets.)

JIMMY. I came across this last night—this'll interest you—in Book Two of Virgil's *Georgics*.[49]

DOALTY. Be God, that's my territory alright.

BRIDGET. You clown you! *(To Sarah)* Hold this for me, would you? *(her mirror.)*

JIMMY. Listen to this, Manus. *"Nigra fere et presso pinguis sub vomere terra . . ."*[50]   ~Ireland~

DOALTY. Steady on now—easy, boys, easy—don't rush me, boys—

(He mimes great concentration.)

JIMMY. Manus?

MANUS. "Land that is black and rich beneath the pressure of the plough . . ."   ~Ireland~

DOALTY. Give *me* a chance!

JIMMY. "And with *cui putre*[51]—with crumbly soil—is in the main best for corn." There you are!

DOALTY. There you are.

JIMMY. "From no other land will you see more wagons wending homeward behind slow bullocks." Virgil! There!

DOALTY. "Slow bullocks"!

JIMMY. Isn't that what I'm always telling you? Black soil for corn. *That's* what you should have in that upper field of yours—corn, not spuds.[52]

DOALTY. Would you listen to that fella! Too lazy be Jasus to wash himself and he's lecturing me on agriculture! Would you go and take a running race at yourself, Jimmy Jack Cassie! *(Grabs Sarah.)* Come away out of this with me, Sarah, and we'll plant some corn[53] together.

MANUS. All right—all right. Let's settle down and get some work done. I know Sean Beag[54] isn't coming—he's at the salmon.[55] What about the Donnelly twins? *(To Doalty)* Are the Donnelly twins not coming any more? *(Doalty shrugs and turns away.)* Did you ask them?

DOALTY. Haven't seen them. Not about these days.

---

48. **Horace** Latin poet (65–8 B.C.)   49. **Virgil's *Georgics*** a didactic poem on agriculture by the Roman poet (70–19 B.C.)   50. *Nigra fere et presso pinguis sub vomere terra* Land that is black and rich beneath the pressure of the plough (BF)   51. *cui putre* crumbly soil (BF)   52. **spuds** potatoes   53. **corn** cereal crops   54. **Sean Beag** Little John   55. **at the salmon** salmon fishing

(Doalty begins whistling through his teeth. Suddenly the atmosphere is silent and alert.)

MANUS. Aren't they at home?

DOALTY. No.

MANUS. Where are they then?

DOALTY. How would I know?

BRIDGET. Our Seamus says two of the soldiers' horses were found last night at the foot of the cliffs at Machaire Buidhe[56] . . . *(She stops suddenly and begins writing with chalk on her slate.)* D'you hear the whistles of this aul slate? Sure nobody would write on an aul slippery thing like that.

MANUS. What headline did my father set you?

BRIDGET. "It's easier to stamp out learning than to recall it."

JIMMY. Book Three, the *Agricola* of Tacitus.[57]

BRIDGET. God but you're a dose.[58]

MANUS. Can you do it?

BRIDGET. There. Is it bad? Will he ate[59] me?

MANUS. It's very good. Keep your elbow in closer to your side. Doalty?

DOALTY. I'm at the seven-times table. I'm perfect, skipper.

(Manus moves to Sarah.)

MANUS. Do you understand those sums?

(Sarah nods: Yes. Manus leans down to her ear.)

MANUS. My name is Sarah.

(Manus goes to Maire. While he is talking to her the others swap books, talk quietly, etc.)

MANUS. Can I help you? What are you at?

MAIRE. Map of America. *(Pause.)* The passage money came last Friday.

MANUS. You never told me that.

MAIRE. Because I haven't seen you since, have I?

MANUS. You don't want to go. You said that yourself.

MAIRE. There's ten below me to be raised and no man in the house. What do you suggest?

MANUS. Do you want to go?

MAIRE. Did you apply for that job in the new national school?

MANUS. No.

MAIRE. You said you would.

MANUS. I said I might.

MAIRE. When it opens, this is finished: nobody's going to pay to go to a hedge-school.

MANUS. I know that and I . . . *(He breaks off because he sees Sarah,*

---

56. **Machaire Buidhe** The Yellow Plain   57. ***Agricola* of Tacitus** a biography of the Roman governor of Britain, written by his son-in-law (37–93 A.D.)   58. **dose** nuisance   59. **ate** eat

obviously listening, at his shoulder. She moves away again.) I was thinking that maybe I could . . .

MAIRE. It's £56 a year you're throwing away.

MANUS. I can't apply for it.

MAIRE. You *promised* me you would.

MANUS. My father has applied for it.

MAIRE. He has not!

MANUS. Day before yesterday.

MAIRE. For God's sake, sure you know he'd never—

MANUS. I couldn't—I can't go in against him.

(Maire looks at him for a second. Then:—)

MAIRE. Suit yourself. *(To Bridget)* I saw your Seamus heading off to the Port fair early this morning.

BRIDGET. And wait till you hear this—I forgot to tell you this. He said that as soon as he crossed over the gap at Cnoc na Mona—just beyond where the soldiers are making the maps—the sweet smell was everywhere.

DOALTY. You never told me that.

BRIDGET. It went out of my head.

DOALTY. He saw the crops in Port?

BRIDGET. Some.

MANUS. How did the tops look?

BRIDGET. Fine—I think.

DOALTY. In flower?

BRIDGET. I don't know. I think so. He didn't say.

MANUS. Just the sweet smell—that's all?

BRIDGET. They say that's the way it snakes in, don't they? First the smell; and then one morning the stalks are all black and limp.

DOALTY. Are you stupid? It's the rotting stalks makes the sweet smell for God's sake. That's what the smell is—rotting stalks.

MAIRE. Sweet smell! Sweet smell! Every year at this time somebody comes back with stories of the sweet smell. Sweet God, did the potatoes ever fail in Baile Beag? Well, did they ever—ever? Never! There was never blight[60] here. Never. Never. But we're always sniffing about for it, aren't we?—looking for disaster. The rents are going to go up again—the harvest's going to be lost—the herring have gone away for ever—there's going to be evictions. Honest to God, some of you people aren't happy unless you're miserable and you'll not be right content until you're dead!

DOALTY. Bloody right, Maire. And sure St. Colmcille[61] prophesied there'd never be blight here. He said:

60. **blight** a fungus which causes potato stalks to wither   61. **St. Colmcille** Donegal-born saint (521–597)

The spuds will bloom in Baile Beag
Till rabbits grow an extra lug.[62]

And sure that'll never be. So we're all right. Seven threes are twenty-one; seven fours are twenty-eight; seven fives are forty-nine—Hi, Jimmy, do you fancy my chances as boss of the new national school?

JIMMY. What's that?—what's that?

DOALTY. Agh, g'way back home to Greece, son.

MAIRE. You ought to apply, Doalty.

DOALTY. D'you think so? Cripes, maybe I will. Hah!

BRIDGET. Did you know that you start at the age of six and you have to stick at it until you're twelve at least—no matter how smart you are or how much you know.

DOALTY. Who told you that yarn?

BRIDGET. And every child from every house has to go all day, every day, summer or winter. That's the law.

DOALTY. I'll tell you something—nobody's going to go near them—they're not going to take on—law or no law.

BRIDGET. And everything's free in them. You pay for nothing except the books you use; that's what our Seamus says.

DOALTY. "Our Seamus." Sure your Seamus wouldn't pay anyway. She's making this all up.

BRIDGET. Isn't that right, Manus?

MANUS. I think so.

BRIDGET. And from the very first day you go, you'll not hear one word of Irish spoken. You'll be taught to speak English and every subject will be taught through English and everyone'll end up as cute[63] as the Buncrana[64] people.

(Sarah suddenly grunts and mimes a warning that the master is coming. The atmosphere changes. Sudden business. Heads down.)

DOALTY. He's here, boys. Cripes, he'll make yella meal out of me for those bloody tables.

BRIDGET. Have you any extra chalk, Manus?

MAIRE. And the atlas for me.

(Doalty goes to Maire who is sitting on a stool at the back.)

DOALTY. Swop you seats.

MAIRE. Why?

DOALTY. There's an empty one beside the Infant Prodigy.

MAIRE. I'm fine here.

DOALTY. Please, Maire. I want to jouk[65] in the back here. *(Maire rises.)*

---

62. **lug** ear   63. **cute** clever   64. **Buncrana** town in north Donegal   65. **jouk** duck

God love you. *(Aloud.)* Anyone got a bloody table-book?[66] Cripes, I'm wrecked. *(Sarah gives him one.)* God, I'm dying about you.

(In his haste to get to the back seat, Doalty bumps into Bridget who is kneeling on the floor and writing laboriously on a slate resting on top of a bench-seat.)

BRIDGET. Watch where you're going, Doalty!

(Doalty gooses Bridget. She squeals. Now the quiet hum of work: Jimmy reading Homer in a low voice; Bridget copying her headline; Maire studying the atlas; Doalty, his eyes shut tight, mouthing his tables; Sarah doing sums. After a few seconds:—)

BRIDGET. Is this "g" right, Manus? How do you put a tail on it?

DOALTY. Will you shut up! I can't concentrate!

(A few more seconds of work. Then Doalty opens his eyes and looks around.)

False alarm, boys. The bugger's not coming at all. Sure the bugger's hardly fit to walk.

(And immediately Hugh enters. A large man, with residual dignity, shabbily dressed, carrying a stick. He has, as always, a large quantity of drink taken, but he is by no means drunk. He is in his early sixties.)

HUGH. *Adsum,*[67] Doalty, *adsum.* Perhaps not in *sobrietate perfecta*[68] but adequately *sobrius*[69] to overhear your quip. Vesperal salutations to you all.

(Various responses.)

JIMMY. *Ave,*[70] Hugh.

HUGH. James. *(He removes his hat and coat and hands them and his stick to Manus, as if to a footman.)* Apologies for my late arrival: we were celebrating the baptism of Nellie Ruadh's baby.

BRIDGET *(innocently).* What name did she put on it, Master?

HUGH. Was it Eamon? Yes, it was Eamon.

BRIDGET. Eamon Donal from Tor![71] Cripes!

HUGH. And after the *caerimonia nominationis*[72]—Maire?

MAIRE. The ritual of naming.

HUGH. Indeed—we then had a few libations to mark the occasion. Altogether very pleasant. The derivation of the word "baptize"?—where are my Greek scholars? Doalty?

DOALTY. Would it be—ah—ah—

HUGH. Too slow. James?

JIMMY. "*Baptizein*"[73]—to dip or immerse.

HUGH. Indeed—our friend Pliny Minor speaks of the "*baptisterium*"[74]—the cold bath.

DOALTY. Master.

66. **table-book** book of mathematical tables 67. *Adsum* I am present (BF) 68. *sobrietate perfecta* complete sobriety (BF) 69. *sobrius* sober (BF) 70. *Ave* hail (BF) 71. **Tor** Towering Rocks, in Donegal 72. *caerimonia nominationis* ceremony of naming (BF) 73. *Baptizein* βαπτίζειν: to dip or immerse (BF) 74. *baptisterium* cold bath, swimming-pool (BF)

HUGH. Doalty?

DOALTY. I suppose you could talk then about baptizing a sheep at sheep-dipping, could you?

(Laughter. Comments.)

HUGH. Indeed—the precedent is there—the day you were appropriately named Doalty—seven nines?

DOALTY. What's that, Master?

HUGH. Seven times nine?

DOALTY. Seven nines—seven nines—seven times nine—seven times nine are—cripes, it's on the tip of my tongue, Master—I knew it for sure this morning—funny that's the only one that foxes me—

BRIDGET *(prompt)*. Sixty-three.

DOALTY. What's wrong with me: sure seven nines are fifty-three, Master.

HUGH. Sophocles from Colonus would agree with Doalty Dan Doalty from Tulach Alainn.[75] "To know nothing is the sweetest life." Where's Sean Beag?

MANUS. He's at the salmon.

HUGH. And Nora Dan?

MAIRE. She says she's not coming back any more.

HUGH. Ah. Nora Dan can now write her name—Nora Dan's education is complete. And the Donnelly twins?

(Brief pause. Then:—)

BRIDGET. They're probably at the turf.[76] *(She goes to Hugh.)* There's the one-and-eight[77] I owe you for last quarter's arithmetic and there's my one-and-six for this quarter's writing.

HUGH. *Gratias tibi ago.*[78] *(He sits at his table.)* Before we commence our *studia*[79] I have three items of information to impart to you—*(To Manus)* A bowl of tea, strong tea, black—

(Manus leaves.)

Item A: on my perambulations today—Bridget? Too slow. Maire?

MAIRE. Perambulare[80]—to walk about.

HUGH. Indeed—I encountered Captain Lancey of the Royal Engineers who is engaged in the ordnance survey of this area. He tells me that in the past few days two of his horses have strayed and some of his equipment seems to be mislaid. I expressed my regret and suggested he address you himself on these matters. He then explained that he does not speak Irish. Latin? I asked. None. Greek? Not a syllable. He speaks—on his own admission—only English; and to his credit he seemed suitably verecund—James?

---

75. **Tulach Alainn** Lovely Little Hill   76. **at the turf** harvesting peat   77. **one-and-eight** one shilling and eight pence   78. *Gratias tibi ago* I thank you (BF)   79. *studia* studies (BF)   80. *Perambulare* to walk through (BF)

JIMMY. *Verecundus*[81]—humble.

HUGH. Indeed—he voiced some surprise that we did not speak his language. I explained that a few of us did, on occasion—outside the parish of course—and then usually for the purposes of commerce, a use to which his tongue seemed particularly suited—*(Shouts)* and a slice of soda bread—and I went on to propose that our own culture and the classical tongues made a happier conjugation—Doalty?

DOALTY. *Conjugo*[82]—I join together.

(Doalty is so pleased with himself that he prods and winks at Bridget.)

HUGH. Indeed—English, I suggested, couldn't really express us. And again to his credit he acquiesced to my logic. Acquiesced—Maire?

(Maire turns away impatiently. Hugh is unaware of the gesture.)

Too slow. Bridget?

BRIDGET. *Acquiesco.*[83]

HUGH. *Procede.*[84]

BRIDGET. *Acquiesco, acquiescere, acquievi, acquietum.*

HUGH. Indeed—and Item B . . .

MAIRE. Master.

HUGH. Yes?

(Maire gets to her feet uneasily but determinedly. Pause.)

Well, girl?

MAIRE. We should all be learning to speak English. That's what my mother says. That's what I say. That's what Dan O'Connell[85] said last month in Ennis.[86] He said the sooner we all learn to speak English the better.

(Suddenly several speak together.)

JIMMY. What's she saying? What? What?

DOALTY. It's Irish he uses when he's travelling around scrounging votes.

BRIDGET. And sleeping with married women. Sure no woman's safe from that fella.

JIMMY. Who-who-who? Who's this? Who's this?

HUGH. *Silentium!*[87] *(Pause.)* Who is she talking about?

MAIRE. I'm talking about Daniel O'Connell.

HUGH. Does she mean that little Kerry politician?

MAIRE. I'm talking about the Liberator, Master, as you well know. And what he said was this: "The old language is a barrier to modern progress."

81. *Verecundus* shame-faced, modest (BF)   82. *Conjugo* I join together (BF)   83. *Acquiesco* to rest, to find comfort in (BF)   84. *Procede* proceed (BF)   85. **Dan O'Connell** the "Liberator," whose signal political achievement was Catholic Emancipation (1829)   86. **Ennis** town in Co. Clare   87. *Silentium!* Silence (BF)

He said that last month. And he's right. I don't want Greek. I don't want
Latin. I want English.

(*Manus reappears on the platform above.*)

I want to be able to speak English because I'm going to America as
soon as the harvest's all saved.

(*Maire remains standing. Hugh puts his hand into his pocket and produces
a flask of whiskey. He removes the cap, pours a drink into it, tosses it back,
replaces the cap, puts the flask back into his pocket. Then:—*)

HUGH. We have been diverted—*diverto—divertere*[88]—Where were we?

DOALTY. Three items of information, Master. You're at Item B.

HUGH. Indeed—Item B—Item B—yes—On my way to the christening this morning I chanced to meet Mr George Alexander, Justice of the
Peace. We discussed the new national school. Mr Alexander invited me to
take charge of it when it opens. I thanked him and explained that I could
do that only if I were free to run it as I have run this hedge-school for the
past thirty-five years—filling what our friend Euripides calls the "*aplestos
pithos*"[89]—James?

JIMMY. "The cask that cannot be filled."

HUGH. Indeed—and Mr Alexander retorted courteously and emphatically that he hopes that is how it will be run.

(*Maire now sits.*)

Indeed. I have had a strenuous day and I am weary of you all. (*He
rises.*) Manus will take care of you.

(*Hugh goes towards the steps. Owen enters. Owen is the younger son, a
handsome, attractive young man in his twenties. He is dressed smartly—a city
man. His manner is easy and charming: everything he does is invested with
consideration and enthusiasm. He now stands framed in the doorway, a travelling bag across his shoulder.*)

OWEN. Could anybody tell me is this where Hugh Mor O'Donnell
holds his hedge-school?

DOALTY. It's Owen—Owen Hugh! Look, boys—it's Owen Hugh!

(*Owen enters. As he crosses the room he touches and has a word for each
person.*)

OWEN. Doalty! (*Playful punch.*) How are you, boy? *Jacobe, quid agis?*[90]
Are you well?

JIMMY. Fine. Fine.

OWEN. And Bridget! Give us a kiss. Aaaaaah!

BRIDGET. You're welcome, Owen.

OWEN. It's not—? Yes, it *is* Maire Chatach![91] God! A young woman!

---

88. *diverto, divertere* to turn away (BF)   89. *aplestos pithos* ἄπληστος πίθος:
unfillable cask (BF)   90. *Jacobe, quid agis?* James, how are you? (BF)   91. **Maire
Chatach** Curly-headed Mary

MAIRE. How are you, Owen?

(Owen is now in front of Hugh. He puts his two hands on his Father's shoulders.)

OWEN. And how's the old man himself?

HUGH. Fair—fair.

OWEN. Fair? For God's sake you never looked better! Come here to me.

(He embraces Hugh warmly and genuinely.)

Great to see you, Father. Great to be back.

(Hugh's eyes are moist—partly joy, partly the drink.)

HUGH. I—I'm—I'm—pay no attention to—

OWEN. Come on—come on—come on— *(He gives Hugh his handkerchief.)* Do you know what you and I are going to do tonight? We are going to go up to Anna na mBreag's . . .

DOALTY. Not there, Owen.

OWEN. Why not?

DOALTY. Her poteen's[92] worse than ever.

BRIDGET. They say she puts frogs in it!

OWEN. All the better. *(To Hugh)* And you and I are going to get footless drunk. That's arranged.

(Owen sees Manus coming down the steps with tea and soda bread. They meet at the bottom.)

And Manus!

MANUS. You're welcome, Owen.

OWEN. I know I am. And it's great to be here. *(He turns round, arms outstretched.)* I can't believe it. I come back after six years and everything's just as it was! Nothing's changed! Not a thing! *(Sniffs.)* Even that smell—that's the same smell this place always had. What is it anyway? Is it the straw?

DOALTY. Jimmy Jack's feet.

(General laughter. It opens little pockets of conversation round the room.)

OWEN. And Doalty Dan Doalty hasn't changed either!

DOALTY. Bloody right, Owen.

OWEN. Jimmy, are you well?

JIMMY. Dodging about.

OWEN. Any word of the big day?

(This is greeted with "ohs" and "ahs.")

Time enough, Jimmy. Homer's easier to live with, isn't he?

MAIRE. We heard stories that you own ten big shops in Dublin—is it true?

OWEN. Only nine.

92. **poteen** illicitly distilled whiskey

[handwritten top margin: Hickey — They Translate through hour (thank god)]

BRIDGET. And you've twelve horses and six servants.

OWEN. Yes—that's true. God Almighty, would you listen to them—taking a hand at me!

MANUS. When did you arrive?

OWEN. We left Dublin yesterday morning, spent last night in Omagh and got here half an hour ago.

MANUS. You're hungry then.

HUGH. Indeed—get him food—get him a drink.

OWEN. Not now, thanks; later. Listen—am I interrupting you all?

HUGH. By no means. We're finished for the day. *[handwritten: — Oh? Just began]*

OWEN. Wonderful. I'll tell you why. Two friends of mine are waiting outside the door. They'd like to meet you and I'd like you to meet them. May I bring them in?

HUGH. Certainly. You'll all eat and have . . .

OWEN. Not just yet, Father. You've seen the sappers working in this area for the past fortnight, haven't you? Well, the older man is Captain Lancey . . .

HUGH. I've met Captain Lancey.

OWEN. Great. He's the cartographer in charge of this whole area. Cartographer—James?

(Owen begins to play this game—his father's game—partly to involve his classroom audience, partly to show he has not forgotten it, and indeed partly because he enjoys it.)

JIMMY. A maker of maps.

OWEN. Indeed—and the younger man that I travelled with from Dublin, his name is Lieutenant Yolland and he is attached to the toponymic department—Father?—*responde*—*responde*! *[handwritten: gram]*

HUGH. He gives names to places. *[handwritten: name]*

OWEN. Indeed—although he is in fact an orthographer—Doalty?—too slow—Manus?

MANUS. The correct spelling of those names.

OWEN. Indeed—indeed!

(Owen laughs and claps his hands. Some of the others join in.)

Beautiful! Beautiful! Honest to God, it's such a delight to be back here with you all again—"civilized" people. Anyhow—may I bring them in?

HUGH. Your friends are our friends.

OWEN. I'll be straight back.

(There is general talk as Owen goes towards the door. He stops beside Sarah.)

OWEN. That's a new face. Who are you?

(A very brief hesitation. Then:—)

SARAH. My name is Sarah.

OWEN. Sarah who?

SARAH. Sarah Johnny Sally.

[handwritten left margin: the translating game (defining game)]

[handwritten bottom right: Identifying the self — who are you]

[handwritten bottom left: knowing difficult word —]

OWEN. Of course! From Bun na hAbhann![93] I'm Owen—Owen Hugh Mor. From Baile Beag. Good to see you. *where Mr. O'Donnell*

(During this Owen–Sarah exchange.)

HUGH. Come on now. Let's tidy this place up. *(He rubs the top of his table with his sleeve.)* Move, Doalty—lift those books off the floor.

DOALTY. Right, Master; certainly, Master; I'm doing my best, Master.

(Owen stops at the door.)

OWEN. One small thing, Father.

HUGH. *Silentium!*

OWEN. I'm on their pay-roll.

(Sarah, very elated at her success, is beside Manus.)

SARAH. I said it, Manus!

(Manus ignores Sarah. He is much more interested in Owen now.)

MANUS. You haven't enlisted, have you?!

(Sarah moves away.)

OWEN. Me a soldier? I'm employed as a part-time, underpaid, civilian interpreter. My job is to translate the quaint, archaic tongue you people persist in speaking into the King's good English. *traitor?*

(He goes out.)

HUGH. Move—move—move! Put some order on things! Come on, Sarah—hide that bucket. Whose are these slates? Somebody take these dishes away. *Festinate!*[94] *Festinate!*

(Manus goes to Maire who is busy tidying.)

MANUS. You didn't tell me you were definitely leaving.

MAIRE. Not now.

HUGH. Good girl, Bridget. That's the style.

MANUS. You might at least have told me. *your new story (Lancey)*

HUGH. Are these your books, James?

JIMMY. Thank you.

MANUS. Fine! Fine! Go ahead! Go ahead!

MAIRE. You talk to me about getting married—with neither a roof over your head nor a sod of ground under your foot. I suggest you go for the new school; but no—"My father's in for that." Well now he's got it and now this is finished and now you've nothing.

MANUS. I can always . . .

MAIRE. What? Teach classics to the cows? Agh—

(Maire moves away from Manus. Owen enters with Lancey and Yolland. Captain Lancey is middle-aged; a small, crisp officer, expert in his field as cartographer but uneasy with people—especially civilians, especially these foreign civilians. His skill is with deeds, not words. Lieutenant Yolland is in his late

93. **Bun na hAbhann!** Mouth of the River 94. *Festinate!* Hurry! (BF)

twenties/early thirties. He is tall and thin and gangling, blond hair, a shy, awkward manner. A soldier by accident.)

OWEN. Here we are. Captain Lancey—my father.

LANCEY. Good evening.

(Hugh becomes expansive, almost courtly, with his visitors.)

HUGH. You and I have already met, sir.

LANCEY. Yes.

OWEN. And Lieutenant Yolland—both Royal Engineers—my father.

HUGH. You're very welcome, gentlemen.

YOLLAND. How do you do.

HUGH. *Gaudeo vos hic adesse.*[95]

OWEN. And I'll make no other introductions except that these are some of the people of Baile Beag and—what?—well you're among the best people in Ireland now. *(He pauses to allow Lancey to speak. Lancey does not.)* Would you like to say a few words, Captain?

HUGH. What about a drop, sir?

LANCEY. A what?

HUGH. Perhaps a modest refreshment? A little sampling of our *aqua vitae*?

LANCEY. No, no.

HUGH. Later perhaps when—

LANCEY. I'll say what I have to say, if I may, and as briefly as possible. Do they speak *any* English, Roland?

OWEN. Don't worry. I'll translate.

LANCEY. I see. *(He clears his throat. He speaks as if he were addressing children—a shade too loudly and enunciating excessively.)* You may have seen me—seen me—working in this section—section?—working. We are here—here—in this place—you understand?—to make a map—a map—a map and—

JIMMY. *Nonne Latine loquitur?*[96]

(Hugh holds up a restraining hand.)

HUGH. James.

LANCEY *(to Jimmy)*. I do not speak Gaelic, sir.

(He looks at Owen.)

OWEN. Carry on.

LANCEY. A map is a representation on paper—a picture—you understand picture?—showing, representing this country—yes?—showing your country in miniature—a scaled drawing on paper of—of—of—

(Suddenly Doalty sniggers. Then Bridget. Then Sarah. Owen leaps in quickly.)

---

95. *Gaudeo vos hic adesse* Welcome (BF)   96. *Nonne Latine loquitur?* Does he not speak Latin? (BF)

OWEN. It might be better if you *assume* they understand you—

LANCEY. Yes?

OWEN. And I'll translate as you go along.

LANCEY. I see. Yes. Very well. Perhaps you're right. Well. What we are doing is this. *(He looks at Owen. Owen nods reassuringly.)* His Majesty's government has ordered the first ever comprehensive survey of this entire country—a general triangulation[97] which will embrace detailed hydrographic[98] and topographic[99] information and which will be executed to a scale of six inches to the English mile.

HUGH *(pouring a drink)*. Excellent—excellent.

(Lancey looks at Owen.)

OWEN. A new map is being made of the whole country.

(Lancey looks to Owen: Is that all? Owen smiles reassuringly and indicates to proceed.)

LANCEY. This enormous task has been embarked on so that the military authorities will be equipped with up-to-date and accurate information on every corner of this part of the Empire.

OWEN. The job is being done by soldiers because they are skilled in this work.

LANCEY. And also so that the entire basis of land valuation can be reassessed for purposes of more equitable taxation.

OWEN. This new map will take the place of the estate agent's map so that from now on you will know exactly what is yours in law.

LANCEY. In conclusion I wish to quote two brief extracts from the white paper which is our governing charter: *(Reads)* "All former surveys of Ireland originated in forfeiture[100] and violent transfer of property; the present survey has for its object the relief which can be afforded to the proprietors and occupiers of land from unequal taxation."

OWEN. The captain hopes that the public will cooperate with the sappers and that the new map will mean that taxes are reduced.

HUGH. A worthy enterprise—*opus honestum*![101] And Extract B?

LANCEY. "Ireland is privileged. No such survey is being undertaken in England. So this survey cannot but be received as proof of the disposition of this government to advance the interests of Ireland." My sentiments, too.

OWEN. This survey demonstrates the government's interest in Ireland and the captain thanks you for listening so attentively to him.

HUGH. Our pleasure, Captain.

LANCEY. Lieutenant Yolland?

97. **triangulation** surveying technique to measure terrain 98. **hydrographic** mapping surface water 99. **topographic** pertaining to the names of places 100. **forfeiture** the surrender of land as a result of judicial punishment 101. *opus honestum!* an honourable task (BF)

YOLLAND. I—I—I've nothing to say—really—

OWEN. The captain is the man who actually makes the new map. George's task is to see that the place-names on this map are ... correct. *(To Yolland.)* Just a few words—they'd like to hear you. *(To class.)* Don't you want to hear George, too?

MAIRE. Has he anything to say? *— "speak for yourself, John"*

YOLLAND *(to Maire)*. Sorry—sorry?

OWEN. She says she's dying to hear you.

YOLLAND *(to Maire)*. Very kind of you—thank you ... *(To class)* I can only say that I feel—I feel very foolish to—to—to be working here and not speak your language. But I intend to rectify that—with Roland's help—indeed I do.

OWEN. He wants me to teach him Irish! *mutiny Owen*

HUGH. You are doubly welcome, sir.

YOLLAND. I think your countryside is—is—is—is very beautiful. I've fallen in love with it already. I hope we're not too—too crude an intrusion on your lives. And I know that I'm going to be happy, very happy, here.

OWEN. He is already a committed Hibernophile[102]—

JIMMY. He loves—

OWEN. All right, Jimmy—we know—he loves Baile Beag; and he loves you all.

HUGH. Please ... May I ... ?

(Hugh is now drunk. He holds on to the edge of the table.)

OWEN. Go ahead, Father. *(Hands up for quiet.)* Please—please.

HUGH. And we, gentlemen, we in turn are happy to offer you our friendship, our hospitality, and every assistance that you may require. Gentlemen—welcome!

(A few desultory claps. The formalities are over. General conversation. The soldiers meet the locals. Manus and Owen meet down stage.)

OWEN. Lancey's a bloody ramrod but George's all right. How are you anyway?

MANUS. What sort of a translation was that, Owen?

OWEN. Did I make a mess of it?

MANUS. You weren't saying what Lancey was saying!

OWEN. "Uncertainty in meaning is incipient poetry"—who said that?

MANUS. There was nothing uncertain about what Lancey said: it's a bloody military operation, Owen! And what's Yolland's function? What's "incorrect" about the place-names we have here?

OWEN. Nothing at all. They're just going to be standardized.

MANUS. You mean changed into English?

OWEN. Where there's ambiguity, they'll be Anglicized.

102. **Hibernophile** lover of Ireland

Owen then is a traitor is betraying family + friends in England's interest in domination. What we did to the native in new ways for power

MANUS. And they call you Roland! They both call you Roland!

OWEN. Shhhhh. Isn't it ridiculous? They seemed to get it wrong from the very beginning—or else they can't pronounce Owen. I was afraid some of you bastards would laugh.

MANUS. Aren't you going to tell them?

OWEN. Yes—yes—soon—soon.

MANUS. But they . . .

OWEN. Easy, man, easy. Owen—Roland—what the hell. It's only a name. It's the same me, isn't it? Well, isn't it?

MANUS. Indeed it is. It's the same Owen.

OWEN. And the same Manus. And in a way we complement each other. *(He punches Manus lightly, playfully and turns to join the others. As he goes.)* All right—who has met whom? Isn't this a job for the go-between?

(Manus watches Owen move confidently across the floor, taking Maire by the hand and introducing her to Yolland. Hugh is trying to negotiate the steps. Jimmy is lost in a text. Doalty and Bridget are reliving their giggling. Sarah is staring at Manus.)

ACT 2

SCENE I

The sappers have already mapped most of the area. Yolland's official task, which Owen is now doing, is to take each of the Gaelic names—every hill, stream, rock, even every patch of ground which possessed its own distinctive Irish name—and Anglicize it, either by changing it into its approximate English sound or by translating it into English words. For example, a Gaelic name like Cnoc Ban could become Knockban or—directly translated—Fair Hill. These new standardized names were entered into the Name-Book, and when the new maps appeared they contained all these new Anglicized names. Owen's official function as translator is to pronounce each name in Irish and then provide the English translation.

The hot weather continues. It is late afternoon some days later.

Stage right: an improvised clothes-line strung between the shafts of the cart and a nail in the wall; on it are some shirts and socks.

A large map—one of the new blank maps—is spread out on the floor. Owen is on his hands and knees, consulting it. He is totally engrossed in his task which he pursues with great energy and efficiency.

Yolland's hesitancy has vanished—he is at home here now. He is sitting on the floor, his long legs stretched out before him, his back resting against a creel,

*his eyes closed. His mind is elsewhere. One of the reference books—a church
registry—lies open on his lap.*

*Around them are various reference books, the Name-Book, a bottle of poteen,
some cups, etc.*

*Owen completes an entry in the Name-Book and returns to the map on the
floor.*

OWEN. Now. Where have we got to? Yes—the point where that stream
enters the sea—that tiny little beach there. George!

YOLLAND. Yes. I'm listening. What do you call it? Say the Irish name
again?

OWEN. Bun na hAbhann.

YOLLAND. Again.

OWEN. Bun na hAbhann.

YOLLAND. Bun na hAbhann.

OWEN. That's terrible, George.

YOLLAND. I know. I'm sorry. Say it again.

OWEN. Bun na hAbhann.

YOLLAND. Bun na hAbhann.

OWEN. That's better. Bun is the Irish word for bottom. And Abha
means river. So it's literally the mouth of the river.

YOLLAND. Let's leave it alone. There's no English equivalent for a
sound like that.

OWEN. What is it called in the church registry?

(Only now does Yolland open his eyes.)

YOLLAND. Let's see . . . Banowen.

OWEN. That's wrong. *(Consults text.)* The list of freeholders calls it
Owenmore—that's completely wrong: Owenmore's the big river at the
west end of the parish. *(Another text.)* And in the grand jury lists it's
called—God!—Binhone!—wherever they got that. I suppose we could
Anglicize it to Bunowen; but somehow that's neither fish nor flesh.

(Yolland closes his eyes again.)

YOLLAND. I give up.

OWEN *(at map)*. Back to first principles. What are we trying to do?

YOLLAND. Good question.

OWEN. We are trying to denominate and at the same time describe
that tiny area of soggy, rocky, sandy ground where that little stream enters
the sea, an area known locally as Bun na hAbhann . . . Burnfoot! What
about Burnfoot?

YOLLAND *(indifferently)*. Good, Roland, Burnfoot's good.

OWEN. George, my name isn't . . .

YOLLAND. B-u-r-n-f-o-o-t?

OWEN. Are you happy with that?

YOLLAND. Yes.

OWEN. Burnfoot it is then. *(He makes the entry into the Name-Book.)*
Bun na h-Abhann—B-u-r-n-

YOLLAND. You're becoming very skilled at this.   *owen is dominah*

OWEN. We're not moving fast enough.

YOLLAND *(opens eyes again)*. Lancey lectured me again last night.

OWEN. When does he finish here?

YOLLAND. The sappers are pulling out at the end of the week. The
trouble is, the maps they've completed can't be printed without these
names. So London screams at Lancey and Lancey screams at me. But I
wasn't intimidated.

(Manus emerges from upstairs and descends.)

"I'm sorry, sir," I said, "But certain tasks demand their own tempo.
You cannot rename a whole country overnight." Your Irish air has made
me bold. *(To Manus)* Do you want us to leave?

MANUS. Time enough. Class won't begin for another half-hour.

YOLLAND. Sorry—sorry?

OWEN. Can't you speak English?

(Manus gathers the things off the clothes-line. Owen returns to the map.)

OWEN. We now come across that beach . . .

YOLLAND. Tra—that's the Irish for beach. *(To Manus)* I'm picking up
the odd word, Manus.

MANUS. So.

OWEN. . . . on past Burnfoot; and there's nothing around here that
has any name that I know of until we come down here to the south end,
just about here . . . and there should be a ridge of rocks there . . . Have
the sappers marked it? They have. Look, George.

YOLLAND. Where are we?

OWEN. There.

YOLLAND. I'm lost.

OWEN. Here. And the name of that ridge is Druim Dubh. Put English
on that, Lieutenant.

YOLLAND. Say it again.

OWEN. Druim Dubh.

YOLLAND. Dubh means black.

OWEN. Yes.

YOLLAND. And Druim means . . . what? a fort?

OWEN. We met it yesterday in Druim Luachra.

YOLLAND. A ridge! The Black Ridge! *(To Manus)* You see, Manus?

OWEN. We'll have you fluent at the Irish before the summer's over.

YOLLAND. Oh, I wish I were. *(To Manus as he crosses to go back upstairs)*
We got a crate of oranges from Dublin today. I'll send some up to you.

MANUS. Thanks. *(To Owen)* Better hide that bottle. Father's just up
and he'd be better without it.

OWEN. Can't you speak English before your man?

MANUS. Why?

OWEN. Out of courtesy.

MANUS. Doesn't he want to learn Irish? *(To Yolland)* Don't you want to learn Irish?

YOLLAND. Sorry—sorry? I—I—

MANUS. I understand the Lanceys perfectly but people like you puzzle me.

OWEN. Manus, for God's sake!

MANUS *(still to Yolland)*. How's the work going?

YOLLAND. The work?—the work? Oh, it's—it's staggering along—I think—*(To Owen)*—isn't it? But we'd be lost without Roland.

MANUS *(leaving)*. I'm sure. But there are always the Rolands, aren't there?

(He goes upstairs and exits.)

YOLLAND. What was that he said?—something about Lancey, was it?

OWEN. He said we should hide that bottle before Father gets his hands on it.

YOLLAND. Ah.

OWEN. He's always trying to protect him.

YOLLAND. Was he lame from birth?

OWEN. An accident when he was a baby: Father fell across his cradle. That's why Manus feels so responsible for him.

YOLLAND. Why doesn't he marry?

OWEN. Can't afford to, I suppose.

YOLLAND. Hasn't he a salary?

OWEN. What salary? All he gets is the odd shilling Father throws him—and that's seldom enough. I got out in time, didn't I?

(Yolland is pouring a drink.)

Easy with that stuff—it'll hit you suddenly.

YOLLAND. I like it.

OWEN. Let's get back to the job. Druim Dubh—what's it called in the jury lists? *(Consults texts.)*

YOLLAND. Some people here resent us.

OWEN. Dramduff—wrong as usual.

YOLLAND. I was passing a little girl yesterday and she spat at me.

OWEN. And it's Drimdoo here. What's it called in the registry?

YOLLAND. Do you know the Donnelly twins?

OWEN. Who?

YOLLAND. The Donnelly twins.

OWEN. Yes. Best fishermen about here. What about them?

YOLLAND. Lancey's looking for them.

OWEN. What for?

YOLLAND. He wants them for questioning.

OWEN. Probably stolen somebody's nets. Dramduffy! Nobody ever called it Dramduffy. Take your pick of those three.

YOLLAND. My head's addled. Let's take a rest. Do you want a drink?

OWEN. Thanks. Now, every Dubh we've come across we've changed to Duf. So if we're to be consistent, I suppose Druim Dubh has to become Dromduff.

(Yolland is now looking out the window.)

You can see the end of the ridge from where you're standing. But D-r-u-m or D-r-o-m? *(Name-Book)* Do you remember—which did we agree on for Druim Luachra?

YOLLAND. That house immediately above where we're camped—

OWEN. Mm?

YOLLAND. The house where Maire lives.

OWEN. Maire? Oh, Maire Chatach.

YOLLAND. What does that mean?

OWEN. Curly-haired; the whole family are called the Catachs. What about it?

YOLLAND. I hear music coming from that house almost every night.

OWEN. Why don't you drop in?

YOLLAND. Could I?

OWEN. Why not? We used D-r-o-m then. So we've got to call it D-r-o-m-d-u-f-f—all right?

YOLLAND. Go back up to where the new school is being built and just say the names again for me, would you?

OWEN. That's a good idea. Poolkerry, Ballybeg—

YOLLAND. No, no; as they still are—in your own language.

OWEN. Poll na gCaorach,

(Yolland repeats the names silently after him.)

Baile Beag, Ceann Balor, Lis Maol, Machaire Buidhe, Baile na Gall, Carraig na Ri, Mullach Dearg—[103]

YOLLAND. Do you think I could live here?

OWEN. What are you talking about?

YOLLAND. Settle down here—live here.

OWEN. Come on, George.

YOLLAND. I mean it.

OWEN. Live on what? Potatoes? Buttermilk?

YOLLAND. It's really heavenly.

OWEN. For God's sake! The first hot summer in fifty years and you think it's Eden. Don't be such a bloody romantic. You wouldn't survive a mild winter here.

103. **Baile Beag, Ceann Balor, Lis Maol, Machaire Buidhe, Baile na nGall, Carraig na Ri, Mullach Dearg** Little Town, Balor's Head, Bare Fort, Yellow Plain, Town of the Foreigners, Rock of the Kings, Red Height

YOLLAND. Do you think not? Maybe you're right.

(Doalty enters in a rush.)

DOALTY. Hi, boys, is Manus about?

OWEN. He's upstairs. Give him a shout.

DOALTY. Manus! The cattle's going mad in that heat—Cripes, running wild all over the place. *(To Yolland)* How are you doing, skipper?

(Manus appears.)

YOLLAND. Thank you for—I—I'm very grateful to you for—

DOALTY. Wasting your time. I don't know a word you're saying. Hi, Manus, there's two bucks down the road there asking for you.

MANUS *(descending)*. Who are they?

DOALTY. Never clapped eyes on them. They want to talk to you.

MANUS. What about?

DOALTY. They wouldn't say. Come on. The bloody beasts'll end up in Loch an Iubhair[104] if they're not capped. Good luck, boys!

(Doalty rushes off. Manus follows him.)

OWEN. Good luck! What were you thanking Doalty for?

YOLLAND. I was washing outside my tent this morning and he was passing with a scythe across his shoulder and he came up to me and pointed to the long grass and then cut a pathway round my tent and from the tent down to the road—so that my feet won't get wet with the dew. Wasn't that kind of him? And I have no words to thank him . . . I suppose you're right: I suppose I couldn't live here . . . Just before Doalty came up time this morning, I was thinking that at that moment I might have been in Bombay instead of Ballybeg. You see, my father was at his wits end with me and finally he got me a job with the East India Company—some kind of a clerkship. This was ten, eleven months ago. So I set off for London. Unfortunately I—I—I missed the boat. Literally. And since I couldn't face Father and hadn't enough money to hang about until the next sailing, I joined the army. And they stuck me into the Engineers and posted me to Dublin. And Dublin sent me here. And while I was washing this morning and looking across the Tra Bhan, I was thinking how very, very lucky I am to be here and not in Bombay.

OWEN. Do you believe in fate?

YOLLAND. Lancey's so like my father. I was watching him last night. He met every group of sappers as they reported in. He checked the field kitchens. He examined the horses. He inspected every single report—even examining the texture of the paper and commenting on the neatness of the handwriting. The perfect colonial servant: not only must the job be done—it must be done with excellence. Father has that drive, too; that dedication; that indefatigable energy. He builds roads—hopping from one

---

104. **Loch an Iubhair** Lake of the Yew Tree

end of the Empire to the other. Can't sit still for five minutes. He says himself the longest time he ever sat still was the night before Waterloo when they were waiting for Wellington to make up his mind to attack.

OWEN. What age is he?

YOLLAND. Born in 1789—the very day the Bastille fell.[105] I've often thought maybe that gave his whole life its character. Do you think it could? He inherited a new world the day he was born—The Year One. Ancient time was at an end. The world had cast off its old skin. There were no longer any frontiers to man's potential. Possibilities were endless and exciting. He still believes that. The Apocalypse[106] is just about to happen . . . I'm afraid I'm a great disappointment to him. I've neither his energy, nor his coherence, nor his belief. Do I believe in fate? The day I arrived in Ballybeg—no, Baile Beag—the moment you brought me in here, I had a curious sensation. It's difficult to describe. It was a momentary sense of discovery; no—not quite a sense of discovery—a sense of recognition, of confirmation of something I half knew instinctively; as if I had stepped . . .

OWEN. Back into ancient time?

YOLLAND. No, no. It wasn't an awareness of *direction* being changed but of experience being of a totally different order. I had moved into a consciousness that wasn't striving nor agitated, but at its ease and with its own conviction and assurance. And when I heard Jimmy Jack and your father swapping stories about Apollo[107] and Cuchulainn[108] and Paris[109] and Ferdia[110]—as if they lived down the road—it was then that I thought—I knew—perhaps I could live here . . . *(Now embarrassed)* Where's the poteen?

OWEN. Poteen.

YOLLAND. Poteen—poteen—poteen. Even if I did speak Irish I'd always be an outsider here, wouldn't I? I may learn the password but the language of the tribe will always elude me, won't it? The private core will always be . . . hermetic,[111] won't it?

OWEN. You can learn to decode us.

(Hugh emerges from upstairs and descends. He is dressed for the road. Today he is physically and mentally jaunty and alert—almost self-consciously jaunty and alert. Indeed, as the scene progresses, one has the sense that he is deliberately parodying himself. The moment Hugh gets to the bottom of the steps Yolland leaps respectfully to his feet.)

HUGH *(as he descends)*

105. **Bastille** Paris prison, captured on July 14, 1789   106. **Apocalypse** end of the world   107. **Apollo** Greek sun-god   108. **Cuchulainn** hero of the Ulster Cycle of Celtic myth   109. **Paris** prince of Troy, abductor of Helen   110. **Ferdia** friend and victim of Cuchulainn   111. **hermetic** concealed, secret

Quantumvis cursum longum fessumque moratur
Sol, sacro tandem carmine vesper adest.[112]

I dabble in verse, Lieutenant, after the style of Ovid. *(To Owen)* A drop of that to fortify me.

YOLLAND. You'll have to translate it for me.

HUGH. Let's see—

> No matter how long the sun may linger on his
>   long and weary journey
> At length evening comes with its sacred song.

YOLLAND. Very nice, sir.

HUGH. English succeeds in making it sound . . . plebeian.

OWEN. Where are you off to, Father?

HUGH. An *expeditio*[113] with three purposes. Purpose A: to acquire a testimonial from our parish priest— *(To Yolland)* a worthy man but barely literate; and since he'll ask me to write it myself, how in all modesty can I do myself justice? *(To Owen)* Where did this *(drink)* come from?

OWEN. Anna na mBreag's.

HUGH *(to Yolland)*. In that case address yourself to it with circumspection. *(And Hugh instantly tosses the drink back in one gulp and grimaces.)* Aaaaaaagh! *(Holds out his glass for a refill.)* Anna na mBreag means Anna of the Lies. And Purpose B: to talk to the builders of the new school about the kind of living accommodation I will require there. I have lived too long like a journeyman tailor.

YOLLAND. Some years ago we lived fairly close to a poet—well, about three miles away.

HUGH. His name?

YOLLAND. Wordsworth—William Wordsworth.[114]

HUGH. Did he speak of me to you?

YOLLAND. Actually I never talked to him. I just saw him out walking—in the distance.

HUGH. Wordsworth? . . . No. I'm afraid we're not familiar with your literature, Lieutenant. We feel closer to the warm Mediterranean. We tend to overlook your island.

YOLLAND. I'm learning to speak Irish, sir.

HUGH. Good.

YOLLAND. Roland's teaching me.

HUGH. Splendid.

YOLLAND. I mean—I feel so cut off from the people here. And I was

112. *Quantumvis cursum . . . adest* No matter how long the sun on his long weary course / At length evening comes with its sacred song (BF) 113. *expeditio* an expedition (BF) 114. **Wordsworth** (1770–1850) the English Romantic poet

trying to explain a few minutes ago how remarkable a community this is. To meet people like yourself and Jimmy Jack who actually converse in Greek and Latin. And your place names—what was the one we came across this morning?—Termon, from Terminus, the god of boundaries. It—it— it's really astonishing.

HUGH. We like to think we endure around truths immemorially pos- ited.

YOLLAND. And your Gaelic literature—you're a poet yourself—

HUGH. Only in Latin, I'm afraid.

YOLLAND. I understand it's enormously rich and ornate.

HUGH. Indeed, Lieutenant. A rich language. A rich literature. You'll find, sir, that certain cultures expend on their vocabularies and syntax acquisitive energies and ostentations entirely lacking in their material lives. I suppose you could call us a spiritual people.

OWEN (*not unkindly; more out of embarrassment before Yolland*). Will you stop that nonsense, Father.

HUGH. Nonsense? What nonsense?

OWEN. Do you know where the priest lives?

HUGH. At Lis na Muc, over near . . .

OWEN. No, he doesn't. Lis na Muc, the Fort of the Pigs, has become Swinefort. (*Now turning the pages of the Name-Book—a page per name.*) And to get to Swinefort you pass through Greencastle and Fair Head and Strandhill and Gort and Whiteplains. And the new school isn't at Poll na gCaorach—it's at Sheepsrock. Will you be able to find your way?

(*Hugh pours himself another drink. Then:—*)

HUGH. Yes, it is a rich language, Lieutenant, full of the mythologies of fantasy and hope and self-deception—a syntax opulent with tomorrows. It is our response to mud cabins and a diet of potatoes; our only method of replying to . . . inevitabilities. (*To Owen*) Can you give me the loan of half-a-crown? I'll repay you out of the subscriptions I'm collecting for the publication of my new book. (*To Yolland*) It is entitled: "The Pentaglot Preceptor or Elementary Institute of the English, Greek, Hebrew, Latin and Irish Languages; Particularly Calculated for the Instruction of Such Ladies and Gentlemen as may Wish to Learn without the Help of a Master."

YOLLAND (*laughs*). That's a wonderful title!

HUGH. Between ourselves—the best part of the enterprise. Nor do I, in fact, speak Hebrew. And that last phrase—"without the Help of a Master"—that was written before the new national school was thrust upon me—do you think I ought to drop it now? After all you don't dispose of the cow just because it has produced a magnificent calf, do you?

YOLLAND. You certainly do not.

HUGH. The phrase goes. And I'm interrupting work of moment. (*He goes to the door and stops there.)* To return briefly to that other matter, Lieutenant. I understand your sense of exclusion, of being cut off from a life here; and I trust you will find access to us with my son's help. But remember that words are signals, counters. They are not immortal. And it can happen—to use an image you'll understand—it can happen that a civilization can be imprisoned in a linguistic contour which no longer matches the landscape of . . . fact. Gentlemen. *(He leaves.)*

OWEN. "An *expeditio* with three purposes": the children laugh at him: he always promises three points and he never gets beyond A and B.

MANUS. He's an astute man.

OWEN. He's bloody pompous.

YOLLAND. But so astute.

OWEN. And he drinks too much. Is it astute not to be able to adjust for survival? Enduring around truths immemorially posited—hah!

YOLLAND. He knows what's happening.

OWEN. What is happening?

YOLLAND. I'm not sure. But I'm concerned about my part in it. It's an eviction of sorts.

OWEN. We're making a six-inch map of the country. Is there something sinister in that?

YOLLAND. Not in—

OWEN. And we're taking place-names that are riddled with confusion and—

YOLLAND. Who's confused? Are the people confused?

OWEN. —and we're standardizing those names as accurately and as sensitively as we can.

YOLLAND. Something is being eroded.

OWEN. Back to the romance again. All right! Fine! Fine! Look where we've got to. *(He drops on his hands and knees and stabs a finger at the map.)* We've come to this crossroads. Come here and look at it, man! Look at it! And we call it crossroads Tobair Vree. And why do we call it Tobair Vree? I'll tell you why. Tobair means a well. But what does Vree mean? It's a corruption of Brian—*(Gaelic pronunciation)* Brian—an erosion of Tobair Bhriain. Because a hundred-and-fifty years ago there used to be a well there, not at the crossroads, mind you—that would be too simple—but in a field close to the crossroads. And an old man called Brian, whose face was disfigured by an enormous growth, got it into his head that the water in that well was blessed; and every day for seven months he went there and bathed his face in it. But the growth didn't go away; and one morning Brian was found drowned in that well. And ever since that crossroads is known as Tobair Vree—even though that well has long since dried up. I know the story because my grandfather told it to me. But ask Doalty—or Maire—or Bridget—even my father—even Manus—why it's

called Tobair Vree; and do you think they'll know? I know they don't
know. So the question I put to you, Lieutenant, is this: what do we do
with a name like that? Do we scrap Tobair Vree altogether and call it—
what?—The Cross? Crossroads? Or do we keep piety with a man long
dead, long forgotten, his name "eroded" beyond recognition, whose trivial
little story nobody in the parish remembers?

YOLLAND. Except you.

OWEN. I've left here.

YOLLAND. You remember it.

OWEN. I'm asking you: what do we write in the Name-Book?

YOLLAND. Tobair Vree.

OWEN. That's what you want?

YOLLAND. Yes.

OWEN. You're certain?

YOLLAND. Yes.

OWEN. Fine. Fine. That's what you'll get.

YOLLAND. That's what you want, too, Roland.

(Pause.)

OWEN *(explodes)*. George! For God's sake! *My name is not Roland!*

YOLLAND. Not Roland?

OWEN. Owen.

YOLLAND. You mean to say—?

OWEN. Owen.

YOLLAND. But I've been—

OWEN. O-w-e-n.

YOLLAND. Where did Roland come from?

OWEN. I don't know.

YOLLAND. It was never Roland?

OWEN. Never.

YOLLAND. O my God!

*(Pause. They stare at one another. Then the absurdity of the situation strikes
them suddenly. They explode with laughter. Owen pours drinks. As they roll
about, their lines overlap.)*

YOLLAND. Why didn't you tell me?

OWEN. Do I look like a Roland?

YOLLAND. Spell Owen again.

OWEN. I was getting fond of Roland.

YOLLAND. O my God!

OWEN. O-w-e-n.

YOLLAND. What'll we write—

OWEN. —in the Name Book?!

YOLLAND. R-o-w-e-n!

OWEN. Or what about Ol-

YOLLAND. Ol- what?

OWEN. Oland!

(And again they explode. Manus enters. He is very elated.)

MANUS. What's the celebration?

OWEN. A christening!

YOLLAND. A baptism!

OWEN. A hundred christenings!

YOLLAND. A thousand baptisms! Welcome to Eden!

OWEN. Eden's right! We name a thing and—bang!—it leaps into existence!

YOLLAND. Each name a perfect equation with its roots.

OWEN. A perfect congruence with its reality. *(To Manus)* Take a drink.

YOLLAND. Poteen—beautiful.

OWEN. Lying Anna's poteen.

YOLLAND. Anna na mBreag's poteen.

OWEN. Excellent, George.

YOLLAND. I'll decode you yet.

OWEN *(offers drink)*. Manus?

MANUS. Not if that's what it does to you.

OWEN. You're right. Steady—steady—sober up—sober up.

YOLLAND. Sober as a judge, Owen.

(Manus moves beside Owen.)

MANUS. I've got good news! Where's Father?

OWEN. He's gone out. What's the good news?

MANUS. I've been offered a job.

OWEN. Where? *(Now aware of Yolland.)* Come on, man—speak in English.

MANUS. For the benefit of the colonist?

OWEN. He's a decent man.

MANUS. Aren't they all at some level?

OWEN. Please.

(Manus shrugs.)

He's been offered a job.

YOLLAND. Where?

OWEN. Well—tell us!

MANUS. I've just had a meeting with two men from Inis Meadhon. They want me to go there and start a hedge-school. They're giving me a free house, free turf, and free milk; a rood of standing corn;[115] twelve drills[116] of potatoes; and—

(He stops.)

OWEN. And what?

---

115. **a rood of standing corn** a quarter acre of uncut cereal   116. **drills** rows

MANUS. A salary of £42 a year!

OWEN. Manus, that's wonderful!

MANUS. You're talking to a man of substance.

OWEN. I'm delighted.

YOLLAND. Where's Inis Meadhon?

OWEN. An island south of here. And they came looking for you?

MANUS. Well, I mean to say . . .

(Owen punches Manus.)

OWEN. Aaaaagh! This calls for a real celebration.

YOLLAND. Congratulations.

MANUS. Thank you.

OWEN. Where are you, Anna?

YOLLAND. When do you start?

MANUS. Next Monday.

OWEN. We'll stay with you when we're there. *(To Yolland)* How long will it be before we reach Inis Meadhon?

YOLLAND. How far south is it?

MANUS. About fifty miles.

YOLLAND. Could we make it by December?

OWEN. We'll have Christmas together. *(Sings)* "Christmas Day on Inis Meadhon . . ."

YOLLAND *(toast)*. I hope you're very content there, Manus.

MANUS. Thank you.

(Yolland holds out his hand. Manus takes it. They shake warmly.)

OWEN *(toast)*. Manus.

MANUS *(toast)*. To Inis Meadhon.

(He drinks quickly and turns to leave.)

OWEN. Hold on—hold on—refills coming up.

MANUS. I've got to go.

OWEN. Come on, man; this is an occasion. Where are you rushing to?

MANUS. I've got to tell Maire.

(Maire enters with her can of milk.)

MAIRE. You've got to tell Maire what?

OWEN. He's got a job!

MAIRE. Manus?

OWEN. He's been invited to start a hedge-school in Inis Meadhon.

MAIRE. Where?

MANUS. Inis Meadhon—the island! They're giving me £42 a year and . . .

OWEN. A house, fuel, milk, potatoes, corn, pupils, what-not!

MANUS. I start on Monday.

OWEN. You'll take a drink. Isn't it great?

MANUS. I want to talk to you for—

MAIRE. There's your milk. I need the can back.
(Manus takes the can and runs up the steps.)
MANUS *(as he goes)*. How will you like living on an island?
OWEN. You know George, don't you?
MAIRE. We wave to each other across the fields.
YOLLAND. Sorry-sorry?
OWEN. She says you wave to each other across the fields.
YOLLAND. Yes, we do; oh, yes; indeed we do.
MAIRE. What's he saying?
OWEN. He says you wave to each other across the fields.
MAIRE. That's right. So we do.
YOLLAND. What's she saying?
OWEN. Nothing—nothing—nothing. *(To Maire)* What's the news?
(Maire moves away, touching the text books with her toe.)
MAIRE. Not a thing. You're busy, the two of you.
OWEN. We think we are.
MAIRE. I hear the Fiddler O'Shea's about. There's some talk of a dance tomorrow night.
OWEN. Where will it be?
MAIRE. Maybe over the road. Maybe at Tobair Vree.
YOLLAND. Tobair Vree!
MAIRE. Yes.
YOLLAND. Tobair Vree! Tobair Vree!
MAIRE. Does he know what I'm saying?
OWEN. Not a word.
MAIRE. Tell him then.
OWEN. Tell him what?
MAIRE. About the dance.
OWEN. Maire says there may be a dance tomorrow night.
YOLLAND *(to Owen)*. Yes? May I come? *(To Maire)* Would anybody object if I came?
MAIRE *(to Owen)*. What's he saying?
OWEN *(to Yolland)*. Who would object?
MAIRE *(to Owen)*. Did you tell him?
YOLLAND *(to Maire)*. Sorry-sorry?
OWEN *(to Maire)*. He says may he come?
MAIRE *(to Yolland)*. That's up to you.
YOLLAND *(to Owen)*. What does she say?
OWEN *(to Yolland)*. She says—
YOLLAND *(to Maire)*. What-what?
MAIRE *(to Owen)*. Well?
YOLLAND *(to Owen)*. Sorry-sorry?
OWEN *(to Yolland)*. Will you go?

YOLLAND *(to Maire).* Yes, yes, if I may. *ouch!*

MAIRE *(to Owen).* What does he say?

YOLLAND *(to Owen).* What is she saying?

OWEN. Oh for God's sake! *(To Manus who is descending with the empty can.)* You take on this job, Manus.

MANUS. I'll walk you up to the house. Is your mother at home? I want to talk to her.

MAIRE. What's the rush? *(To Owen)* Didn't you offer me a drink?

OWEN. Will you risk Anna na mBreag?

MAIRE. Why not.

(Yolland is suddenly intoxicated. He leaps up on a stool, raises his glass and shouts.)

YOLLAND. Anna na mBreag! Baile Beag! Inis Meadhon! Bombay! Tobair Vree! Eden! And poteen—correct, Owen?

OWEN. Perfect.

YOLLAND. And bloody marvellous stuff it is, too. I love it! Bloody, bloody, bloody marvellous!

(Simultaneously with his final "bloody marvellous" bring up very loud the introductory music of the reel. Then immediately go to black. Retain the music throughout the very brief interval.)

SCENE 2

The following night.

This scene may be played in the schoolroom, but it would be preferable to lose—by lighting—as much of the schoolroom as possible, and to play the scene down front in a vaguely "outside" area.

The music rises to a crescendo. Then in the distance we hear Maire and Yolland approach—laughing and running. They run on, hand-in-hand. They have just left the dance. Fade the music to distant background. Then after a time it is lost and replaced by guitar music. Maire and Yolland are now down front, still holding hands and excited by their sudden and impetuous escape from the dance.

MAIRE. O my God, that leap across the ditch nearly killed me.

YOLLAND. I could scarcely keep up with you.

MAIRE. Wait till I get my breath back.

YOLLAND. We must have looked as if we were being chased.

(They now realize they are alone and holding hands—the beginnings of embarrassment. The hands disengage. They begin to drift apart. Pause.)

MAIRE. Manus'll wonder where I've got to.

YOLLAND. I wonder did anyone notice us leave.

Whoa — they don't know each other's language

(Pause. Slightly further apart.)

MAIRE. The grass must be wet. My feet are soaking.

YOLLAND. Your feet must be wet. The grass is soaking.

(Another pause. Another few paces apart. They are now a long distance from one another.)

YOLLAND *(indicating himself)*. George.

(Maire nods: Yes-yes. Then:—)

MAIRE. Lieutenant George.

YOLLAND. Don't call me that. I never think of myself as Lieutenant.

MAIRE. What-what?

YOLLAND. Sorry-sorry? *(He points to himself again.)* George. *(Maire nods: Yes-yes. Then points to herself.)*

MAIRE. Maire.

YOLLAND. Yes, I know you're Maire. Of course I know you're Maire. I mean I've been watching you night and day for the past—

MAIRE *(eagerly)*. What-what?

YOLLAND *(points)*. Maire. *(Points.)* George. *(Points both.)* Maire and George.

(Maire nods: Yes-yes-yes.)

I—I—I—

MAIRE. Say anything at all. I love the sound of your speech.

YOLLAND *(eagerly)*. Sorry-sorry?

(In acute frustration he looks around, hoping for some inspiration that will provide him with communicative means. Now he has a thought: he tries raising his voice and articulating in a staccato style and with equal and absurd emphasis on each word.) Every-morning-I-see-you-feeding-brown-hens-and-giving-meal-to-black-calf—*(The futility of it)*—O my God.

(Maire smiles. She moves towards him. She will try to communicate in Latin.)

MAIRE. *Tu es centurio in—in—in exercitu Britannico*—[117]

YOLLAND. Yes-yes? Go on—go on—say anything at all—I love the sound of your speech.

MAIRE. —*et es in castris quae—quae—quae sunt in agro*[118]—*(The futility of it)*—O my God. *(Yolland smiles. He moves towards her. Now for her English words.)* George—water.

YOLLAND. "Water"? Water! Oh yes—water—water—water—very good—water—good—good.

MAIRE. Fire.

YOLLAND. Fire—indeed—wonderful—fire, fire, fire—splendid—splendid!

---

117. *Tu es centurio in exercitu Britannico* You are a centurion in the British Army (BF) 118. *et es in castris quae sunt in agro* And you are in the camp in the field (BF)

MAIRE. Ah . . . ah . . .

YOLLAND. Yes? Go on.

MAIRE. Earth.

YOLLAND. "Earth"?

MAIRE. Earth. Earth. *(Yolland still does not understand. Maire stoops down and picks up a handful of clay. Holding it out.)* Earth.

YOLLAND. Earth! Of course—earth! Earth. Earth. Good Lord, Maire, your English is perfect!

MAIRE *(eagerly)*. What-what?

YOLLAND. Perfect English. English perfect.

MAIRE. George—

YOLLAND. That's beautiful—oh, that's really beautiful.

MAIRE. George—

YOLLAND. Say it again—say it again—

MAIRE. Shhh. *(She holds her hand up for silence—she is trying to remember her one line of English. Now she remembers it and she delivers the line as if English were her language—easily, fluidly, conversationally.)* George, "In Norfolk we besport ourselves around the maypoll."

YOLLAND. Good God, do you? That's where my mother comes from—Norfolk. Norwich actually. Not exactly Norwich town but a small village called Little Walsingham close beside it. But in our own village of Winfarthing we have a maypole too and every year on the first of May— *(He stops abruptly, only now realizing. He stares at her. She in turn misunderstands his excitement.)*

MAIRE *(to herself)*. Mother of God, my Aunt Mary wouldn't have taught me something dirty, would she?

(Pause. Yolland extends his hand to Maire. She turns away from him and moves slowly across the stage.)

YOLLAND. Maire.

(She still moves away.)

Maire Chatach.

(She still moves away.)

Bun na hAbhann? *(He says the name softly, almost privately, very tentatively, as if he were searching for a sound she might respond to. He tries again.)* Druim Dubh?

(Maire stops. She is listening. Yolland is encouraged.)

Poll na gCaorach. Lis Maol.

(Maire turns towards him.)

Lis na nGall.

MAIRE. Lis na nGradh.

(They are now facing each other and begin moving—almost imperceptibly—towards one another.)

MAIRE. Carraig an Phoill.

the sounds of words & love —
4. Cyrano & Roxane
— Romeo & Juliet

YOLLAND. Carraig na Ri. Loch na nEan.

MAIRE. Loch an Iubhair. Machaire Buidhe.

YOLLAND. Machaire Mor. Cnoc na Mona.

MAIRE. Cnoc na nGabhar.

YOLLAND. Mullach.

MAIRE. Port.

YOLLAND. Tor.

MAIRE. Lag.

(*She holds out her hands to Yolland. He takes them. Each now speaks almost to himself/herself.*)

YOLLAND. I wish to God you could understand me.

MAIRE. Soft hands; a gentleman's hands.

YOLLAND. Because if you could understand me I could tell you how I spend my days either thinking of you or gazing up at your house in the hope that you'll appear even for a second.

MAIRE. Every evening you walk by yourself along the Tra Bhan and every morning you wash yourself in front of your tent.

Poetic Juxtaposition

YOLLAND. I would tell you how beautiful you are, curly-headed Maire. I would so like to tell you how beautiful you are.

MAIRE. Your arms are long and thin and the skin on your shoulders is very white.

YOLLAND. I would tell you . . .

MAIRE. Don't stop—I know what you're saying.

YOLLAND. I would tell you how I want to be here—to live here—always—with you—always, always.

MAIRE. "Always"? What is that word—"always"?

YOLLAND. Yes-yes; always.

MAIRE. You're trembling.

YOLLAND. Yes, I'm trembling because of you.

MAIRE. I'm trembling, too.

(*She holds his face in her hand.*)

YOLLAND. I've made up my mind . . .

MAIRE. Shhhh.

YOLLAND. I'm not going to leave here . . .

Closer trans. than his

MAIRE. Shhh—listen to me. I want you, too, soldier.

YOLLAND. Don't stop—I know what you're saying.

universal language of look & gesture

MAIRE. I want to live with you—anywhere—anywhere at all—always—always.

YOLLAND. "Always"? What is that word—"always"?

MAIRE. Take me away with you, George.

(*Pause. Suddenly they kiss. Sarah enters. She sees them. She stands shocked, staring at them. Her mouth works. Then almost to herself.*)

SARAH. Manus . . . Manus!

(*Sarah runs off. Music to crescendo.*)

ACT 3

The following evening. It is raining.

Sarah and Owen alone in the schoolroom. Sarah, more waiflike than ever, is sitting very still on a stool, an open book across her knee. She is pretending to read but her eyes keep going up to the room upstairs. Owen is working on the floor as before, surrounded by his reference books, map, Name-Book, etc. But he has neither concentration nor interest; and like Sarah he glances up at the upstairs room.

After a few seconds Manus emerges and descends, carrying a large paper bag which already contains his clothes. His movements are determined and urgent. He moves around the classroom, picking up books, examining each title carefully, and choosing about six of them which he puts into his bag. As he selects these books:—

OWEN. You know that old limekiln beyond Con Connie Tim's pub, the place we call The Murren?—do you know why it's called The Murren?

(Manus does not answer.)

I've only just discovered: it's a corruption of Saint Muranus. It seems Saint Muranus had a monastery somewhere about there at the beginning of the seventh century. And over the years the name became shortened to the Murren. Very unattractive name, isn't it? I think we should go back to the original—Saint Muranus. What do you think? The original's Saint Muranus. Don't you think we should go back to that?

(No response. Owen begins writing the name into the Name-Book. Manus is now rooting about among the forgotten implements for a piece of rope. He finds a piece. He begins to tie the mouth of the flimsy, overloaded bag—and it bursts, the contents spilling on the floor.)

MANUS. Bloody, bloody, bloody hell!

(His voice breaks in exasperation: he is about to cry. Owen leaps to his feet.)

OWEN. Hold on. I've a bag upstairs.

(He runs upstairs. Sarah waits until Owen is off. Then:—)

SARAH. Manus . . . Manus, I . . .

(Manus hears Sarah but makes no acknowledgement. He gathers up his belongings. Owen reappears with the bag he had on his arrival.)

OWEN. Take this one—I'm finished with it anyway. And it's supposed to keep out the rain.

(Manus transfers his few belongings. Owen drifts back to his task. The packing is now complete.)

MANUS. You'll be here for a while? For a week or two anyhow?

OWEN. Yes.

MANUS. You're not leaving with the army?

OWEN. I haven't made up my mind. Why?

MANUS. Those Inis Meadhon men will be back to see why I haven't turned up. Tell them—tell them I'll write to them as soon as I can. Tell them I still want the job but that it might be three or four months before I'm free to go.

OWEN. You're being damned stupid, Manus.

MANUS. Will you do that for me?

OWEN. Clear out now and Lancey'll think you're involved somehow.

MANUS. Will you do that for me?

OWEN. Wait a couple of days even. You know George—he's a bloody romantic—maybe he's gone out to one of the islands and he'll suddenly reappear tomorrow morning. Or maybe the search party'll find him this evening lying drunk somewhere in the sandhills. You've seen him drinking that poteen—doesn't know how to handle it. Had he drink on him last night at the dance?

MANUS. I had a stone in my hand when I went out looking for him—I was going to fell him. The lame scholar[119] turned violent.

OWEN. Did anybody see you?

MANUS *(again close to tears)*. But when I saw him standing there at the side of the road—smiling—and her face buried in his shoulder—I couldn't even go close to them. I just shouted something stupid—something like, "You're a bastard, Yolland." If I'd even said it in English . . . 'cos he kept saying "Sorry-sorry?" The wrong gesture in the wrong language.

OWEN. And you didn't see him again?

MANUS. "Sorry?"

OWEN. Before you leave tell Lancey that—just to clear yourself.

MANUS. What have I to say to Lancey? You'll give that message to the islandmen?

OWEN. I'm warning you: run away now and you're bound to be—

MANUS *(to Sarah)*. Will you give that message to the Inis Meadhon men?

SARAH. I will.

(Manus picks up an old sack and throws it across his shoulders.)

OWEN. Have you any idea where you're going?

MANUS. Mayo,[120] maybe. I remember Mother saying she had cousins somewhere away out in the Erris Peninsula. *(He picks up his bag.)* Tell Father I took only the Virgil and the Caesar and the Aeschylus because they're mine anyway—I bought them with the money I got for that pet lamb I reared—do you remember that pet lamb? And tell him that Nora Dan never returned the dictionary and that she still owes him two-and-six for last quarter's reading—he always forgets those things.

OWEN. Yes.

MANUS. And his good shirt's ironed and hanging up in the press and his clean socks are in the butter-box under the bed.

119. **scholar** student 120. **Mayo** western county

OWEN. All right.

MANUS. And tell him I'll write.

OWEN. If Maire asks where you've gone . . . ?

MANUS. He'll need only half the amount of milk, now, won't he? Even less than half—he usually takes his tea black. *(Pause.)* And when he comes in at night—you'll hear him; he makes a lot of noise—I usually come down and give him a hand up. Those stairs are dangerous without a bannister. Maybe before you leave you'd get Big Ned Frank to put up some sort of a handrail. *(Pause.)* And if you can bake, he's very fond of soda bread.

OWEN. I can give you money. I'm wealthy. Do you know what they pay me? Two shillings a day for this—this—this—

(Manus rejects the offer by holding out his hand.)

Goodbye, Manus.

(Manus and Owen shake hands. Then Manus picks up his bag briskly and goes towards the door. He stops a few paces beyond Sarah, turns, comes back to her. He addresses her as he did in Act One but now without warmth or concern for her.)

MANUS. What is your name? *(Pause.)* Come on. What is your name?

SARAH. My name is Sarah.

MANUS. Just Sarah? Sarah what? *(Pause.)* Well?

SARAH. Sarah Johnny Sally.

MANUS. And where do you live? Come on.

SARAH. I live in Bun na hAbhann.

(She is now crying quietly.)

MANUS. Very good, Sarah Johnny Sally. There's nothing to stop you now—nothing in the wide world. *(Pause. He looks down at her.)* It's all right—it's all right—you did no harm—you did no harm at all.

(He stoops over her and kisses the top of her head—as if in absolution. Then briskly to the door and off.)

OWEN. Good luck, Manus!

SARAH. *(Quietly)* I'm sorry . . . I'm sorry . . . I'm so sorry, Manus . . .

(Owen tries to work but cannot concentrate. He begins folding up the map. As he does:—)

OWEN. Is there a class this evening?

(Sarah nods: yes.)

I suppose Father knows. Where is he anyhow?

(Sarah points.)

Where?

(Sarah mimes rocking a baby.)

I don't understand—where?

(Sarah repeats the mime and wipes away tears. Owen is still puzzled.)

It doesn't matter. He'll probably turn up.

(Bridget and Doalty enter, sacks over their heads against the rain. They are self-consciously noisier, more ebullient, more garrulous than ever—brimming over with excitement and gossip and brio.)[121]

DOALTY. You're missing the crack,[122] boys! Cripes, you're missing the crack! Fifty more soldiers arrived an hour ago!

BRIDGET. And they're spread out in a big line from Sean Neal's over to Lag and they're moving straight across the fields towards Cnoc na nGabhar!

DOALTY. Prodding every inch of the ground in front of them with their bayonets and scattering animals and hens in all directions!

BRIDGET. And tumbling everything before them—fences, ditches, haystacks, turf-stacks!

DOALTY. They came to Barney Peter's field of corn—straight through it be God as if it was heather!

BRIDGET. Not a blade of it left standing.

DOALTY. And Barney Petey just out of his bed and running after them in his drawers: "You hoors[123] you! Get out of my corn, you hoors you!"

BRIDGET. First time he ever ran in his life.

DOALTY. Too lazy, the wee get,[124] to cut it when the weather was good. *(Sarah begins putting out the seats.)*

BRIDGET. Tell them about Big Hughie.

DOALTY. Cripes, if you'd seen your aul fella, Owen.

BRIDGET. They were all inside in Anna na mBreag's pub—all the crowd from the wake—

DOALTY. And they hear the commotion and they all come out to the street—

BRIDGET. Your father in front; the Infant Prodigy footless[125] behind him!

DOALTY. And your aul fella, he sees the army stretched across the countryside—

BRIDGET. O my God!

DOALTY. And Cripes he starts roaring at them!

BRIDGET. "Visigoths! Huns! Vandals!"[126]

DOALTY. *"Ignari! Stulti! Rustici!"*[127]

BRIDGET. And wee Jimmy Jack jumping up and down and shouting, "Thermopylae! Thermopylae!"[128]

DOALTY. You never saw crack like it in your life, boys. Come away on out with me, Sarah, and you'll see it all.

121. *brio* vivacity   122. **crack** fun   123. **hoors** whores, general term of abuse   124. **get** child   125. **footless** drunk   126. **Visigoths! Huns! Vandals!** barbarian tribes who invaded Europe in the fourth century   127. *Ignari! Stulti! Rustici!* Ignoramuses! Fools! Peasants! (BF)   128. **Thermopylae** a narrow pass where Leonidas and 300 Spartans heroically defended Greece against the huge Persian army of Xerxes in 480 B.C.

BRIDGET. Big Hughie's fit to take no class. Is Manus about?

OWEN. Manus is gone.

BRIDGET. Gone where?

OWEN. He's left—gone away.

DOALTY. Where to?

OWEN. He doesn't know. Mayo, maybe.

DOALTY. What's on in Mayo?

OWEN *(to Bridget)*. Did you see George and Maire Chatach leave the dance last night?

BRIDGET. We did. Didn't we, Doalty?

OWEN. Did you see Manus following them out?

BRIDGET. I didn't see him going out but I saw him coming in by himself later.

OWEN. Did George and Maire come back to the dance?

BRIDGET. No.

OWEN. Did you see them again?

BRIDGET. He left her home. We passed them going up the back road—didn't we, Doalty?

OWEN. And Manus stayed till the end of the dance?

DOALTY. We know nothing. What are you asking us for?

OWEN. Because Lancey'll question me when he hears Manus's gone. *(Back to Bridget.)* That's the way George went home? By the back road? That's where you saw him?

BRIDGET. Leave me alone, Owen. I know nothing about Yolland. If you want to know about Yolland, ask the Donnelly twins.

(Silence. Doalty moves over to the window.)

(To Sarah) He's a powerful fiddler, O'Shea, isn't he? He told our Seamus he'll come back for a night at Hallowe'en.

(Owen goes to Doalty who looks resolutely out the window.)

OWEN. What's this about the Donnellys? *(Pause.)* Were they about last night?

DOALTY. Didn't see them if they were.

(Begins whistling through his teeth.)

OWEN. George is a friend of mine.

DOALTY. So.

OWEN. I want to know what's happened to him.

DOALTY. Couldn't tell you.

OWEN. What have the Donnelly twins to do with it? *(Pause.)* Doalty!

DOALTY. I know nothing, Owen—nothing at all—I swear to God. All I know is this: on my way to the dance I saw their boat beached at Port. It wasn't there on my way home, after I left Bridget. And that's all I know. As God's my judge. The half-dozen times I met him I didn't know a word he said to me; but he seemed a right enough sort . . . *(With sudden excessive interest in the scene outside.)* Cripes, they're crawling all over the place! Cripes, there's millions of them! Cripes, they're levelling the whole land!

(Owen moves away. Maire enters. She is bareheaded and wet from the rain; her hair in disarray. She attempts to appear normal but she is in acute distress, on the verge of being distraught. She is carrying the milk-can.)

MAIRE. Honest to God, I must be going off my head. I'm halfway here and I think to myself, "Isn't this can very light?" and I look into it and isn't it empty.

OWEN. It doesn't matter.

MAIRE. How will you manage for tonight?

OWEN. We have enough.

MAIRE. Are you sure?

OWEN. Plenty, thanks.

MAIRE. It'll take me no time at all to go back up for some.

OWEN. Honestly, Maire.

MAIRE. Sure it's better you have it than that black calf that's . . . that . . . *(She looks around.)* Have you heard anything?

OWEN. Nothing.

MAIRE. What does Lancey say?

OWEN. I haven't seen him since this morning.

MAIRE. What does he *think*?

OWEN. We really didn't talk. He was here for only a few seconds.

MAIRE. He left me home, Owen. And the last thing he said to me—he tried to speak in Irish—he said, "I'll see you yesterday"—he meant to say "I'll see you tomorrow." And I laughed that much he pretended to get cross and he said "Maypoll! Maypoll!" because I said that word wrong. And off he went, laughing—laughing, Owen! Do you think he's all right? What do *you* think?

OWEN. I'm sure he'll turn up. Maire.

MAIRE. He comes from a tiny wee place called Winfarthing. *(She suddenly drops on her hands and knees on the floor—where Owen had his map a few minutes ago—and with her finger traces out an outline map.)* Come here till you see. Look. There's Winfarthing. And there's two other wee villages right beside it; one of them's called Barton Bendish—it's there; and the other's called Saxingham Nethergate—it's about there. And there's Little Walsingham—that's his mother's townland. Aren't they odd names? Sure they make no sense to me at all. And Winfarthing's near a big town called Norwich. And Norwich is in a county called Norfolk. And Norfolk is in the east of England. He drew a map for me on the wet strand and wrote the names on it. I have it all in my head now: Winfarthing—Barton Bendish—Saxingham Nethergate—Little Walsingham—Norwich—Norfolk. Strange sounds, aren't they? But nice sounds; like Jimmy Jack reciting his Homer. *(She gets to her feet and looks around; she is almost serene now. To*

Checkhovian — DISconnected connections wandering together in his voice [handwritten annotations]

Sarah) You were looking lovely last night, Sarah. Is that the dress you got from Boston? Green suits you. *(To Owen)* Something very bad's happened to him, Owen. I know. He wouldn't go away without telling me. Where is he, Owen? You're his friend—where is he? *(Again she looks around the room; then sits on a stool.)* I didn't get a chance to do my geography last night. The master'll be angry with me. *(She rises again.)* I think I'll go home now. The wee ones have to be washed and put to bed and that black calf has to be fed . . . My hands are that rough; they're still blistered from the hay. I'm ashamed of them. I hope to God there's no hay to be saved in Brooklyn. *(She stops at the door.)* Did you hear? Nellie Ruadh's baby died in the middle of the night. I must go up to the wake. It didn't last long, did it?

(Maire leaves. Silence. Then.)

OWEN. I don't think there'll be any class. Maybe you should . . .

(Owen begins picking up his texts. Doalty goes to him.)

DOALTY. Is he long gone?—Manus.

OWEN. Half an hour.

DOALTY. Stupid bloody fool.

OWEN. I told him that.

DOALTY. Do they know he's gone?

OWEN. Who?

DOALTY. The army.

OWEN. Not yet.

DOALTY. They'll be after him like bloody beagles. Bloody, bloody fool, limping along the coast. They'll overtake him before night for Christ's sake.

(Doalty returns to the window. Lancey enters—now the commanding officer.)

OWEN. Any news? Any word?

(Lancey moves into the centre of the room, looking around as he does.)

LANCEY. I understood there was a class. Where are the others?

OWEN. There was to be a class but my father—

LANCEY. This will suffice. I will address them and it will be their responsibility to pass on what I have to say to every family in this section.

(Lancey indicates to Owen to translate. Owen hesitates, trying to assess the change in Lancey's manner and attitude.)

I'm in a hurry, O'Donnell.

OWEN. The captain has an announcement to make.

LANCEY. Lieutenant Yolland is missing. We are searching for him. If we don't find him, or if we receive no information as to where he is to be found, I will pursue the following course of action. *(He indicates to Owen to translate.)*

OWEN. They are searching for George. If they don't find him—

LANCEY. Commencing twenty-four hours from now we will shoot all livestock in Ballybeg.

(Owen stares at Lancey.)

At once.

OWEN. Beginning this time tomorrow they'll kill every animal in Baile Beag—unless they're told where George is.

LANCEY. If that doesn't bear results, commencing forty-eight hours from now we will embark on a series of evictions and levelling of every abode in the following selected areas—

OWEN. You're not—!

LANCEY. Do your job. Translate.

OWEN. If they still haven't found him in two days time they'll begin evicting and levelling every house starting with these townlands.

(Lancey reads from his list.)

LANCEY. Swinefort.

OWEN. Lis na Muc.

LANCEY. Burnfoot.

OWEN. Bun na hAbhann.

LANCEY. Dromduff.

OWEN. Druim Dubh.

LANCEY. Whiteplains.

OWEN. Machaire Ban.

LANCEY. Kings Head.

OWEN. Cnoc na Ri.

LANCEY. If by then the lieutenant hasn't been found, we will proceed until a complete clearance is made of this entire section.

OWEN. If Yolland hasn't been got by then, they will ravish the whole parish.

LANCEY. I trust they know exactly what they've got to do. *(Pointing to Bridget.)* I know you. I know where you live. *(Pointing to Sarah.)* Who are you? Name!

(Sarah's mouth opens and shuts, opens and shuts. Her face becomes contorted.)

What's your name?

(Again Sarah tries frantically.)

OWEN. Go on, Sarah. You can tell him.

(But Sarah cannot. And she knows she cannot. She closes her mouth. Her head goes down.)

OWEN. Her name is Sarah Johnny Sally.

LANCEY. Where does she live?

OWEN. Bun na hAbhann.

LANCEY. Where?

OWEN. Burnfoot.

LANCEY. I want to talk to your brother—is he here?

OWEN. Not at the moment.

LANCEY. Where is he?

OWEN. He's at a wake.

LANCEY. What wake?

(Doalty, who has been looking out the window all through Lancey's announcements, now speaks—calmly, almost casually.)

DOALTY. Tell him his whole camp's on fire.

LANCEY. What's your name? *(To Owen)* Who's that lout?

OWEN. Doalty Dan Doalty.

LANCEY. Where does he live?

OWEN. Tulach Alainn.

LANCEY. What do we call it?

OWEN. Fair Hill. He says your whole camp is on fire.

(Lancey rushes to the window and looks out. Then he wheels on Doalty.)

LANCEY. I'll remember you, Mr Doalty. *(To Owen)* You carry a big responsibility in all this. *for telling him – for naming it*

(He goes off.)

BRIDGET. Mother of God, does he mean it, Owen?

OWEN. Yes, he does.

BRIDGET. We'll have to hide the beasts somewhere—our Seamus'll know where. Maybe at the back of Lis na nGradh—or in the caves at the far end of the Tra Bhan. Come on, Doalty! Come on! Don't be standing about there!

(Doalty does not move. Bridget runs to the door and stops suddenly. She sniffs the air. Panic.)

The sweet smell! Smell it! It's the sweet smell! Jesus, it's the potato blight! *in 15 years*

DOALTY. It's the army tents burning, Bridget.

BRIDGET. Is it? Are you sure? Is that what it is? God, I thought we were destroyed altogether. Come on! Come on!

(She runs off. Owen goes to Sarah who is preparing to leave.)

OWEN. How are you? Are you all right?

(Sarah nods: Yes.)

OWEN. Don't worry. It will come back to you again.

(Sarah shakes her head.)

OWEN. It will. You're upset now. He frightened you. That's all's wrong.

(Again Sarah shakes her head, slowly, emphatically, and smiles at Owen. Then she leaves. Owen busies himself gathering his belongings. Doalty leaves the window and goes to him.)

DOALTY. He'll do it, too.

OWEN. Unless Yolland's found.

DOALTY. Hah!

OWEN. Then he'll certainly do it.

DOALTY. When my grandfather was a boy they did the same thing. *(Simply, altogether without irony)* And after all the trouble you went to, mapping the place and thinking up new names for it. *(Owen busies himself. Pause. Doalty almost dreamily.)* I've damned little to defend but he'll not put me out without a fight. And there'll be others who think the same as me.

OWEN. That's a matter for you.

DOALTY. If we'd all stick together. If we knew how to defend ourselves.

OWEN. Against a trained army.

DOALTY. The Donnelly twins know how.   *The o'leary's famine*

OWEN. If they could be found.

DOALTY. If they could be found. *(He goes to the door.)* Give me a shout after you've finished with Lancey. I might know something then.

(He leaves.)

(Owen picks up the Name-Book. He looks at it momentarily, then puts it on top of the pile he is carrying. It falls to the floor. He stoops to pick it up—hesitates—leaves it. He goes upstairs. As Owen ascends, Hugh and Jimmy Jack enter. Both wet and drunk. Jimmy is very unsteady. He is trotting behind Hugh, trying to break in on Hugh's declamation. Hugh is equally drunk but more experienced in drunkenness: there is a portion of his mind which retains its clarity.)

HUGH. There I was, appropriately dispositioned to proffer my condolences to the bereaved mother . . .

JIMMY. Hugh—

HUGH. . . . and about to enter the *domus lugubris*[129]—Maire Chatach?

JIMMY. The wake house.

HUGH. Indeed—when I experience a plucking at my elbow: Mister George Alexander, Justice of the Peace. "My tidings are infelicitous," said he—said he—Bridget? Too slow. Doalty?

JIMMY. *Infelix*[130]—unhappy.

HUGH. Unhappy indeed. "Master Bartley Timlin has been appointed to the new national school." "Timlin? Who is Timlin?" "A schoolmaster from Cork. And he will be a major asset to the community: he is also a very skilled bacon-curer!"

JIMMY. Hugh—

HUGH. Ha-ha-ha-ha-ha! The Cork bacon-curer! *Barbarus hic ego sum quia non intelligor ulli*[131]—James?

---

129. *domus lugubris* house of mourning (BF)   130. *Infelix* unlucky, unhappy (BF)   131. *Barbarus hic ego sum quia non intelligor ulli* I am a barbarian here because I am not understood by anyone (BF)

JIMMY. Ovid.

HUGH. *Procede.*[132]

JIMMY. "I am a barbarian in this place because I am not understood by anyone."

HUGH. Indeed—*(Shouts)* Manus! Tea! I will compose a satire on Master Bartley Timlin, schoolmaster and bacon-curer. But it will be too easy, won't it? *(Shouts)* Strong tea! Black!

(The only way Jimmy can get Hugh's attention is by standing in front of him and holding his arms.)

JIMMY. Will you listen to me, Hugh!

HUGH. James. *(Shouts)* And a slice of soda bread.

JIMMY. I'm going to be married.

HUGH. Well!

JIMMY. At Christmas.

HUGH. Splendid.

JIMMY. To Athene.

HUGH. Who?

JIMMY. Pallas Athene.

HUGH. *Glaukopis Athene?*

JIMMY. Flashing-eyed, Hugh, flashing-eyed!

(He attempts the gesture he has made before: standing to attention, the momentary spasm, the salute, the face raised in pained ecstasy—but the body does not respond efficiently this time. The gesture is grotesque.)

HUGH. The lady has assented?

JIMMY. She asked *me—I* assented.

HUGH. Ah. When was this?

JIMMY. Last night.

HUGH. What does her mother say?

JIMMY. Metis from Hellespont? Decent people—good stock.

HUGH. And her father?

JIMMY. I'm meeting Zeus tomorrow. Hugh, will you be my best man?

HUGH. Honoured, James; profoundly honoured.

JIMMY. You know what I'm looking for, Hugh, don't you? I mean to say—you know—I—I—I joke like the rest of them—you know?—*(Again he attempts the pathetic routine but abandons it instantly.)* You know yourself, Hugh—don't you?—you know all that. But what I'm really looking for, Hugh—what I really want—companionship, Hugh—at my time of life, companionship, company, someone to talk to. Away up in Beann na Gaoithe—you've no idea how lonely it is. Companionship—correct, Hugh? Correct?

HUGH. Correct.

132. *Procede* proceed (BF)

JIMMY. And I always liked her, Hugh. Correct?

HUGH. Correct, James.

JIMMY. Someone to talk to.

HUGH. Indeed.

JIMMY. That's all, Hugh. The whole story. You know it all now, Hugh. You know it all.

(As Jimmy says those last lines he is crying, shaking his head, trying to keep his balance, and holding a finger up to his lips in absurd gestures of secrecy and intimacy. Now he staggers away, tries to sit on a stool, misses it, slides to the floor, his feet in front of him, his back against the broken cart. Almost at once he is asleep. Hugh watches all of this. Then he produces his flask and is about to pour a drink when he sees the Name-Book on the floor. He picks it up and leafs through it, pronouncing the strange names as he does. Just as he begins, Owen emerges and descends with two bowls of tea.)

HUGH. Ballybeg. Burnfoot. King's Head. Whiteplains. Fair Hill. Dunboy. Green Bank.

(Owen snatches the book from Hugh.)

OWEN. I'll take that. *(In apology.)* It's only a catalogue of names.

HUGH. I know what it is.

OWEN. A mistake—my mistake—nothing to do with us. I hope that's strong enough *(tea)*. *(He throws the book on the table and crosses over to Jimmy.)*

Jimmy. Wake up, Jimmy. Wake up, man.

JIMMY. What—what-what?

OWEN. Here. Drink this. Then go on away home. There may be trouble. Do you hear me, Jimmy? There may be trouble.

HUGH *(indicating Name-Book)*. We must learn those new names.

OWEN *(searching around)*. Did you see a sack lying about?

HUGH. We must learn where we live. We must learn to make them our own. We must make them our new home.

(Owen finds a sack and throws it across his shoulders.)

OWEN. I know where I live.

HUGH. James thinks he knows, too. I look at James and three thoughts occur to me: A—that it is not the literal past, the "facts" of history, that shape us, but images of the past embodied in language. James has ceased to make that discrimination.

OWEN. Don't lecture me, Father.

HUGH. B—we must never cease renewing those images; because once we do, we fossilize. Is there no soda bread?

OWEN. And C, Father—one single, unalterable "fact": if Yolland is not found, we are all going to be evicted. Lancey has issued the order.

HUGH. Ah. *Edictum imperatoris.*[133]

133. *Edictum imperatoris* the decree of the commander (BF)

OWEN. You should change out of those wet clothes. I've got to go. I've got to see Doalty Dan Doalty.

HUGH. What about?

OWEN. I'll be back soon.

(As Owen exits.)

HUGH. Take care, Owen. To remember everything is a form of madness.

(He looks around the room, carefully, as if he were about to leave it forever. Then he looks at Jimmy, asleep again.)

The road to Sligo. A spring morning. 1798.[134] Going into battle. Do you remember, James? Two young gallants with pikes[135] across their shoulders and the *Aeneid*[136] in their pockets. Everything seemed to find definition that spring—a congruence, a miraculous matching of hope and past and present and possibility. Striding across the fresh, green land. The rhythms of perception heightened. The whole enterprise of consciousness accelerated. We were gods that morning, James; and I had recently married *my* goddess, Caitlin Dubh Nic Reactainn, may she rest in peace. And to leave her and my infant son in his cradle—that was heroic, too. By God, sir, we were magnificent. We marched as far as—where was it?—Glenties![137] All of twenty-three miles in one day. And it was there, in Phelan's pub, that we got homesick for Athens, just like Ulysses. The *desiderium nostrorum*[138]—the need for our own. Our *pietas*,[139] James, was for older, quieter things. And that was the longest twenty-three miles back I ever made. *(Toasts Jimmy.)* My friend, confusion is not an ignoble condition.

(Maire enters.)

MAIRE. I'm back again. I set out for somewhere but I couldn't remember where. So I came back here.

HUGH. Yes, I will teach you English, Maire Chatach.

MAIRE. Will you, Master? I must learn it. I need to learn it.

HUGH. Indeed you may well be my only pupil.

(He goes towards the steps and begins to ascend.)

MAIRE. When can we start?

HUGH. Not today. Tomorrow, perhaps. After the funeral. We'll begin tomorrow. *(Ascending)* But don't expect too much. I will provide you with the available words and the available grammar. But will that help you to interpret between privacies? I have no idea. But it's all we have. I have no idea at all.

(He is now at the top.)

MAIRE. Master, what does the English word "always" mean?

134. **1798** the year of widespread peasant insurrection   135. **pikes** a pole with a sharp, steel-tipped end   136. ***Aeneid*** Virgil's epic poem   137. **Glenties** in south Donegal   138. ***desiderium nostrorum*** longing/need for our things/people (BF)   139. ***pietas*** piety (BF)

HUGH. *Semper—per omnia saecula.*[140] The Greeks called it "*aei.*"[141] It's not a word I'd start with. It's a silly word, girl.

(He sits. Jimmy is awake. He gets to his feet. Maire sees the Name-Book, picks it up, and sits with it on her knee.)

MAIRE. When he comes back, this is where he'll come to. He told me this is where he was happiest.

(Jimmy sits beside Maire.)

Calm words that the si...

JIMMY. Do you know the Greek word *endogamein?*[142] It means to marry within the tribe. And the word *exogamein*[143] means to marry outside the tribe. And you don't cross those borders casually—both sides get very angry. Now, the problem is this: Is Athene sufficiently mortal or am I sufficiently godlike for the marriage to be acceptable to her people and to my people? You think about that.

HUGH. *Urbs antiqua fuit*[144]—there was an ancient city which, 'tis said, Juno loved above all the lands. And it was the goddess's aim and cherished hope that here should be the capital of all nations—should the fates perchance allow that. Yet in truth she discovered that a race was springing from Trojan blood to overthrow some day these Tyrian towers—a people *late regem belloque superbum*[145]—kings of broad realms and proud in war who would come forth for Lybia's downfall[146]—such was—such was the course—such was the course ordained—ordained by fate ... What the *Future/Name* hell's wrong with me? Sure I know it backwards. I'll begin again. *Urbs antiqua fuit*—there was an ancient city which, 'tis said, Juno[147] loved above all the lands. *Ireland —*

(Begin to bring down the lights.)

And it was the goddess's aim and cherished hope that here should be the capital of all nations—should the fates perchance allow that. Yet in truth she discovered that a race was springing from Trojan blood to overthrow some day these Tyrian towers—a people, kings of broad realms and proud in war who would come forth for Lybia's downfall ...

Lybia = ?

The Irish —? The hope y Revolution — the closing events unresolved — Manus? Yolland? even the funeral

BLACK

140. *Semper—per omnia saecula* Always—for all time (BF)   141. *aei* ἀεί: always (BF)   142. *endogamein* ἐνδογαμεῖν: to marry within the tribe (BF)   143. *exogamein* ἐξογαμεῖν: to marry outside the tribe (BF)   144. **Urbs antiqua fuit** There was an ancient city (BF)   145. *late regem belloque superbum* kings of broad realms and proud in war (BF)   146. **Lybia's downfall** the destruction of Carthage in 146 B.C. (Virgil, *Aeneid* I)   147. **Juno** wife of Jupiter, mistress of heaven and earth

General Bibliography
of Sources on Irish Drama

Bell, Sam Hanna. *The Theatre in Ulster.* Dublin: Gill and Macmillan, 1972.

Boyd, Ernest A. *The Contemporary Drama of Ireland.* Dublin: Talbot Press/London: Unwin, 1918.

———. *Ireland's Literary Renaissance.* Dublin: Maunsel, 1916; New York: Barnes and Noble, 1968; Dublin: Allen Figgis, 1969.

Browne, Ray Broadus, William John Roscelli, and Richard Loftus. *The Celtic Cross: Studies in Irish Culture and Literature.* West Lafayette, IN: Purdue University Studies, 1964.

Coxhead, Elizabeth. *Daughters of Erin: Five Women of the Irish Renascence.* London: Secker and Warburg, 1965.

Deane, Seamus. *Celtic Revivals: Essays in Modern Irish Literature, 1880–1980.* London: Faber, 1985; Wake Forest, NC: Wake Forest University Press, 1985.

Edwards, Philip. *Threshold of a Nation: A Study of English and Irish Drama.* Cambridge: Cambridge University Press, 1979.

Ellis-Fermor, Una. *The Irish Dramatic Movement.* London: Methuen, 1939; revised 1954.

Fallis, Richard. *The Irish Renaissance.* Syracuse, NY: Syracuse University Press, 1977.

Fay, Frank. *Towards a National Theatre: Dramatic Criticism.* Ed. and intro. Robert Hogan. Dublin: Dolmen, 1970.

Fay, William G., and Catherine Carswell. *The Fays of the Abbey Theatre: An Autobiographical Record.* New York: Harcourt, Brace, 1935.

Finneran, Richard J., ed. *Anglo-Irish Literature: A Review of Research.* New York: MLA, 1976; Supplement, 1982.

Fitz-Simon, Christopher. *The Irish Theatre.* London: Thames and Hudson, 1983.

Gregory, Isabella Augusta. *Lady Gregory's Journals, 1916–1930.* Ed. Lennox Robinson. London: Putnam, 1946.

———. *Our Irish Theatre.* Dublin: Dolmen, 1970.

Gwynne, Stephen. *Irish Literature and Drama.* Gerrards Cross, Bucks.: Colin Smythe, 1973.

Harmon, Maurice. *Select Bibliography for the Study of Anglo-Irish Literature and its Backgrounds.* Dublin: Wolfhound Press, 1977.

Hogan, Robert. *After the Irish Renaissance.* Minneapolis: University of Minnesota Press, 1967; London: Macmillan, 1968.

———, ed. *Dictionary of Irish Literature.* Westport, CT: Greenwood Press, 1979.

———, and James Kilroy. *The Irish Literary Theatre, 1899–1901.* Vol. 1 of *The Modern Irish Drama.* Dublin: Dolmen Press, 1975.

———. *Laying the Foundations, 1902–1904.* Vol. 2 of *The Modern Irish Drama.* Dublin: Dolmen Press, 1976.

———, Richard Burnham and Daniel Poteet. *The Abbey Theatre, 1905–1909.* Vol. 3 of *The Modern Irish Drama.* Dublin: Dolmen Press, 1978.

———. *The Rise of the Realists, 1910–1915.* Vol. 4 of *The Modern Irish Drama.* Dublin: Dolmen Press, 1979.

Holloway, Joseph. *Joseph Holloway's Abbey Theatre: A Selection from His Unpublished*

Journal "*Impressions of a Dublin Playgoer.*" Ed. Robert Hogan and Michael J. O'Neill. Carbondale, IL: Southern Illinois University Press, 1967. (Covers 1899–1926)

———. *Joseph Holloway's Abbey Theatre.* 3 vols. Ed. Robert Hogan and Michael J. O'Neill. Dixon, CA: Proscenium Press, 1968–70. (Covers 1926–31, 1932–37, 1938–44)

Howarth, Herbert. *The Irish Writers: Literature and Nationalism, 1880–1940.* New York: Hill and Wang/London: Rockliff, 1958.

Hunt, Hugh. *The Abbey: Ireland's National Theatre, 1904–1979.* Dublin: Gill and Macmillan/New York: Columbia University Press, 1979.

Irish Literary Studies 15. Totowa, NJ: Barnes and Noble, 1983.

Jochum, K. P. S. *W. B. Yeats: A Classified Bibliography of Criticism.* Urbana, IL: University of Illinois Press, 1978. (Has extensive general bibliographies)

Kilroy, James. *The 'Playboy' Riots.* Dublin: Dolmen Press, 1971.

Kosok, Heinz, ed. *Studies in Anglo-Irish Literature.* Bonn: Bouvier Verlag, Herbert Grundmann, 1982.

Krause, David. *The Profane Book of Irish Comedy.* Ithaca, NY: Cornell University Press, 1982.

Maxwell, D. E. S. *A Critical History of Modern Irish Drama, 1891–1980.* Cambridge, England: Cambridge University Press, 1984.

McCann, Sean, ed. *The Story of the Abbey.* London: New English Library, 1967.

McHugh, Roger, and Maurice Harmon. *A Short History of Anglo-Irish Literature.* Dublin: Wolfhound Press/Totowa, NJ: Barnes and Noble, 1982.

MacLiammoir, Michael. *All for Hecuba.* London: Methuen, 1946.

———. *Theatre in Ireland.* Dublin: Cultural Relations Committee, 1964.

Malone, Andrew E. *The Irish Drama.* London: Constable, 1929.

Mikhail, E. H. *A Research Guide to Modern Irish Dramatists.* Troy, NY: Whitston, 1979.

Moore, George. *Hail and Farewell!* 3 vols. London: Heinemann, 1920–1931.

Murray, Christopher. "Irish Drama in Transition, 1966–78." *Etudes Irlandaises,* 1979: 287–308.

O'Connor, Frank. *The Backward Look: A Survey of Irish Literature.* London: Macmillan, 1967. (Published in U.S.A. as *A Short History of Irish Literature: A Backward Look.* New York: Putnam, 1967.)

Ó hAodha, Mícheál. *Theatre in Ireland.* Oxford: Basil Blackwell, 1974.

Robinson, Lennox. *Ireland's Abbey Theatre: A History, 1899–1951.* London: Sidgwick and Jackson, 1951.

———, ed. *The Irish Theatre.* Lectures delivered during the Abbey Theatre Festival held in Dublin in August 1938. London: Macmillan, 1939.

Ronsley, Joseph, ed. *Myth and Reality in Irish Literature.* Waterloo: Wilfred Laurier Press, 1977.

Simpson, Alan. *Beckett and Behan and a Theatre in Dublin.* London: Routledge and Kegan Paul, 1962.

Waters, Maureen. *The Comic Irishman.* Albany, NY: SUNY Press, 1984.

Weygandt, Cornelius. *Irish Plays and Playwrights.* Port Washington, NY: Kennikat, 1966 (reprint of 1913 ed.).

Worth, Katherine. *The Irish Drama of Europe from Yeats to Beckett.* Atlantic Highlands, NJ: Humanities Press, 1978.